INTELLECTUAL PROPERTY DAMAGES

INTELLECTUAL PROPERTY DAMAGES

Guidelines and Analysis

Mark A. Glick

Lara A. Reymann

Richard Hoffman

John Wiley & Sons, Inc.

For general information on our other products and services, or technical support, please contact our Customer Care Department within the United States at 800-762-2974, outside the United States at 317-572-3993 or fax 317-572-4002.

Wiley also publishes its books in a variety of electronic formats. Some content that appears in print may not be available in electronic books.

Library of Congress Cataloging-in-Publication Data

Glick, Mark A.
  Intellectual property damages : guidelines and analysis / Mark A. Glick,
Lara A. Reymann, Richard R. Hoffman.
     p. cm.
Includes index.
  ISBN 0-471-23719-1 (cloth : acid-free paper)
 1. Intellectual property—United States. 2. Actions and
defenses—United States. 3. Damages—United States. I. Reymann, Lara A.
II. Hoffman, Richard R. III. Title.
  KF2983 .G58 2003
    346.7304′8—dc21

                                                        2002014438

Printed in the United States of America

10 9 8 7 6 5 4 3 2 1

ABOUT THE AUTHORS

Mark A. Glick has a Ph.D. in economics and a J.D. in law. He is a professor of economics at the University of Utah Department of Economics, where he teaches law and economics and industrial organization. He also serves as Of Counsel with the law firm Parsons Behle & Latimer, where he practices in the areas of intellectual property and antitrust. He is a graduate of UCLA, The New School for Social Research, and Columbia University.

Lara A. Reymann is a member of the Litigation Department at Parsons Behle & Latimer, where she practices intellectual property law. Ms. Reymann graduated *cum laude* from Dartmouth College with a B.A. in government and a minor in philosophy. She received her J.D. with honors from the University of Chicago Law School, where she worked in the Mandel Legal Aid Clinic for several years.

Richard Hoffman is a director at LECG with over 12 years of experience in accounting and consulting. He is a CPA and is Accredited in Business Valuations. Rick worked at international accounting firms for approximately 10 years before joining LECG in 2000. He also has been an adjunct professor at the University of Utah.

Acknowledgments

The authors acknowledge the contribution of several colleagues, academics, experts, and lawyers. The IP/Antitrust group at Parsons Behle & Latimer provided valuable input into the chapters on litigation and the patent and antitrust interface. In particular, Raymond Etcheverry, David Mangum, and Kevin Speirs have been mentors and helped the authors appreciate the importance of damages in intellectual property cases. Also, several patent lawyers and specialists in trademark and copyright law reviewed and commented on the substantive chapters on IP law, in-cluding Margaret McGann, Bill Evans, and Vanessa Pierce. Moreover, we are indebted to individuals outside our respective firms who reviewed chapters within their substantive specialties and provided vital insights. These individuals include Dr. Duncan Cameron, economist with LECG's Los Angeles office; Dr. Mike Lemmon, finance professor at the University of Utah; and Steve Stauffer of PricewaterhouseCoopers. Ted Tatos, Dianna Gibson, Roger Smith, and Laura McNichols also assisted in the development and revision of the book. The authors also express appreciation to Robert Goldscheider for his valuable help and thoughtful introduction. Any mistakes or errors are our own.

Finally, the authors thank their respective spouses, without whose extreme tolerance and support there would be no book.

Contents

Preface

This book arises from the authors' collective experience acting as damage experts and managing damage experts in intellectual property (IP) cases. In case after case we have observed that the damage portion of IP litigation is treated as a neglected stepchild. This failure to prioritize construction of a damage theory is curious since so much rides on each side's evaluation of damages, both for settlement purposes and for trial preparation. Since it is so typical to allocate insufficient resources and inadequate attention to damages, lawyers know little about how to effectively use their own experts and undermine opposing experts, and the experts themselves do not possess the necessary background in IP to be effective. This uneducated state precludes informed analysis of IP litigation, including the decision of whether to litigate at all, what possible outcomes to anticipate, and what terms or financial compensation might constitute a reasonable settlement.

Over the years the authors have sought to fill this vacuum, first within their (two authors) own law firm and then more generally. We have taught IP damages classes for the National Association of Valuation Analysts, given presentations to numerous law firms, and instructed economists at the University of Utah in the law and economics program where Mark Glick is a professor. This book represents our attempt to systematize the general knowledge that experts and lawyers need to have in order to be effective in evaluating, presenting, and opposing damage claims in IP cases.

There are several implicit themes that run throughout this text. It may be useful to recognize these themes at the outset to establish a context for the following chapters. Initially, we are not concerned at all with issues such as how to answer questions in a deposition. An informed, honest expert will have little problem with learning basic litigation skills. Of greater moment for any expert is a firm grasp of the necessary substantive knowledge. The deficiencies experts often display are, in part, a consequence of the departmentalization of most business schools in the United States. For example, there is not one question concerning calculating future sales on the CPA exam, and standard accounting programs do not offer any courses that prepare their majors for litigation support. However, there is a vast industry of accountants in the litigation support area, and lawyers typically uncritically rely on these experts for their damages cases. In contrast, economists are trained in microeconomics and econometrics (statistics applied to economics), a skill set remarkably compatible with judicial precedent on damages. Yet nothing in an economics Ph.D. program will prepare an economist to effectively guide attorneys in the discovery process, or understand the structure of the books and records of the company, or even how to apply their economic training in the specific IP context. Financial economists are yet another breed. Finance programs teach valuation principles, discounting, and risk analysis (i.e., all of the mechanics of the damage calculation). But none of these skills will have any value in litigation unless the attorneys provide the right information, effectively relate to the expert the judicial requirements for the analysis, and manage and combine the right skill sets for each case situation. In short, our experience is that success in an intellectual property damage case requires experts with complementary skills, combined with attorney instruction and management.

In the chapters that follow, we hope to provide experts and lawyers with what they need to know about intellectual property law and intellectual property litigation in order to be effective in their roles. Some chapters will be more relevant for some than others. For example, Chapters 1 and 2 on litigation and *Daubert* cover material many attorneys are likely to be familiar with, while nonlawyer experts are less likely to have been exposed to these topics. Experts, on the other hand, may consider skipping some of the chapters on economics, finance, and accounting, while lawyers should read those chapters carefully in order to understand what information and evidence their experts will require in order to be effective. Attorneys also may be more interested in the factors that determine potential damages than in the equations necessary for the actual calculations. In short, the chapters will vary in their direct applicability to the roles of experts and attorneys in an intellectual property damage case. However, gaining an increased understanding of the skills and knowledge that each team member will bring to the table can only benefit the entire litigation enterprise. Finally, because this book cannot substitute for formal training and experience, we provide suggestions for additional reading so that any specific topic can be studied in greater depth.

Introduction

It is a pleasure and an honor for me to write some introductory remarks about this book, which deals with the fruits of innovation and which is, itself, innovative.

As an active practitioner for over 40 years in the law and business based on intellectual property, and someone who believes that professionals should make scholarly contributions to their chosen specialties, I am able to appreciate this excellent collaborative effort. In my opinion, this is an important new source of insights and information about this dynamic subject.

This has been an ambitious project with a broader focus than most works in this area. It contains the most complete and lively analysis about damages from patent infringements. In addition, it is the only book I know that contains parallel analysis of the key issues in assessing damages for the misuse of copyrights, trademarks, and trade secrets. Inasmuch as the majority of technology-related business today involves the employment of many, if not all, of these intellectual property rights, this multifaceted commentary is very pertinent.

The authors do not address these core issues in a vacuum. They provide a succinct and well-written historical background about intellectual property and the arenas in which disputes are litigated and resolved. They also discuss the antitrust laws and their interface with intellectual property. Furthermore, their methodology combines theoretical—sometimes rising to philosophical—discussions of many relevant matters, together with "nuts and bolts" solutions and vivid examples.

Because of his background as a university professor of economics as well as a litigating lawyer, Mark Glick has the qualifications to discuss current legal and economic issues in combination, taking into account his firsthand practical experience. Accounting skills to help determine lost profits and reasonable royalties are invariably necessary in these disputes. It was therefore astute that Richard Hoffman, an able CPA who specializes in these matters, has been included in the team of authors. Mark and Richard frequently collaborate successfully on matters of this sort. Their integrated inputs are much appreciated. Lara Reymann, who combines youth, enthusiasm, thoroughness, and high intelligence, has also played a continually catalytic role in this project.

Since this book covers legal, business, and accounting matters, it should be appreciated by a wide audience. I believe senior corporate executives, IP litigating attorneys, whether or not they are patent lawyers, and students should all be able to gain considerable knowledge from exposure to this work product. Other members of the bar and bench will also find useful material herein.

This book is well organized and capable of being read through by someone new to intellectual property who is motivated to get more than a superficial grasp of IP. The book can also be effectively employed as a reference and research tool.

Without wanting to sound avuncular, I believe that Mark, Rick and Lara have succeeded in creating a fine addition to the literature in their chosen field. I therefore hope that these three ambitious people will not relax their grip on the "controls" of the "vehicle" they have worked so hard to research, write, and edit. I look forward to regular updates of their scholarship in the future.

Robert Goldscheider
East Hampton, New York
July 2002

Part One

Legal, Economic, and Financial Foundations of Intellectual Property Damages

1

The Litigation Process

Although litigators will be familiar with much of the content of this chapter, nonlawyers often have only a vague understanding of the legal process involved in enforcing intellectual property (IP) rights. Economists, accountants, and financial economists who wish to increase their value as members of an IP litigation team should understand the general structure and chronology of the litigation process to anticipate how they will be involved at each stage. An expert who understands the overall theory of the case, as well as the means of developing and presenting that theory at various stages of litigation, exponentially increases his or her value to the litigation team. A basic knowledge of the litigation process is therefore integral to an expert's ability to contribute effectively throughout litigation.

Intellectual property litigation involves teams of individuals with various areas of expertise. A typical IP case might require attorneys, economists, accountants, experts in the relevant field (e.g., computer science), and the necessary support staff. The more that each participant understands about his or her role and the expected contributions of the other team members, the more effective each participant will be during litigation. Commonly, there will be an overlap between the individual roles, and team members should be ready to question and supplement each others' theories as the case progresses.

STRUCTURE OF THE COURT SYSTEM

Litigation can take place either in state court or in federal court. Intellectual property cases (with the exception of trade secret cases) typically occur in federal court, primarily because patents, copyrights, and, to a large extent, trademarks are governed by federal statutes. Since there is no federal trade secret statute, trade secret law varies from state to state and is litigated in both federal court and state court. The litigation process in federal court is governed by the Federal Rules of Civil Procedure (FRCP). This means that the admissibility and form of depositions and live testimony are determined under the FRCP and the Federal Rules of Evidence (FRE). Each state has its own rules of civil procedure and evidence that govern actions filed in state court. Typically, these state rules are similar (but not identical) to their federal counterparts.

Federal litigation begins at the district court level, often referred to as the trial courts. District courts can hear both criminal and civil cases. There are 93 federal judicial districts in the United States; each state has at least 1 federal district court, and the states that tend to have more federal litigation have several districts. For example, New York has 4 federal districts. Moreover, each district may have multiple judges. The bench for the Southern District of New York, one of the busiest districts in the country, has 25 judges. In contrast, the bench for the District of Wyoming has 3 judges.

State court structures are less uniform. State trial courts are known by various names, depending on the particular state. Many states refer to their trial courts as district courts, while other states have titled their lowest level of courts superior courts (California) or even supreme courts (New York). Generally, state trial courts are organized along county lines, with the number of courts varying according to the population and litigation needs of the relevant geographic area.

If either party decides to appeal a final judgment from the trial court, the litigation proceeds to the appellate courts. Unlike trial courts, which almost always consist of a single judge and possibly a jury, appellate courts are made up of a panel of judges and never involve a jury. The federal appellate courts are divided into 13 circuits, 10 sequentially numbered circuit courts, plus the circuit court for the District of Columbia; each circuit handles the appeals for a geographic region of the country. For example, the Court of Appeals for the Tenth Circuit (referred to simply as the Tenth Circuit) hears appeals from federal district courts in Utah, Wyoming, Colorado, New Mexico, Kansas, and Oklahoma. A circuit court typically will have a panel of three judges decide a case, although the entire court may hear the appeal for particularly significant cases. When all of the circuit judges hear a case, the resulting decision is referred to as an en banc ruling.

Patent appeals are handled by a specialized federal appeal court known as the United States Court of Appeals for the Federal Circuit, or simply the Federal Circuit. In 1909, the Court of Customs and Patent Appeals was created to handle certain customs and patent matters. The Court of Customs and Patent Appeals was abolished in 1982 and was completely replaced by the Federal Circuit. According to federal statute, the Federal Circuit is the exclusive court of appeals for patent decisions from district courts.[1] Federal district court opinions in patent cases are appealed directly to the Federal Circuit, bypassing the normally assigned circuit court for that region. Opinions issued by the Federal Circuit are binding on all federal district courts, regardless of where they are located. Additionally, the Federal Circuit has exclusive jurisdiction of appeals from decisions of the Patent and Trademark Office (PTO) Board of Patent Appeals and Interferences relating to patent applications and interferences.[2] For example, the Federal Circuit can hear appeals from the PTO Board's rejection of certain claims. The Federal Circuit's decisions can be reviewed only by the United States Supreme Court.

The Federal Circuit (and the Court of Customs and Patent Appeals before it) was created because of a perceived need for patent disputes to be heard on appeal by judges well versed in the technical aspects of patent law. By providing a single forum for appeals of patent matters, the Federal Circuit strives to achieve uniformity in the exposition and application of substantive patent law. Although patent appeals are heard only by the Federal Circuit, the Federal Circuit's appellate review is not limited to patent issues. In fact, many nonpatent issues are heard on appeal by the Federal Circuit, primarily when such issues are present as a separate question within a patent case.[3]

Like all appellate courts, the Federal Circuit is not bound by the trial court's reasoning in evaluating the judgment being appealed.[4] A flaw in the trial court's reasoning is insufficient grounds for reversal when the court ultimately reached the correct result.[5] Generally, appellate courts will not second-guess the trial court's determinations on issues exclusively within the trial court's discretion, such as evaluations of witness credibility.[6] A trial court's determination that one expert's testimony and analysis is more credible than that of the opposing expert is a matter within the discretion of the trial court.[7] The Federal Circuit repeatedly emphasizes in its opinions that it reviews decisions, not phrases in an opinion, expressions, passing comments, or mere dicta (statements within an opinion that are not relied on in the court's findings). A difference in opinion as to the correct philosophical approach is not critical unless it has resulted in an improper result. However, if the analysis reflected in an opinion is so hopelessly flawed that the true basis for the judgment cannot be determined, or if it appears to have a clearly erroneous factual basis, then the lower court's opinion may be reversed.[8]

The Federal Circuit's review of PTO Board decisions is based on the record testimony and evidence presented to the PTO. If the PTO Board's decision affirmed a patent examiner's rejection of an application generally, without identifying or reviewing a particular ground on which the examiner relied, that ground is assumed to be affirmed. Accordingly, the Federal Circuit will consider such a ground in its review.

All appellate courts have the authority to affirm, modify, or vacate a trial court's decision. Moreover, if the appellate court determines that additional action must be taken, the appellate court may remand the case to the trial court with specific directions or guidelines as to the necessary findings or calculations that must be done. A remand returns the case to the lower court's jurisdiction. Because a remand involves an additional commitment of judicial resources at the trial court level, it is not a decision that is taken lightly by appellate courts. Ordinarily, where a trial court errs in applying a legal standard (such as a stricter burden of proof than is warranted), the appellate court may remand to permit reconsideration under the proper standard. However, if the record before the appellate court indicates that there is no question as to what the result would be on remand, the appellate court can simply correct the error and issue a final decision itself. In contrast, if the lower court must make additional findings of fact to support the decision, remand is appropriate. For example, if a district court determines that attorneys' fees are not appropriate, but the appellate court concludes that the prevailing party should be awarded attorneys' fees, a remand probably is necessary for the trial court to determine the proper amount of attorneys' fees. In general, a remand is required if the information necessary for the appellate court's decision is not apparent from or contained in the record.

Appeals from the state trial courts progress to the appellate courts, or courts of appeal. Some states only have one level of appellate review—typically the state supreme court. However, at least one-third of the states now have two levels of appellate review, that is, an intermediate appellate court that hears appeals from the trial courts and a higher court that selectively hears appeals from intermediate court decisions. The initial appeal is called an appeal "as of right," while an appeal to the higher court generally is a "discretionary" right to judicial review.

The culmination of the federal and state appeals process is the United States Supreme Court. The United States Supreme Court has discretion to review certain appeals from both the highest level of state courts and the federal appellate courts. If the Court decides to hear an appeal, it is said to have "granted cert.," a shorthand reference for the decision to review a lower court's decision. There are nine justices on the United States Supreme Court, and all of them hear each appeal (unlike the panels that hear appeals on the circuit court level). Most cases never reach the United States Supreme Court, due in part to the low odds of the Court deciding to hear an appeal. The odds of the Court granting "cert." on a particular case hover around 1 in 10.[9] This does not take into account the external factors that affect the number of cases submitted to the Court for review, such as limited resources to fund the expense of protracted litigation, mootness of particular issues after the length of time it would take to reach the highest court, and sheer frustration with the litigation process.

THE COMPLAINT

An IP lawsuit, like any other litigation, begins with the filing of a complaint. The party who files the complaint with the court is known as the plaintiff, while the party against whom the complaint is filed is the defendant. There may be multiple defendants and/or multiple plaintiffs in any particular case.

In some instances, multiple plaintiffs may desire to join their claims together in what is known as a "class action." A "class" of plaintiffs must satisfy four primary legal requirements before they can be certified by a trial court to proceed as a single action: (1) numerosity (there must be a substantial number of class members, too many to deal with by simply joining them as additional plaintiffs); (2) commonality (common questions of law or fact must exist and, in some types of class actions, predominate over any questions affecting only individual class members); (3) typicality (the class representative, i.e., the plaintiff present in the courtroom whose identity is known, must be part of the class and must possess the same interest and suffer the same injury as the class members); and (4) representativeness (the parties present must adequately represent the interests of absent class members who may be bound by the judgment reached therein). Additionally, the plaintiffs must satisfy the court that the class is adequately defined, that is, the class must be defined clearly enough that the court and the parties understand who would fall within the class, even if the exact identities and number of persons within the class are not yet known. Class actions are more common in tort cases, such as litigation over a defective product that may have injured a class of persons including all purchasers of that product, than in IP cases. The reason is simple—seldom will there be an entire class of individuals, known and unknown, with an ownership interest in a particular piece of IP.

The complaint must detail the facts of the case sufficient to "plead" every element of each alleged cause of action. It is not necessary for the complaint to contain every factual detail known to the plaintiff. The courts require only that the plaintiff provide sufficient detail to put the defendant on notice as to the basis for the claims against him or her. The United States Supreme Court, in the seminal case *Conley v. Gibson*, held that a complaint only needs to include a short plain statement of the claim, sufficient to show that the plaintiff is entitled to relief.[10] The statement is sufficient if it "give[s] the defendant fair notice of what the plaintiff's claim is and the grounds upon which it rests."[11] This standard for pleadings is known as notice pleading. Accordingly, a complaint may sketch the basis of the wrongful act in fairly broad terms, because the plaintiff likely has not yet had the opportunity to obtain all of the relevant factual details from the defendant. For example, a typical complaint alleging patent infringement might identify the patent being infringed and the defendant's product or process that is accused of infringing that patent, but it may refrain from detailing the other particulars of the infringement. Notice pleading allows a plaintiff the flexibility to develop a theory of the case as he or she learns more facts about the defendant's use of the infringing technology or design.

Generally, a complaint must state the causes of action and then "pray" for some item of relief from the court. For example, the elements of a negligence tort, like a car accident, are negligence (not meeting a standard of care), causation, and damages. A complaint alleging negligence probably would detail what happened in the accident, the facts allegedly establishing the defendant's negligence (e.g., the defendant failed a sobriety test at the scene of the accident), how the defendant's negligence caused the plaintiff to break a leg, and what amount of money will be required to compensate the plaintiff for the damage. Some complaints opt to leave the amount of damages unspecified, simply asking for an award of damages "in an amount to be determined at trial." Detailing the amount of damages sought is not necessary to satisfy the requirements of notice pleading.

THE ANSWER

After being served with the complaint, the defendant must either answer or move for dismissal of the case, typically within 20 days. In an answer, the defendant will admit or deny, in summary fashion, each fact alleged in the complaint. The answer is also the defendant's first opportunity to articulate the defenses and counterclaims[12] that he or she wishes to raise in the litigation. Everyone on the litigation team should read the answer, as the admissions may significantly narrow the issues presented for litigation. Taken together, the admissions and denials frame the issues that will be fought over in discovery, in motions, and ultimately at trial.

In lieu of an answer, a defendant may choose to file a motion to dismiss the case. However, at this stage, motions to dismiss face a very high standard, as the court must assume that each allegation pled in the complaint is true. However, the defendant may ask the court to dismiss the complaint for failing to meet certain requirements necessary for the suit to proceed, such as if the plaintiff has filed the complaint in the wrong court (resulting in lack of jurisdiction) or failed to state a claim for which relief can be granted.[13] For example, a plaintiff alleging negligence would fail to state a claim if the plaintiff failed to provide any facts or allegations that he or she was injured by the defendant. In that case, one of the essential elements of a negligence claim (causation) would be missing and the trial court could not allow the case to proceed. Like answers, motions to dismiss are almost exclusively the attorney's responsibility to draft—expert analysis is universally unnecessary for judicial evaluation at this point.

ATTORNEYS' MEETING AND PROTECTIVE ORDERS

Rule 26 of the FRCP requires the parties' attorneys to meet and develop a discovery plan.[14] This meeting must occur at least 14 days before a scheduling conference is held with the judge. The discovery plan will set cutoff dates for document requests, expert reports, interrogatories, and depositions.[15] Rule 26 also requires each party to provide the opposing party with initial disclosures concerning their witnesses, relevant documents, and damages. Finally, Federal Rule of Civil Procedure 26(a)(2) sets forth what must be contained in your expert report. This section of the rules should be required reading for any expert.

The attorneys' meeting may also be the first time that the parties discuss drafting a stipulated protective order to govern discovery. Particularly in IP litigation, the documents likely to be produced during discovery may contain highly sensitive information concerning research and development, confidential technology, marketing plans, and customer lists. Given the likelihood that such documents will be relevant to the ongoing litigation, the parties often agree to produce documents subject to certain restrictions on their use by the other side. Under Federal Rule of Civil Procedure 26(c)(7), confidential commercial information warrants special protection. A protective order does not eliminate the requirement that the information be relevant or that the request for documents must not be overly broad and burdensome. However, a stipulated protective order does provide some security for sensitive documents without requiring the parties to seek judicial rulings on each particular document.

Commonly, a stipulated protective order will permit any producing party to designate information that is "believed to be subject to protection under Federal Rule of Civil Procedure 26(c)(7)" as confidential and limit disclosure of all documents so designated. For example, many protective orders provide that documents stamped "confidential" may be shown only to counsel and expert witnesses, but not to anyone in-house at the competing business, possibly including the attorney's client. Some protective orders contain degrees of protection, such as "confidential" and "confidential—attorneys' eyes only," where the latter designation may be shown only to an even narrower class of individuals. Protective orders also may limit the use of the disclosed information to the litigation at hand and require the destruction or return of such information after the conclusion of the lawsuit. In order to have a fallback position, attorneys frequently include in the protective order provisions regarding "inadvertent disclosure" (i.e., production of information without the appropriate designation, which nevertheless should be treated as confidential). Commonly, this provision simply allows an attorney to remedy the situation if it is addressed within a certain period after the error is discovered by retrieving the documents or retroactively designating them as confidential. Because the particulars may vary, attorneys may agree to exchange drafts of a proposed protective order, tailored to the facts of the case, until they can stipulate to a mutually agreeable form for the order.

If the parties do not stipulate to a protective order, either party may still ask the court to grant a protective order at some point in the litigation. The party seeking a protective order must establish that the information sought is confidential and that the disclosure of that information has the potential to harm the party or the party's business.[16] The party opposing the protective order must then show that the disclosure of such information is neither necessary nor relevant to the case.[17] For example, the Federal Circuit has held that an infringer's sales information is relevant because it tends to show commercial success, which may support patentability.[18] However, the party opposing such discovery (or a nonparty objecting to a subpoena) may argue that sales information is neither relevant nor necessary to the case.[19] Alternatively, the resisting party may seek to delay their disclosure of such information until liability first has been established.[20]

The Supreme Court has considered and approved the use of protective orders to control discovery in civil litigation. Early cases have indicated that the restrictions on the use of information produced subject to protective orders might conflict with the rights of free speech protected under the First Amendment.[21] However, in *Seattle Times Co. v. Rhinehart*, the Supreme Court clarified the interaction of those principles and indicated its support for judicial regulation of the discovery process.

Seattle Times Co. v. Rhinehart[22]

This United States Supreme Court case addressed whether parties to civil litigation have a First Amendment right to disseminate, in advance of trial, information gained through the pretrial discovery process. Rhinehart was the spiritual leader of the Aquarian Foundation, an organization whose beliefs included the ability to communicate with the dead through a medium, primarily Rhinehart. The *Seattle Times* published a series of articles about the Aquarian Foundation that became the basis for litigation between the parties. Rhinehart alleged defamation and invasion of privacy. During the litigation, the *Seattle Times* sought lists of donors and members of the foundation and certain financial information about the foundation.

The trial court granted a protective order forbidding the use of the financial and membership information obtained through discovery for any purpose except preparation for trial. The *Seattle Times* appealed, and ultimately the Supreme Court affirmed the lower court's decision. The Supreme Court cited the "significant potential for abuse" of pretrial discovery by litigants as a substantial government interest unrelated to the suppression of speech, and therefore a legitimate justification for protective orders issued by trial courts.

In short, when a protective order is entered on a showing of "good cause" as required by Federal Rule of Civil Procedure 26(c), is limited to the context of pretrial civil discovery, and "does not restrict the dissemination of the information if gained from other sources," it will not be struck down under the First Amendment.

If the parties reach an agreement, the protective order will be submitted to the court with the signatures of both parties to create an enforceable agreement should the parties later disagree about the treatment of certain information. One can imagine how important this would be in a trade secret case. Experts typically are asked to sign the agreement before obtaining access to confidential information. It is vital that an expert understand the conditions attached to his or her access, use, and retention of information that falls under the protective order. Attorneys and experts should take great care to see that they comply with the terms of the protective order, specifically the process for designating information "confidential" and the appropriate use of such designated information received from the other side.

DISCOVERY

The confidentiality agreement is a prelude to discovery. Typically, discovery begins with document requests and interrogatories (written questions). Document requests ask the other side to produce copies of relevant information in any form. Interrogatories ask the other side to provide written answers to certain questions about their arguments in the case, their account of certain events, and the possible witnesses that they may use at trial. In general, a party has 30 days to respond or object to a discovery request. The FRCP defines the scope of discovery as follows:

Federal Rule of Civil Procedure 26(b)(1)

Parties may obtain discovery regarding any matter, not privileged, that is relevant to the claim or defense of any party, including the existence, description, nature, custody, condition, and location of any books, documents or other tangible things and the identity and location of persons having knowledge of any discoverable matter. For good cause, the court may order discovery of any matter relevant to the subject matter involved in the action. Relevant information need not be admissible at the trial if the discovery appears reasonably calculated to lead to the discovery of admissible evidence.

Clearly, the scope of discovery is intended to be broad, with the understanding that not everything discoverable may ultimately be admissible at trial. Written discovery is an area where expert input is critical in an IP case. A sample discovery request is included in Appendix B.

Experts can play a critical role in helping the attorney ask for the right documents and ask the right questions to establish the damage case. A common mistake made by attorneys is underutilizing their experts during the discovery process. Not only can experts assist with framing discovery requests, but the experts also should begin fleshing out their damages theories as early as possible while there is still time to develop and revise the theories based on the information that comes to light. Each scheduling order will contain a deadline for concluding fact discovery; after that cutoff, attorneys and experts will be unable to request additional information from the other side.

Several objections are available to the party who does not wish to produce responsive documents. Generally, the responding party will identify several general objections (such as "vague and ambiguous," "overly broad," and "irrelevant") and then nevertheless offer to produce the responsive documents "subject to and without waiving the foregoing objections." However, there also are grounds on which a party might refuse to produce anything at all. These objections include:

1. The discovery request is unreasonably duplicative.
2. The discovery sought is available from some other source that is more convenient, less burdensome, or less expensive.
3. The party seeking the discovery is better situated to obtain the information sought.

4. The burden or expense of the proposed discovery outweighs its likely benefit, taking into account the needs of the case, the amount in controversy, the parties' resources, the importance of the issues at stake, and the importance of the proposed discovery in resolving the issues in the litigation.
5. The material sought is privileged (usually because it consists of communications between an attorney and a client, or because it represents the "work product" of the attorney, i.e., part of the attorney's preparation for litigation).[23]

If a party claims privilege as the grounds for withholding certain information, it must produce a "privilege log" describing each document withheld (without revealing the contents) and identifying the reason for the assertion of privilege.[24] Generally, the document descriptions will include the date of the document, the author of the document, and sometimes the length of the document.

Privilege generally is claimed most frequently for two types of information: attorney–client communications and work product. Both of these privileges are the subject of many treatises, articles, and legal opinions. The following section merely provides a brief overview of the basis for asserting the privileges.

Attorney–Client Privilege

The attorney–client privilege generally applies to and protects communications between a client and an attorney made for the purpose of furnishing or obtaining professional legal advice.[25] The purpose of the attorney–client privilege is to encourage full and frank communication between attorneys and their clients by ensuring that such communications will be held in confidence.[26] Accordingly, the attorney–client privilege belongs to the client, not the attorney, and only the client may disclose the communications.[27]

The communication may be oral or written, but it must be made with a reasonable expectation of privacy. For example, if the client yells something to counsel across a room full of people, the privilege has been waived as to that communication. Moreover, the attorney–client privilege attaches only to the contents of the communication itself, not the underlying facts. This means that a client cannot claim privilege over certain facts sought to be discovered by the other side simply because the client also communicated those facts to the attorney.[28] The communication itself is protected even if the information may be discovered through other sources.[29] Finally, acts that are simply observed by the attorney, and not directly conveyed by the client, are not necessarily privileged. In evaluating that issue, the courts examine whether what the lawyer observed (e.g., the client's attitude or actions) could be deemed confidential in nature.[30]

Work Product Privilege

The work product privilege applies to those documents and tangible things "prepared in anticipation of litigation or for trial" by a party or that party's representative, including the party's "attorney, consultant, surety, indemnitor, insurer or agent."[31] The party seeking discovery as to those materials must show that the party has "substantial need of the materials in the preparation of the party's case and that the party is unable without undue hardship to obtain the substantial equivalent of the materials by other means."[32] Even if the court finds that those requirements have been met, the court must still, where feasible, redact certain information or otherwise "protect against disclosure of the mental impressions, conclusions, opinions, or legal theories of an attorney or other legal representative of a party concerning the litigation."[33] Accordingly, in ordering discovery of work product, the court may redact such information.

The FRCP makes clear that documents indicating a party's legal strategy, assessment of the strength of various claims, or other preparation for trial are core work product and generally will be outside the bounds of discovery.[34] The more the materials reflect the attorney's mental processes and nature or direction of the investigation, the greater the burden will be on the requesting party to show good cause for disclosure.[35] Just as with attorney–client privilege, work product protection does not prevent the underlying information from being discovered; it only precludes production of particular materials absent a showing of substantial need and inability to obtain that information without undue hardship. For example, the notes taken by an attorney during or after his interview of a particular witness may qualify as work product. However, the other party is entitled to interview that witness and may even be able to require the first attorney to disclose the identity of that witness.[36] Moreover, should that witness become ill and unable to communicate, the other party could argue that the facts warrant disclosure of the attorney's notes to avoid undue hardship on him or her based on the practical unavailability of the information possessed by that witness. In such case, the court could require a factual summary, redacted of all mental impressions and legal strategy, to be turned over to the opposing party.

Electronic Discovery

An important area of discovery that recently is receiving new interest from courts and attorneys is the discovery of electronically stored information.[37] Although the definition of a "document" under the FRCP has included a reference to electronic data since 1970, it is only recently that litigators have begun aggressively pursuing the full extent of the electronic data available in most companies. The volume of data available in electronic form is staggering. In 1998, 3.4 trillion e-mail messages were sent worldwide, including approximately 343 billion in the United States.[38] Currently, approximately 93 percent of the world's information is being generated and stored in digital form, while only 7 percent is stored in other media such as paper and film.[39] This means that the attorney (or expert) who ignores the relevant electronic information that potentially exists in a case is missing the lion's share of the evidence.

Moreover, attorneys should not be content with paper versions or "hard copies," of the electronic files. Electronic documents have embedded information known as "metadata," information that is attached to the file and can conclusively resolve conflicting testimony concerning such issues as the date that a file was created and the author of that file. For example, a date in a printed document may reflect simply the date that it was printed rather than the date the document was created. Additionally, electronic versions of documents may indicate the last date that the document was edited, the last person to edit it, and possibly even the changes made. None of these factors is apparent from the printout of the same document.

Not only do electronic documents offer *more* information, but also they often are easier to review for relevant information. For instance, a collection of electronic documents can be combined within a database enabling efficient data analysis. Attorneys, experts, and their assistants can explore electronic data through text searches rather than being forced to peruse thousands of pages for a minimal return. Electronic databases, depending on their particular format, can be searched using key words or phrases, Boolean requests, fuzzy logic, proximity, and thesaurus-based search methods to extract relevant information.

Depositions

Discovery also involves taking and defending depositions. Each side will seek to take the deposition of the witnesses identified by the other party as being their primary witnesses on certain topics. A deposition involves oral questions asked by an attorney of a witness who is sworn in as if he or she were giving testimony at trial. The witness's testimony will be recorded by a court reporter and will provide valuable insight into the witness's likely testimony at trial. In fact, deposition testimony may come back to haunt the sloppy witness who alters his or her testimony at trial; attorneys will be prepared to present the earlier testimony as impeachment of the expert's credibility where it conflicts or contrasts with the most recent evolution of the expert's opinion. Expert depositions are always important, but the expert's contribution need not be limited to his or her actual testimony at deposition. Experts can assist in creating a strategy for questioning the opposing experts and may even attend the depositions to suggest follow-up questions of which the attorney may not be aware.

EXPERT DISCLOSURES

During discovery, in addition to helping frame the discovery requests made of the opposing party, expert witnesses must disclose certain information about themselves and the information that they have reviewed in reaching their opinions. The FRCP requires all testifying experts to disclose "a complete statement of all opinions to be expressed and the basis and reasons therefore; [and] the *data or other information considered by the witness* in forming the opinions."[40] Some federal courts have interpreted these requirements quite broadly.

In re Pioneer Hi-Bred Int'l, Inc.[41]

In *Pioneer Hi-Bred*, the Federal Circuit held that documents and information disclosed to a testifying expert are subject to mandatory disclosure "whether or not the expert relies upon the documents and information in preparing his report." The court noted that "fundamental fairness requires disclosure of all information supplied to a testifying expert in connection with his testimony," including documents and information that might be classified as privileged. The court emphasized that the 1993 amendments to the rule were meant to eliminate the argument that information disclosed to testifying experts could be withheld from discovery on the basis of work product or attorney–client privilege.

Johnson v. Gmeinder[42]

In *Johnson*, the court held that simply reading or reviewing materials before or in connection with formulating expert opinions would be deemed "consideration" of the information for purposes of mandatory disclosures. In this case, the expert testified at the hearing that he had merely read, but not "considered" certain materials in preparing for his expert report. The court rejected that argument, holding that mandatory disclosures would even include information that the expert had evaluated, but then rejected as a basis for his ultimate conclusions.

The requesting party has a right to the contents of a testifying expert's communications with counsel, including the attorney's mental impressions and legal theories, because such communications could influence the expert's substantive consideration of the issues as well as the form of the expert's opinions. Moreover, a recurring theme in cases addressing this issue is that the judge has a right "to know who is testifying" (i.e., how much of the opinion originated with the expert and how much was spoon-fed by counsel). Accordingly, attorneys and experts should be aware that all information reviewed by a testifying expert may be the subject of mandatory disclosures, specific discovery requests, and lines of questioning at the expert's deposition.[43]

Furthermore, mandatory disclosures may require the production of draft versions of the expert's report. Draft reports that are exchanged between an expert and an attorney and contain written comments or notes arguably are additional materials considered by the expert in reaching his or her opinion.[44] *Trigon Ins. Co. v. United States* took an extremely strict approach to this requirement and stands as a warning for both counsel and experts.

Trigon Ins. Co. v. United States[45]

In *Trigon*, the documents in question were drafts of expert reports that were not "solely the product of the expert's own thoughts and work." The court found that parties were required to retain and produce draft reports sent to and from the experts. The plaintiff had only requested the draft reports informally (apparently at least once by letter), but the court found that a formal discovery request was not necessary to trigger the obligation to retain copies of the drafts. Since the defendant had failed to retain copies of the draft reports, the court found that the plaintiff was entitled to recover attorneys' fees and costs related to the issue and an adverse inference against the expert's testimony at trial. This adverse inference is an extremely severe sanction, as it would substantially undermine the expert's credibility to a jury or the court. The court considered precluding the expert from testifying at all, but decided to allow the testimony only because a forensic inspection of the defendant's computers had recovered some portion of the missing documents. The defendant also was required to pay for the cost of the forensic inspection.

The court did not address whether retention and disclosure would be required where the testifying experts worked alone (which were not the facts presented by the case), but that distinction may be meaningless in any practical sense given the frequent occurrence of experts and attorneys working closely together on the expert report.

EXPERT REPORTS

The scheduling order will contain due dates for expert reports. Typically, the plaintiff's expert report is due first, followed a month or so later by the defendant's expert report. Sometimes initial reports from both sides are due simultaneously, followed by rebuttal reports. Many different schedules can exist. An expert should have copies of all the pleadings and the scheduling order prior to preparing and serving his report. Much can be said about how to structure and write an effective expert report, but that topic is beyond the scope of this book. A sample expert report is included in Appendix B as an example of a format and organizational structure that the authors have found particularly effective in litigation.

EXPERT DEPOSITIONS

Sometime after the expert reports are filed, the experts on both sides usually will be deposed.[46] Testimony given at a deposition is made under oath, subject to the penalties of perjury. Depositions are always recorded, usually by a stenographer, although videotaping a deposition is gaining popularity. Support among litigators for videotaping depositions has been driven in part by experienced experts who have attempted to evade clear and honest answers to questions. Videotaping makes evasive tactics in a deposition difficult.

In a deposition, the person being deposed (the deponent) is asked questions by an attorney and given an opportunity to answer. At times, the attorneys present may object either to the form of a question or to the subject matter to which the question pertains. The deponent should always pause briefly before answering in order to give counsel the opportunity to object, then listen carefully to the particular objection being made because the objection may provide a clue as to the goal of the questioning attorney. After an objection has been made, an expert should resume testifying only after counsel instructs the expert to continue. Under certain narrow circumstances, an expert may be instructed by the attorney not to answer. Under the FRCP, an attorney may instruct the deponent not to answer only: (1) where the question seeks privileged information; (2) where the question (or probable answer) violates a court-directed limitation on evidence; or (3) where it becomes apparent that the deposition is being conducted "in bad faith or in such a manner as unreasonably to annoy, embarrass or oppress."[47]

Experts are deposed primarily for three reasons: (1) to gain a more complete understanding of the expert's opinions and likely testimony at trial than is possible from the expert report, (2) to confront the expert with potential oversights and weaknesses in his opinion or qualifications that may undermine his reliability as an expert, and (3) to test the expert's commitment to certain opinions. Experts can be confronted with their deposition testimony when they are on the witness stand, so it is very important for the deposition to go well.

As an expert, there is very little real art to being deposed. The expert's best defense is to know the case, know the topic of inquiry, and formulate opinions that are defensible and not exaggerated. Substantive knowledge about IP law and damages theories can expose the goals of the questioning attorney, as well as the purpose of certain questions and how an expert's statements can affect the outcome of the litigation. The Additional Reading section at the end of this chapter identifies additional materials that provide more detailed discussions of deposition tactics and procedures.

MOTION PRACTICE

After expert depositions, the parties may file motions to limit the issues for which trial is necessary and restrict the evidence that will be heard at trial. These motions generally take the form of either motions for summary judgment or motions in limine.[48]

In essence, a motion for summary judgment means that the judge can determine the outcome of the case because discovery has revealed either that the issues in dispute are purely legal (judges decide law, whereas juries decide facts) or that the evidence is so one-sided that no reasonable juror could find in favor of a particular party on an essential element of a claim. A party moving for summary judgment must establish that there are no disputes as to "genuine issues of material fact."[49] Moreover, the court will construe the pleadings and factual record strictly against the party moving for summary judgment, essentially giving the opposing party the benefit of the doubt where there is a basis for such doubt.[50] In short, a party seeking summary judgment faces a very high evidentiary standard. In light of this significant burden, parties often move for *partial* summary judgment. A motion for partial summary judgment asks the court to rule on a limited issue that will further the efficient resolution of the case (sometimes by increasing pressure to settle), although it does not aim to decide the case completely. For example, a plaintiff in a patent infringement case might find it strategically wise to file for partial summary judgment solely on the issue of infringement or validity. Neither one of those issues resolves the question of damages or ends the case, but it might effectively limit the amount of time and resources required for trial.

"Motion in limine" simply means a motion "to exclude" certain evidence or testimony. Since the parties will have deposed each other's primary witnesses and exchanged witness and exhibit lists before trial, each side should have a reasonable idea of what to anticipate hearing at trial. A party may move to exclude evidence that he or she anticipates the other side will use at trial because that evidence is irrelevant to the issues that will be tried or because the evidence is more prejudicial than probative of the issues.[51] The FRE broadly defines "relevance" as "evidence having any tendency to make the existence of any fact that is of consequence to the determination of the action more probable or less probable than it would be without the evidence."[52] Even if the court is satisfied that the evidence is relevant, the evidence may still be excluded for a host of reasons, including "if its probative value is substantially outweighed by the danger of unfair prejudice, confusion of the issues, or misleading the jury, or by considerations of undue delay, waste of time, or needless presentation of cumulative evidence."[53] Additionally, a party may object to the admission of testimony that will consist of nothing more than hearsay evidence.[54] Basically, any of the rules of evidence could provide the basis for a motion in limine, although relevance and lack of adequate probative value are two of the most common grounds for moving to exclude certain evidence from trial.

Experts often play an important role during motion practice by helping the lawyers formulate the theories of the case. In the context of motions for summary judgment, experts often provide affidavits on issues that are submitted as supporting attachments to the motion for summary judgment or legal memorandum opposing summary judgment. Additionally, an expert or portions of the expert's testimony may be the subject of a motion in limine. Motions in limine regarding experts are commonly referred to as "*Daubert* motions" and they are discussed in detail in Chapter 2.

TRIAL

If a plaintiff's case survives summary judgment, then the dispute will be decided at trial. The trial is a complicated process in which the expert plays a small but important role. Although this book does not include a discussion of how to testify at trial, the fundamentals of knowledge, preparation, and accuracy are just as critical at trial as during deposition. When possible, an expert should be present during the trial to hear the testimonies of fact witnesses prior to giving his or her own testimony. An expert generally is not subject to the exclusionary rule that can bar fact witnesses other than the corporate representative from the courtroom prior to giving their testimony.

COURT OPINIONS

Courts may issue rulings, or opinions, at several points during litigation. Rulings may address the admissibility of evidence, the propriety of certain discovery tactics, the relevance of certain issues, and the use of expert testimony. A court may issue various orders to govern the conduct of the parties in a particular case. Published court opinions (as opposed to merely oral rulings) also can have weight in unrelated litigation. An opinion from a higher court (e.g., a circuit court that hears appeals from the particular district court at issue) is described as "binding precedent." Binding precedent must be followed by all lower courts. However, not all circuit court opinions are binding on all lower courts. For instance, an opinion issued from a higher court that is not in the same circuit as the district court might be persuasive but is not binding on the lower court's decision. The closer the factual parallel between cases, the more likely a court might be to find another judge's opinion instructive, even if it comes from a different jurisdiction. Of course, United States Supreme Court opinions are binding on all courts.

Commonly, judicial interpretation of statutes and existing law offers better guidance for lawyers and experts in litigation than the statutes themselves. Different jurisdictions may interpret the same statute in different and possibly conflicting ways. The outcome of any particular litigation may depend on the attitude of courts in the relevant jurisdiction, rather than on some absolute answer that would apply regardless of location. Where certain issues have not yet been addressed in a specific jurisdiction (as is commonly the case in less populated areas), the opinions of other courts from around the country can serve both as predictors of potential outcomes in litigation and as support for particular arguments.

A final judgment in the case can become the basis for an appeal. Until a final judgment has been entered, other rulings by the court generally cannot be appealed. Some intermediate decisions may significantly impact the case, but if the litigation were interrupted for appeals of every ruling, litigation would be even more protracted and resolution even harder to obtain.

LITIGATION VERSUS ALTERNATIVE DISPUTE RESOLUTION

After the decision to take action, often the first choice that must be made is whether to litigate in court or pursue one of the alternative means of dispute resolution. Litigation in court is what people typically think of when they imagine suing or being sued, and the process has been discussed in detail. However, alternative dispute resolution (or

ADR) has been increasing steadily in popularity as an alternative, or sometimes a precursor, to traditional litigation.

Alternative dispute resolution may be particularly appropriate in the context of IP litigation, given the typical expenditures of time and resources on the litigation process. Recent statistics indicate that 76 percent of patent suits settle, but not before each side has incurred over $1 million in legal fees and indirect legal expenses.[55] Moreover, litigating a patent case through the trial stage costs each side an average of approximately $2 million in legal fees and related expenses, and the average costs have been increasing about 15 percent per year over the last five years.[56] The theoretical advantages of ADR include speed, economy, expertise of the decision maker, privacy, greater informality, convenience related to selecting the time and place of the proceedings, and finality without recourse to appeal.

However, extremely complex IP cases may benefit from the formal procedures used in federal court rather than the simplified, potentially less sophisticated approaches of ADR. Intellectual property cases typically require significant investigation and exchange of information, perhaps best accomplished through the formal discovery procedures used in federal courts. Similarly, the parties often will not move toward settlement until the issues have been narrowed and both parties have been assured that they have all relevant information. By the time both parties have conducted the necessary factual investigation, hired and prepared expert witnesses, and identified the linchpin issues, they may have already invested sufficient resources to void any cost savings through ADR.

Alternative dispute resolution consists primarily of mediation and arbitration. Essentially, mediation consists of settlement discussions facilitated by the perspective of a neutral third party (often someone with experience as a judge or expertise in the relevant area). Mediation is a meeting of the parties before a mutually selected mediator who attempts to mediate the differences between the parties and facilitate settlement. The mediation can last as long as the parties believe that it is serving a useful purpose, but it generally does not last more than a couple days. The mediator generally will listen to both sides' presentations of their arguments, and then may separate the parties and speak to each side about the perceived strengths and weaknesses in their arguments. The mediator can present various settlement options to the opposing sides and discuss the merits of the proposals with each side. A mediator's goal is to enable the parties to find a mutually satisfactory resolution to their dispute, given the facts and the law. Although the mediator's opinions and findings can sway one or both of the parties toward a settlement, the parties typically agree that the findings of the mediator will not be binding, so mediation does not preclude seeking a resolution in court or through binding arbitration.

Arbitration, on the other hand, is conducted very much like courtroom litigation, and the arbitrator's decision, like a judge's ruling, generally is binding and final for the parties.[57] Generally, the arbitration process moves faster than traditional litigation and can save the parties significant amounts in fees and costs. Moreover, the ability to select your arbitrator, in effect tailoring him or her to the nature of your case, proffers an advantage over the random assignment of judges in the federal and state court systems. Both forms of ADR involve attorneys, witnesses, and rules of evidence. However, the technical rules governing the admissibility of evidence often are modified, either through mutual stipulation of the parties beforehand or because the ADR is conducted under the rules of a particular organization, such as the American Arbitration Association (AAA). Generally, at a hearing, the arbitrator will receive all relevant evidence without applying strict rules of evidence. Both parties have the option of being represented by counsel and to present their cases in a manner possibly very similar to the organization and structure of a court case. After the hearing, the arbitrator will have a certain amount of time within which to render his or her final decision. The length of time that an arbitrator has to issue a decision can be predetermined by the organization's rules or by an agreement between the parties. For example, under the AAA rules, the arbitrator renders a final decision within 30 days of the hearing's conclusion. This timing can be in marked contrast to the lengthy time lines of many federal courts.

By law, even "final" or "binding" decisions of an arbitrator may be appealed to a court in limited circumstances. However, courts have adopted a standard of review (in other words, the standard to which they will hold the other forum, in this case the arbitrator) that virtually guarantees that such appeals will be unsuccessful unless the decision was truly arbitrary or capricious. An arbitration decision, unlike a judicial ruling, is not subject to reversal by the courts based on the argument that it was legally erroneous. Under section 10 of the Federal Arbitration Act (FAA),[58] the arbitrator's decision may be set aside by a court only for such reasons as bias or corruption of the arbitrator, misconduct by the arbitrator, or action in excess of his or her power.[59] Clearly, the courts have an interest in decreasing their own caseload by encouraging dispute resolution outside the courtroom. If every ADR decision could be essentially reheard on appeal, the lack of finality would discourage potential litigants from pursuing that form of dispute resolution. Therefore, the courts will only address the merits of an arbitrated case where it appears that the arbitrator's actions were nearly inexcusable.

The courts may, however, at the request of one of the parties, intervene before the arbitration begins. Courts may stay the arbitration, order that the arbitration proceed, or stay related judicial proceedings in favor of arbitration. The arbitration process generally begins with a written "demand for arbitration" or other form of notice sent by one party to the other alerting them of their intention to arbitrate certain issues. The recipient of such a demand may ignore the letter and bring suit in court. The party seeking arbitration may then apply for a stay of the judicial proceedings in favor of arbitration.[60] If the party seeking arbitration can satisfy a court that the issue involved in the lawsuit is covered by a valid and binding arbitration agreement between the parties (frequently found in the contract at the heart of the dispute), then the court must stay the lawsuit.[61] Similarly, the party seeking arbitration may ask a court for an order "directing that such arbitration proceed in the manner provided for" in the parties' arbitration agreement if the other party simply refuses to participate in the arbitration, without bringing an independent suit.[62] To issue such an order, the court must determine the existence of a valid arbitration agreement. Finally, the party who wishes to avoid arbitration may seek a court order staying the arbitration pending a judicial determination of whether a valid agreement to arbitrate exists. The federal courts are limited to these forms of injunctive relief related to arbitration; they will not intervene merely to address evidentiary issues or other intermediate issues within the arbitration.

SUMMARY

Chapter 1 explained the basic structure of the U.S. court system and generally outlined the essential chronology of litigation. This background information should provide a helpful context for participants in the litigation process. By understanding the various stages of litigation and anticipating your role in those stages, you can be better prepared and more capable of contributing valuable input to the development of an IP damages theory. Early involvement and comprehension of the standards that will be applied to your theory will improve both your work product and the work product of other team members who could benefit from your perspective.

ENDNOTES

[1]   *See* 28 U.S.C. § 1295(a)(4)(C).

[2]   *See* 28 U.S.C. § 1295(a)(4)(A).

[3]   In fact, the Federal Circuit's application of its own law to issues outside the patent area has sparked some controversy. *See* Ronald Katz and Adam Safer, *Should One Patent Court Be Making Antitrust Law for the Whole Country,* 69 Antitrust L. J. 687 (2002).

[4]   *See, e.g., Forsley v. Principi,* 284 F.3d 1355 (Fed. Cir. 2002) (stating that appellate courts must apply the correct law, even if not presented by the parties or considered by the lower court (citing *Kamen v. Kemper Fin. Servs., Inc.,* 500 U.S. 90, 99 (1991))).

[5]   *See, e.g., Glaxo, Inc. v. Torpharm, Inc.,* 153 F.3d 1366, 1370 (Fed. Cir. 1998) ("We must reverse a summary judgment if any errors of law were made, unless an independent legal ground exists in the record upon which we can affirm." (citations omitted)).

[6]   *See, e.g., Molins PLC, v. Textron, Inc.,* 48 F.3d 1172, 1181 (Fed. Cir. 1995) ("We accord deference to the fact finder's assessment of a witness's credibility and character."); *DeSarno v. Dep't of Commerce,* 761 F.2d 657, 661 (Fed. Cir. 1985) ("It is not our function to second-guess the credibility determinations of the presiding official, which were based on the demeanor of the witnesses during the hearing.").

[7]   *See, e.g., Gould v. Quigg,* 822 F.2d 1074, 1077–78 (Fed. Cir. 1987) (affirming trial court's resolution of conflicting expert testimony based on credibility assessments).

[8] *See, e.g., Smiths Indus. Med. Sys., Inc. v. Vital Signs, Inc.*, 183 F.3d 1347, 1354–55 (Fed. Cir. 1999) (reversing trial court's legal determination of obviousness based on the court's erroneous claim construction and flawed analysis of the differences between the claimed invention and the prior art).

[9] The Supreme Court may review any decision of a court of appeals, including the Federal Circuit, by granting a discretionary "writ of certiorari." Unlike the Supreme Court's jurisdiction in appeals from state court decisions, which is limited to questions of federal law, the Court may decide *any legal question*, whether state or federal, in cases appealed from lower federal courts. However, the Court generally limits itself to reviewing important questions of federal law.

[10] *Conley v. Gibson*, 355 U.S. 41 (1957).

[11] *Id.* at 47.

[12] Counterclaims are simply the affirmative claims that a defendant raises against the plaintiff. In other words, where the defendant believes that not only is she without blame, but also that in fact the plaintiff has harmed *her*, she can raise a counterclaim seeking damages or some other remedy.

[13] *See* Fed. R. Civ. P. 12.

[14] *See* Fed R. Civ. P. 26.

[15] *Id.*

[16] *See, e.g., American Standard Inc. v. Pfizer, Inc.*, 828 F.2d 734, 741 (Fed. Cir. 1987).

[17] *Id.*

[18] *In re: Huang,* 100 F.3d 135, 139–40 (Fed. Cir. 1996) (noting that sales information may be relevant to commercial success, although such information alone is not dispositive).

[19] *See, e.g., Micro Motion, Inc. v. Kane Steel Co., Inc.*, 894 F.2d 1313, 1326 (Fed. Cir. 1990) (holding sales information from a nonparty to be irrelevant).

[20] Fed. R. Civ. P. 26(d).

[21] *See In re Halkin,* 598 F.2d 176 (D.C. Cir. 1979) (overturning a protective order because the "inherent value of speech in terms of its capacity for informing the public does not turn on how or where the information was acquired"), *overruled by Seattle Times Co. v. Rhinehart,* 467 U.S. 20, 32 & n. 18 (1984). At issue in *Halkin* were copies of documents relating to Operation Chaos, the CIA's program with regard to antiwar activities during the Vietnam War. The plaintiffs intended to release several of them at a press conference. It may be that the inherent appeal of society's interest in government information about private citizens protesting an unpopular war played a role in this decision, where financial documents about a company offer less intuitive value as a First Amendment argument.

[22] *Seattle Times Co. v. Rhinehart,* 467 U.S. 20, 32–37 (1984).

[23] *See* Fed. R. Civ. P. 26(b)(2).

[24] *See* Fed. R. Civ. P. 26(b)(5).

[25] *See, e.g., American Standard, Inc. v. Pfizer,* 828 F.2d 734, 744–45 (Fed. Cir. 1987).

[26] *Id.*

[27] *Id.; see also* 8 I. Wigmore, Evidence, § 2321 (McNaughton, rev. ed., 1961).

[28] *See, e.g., In re Grand Jury Subpoena Duces Tecum (Rich),* 731 F.2d 1032, 1037 (2d Cir. 1984) (finding that attorney–client privilege protects communications, not underlying information); *J.P. Foley & Co., Inc. v. Vanderbilt,* 65 F.R.D. 523, 526 (S.D.N.Y. 1974) (noting that privilege pertains solely to substance of communications, it does not "preclude inquiry into the subject matter of communications").

[29] *See, e.g., United States v. O'Malley,* 786 F.2d 786, 794 (7th Cir. 1986) (rejecting argument that witness's communications to counsel were not privileged because he had given the same information to the FBI).

[30] *In re Grand Jury Proceedings,* 791 F.2d 663, 665 (8th Cir. 1986) (requiring attorney to authenticate certain signatures and photographs allegedly of the client who was being investigated by a grand jury because appearance and handwriting generally are not confidential communications as others could observe them as well); *United States v. Weger,* 709 F.2d 1151, 1154–56 (7th Cir. 1983) (affirming lower court's admission of letter to counsel purely for the purpose of comparing the typeset with that of another letter typed on the defendant's typewriter); *In re Walsh,* 623 F.2d 489, 494 (7th Cir.), *cert. denied,* 449 U.S. 994 (1980) (finding that privilege does not apply to attorney's observations about client's physical appearance, demeanor, and dress).

[31] Fed. R. Civ. P. 26(b)(3).

[32] *Id.*

[33] *Id.*

[34] *See Hickman v. Taylor,* 329 U.S. 495 (1947) (finding that work product includes "interviews, statements, memoranda, correspondence [and] briefs" of lawyers and indicating a strong reluctance to force an attorney to become a witness); *Ford v. Philips Elec. Instruments Co.,* 82 F.R.D. 359, 360 (E.D. Pa. 1979) (lawyer's discussion with a third-party witness concerning the lawyer's evaluation of the case were not discoverable at the witness's deposition); *In re Grand Jury Proceedings (Duffy),* 473 F.2d 840, 848 (8th Cir. 1973) (holding that lawyer's recollection of conversations with a witness were privileged as work product); *Harper & Row Publishers, Inc. v. Decker,* 423 F.2d 487, 492 (7th Cir. 1970), *aff'd* 400 U.S. 348 (1971) (holding that law firm's memoranda of interviews with witnesses were protected).

[35] *Harper & Row Publishers, Inc. v. Decker,* 423 F.2d 487, 492 (7th Cir. 1970), *aff'd,* 400 U.S. 348 (1971).

[36] *See United States v. Int'l Business Mach. Corp.,* 79 F.R.D. 378, 380 (S.D.N.Y. 1978) (noting that Supreme Court has never indicated that opposing counsel "could not subsequently inquire of the witnesses themselves what they said at the interview); *Lauritzen v. Atlantic Greyhound Corp.,* 8 F.R.D. 237, 238 (E.D. Tenn. 1948), *aff'd,* 182 F.2d 540 (6th Cir. 1950) (requiring defendants to produce lists of witnesses to a bus accident, despite objection that such lists were work product); *United States v. Exxon Corp.,* 87 F.R.D. 624, 638 (D.D.C. 1980) (finding that work product protection does not preclude answering questions as to whether protected documents even exist). *But see In re Grand Jury Impanelled Oct. 18, 1979 (Malfitano),* 744 F.2d 1464, 1467 (11th Cir. 1984) (holding that a list of potential witnesses interviewed by the attorney was work product because it revealed the litigation strategy, although disclosure could be made upon a relatively low showing of need and hardship).

[37] *See generally* Kenneth J. Withers, *Computer-Based Discovery in Federal Civil Litigation,* Fed. Cts. L. Rev. (Oct. 2000).

[38] *See* Kenneth J. Withers, *The Real Cost of Virtual Discovery,* Federal Discovery News (February 2001).

[39] *Id.*

[40] Fed. R. Civ. P. 26(a)(2)(B) (emphasis added). These disclosures must be made at least 90 days before the trial date or upon the date directed by the court or stipulated to by the parties. *See* Fed. R. Civ. P. 26(a)(2)(C).

[41] 238 F.3d 1370 (Fed. Cir. 2001); *see also Aniero Concrete Co. v. New York City School Constr. Auth.,* 94 Civ. 9111, 2002 U.S. Dist. LEXIS 2892 (S.D.N.Y. Feb. 22, 2002) (concluding that the majority of courts agree that reliance by the expert on the information is not necessary for the information to be subject to mandatory disclosure).

[42] 191 F.R.D. 638, 641 (D. Kan. 2000).

[43] For more judicial treatment of the privilege argument in the context of expert disclosures, *see B.C.F. Oil Ref., Inc. v. Consol. Edison Co.,* 171 F.R.D. 57, 66 (S.D.N.Y. 1997) (disclosures must include attorney opinions given to the expert); *W.R. Grace & Co. v. Zotos Int'l, Inc.,* No. 98-CV-838S(F), 2000 U.S. Dist. LEXIS 18096 (W.D.N.Y. Nov. 2, 2000) (availability of cross-examination at trial is not an adequate substitute for pretrial disclosures of information considered).

[44] *See W.R. Grace,* 2000 U.S. Dist. LEXIS 18096 (finding that drafts of expert report faxed to counsel must be disclosed).

[45] 204 F.R.D. 277 (E.D. Va. 2001).

[46] *See* Fed. R. Civ. P. 26(b)(4).

[47] Fed. R. Civ. P. 30(d).

[48] *See* Fed. R. Civ. P. 56; Fed. R. Evid. 401–403.

[49] *See Anderson v. Liberty Lobby, Inc.,* 477 U.S. 242, 250–51 (1986) (mandating summary judgment if a party fails to establish the existence of an element essential to that party's claim and on which it bears the burden of proof).

[50] *See, e.g., Suntinger, Inc. v. Scientific Research Funding Group,* 189 F.3d 1327, 1334 (Fed. Cir. 1999) (viewing evidence in a light most favorable to the nonmovant and drawing all reasonable inferences in its favor).

[51] *See* Fed. R. Civ. P. 401, 402, 403.

[52] Fed. R. Civ. P. 401.

[53] Fed. R. Civ. P. 403.

[54] *See generally* Fed. R. Evid. 801, 802, 803.

[55] Robert Goldscheider, *ADR Focused on Licensing and Intellectual Property,* working paper; 5 Eckstorm's Licensing in Foreign and Domestic Operations: The Forms and Substance of Licensing § 21:2 (April 2002).

[56] *See id.*

[57] The binding nature of the arbitration or mediation, like many procedural aspects of ADR, is subject to the stipulation of the parties, either in a pre-existing contract or through an agreement reached subsequent to the conflict. However, most parties believe that any efficiency advantages of arbitration are lost if the parties can simply pursue the case in court once arbitration has concluded. Therefore, arbitration clauses in contracts typically

require the arbitration to take place within a certain time frame and for the parties to accept the arbitrator's decision as final.

[58] *See* 9 U.S.C.A. §§ 1–14 (1999).

[59] *See* 9 U.S.C.A. § 10(a) (1999).

[60] *See* FAA, 9 U.S.C.A. § 3 (1999); Uniform Arbitration Act § 2(d).

[61] *See* FAA, 9 U.S.C.A. § 3.

[62] *See* FAA, 9 U.S.C.A. § 4; Uniform Arbitration Act § 2(a).

ADDITIONAL READING

Walter D. Alley, *Electronic Discovery Tools for Litigators*, LJN Legal Tech Newsletter (Oct. 2001).

Steven Babitsky and James J. Mangraviti, Jr., *How to Excel During Depositions: Techniques for Experts That Work*, SEAK, Inc. (1999).

Margaret Berger, *Evidentiary Framework, Reference Manual on Scientific Evidence* 37 (1994).

Morgan Chu, *Discovery of Experts*, 8 Litigation 13 (Winter 1982).

Theodore C. Hirt, *Expert Reports*, 22 Litigation 46 (Summer 1996).

William Iscle, *Under Oath: Tips for Testifying*, LRP Pub. (1995).

Steven Lubet, *Expert Testimony: A Guide for Expert Witnesses and the Lawyers Who Examine Them*, NITA (1998).

Joan A. Lukey and Elizabeth A. Rowe, *Electronic Discovery: An Overview*, www.abanet.org/litigation/home.html.

David Malone and Paul Zwier, *Effective Expert Testimony*, NITA (2000).

Marc Rabinoff and Stephen Holmes, *The Forensic Expert's Guide to Litigation: The Anatomy of a Lawsuit*, LRP Pub. (1996).

Mark D. Robins, *Computers and the Discovery of Evidence—A New Dimension to Civil Procedure*, 17 J. Marshall J. Computer Info. L. 411 (Winter 1999).

Michael Sacks, *A Guide for Testifying and Consulting Experts*, LRP Pub. (1995).

Kenneth J. Withers, *The Real Cost of Virtual Discovery*, Federal Discovery News (Feb. 2001).

Kenneth J. Withers, *Computer-Based Discovery in Federal Civil Litigation*, Federal Courts Law Review (Oct. 2000).

2

Damage Principles and *Daubert*

The plight of the expert in an intellectual property (IP) case brings to mind the statement by English author Samuel Butler, "Life is the art of drawing sufficient conclusions from insufficient premises." Although Butler's assessment may not have held up under the standards applicable to a testifying expert's opinions, the fact is that a case seldom presents complete documentation or an opportunity for perfect knowledge of all relevant facts. Moreover, experts often are privy to only a portion of the evidence and are instructed to operate under a certain set of factual and/or legal assumptions. In essence, both attorneys and experts are seeking to draw "sufficient conclusions" from the hand they are dealt. The manner in which they do so is the subject of great debate, both between opposing parties in litigation and in the judiciary's continuing attempt to derive a single set of standards that would apply equally to all expert testimony and provide a fail-safe measure of reliability. The authors believe that this attempt has been only partially successful and that the applicable rules are still evolving. Nonetheless, attorneys and experts must be aware of and play by the present rules set out by the courts. This chapter explains the current standards for admissibility of expert opinions.

DAUBERT ISSUES

Federal Rules of Evidence 702 and 703 govern expert testimony. The traditional standard for admissibility of expert testimony under Rule 702 was whether the testimony would assist the triers of fact, rather than confuse or mislead them. Rule 703 sets forth the standard for admissibility of the underlying data relied on by the expert in formulating his or her opinion. Rules 702 and 703 were recently revised and the new text became effective on December 1, 2000. The revisions are intended to codify and clarify the standards that have evolved under a line of Supreme Court cases that set forth guidelines for judging when expert testimony is reliable. This line of cases is known as the *Daubert* trilogy, and the committee notes that accompany the revised rules re-affirm the trilogy's continued importance.[1] The three cases in the *Daubert* trilogy are described in the boxes below.

Daubert v. Merrell Dow Pharmaceuticals, Inc.[2]

In *Daubert*, the Supreme Court stated that the judge must act as a gatekeeper to determine in advance of trial whether expert testimony is reliable. The judge must exclude unreliable testimony from consideration by the court or the jury. The Court adopted a four-factor test: (1) is the expert opinion testable, (2) has the methodology been subject to peer review, (3) is there a known error rate for the method, and (4) is the method generally accepted in the scientific community? These four criteria became the foundation for judicial evaluations of expert testimony.

General Electric Co. v. Joiner[3]

In *Joiner*, the Supreme Court resolved a disagreement among the circuits concerning the standard for reviewing a district court's exclusion of expert testimony. The Court held that a stringent standard of "abuse of discretion" should be applied, giving district court judges significant leeway in decisions concerning the admissibility of expert testimony. Discretionary decisions are extremely difficult to overturn on appeal. The effect of this decision was to encourage district court judges to perform their role as a gatekeeper, rather than simply admitting everything and letting disputes about the evidence go merely to weight rather than admissibility.

Kumho Tire, Ltd. v. Carmichael[4]

In *Kumho Tire*, the Supreme Court expressly expanded the *Daubert* inquiry to *all experts*. Before *Kumho Tire*, it was unclear whether *Daubert* applied to experts other than scientists. *Kumho Tire* applied the gatekeeping analysis to any expert, whether the expert's field of expertise was chemistry, accounting, economics, or drywall repair. The Court also explained that the district court should have flexibility in the application of the *Daubert* factors to the facts of the case and the expert at issue. The flexibility of a case-by-case analysis was a natural extension of *Joiner* granting the district courts discretion in the decision to admit or exclude expert testimony.

All experts in IP cases must be careful not to run afoul of the *Daubert* principles, or they risk having their opinions, reports, and testimony excluded. The *Daubert* trilogy anticipates removing an expert from litigation entirely, not merely questioning the weight or credibility that should be given to the expert's opinions.

MAKING SENSE OF *DAUBERT*

The Supreme Court's concern in *Daubert* was to establish the trial court judge as a gate-keeper to keep "junk science" out of the courtroom. The danger of "junk science" is that an unsophisticated jury could be persuaded by a well-polished expert or a person with impressive credentials and could base a jury verdict on evidence that is not truly competent. Essentially, the Supreme Court in *Daubert* desired to eliminate from the courtroom "systems of knowledge" that have a fundamental nature different from "scientific knowledge." Of course, scientific knowledge is not limited to chemistry, physics, biology, and the other fields one might consider to be traditional sciences. Scientific knowledge simply refers to one particular means of establishing knowledge. For example, scientific knowledge is knowledge that is acquired through the scientific method, whether the information itself pertains to traditional fields of science, economics, or architecture.

The four *Daubert* factors that the Supreme Court introduced to differentiate science from nonscience are (1) testability, (2) peer review, (3) error rates, and (4) acceptance by the scientific community.[5] These guidelines were supposed to aid the trial court in separating scientific systems of knowledge from other types of knowledge. The assumption of the Court was that scientific systems of knowledge were inherently more reliable and thus preferable to other means of establishing knowledge. In our view, the *Daubert* factors are not adequate for the task, particularly after the Court's expansion of the criteria to cover social science in its opinion in *Kumho Tire*. Instead, the drafters of the amendment to Federal Rule of Evidence 702 properly expanded the inquiry by adding other traditional judicial guidelines relevant to social science and damage experts in particular. These factors are discussed in subsequent sections.

It is useful to first illustrate the logical underpinnings of several systems of knowledge and then determine whether the *Daubert* factors alone are useful in distinguishing between the systems of knowledge or identifying which types of knowledge are reliable. One important differentiating characteristic of systems of knowledge pertains to how each system connects unobservable core concepts to observable or empirical events. We will refer to the unobservable conceptual theory as the "theoretical" level and the empirical world (i.e., the phenomena we experience through our physical senses) as the "observable" level. Exhibit 2-1 depicts two types of knowledge that the *Daubert* opinion aimed at filtering out of a case during the pretrial period.[6]

In religious thought, the power of the analysis resides at the theoretical level alone. There is no connecting relationship between observable reality and explanatory concepts. The concepts originate elsewhere (e.g., in sacred texts or proclamations of religious leaders). The litigation equivalent of religious thought is the expert who bases his

	Mysticism	Religion
Observational Knowledge	x	y
Theoretical Analysis	y	x

EXHIBIT 2-1   Theoretical and Observational Knowledge

or her conclusions on theory that cannot be challenged by resorting to observation in the discovery process or through independent analysis. In contrast, what is labeled mysticism in Exhibit 2-1 involves pure abstraction from observation without the development of a system of theoretical concepts that offers an explanation for association of events and a consistency with other theories. The analogy in litigation is the expert whose opinion is based purely on his "20 years of experience."

One can view the *Daubert* opinion as an effort to eliminate religious and mystical systems of thought as possible bases for a jury's verdict in complicated litigation situations. The weakness of the *Daubert* four-factor approach is that it is both under-inclusive and overinclusive. In *Daubert*, the Court explicitly referred to Carl Hempel, an extreme advocate of the empiricist view of science. Hempel, along with other logical empiricists such as Karl Popper and Rudolph Carnap, narrowly defined the scientific inquiry as encompassing solely a set of what Hempel called "deductive nomological" explanations. The empiricist approach to accumulating scientific knowledge involves the use of deductive logic to move from premises based on empirical generalization to an observational conclusion, such as an explanation of a recurring event that enables a prediction of its recurrence. Such observational predictions are testable, and testing can directly verify or falsify the prediction. Using the same illustrative approach as adopted in Exhibit 2-1, Exhibit 2-2 depicts the "empiricist" approach to science.

The "testability" prong of the *Daubert* approach is a core feature of the empiricist critique. Unfortunately, most philosophers of science believe it goes too far and throws the baby out with the bathwater. As many scientists will admit, there is "no exact way

	Empirical Knowledge
Observational Knowledge	x ⟶ y
Theoretical Analysis	

EXHIBIT 2-2   The "Empiricist" Approach to Science

to define anything outside pure mathematics and logic, and even there some basic terms have extremely shaggy edges.[7] For example, under certain conditions, such as high speeds, Newton's laws no longer apply. Yet such observations typically result in modifications and a theory of broader scope (in Newton's case the theory of relativity), not complete rejection of the underlying theory because it failed an empirical test. Results of experiments inconsistent with atomic theory have led to postulation of new particles, not rejection of the entire atomic theory. Dark matter is the result of observational anomalies in astronomy, not theoretical rejection. Causation itself is surprisingly vague; the modern liability expert defines cause by what courts think they can control, resulting in something that has "little to do with scientific fact and much to do with society, culture, and legal will. Much like the law itself, one is told."[8]

Although the testability prong of *Daubert* does appear to accomplish the task of eliminating religious types of thought from the courtroom, the test still is both overinclusive and underinclusive. It is overinclusive because the testability prong alone would not exclude mysticism, the expert whose opinion is based on "experience" but not grounded in particulars. It is underinclusive because scientific theory, particularly in such social sciences as economics and finance, cannot strictly meet the empiricist criteria. Exhibit 2-3 illustrates the complicated nature of scientific theory.

In science, a complex interaction exists between the observational and the theoretical. Theories are modified in response to testing. Testing often cannot reach core concepts of a theory, but is instead performed on a theory's implications.

The *Daubert* line of cases does not provide a philosophical justification for the assumption that the empiricist approach produces inherently more reliable conclusions than other theories of knowledge. There seems to be a logical disconnect between testability and reliability; the mere ability to test a conclusion by reference to observable phenomena does not necessarily ensure that the resulting opinions will be more reliable than those opinions based on the more complex (and common) merger of theoretical and observable knowledge. As set forth in Exhibit 2-3, the scientific approach itself is a process involving comparison of theory and observable phenomena, with the two being interdependent elements of the overall scientific conclusion. For example, econometricians are extremely wary of what they call "data mining." Data mining involves

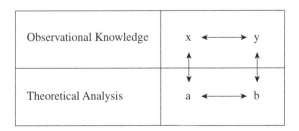

EXHIBIT 2-3   Scientific Theory

simply discovering the relationships between variables and then telling a story about these relationships ex post facto. This is an example of empiricism, even though the results are testable. In contrast, the scientific approach is to conceptually develop theoretical relationships, test these relationships, and adjust the theory when testing reveals flawed assumptions.

Damage experts in litigation rely on social science, specifically the fields of accounting, economics, and finance, for their opinions. Unlike natural science, social science is based on a body of core nonobservable concepts that are articulated into theories amenable to empirical verification. The core conceptual aspects of social science are not falsifiable by empirical testing. Although this is true of the natural sciences as well, it is true to a lesser extent, a fact that appears to be readily accepted by courts. The conceptual aspects of many natural sciences can be expressed in sets of equations that make them more, albeit not completely, subject to refutation. In economics, by contrast, there is no unifying set of equations, but instead a variety of the basic principles linked to models. The models themselves are testable, but empirical falsification of a model does not invalidate basic principles, because these principles are only loosely related to the models, mediated by layers of specific assumptions. For example, economics and finance are grounded in assumptions about human preferences that allow for the existence of a "utility function." A utility function can then be used to establish other concepts such as "demand" in economics or "risk aversion" in finance. These latter concepts are testable, but their utility foundations are not. To the extent that *Daubert* requires testability of basic theory, social science cannot clear the hurdle. Yet this certainly is not the result desired by the *Daubert* Court, particularly in light of *Kumho Tire*.

Another ambiguity in *Daubert* arises over how to apply the testability factor. Is testability applied to the theory, the expert's model, or is the expert's model applied to the facts of the case? The judicial answers to these questions are not clear or consistent. Moreover, use of the word *methodology* is not helpful. All of these levels or any subset thereof could be included in the term *methodology*.

Leaving aside the issue of the error rate, which again relates to testability, the *Daubert* factors pertaining to peer review and acceptance in the scientific community are helpful methods of ferreting out scientific thought from nonscientific knowledge within the natural sciences. Scientists appear to know science when they see it. Thomas Kuhn, in his book *The Structure of Scientific Revolutions*, is a dissenter in this regard, but today his relativist view is held by only a minority. Kuhn contended that acceptance by the community of scientists was what made a theory survive, not its ability to generate knowledge. Kuhn himself revised his radical view in a postscript, and few scientists hold such a skeptical view of science. Nonetheless, academics are well aware that peer review and professional acceptance are not foolproof criteria for good science, and Kuhn's criticism contains a kernel of truth, especially in the social sciences. For example, no one can argue persuasively that economic theory evolves solely through a series of falsifications. Instead, social science is closely tied to events outside of its discipline. In the economics profession, the Great Depression gave rise to Keynesianism and the inflation of the 1970s led to monetarism. Moreover, there are numerous examples of prominent theories that fail to yield empirically verifiable results yet survive and thrive in the social sciences. In finance, the capital asset pricing theory (CAPM) is an example. Although several prominent papers empirically have raised doubts about CAPM, it remains the leading theory of asset pricing in finance.[9] Accordingly, while reliance on peer review in the social sciences is important, if taken to extreme, it merely delegates issues of admissibility to a small group of journal referees (with possible political biases).

The *Kumho Tire* case and the commentary to Rule 702 provide a marked shift away from the *Daubert* factors to a much more workable basis for the Court's gatekeeper function. In *Kumho Tire*, the Supreme Court clarified that all expert testimony is admissible only if it is both relevant and reliable.[10] The criteria of reliability and relevance avoid the pitfalls of the strict four-factor *Daubert* approach and allow a plaintiff or defendant to challenge the viability of an opposing theory on scientific grounds in the specific context of the case in which it is being proffered. By "relevant," the Court meant that the expert opinion must "fit" the facts of the case and "aid the trier of fact."[11] An expert cannot simply ferret out facts from the record that are consistent with his or her opinion and ignore others. Nor will "canned" analysis be acceptable under Rule 702. As an example, in *Concord Boat Corp. v. Brunswick*,[12] the Eighth Circuit overturned a $44 million verdict on the grounds that the expert opinion should not have been admitted under *Daubert*. In part, the court concluded that the expert's opinion lacked relevance because the expert did not "segregate any lawful acts and unrelated market events . . . in order to enable the jury to assign damages only for illegal actions taken by [the defendant]."[13] Disaggregation is connected to relevance because without disaggregating damages, an expert opinion does not "aid the trier of fact." Following *Concord Boat* (which is in accord with a series of Ninth Circuit cases), experts are required on relevance grounds to segregate damages by each alleged cause. One lump-sum number for the amount of damages allegedly caused by a variety of conduct (potentially both legal and illegal acts) likely will not pass the relevance prong of Rule 702.

Rule 702 also requires that an expert opinion be reliable. Reliability is a difficult concept that combines the four *Daubert* factors with traditional concerns about speculation, lack of mitigation, and logical consistency of a damage analysis. The 2000 commentary to Rule 702 is very helpful in elucidating several factors that could be considered in a reliability analysis. We quote from the commentary at length:

> Courts both before and after *Daubert* have found other factors relevant in determining whether expert testimony is sufficiently reliable to be considered by the trier of fact. These factors include:
>
> (1) Whether experts are "proposing to testify about matters growing naturally and directly out of research they have conducted independent of the litigation, or whether they have developed their opinions expressly for purposes of testifying." *Daubert v. Merrell Dow Pharmaceuticals, Inc.*, 43 F.3d 1311, 1317 (9th Cir. 1995).

(2) Whether the expert has unjustifiably extrapolated from an accepted premise to an unfounded conclusion. *See General Elec. Co. v. Joiner,* 522 U.S. 136, 146 (1997) (noting that in some cases a trial court "may conclude that there is simply too great an analytical gap between the data and the opinion proffered).

(3) Whether the expert has adequately accounted for obvious alternative explanations. *See Claar v. Burlington N.R.R.,* 29 F.3d 499 (9th Cir. 1994) (testimony excluded where the expert failed to consider other obvious causes for the plaintiff's condition). *Compare Ambrosini v. Labarraque,* 101 F.3d 129 (D.C. Cir. 1996) (the possibility of some uneliminated causes presents a question of weight, so long as the most obvious causes have been considered and reasonably ruled out by the expert).

(4) Whether the expert "is being as careful as he would be in his regular professional work outside his paid litigation consulting." *Sheehan v. Daily Racing Form, Inc.,* 104 F.3d 940, 942 (7th Cir. 1997). *See Kumho Tire Co. v. Carmichael,* 119 S. Ct. 1167, 1176 (1999) (*Daubert* requires the trial court to assure itself that the expert "employs in the courtroom the same level of intellectual rigor that characterizes the practice of an expert in the relevant field").

(5) Whether the field of expertise claimed by the expert is known to reach reliable results for the type of opinion the expert would give. *See Kumho Tire Co. v. Carmichael,* 119 S. Ct. 1167, 1175 (1999) (*Daubert*'s general acceptance factor does not "help show that an expert's testimony is reliable where the discipline itself lacks reliability, as, for example, do theories grounded in any so-called generally accepted principles of astrology or necromancy."); *Moore v. Ashland Chemical, Inc.,* 151 F.3d 269 (5th Cir. 1998) (en banc) (clinical doctor was properly precluded from testifying to the toxicological cause of the plaintiff's respiratory problem, where the opinion was not sufficiently grounded in scientific methodology); *Sterling v. Velsicol Chem., Corp.,* 855 F.2d 1188 (6th Cir. 1988) (rejecting testimony based on "clinical ecology" as unfounded and unreliable).

All of these factors remain relevant to the determination of the reliability of expert testimony under the Rule as amended.[14]

In sum, the standards for admissibility of expert testimony have become more stringent. The Supreme Court's opinions in the *Daubert* trilogy marked a good first step toward the development of guidelines for admissibility, but in the long run the current guidelines will not be workable. However, the revisions to Rule 702 have made the inquiry more realistic and flexible. Both lawyers and experts must understand and meet the standards for admissibility as these standards continue to evolve.

DAMAGE ANALYSIS IN GENERAL IN LIGHT OF THE SUBSTANTIVE CASE LAW ON DAMAGES

An expert can be excluded under a *Daubert* inquiry or because of a more traditional failure to satisfy the proper case law standards for computing damages. The core principle of compensatory damages requires awarding the smallest monetary amount required to put the plaintiff in the pecuniary position he or she would have been in had the alleged "bad act" not occurred. In order to comport with this basic standard, the expert must have a good grasp of the plaintiff's actual economic situation. The expert must then construct the hypothetical "but for" world, that is, the hypothetical situation that the plaintiff would have been in had the defendant's bad conduct not happened.

$$\boxed{\text{Compensation}} \quad = \quad \boxed{\text{"But For" World}} \quad - \quad \boxed{\text{"Actual" World}}$$

The case law puts specific limits on how experts can construct the "but for" world, and violation of these limitations expose the expert's analysis to a possible *Daubert* challenge on reliability grounds. Being familiar with some of the judicial ground rules for damages calculations can be as important as having a working knowledge of the economic or financial basics necessary to reach a reliable conclusion. The most carefully constructed damage theory may become worthless if it does not comply with the following judicial principles.

The "But For" World Is Restricted to Constructions Based on Information Known with "Reasonable Certainty"

Regardless of the expert's intuition or the plaintiff's judgment about the "but for" world, the expert is limited to record evidence, or other evidence conforming to Rule 703, that is known with "reasonable certainty." For example, an expert cannot speculate about future growth rates without a sound basis in past performance, industry growth rates, or comparable business growth rates. A plaintiff's confidence that sales were about to increase ten-fold will not be adequate foundation for projecting lost profits. Absent use of information known with reasonable certainty, the damage analysis is speculative and subject to dismissal.

Bigelow v. RKO Productions[15]

Bigelow involved a suit for treble damages under the Sherman Antitrust Act by an independent movie theater against distributors of films and their affiliated theaters. The jury found that there had been an unlawful conspiracy among the distributors and their affiliated theaters to leave the independent exhibitor with nothing but second-run films. The jury awarded damages based on the discriminatory operation of the release system and the resulting decrease in the independent theaters' ticket sales. The Supreme Court held that it is proper for a jury to *infer* that the plaintiffs had been damaged based on certain circumstantial facts, including the defendants' wrongful acts, the tendency of the wrongful acts to injure plaintiff's business, and evidence of a decline in profits. The Court

(continues)

Bigelow v. RKO Productions (continued)

recognized that the bad acts themselves had made it impossible to ascertain precisely what profits would have been in the but-for world, but found that the jury could make a "just and reasonable estimate of the damage based on relevant data . . . [including] probable and inferential as well as . . . direct and positive proof."

The Court stated that a jury verdict cannot be based on "speculation or guesswork," but that comparison of plaintiff's receipts before and after the unlawful acts afforded an adequate basis for the jury's computation of the damages.

The "But For" World Must Have Been Foreseeable by the Parties

Courts limit the "but for" world to situations that either were foreseen by the parties in the lawsuit or would have been generally foreseeable at the time of the contract or the tort. Subsequent exotic or remote circumstances, even if known with reasonable certainty, cannot be used in constructing the "but for" world.

Hadley v. Baxendale[16]

Although *Hadley v. Baxendale* is a case from the English courts in the nineteenth century, it established a principle of damage calculation, the foreseeability requirement, that remains extremely important today. In *Hadley*, the owners of a flour mill sent a broken shaft to the defendant—a nineteenth century equivalent of a FedEx office—to be shipped for repairs. Due to some errors on the defendant's part, the shipment of the shaft was significantly delayed. The mill owner sued the shipper, seeking the lost profits that he incurred from shutting down his mill while waiting for the replacement part. The court held that damages should be restricted to foreseeable damages, i.e., those damages that the parties might reasonably anticipate at the time that they made the contract. In this case, the court found that the shipper could not have reasonably foreseen that a delay in shipping the part would force the miller to cease all business during the interim.

"[I]t is obvious that, in the great multitude of cases of millers sending off broken shafts to third persons by a carrier under ordinary circumstances, such consequences would not, in all probability, have occurred. . . . It follows, therefore, that the loss of profits here cannot reasonably be considered such a consequence of the breach of contract as could have been fairly and reasonably contemplated by both parties when they made this contact."

The "But For" World Must Be Constructed Using the "Least Cost Avoidance Principle"

When the expert constructs the "but for" world, he or she must construct it by taking into account how the plaintiff could have adjusted or did adjust to the changed circumstances. Optimizing behavior should be assumed on the part of the injured party. For example, in a case involving the failure to lend money, the "but for" world should assume that the plaintiff can borrow money at a higher rate from another source. The expert cannot skip to the assumption of devastating losses unless it can be demonstrated that no other lender was reasonably available. In short, irrational failures to mitigate and minimize damages will be held against the injured party when it comes time to calculate the appropriate remedy.

Only the "Bad Acts" of the Defendant Can Be Subtracted in Constructing the "But For" World

The defendant is responsible for only his or her bad acts. A bad act is a violation of the law, such as a breach of a contract or an infringement of a valid patent. The expert must construct the "but for" world by assuming that the defendant did not behave in the manner that caused the violation, but that all other factors remained constant. For example, an expert cannot construct the "but for" world under the assumption that if the defendant had not breached the contract he or she also would have entered and performed on a second contract. In addition, the "but for" world must acknowledge shortcomings in the profit structure of the plaintiff that cannot be attributed to the bad act of the defendant.

Risk and Reward Must be Matched

Because the violation virtually always occurs at a time earlier than the date of the damage analysis, the difficulty lies in determining how to measure the stream of benefits that would have occurred in the "but for" world after the date of the violation. This is an issue of significant controversy. It is clear that when a plaintiff is awarded damages, he or she is relieved of the risk of the receipt of the benefit stream. Hence, it is inappropriate to construct a "but for" world in which the plaintiff is compensated for risk that was reduced by the actions of the defendant. For example, suppose a business contracts to provide a particular asset (possibly a type of technology) to another business. The asset is never provided, and as a result, the purchaser loses a potentially valuable opportunity because of the absence of the asset. Sometime later, when liability issues are no longer in dispute, the expert is asked to calculate the damages resulting from the breach of the contractual promise to provide the asset several years earlier. Two important issues must be addressed. First, what would have been the plaintiff's position at the time of the bad act had the bad act not occurred (i.e., what was the value of the opportunity)? Second, how should the passage of time between when the wrong occurred and the resolution of the case be treated? A large body of economic literature addresses these issues.[17] The answers to both of these questions, in the authors' view, require the use of the real option theory.[18]

Unrealistic Reliance on Market Imperfections Should Be Avoided

To the extent that damages depend on significant market imperfections, such damages must be factually justified. In the absence of facts to the contrary, courts require that competitive responses in the "but for" world be taken into account. For example, it cannot be assumed that a firm in a competitive market would receive substantial economic rents for long periods without encouraging entry by other participants. Moreover, if the expert assumes that positive net present value opportunities exist in the "but for" world, this assumption must be justified in light of the available facts. As a last example, strong factual justifications must be present before damages can exceed a company's market cap or total value.

Courts have excluded from evidence damage analyses that fail to account for competitive responses. For example, the Ninth Circuit in *Murphy Tugboat Co. v. Crowley*[19] stated as follows:

> The expert witness's testimony as to Murphy's expected share in the large vessel and flat tow market segment depended upon an assumption that Red Stack would not cut its prices in reaction, even to a loss of over one-quarter of its prior share of . . . the market. . . . A reasonable jury could not, however, indulge in the assumption that a competitor would follow a course of behavior other than that which it believed would maximize its profits. . . . In a hypothetical economic construction, such as the one underlying Murphy's theory on lost past profits, economic rationality must be assumed for all competitors, absent the strongest evidence of chronic irrationality. Otherwise, it will be impossible to keep chronic speculation in check.

Other cases have reached similar conclusions.[20]

Where Possible, Damages Must Be Constructed Cause by Cause (Disaggregation)

A failure to disaggregate damages by the various causes at work can be fatal to an expert opinion. Experts must link, or segregate, their claimed damages according to the identified causal factors. Where an expert asserts an assortment of separate business practices or a variety of conduct as the proximate cause of the claimed damages, the expert also must particularize their damage proof to the fullest extent possible. In other words, specific damages must be attributed to particular causes.

The impetus for requiring disaggregation wherever possible is the scenario in which a finder of fact (either the judge or the jury) determines that only some of the challenged acts were illegal and holds that the remainder of the alleged conduct was lawful. Without particularized chains of cause and effect, the trier of fact is left with no rational basis for determining the amount by which to reduce the plaintiff's damages. Yet, if the damages are not reduced by some amount, they likely are insufficiently tied to the challenged conduct and fail to account for the effect of legitimate market competition. Courts want neither to give a windfall to plaintiffs damaged by legal conduct nor to force a defendant to "compensate" for more than the damages proximately caused by their illegal acts.

MCI Communications Corp. v. AT&T[21]

In *MCI*, the court held that plaintiff's damage theory failed because it did "not establish any variation on the outcome depending on which acts of AT&T were held to be legal and which illegal." At trial, the jury found that some of AT&T's conduct constituted legitimate competition. However, the jury was left without a means to adjust the amount of damages to reflect lawful competition, other than purely "guessing" at the appropriate reduction. Leaving the jury in such a position does not "assist the trier of fact" as required by Federal Rule of Evidence 702, and therefore the damage theory could not be admissible.

Damages Should Be Discounted to Account for Risk and the Time Value of Money

In some cases, an award of monetary damages should be adjusted to reflect the economic consequences of the alleged bad act. The actual calculations required to discount economic damages are discussed in Chapters 5 and 14. However, it is important for the attorney to understand when such a calculation is necessary or appropriate. Essentially, damages can be discounted for two reasons: First, where the plaintiff did not bear the risk related to the profits or opportunity lost as a result of a defendant's bad act; and second, where the damages resulting from the bad act are long-lasting.

The theory behind discounting damages in the first scenario is that one component of lost profits is a return for bearing risk. Where a plaintiff lost the opportunity to earn profits, he did not bear risk and should not receive a return as if he had borne the risk. Accordingly, lost profits can be discounted at a rate that includes a risk premium. This rationale might apply where a defendant is accused of breaching a commercial contract and that breach prevented the plaintiff from doing business.

The second reason to discount involves the time value of money. In accordance with well-established economic principles, long-lasting damages should be discounted to take into account the declining value of money over time. Damages can be long-lasting, either because they stem from a single wrongful act that had significant consequences or because they stem from a series of wrongful acts, each of which directly damaged the plaintiff for a short period. With the first type of bad act, the defendant may have destroyed an asset that would have yielded a stream of profits for many years. The damages would last as long as the stream of profits would have lasted, but they would need to be discounted each year back to the time of the wrongful act. Similarly, if the defendant's wrongful act resulted in delaying the plaintiff's opportunity to make profits, the lost profits attributable to the delay would be discounted for each period of delay. For example, a stream of lost profits resulting from one year's delay would be discounted back to the year when the wrongful act began to inflict damages; a stream of additional lost profits resulting from an 18-month delay also would be discounted back to the time of the bad act.

In determining the need to discount the damage award, the duration of the damages themselves is more important than the duration of the alleged wrongful act or acts. In essence, courts determine whether a particular set of damages is long-lasting by evaluating whether and how quickly the plaintiff's stream of profits could be restored by the cessation of the bad act.

These basic principles of damages apply in the context of each of the specific areas of IP law that we discuss in Chapters 6, 7, 10, 11, and 13. It is important to consider the basic tenets when evaluating your options for damage calculations. Some means of calculating damages may offer potentially greater recovery than others, but they would be harder to construct in a manner that coheres with the judicial rules for admissible damage theories previously discussed. Keep these basic principles of damage calculations in mind when evaluating the remedies available in particular areas of IP.

SUMMARY

This chapter examined the judicial standards that expert testimony must satisfy to be admissible for any purpose in court. Specifically, this chapter analyzed the means of establishing (or attacking) an expert's opinions as both reliable and relevant under the *Daubert* trilogy and the FRE. Additionally, the chapter introduced some general principles that apply to all damage theories and outlined their particular application in IP litigation. The information in this chapter provides a basic foundation for discussions of any potential damage theory and the evidence that will be necessary to support it.

ENDNOTES

[1] *See* Fed. R. Evid. 702 Advisory Committee Notes, 2000 Amendments.

[2] *Daubert v. Merrell Dow Pharms., Inc.,* 509 U.S. 579 (1993).

[3] *General Elec. Co. v. Joiner,* 522 U.S. 136 (1997).

[4] *Kumho Tire, Ltd. v. Carmichael,* 526 U.S. 137 (1999).

[5] *See Daubert,* 509 U.S. at 593–94.

[6] *See generally* David Willer and Judith Willer, *Systematic Empiricism: Critique of a Pseudoscience,* Englewood Cliffs, N.J.: Prentice-Hall (1973).

[7] Martin Gardner, *Science: Good, Bad and Bogus,* Buffalo, NY: Prometheus Books (1989), xii.

[8] Peter W. Huber, *Galileo's Revenge: Junk Science in the Courtroom,* New York: Basic Books (1989), at 215–16.

[9] *See* Richard Roll, *A Critique of the Asset Pricing Theory's Tests,* J. Fin. Econ. 4 (1977); Eugene Fama and Kenneth French, *The Cross-Section of Expected Stock Returns,* J. Fin. 427 (1992).

[10] *See Kumho Tire,* 526 U.S. at 150–51.

[11] *See id.*

[12] 207 F.3d 1039 (8th Cir. 2000).

[13] *Id.* at 1055.

[14] Fed. R. Evid. 702 Advisory Committee Notes, 2000 Amendments.

[15] *Bigelow v. RKO Prods.,* 327 U.S. 251 (1946).

[16] *Hadley v. Baxendale,* 9 Ex. 341, 354, 156 Eng. Rep. 145, 151 (1854).

[17] Franklin Fisher and R. Craig Romaine, *Janis Joplin's Yearbook and the Theory of Damages,* 5 J. Acct., Aud. Fin. 145 (1990). *See, e.g.,* William Tye, Stephen Kabor, and A. Lawrence Kolbe, *How to Value a Lost Opportunity from Market Foreclosure,* 12 Res. L. Econ. 83 (1995); Konrad Bonsack, *Damages Assessment, Janis Joplin's Yearbook, and the Pie-Powder Court,* 13 Geo. Mason U.L. Rev. 1 (1990); Tyler Bowles and W. Chris Lewis, *Unsettled Issues in Measuring Lost Profits,* 9 J. Legal Econ. 19 (2000); James Patell, Roman Weil, and Mark Wolfsen, *Accumulating Damages in Litigation: The Roles of Uncertainty and Interest Rates,* 11 J. of Legal Studies 341 (1982); R. F. Lanzillotti and A.K. Esquibel, *Measuring Damages in Commercial Litigation: Present Value of Lost Opportunities,* S.J. Acct., Aud. Fin. 125 (1990); Kenneth Kolaski and Mark Kuga, *Measuring Commercial Damages Via Lost Profits or Loss or Business: Are These Measures Redundant or Distinguishable?* 18 J.L. Com. 1 (1998); John D. Taurman and Jeffrey C. Bodington, *Measuring Damage to a Firm's Profitability: Ex Ante or Ex Post,* 37 Antitrust Bull. 57 (1992); Andrew Simmonds, *Indirect Causation: A Reminder from the Biblical Goring Ox Rule for Fraud on the Market Securities Litigation,* 88 Ky. L.J. 641 (1999–2000); Janet Kiholm Smith, *Reference Guide on the Estimation of Economic Losses: The Economic Approach to Evaluating Damage Awards,* 36 Jurimetrics J. 217 (1996); Robert Fuhrman, *A Discussion of Technical Problems with EPA's Ben Model,* 1 Envtl. Law 561 (1995).

[18] This issue is beyond the scope of this book, but the authors plan to address it in some detail in the first supplement to this book.

[19] 658 F.2d 1256, 1262 (9th Cir. 1981) *cert. denied,* 455 U.S. 1018 (1982).

[20] *See, e.g. Park v. El Paso Bd. of Realtors,* 764 F.2d 1053 (5th Cir. 1985), *cert. denied,* 474 U.S. 1102 (1986); *Coleman Motor Co. v. Chrysler Corp.,* 525 F.2d 1338 (3rd Cir. 1975).

[21] 708 F.2d 1081, 1163 (7th Cir. 1982).

ADDITIONAL READING

Margaret A. Berger, *Procedural Paradigms for Applying the Daubert Test,* 78 Minnesota Law Review 1345 (June 1994).

Judge Harvey Brown, *Eight Gates for Expert Witnesses,* 36 Houston Law Review 743 (Fall 1999).

David L. Faigman et al., *How Good Is Good Enough? Expert Evidence Under Daubert and Kumho*, 50 Case Western Reserve Law Review 645 (2000).

Shubha Ghosh, *Fragmenting Knowledge, Misconstruing Rule 702: How Lower Courts Have Resolved the Problem of Technical and Other Specialized Knowledge in Daubert v. Merrell Dow Pharmaceuticals, Inc.*, 1 Journal of Intellectual Property 1 (Spring 1999).

Robert J. Goodwin, *The Hidden Significance of Kumho Tire Co. v. Carmichael: A Compass for Problems of Definition and Procedure Created by Daubert v. Merrell Dow Pharmaceuticals, Inc.*, 52 Baylor Law Review 603 (2000).

Michael H. Graham, *The Expert Witness Predicament: Determining "Reliable" Under the Gatekeeping Test of Daubert, Kumho, and Proposed Amended Rule 702 of the Federal Rules of Evidence*, 54 University of Miami Law Review 317 (2000).

D. Bruce Johnsen, *Daubert, The Scientific Method, and Economic Expert Testimony*, 9 Kansas Journal of Law & Public Policy 149 (1999).

Joseph A. Kuiper, *The Courts, Daubert, and Willingness-to-Pay: The Doubtful Future of Hedonic Damages Testimony Under the Federal Rules of Evidence*, University of Illinois Law Review 1197 (1996).

Mark Lewis and Mark Kitrick, *Kumho Tire v. Carmichael: Blowout From the Over-inflation of* Daubert *v. Merrell Dow Pharmaceuticals*, 31 University of Toledo Law Review 79 (Fall 1999).

Robert F. Reilly, *Implications of Recent Daubert-Related Decisions on Valuation Expert Testimony*, 18 American Bankruptcy Institute Journal 28 (June 1999).

Nicholas Targ and Elise Feldman, *Courting Science: Expert Testimony After Daubert and Carmichael*, 13 Natural Resources & Environment 507 (Spring 1999).

Jeanne Wiggins, *Kumho Tire Co. v. Carmichael: Daubert's Gatekeeping Method Expanded to Apply to All Expert Testimony*, 51 Mercer Law Review 1325 (2000).

David Willer and Judith Willer, *Systematic Empiricism: Critique of a Pseudoscience*, Englewood Cliffs, N.J.: Prentice-Hall (1973).

3

Introduction to the Economics
of Intellectual Property
Damage Calculations

Intellectual property (IP) damage analysis is significantly informed by the disciplines of industrial organization economics, law and economics, accounting, and the financial principles of valuation. Chapters 3, 4, and 5 address these topics. In particular, the legal framework for calculating damages in IP cases is remarkably amenable to economic and financial principles. Chapter 3 begins by developing the basic economics used in IP damage analysis. Chapters 4 and 5 address accounting and valuation principles.

A BRIEF REVIEW OF BASIC ECONOMICS

Assumptions are simply inescapable, in both economic and legal matters. "Economists make assumptions for the obvious reason that the world, viewed economically, is too complicated to understand without abstraction. . . . The art of economics is picking assumptions to better understand certain features of it, without inevitably causing those features to be unimportant ones."[1] If one were to summarize the foundations of micro-economics in the tersest fashion, one might focus on three assertions: (1) consumers maximize utility, (2) firms maximize profit, and (3) the market seeks equilibrium. The first assumption, that consumers maximize utility, is called consumer rationality, and it leads to the concept of the demand curve. The demand curve is simply a summary of the amounts of a product that consumers as a whole will be willing to purchase at different prices. In contrast, the supply curve describes how much output firms will produce as their output prices increase. This follows from the second assumption because firms produce the quantity of output that maximizes profit. Finally, market equilibrium is the point at which neither producers nor consumers have incentives to change prices or output. Clearly, microeconomic behavior is more complicated in the real world. The method used in economics is to first assume perfect markets and in that context model economic outcomes. Then, after studying perfect markets, assumptions are weakened and the impact of market imperfections are studied. The latter process has resulted in much of the useful economic theory for IP damage analysis.

Demand

Demand is essentially a multivariate relationship that depends not only on the price of the commodity in question, but also on the prices of other goods that may be substitutes or complements, the subjective tastes and preference of the individual consumers, their incomes, and a host of other variables. The demand function relates the quantity that consumers demand to these determining factors. A sample demand function can be expressed as:

$$Q = F\left(P_1, \overline{P}_2, \overline{I}, \overline{T}\right)$$

where

P₁ is the price of the commodity concerned

P₂ is the price of another commodity (constant)

I is the income of the consumer (constant)

T is the tastes and preferences of the consumer (constant)

When a demand function is plotted, as in Exhibit 3-1, it displays a negative slope implying that lower quantities are demanded at high prices and vice versa.

Supply

The supply function is also a multivariate function that depends on factors such as the market price of the commodity at issue; the prices of the labor, capital, and raw materials; the level of technology; the taxation or subsidy policy of the government; and so

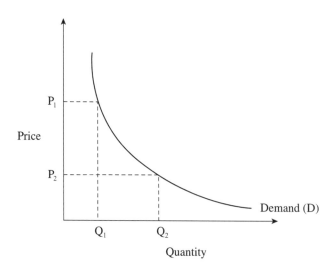

EXHIBIT 3-1   Demand Function

on. The supply curve illustrates how the quantity produced changes with the prices of the commodity in question. In general, producers will be willing to produce more when their output prices are higher because it increases their profits. Higher profits from the sale of one particular product encourage the firm to increase the output of this product, as opposed to other products or engaging in other activities. The supply curve is positively sloped, as shown in Exhibit 3-2. A simple supply function can be denoted as:

$$Q = G\left(P_1, \overline{K}, \overline{L}, \overline{R}, \overline{G}\right)$$

where

P_1 is the price of the commodity concerned
K is the amount of capital employed
L is the amount of labor employed
R is the amount of raw materials employed
G represents government taxes or subsidies

Market Equilibrium

Given a supply and a demand function, it becomes relatively simple to determine the level of output that would be steady state position for producers and consumers alike. Superimposing the two curves determines the equilibrium level of output and price Q* and P* (see Exhibit 3-3).

At price P*, the producers are willing to supply Q* amount of the commodity; likewise; the consumers are willing to pay P* for the same amount of the commodity, making P* the equilibrium price and Q* the equilibrium quantity. At P* and Q*, there is no incentive to change position. In contrast, at any P > P*, there will be more supply

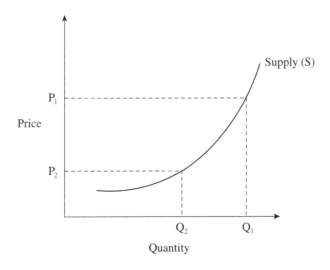

EXHIBIT 3-2   Supply Curve

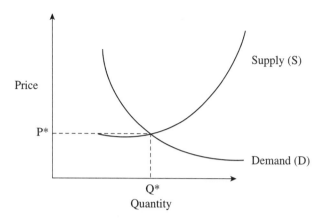

EXHIBIT 3-3   Market Equilibrium

than demand. This will cause inventories to build up, and firms will lower prices to sell their excess stock. Likewise, at P < P*, demand will exceed supply, and firms will bid up prices to achieve higher profits. As a result, only at P*, Q* is there no incentive to change price and output. We call this pair the equilibrium price and output. We now turn (or abruptly jump) from the very basic microeconomic model to more specialized analyses that are useful in IP damage cases. The reader who is not well versed in economics should be aware that we now intend to skip several layers of basic concepts to go directly to the operational economic principles useful for our topics.

THE INDUSTRIAL ORGANIZATION FOUNDATIONS OF INTELLECTUAL PROPERTY DAMAGES

Competent analysis of damages requires a working knowledge of industrial organization. Industrial organization is a branch of applied microeconomics that addresses such issues as the relationship between market structure, prices and output, market power, defining the relevant market, imperfect competition, and innovation. Numerous economics textbooks are available that set forth the basic concepts in this area. This chapter first focuses on a limited number of specific concepts that are critical for conducting damage analysis in an IP case.

The fundamental question in IP damage analysis is what would the "market" look like "but for" the infringement of a patent, copyright, trademark, or trade secret. Therefore, an important issue for analyses of lost profits, reasonable royalties, and the causation of infringer profits relates to how consumers react to the absence of the infringer's product or service in the market. Consumer reaction can be studied directly through econometric techniques when adequate data are available or more typically through inferences based on market analysis.

In this section, we focus on building the economic apparatus for market analysis. Economists have developed two exemplifying paradigm market structures used as a starting point by students of economics: perfect competition and monopoly. Readers who are unfamiliar with these basic economic tools are referred to the Additional Reading at the end of the chapter. Exhibit 3-4 illustrates both paradigm types of market structures.

Under perfect competition, each firm sets prices equal to marginal cost. This is evident in Exhibit 3-4, where P_c equals MC. This means that the firm achieves average profitability (sometimes referred to as the opportunity cost of capital because it is no more than the profits that could be achieved by the next most productive use of the capital). The conditions that support perfect competition are extreme and exacting. Formally, these conditions would be: (1) no differences among products; (2) infinitely many, infinitely small firms; (3) no barriers to entry; and (4) perfect consumer and producer information.

At the other extreme, in the absence of competition, a firm will set its price at the monopoly price. The monopoly price is always higher than the competitive price and occurs where marginal cost equals marginal revenue. Considering the difference between the monopoly model and the competitive model provides some flavor for how economics can be useful in calculating differences between an actual world and a "but for" world in, for example, a patent infringement case. Assume that a market consists of only two firms, the patent owner and the infringer. In competition, under fairly general assumptions, the patent owner would set price at P_c and obtain sales of Q_c. However, if the infringer did not exist, the patent owner would set price at P_M and sell Q_M. The lost profits arising from the difference between the actual world and the "but for" world in this simple case is the area B. Real-world situations are much more complex than this simple case. Nonetheless, if the economist has sufficient information, the equilibrium prices and quantities in the "but for" world can be calculated.

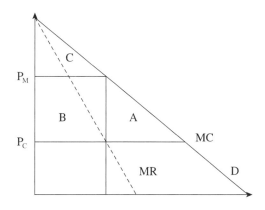

EXHIBIT 3-4   Paradigm Market Structures

In most situations, markets in which infringement occur consist of more than two competitive products. In these more typical situations, economists employ more complex oligopoly models to study the impact of hypothetical market changes arising from the removal of an infringing product from the market.

Models of competition and monopoly exhibit an important relationship between market power and elasticity of demand. Elasticity is the economist's measure of the responsiveness of output, or degree of consumer switching, to changes in price. Elasticity is a ratio of percentage changes, and therefore is unitless, so that its measure is not affected by the units of measure for prices or quantities. More formally:

$$\text{Elasticity} = \frac{\dfrac{\Delta Q}{Q}}{\dfrac{\Delta P}{P}} = \frac{\Delta Q}{\Delta P} \times \frac{P}{Q} = \frac{dQ}{dP} \times \frac{P}{Q}$$

The inverse slope of the demand curve is dQ/dP. The additional term P/Q indicates that elasticity typically changes at each point on the demand curve. As a firm raises its price, elasticity generally increases because other competing products appear more competitive to consumers. As a result, it would be incorrect to simplistically infer a lack of market power from the observation that consumers freely substitute between a variety of products.[2]

A monopolist who maximizes profit will raise its price until it faces sufficient restraints from substitute products to make further increases unprofitable. The monopolist maximizes profits by balancing the greater profit margin on all sales that results from raising its price against the potential lost sales due to consumers defecting to competing products because of the high price (this is precisely what elasticity measures). The firm can achieve its optimal profit maximizing price by setting its marginal revenue (the revenue it receives for an additional unit) equal to its marginal cost (the variable cost of producing the additional unit of output).

The marginal revenue that a firm receives can be written in terms of elasticity:

$$MR = \frac{d(PQ)}{dQ} = (P)\frac{dQ}{dQ} + (Q)\frac{dP}{dQ}$$

Algebraic manipulation of the right-hand side of the above equation yields:

$$= P\left(1 + \frac{Q}{P}\frac{dP}{dQ}\right)$$

$$= P\left(1 - \frac{1}{e}\right)$$

where "e" is the elasticity measure. When the firm attempts to set price optimally to maximize its profits, it will set marginal cost equal to marginal revenue:

$$MC = MR = P\left(1 - \frac{1}{e}\right)$$

Manipulating this equation leads to the following important relationship.[3]

$$\frac{P - MC}{P} = \frac{1}{e}$$

Accordingly, as the equation above demonstrates, there is a very strong general relationship between the optimal markup over cost (market power) and the inverse of the elasticity of demand facing the firm.

The economic concept of relevant market attempts to link the concepts of market power and market share. Market power is defined as the ability to profitably raise price above competitive levels (i.e., above marginal cost). Courts in antitrust cases have for several decades equated "monopoly" with large market shares. Indeed, to measure market share it is necessary to define the relevant market in which market share is measured. The necessity of defining the relevant market in turn begs the question of the theoretical basis for equating market share and market power. Two oligopoly models provide a direct link between market power and market share that does not depend on the existence of overt collusion. The theoretical establishment of this link provides the basis for defining the relevant market in a coherent fashion.

The two oligopoly models linking market share and market power are the dominant firm/fringe model and the Cournot model. For purposes of defining the relevant market, economists have focused largely on the Cournot model, and the Cournot model can be justified by its computational simplicity, a strong correspondence with the "Nash" equilibrium concept for noncooperative strategic interaction, and accepted intuition about concentrated market structures.[4] The Cournot model assumes that several large firms are involved in competitive rivalry and that little or no new entry exists. Each firm reacts to the output of its rivals, but under the simplifying assumption that each firm assumes that its own output change will not impact rivals' reactions. These assumptions result in a set of reactions between rivals that culminate in an equilibrium point that is an example of a "Nash equilibrium."

To show the relationship between market share and market power in the Cournot model, assume that n firms in an industry are engaged in Cournot rivalry. Each firm seeks to maximize its own profits, π_i, where profits are defined as the difference between revenue and costs. Revenue, in turn, is equal to the market price multiplied by firm i's output, and the cost also depends on the output of firm i:

$$\pi_i = P(Q) \, q_i - C_i(q_i)$$

Maximizing profits requires that the first derivative of the profit function is set equal to zero:

$$\frac{d\pi_i}{dq_i} = O = P + q_i\left(\frac{dP}{dQ}\right) - MC_i$$

Manipulating this result leads to the following:

$$MC_i = P\left[1 - \left(\frac{q_i}{Q}\right)\left(\frac{dP}{dQ}\right)\left(\frac{Q}{P}\right)\right]$$

This can be rewritten as:

$$MC = P - S_i\frac{P}{E}$$

This expression leads to the result that we seek:

$$\frac{P - MC}{P} = \frac{S_i}{e}$$

where S_i is the quantity market share of firm i. The Cournot assumptions therefore lead to a straightforward relationship between market power and market share parameterized by the inverse of the market elasticity.

To operationalize this relationship requires a definition of the relevant market that allows for comparability of market share based on measures of market power across industries. The 1992 Horizontal Merger Guidelines Definition promulgated by the Department of Justice and the Federal Trade Commission (the Guidelines) does precisely this by defining the relevant market in a manner that forces the analyst to select a market that leads to a common market elasticity among industries[5]:

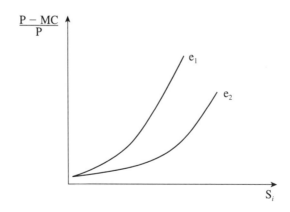

Put differently, the market definition test forces the analyst to choose a single market elasticity, such as e_2, for example, to facilitate cross-market comparisons of market power. With this background in mind, we now turn to the Guidelines' market test that incorporates an economically grounded method for selecting competing products for inclusion or exclusion in the relevant market. This will be a critical decision point in any lost profits analysis in an infringement case.

Relevant Markets

A rigorous and operational yet accessible approach to market definition appears in the 1994 Federal Trade Commission and Department of Justice Horizontal Merger Guidelines.

The stated purpose of the Guidelines is to identify economic dangers posed by mergers that may "create or enhance 'market power' or . . . facilitate its exercise."[6] "Market power" is defined as the ability to profitably raise price above competitive levels.[7] That "market power" could result either from an increased unilateral ability to raise price or from an industry structure more conducive to collusive activities. It has long been recognized that market power is constrained by the ability of customers to switch away from a price increase by buying different products, or the same products from more distant suppliers (demand substitution), or by buying from additional sellers attracted by the increased price (supply substitution). The Guidelines set out an integrated multistep procedure designed to analyze these issues.

As the first step in the analytical process designed to determine when market power may be created or enhanced by a proposed merger, the Guidelines call for defining the relevant markets. According to the guidelines, a market:

> is defined as a product or group of products and a geographic area in which it is sold such that a hypothetical, profit-maximizing firm, not subject to price regulations, that was the only present and future seller of those products in that area would impose a small but significant and nontransitory increase in price above prevailing or likely future levels.[8]

That is, the relevant market has both a geographic component and a product component. If, in a given geographic area, a sole provider of a particular product could profitably raise its price a "small but significant" amount (e.g., 5 percent), then that product is a relevant market for that geographic area.

The Narrowest Market Concept. The procedure set forth in the Guidelines is as follows: starting with a particular product of one of the merging firms, the analyst asks whether a hypothetical monopolist would find it profitable to increase prices of that product above the current levels by approximately 5 percent.[9] If the answer is yes, that product is deemed a relevant market for further consideration.[10] If the answer is no, the product, in and of itself, is deemed too narrow to constitute a relevant market, and the set of products is broadened to include the next-best set of substitutes and the process is repeated. The analyst inquires whether a sole provider of both the product and the next-best set of substitutes could profitably increase price by 5 percent. If the answer is yes, that set of products is deemed a relevant market. If the answer is no, the next-best set of substitutes is again added and the process is repeated.[11] Thus, a relevant product market is the *smallest* set of products for which a hypothetical monopolist would find it profitable to increase prices by 5 percent. The analysis continues until markets are delineated around each of the products of each of the merging firms. The two sets of product markets are then compared to determine whether the two merging firms are participants in any of the same product markets. If they are, the merger is deemed "horizontal," and analysis of any potential anticompetitive effects resulting from the merger continues.

Geographic markets are defined in an analogous manner. Beginning with the location of each merging firm, the analyst asks whether a sole provider of the relevant product could raise its price by 5 percent. If not, the geographic area is expanded to include the next-best substitute for production and the analysis is repeated.[12] This process continues until the test is satisfied. For any given merger, there can be multiple relevant product and geographic markets, each addressing a different possible exercise of market power.

Supply-Side Substitution. The Guidelines' mechanism for dealing with potential supply-side responses to an exercise of market power is also noteworthy. In defining the relevant product market, the Guidelines focus directly on demand-side substitution—the reaction of the consumer to an increase in price. Supply-side substitution responses to attempted exercises of market power—supplier reactions to price increases—are considered in separate sections of the Guidelines dealing with the identification of firms in the relevant market and the likelihood of new entry.[13] This is accomplished by including among the participants in the defined market not only those firms presently producing products in the relevant market but also those firms that are "uncommitted entrants."[14] Uncommitted entrants are firms that, in response to a 5 percent price increase and without the expenditure of significant sunk costs, would likely supply the relevant product within one year. The likelihood, timeliness, and sufficiency of longer-term supply responses (i.e., within two years) are addressed in the entry section of the Guidelines. This longer-term supply response is also considered because, as recognized in the Guidelines:

> A merger is not likely to create or enhance market power or to facilitate its exercise, if entry into the marketplace is so easy that market participants, after the merger, either collectively or unilaterally could not profitably maintain a price increase above premerger levels. Such entry likely will deter an anticompetitive merger in its incipiency, or deter or counteract the competitive effects of concern.[15]

Calculation of Market Shares. Once the firms that participate in the relevant markets have been identified, each firm's market share is calculated. Market shares typically are calculated as each firm's share of total sales or current capacity in the market. Capacity measures are recommended when goods are homogeneous. Sales are appropriate when products are subject to some differentiation by product characteristics, brand name, or other features.

The merger guidelines approach operationalizes results from the industrial organization literature that allow the economist to make inferences about consumer behavior where an infringer is to be removed from the market. For example, in such a case, one plausible assumption is that the infringer's sales would be distributed according to market share. It is critical when such an approach is used that the boundaries of the relevant market and the market shares in the market be determined properly.

Information Used to Implement the Merger Guidelines Market Test. The market test requires an assessment of consumer reaction to a small but significant increase in price of one or more products. Indirect information about such reactions typically are available from the party's documents and third-party sources. The Merger Guidelines themselves refer to four categories of information:

1. evidence that buyers have shifted or have considered shifting purchases between products in response to relative changes in price or other competitive variables;
2. evidence that sellers base business decisions on the prospect of buyer substitution between products in response to relative changes in price or other competitive variables;
3. the influence of downstream competition faced by buyers in their output markets; and
4. the timing and costs of switching products.[16]

In addition, other relevant information would include:

5. the parties' pricing documents describing how prices are set;
6. the parties' views of their competitors and the market;
7. third-party views of the market;
8. vendor's views of the market;
9. information concerning how the parties position their products in their advertising.

One important weakness of a market share approach to lost profits is that each product is treated in a binary "in or out" of the market fashion. Most markets consist of differentiated products, where some products are closer substitutes than others. Such differentiation can be inferred from the same types of information described above. To the degree that products are differentiated, close substitutes to the infringer's product likely would receive more sales that its market share if the infringer were eliminated; more distant substitutes would receive fewer sales. It is appropriate to gather as much information on product differentiation as possible even when adopting the market share approach to determine whether adjustments to market share are in order.

THE DIRECT APPROACH: ECONOMETRICS

When detailed data are available, market analysis can be performed directly by using econometrics to estimate a demand function. Empirically, a market demand function is generally estimated using techniques associated with regression analysis. Regression analysis, in its most common form, is referred to in the statistical vernacular as ordinary least squares (OLS), because operationally, regression minimizes the squares of the differences between the actual value and the "fitted" value of the variable that is being studied (the dependent variable). Regression analysis is a statistical method used to relate changes in a dependent variable Y to changes in other variables, known as independent, or explanatory, variables. Ordinary least squares sometimes can be useful in extrapolating trends or testing the significance of market structure changes (e.g., the presence of an infringing product).

In IP damage analysis, we frequently are concerned with estimating demand and elasticity of demand for market analysis. However, estimating demand functions requires econometric techniques and considerations that are significantly more sophisticated than OLS. In the case of a demand function (see preceding), the quantity demanded is estimated as a function of several variables, usually the following (we now switch notation slightly to remain consistent with econometrics textbooks):

$$Q_x = f\,(P_x, I, P_y)$$

where
Q_x = quantity demanded of good X
P_x = price of good X
I = income of consumers
P_y = vector of prices of related goods

Once we have a functional form of the model, the particular econometric technique that is appropriate for the model specified must be chosen. Unfortunately, the expert often has little or no a priori knowledge of the true functional form of the demand function. Consequently, the researcher must rely on experience, previous literature on the subject, market analyses, and attempts to use "flexible" specifications. Often, the results of regression analysis using a particular functional form specification will signal a mis-specification problem. For example, lack of statistical significance in all or a majority of explanatory variables, poor fit, or incorrect signs (e.g., negative signs on prices of well-established substitute goods) may indicate a problem with the functional form of the model. When this happens, the expert should estimate several models with various functional forms to arrive at a satisfactory solution. A good place to start is to examine the data using simple descriptive statistics. Although such data sometimes are regarded by theoreticians as operationally problematic, some data analysis is standard practice, because theory alone often cannot cull market inconsistencies that may be illuminated only by analysis of the actual data. Naturally, care must be taken in applying such techniques to ensure robustness of the results and to avoid violations of the basic assumptions underlying regression analysis.[17]

In practice, the simplest demand function to specify and estimate is the linear demand function. In this case, the term *linear* refers to linearity in the coefficients. The variables themselves are free to take any functional form (e.g., quadratic, natural log, inverse, etc.) specified by the researcher. Such a function would be represented as:

$$Q_x = \alpha + \beta P_x + \gamma I + \Sigma \lambda_y P_y + \varepsilon$$

where α, β, γ, and λ, are unknown parameters to be estimated and ε is a stochastic error term. Estimating a regression model can be accomplished using any readily available commercial statistical analysis software such as SAS®, Stata, E-Views, and so on, and even MS Excel. Statistical significance of these coefficient estimates is then performed using t-tests.[18]

Determining own-price, income, and cross-price elasticities is one important by-product of estimating a demand function. Own-price elasticity is defined as the percentage increase in demand of good X associated with a given percentage increase in the price of good X. Income elasticity is the percentage increase in the demand for commodity X associated with a given percentage increase in consumer income. Cross-price elasticity is the percentage increase in the demand for commodity X associated with a given percentage increase in the price of a related commodity. Elasticities can be easily calculated from the demand model specification as:

$$E_x = -(\Delta Q_x/\Delta P_x) \times P_x/Q_x \quad \text{(own-price elasticity)}$$
$$E_i = (I/Q_x) \times \gamma \quad \text{(income elasticity)}$$
$$E_{xy} = (P_y/Q_y) \times \lambda_y \quad \text{(cross-price elasticity)}[19]$$

Obviously, one problem associated with the linear demand model is that the elasticities are variable. That is, as described earlier, the elasticities are not constant across the demand curve, but instead vary along the demand curve. A more commonly used and more flexible specification is a nonlinear demand function, which has constant elasticity along the demand curve:

$$Q_x = \alpha P_x^{\beta} I^{\gamma} \Pi P_y^{\gamma}$$

Although this model is nonlinear in the coefficients, simple algebraic manipulation yields a linear model that can be estimated using linear techniques. Taking the natural log of both sides of the equation, one obtains:

$$\log Q_x = \log \alpha + \beta \log P_x + \gamma \log I + \lambda_y \log(\Sigma P_y) + \log \varepsilon$$

This model yields a constant elasticity estimate along the demand curve.

Unfortunately, the estimation of a market demand function is not resolved once an appropriate functional form is chosen. The more serious empirical problem of simultaneity arises with such market demand functions. As in many significant economic models, a simultaneous relationship exists between the supply and demand variables in the model. To illustrate the problem, consider the linear model equation previously shown. We hypothesized that the price of good X influences its demand, but we also know that the quantity demanded of a good also influences its price. The question that naturally arises is: Which comes first? Does demand influence price first, or does price influence demand? The answer to this question is that both variables influence each other at the same time. That is, they are simultaneously determined, or in the parlance of econometrics, they are endogenous. Given the simultaneous relationship that defines them, endogenous variables must be modeled using systems of interdependent equations. Each endogenous variable is a function of other endogenous variables and exogenous variables (i.e., variables that are not simultaneously determined). To examine how feedback loops work within the entire model, the entire system must be considered together, rather than each equation separately. Consider, for example, the following system:

$$Q_x = \alpha + \beta P_x + \gamma I + \Sigma \lambda_y P_y + \varepsilon_1$$
$$P_x = \phi + \varphi Q_x + \delta S_x + \Sigma \eta_y P_y + \varepsilon_2$$

where the variables are the same as defined previously, and S_x is a vector of supply-side effects, such as production costs. Note that in the first equation, the dependent variable is quantity, while price is included as an independent variable. In the second equation, price is explained as a function of quantity and a series of other exogenous variables.

Two-Stage Least Squares

The above demand system generates additional empirical concerns. The OLS method discussed previously can no longer be applied to such systems. Ordinary least squares regressions are predicated on the assumptions of the Gauss–Markov theorem, which states that, if its assumptions are satisfied, the OLS coefficients are the best linear unbiased estimates (BLUE) of the true population parameters. The above Equations violate one of these assumptions, that orthogonality must exist between the stochastic error term and the independent variables cannot be correlated with one another. That is, the error term and the independent variables must be uncorrelated. The reason for this assumption is that, if the error term is correlated with any independent variable in the model, the OLS coefficients will incorrectly attribute some of the effect of the error term to the independent variable(s) with which it is correlated. As a result, the OLS coefficients will not be unbiased (centered on the true value) and the BLUE property of Gauss–Markov will not apply. This phenomenon is commonly known as simultaneity equation bias. Unfortunately, this is precisely the problem that affects equations that are simultaneous in nature, such as the demand function. To see how this works, consider an increase in the error term ε_1 in the first equation above. If ε_1 increases, it will cause an increase in Q_x. If Q_x increases, it will cause an increase in P_x in the second equation. But, if P_x increases in the second equation, it will in turn effect an increase in Q_x in the first equation. Thus, the error term in the first equation is correlated with P_x in the same equation, generating biased coefficients and therefore violating the Gauss–Markov assumptions.

Although OLS is no longer an appropriate tool to estimate such simultaneous equation models, a variety of statistical tools have been developed that solve this problem. Most tools can be classified according to two principal methodologies: the generalized method of moments (GMM) and the method of maximum likelihood (ML). Each of these methods consists of a series of techniques that can be applied to systems of equations, and numerous econometrics textbooks describe how to employ the methods.

In practice, the most popular tool for dealing with simultaneous equation systems falls under the GMM methodology and is an instrumental variable technique known as two-stage least squares (2SLS or TSLS).[20] For the purposes of this discussion, 2SLS is used as the tool of choice.[21]

Two-stage least squares attempts to find a variable that is both uncorrelated with the error term and highly correlated with the dependent variable. Considering Equations described previously, 2SLS would substitute for P_x an *instrumental* variable that meets both of these conditions. Although such a variable may seem difficult to find, 2SLS provides a systematic method to accomplish the task. The steps are as follows:

1. *Identify the demand and supply functions.* The parameters of a demand system can be estimated only if the system is "identified." Identification refers to the ability to algebraically recover unique values of the parameters in question. In practice, identification requires a sufficient number of exogenous variables in each equation of the system. The reader is referred to the econometrics texts in the Additional Reading section for the appropriate tests for identification.

2. *Generate reduced-form equations.* Reduced-form equations express each endogenous variable as a function of the error term, exogenous variables, and possibly lagged endogenous variables. In this case, separate equations would be generated for Q_x and P_x.

3. *Perform OLS on the reduced-form equations.* An OLS equation is estimated for each endogenous variable that was included in the right-hand side of the system of equations as a function of the exogenous variables in the system. In our demand function example, a separate reduced-form regression would be run for Q_x and P_x.

4. *Substitute predicted values in the model and run OLS.* Each equation estimated in Step 3 will generate predicted values for Q_x and P_x that are orthogonal to the error terms. These predicted values now become instrumental variables and are substituted for the original endogenous variables. In the equations estimated in Step 4, predicted values would be generated for Q_x and P_x. These in turn would be used to reestimate the original system of equations.

Although 2SLS provides a solution for the endogeneity problem, it is by no means a complete cure. The effects of 2SLS are essentially that the t-tests are more reliable and the coefficient estimates are consistent and asymptotically unbiased in large samples. However, 2SLS estimates are still biased, particularly in small samples, and great care should be taken when drawing any statistical inferences in situations where the sample size used to estimate the system of equations is small.

The Almost Ideal Demand System (AIDS) Model

As mentioned previously, economic researchers have explored a variety of models to estimate own-price and cross-price elasticities in order to examine the effects of mergers. These techniques can be used for market analysis in IP damage cases. Linear, log-linear (constant-elasticity), and logit models are three useful techniques. Each of these approaches has a set of idiosyncratic characteristics that differentiate them according to the criteria sought by the expert: computational tractability, operational flexibility, ability to explain the data at hand, and intuitive appeal.

The AIDS model, originally proposed by Denton and Muellbauer (1980),[22] has gained a level of acceptance and popularity due to certain desirable characteristics and is useful in IP cases for its simplicity. The AIDS model specifies the share of a brand in a given market as a function of the prices of the other competing brands in the market. For example, the market share of Pepsi-Cola would be modeled as a function of the price of Coca-Cola, Mountain Dew, and other branded soda products. The model is sensitive to the market definitions assumed. The expert must be careful because omitting relevant variables, such as other products, can have a serious impact on the results.

The AIDS model specification for an *n*-good system is:

$$S_i = \alpha_i + \sum_{j=1}^{n} \beta_{ij} \ln p_i + \lambda \ln(X/P)$$

where

α_i = constant term in the ith equation
S_i = the market share of the ith brand
β_{ij} = coefficients for the jth brand in the ith equation
p_j = the price vector for the jth brand
λ_i = the parameter associated with the aggregate expenditure terms
X = industry (aggregate) expenditure
P = price index

In practice, the aggregate expenditure term can be omitted, leaving the equation as:

$$S_i = \alpha_i + \sum_{i=1}^{n} \beta_{ij} \ln p_j$$

Omitting this term requires the assumption of homotheticity, meaning that changes in the aggregate expenditure are hypothesized to have no influence on the size of the market shares themselves. More specifically, a change in industry expenditure is presumed to filter down to each brand in direct proportion to its market share, such that, while the quantities purchased of a particular brand may change, its individual market share will remain unaffected. In merger analysis, the constant terms fall out of the equation as well, because the metrics of interest are the market share changes created by the merger.

The AIDS model also requires that all market shares sum to 1. This is commonly referred to as the "adding up" property of the AIDS model. Since $\sum_{i=1}^{n} S_i = 1$, the N equations can be reduced to $N-1$, with prices expressed relative to the "numeraire" product in the omitted equation, because the last equation can be completely determined by subtracting the $N-1$ market shares from 1. The "adding up" property holds for any set of price changes, which in turn implies that:

$$\sum_{i=1}^{n} \beta_{ij} = 0 \text{ for any } j$$

That is, the own price coefficients β_{ij} (where $i = j$) and cross-price coefficients β_{ij} (where $i \neq j$) for any good j equal zero. This is known as the assumption of homogeneity implied by economic theory. That is, equal proportional changes in the prices of individual brands have no impact on their market share. Thus, in a market where homogeneity exists, a marketwide 5 percent price increase would leave the individual market shares of the brands operating in that market unaffected because relative prices would be unchanged. Another assumption of economic theory that is easily implemented within the AIDS model is symmetry (i.e., that $\beta_{ij} = \beta_{ji}$). That is, the effect of a change in brand j's price should influence brand i's market share by the same amount that a change in brand i's price will influence brand j's market share. It is important at this point not to confuse the β coefficients with the elasticities. The elasticities are computed from the β coefficients, as will be shown subsequently, but for now it is important to understand that these terms are not synonymous.

An attractive feature of the AIDS model is that the assumptions of homogeneity and symmetry can be directly tested within the model. Consider a hypothetical market with four brands. The AIDS model would specify the following equations, based on the assumptions described:

$$S_1 = \beta_{11} \ln(p_1) + \beta_{12} \ln(p_2) + \beta_{13} \ln(p_3) + \beta_{14} \ln(p_4)$$
$$S_2 = \beta_{21} \ln(p_1) + \beta_{22} \ln(p_2) + \beta_{23} \ln(p_3) + \beta_{24} \ln(p_4)$$
$$S_3 = \beta_{31} \ln(p_1) + \beta_{32} \ln(p_2) + \beta_{33} \ln(p_3) + \beta_{34} \ln(p_4)$$
$$S_4 = \beta_{41} \ln(p_1) + \beta_{42} \ln(p_2) + \beta_{43} \ln(p_3) + \beta_{44} \ln(p_4)$$

In this system, the β_{ij} (where $i = j$) indicate the effect of a change in an individuals brand's price on its market share. These coefficients are expected to be negative, because an increase in a brand's own price would be expected to decrease its market share, all other things being equal. The cross-price coefficients β_{ij} (where $i \neq j$) indicate the effects of changes in other brands' prices on an individual brand's market share. Conversely, these signs would be expected to be positive in the case of substitutes, because an increase in the price of competing brands would make a rival brand more attractive to consumers, thereby increasing its market share. In the model estimation, it is relatively straightforward to test the homogeneity and symmetry assumptions using a likelihood ratio test (LRT). Most statistical software packages, such as SAS®, perform such tests.

The system described reveals a complication of the AIDS model. In the four-brand market example, the model must estimate 16 parameters. Consider now a market with 100 brands. The model would then be required to estimate 10,000 parameters. That is, for n goods, the model estimates n^2 parameters: n own-price coefficients and $n(n - 1)$ cross-price coefficients. As n is increased, the computational tractability of the approach becomes an issue of concern, because a very large number of observations would be needed to ensure that the model retains sufficient degrees of freedom for estimation.[23] Furthermore, the more parameters estimated, the greater the probability of obtaining imprecise measurements of the coefficients or algebraic signs on the coefficients that are inconsistent with economic theory. Several methods of alleviating this problem can be used, among them is reducing the number of parameters estimated by specifying a model produced by a multilevel decision process.[24]

The estimated coefficients of an AIDS model are not elasticities, and we now turn to converting these coefficients to elasticities. The equation for the elasticities is:

$$\varepsilon = ((\beta_{ij} + \lambda_i(S_j - \lambda_j \ln (X/P)) \div S_i) - \delta_{ij}$$

where $\delta_{ij} = 1$ when $i = j$ and 0 otherwise and the rest of the variables are as defined previously.

The AIDS model has been used extensively in demand analysis, especially in merger simulation. Other econometric models exist, as mentioned previously, and often the choice of the model depends on the issue addressed by the researcher. For example, in the fields of transportation and environmental economics, the random utility model (RUM) developed by Daniel McFadden, whose work on the subject earned him the Nobel Prize in economics, has been widely used to estimate demand for modes of transport or recreation sites. Operational familiarity with several models is a valuable advantage to the researcher, as multiple arrows in the quiver can be used to address a wider array of economic issues.

This section does not contain a full discussion of econometrics. It is meant instead to alert experts and lawyers dealing with IP damages that economists have developed powerful statistical tools that can be drawn on in cases in which high-quality data are available.

THE LAW AND ECONOMICS OF BARGAINING

The economics of bargaining and the principles of game theory are foundational principles in the analysis of reasonable royalties. This is another topic we do not address, but again, we alert the expert to the existence of relevant literature. Courts have imposed the legal fiction that a reasonable royalty is the outcome of a hypothetical negotiation between the parties at the onset of infringement. The outcomes of negotiations are the focus of the economics of cooperative game theory.

In a cooperative game, both parties understand that exchange is mutually beneficial; that is, both parties benefit from cooperating with each other. Suppose Mark owns a car that he values at $1,000 and Rick values the same car at $2,000. Moving the resource (in this case the car) from Mark to Rick creates $1,000 of "surplus." The buyer will never pay more than the value he places on the resource (typically determined by the next-best substitute) and the seller will never accept less than his current value of the resource (typically determined by the next-best employment of the resource). The difference between these two limits is called the "bargaining range."

The parties typically will bargain over the transaction price within the bargaining range. The final price will determine how the surplus is distributed. As long as the game remains cooperative, economics has little to say on how the final negotiation ends, except that it will remain within the bargaining range. The final transaction price within the bargaining range depends on the art of bargaining and the parties' skill and ability at negotiating.[25]

THE ECONOMICS OF INTELLECTUAL PROPERTY

Patents

Economists have written extensively about the economics of patents. The originating assumption for economists is that ideas differ from physical property in several important respects. First, ideas are what economists call a *public good*. As Thomas Jefferson wrote, "He who receives an idea from me, receives instructions himself without lessening mine; as he who lights his taper at mine, receives light without darkening me." In contrast to physical property, where establishing property rights arguably increases the public welfare by creating incentives to maintain and efficiently use the property, *diffusion* of ideas among the members of society produces the greatest public benefit.

Second, it generally is the case that it is less costly to copy an idea than to develop the idea in the first instance. Think of reverse engineering a product or, more dramatically, downloading digital music or software files. This means that it frequently will be remarkably difficult to exclude others from using an idea.

Establishing property rights to IP is a way to provide a reward in exchange for developing new ideas. By allowing a patent owner to exclude others from using an idea, a patent owner can earn profits by exclusively selling products that incorporate the idea or by licensing the use of the idea to others. Thus, IP rights, such as patents, allow a return to innovation notwithstanding the ease of copying ideas.

There is a basic conflict between the benefits of diffusion of ideas and the incentives to create new ideas. Although the greatest public benefit would result from making ideas freely available to the public, this would provide little or no incentive to innovate because the private returns to innovation would be much less than the public benefit. Conversely, granting property rights to ideas provides incentives to develop new ideas, but limits the benefits from diffusion. The important public policy issues regarding patents involve a balancing of benefits from increased innovation against costs of interfering with the free use of ideas.

The patent system grants an exclusive right to exclude others from using an idea without permission for a specified period of time (now 20 years). After the patent has expired, the idea can be used by anybody. This represents a trade-off between providing incentives to develop technologies and promoting diffusion of ideas that are developed. In addition, since it is not necessary to provide rewards for all innovations, patent protection is limited to ideas that have utility, are previously unknown, and are nonobvious.

The fundamental point of IP rights is to create incentives for research and development (R&D). Studies by economists have established that technological progress is surprisingly critical to economic welfare. Economic welfare, for economists, thus can be increased two ways. First, "dynamic efficiency" refers to the increase in consumer welfare from innovation in new cost-reducing processes and new products. Second, "static efficiency" refers to the increased benefit that consumers obtain from lower prices and increased output. Until publication of the seminal papers by Robert Solow and Edward Dennison,[26] economists focused largely on static efficiency concerns. Solow and Dennison showed that approximately 68 to 81 percent of the growth in U.S. output has been a result of technological advance as opposed to increased labor and capital. This was a significant result that caused renewed interest among economists in the issue of innovation and its causes.

According to economists, the primary problem faced by potential innovators is that technical changes, in the form of new products and processes, are largely "public goods." This means, unlike with other forms of property, inventors and authors cannot prevent others from appropriating or using their inventions without the intervention of the legal system. For example, you can prevent others from using your car by locking it in your garage. You cannot prevent someone from copying software you have invented after sale without copyright protection. Mansfield, for example, studied the cost of imitating or copying inventions compared to the innovator's original costs. He found that an imitator's costs are approximately 65 percent of the innovator's costs. Moreover, imitation can occur quickly. Mansfield found that information about most R&D efforts are in the hands of rivals within 12 to 18 months of their invention, and the imitation of a new invention can occur within months.[27]

As a result, absent some legal protection for innovation, the incentives for investment in new technology would be severely dampened because inventors and authors would be unable to capture any of the economic benefits of their inventions.

Market Structure and Innovation. Economists have debated whether firms with market power or competitive firms will engage in more innovating activities. A number of models have been developed that indicate that the incentive to innovate is stronger under competition than under monopoly. These results are straightforward and easy to understand. The incentive for the monopoly firm to innovate is the additional profit gained from the innovation. The monopolist is already making profits in the preinnovation stage. Therefore, in the postinnovation stage, the additional profits are due to the cost savings themselves on the monopoly output. In contrast, the competitive firm begins from a situation of no economic profits. The innovation potentially provides the competitive firm with lower costs or greater market power. Thus, the additional profits from innovation are likely to be higher to the competitive firm than to the monopolist.

In contrast, Joseph Schumpeter[28] contended that innovation is likely to be larger for firms with market power than for competitive firms. This is because firms with large profits will have a greater ability to release free cash flow for use in R&D activities. Moreover, R&D activities may be subject to significant economies of scale. In this case, large firms will also be much more efficient at innovating.

The empirical evidence addressing this controversy is mixed. Some studies have found that spending on R&D and number of patents is positively related to firm size or concentration. Other studies have found more innovation among competitive firms. Several empirical studies have found an inverted U-shaped relationship between market concentration and spending on R&D activities. This result, although criticized by several other studies, suggests that R&D spending is discouraged by either too much or too little competition. Still other studies question the relationship between R&D and innovation and the relationship between R&D and economic growth.

Dynamic Versus Static Efficiency.   An issue that lies at the heart of the interplay between the IP laws and the antitrust laws is the apparent trade-off between incentives for dynamic efficiency and incentives for static efficiency.

The Trade-Off.   Ultimately, the goal of the IP laws can be viewed as maximizing the difference between the total social benefit from innovation less the total social cost of innovation. The benefit from innovation consists of lower cost processes and new or better products. The costs are twofold. First, expenditure on innovation consumes resources that could be put to other uses. Second, to the extent that the IP laws grant exclusive rights, static efficiency is reduced because consumers pay higher prices, and the market has less output. In addition, stringent IP laws can reduce incentives for follow-on improvement inventions.

Optimal Patent Life.   Nordhaus was one of the first economists to formally address this trade-off.[29] Nordhaus considered the issue of the optimal patent life, the one variable impacting the dynamic efficiency–static efficiency trade-off that Congress can control. Nordhaus attempted to find the optimal patent life by comparing the size of the lost consumer surplus due to the monopoly (the deadweight loss), the impact of its deferral measured by the discount rate, and the increasing R&D costs stimulated by the greater monopoly profits against the increasing amount of cost reduction (and hence profit and consumer surplus stimulated by the longer patent life). He found that, as the amount of induced cost reduction from innovation from longer patent life increases, society must wait longer to appropriate the full benefits of the innovation. At the same time, monopoly profits in the future are discounted more heavily, resulting in less innovation. The optimal length of the patent thus depends on several factors, including: (1) the elasticity of demand (the greater the demand elasticity, the greater the cost to society from the patent monopoly); (2) how easy it is to achieve the cost reduction (when bid cost reductions are easily obtained, society is less willing to sacrifice consumer surplus to obtain them); (3) the impact of the patent length on inventiveness; and (4) the discount rate.

The following equation relates these factors:

$$NSB(t) = [(CSm + \pi m) \int e^{-rs} ds + CS_c \int e^{-rs} ds] \, P(N) - M(N)$$

where
   CSm is consumer surplus with the patent
   πm is the patentor's profits
   CS_c is the competitive consumer surplus absent the patent
   $P(N)$ is the probability of an invention based on expenditure of N firms
   $M(N)$ is the cost of R&D by N firms

Economists believe that it is likely that the optimal patent length will differ by industry. For example, in less competitive markets, short patents may be best because deadweight loss can be large, whereas the opposite is true in more competitive markets. Because of the difficulty of obtaining the required information and the costs of non-uniformity in the patent system, policy has dictated an across-the-board 20-year patent length in most of the world.

Optimal Patent Breadth.   Unfortunately, little work has addressed the issue of optimal patent breadth. The breadth of patent protection is a key variable in creating incentives for the size and type of future innovations. Unlike patent length, the interpretation of the breadth of a patent claim is a matter of law determined by the federal courts. To understand the trade-off inherent in determining the breadth of a patent claim, consider two patents with the following independent claims:

PATENT 1	PATENT 2
Element *A*	Element *A*
Element *B*	Element *B*
Element *C*	Element *C*
	Element *D*

Patent 1 might be considered a basic research patent. Patent 2 is an improvement patent. Anyone practicing an invention that is covered by claims *A*, *B*, *C*, and *D* would be obligated to pay a royalty to the owner of patent 2 for the combination of elements *A*, *B*, *C*, and *D*, and to the owner of patent 1 for elements *A*, *B*, and *C*. As a result, the incentive to produce improvement or second-generation patents is dampened to the extent that patent 2 "reads on" patent 1. However, if the claims of patent 1 are interpreted narrowly, patent 2 is less likely to read on its claims and the incentives for follow-on research is increased, albeit at the expense of the incentive for basic research.

This problem may be solved privately through joint ventures and patent pools or cooperative research. However, such collaboration among competitors can raise other antitrust concerns.

The Economics of Copyrights

The economic literature on copyright protection has essentially focused on two issues. The first issue is whether copyright protection is really necessary to create sufficient incentives for authors. The second issue is an attempt to explain how copyright law has evolved by considering the trade-off between incentives for current increased production in artistic work and future increases in artistic work plus reductions in static output from the copyright monopoly.

Supreme Court Justice Stephen Breyer's article "The Uneasy Case for Copyright: A Study of Copyright in Books, Photocopies and Computer Programs" is a leading article that addresses the first issue. Justice Breyer contends that the case for copyright protection generally may not be as strong as conventional wisdom suggests. This is because market forces may be sufficient to create the necessary incentives for current investment by authors. If this is the case, the disincentives copyright protection creates for future expression and reductions in static efficiency could offset the social gains. Justice Breyer considers several market mechanisms that create incentives for authors. Among these incentives are the fact that there is a cost to copying, copying takes time, and the result may be a poor substitute. In such cases, the author's profits may not be significantly diluted by the copier. Moreover, in the case of textbooks, authors receive several external benefits, such as prestige, tenure, and higher salaries, which may alone create sufficient incentives for scholarly works. In addition, Justice Breyer suggests that potential textbook and software buyers could enter into executory contracts that could ensure an adequate return to the author.

Landes and Posner[30] have attempted the more comprehensive exercise of trying to interpret copyright law as optimally balancing two competing interests. On one side of the ledger are the incentives for the first generation of authors to create expressive works. On the other side of the balance are the difficulty copyright protection poses for future generations of authors who have less public domain art to build on, as well as the static efficiency costs (proxied by Landes and Posner using an output variable) from precluding consumers from purchasing less expensive unauthorized copies. After a formal presentation of the trade-off, Landes and Posner attempt to draw out several implications of their analysis:

- The rule that independent recreation is not actionable is explained by the fact that it would be too costly to search the prior art (as done after a patent application) because the copyrighted literature is too vast.

- Ideas are not protected because taking ideas out of the public domain would increase the costs of future authors (who would have to develop the idea and the expression) compared to the benefit of the output of first-generation authors.
- The rationale for giving authors a copyright on their derivative work is not to create more profits on the original work. Landes and Posner contend that derivative works typically are not close substitutes for original works (like a movie based on a book). Instead, they argue that the rights in the derivative work (like a translation) create incentives to create more derivative works. The right should be given to the original author to prevent delay in original publication until the derivative work is created. The derivative work's author (who is not the original author) also has a known person to go to for a license reducing transactions costs, and where no copyright exists on the original work, the derivative work's author can obtain protection.
- The case for fair use is based on transaction costs. Authors benefit by the publicity received from reviews, quotations, and parody. Works of art are often "experience goods" requiring "free samples." Without fair use rules, each such quotation would require a costly licensing negotiation that might discourage its publication.
- Tying the copyright duration to the death of the author makes tracing easier because all of an author's works lose protection at the same time.

The Economics of Trademarks

Economists view the analysis of trademarks as a branch of the economics of information. The development of economic thought concerning information can be traced to Stigler's pioneering work on the economics of information.[31] Stigler recognized that information about the price and quality characteristics of goods and services is a scarce resource. Information is demanded by consumers as an input to market decisions, and real resources must be expended to obtain such information. The necessary expenditure on such information is called "search costs." The purpose of a trademark is to reduce consumer search costs.

To perform this function, a trademark or a brand name must be exclusive. That is, the consumer must be confident that the name "McDonald's" applies only to a set of fast-food restaurants with particular characteristics that the consumer has sampled in the past.

Moreover, exclusive trademarks encourage investment in quality and implicit warranties by producers. A firm has an important stake in how consumers judge their brand and will invest resources in ensuring that consumers associate their brand with a high-quality product. Furthermore, firms recognize that high-quality products can be sold at higher prices. To the extent that a trademark is not exclusive or is inconsistent or ambiguous, the return on investment in brand quality is diluted and firms will have a weaker incentive to invest in quality and consistency.

There is a growing consensus among economists that strong brands lower search costs and do not create market power (like a patent or a copyright does). Trademark law appears to recognize this benefit and has evolved in the direction of protecting trademarks to the extent that they do not distort consumer information (deceptive marks) or impede competition by monopolizing the availability of similar marks for competitors (the ban on generic or descriptive marks without secondary meaning).[32]

The Economics of Trade Secrets

Very little has been written about the economics of trade secrets. One exception is the paper by Friedman, Landes, and Posner.[33] In that paper, the authors address two questions. First, why is a choice between patent and trade secret allowed? Second, why does trade secret law not protect against accidental disclosure or reverse engineering?

The Choice Between Patent Law and Trade Secret Law.   The answer to the first quesiton, according to Friedman, Landes, and Posner, is that inventors choose trade secret protection when they believe that the secret is worth less than the patent process costs (typically in the range of $10,000 to for a U.S. patent), the invention might lack the required novelty for patentability, or the secret is so valuable (like Coca-Cola's formula) that patent protection is insufficient in duration. The trade secret alternative may also have social benefits because it discourages excessive effort in a race to the patent office.

Why Does Trade Secret Law Only Prevent Improper Misappropriation?   There is no "finders keepers" rule with other types of personal property unless the property is abandoned. Friedman, Landes, and Posner suggest that the answer is that the level of protection is reciprocal. Every producer of business information is also a consumer of its competitors' information. The law strikes a balance by prohibiting only the most costly means of information retrieval. If innocent appropriation were illegal, like reverse engineering or public searches of data, then too much would have to be expended by companies seeking to conduct business but avoid lawsuits for inadvertent discoveries of others' trade secrets. Moreover, a firm would have no way of knowing whether it came across a trade secret. Refusal to enforce agreements not to disclose trade secrets, however, would cause the trade secret holders to take unduly expensive precautions.

The case for reverse engineering is more difficult. Friedman, Landes, and Posner argue that it would be too difficult to distinguish independent research from reverse engineering if reverse engineering were illegal.

In sum, economists not only have developed tools in many contexts that can be used in IP damage analysis, but also, to a more limited extent, they have directly attempted to explain IP law itself using economic precepts.

SUMMARY

This chapter focused on the basic economic tools needed for calculation of IP damages. One such tool that is critical is an understanding of how to define the relevant product market. When sufficient data are available, econometrics can be a helpful tool for obtaining the inputs to an IP damage analysis. This chapter further addressed how economists think about and understand IP. This latter discussion can help both lawyers and experts to structure their thinking about an IP case at its initial stages.

ENDNOTES

[1] A. Mitchell Polinsky, *An Introduction to Law and Economics*, 2nd ed., New York: Aspen Publishers (1989), 2, 4.

[2] Inferring lack of market power solely from evidence of substitution is known as the "cellophane trap."

[3] The algebra is:

$$MC = P - \frac{P}{e} \longrightarrow P - MC = \frac{P}{e}$$

[4] For a justification of the Cournot output and conjectural variation assumptions, *see* Carl Shapiro, "Theories of Oligopoly Behavior," *Handbook of Industrial Organization*, Vol. I, Schalensee and Willig, eds., Amsterdam: North Holland (1990), 329–414.

[5] The Guidelines represent an attempt to bring merger analysis under section 7 of the Clayton Act more in line with modern economic thinking. The Guidelines were authored in large part by economists employed at the antitrust enforcement agencies. *See* Gregory J. Werden, *Market Delineation and the Justice Department's Merger Guidelines*, Duke L.J. 514 (1983).

[6] *See* Guidelines § 0.1.

[7] *Id.*

[8] *Id.* § 2.0.

[9] In fact, the Guidelines use the term "small but significant and nontransitory" increase in price. We use 5 percent as a shorthand.

[10] *See* Guidelines § 1.11.

[11] *Id.*

[12] *Id.* § 1.21.

[13] *Id.* §§ 1.3 and 3.0.

[14] *Id.* § 1.32.

[15] *Id.* § 3.0.

[16] Merger Guidelines § 1.11.

[17] For a more rigorous discussion of such methods and their statistical implications, the expert is referred to W. H. Greene, *Econometric Analysis*, Englewood Cliffs, N.J.: Prentice-Hall (1999).

[18] T-tests are based on the assumption of asymptotic normality. In small samples, t-tests may be unreliable and should not be relied on as prima facie evidence of statistical significance.

[19] Cross-price elasticities can thus be estimated for each good in the vector P_y.

[20] Although some texts paraphrase two-stage least squares as TSLS, the reader should be aware of three-stage least squares, whose existence may cause some confusion when using the TSLS acronym.

[21] An alternative called limited information maximum likelihood (LIML) is not discussed here, but the reader is referred to W. H. Greene, *Econometric Analysis* (Upper Saddle River, N.J.: Prentice-Hall (1999)) for a rigorous discussion of the subject as well as a more in-depth treatment of 2SLS.

[22] *See* A. Deaton and J. Muellbauer, *An Almost Ideal Demand System*, Am. Econ. Rev. 70 (1981).

[23] Note that imposing constraints on the parameters, such as the homogeneity and symmetry properties implied by economic theory, and eliminating one equation by virtue of the "adding up" property, reduces the number of parameters to be estimated. The ease of imposing these parameter-saving constraints is another desirable feature of the AIDS formulation.

[24] *See* Daniel L. Rubinfeld, *Market Definition with Differentiated Products: The Post/Nabisco Cereal Merger,* 68 Antitrust Law J. 163, 173–176 (2000), for a discussion of this approach.

[25] Economists can say much more about the outcome of noncooperative negotiation. In these situations, game theory concepts apply. *See* Robert Gibbons, *Game Theory for Applied Economists*, Princeton, N.J.: Princeton University Press (1992).

[26] Robert M. Solow, *Technical Charge and the Aggregate Production Function,* 39 Rev. Econ Stat. 312 (1957); Edward Dennison, *Accounting for United States Economic Growth: 1929–1969*, Washington, D.C.: Brooking Institution (1974).

[27] Edwin Mansfield et al., *The Production and Application of New Industrial Technology*, New York: W. W. Norton (1977).

[28] Joseph Schumpeter, *The Theory of Economic Development,* Cambridge: Harvard University Press (1934).

[29] William Nordhaus, *An Economic Theory of Technological Change,* 59 Am. Econ. Rev. 18 (1969).

[30] W. Landes and R. Posner, *An Economic Analysis of Copyright Law,* 18 J. Legal Studies 3LS (1989).

[31] George S. Stigler, *The Economics of Information,* 69 J. Pol. Econ. 213 (1961).

[32] W. Landes and R. Posner, *The Economics of Trademark Law,* 78 Trademark Rep. 267 (1988), develop the analysis of the various aspects of trademark law based on the economics of information.

[33] Friedman, W. Landes, and R. Posner, *Some Economics of Trade Secret Law*, 5 Journal of Economic Perspectives 61 (1991).

ADDITIONAL READING

Roger L. Beck, *The Prospect Theory of the Patent System and Unproductive Competition*, 5 Research in Law & Economics 193 (1983).

Stanley M. Besen and Leo J. Raskind, *An Introduction to the Law and Economics of Intellectual Property*, 5 Journal of Economic Perspectives 3 (Winter 1991).

Richard Gilbert and Carl Shapiro, *Optimal Patent Length and Breadth*, 21 RAND Journal of Economics 106 (Spring 1990).

Paul Klemperer, *How Broad Should the Scope of Patent Protection Be?* 21 RAND Journal of Economics 113 (Spring 1990).

Janusz A. Ordover, *A Patent System for Both Diffusion and Exclusion*, 5 Journal of Economic Perspectives 43 (Winter 1991).

Suzanne Scotchmer, *Standing on the Shoulders of Giants: Cumulative Research and the Patent Law*, 5 Journal of Economic Perspectives 29 (Winter 1991).

David L. Kaserman and John W. Mayo, *Government and Business: The Economics of Antitrust and Regulation*, The Dryden Press (1995).

Luis M.B. Cabral, *Introduction to Industrial Organization*, Cambridge: The MIT Press (2000).

Mark Seidenfeld, *Microeconomic Predicates to Law and Economics*, Anderson Publishing Co. (1996).

Stephen Martin, *Industrial Economics: Economic Analysis and Public Policy*, 2nd ed., New York: Macmillan Publishing Company (1994).

Jeffrey L. Harrison, *Law and Economics: In a Nutshell*, New York: West Publishing Co. (1995).

Nicholas Mercuro and Steven G. Medema, *Economics and the Law: From Posner to Post-Modernism*, Princeton, N.J.: Princeton University Press (1997).

A. Mitchell Polinsky, *An Introduction to Law and Economics*, 2nd ed., Boston: Little, Brown (1989).

Eric A. Posner, general editor, *Chicago Lectures in Law and Economics*, New York: Foundation Press (2000).

Werner Z. Hirsch, *Law and Economics: An Introductory Analysis*, 3rd ed., San Diego: Academic Press (1999).

Robin Paul Malloy, *Law and Economics: A Comparative Approach to Theory and Practice*, New York: West Publishing Co. (1990).

Richard A. Posner, *Economic Analysis of Law*, 4th ed., Boston: Little, Brown (1992).

Robert Cooter and Thomas Ulen, *Law and Economics*, 3rd ed., Menlo Park: Addison-Wesley-Longman (2000).

Don E. Waldman and Elizabeth J. Jensen, *Industrial Organization: Theory and Practice*, 2nd ed., Boston: Addison-Wesley-Longman (2001).

William F. Shughart II, *The Organization of Industry*, Chicago: Richard D. Irwin (1990).

Stephen Martin, *Advanced Industrial Economics*, Oxford: Blackwell Publishers (1993).

F. M. Scherer and David Ross, *Industrial Market Structure and Economic Performance*, Boston: Houghton Mifflin (1990).

W. Kip Viscusi, John M. Vernon, and Joseph E. Harrington, Jr., *Economics of Regulation and Antitrust*, 3rd ed. Cambridge: The MIT Press (2000).

Dennis W. Carlton and Jeffrey M. Perloff, *Modern Industrial Organization*, 3rd ed., Menlo Park: Addison-Wesley-Longman (2000).

Lynne Pepall, Daniel J. Richards, and George Norman, *Industrial Organization: Contemporary Theory and Practice*, Cincinnati: South-Western College Publishing (1999).

Fred S. McChesney, *Economic Inputs, Legal Outputs: The Role of Economists in Modern Antitrust*, New York: John Wiley & Sons (1996, 1998).

Richard Schmalensee and Robert D. Willig, *Handbook of Industrial Organization*, Vol. I, Amsterdam: Elsevier Science Publishing Company (1989).

Jan Kmenta, *Elements of Econometrics*, Ann Arbor: University of Michigan Press (1997).

W. H. Greene, *Econometric Analysis*, Upper Saddle River, N.J., Prentice-Hall (1999).

G. S. Maddala, *Introduction to Econometrics*, New York: Macmillan (1992).

George C. Judge, R. Carter Hill, William E. Griffiths, Helmut Lütkepohl, and Tsoung-Chao Lee, *Introduction to the Theory and Practice of Econometrics*, New York: John Wiley & Sons (1988).

A. H. Studenmund, *Using Econometrics: A Practical Guide*, 4th ed., Boston: Addison-Wesley-Longman (2001).

4

Introduction to
Accounting Principles in
Intellectual Property Damages

In addition to economics, competent intellectual property (IP) analysis requires an understanding of both the IP owner's and the infringer's books and records. A background in accounting principles is required to accurately identify the financial information necessary for translating abstract economic theories into factually supported positions. Moreover, an understanding of the accounting system is needed for efficient and effective document discovery. While this book does not try to teach a complete accounting course, this chapter provides an overview that we believe will help the reader identify the most important records.

INTRODUCTION TO FINANCIAL STATEMENTS

Understanding the financial statements of the relevant companies in a case is critical to calculating damages. In most cases, the financial records of both parties must be scrutinized. A lost profits analysis, for example, requires an analysis of the plaintiff's financial statements (financials) to determine the profitability of the infringed technology. Any "unjust enrichment" or "reasonable royalty" calculation also requires an understanding of the defendant's financials. The documents sought through discovery will vary depending on the theory of damages. All too often, attorneys simply will ask the other side for the same documents that have been requested from their own client. Such overly simplistic thinking is likely to leave damage experts at a disadvantage. Furthermore, ineffective discovery can result in additional legal fees as subsequent requests are necessary to capture the information that should have been included in the initial set of discovery requests. Finally, because recent trends in the federal rules and most state rules favor limiting the total number of document requests allowed to each party, it is increasingly necessary for document requests to be efficient and gather the necessary information on the first try, where possible.

Accordingly, the purpose of this chapter is to sufficiently educate those with very little accounting knowledge to enable them to conduct effective discovery requests and to understand useful accounting techniques generally. Be aware that because the particular accounting data may vary greatly (even for businesses within the same industry), the formal assistance of an accountant is likely to be necessary, or at least very helpful, in completing discovery. The best financial discovery often is performed over at least two document requests. The first request usually should be relatively small, focusing on macro-type documents (e.g., tax returns, balance sheets, business plans, private placement memoranda, etc.). This request most often is made with a relatively large range of dates in mind, such as tax returns for the last five years. The purpose of the request is to obtain sufficient information about the opposing party to ensure that a second request is on point and will result in the best available useful evidence. The second document request generally is aimed at the most detailed data regarding the heart of the litigation. For example, a second request might ask for customer lists, invoices, account details, sales by product number, and so on. Ideally, the second request will provide the type of information that will allow the damage expert to use company-related documents rather than industry estimates in performing the analysis. Again, the actual documents requested will change from case to case, as will the ability to narrow the requests at an early stage.

Perhaps the biggest factor affecting this two-step discovery process is the method of accounting used by the company. There are two primary methods of accounting: (1) cash basis and (2) accrual basis. As discussed in the following section, the practitioner can make some assumptions about the opponents' accounting methodology based on generalizations that empirically function as good indicators. For example, the tax return of a business contains a box that is checked by the filer to indicate which method of accounting the taxpayer used. Thus, if you already have your opponent's tax return, you can definitively determine the methodology prior to using up any of your document requests. As a general rule, companies that are either large or publicly held use the accrual method. Small or private companies tend to operate on a cash basis.

CASH BASIS

The cash basis of accounting is employed by many small businesses in the United States. For example, many sole proprietors, multilevel marketers, and businesses operated as a second job use the cash method of accounting. The cash basis of accounting is similar to the way most individuals maintain their own checking account. On the day that a company pays a bill (or cuts a check), they record it. On the day the company actually deposits revenue, they record it. Cash accounting ignores checks and bills that have not yet arrived, even if the company knows that they are coming. The cash basis approach even ignores bills that have arrived but have not been paid, as well as checks that have been received but not deposited. This system of accounting is regarded as less sophisticated than the accrual method (discussed in the next section). The cash method is similar to an ostrich with its head in the sand, because cash basis companies act as if a bill that has not arrived does not exist. Thus, accounting records maintained on the cash basis of accounting are much less likely to accurately reflect the entire business situation than if the accrual method had been used. It is impossible to anticipate whether a cash basis company is in better or worse financial condition than is indicated by its financial statements than if the company used the accrual basis of accounting.

A simple example illustrates the difficulties associated in the cash basis methodology. Imagine that you are evaluating two businesses that are both using the cash basis of accounting. Assume that the date is December 31 and you are trying to determine which business is in better condition as of that date. The first company is a construction firm that has worked since last January 1 on a $5 million construction project. The company completed construction on December 29. During the last year (over the life of the project), the company paid out $4.5 million in expenses related to the project. The contract called for the company to be paid the final 20 percent of the $5 million within 30 days after completion of the project. The company received partial payments of $4 million during the year.

The second business is a construction company that also has worked since last January 1 on a $5 million construction project. This company is not yet finished with the project. In fact, the company expects to spend $500,000 in January to complete the project. This is in addition to the $4.6 million the company has already spent since it began working on the project. This company did manage to negotiate a better contract than the first company negotiated, as the second company has already received all of the $5 million.

Which company is in better financial condition? The first company is more financially sound. After all, the company spent a total of $4.5 million to complete the work, netting a $500,000 profit. The second company was paid $5 million on a project that will ultimately cost $5.1 million ($4.6 million + $500,000), resulting in a net loss of $100,000. However, the financial statements for the two firms might lead you to the opposite conclusion. For the year ending December 31, the first company will report only the $4 million of revenue *it received* and the $5 million worth of expenses *it has already paid*. Thus, the company showed a net *loss* of $1 million. In contrast, the second company reported the $5 million of revenue it received and the $4.6 million of expenses it paid. Thus, the second company showed a net *gain* of $400,000.

As this example illustrates, the practitioner cannot predict whether a company's use of the cash basis method of accounting will overstate or understate the company's financial position. Neither can the practitioner assume that the financial condition is in fact misstated. However, when a firm uses the cash basis of accounting, the practitioner can assume that he or she likely will need to spend time making sure he or she knows about revenues earned but not yet deposited and expenses incurred but not yet paid. The discovery requests should take this into account.

THE ACCRUAL METHOD

If the cash method is like an ostrich with its head in the sand, seeing neither approaching danger nor friends, the accrual method can be compared to Chicken Little's pessimistic outlook—"the sky is falling." The accrual method attempts to include all conceivable expenses while recognizing only the most conservative estimate of revenues. The theory behind the accrual method is based largely on the "matching principle." Accountants attempt to match revenues with the expenses incurred in generating those revenues, regardless of when the expenses are actually paid. An example illustrates the thought process. Imagine that a company engaged in oil and gas development plans to produce oil over the next five years. At the end of the five years, the company expects to pay $500,000 to repair the land to make it conform to environmental laws. Under the accrual method, the company would record $100,000 of environmental remediation expenses in each of the next five years. This treatment matches the expense with the revenue, even though the actual remediation payments will not be made until after the development, some five years from now.

The accrual method is the more commonly used method among large companies. In practice, many companies use the cash basis throughout the year until the last month of the reporting cycle. At that point, they make the accounting entries necessary to conform to the accrual method of accounting. Thus, the expert could receive two statements for the same company that are not prepared on a consistent basis. An indication of such a situation is an inventory balance that does not change throughout the year or a balance sheet that is void of accounts payable. When faced with such a situation, the damage expert must inquire into the "accounting cycle" to identify information that is fairly compared to the data in hand. The accounting cycle is discussed in more detail later in this chapter.

A significant advantage of analyzing a business that uses the accrual method is that there is a high likelihood that all expenses are identified. However, a disadvantage of the accrual method is that it is easy to overstate a company's *incremental costs*. As discussed in detail in Chapter 14, "incremental costs" are one of the primary tools used in preparing a damage analysis. This can be illustrated using the same oil and gas company described previously. Assume that the company is infringing protected technology that allows the company to get oil out of the ground for less money than it is able to without the technology. Further assume that the technology at issue does not affect the expected remediation costs. The expert must remove the remediation expense from his or her analysis to avoid overstating *incremental expenses*. In sum, when analyzing a cash basis firm, the practitioner must make sure that relevant expenses are not left out of the analysis. Conversely, when analyzing a firm that uses the accrual method, the expert must be certain not to include expenses that should be left out of the analysis.

THE FINANCIAL STATEMENTS

The first document request usually is more general in nature and broader in scope than subsequent document requests. The first request typically asks for the high-level financial statements for a period of time before the alleged infringement (often 3 to 5 years) through the date of the request. When accountants use the term *financial statements*, they typically are referring to a set of documents consisting of (1) income statement, (2) balance sheet, and (3) statement of cash flows. Each of the three types of documents is designed to serve a distinct purpose, and each can be useful for different aspects of the IP damage analysis.

THE INCOME STATEMENT—ALSO CALLED A "PROFIT/LOSS STATEMENT"

The income statement is called a "period" document because it relates to a specific period of time. Most companies prepare monthly, quarterly, and annual income statements. It is most common for the income statement to have a "Year to Date" column as well as a column that is for the same period of time during the previous year. Exhibit 4-1 is an example of an income statement for the hypothetical company ABC, Inc.

The income statement is the most useful document for determining the *incremental margin* on additional products sold. The incremental margin is the appropriate profit stream to use when determining a lost profit damage calculation. To obtain the incremental profit margin, one must begin with the income statement. The income statement lists the revenues and the expenses of the business. Revenues from the company's operating activities are listed at the top. Frequently, the revenues are "net," meaning net of returns. For example, in the sample income statement (Exhibit 4-1), "Net product sales" is listed. This amount is "net" of customer returns. In most cases, the difference between gross revenues (before returns) and net revenues (after returns) is insignificant. However, for certain industries, such as in the health care industry, the difference can be quite large. This is intuitive because hospitals typically charge much more than the insurance companies pay, which results in the large difference. For companies that are in an industry that usually does not have such a large difference, the presence of significant returns can be evidence of poor manufacturing quality.

Next, the cost of goods sold (COGS) is listed on the income statement. The COGS typically includes direct costs incurred in making the sale. For instance, COGS includes the material and the labor costs needed to make a widget. Of course, the applicable costs change from industry to industry. For instance, in a law firm, the COGS is the cost of the attorneys' labor. In contrast, an automated widget manufacturer may not include any labor costs in its COGS. The COGS is nearly always incremental and represents the typical starting point for the determination of the total incremental costs.

Next, the income statement typically lists the company's *operating expenses*. Operating expenses are necessary to conduct the business's operations. Typically, the operating expenses include some costs that are incremental and some that are not. By using a combination of statistical analysis and intuition, the practitioner can estimate the portion of operating expenses that are incremental. In other words, if the plaintiff had made the lost sale, they would have incurred the incremental costs.

The operating expenses commonly are followed on the income statement by the business's selling general and administrative (SG&A) expenses. Frequently, a portion of the selling costs are incremental (e.g., commissions, etc.). Conversely, general and administrative expenses consist of items such as the CEO's salary and usually are not incremental.

Generally, the remaining listed income or expenses are ignored as irrelevant to a damage calculation. These recorded but irrelevant items may include gains or losses from discontinued operations, other income/expense, and extraordinary income and expenses at the very bottom of the income statement. It is very rare that such amounts would be applicable to a damage analysis.

| | Years Ended December 31, | |
	2000	1999
REVENUES		
Net product sales	$ 5,930	$ 6,292
Research grants	198	—
Total revenues	$ 6,128	$ 6,292
COST OF GOODS SOLD	4,530	5,250
Profit from sales	$ 1,598	$ 1,042
OPERATING COSTS AND EXPENSES		
Selling, general, and administrative	$ 4,068	$ 5,320
Research and development	10,398	14,669
Total operating costs and expenses	$14,466	$19,989
Loss from operations	($12,868)	($18,947)
OTHER INCOME (EXPENSE)		
Interest income	$ 2,941	$ 901
Interest expense	(762)	(221)
Other income	—	—
Total other income (expense)	$ 2,179	$ 680
Net and other comprehensive loss	($10,689)	($18,267)
Basic and diluted net loss per share	($0.49)	($0.82)
Shares used in calculation of basic and diluted net loss per share	21,801	15,842

EXHIBIT 4-1   **Income Statement for ABC, Inc.**

BALANCE SHEET

The balance sheet represents a "snapshot" of a company's assets, liabilities, and equity as of a particular day. Although the specific items listed on the balance sheet differ from company to company, certain aspects are always the same; assets are always listed first, followed by liabilities, and finally equity. Within the assets, those that are most easily and quickly converted to cash are listed first. The amounts on the balance sheet are called "book value" and generally represent the amount spent on acquiring the account. Exhibit 4-2 represents a sample balance sheet for ABC, Inc.

	December 31,	
	2000	**1999**
ASSETS		
Current assets:		
Cash and cash equivalents	$ 14,153	$ 881
Short-term debt securities held to maturity		
and time deposits, partially restricted	109,089	20,630
Receivables	1,526	316
Note receivable from related party	278	278
Other current assets	502	547
Total Current Assets	$125,548	$22,652
Property and equipment	$ 9,961	$ 9,562
Accumulated depreciation	$ (8,938)	$ (8,452)
Net Fixed Assets	$ 1,023	$ 1,110
Debt issuance costs	108	127
Long-term debt securities held to maturity	$ 12,343	
TOTAL ASSETS	$139,022	$23,889
LIABILITIES AND STOCKHOLDERS' EQUITY		
Current Liabilities	$ 1,082	$ 993
Accounts Payable	1,663	1,167
Accrued Liabilities	256	214
Total Current Liabilities	$ 3,001	$ 2,374
Convertible notes payable	$ 10,958	$10,215
Deferred revenue	130	25
Stockholders' equity		
Common stock, .001 par value, 50,000,000 shares		
authorized: issued and outstanding 27,352,000		
shares in 2000 and 17,503,000 shares in 1999	27	17
Additional paid-in capital	226,465	102,128
Accumulated deficit	(101,559)	(90,870)
Total Stockholders' Equity	$124,933	$11,275
TOTAL LIABILITIES AND		
STOCKHOLDERS' EQUITY	$139,022	$23,889

EXHIBIT 4-2   Sample Balance Sheet for ABC, Inc.

Assets

The entry titled "Total Current Assets" ($125,548 for ABC) represents the assets that the company expects to use over the next 12 months. The most common current assets are cash, accounts receivable, inventory, and prepaid assets. Often, the fair market value of current assets is very similar to their book value. An asset is considered "current" if it is likely to be used during the next year.

Fixed assets (here $1,023 for property, plant, and equipment) usually are listed next. Fixed assets consist of assets that are expected to remain in use for more than one year. Typical fixed assets include buildings, vehicles, property, and equipment. Additionally, purchased patents and goodwill are fixed assets. In fact, only *purchased* IP is listed. Internally developed IP, whether it be a patented process or copyrighted software code, is not typically reflected anywhere on the balance sheet. The fixed assets, including the IP, are recorded at their cost and depreciated over their useful life during subsequent periods.

Accumulated depreciation is a line item under fixed assets that *reduces* the book value of the fixed assets to reflect the wear and tear on the asset. The accumulated depreciation account is a negative amount within the fixed asset section of the balance sheet. At the bottom of the fixed asset section is a line item titled "Net Fixed Assets." The net fixed assets represent the cost of the assets "net" of depreciation. As each year passes, the fixed asset balance remains the same, the accumulated depreciation increases, and the net fixed assets decrease.

For instance, assume that a company buys a building for $600,000. Further assume that the company expects the building to be used for 30 years. The balance sheet will include a line item under fixed assets titled "Building" with a corresponding amount of $600,000. Each year $20,000 ($600,000 ÷ 30 years = $20,000/year) will be added to the accumulated depreciation account. Thus, in the first year the account balances are as follows:

Building	$600,000
Accumulated depreciation	($ 20,000)
Net fixed assets	$580,000

The second year would show account balances as follows:

Building	$600,000
Accumulated depreciation	($ 40,000)
Net fixed assets	$560,000

This process would be repeated until the 30th year when the accounts would be:

Building	$600,000
Accumulated depreciation	($600,000)
Net fixed assets	$ 0

Of course, real businesses typically have more than one fixed asset (i.e., buildings, delivery trucks, equipment, purchased patents, etc.). However, they usually have only one accumulated depreciation account. Thus, a more typical fixed asset account looks like the following:

Trucks	$ 120,000
Equipment	80,000
Building	600,000
Patents	500,000
Accumulated depreciation	(300,000)
Net fixed assets	$1,000,000

As opposed to current assets, there rarely is a close relationship between the book value of fixed assets and the fair market value of the fixed assets. The explanation for this observation is easy to understand. Recall the previous example. Over a 30-year period, it is likely that the fair market value of the building increases. Yet, after 30 years, the balance sheet shows net fixed assets of zero. It is precisely for this reason that the book value of assets is rarely used to value a business.

Liabilities

The liabilities of a company represent debts incurred to partially finance the purchase of the assets. Like the assets, liabilities are classified as either current (due within one year) ($3,001 for ABC) or long-term (due on a date later than one year from the balance sheet date) (for ABC, $10,958 plus $130 ($11,088 total)). Some of the borrowed amounts are via formal loans, whereas other borrowings are through more "informal" means. Generally, the formal loans are part of *long-term liabilities*, whereas the informal loans are part of the current liabilities. The formal loans typically are made to the company by banks via a note. The balance sheet typically lists the interest rate of the note and often the date on which it must be repaid to the bank. Informal loans consist of accrued expenses, accounts payable, and so on. These types of borrowings usually are interest-free and for a very short term. As can be surmised from the preceding explanation, the liabilities section of the balance sheet usually is very straightforward and easy to understand. There are, however, a couple of relevant exceptions.

Deferred Revenue.   Deferred revenue is a liability ($130 for ABC) that indicates that the company has received cash that it has not yet earned. This is not an uncommon occurrence. For example, assume that the construction company described previously had received 25 percent of the contract price as a down payment. The down payment would be recorded as deferred revenue until the construction company completed 25 percent of the work (at which point it would be revenue or sales). The deferred revenue account may be relevant to IP damage calculations. It is particularly relevant in disputes involving software companies. Many times, software companies receive cash before they deliver the software according to their contract. Since the proper accounting for such revenue is a complex portion of accounting rules, many companies that are not audited classify the amount as *revenue* when in fact it is *deferred revenue*. The result is that the company looks as if it has higher sales (revenue) than it actually does. It also appears to have less debt than it actually owes (because the deferred revenue is actually a debt).

Deferred Tax Liability.   Deferred tax liability results from legally deferring taxes. It arises as a result of a taxpayer taking advantage of the tax laws. Companies legally may use one method of accounting for tax treatment and another accounting method for their own financial reporting. The different methods may allow the company to pay less in taxes, resulting in a tax savings to the company. The tax savings are considered a liability, as the savings are only temporary and ultimately must be paid to the taxing authority. For instance, assume that a company depreciates $100,000 of equipment over a 10-year period ($10,000 per year). Further assume that the tax laws allow the company to depreciate the equipment over five years ($20,000 per year). In the first year, the tax return will show $10,000 less profit than the company's income statement shows. As a consequence, the taxes paid by the company will be smaller than if the company had paid taxes on the income in its income statement (because the profits are less). The savings are booked as a deferred tax liability. The company ultimately will pay the difference in taxes. Most valuation experts ignore this "liability."

Equity

The equity section is perhaps the most confusing portion of the balance sheet. The equity section is not related to the fair market value of a company. The equity on the balance sheet is referring to book equity, which is simply the difference between the total assets and the total liabilities. This amount often is much less than fair value. Perhaps the easiest way to gain a general understanding of the equity section of a balance sheet is to describe how it evolves over a company's lifetime. Imagine that a company is formed and has 100 shares with a par value of one dollar. Further assume that the company sells the shares to the original investors for $10 each for a total of $1,000. The equity section begins with such transactions. The first line item in the example reflects $100 for common stock. The amount is calculated as the par value times the number of shares ($1 × 100). The next line item is "paid-in capital." The paid-in capital amount is calculated as the difference between the original purchase price and the par value times the number of shares [(10 − 1) × 100 = 900].

Assume next that the company generated $200 of net income during the year and paid shareholders dividends of $100. The equity section would have increased by a total of $100. This amount reflects the increase from the net income ($200) less the amount paid out as dividends ($100). This discussion is intended to provide a very high level review of the equity section. It usually is not necessary to deal with the equity section during an IP analysis. Even if it were necessary to determine the true "equity" in a firm, the practitioner would use valuation techniques to calculate the value rather than use the equity section of the balance sheet.

CASH FLOW STATEMENT

The primary purpose of the cash flow statement is to provide information about a company's inflows and outflows of cash. This information can help project the future net cash flows of the company. Cash flows are derived through three types of business activities: cash flows from (used in) operating activities, cash flows from (used in) investing activities, and cash flows from (used in) financing activities. Additionally, the cash flow statement reports the effect of foreign exchange rates on the company as well as the increase or decrease in cash during the period and the noncash investing and financing activities. There are two formats in which cash flow information may be displayed: the direct method and the indirect method. Both methods compute and present the information pertaining to the investing and financing activities, but they differ in the approach used to calculate net cash flows from operating activities. More important, both methods result in providing the user with the same valuable information (e.g., where the cash went or came from).

An example of the indirect method for ABC, Inc. is shown in Exhibit 4-3.

For more detailed analysis on particular financial statements, it may be necessary to read accounting literature. As there is an enormous amount of it, the following section is intended to help the reader determine the best source of information.

THE ROLE OF STANDARDS IN FINANCIAL STATEMENTS

Over the years, the accounting profession has developed a structure of accounting practice standards to address the comparability of financial statements. The chief body of practice standards is a set of generally accepted accounting principles (GAAP), which is intended both to guide and to govern the preparation of financial statements. "Generally accepted" means either that an authoritative accounting rule-making body has established a principle of reporting or a principle has achieved general acceptance through practice and universal application.

Several major organizations are involved in the development of financial accounting standards in the United States. These organizations are:

- Securities and Exchange Commission (SEC)—the government body that regulates public companies
- American Institute of Certified Public Accountants (AICPA)—the entity that regulates and licenses accountants
- Financial Accounting Standards Board (FASB)—an organization that creates accounting policy (referred to as GAAP)
- Governmental Accounting Standards Board (GASB)—the body that governs governmental accounting

The SEC was created by the federal government in the 1930s as a direct result of the 1929 stock market crash, which was blamed partially on inadequate financial disclosure. The SEC is an independent regulatory agency of government. Companies issuing publicly traded stock or listed on stock exchanges are required to file annual audited reports with the SEC, and the SEC is charged with the responsibility of establishing the accounting practices and policies that the companies under its jurisdiction must follow. Initially, the SEC relied on the AICPA to create and enforce accounting standards. In response, the AICPA created the Committee on Accounting Procedure (CAP) in the 1930s to set reporting requirements. The CAP was replaced by the Accounting Principles Board (APB), which was then replaced by the FASB in the early 1970s. The upshot of all these bureaucratic transitions is that the FASB is the major operating organization of the standard-setting structure.

| | Years ended December 31, | | |
	2000	1999	1998
CASH FLOWS FROM OPERATING ACTIVITIES:			
Net loss	($10,689)	($13,017)	($ 8,104)
Adjustments to reconcile net loss to net cash used in operating activities:			
Depreciation and amortization	486	546	604
Amortization of premiums and discounts on investments	(15)	(725)	(819)
Amortization of debt issuance costs	19	—	—
Noncash interest expense on convertible notes payable	743	221	—
Stock compensation expense	59	760	124
(Gain)/loss on disposal of property and equipment		74	(128)
Changes in assets and liabilities:			
(Increase) decrease in receivables	(1,210)	(65)	38
(Increase) decrease in other current assets	45	(136)	(71)
Increase in accounts payable, accrued	—	—	—
Liabilities and accrued vacation	627	848	413
Increase in deferred rent	105	25	
Decrease in deferred revenue			(4,656)
Net cash used in operating activities	($ 9,830)	($11,469)	($12,599)

EXHIBIT 4-3   Indirect Method for ABC, Inc.

THE ACCOUNTING CYCLE

As discussed at the beginning of this chapter, the second, more detailed discovery request aims at obtaining very specific information necessary to make the most objective damage analysis possible. To make a pointed second request, it is important to understand the accounting cycle. The accounting cycle consists of the procedures that firms use to record transactions and ultimately prepare the financial statements. In other words, the accounting cycle contains the raw information that is summarized by the financial statements. Exhibit 4-4 illustrates the steps in the accounting cycle.

Each step in the accounting cycle contributes to the ultimate goal—-the generation of the financial statements. Accordingly, understanding the nature of the steps involved in the accounting cycle prepares the damage expert or attorney to go beyond the financial statements and address the underlying data with more precision.

Step 1: Identification and Measurement of Transactions or Events to Be Recorded

In the first step of the accounting cycle, events that change a firm's resources or obligations should be identified and relevant data about those events should be gathered. These

| | Years ended December 31, | | |
	2000	1999	1998
CASH FLOWS FROM INVESTING ACTIVITIES:			
Purchase of investments held to maturity and time deposits	($238,848)	($30,812)	($39,462)
Proceeds from maturity of investments held to maturity	127,852	27,903	47,355
Proceeds from sale of investments held to maturity	10,209		
Purchase of property and equipment	(399)	(246)	(857)
Proceeds from sale of property and equipment			209
Loan to related party	—	(125)	—
Net cash provided by (used in) investing activities	($101,186)	($ 3,280)	$ 7,245
CASH FLOWS FROM FINANCING ACTIVITIES:			
Net proceeds from issuance of common stock	$121,727	$ 5,146	$ 3,921
Net proceeds from issuance of convertible notes payable	—	9,873	—
Capital contribution	2,561	—	—
Net cash provided by financing activities	$124,288	$15,019	$ 3,921
Increase (decrease) in cash and cash equivalents	13,272	270	(1,433)
And cash equivalents at beginning of period	881	611	2,044
And cash equivalents at end of period	14,153	881	611

EXHIBIT 4-3 (continued)

types of events fall into two categories: (1) internal events that occur within the entity and do not involve external parties; and (2) external events that involve either interactions with a third party or environmental events that are beyond the control of the enterprise. Examples of internal events include the use of inventory for production and the recognition of depreciation and amortization of fixed assets. External events include losses caused by an earthquake or fire and changes in the price of a product bought or sold by the enterprise. All such events are referred to as transactions and often are accompanied by a "source document," which is important to the initial recording of transactions in a journal. A source document is the most detailed form of accounting record that exists. For instance, invoices, sales slips, check copies, bank slips, and contracts are all source documents. Other events, such as the accrual of interest, are not signaled by a new source document. For example, the source document for the accrual of interest typically is the original loan document. The objective of a firm's accountant is to accumulate and record as many events as possible that affect the financial position of the enterprise.

As an example of when the first step of the accounting cycle may be important to the discovery process, imagine a case in which the plaintiff alleges that the defendant misappropriated the plaintiff's trade secret, a secret formula for making incredibly tasty barbecue sauce. The source documents (in this case, invoices) could be used to show that the defendant had never purchased the secret ingredients for the sauce prior to the time of the alleged theft, but began buying the ingredients shortly thereafter. Accordingly, the source documents reflecting the external event commonly known as buying supplies could be used as evidence supporting the plaintiff's theory of misappropriation.

Step 2: Journalize Transactions and Events

The next step in this process measures and records the economic effect of the transactions. In other words, it reflects when an accountant actually wrote something down. The transactions are categorized and collected in "accounts." The seven major types of

Step 1	Identification and Measurement of Transactions or Events to Be Recorded
Step 2	Journalize Transactions and Events
Step 3	Posting from Journals to the Ledger
Step 4	Trial Balance Preparation
Step 5	Journalize and Post Adjusting Journal Entries
Step 6	Adjusted Trial Balance
Step 7	Financial Statement Preparation

EXHIBIT 4-4   Accounting Cycle Steps

accounts are assets, liabilities, owners' equity, revenue, expenses, gains, and losses. Transactions are recorded via "journal entries" that are kept in chronological order. Journal entries are recorded in "journals," usually an actual book or a computer file. Each journal entry includes the date, the account amounts, and a description of the transaction. A journal entry looks like this:

> Cash . . . 100
>> Accounts Receivable . . . 100
>> To record the collection of the Smith receivable

Accounting systems usually have two types of journals: general journals and specialized journals. General journals are used to record all of the journal entries. Specialized journals are used to summarize transactions with common characteristics. Specialized journals include cash receipts journals, sales journals, purchases journals, and cash payments journals.

To see the utility of journal entries, imagine a case in which a patent owner is claiming that its patent is very valuable. Assume that the patent owner purchased the patented technology around the time that infringement allegedly began. The defense could request the journal entry created when the plaintiff purchased the technology. The entry would reveal the fair market value (per the plaintiff) as of the date of the purchase. It would be difficult for the plaintiff to argue that the patent had more value at that time than was recorded in its journal entry.

Step 3: Posting from Journals to the Ledger

The next step in the accounting cycle is to transfer the transaction data from the journal to the general ledger. This process is called "posting." Posting reclassifies the data from the journal's chronological format to an account classification format in the ledger. This step creates a single place to find all of the transactions that took place in a similar account. An account is simply a detailed category of assets, liabilities, equity, revenue, or expenses. For example, "sales," "costs of goods sold," "auto expenses," "vehicles," and "accounts payable" might all be separate accounts in a general ledger.

General ledger information is most useful in situations such as the following scenario. Imagine a defendant who allegedly has violated a noncompete agreement with his former employer. The defendant's sales ledger would give a detail of sales (usually organized by customer name). The ledger could be used to identify the customers that were previously customers of his prior employer (the plaintiff).

Step 4: Trial Balance Preparation

Once the transaction entries have been recorded in the journals and posted to the ledger, an unadjusted trial balance is prepared. Despite its litigious-sounding name, the trial balance is a standard step in the accounting cycle that takes place regardless of whether the firm's legal department is particularly busy. The unadjusted trial balance lists all of the accounts and their totals in one document. Basically, the unadjusted trial balance is a more detailed version of the income statement and balance sheet.

An unadjusted trial balance could be used in a case in which the defendant is accused of selling infringing hardware and the defendant is known to sell noninfringing software as well as the allegedly infringing hardware. The trial balance will show the hardware sales independent of the software sales. In contrast, the income statement may simply lump all sales together, which would be less than helpful to the plaintiff's damage expert.

Step 5: Journalize and Post Adjusting Journal Entries

As discussed at the beginning of this chapter, many privately held firms use the cash method of accounting during the year but report their financials using the accrual method. At the end of the year, these firms convert from the cash basis to the accrual basis. This conversion is done by "adjusting journal entries." This step comes into play for a damage expert where it is necessary to compare a firm's financials in June (calculated on a cash basis) to its December financial statements (done on an accrual basis). In that case, the damage expert would want the adjusting entries in order to make a similar type of adjustment to the June financials. With the adjusting entries, the damage expert can reasonably compare the financial statements from the two periods. In other words, the journal entries reflecting the "adjustment" may be necessary to ensure that your damage calculations are not comparing apples to oranges.

Step 6: Adjusted Trial Balance

Once the adjusting journal entries are made, an adjusted trial balance is prepared. Thus, the adjusted trial balance is more detailed than the financial statements and represents accounts that are stated under the accrual method. This document should be requested whenever litigation requires a detailed summary under the accrual method of accounting.

Exhibit 4-5 depicts the six steps previously discussed, as laid out in a typical accounting document.

1. Under the column "Journal Entries," you can see the entries made to record six different sales. The entries are organized in the order in which the sales were made (Steps 1 and 2).
2. The next column, "General Ledger," lists all of the transactions, still in chronological order. However, all of the sales are in one place and all of the receivables are in another location (Step 3).
3. The "Sales Ledger" column sorts the sales by the type of sale. If the accounts receivable ledger were shown, it would sort the receivables by customer name (Step 3).

Journal Entries

Account Receivable—Williams		100	
	Hardware Sale (1)		100
Account Receivable—Mackenzie		100	
	Software Sale (2)		100
Account Receivable—Smith		200	
	Maintenance Sale (3)		200
Account Receivable—Kennedy		200	
	Hardware Sale (4)		200
Account Receivable—McNichols		300	
	Software Sale (5)		300
Account Receivable—Tatos		300	
	Maintenance Sale (6)		300

General Ledger			Sales Ledger		
Sales			**Sales**		
1	Hardware Sale	100	1	Hardware Sale	100
2	Software Sale	100	4	Hardware Sale	200
3	Maintenance Sale	200		Total Hardware Sales	300
4	Hardware Sale	200			
5	Software Sale	300	3	Maintenance Sale	200
6	Maintenance Sale	300	6	Maintenance Sale	300
	Total Sales			Total Maintenance Sales	500
Accounts Receivable					
1	Account Receivable—Williams	100	2	Software Sale	100
2	Account Receivable—Mackenzie	100	5	Software Sale	300
3	Account Receivable—Smith	200		Total Software Sales	400
4	Account Receivable—Kennedy	200			
5	Account Receivable—McNichols	300			
6	Account Receivable—Tatos	300			
	Total Account Receivable	1200			

(continues)

EXHIBIT 4-5   Accounting Documentation of Steps

4. The "Unadjusted Trial Balance" lists the totals from the Sales Ledger. It also has the total accounts receivable balance (Step 4).

5. The "Adjustments" column shows the adjustments necessary to make the financial statements conform to GAAP. In this case, it has been determined that the Smith receivable is bad debt. As such, it is necessary to reserve an amount in the account "Allowance for Doubtful Accounts." Note that the adjustment is in a similar form as the journal entry made to create the account receivable in the first place (Step 5).

6. The "Adjusted Trial Balance" reflects the trial balance after the adjusting journal entries have been made. Of course, for a real company, the sales and bad

Unadjusted Trial Balance		Adjustments		
Hardware Sale	300	Bad Debt Expense	200	
Maintenance Sale	500	Allowance for Doubtful Accounts		200
Software Sale	400			
Total Sales	1200	To reflect the bad debt of Smith		
Account Receivables	1200			

Adjusted Trial Balance		Financials	
		Income Statement	
Hardware Sale	300	Sales	1200
Maintenance Sale	500	Less: Bad Debt	−200
Software Sale	400		
Total Sales	1200	**Balance Sheet**	
		Accounts Receivable (net)	1000
Account Receivables	1200		
Allowance for D.A.	−200		
	1000		

EXHIBIT 4-5   (continued)

debt would be recorded on the income statement, whereas the accounts receivable and allowance for doubtful accounts would be recorded on the balance sheet (Step 6).

After completing the six steps, the financials are complete and need only to be prepared (Step 7). The "Financials" column reveals the information that became available via the first document request. Note that the accounts receivable balance is "net" of the allowance for doubtful accounts and that all sales are lumped together. While this type of consolidation makes it easier to read the financial statements, it often is too generic for an expert to use effectively in preparing a sophisticated damages report.

In summary, these seven steps constitute the portions of the accounting cycle that are most useful to damage experts. The steps typically are performed every fiscal period to prepare the financial statements.

ALL FINANCIAL STATEMENTS ARE NOT CREATED EQUAL

The problem with a good discovery request is that once made, the practitioner has to decipher the documents. The following section is intended to assist in that process. As it is typical to receive more than one document with the same information, one must be able to determine the best of those documents.

Unreliable financial statements result in a problematic basis for a damage calculation. Fortunately, accountants make it easy to determine the relative reliability of financial statements. Accountants include a written explanation of the work they have done with regard to preparing the financial statements. In that explanation, accountants indicate whether they have "compiled," "reviewed," or "audited" the financial statements. If there is no explanatory paragraph, it is likely that no independent accountant has done any work at all on the financials. In other words, if there is no written explanation, the financial statements are only as good as the ability of the firm's management.

Compiled Financial Statements

When a CPA "compiles" financial statements, he or she simply takes the information from the client and puts it into a conventional format. He or she does not do any work or opine on the appropriateness of the amounts within the categories.

Reviewed Financials Statements

When a CPA "reviews" financial statements, he or she performs a very limited set of analytical procedures. While reviewed financial statements are often reliable, they usually do not contain all of the information that is provided in audited financial statements.

Specifically, they do not contain all of the footnotes to the financials; these footnotes can be very significant to a damages analysis.

AUDITED FINANCIALS

Audited financial statements are the most reliable financial statements available. You can tell that an audit has been performed by the existence of an audit opinion. The audit opinion is in a letter format from the auditor and is attached to the front of the financial statements. There are two primary reasons an audit opinion is beneficial. First, the existence of an audit opinion means that the financial statements probably conform to GAAP. Second, auditors create documents that can be extremely useful in preparing a damage claim. To most effectively take advantage of audited financial statements, the practitioner should have a fundamental understanding of: (1) the significance of the dates identified in the audit report, (2) the different opinions issued by auditors, and (3) which documents created by auditors are the most useful for damage calculations.

SIGNIFICANT DATES IDENTIFIED IN THE REPORT

There are two dates contained within all audit opinions that are significant to the damage expert: (1) the report date and (2) the date of the opinion.

Report Date

The report date refers to the last day of the accounting period. After the company name, the heading of the financial statement says one of two things: either (1) the balance sheet states "As of December 31, 2002," indicating the date of the "snapshot"; or (2) the income statement and statement of cash flows state "For the Period Ending December 31, 2002," indicating that the document covers a specific period (usually one year). Thus, when making a discovery request for the income statement, the practitioner should request the "Income Statement for the Period Ending December 31, 2002." Conversely, when making a request for a balance sheet, the practitioner should ask for the "Balance Sheet as of December 31, 2002."

Date of the Opinion

The accounting firm that conducted the audit signs and dates the audit opinion. The date is sometimes useful in a damage case. For example, if the auditors are aware of a significant event that occurred after the report date but before the date of their opinion, they will disclose the event in the footnotes. The event is significant if it would reasonably be expected to affect the financial statements (i.e., a fire at the headquarters, a strike, a loss of financing, etc.). Imagine a situation in which the plaintiff claims that your client stole their trade secret on January 9. They claim that their business was totally destroyed as a result. Assume that their expert calculates damages based on the premise that the business was destroyed the day of the theft. However, the December 31 audit report (issued January 31) is done *without* a footnote regarding subsequent events. The lack of a significant event footnote about the theft is strong evidence that, as of January 31, the plaintiffs did not have reason to think that their business was destroyed.

DIFFERENT AUDIT OPINIONS

Nearly all audits result in the same type of opinion—an unqualified opinion. However, since there are various types of opinions, the practitioner should be aware of the different possible types. The following discussion outlines the main types of audit opinions.

Unqualified Opinion

An unqualified opinion, also called a "clean" opinion, is the most common opinion issued. A clean opinion generally means that the auditor believes that the financial statements are *materially* in compliance with GAAP. In other words, there may be *known* problems in the financial statements that are not material. "Material" generally is considered to be the amount that would influence a reasonable user of the financial statements. The amount that is considered "material" changes based on the size of the company. It is easy to appreciate why this is the case. A $500,000 overstatement of revenues in a company that has $1 billion in revenues is not likely to influence a user. However, a $500,000 overstatement of revenues in a company with $1 million of revenue is likely to be very "material" to the user.

Qualified Opinion

A qualified opinion is issued when the auditor does not believe that the financial statements conform to GAAP. It is rare for an auditor to issue a qualified opinion. While auditors often find portions of the financial statements that do not conform to GAAP, they typically bring the problem to management. Management then generally corrects the problem, allowing the auditor to issue a clean opinion.

Going-Concern Opinion

A going-concern opinion is issued when the auditor believes the company may not survive for one more year. It is somewhat common among businesses that, in fact, ultimately fail. Such an opinion often can be very useful to an attorney or an expert. Imagine that your client is sued for stealing a trade secret. Further assume that the plaintiff claims that the alleged theft caused his business to fail. As proof, the plaintiff points out the fact that the business failed within three months of the theft. The plaintiff also offers up the fact that the company had existed for 50 years prior to the theft as another indicator of the impact of the loss of the trade secret. However, the defense discovers that the trade secret allegedly was stolen nine months *after* the plaintiff's auditors issued a "going-concern" opinion. The existence of a "going-concern" opinion is very strong evidence that the company's failure was looming long before the alleged theft. The additional documents that would help demonstrate this defense are described in subsequent sections.

Scope Opinion

A scope opinion is another rare opinion. Generally, this opinion means that after considering the evidence provided, the auditor believes that the company's financial statements comply with GAAP. However, it also indicates that the auditor was not able to analyze everything it asked the client to provide (i.e., the auditor's scope was limited). A common scenario in which a scope opinion is issued involves a company that has been in existence for many years, but has never before had an audit. Such a client often has lost track of the documents needed by the auditor. As a result, the auditor must issue a "scope limitation."

While an opinion can be helpful on its own, the more likely benefit of audited financial statements is related to the documents that *must* be created during the course of the auditors completing their audit. The following section describes some of the most useful documents that are kept by the auditors. It should be noted that usually *only the auditors* keep a copy of these documents. Thus, it often is necessary to subpoena the auditors to obtain the desired documentation.

MANAGEMENT REPRESENTATION LETTER

Management often does not want to live with their previously audited financial statements during litigation. All auditors obtain a management representation letter (MRL) as part of their steps in completing the audit. In short, the MRL is a letter written by the management to the auditors telling the auditors that management has disclosed everything that is *material* to readers of the financial statements. In the course of conducting an audit, the company's management typically represents the following facts:

1. Management has told the auditors the truth.
2. Management has told the auditors about all transactions that have occurred.
3. Management has told the auditors about all existing liabilities (including lawsuits).
4. There have been no significant events that have happened during the time period between the report date and the opinion date.

5. Management is in compliance with laws, debt covenants, etc.
6. The financial information is the responsibility of the company's management.

The actual letters include many more representations. However, the significance of all the representations is that the MRL makes it very difficult for management not to take responsibility for the accounting and financial statements contained within the audited statements.

SUMMARY OF PROPOSED ADJUSTMENTS

Although the name of the actual worksheet varies from firm to firm, all audit firms maintain the same type of information regarding their proposed adjustments. The proposed adjustments schedule is a list of all adjustments that were proposed by the auditors. In other words, the schedule discusses all of the problems the auditors found during the course of conducting the audit. When auditors find such problems, they discuss them with management. The typical schedule of proposed adjustments also discusses management's response to the auditor's proposed correcting journal entries. Finally, the schedule details the resolution. The schedule is the fastest mechanism by which to identify the company's accounting weak spots. Since the worksheet does not have a standard name, a subpoena should request something like, "Provide all work papers depicting proposed journal entries to the financial statements of ABC Company for the period ending December 31, 2002, including adjustments, reclassifications, and/or eliminating entries."

ADJUSTED TRIAL BALANCE

An adjusted trial balance is a document that all auditors will keep and most of their clients will keep as well. As discussed earlier in this chapter, the adjusted trial balance provides a summary of the accounts that is more detailed than the financial statements. The adjusted trial balance is to an accountant what the Rosetta stone is to a historian. This is because the financial statements employ large general categories, whereas the adjusted trial balance uses detailed summaries. Most auditors use the term *adjusted trial balance*, so discovery requests should be able to target the desired documents fairly easily.

DEBT COVENANT COMPLIANCE

One of the steps required to complete an audit relates to the classification of debt. As discussed previously, a debt that is due within one year is a current liability. A debt that is due later than one year from the date of the financial statements is classified as a long-term liability. Virtually all loans have covenants with which the debtor must comply. If the debtor does not comply with the covenants, it is typical for the loan to become due immediately. In other words, failure to comply with certain provisions can transform a long-term loan into a current obligation. This would devastate most firms. Accordingly, auditors always check to see if the firm is in compliance with its debt covenants. Since bankers are concerned with many of the same issues as damage experts (i.e., profitability, expectations of future earnings, etc.), a request for the auditors' work papers regarding compliance with debt covenants is often a fruitful request.

FINANCIAL STATEMENT TREND ANALYSIS

As a standard part of most audits, the auditor performs trend analysis on the company's financial statements. The auditor spots material changes and inquires of management the cause of such changes. The auditor then documents the response from management in their trend analysis. This schedule has no standard, industry-wide name. A document request for "ratio analysis performed on any of the financial statements for the period ending December 31, 2002" or "trend analysis performed on any of the financial statements for the period ending December 31, 2002" should produce such schedules.

Imagine that a plaintiff claims that your client's patent infringement caused the plaintiff to suffer lost sales. Assume that you obtained a subpoena requiring the plaintiff's auditor to produce its trend analysis on the audit conducted one year before the alleged infringement and one year after the alleged infringement. Further assume that you learn that the auditors analyzed the decrease in sales. Finally, assume that the auditors' analysis indicates that management told the auditors that the sales decrease was related to the loss of a major customer. The auditors' schedules facilitate identifying and interviewing the proper fact witnesses and possibly result in a determination that the loss was unrelated to the alleged infringement. Obviously, this information would greatly reduce damages and may even help with establishing liability.

Ratio analysis also can be used to assess the health or performance of a company. Ratio analysis helps to expose a company's strengths and weaknesses by creating percentages, rates, or proportions from a company's financial statements. These ratios express the mathematical relationship between one quantity and another and can be used to chart a company's performance over time or to compare two competitors.

Four general categories of ratio analysis exist: (1) liquidity ratios, (2) activity ratios, (3) profitability ratios, and (4) coverage ratios. Each category evaluates a particular area of performance.

For example, *liquidity ratios* measure the enterprise's short-term ability to pay its maturing obligations. One such ratio, the current ratio, is defined as current assets divided by current liabilities. Companies with a higher current ratio have better short-term debt-paying ability than companies with a lower current ratio. Another type of ratio analysis, *activity ratios*, measures how effectively the enterprise is using their employed assets (e.g., how efficiently assets are used to generate sales). *Profitability ratios* measure how successful a company is in a given period; these ratios measure such things as a company's profit margin on sales or their rate of return on assets. Finally, *coverage ratios* measure the degree of protection and security for long-term creditors and investors. For instance, debt to total assets measures the percentage of total assets provided by creditors.

Exhibit 4-6 illustrates ratios often used in ratio analysis.[1] Ratio analysis is most useful in implementing the income approach and the market approach, and in analyzing the firm's capacity, which is necessary to recover lost profits, as discussed in Chapter 14.

DETAIL OF ACCOUNTS

In the course of conducting an audit, an auditor details the most significant accounts. For instance, sales most often are detailed by geography, channel, or customer. Likewise, the most significant expenses, assets, and liabilities are also analyzed on a very detailed level. Using the previous example, a request for the "audit work papers related to the revenue account" would likely have resulted in evidence that the infringement did not cause the lost sales. Again, there is no term of art for the appropriate schedules. However, a request for the work papers associated with the desired account(s) should suffice.

Fortunately, an audit also produces valuable information that does not have to be obtained from the auditor. The most useful information often is contained in the footnotes to the financial statements. Footnotes are perhaps the most difficult part of the financial statements to appreciate, yet they also can provide valuable information. The footnotes are located just following the financial statements. Some footnotes appear in all financial statements. However, most footnotes change depending on the type of business and its particular characteristics. The following footnotes frequently have been found useful in performing IP damage analysis.

Purchase Price Allocation

When the audited company acquires another company, the purchase price of the acquired company must be allocated across the various asset categories. All of the amounts listed in the purchase price allocation are stated at "fair market value." Patents, trademarks, trade secrets, goodwill, and other identifiable assets (both tangible and intangible) are analyzed separately from the other assets. The footnotes to the financial statements discuss the purchase price allocation. However, for more detailed information, you may need to obtain the underlying work papers from the company.

RATIO	FORMULA	PURPOSE
Liquidity		
Current ratio	Current Assets/ Current Liabilities	Measures short-term debt-paying ability
Quick or acid-test ratio	Cash, Marketable Securities, and Net Receivables/ Current Liabilities	Measures immediate short-term liquidity
Current cash debt coverage ratio	Net Cash Provided by Operating Activities/ Average Current Liabilities	Measures a company's ability to pay off its current liabilities in a given year from its operations
Activity		
Receivable turnover	Net Sales/Average Trade Net Receivables	Measures liquidity of receivables
Inventory turnover	Cost of Goods Sold/Average Inventory	Measures liquidity of inventory
Asset turnover	Net Sales/Average Total Assets	Measures how efficiently assets are used to generate sales
Profitability		
Profit margin on sales	Net Income/Net Sales	Measures net income generated by each dollar of sales
Rate of return on assets	Net Income/Average Total Assets	Measures overall profitability of assets
Rate of return on common stock equity	Net Income Minus Preferred Dividends/Average Common Stockholders Equity	Measures profitability of owners' investment
Earnings per share	Net Income Minus Preferred Dividends/ Weighted Shares Outstanding	Measures net income earned on each share of common stock
Price earnings ratio	Market Price of Stock/ Earnings per Share	Measures the ratio of the market price per share to earnings per share
Payout ratio	Cash Dividends/Net Income	Measures percentage of earnings distributed in the form of cash dividends
Coverage		
Debt to total assets	Total Debt/Total Assets or Equity	Measures the percentage of total assets provided by creditors
Times interest earned	Income Before Interest and Taxes/ Interest	Measures the ability to meet interest payments as they come due
Cash debt coverage	Net Cash Provided by Operating Activities/Average Total Liabilities	Measures a company's ability to repay total liabilities in a given year from its operations
Book value per share	Common Stockholders' Equity/ Outstanding Shares	Measures the amount each share would receive if the company were liquidated at the amounts reported on the balance sheet

EXHIBIT 4-6   Ratios

Goodwill Valuation

Accounting rules recently have changed to require companies to make an annual determination of whether their goodwill is "impaired." Goodwill is considered to be "impaired" if the fair market value of the goodwill is less than its book value (amount on the balance sheet). However, the reverse is not true. If the fair market value is expected to be greater than the book value, the goodwill is left on the books at its cost, as accountants are loath to risk overstating assets. The footnotes to the financial statements typically will provide significant details regarding the impairment analysis. Again, the footnotes will be supported by more detailed analyses that may be obtained via subpoena.

Related Party Transactions

Another frequently used footnote relates to disclosing any transactions between the company and related parties. Related parties generally are described as owners, directors, officers, spouses of the preceding, and so on. It is common for privately held companies to have several related party transactions. Furthermore, the related transactions frequently are not being conducted at their fair market value. To properly analyze the company, it is common for practitioners to adjust the financial statements to account for the related party transactions. Such adjustments are made by adjusting the affected accounts to make them reflect the amount that would be reported if the expense had been done at fair market value.

SUMMARY

This chapter addressed the basic accounting principles that attorneys and experts must understand to conduct effective discovery. Moreover, the accounting principles discussed herein enable the analysis of the relevant financial information. In most IP damages cases, the financial information of both parties should be analyzed to determine the existence and extent of damages. Therefore, the effective utilization of accounting skills facilitates understanding the financial information retrieved and reaching a proper value for IP.

ENDNOTE

[1] D.E. Kieso and J.J. Weygandt, *Intermediate Accounting,* New York: John Wiley & Sons (1998).

ADDITIONAL READING

Thomas R. Dyckman, Roland E. Dukes, and Charles J. Davis, *Intermediate Accounting*, Chicago: Irwin (1995).

Ernst & Young, *Understanding and Using Financial Data*, New York: John Wiley & Sons (1996).

Andrew A. Haried, Leroy F. Imdieke, and Ralph E. Smith, *Advanced Accounting*, New York: John Wiley & Sons (1994).

Donald Kieso and Jerry Weygandt, *Intermediate Accounting*, New York: John Wiley & Sons (1998).

George Mundstock, *A Finance Approach to Accounting for Lawyers*, New York: Foundation Press (1999).

K. Fred Skousen, Harold Q. Landerderfer, and W. Steve Albrecht, *Accounting Principles and Applications*, Cincinnati: South-Western Publishing (1993).

Clyde P. Stickney, Roman L. Weil, and Sidney Davidson, *Financial Accounting: An Introduction to Concepts, Methods, and Uses*, Englewood Cliffs, N.J.: Academic Press (1991).

Ciaran Walsh, *Key Management Ratios*, Englewood Cliffs, N.J.: Prentice-Hall99 (1996).

Gerald White, Ashwinpaul Sondhi, and Dov Fried, *The Analysis and Use of Financial Statements*, New York: John Wiley & Sons (1998).

5

Financial Principles Used in Intellectual Property Damages

A third scientific discipline useful in intellectual property (IP) damage analysis is financial economics. The field of financial economics has a very broad scope, similar to but distinct from the related fields of accounting and microeconomics. Financial economists study primarily three topics: investments, option theory, and corporate finance. The area of financial economics that is most useful to constructing a sophisticated damage analysis in an IP case is the portion that addresses business valuation. The tools used in business valuation are required to properly perform the mechanics of the IP damage calculation. We use these tools in Chapter 14 on the mechanics of damage analysis. This chapter discusses the general principles of valuation, a critical topic for understanding a damage analysis because of the many ways in which general valuation principles overlap damage calculations and theories.

PRELIMINARY ISSUES

Standard of Value

It is essential for both the attorney and the damage expert to have a clear understanding of the appropriate standard of value in a business valuation. In the United States, the most common standard of value used is fair market value. Fair market value is defined by the American Society of Appraisers as "the amount at which property would change hands between a willing seller and a willing buyer when neither is acting under compulsion and when both have reasonable knowledge of the relevant facts."[1] This standard of value commonly is applied in valuations for mergers and acquisitions, estate and gift tax purposes, charitable contributions, buy–sell agreements, property taxes, as well as in litigation.

Another concept of value, investment value (also called strategic value), represents the value ascribed to an asset from a specific investor's point of view. For example, if a potential buyer views a purchase as a synergistic purchase, the buyer may offer a premium over and above the price that another independent investor would offer for the same company. Consider the following scenario. An office building with inadequate parking is located next to a vacant lot. The owner of the office building is likely to pay more than fair market value for the lot because the lot has a specific utility to him (providing the necessary parking space) that is worth paying a premium. In other words, the investment value of the lot from the building manager's perspective is higher than the amount that might be accorded the lot under a more objective fair market value. In the litigation context, investment value generally is closer to the concept captured by a reasonable royalty damage calculation.

Finally, fair value usually is a statutorily defined standard of value that varies from state to state. An example of fair value is a value that does not consider discounts for lack of marketability and/or control. Fair value is a common standard of value for dissenting stockholder actions and for divorce settings, but it is less useful in IP litigation.

Law of One Price

The law of one price is a basic concept in financial economics that provides a basis for performing valuations. The law of one price states that assets that have identical future payoffs must trade at the same price. This is the case because different prices for identical assets create arbitrage opportunities. While initially this seems obvious, the law of one price goes on to state that two different assets must be valued equally after adjusting for all relevant differences. In other words, a stock that is slightly more risky than its counterpart stock must have a slightly lower price than the counterpart stock to compensate for the additional risk. A much riskier stock must have a much lower price. By making this type of adjustment, the two stocks are valued equally, while accounting for differences in risk. This is helpful only if the practitioner knows the value of the counterpart stock. Yet, by applying this thought process to the investments whose value is known and agreed upon, the expert can effectively use a variation of the law of one price (because the payoffs on each side of the equation are not identical) to perform a reasonableness check on a valuation. The variation can be algebraically performed as:

$$(RFR)(RFI)^t = (VU)(PU)^t + (VD)(PD)^t$$

where

> RFI = risk-free investment
> RFR = risk-free return
>   t = time periods over which the investment is measured
> VU = investment's value in the up stage
> PU = probability of the investment going to the up stage
> VD = investment's value in the down stage
> PD = probability of the investment going to the down stage

The following example illustrates the principle. Assume that the valuation is related to the value of a biotechnology firm. The firm is performing clinical tests that have a 2 percent chance of great success, a 38 percent chance of mediocre results, and a 60 percent chance of failure. Accordingly, based on the results of clinical tests, the firm has a 2 percent chance of being worth $20 million. It is determined that if the product fails or gets very poor clinical results, it has a 60 percent chance of being valueless. Finally, if the results are mediocre, the product has a 38 percent chance of being worth $5 million. In other words, an investor can choose to take the following risk: $(.02)(20,000,000) + (.60)(0) + (.38)(5,000,000) = \$2,300,000$ (in one year), or the investor can buy a risk-free bond from the government. If we assume that the risk-free rate of return currently is 5 percent, the investor would need to buy $2,196,476 worth of bonds to be certain of having $2.3 million one year from today. Thus, the value of the business is $2,196,476.

This exercise is still useful when there is insufficient evidence about the probability of an event. For instance, assume that you are valuing the aforementioned biotech firm. However, this time there is no information regarding the probability of the firm's succeeding in its clinical trials. The opposing expert prepares a valuation that results in a value of $15 million. You determine that the most successful project is likely to lead to a value of $20 million, whereas a failure leads to a worthless project. Next, you perform the following calculation as a reasonableness check of their conclusion[2]:

$$\$15,000,000 = (x)(20,000,000) + (1 - x)(0) =$$
$$\$15,000,000 = (x)(20,000,000) + (0) =$$
$$\$15,000,000 \, / \, \$20,000,000 = x$$
$$75\% = x$$

In other words, the opposing expert's valuation implies that there is a 75 percent chance of the project's being successful. Even though you were unable to determine the probability of successful clinical trials, it is likely that you can gather information that proves the true probability is much less than a 75 percent chance. If there is less than a 75 percent chance, the opposing expert's value is overstated because it does not comply with the law of one price. Although the law of one price is often a useful reasonableness check, more rigorous analyses are needed to actually determine a proper estimate of value.

Valuation theory includes three conventional approaches for determining the value of a company's stock: the income approach, the market approach, and the cost approach (asset-based approach). If performed properly, all three approaches will indicate a similar range of value. It is precisely for that reason that the expert must consider undertaking all three approaches where possible. Since each of the three approaches includes subjective steps, an expert can use the various methods of valuation to act as "sanity" checks for the other calculations (see Exhibit 5-1).

VALUATION APPROACHES

There are three conventional approaches to valuation that may apply in estimating damages for an IP case. These approaches are (1) the income approach, (2) the market approach, and (3) the cost approach.

Income Approach

The income approach estimates the value of a business or IP based on future cash-generating ability. This approach quantifies the expected value of the future economic benefits that accrue to the owners of the IP. These benefits, or future cash flows, are discounted to the present or (if constant over time or growing at a constant rate) capitalized at a rate of return that is commensurate with the risk associated with the future cash flow and the time value of money.

The four steps typically conducted in performing the income approach are:

1. Estimate the expected future cash flows for a certain discrete projection period.
2. Discount these future cash flows to present-value dollars at a rate of return that considers the relative risk of achieving the future cash flows and the time value of money.

Let n = years, r = interest rate, F = future value, P = present value, A = annuity payment, g = growth rate

(1) Future value:

$$F = P(1 + r)^n$$

(2) Present value:

$$P = \frac{F}{(1 + r)^n}$$

(3) Present value of an annuity:

$$P = A\left[\frac{1 - \left(\frac{1}{1 + r}\right)^n}{r}\right]$$

(4) Present value of a perpetual annuity:

$$P = \frac{A}{R}$$

(5) Present value of F growing at rate g indefinitely:

$$P = \frac{F}{r - g}$$

EXHIBIT 5-1   Some Useful Financial Formulas

3. Estimate the residual value of cash flows (if any) subsequent to the discrete projection period.
4. Combine the present value of the residual cash flows (if any) with the present value of the discrete projection period cash flows.

The methodology for each of these steps is discussed in the following sections.

Step 1: Project the Expected Future Cash Flows of the Subject Intellectual Property.
The first step in the income approach is to create a projection of the expected future benefit stream of the asset. Whenever possible, cash flow should be used as the appropriate benefit stream. Investors are concerned with the actual cash that they will receive from an investment and the timing and risk associated with those cash flows. Not only is this principle accepted in theory, but also the proposition has growing empirical support. Most studies of accounting changes that impact cash and earnings differently find that security prices are determined by the change in cash flows.[3] Earnings, or the net income on a firm's income statement, is not the most appropriate measure of the benefit stream if cash flows are known or can be reasonably predicted and are significantly different from net income.[4] As discussed earlier, net income is defined according to the accounting principles of matching and conservatism, which can be independent of the true time of payment. Moreover, empirical work on investor perceptions of value tend to confirm that investors see through accounting conventions and react to underlying changes in cash flow.[5] However, when informational problems exist, earnings can be a better measure of future cash than current cash flows. For example, if information concerning cash flow is known only for two years and during those two years the firm has significant capital investments that are not expected to yield returns until more than two years in the future, the matching principle that is used to construct earnings may provide a better measure of future cash flow than present cash flows. When earnings are used to proxy cash flows, an appropriate earnings model (which has an equivalence to the dividend discount model or discounted cash flow model) should be adopted.[6]

Once a benefit stream is selected, it is important to determine whether the valuation should relate to total invested capital (i.e., interest-bearing debt holders and equity holders) or just equity holders. Assuming that cash flow is used, the net cash flow to total invested capital is computed using the following formula:

Earnings Before Interest and Taxes (EBIT)

−	Estimated federal and state tax expense
+	Noncash expenses (e.g., depreciation, deferred taxes, etc.)
±	Requirements to fund working capital
−	Capital expenditures
+	Preferred dividends, if any
=	Net cash flow to invested capital

Net cash flow to equity is computed using the following formula:

	Net income
+	Noncash expenses (e.g., depreciation, deferred taxes, etc.)
±	Requirements to fund working capital
−	Capital expenditures
±	Changes in long-term debt
=	Net cash flow to equity holders

After the appropriate future cash flow benefit stream is identified, it is appropriate to begin the projection analyses. The projection should approximate the expected value of the future cash flows. The expected value is not the expert's subjective intuition about the future. Rather, it represents the weighted value of all future possible cash flow scenarios weighted by their probabilities. This expected future cash flow must take account of both the probability of a project's utter failure and the probability of miraculous success. To be consistent, the expected value of the future cash flows is the place in the valuation procedure where the unsystematic or the unique risk faced by the company should be taken into account. The benefit stream should be an expected value of several possible future scenarios.

Projections are estimated most easily in situations where the subject IP has established a long track record. The historical results often are very useful in predicting the future performance of the property. However, the historical results should not be the sole basis for establishing the projections. The projections also must consider the asset's situation at the date of the valuation, the outlook for the relevant industry, and any relevant expected changes in the law, new competition, and so on.

Projections usually are best determined by starting with the revenues. Ideally, a relationship between sales and an identifiable independent variable can be established. For example, it is possible that there will be a relationship between new home sales in a particular city and the revenue for furniture companies in the same city. Other factors that must be considered include new competitors moving into the city, interest rates, new technology, price changes, and so on. Although a certain portion of the revenue projection is subjective, reasonable projections must conform to considerations of the particular subject property. For instance, the revenue must be based on manufacturing, sales, and financial limitations specific to the firm at issue as well as market developments outside the firm.

Once the revenue has been projected, all of the expenses that must be incurred to generate this specific revenue should be calculated. Many practitioners use econometric analysis to assist in this calculation. Additionally, the expenses should include amounts that may not historically have changed with sales but would be necessary to produce the projected revenue. For example, if the projected revenues are based on adding a third shift, the required expenditures for the additional supervisors, management, and so on required for adding a third shift must be determined.

Finally, any required costs for capital expenditures and working capital must be considered. Although neither capital expenditures nor working capital is an expenditure in the true sense of the word, both categories reduce cash flows and therefore must be considered.

Working capital typically reduces the cash flows in periods of growth. Working capital represents the value of the current assets less current liabilities. Current assets include items such as cash, receivables, and inventory that are partially used to finance the short-term liabilities. The short-term liabilities generally include the accounts payable, accrued expenses, and so on. The necessity of accounting for the investment in working capital can be illustrated by the following example. Assume that a firm begins business on January 1. Although the company makes sales on the first business day, it offers credit to its customers and does not begin to collect on its receivables for 30 days. The employees must be paid before the 30 days have elapsed. Thus, the firm must have capital (either from borrowing it or from an additional investment by the owners) to pay the employees. This capital is called working capital. Just as a new firm needs working capital funds, nearly all firms that are growing their revenues require working capital investment. If a firm's revenues are decreasing, the change in working capital may actually contribute to cash flows.

Capital expenditures are also an investment that typically reduce cash flows. The relevant capital expenditures represent the cost of buying buildings, office space, computers, trucks, and so on that are required to make the projected sales. Capital expenditures are usually required for firm growth. However, some firms can experience enormous growth with very little investment in capital expenditures. For instance, many Internet-based firms require very little additional capital expenditure beyond what is needed to make the first sale. In contrast, even firms that are experiencing stabilized revenues may have significant required capital expenditures. For instance, airlines must continually invest in new airplanes or airplane maintenance, even if sales are low.

Finally, some reasonable economic theory must guide the benefit projection process. Experts should not assume that a firm will receive returns above the competitive average for an extended period unless there is a very good explanation for that assumption. This caution is empirically justified because high returns induce entry and, in the case of IP, significant design-around efforts by competitors. These consequences in turn should reduce the original firm's returns until the market stabilizes.

Step 2: Determine the Discount Rate Applicable for the Projected Cash Flows. The discount rate is a mechanism for reflecting the systematic risk and the time value of the future estimated cash flow streams. Once an expert determines the expected future cash flow from the asset being valued, he or she must construct the proper discount rate.

The Time Value of Money. The adjustment for time value of money results from the fact that investors value a dollar received today more than they value a dollar received in the future. Thus, to value future cash flows from a business, a security, or an asset such as IP, the expected future cash flow must be converted to an equivalent value today, or into its "present value." The present value represents what investors are willing to pay today for each dollar received in the future, abstracting from any risk. This present value represents the opportunity cost of funds invested today at a risk-free rate of return for the number of periods involved. To determine the opportunity cost of funds at a risk-free rate, it is necessary to find the spot rate or interest rate on a risk-free asset. The set of spot rates for each period can change, and the term structure of interest rates represents the entire set of spot rates on risk-free assets for different holding periods. The term structure of interest rates generally (but not always) is upward-sloping. Because the term structure of interest rates can change and there is no consensus on the factors determining the term structure, it often is appropriate to assume a flat term structure and use a single interest rate, such as the interest rate on a 20-year government note, as a proxy for the risk-free rate of return in all periods.

Adjusting for Risk.   Risk simply refers to variability in expected returns. For example, asset *A* may be certain to generate $10 in cash flow in one year, whereas asset *B* may generate a 50 percent chance of receiving $20 in one year and a 50 percent chance of receiving $0 in one year. The expected returns on both assets are the same (10 percent), yet asset *B* is more risky. To understand why asset *B* is less desirable, financial economists have constructed a theory of investor preferences over uncertain outcomes. The basic assumption of the theory is that investors are "risk-averse," meaning that where possible, investors like to avoid risks. This assumed aversion implies that investors have a utility function[7] with the following characteristic:

$$\frac{-U''(W)}{U'(W)} > 0$$

U'' is the second derivative of the utility function with respect to W, or wealth, and U' is the first derivative with respect to W. A utility function with risk aversion can be depicted as:

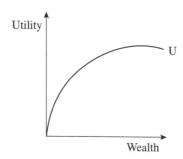

As an investor's wealth increases, his utility increases, albeit at a decreasing rate. The impact of such a utility function is that reductions in wealth result in a greater loss of utility than increases in wealth yield increases in utility. Therefore, investors lose utility overall by variation in returns. As a result, all other factors being equal, investors dislike variation in returns.

Investment theory assumes that the risk-averse utility function is described by the mean and variance, $\sigma,^2$ of the asset's return. The typical assumption is that asset returns are multivariate normally distributed, so even if investors cared about other aspects of the asset's return, such concerns would not impact investment behavior because normally distributed returns are fully defined by the mean and variance alone.

If μ is the mean return, then the variance is:

$$\sigma^2 = \sum_{i=1}^{n} (X_i - \mu)^2$$

That is, the variance is simply the sum of the squared deviations of the asset's returns from the mean return. One important characteristic of the variance is that the sum of several variances will yield a lower variance to the extent that the returns of the assets being summed are not perfectly positively correlated. This observation has led modern portfolio theory to theorize about how investors will select an optimal portfolio. For example, the capital asset pricing model (CAPM) uses this observation to develop appropriate risk premiums. Under CAPM, investors are interested in minimizing risk per unit of expected return. Because of the characteristic of the variance described previously, investors optimize by holding diversified portfolios. The result is that the total risk of an asset can then be divided into two components: (1) the unsystematic or unique risk that can be diversified away, and (2) the systematic or market risk, which is related to the economy as a whole and cannot be reduced by diversification. In the CAPM model, only systematic risk or market risk is the risk for which investors are compensated in the form of a risk premium. This systematic risk can be measured by the variable beta. Beta, β_i, measures the contribution of an asset to the total risk of a well-diversified portfolio; stated differently, beta is the variability in the price of the asset in relation to the total market variability.

$$r_i = r_f + \beta_i \, [E(r_m) - r_f]$$

where r_i is the risk-adjusted discount rate, r_f is the risk-free rate of return, and the last term represents the systematic risk premium, $E(r_m) - r_f$. In the income method, the unique risk is captured by the expected value of future cash flows in the numerator, and only systematic risk is considered in determining the discount rate.

It should be noted that discount rates developed in the CAPM model are based on data derived from publicly traded securities. Consequently, the resultant value derived from using this discount rate represents value attributable to a noncontrolling investor of a marketable investment. As such, the analyst should consider, based on the interest being valued, whether a control premium and/or a discount for lack of marketability are applicable.

The Build-Up Approach.   An alternative approach to determining the risk premium that strays from financial theory and instead relies on empirical findings is called the "build-up" method. The build-up approach estimates the cost of equity by "building up" the required rate of return on equity. The build-up method is performed by estimating each of the risks. The components most often considered are:

$$\begin{array}{l} \text{Risk-free rate} \\ + \;\; \text{Equity premium} \\ + \;\; \text{Size premium} \\ \underline{+ \;\; \text{Specific company premium}} \\ = \;\; \text{Total cost of equity} \end{array}$$

A comparison of the CAPM approach and the build-up approach reveals that both calculations consider similar risks. One difference is that in the CAPM the only source of risk is completely captured by beta, whereas the build-up method relies on the expert's judgment. The build-up method deviates from the CAPM assumption in that the CAPM assumes that only systematic risk is priced by diversified investors. A frame of reference regarding required rates of return can be found in the next section. Historically, small firms have had higher rates of return than large firms. This belief is widely held among the valuation community. There have been several studies demonstrating that this relationship holds true empirically, although there is no consensus regarding the theoretical explanation for this effect, or whether it is true at present.[8] Thus, if the business is a very small firm, the cost of its equity probably should be high.

The Weighted Average Cost of Capital.   In certain situations, it is appropriate to value more than the portion of the business owned by the equity holders. For example, if one is valuing a controlling interest of a company where the owner has to incur debt, it may be appropriate to value the business on a total invested capital basis (i.e., interest-bearing debt and equity), assuming the industry's capital structure, to properly reflect value. In that type of situation, it may be appropriate to value the company based on its weighted average cost of capital (WACC).

The discount rate for a firm or asset that is not all equity financed is the WACC. The WACC is calculated by weighting the required returns on interest-bearing debt and common equity capital in proportion to their estimated percentages in an expected capital structure.

Several possible methods are used in the determination of the appropriate WACC rate. The general formula for calculating the WACC rate is:

$$WACC = Kd \times (d\%) + Ke \times (e\%)$$

where

WACC	=	weighted average cost of capital
Kd	=	after-tax rate of return on debt capital
d%	=	debt capital as a percentage of the sum of the debt, preferred and common equity capital (total invested capital) measured in market terms
Ke	=	required rate of return equity capital
e%	=	common equity capital as a percentage of the total invested capital, measured in market terms

We have discussed two alternative methods of determining the required return on equity, CAPM and the build-up approach. In contrast, the rate of return on debt capital is the rate a prudent debt investor would require on interest-bearing debt. Since the interest on debt capital is deductible for income tax purposes at the corporate level, the after-tax interest rate is most often used in the WACC calculation. The effective income tax rate is the federal income tax rate plus the effective state income tax rate (adjusted for federal income tax deductibility).[9]

The after-tax rate of return on debt capital is typically calculated using the formula:

$$K_d = K \times (1 \times t)$$

where

K_d	=	after-tax rate of return on debt capital
K	=	pretax rate of return on debt capital
t	=	effective federal and state income tax rate

Combining the discount rates for debt and equity with the WACC identity provides a discount rate for valuing the total assets of a firm, thus removing any specific financing decisions from the valuation.

Step 3: Estimate the Residual Value of Cash Flows (If Any) Subsequent to the Discrete Projection Period.   Since businesses, and occasionally IP, are unlike humans in that they do not have to die (but they do pay taxes), the expert faces a problem with establishing the number of years to project revenues. Experts project the cash flows to the point that a reliable terminal value can be determined. The terminal value is the nomenclature used for the valuation of the firm for all of the years that are beyond the last year of the projections. It is reflected in a lump-sum amount that usually is calculated via the Gordon growth model or via application of a market-based multiple of earnings or sales.

The Gordon growth formula is:

$$PV = \frac{CF_0(1 + g)}{K - g}$$

where

PV	=	present value at time 0
CF_0	=	prior periods projected cash flow (or other economic benefit stream)
g	=	projected growth, compounded annually into infinite future
K	=	required rate of return

Thus, the projections are made for the number of years necessary to do one of the following:

1. The revenue growth levels off to a point at which it will remain relatively steady for the future.
2. The firm grows to the point of having public firms/private transactions that are suitable comparisons.

Once the revenue growth rate subsides to a long-term sustainable rate, the Gordon Growth Model can effectively be applied. Even if the firm is still growing at a rate that is too fast to sustain on a long-term basis, it is appropriate to end the projections if a reliable comparative firm or transaction can be used to value the firm.

Regardless of the method used to calculate the terminal value, the value must be discounted back to the present from the date at which the terminal value is calculated.

Step 4: Other Adjustments. Several other adjustments may be necessary when valuing an asset. The first potential adjustment concerns inflation. The valuation equation must be consistent. Both the numerator and the denominator should be measured consistently in either real terms or nominal terms. When a conversion from nominal terms to real terms is required, an approximation to the Fisher equation is often used. The approximation formula is:

$$r \text{ (nominal)} = r \text{ (real)} + i$$

where i represents the inflation rate. Quoted interest rates are nominal interest rates. The key is ensuring that cash flow projections are also in nominal terms when using nominal discount rates.

Step 5: Combine the Present Value of the Residual Cash Flows (If Any) with the Discrete Projection Period Cash Flows.   Next, the present value of the projected cash flows is added to the present value of the terminal value to arrive at the total value, incorporating all adjustments. A further adjustment may concern marketability (liquidity) and control. For example, shares in a closely held corporation are more difficult to sell than publicly traded assets. To adjust for these differences, a marketability discount often is applied to the underlying asset value.

THE MARKET APPROACH

The market approach is a conventionally accepted valuation method that leads to a value estimate based on the transactions of other purchasers and sellers in the marketplace. This approach is based on the principle of substitution. The principle of substitution states that the limit of prices, rents, and rates tends to be set by prevailing prices, rents, and rates for equally desirable substitutes. Use of the market approach results in an indication of value based on an estimate of the price one may reasonably expect to realize on the sale of the subject asset.

This concept is largely intuitive. Many people have employed the same technique during the process of buying a house. For example, assume that a person wanted to buy a house in an exclusive neighborhood ("subject" home). The person would obtain the recent actual sales prices of similar homes. Ideally, the similar homes would be located in the same neighborhood ("comparative" homes). The person would also consider the physical differences between the "subject" home and the "comparative" homes. For instance, if a "comparative" home had a swimming pool and the "subject" home did not, an adjustment would be made to reflect the anticipated difference in the value of each home. Similarly, the person may make price adjustments for other significant features, such as size, style, and so forth.

The market approach is performed in the same manner when valuing a business. The approach generally is accomplished through the following steps:

Establish Criteria for Identifying Comparative Transactions

As with the preceding example, the starting point for this method is identifying "comparative" firms. The advent of the Internet has provided many web sites that are dedicated to providing financial data to the valuation community. Nearly all of the web sites have a search function that facilitates the identification of companies that can be used as comparative firms. Depending on the nature of the engagement, it may be more beneficial to use a database of privately held firms.

Regardless of the database searched, the most common way of locating suitable comparative firms is by searching based on industry (standard industrial classification code) and/or size, usually revenue, total assets, or market capitalization (number of shares multiplied by the share price). Factors that should be considered include company size, growth, liquidity, leverage, and profitability, among others.

The most useful data are gathered from the same period as the date of the damage date. Additionally, as the comparative firms become more similar to the subject business, fewer comparative companies are needed. Conversely, a larger sample of firms can "smooth" differences between the comparative firms and the subject firm. Revisiting the example regarding the price of a home discussed previously illustrates this point. Imagine that the comparative home sales took place three years earlier. Such comparative sales may yield a poor analysis depending on how the market changed during the period between the date of the comparative sale and the valuation date of the subject home. Next, imagine that the comparative home sales involved homes of the same size, sold on the same date, and of the same style as the subject home. However, the comparative homes were in a neighborhood with a view of the ocean, whereas the subject home had no such view. Again, without adjustment, the expert is likely to come to a poor conclusion of value.

If Necessary, Refine the Search by Adding More Criteria and Thus Reduce the List to Those That Are the Most Comparative

Because of the importance of identifying the best comparative firms, it is most common to make initial searches that are rather broad and then refine the search. When the search criteria produce too many comparative companies, it is necessary to refine the search. Shannon Pratt's book on performing business valuations discusses the process under a section called "How Many Guideline Companies." The book suggests that "the answer depends on a number of factors:

- Similarity to the subject—the more similar, the fewer needed.
- Trading activity—again, the more actively traded, the fewer needed.
- Dispersion of value measure data points—the wider the range of relevant measure data points, the more companies it takes to identify a pattern relevant to the subject company."

Further insight is found in *Corporate Finance: A Valuation Approach,* which also discusses the refining step:

> Since we scale prices of other firms to value the firm being analyzed, we would like to use data of firms that are as similar as possible to the firm we value. The flip side of this argument, however, is that by specifying too stringent criteria for similarity, we end up with too few firms to which we can compare. With a small sample of comparable firms, the idiosyncrasies of individual firms affect the average multiples too much so that the average multiple

is no longer a representative multiple. In selecting the sample of comparable firms, you have to balance these two conflicting considerations. The idea is to obtain as large a sample as possible so that the idiosyncrasies of a single firm don't affect the valuation by much, yet not to choose so large a sample that the "comparable firms" are not comparable to the one that you value.[10]

Additional rigor can be added to this step by using econometric analysis. For instance, a large initial search can be refined using cluster analysis, factor analysis, or other statistical techniques.

Rather than relying on intuition, these techniques can identify how close comparable companies are based on predetermined factors. This will be a fruitful area of future analysis by financial analysts. Sometimes it is useful to identify two or more groups of comparative firms. Revisiting the home price example, imagine that the subject home is unusually small and has a view of the ocean. Assume that you are unable to find homes of a similar size that have a view of the ocean. Instead, you find a group of home sales that are very similar in the date of the sale, their style, and size; however, this group of comparative sales does not have a view of the ocean. You also identify a second group of home sales that are similar to each other in size, have an ocean view, yet are different from the subject home's size. Finally, you find a third group of sales that are similar to the size of the homes in the second group and similar to the location of the first group of smaller homes. You can use the difference between the second group and the third group to estimate the value of the view, then add that to the value established by the first group for homes of the same size as the subject home. Such a process is not uncommon when valuing a business. Many firms have segments or components of the business that are more easily valued individually rather than based on the entire business.

Obtain Appropriate Financial Data for the Comparative Companies

Once the comparative firms have been identified, their financial data must be obtained. This typically is an easy step to perform because the same web sites that perform the searches typically provide the financial statements. The most common data obtained are the income statement, balance sheet, and statement of cash flows. Additionally, it is useful to obtain any projections or analysts' reports. Finally, the number of shares and the respective share price must be obtained. It is important that all of these data be the financial information *as of the date of the valuation.*

A valuation generally occurs as of a specific date. The value of a company changes daily. In fact, it is not uncommon for the value of a company to change dramatically in a very short period. Experts and attorneys must always keep the valuation date in mind in the course of gathering discovery and conducting their analyses. Generally, valuation experts believe that the only information that should be considered is the information that is known or knowable as of the date of the valuation. This is particularly important when valuing IP. For example, there can be a great deal of uncertainty as to the rate of a technology's adoption. Frequently, after a claim is filed, both parties gain a much better understanding as to the actual rate of adoption. Generally, it is inappropriate to value the technology based on the information that has been learned subsequent to the date of valuation. This convention can be segregated into two situations:

1. **Event-Specific**—The practitioner should ignore event-specific information that has become known after the date of valuation. For instance, a fire that burned down a manufacturing plant or terrorist acts that changed the industry generally should not be relied on when performing a valuation if they occurred after the valuation date.

2. **Information Regarding the Parties' Expectations**—Since value is ultimately based on the expectations of a business at a particular point in time, it is important to base value on projections that would have been made at the time of the valuation. Practitioners typically begin their analysis with the parties' *projections* (created at or around the valuation date) rather than *actual* results. However, it would be careless to ignore the actual results because projections may be found to consistently be very optimistic (or pessimistic). The actual results sometimes can be used to indicate a proxy that represents reasonable expectations the parties' would have had at the valuation date.

Once the data have been gathered, it is typical to perform ratio analysis on the financial statements. The purpose of the ratio analysis is twofold. First, the analyst is trying to identify similarities between firms. As more similarities are found, the practitioner gains confidence that the comparative firms are suitable. Second, the analysts are looking for differences. Differences indicate either that the firm may not be a suitable comparison on which to base a valuation or that there are accounting differences between the firms. As unsuitable companies are identified, they should no longer be considered (or at least they should be given less weight). To the extent that there are significant accounting differences, the financial statements must be adjusted so that the ratio analysis (and the financial statements) is comparable. This process is discussed in the next step.

Consider Adjusting or Normalizing Financial Data of the Comparative Companies

In certain instances, generally accepted accounting procedures (GAAP) allow two firms to use different methods of accounting for the same type of transaction. If the transaction is prevalent in the firm's financial statements, the different accounting methods could cause material differences between the financial results of the two firms. Furthermore, two firms may also make operational decisions that affect the financial statements but really do not affect the firm's value. Examples of such differences are the following:

Accounting for Inventory.   Firms typically choose between one of two methods—LIFO (last in first out) and FIFO (first in first out). For example, assume that there are two businesses that are the same in all respects except their inventory accounting. The firm using the LIFO method will look less profitable than the other business. Additionally, the LIFO firm will appear to have less valuable inventory. Of course, the firms have the same value. However, failing to adjust for such differences in accounting methods will yield an analysis that indicates deceptively different values for the two firms.

Owning a Building Versus Renting a Building.   Again, assume that the two businesses differ only with respect to their property interest in the building. The building owner is likely to have a lower level of profitability (due to depreciation, debt, insurance, etc.) than the identical business that rents its space. Thus, the financial statements must be adjusted.

Even more common, it is necessary to make such adjustments when comparing a private firm with a public company. For instance, owners of privately held firms frequently have the business pay for many items that may otherwise be considered personal (car allowance, gym fees, etc.). Similarly, owners of private firms often pay family members something other than the fair market rate as a wage.

Select the Valuation Multiples That Are the Most Appropriate to Measure the Comparative Companies and Calculate the Multiples for the Comparative Companies

The valuation multiples that have been used by practitioners are nearly limitless. Some of the most commonly used valuation multiples include price to earnings, price to sales, price to EBIT, price to earnings before interest, taxes, depreciation, and amortization (EBITDA), and so on. Most analysts tend to select several multiples. Next, they look at the variance of the multiples. Ideally, a multiple that is consistent across several firms gives an indication that it is a good proxy for establishing value. For example, if the following multiples were calculated, it is likely that the analyst would conclude that price to sales is an appropriate proxy.

	COMPANY A	COMPANY B	COMPANY C
Price to sales	1.9	1.7	1.7
Price to EBIDTA	12	7	18
Price to earnings	16	10	31

Econometrics also can be helpful in performing this step because techniques are available that can identify the most significant multiples among firms.

When making the necessary subjective portion of this assessment, the most important point to keep in mind is ensuring that investors actually trade on the multiple. This point is highlighted by the main drawback of this approach, which is that a multiple of *anything* can be calculated. For instance, a multiple of price to numbers of letters in the company's name can be calculated. Obviously, such a multiple has nothing to do with the value of a firm. Accordingly, evidence of the proper multiple is the multiple's applicability across different firms that have been determined to be suitable comparisons.

Select and Adjust Multiples to Make Them Appropriate to Apply to the Subject Company

Often the multiples will be further adjusted to account for remaining differences between the comparison companies and the subject firm. The most common type of adjustment is based on size. There is significant evidence that investors pay less for smaller companies than they pay for larger companies. Many times the comparison firms are much larger than the subject firm and the multiple must be adjusted accordingly.

Apply the Multiples to the Subject Company

The last step in the market approach is the application of the multiple(s) to the subject company. The primary thing to keep in mind while implementing this step is to apply the multiple to the subject company in the same way that it was calculated. Upon application of the multiple, the expert has completed the market approach (before consideration of any applicable discounts and/or premiums).

THE COST APPROACH

The cost approach estimates the fair market value of an asset using the concept of replacement cost as an indicator of fair market value. The premise of the cost approach is that a prudent investor would pay no more for an asset than the amount for which the asset could be replaced. Replacement cost new, which refers to the cost to replace the property with like utility using current material and labor rates, establishes the highest amount a prudent investor would pay. To the extent that an existing asset will provide less utility than a new one, the value of that asset is less. Accordingly, replacement cost is adjusted for loss in value due to physical deterioration, functional obsolescence, and economic obsolescence.

Physical deterioration is the loss in value brought about by wear and tear, action of the elements, disintegration, use in service, and all physical factors that reduce the life of an asset. Functional obsolescence is the loss in value due to changes in technology, discovery of new materials, and improved manufacturing processes. Economic obsolescence is the loss in value caused by external forces such as legislative enactments, overcapacity in the industry, changes in supply and demand relationships in the market, and so on. Obsolescence typically is measured by identifying excess operating costs, overcapacities, or the inadequacies of an asset.

Although the cost approach should yield the same valuation conclusion that the other two approaches yield, the underlying data needed to perform the cost approach often are more subjective and more difficult to find than the supporting evidence for the other two methods. Accordingly, the market approach and the income approach are used more frequently than the cost approach. However, the cost approach can be the best approach when valuing certain intangible assets such as research libraries, partially completed software code, and so on.

SUMMARY

Calculation of IP damages requires the successful implementation of valuation principles. Such calculations often require the effective utilization of finance, economic, and accounting skills to properly consider the various factors surrounding the subject property. As a result of the significant disagreement regarding IP damages, experts often are employed to value and explain the damages to the judge and jury.

To properly estimate IP damages, it is essential to determine what is being valued and to specify the valuation date. Then it is appropriate to consider the three common valuation approaches: the income approach, the market approach, and the cost approach. Each of these approaches, if determined to be applicable, not only will indicate the value of the property in dispute, but also will act as a sanity check on the conclusions derived under any of the other approaches.

This chapter set forth the basic financial concepts involved in the valuation of an asset. Valuation concepts are often present in expert damage analysis in IP cases, and in trade secret cases in particular. We use many of the concepts developed in this chapter in our discussion of the mechanics of IP damage analysis.

ENDNOTES

[1] American Society of Appraisers, Business Valuation Standards, Definitions.

[2] In practice, one should also include an intermediate state.

[3] *See* review in Tom Copeland, Tim Koller, and Jack Murrin, *Valuation Measuring the Value of Companies* at 62–87.

[4] Accountants have developed a model of "abnormal earnings" which is mathematically equivalent to a cash flow model but uses accounting earnings as an input. We plan to address such models in the first supplement to this text.

[5] *See, e.g.,* Gary C. Biddle and Fredrick W. Lindahl, *Stock Price Reactions to UFO Adoptions: The Association Between Excess Returns and UFO Tax Savings,* 20 J. Acctng. Res., 551 (1982); E. Lindberg and M. Russ, *To Purchase or to Pool: Does It Matter?* 12 J. Applied Corp. 23 (1999); Bradford Cornell, *Corporation Valuation,* at 104–108 (1993).

[6] *See* discussion in Gerald White, Ashwinpaul Sondi, and Dov Fried, *The Analysis and Use of Financial Statements*, at 1062 et seq. (1998).

[7] A utility function is merely a function in which preferences are converted to real numbers.

[8] For a discussion of this point, *see* Zvi Bodie, Alex Kane, and Alan Marcus, *Investments*, New York: McGraw-Hill (1999) at Chapter 13.

[9] Personal taxes can also have an impact on rates of return required by debt and equity investors. We will discuss this in more depth in the first supplement.

[10] Simon Benninga and Oded Sarig, *Corporate Finance: A Valuation Approach*, New York: McGraw-Hill (1977).

ADDITIONAL READING

Bradford Cornell, *Corporate Valuation*, New York: McGraw-Hill (1993).

Krisha Palepu, Paul Healy, and Victor Bernard, *Business Analysis & Valuation*, Cincinnati: South-Western College Publishing (2000).

Simon Benninga and Oded Sarig, *Corporate Finance: A Valuation Approach*, New York: McGraw-Hill (1997).

Tom Copeland, Tim Kuller, and Jack Murrin, *Valuation: Measuring and Managing the Value of Companies*, New York: John Wiley & Sons (2000).

Shannon Pratt, Robert Reilly, and Robert Schweihs, *Valuing Small Business & Professional Practices*, New York: McGraw-Hill (1998).

F. Peter Boer, *The Valuation of Technology: Business and Financial Issues in R&D*, New York: John Wiley & Sons (1999).

Richard Razgaitis, *Early Stage Technologies: Valuation and Pricing*, New York: John Wiley & Sons (1999).

Shannon P. Pratt, Robert F. Reilly, and Robert P. Schweihs, *Valuing a Business: The Analysis and Appraisal of Closely Held Companies*, 3rd ed., New York: McGraw-Hill (1996).

Robert F. Reilly and Robert P. Schweihs, *Valuing Intangible Assets*, New York: McGraw-Hill (1998).

Part Two

Patent Infringement Damages

6

Introduction to Patent Law

A BRIEF HISTORY

The American patent tradition derives from the "letters patent" issued by England's monarchs, which granted 14 years of exclusive use to the "first and true inventor" of new manufactures. The Statute of Monopolies of 1623 required letters patent only to issue with respect to new devices that were "not contrary to law, nor mischievous to the State, by raising prices of commodities at home, or hurt of trade, or generally inconvenient."[1] Interestingly, the American patent system never adopted standards that so explicitly referenced the potential economic disadvantages to these limited-term monopolies.

The U.S. Constitution, art. I, sec. 8, gives Congress the power "to promote the Progress of Science and useful Arts, by securing for Limited Times to Authors and Inventors the exclusive Right to their respective Writings and Discoveries." Although the term *patent* is not used in the Constitution, the Constitutional Convention's records make clear that the clause was intended to authorize the granting of patents.

The first U.S. patent statute was passed in 1790 (authored by Thomas Jefferson). It called for patent applications and a 14-year term of exclusive use by the inventor if the invention was deemed "sufficiently useful and important." The statute granted a 14-year monopoly on the invention in exchange for disclosure sufficient to enable someone skilled in the art to construct or use the invention.

The U.S. patent law has been revised several times. In 1836, the U.S. Patent Office was established to review patent applications. In 1861, the patent term was extended to 17 years, and three criteria were established for patentability: "novelty," "usefulness," and "priority." In other words, the invention must be a new and useful improvement over existing devices or processes, while "priority" requires that the inventor be the first and true inventor. These requirements are discussed in more detail in the following sections.

The current patent law was passed in 1952 (the Patent Act) and is located in Title 35 of the United States Code (U.S.C.). The Patent Act was partially revised in 1995, extending the patent term to 20 years from the date of filing[2] and classifying "offers to sell" as infringement.[3] The legal standards applied in patent cases are rooted in the statutory language, as interpreted by federal courts. It is important to understand how courts have developed the requirements for patentability because many vital principles cannot be found in the Patent Act alone.

Charles Duell, the American Commissioner of Patents, is widely credited with the statement, "Everything that can be invented has been invented." Duell supposedly made this statement in 1899.[4] Regardless of the accuracy of the quotation, no one could have forecast the spectacular increases in the number of patent applications. On December 10, 1999, the U.S. Patent and Trademark Office (PTO) granted its six millionth patent.[5] In fiscal year 2001, the PTO expected to receive 335,000 patent applications—a 12 percent increase in applications over the filings received in fiscal year 2000.

DESCRIPTION OF A PATENT

Patents may be identified by their titles or by patent number. All patents are assigned numerical identifications. Patent numbers are sequential, so a higher number indicates a more recently issued patent. Because the titles can be cumbersome, a patent often is reduced to three numbers for quick reference, especially in litigation. Those three numbers are the last three digits of a patent number. For example, U.S. Patent No. 1,234,567 would be referred to as "the '567 patent."

The body of a patent has two main parts: the "specification" and the "claims." The specification follows the cover page; it contains a description of the invention, including drawings when necessary. The specification should also describe related art and the relevant prior art (i.e., similar inventions or techniques that precede the patent). The specification further must describe how to make and use the invention ("enabling" the invention) and the "best mode" of carrying out the invention known to the inventor at the time of filing the patent application.[6]

The claims are the most important part of a patent. The claims identify the scope of what is "claimed" for the inventor's exclusive use during the term of the patent. Generally, claims are broader than what is described in the specification in order to include obvious alterations within the scope of the invention. Claims are either "independent" or "dependent"; an "independent claim" refers to a relatively broad claim that is not a subset of another claim. Narrower, "dependent claims" typically follow and incorporate material from an independent claim. The aim of the patent's drafter is to ensure that if the broader independent claim is held invalid, the narrow dependent claims may survive. Dependent claims generally are also attempts by the drafter to preclude small variations on the invention from being patentable.

Each claim usually has three parts: a preamble, a transition, and the body. The preamble generically defines an invention, for example, "an apparatus for writing." A process patent typically begins with "a method for." The transition uses language like "comprising" or "consisting of."[7] The body limits the invention to certain elements (e.g., "an apparatus for writing comprising a wood shaft and a graphite core").

THE SUBJECT MATTER OF UTILITY PATENTS

There are three types of patents: design, plant, and utility patents. We consider only utility patents—the category of patents one is most likely to encounter as a damage expert.[8]

To be patentable, an invention must come within one of the four categories set forth in section 101 of the Patent Act:

> Whoever invents or discovers any new and useful process, machine, manufacture, or composition of matter, or any new and useful improvement thereof, may obtain a patent therefore, subject to the conditions and requirements of this title.[9]

Thus, only four types of inventions can be patented: (1) a process, (2) a machine, (3) a manufacture, and (4) a composition of matter.[10] A process is a new means of achieving a goal or product. Categories (2), (3), and (4) cover types of products made from patentable subject matter. A composition of matter consists of a combination of known things, where the combination itself is the invention. For example, a new combination of known chemicals is patentable as a "composition of matter." A manufacture is an object made by human labor, such as a chair. It does not include products that exist in nature. A machine is an invention that embodies a process. The machine itself is the invention under this category, not the process.

Courts also have excluded certain categories of things or discoveries from patentable subject matter. These excluded categories include printed matter, laws of nature, mathematical algorithms, natural forces, natural principles, methods of calculation, and abstract ideas. As the following cases illustrate, inventions that include elements from some of these categories are not absolutely precluded from constituting patentable subject matter (e.g., mathematical algorithms may be used in patentable applications).

The accepted justification for the categorical exclusions is that patenting such fundamental categories would impede rather than advance innovation and technological progress. Theoretically, awarding exclusive rights to a very broad concept or fundamental principle precludes varied approaches to development, improvements, and applications. However, without the incentive of at least a limited-term monopoly, the inventor lacks the motivation to invest significant time and resources in research and development at all. Moreover, a process or thing that is present in nature supposedly does not require as significant an investment of resources by the inventor, and therefore less reward is necessary to compensate the inventor and preserve his incentive to invent. Patent law is a perpetual attempt to balance the competing interests of diversity of development and inventor incentives. This delicate balancing test is a recurring theme that guides, either explicitly or implicitly, judicial decisions in many areas of patent law, including the scope of patentable subject matter, the breadth of the patent, and the relationship between prior art and the allegedly new invention.

To understand patent law (or any area of intellectual property), it is necessary to gain a familiarity with some judicial opinions. Because reading entire cases can be tedious, difficult, and time-consuming, throughout this book we present the highlights of certain cases. The selected cases were included either because they establish precedent on a particular issue or because they offer a particularly helpful explanation of a legal principle. On certain topics, courts have reached apparently conflicting results; being aware of the potential for varying outcomes and the factors that influence those decisions can be as valuable as learning a straightforward answer.

Several cases epitomize the current analysis of patentable subject matter. *Diamond v. Chakrabarty* is well known for its description of the breadth of the standard for patentable subject matter and its application to modern inventions. *State Street Bank & Trust Co. v. Signature Financial* marks a relatively recent shift in the law that permits the patenting of business methods and transformative applications of mathematical algorithms.

Diamond v. Chakrabarty[11]

Diamond v. Chakrabarty should help you understand how courts analyze the question of patentable subject matter. The Chakrabarty court famously described the scope of patentable subject matter as "anything under the sun that is made by man." *Chakrabarty* held that the inventor must *change* the product's naturally occurring physical properties, not merely take advantage of inherent qualities. Chakrabarty developed a bacterium that broke down crude oil; the genetically altered bacteria were useful for cleaning up oil spills. In upholding the patent, the court emphasized that, although a natural biological phenomenon would not be patentable, a man-made biological product, even a living creature, can be patented.

State Street Bank & Trust Co. v. Signature Financial Group, Inc.[12]

The patented invention in this case was a data processing system that allowed a user to record financial information and make calculations necessary for maintaining a particular financial service called a "partner fund" for mutual funds. The

State Street Bank & Trust Co. v. Signature Financial Group, Inc. (continued)

district court found that the claimed invention fell into one of two judicially created exceptions to statutory subject matter: the mathematical algorithm exception or the business method exception. However, the Federal Circuit held that neither of those categories is necessarily unpatentable subject matter. First, the transformation of data by a machine using algorithms is patentable where it produces a "useful, concrete and tangible result." The court cited to earlier cases such as *Diamond v. Diehr* and *In re Alappat* for the rule that computer software code alone is not patentable, but a machine or manufacture that embodies both hardware and software elements can be patented. This results-oriented analysis means that practical applications of purely mathematical algorithms merit patent protection. Second, the court found that "business methods" are statutory subject matter for patents.

In short, the court held that patentable subject matter should be evaluated not by which of the four statutory categories it most closely matches, but by its "essential character," particularly the inventor's "practical utility." This holding opens the door to a wide range of business methods and activities as patentable subject matter.

These two cases represent a pragmatic and expansive approach to patentability. This approach is particularly relevant for Internet companies today. Internet companies have been awarded patents for fairly traditional business methods, simply because they are "new" and original in the context of e-commerce. These patents are controversial and often are the subject of current litigation.

THE STANDARDS OF PATENTABILITY

Qualifying as patentable subject matter is necessary, but not sufficient, for patentability; the invention must also possess certain specific characteristics. In addition to falling within the scope of patentable subject matter, an invention must meet three statutory criteria. A patentable invention must be novel, have utility, and be nonobvious. Section 101 requires novelty and utility.[13] Section 103 requires an invention to be a nonobvious development compared to prior art.[14]

Utility

Section 101 of the Patent Act provides that a patentable invention must be "useful." The courts require an invention to have a specific beneficial use. It need not be a successful commercial product, but the value of the invention cannot be purely hypothetical. In the vast majority of cases, courts require only a very low threshold of proof of utility. Typically, usefulness is only an issue for chemical combinations, as illustrated by *Brenner v. Manson*.

Brenner v. Manson[15]

Brenner emphasizes that patents are related to the world of commerce, not philosophy or pure science. The invention at issue was a new chemical process for making a known steroid. There was presently no use for the steroid, but the inventor asserted that potential future uses existed. The Court held that vague potential utility is insufficient to satisfy section 101. The Court stated, "a patent is not a hunting license. It is not a reward for the search, but compensation for its successful conclusion." The patent system grants a monopoly in exchange for disclosure of a specific useful invention that benefits the public. If there is no present use, then the monopoly not only does not benefit the public, but it can discourage subsequent discovery of additional uses.

Clearly, the *Brenner* court's opinion relies heavily on the balancing test described above. Awarding the *Brenner* inventor a patent would have been equivalent to granting a monopoly on knowledge for which the inventor had not yet figured out a useful application, and would have excessively preempted other inventors from developing a method *and* a beneficial use for the method.

Novelty

Sections 101 and 102(a), (b), (e), and (g) require that an invention be "new" or novel before it can be patented. These sections work together to ensure that the first person to *invent* the product, not necessarily the first person to file for a patent, receives the patent. Under section 102, an invention cannot be novel if there was "anticipation" of the invention. In the United States, any of the following events, for example, could constitute anticipation of the claimed invention: (1) each and every element of the invention was described in a prior patent or printed publication, (2) all claimed elements existed in an unabandoned and unconcealed invention by others, or (3) the claimed invention was used by others in the United States before the person applying for the patent invented it. In other countries, each and every element must be described in a prior patent or printed publication in order to anticipate a claimed invention. A product or process that would infringe the applicant's invention if it came later in time anticipates the invention if it came before.

When discussing "anticipation" and other issues relating to inventions preceding the allegedly patentable invention, we often use the term *prior art*. Prior art simply refers to the state of knowledge and known discoveries that existed in the relevant field of art before the invention in question. Prior art can encompass published articles, theses, machines, models, other products, and so on. Experts commonly are called on to distinguish the supposedly new invention from the prior art or to discuss the scope of the prior art.

Scripps Clinic & Research Found., Inc. v. Genentech, Inc.[16]

Scripps analyzes the extent to which a prior disclosure may put the invention in the hands of the public. The invention in this case involved a method for making a protein related to the clotting of blood. One issue in the case was whether the claims under which infringement was alleged were anticipated by a Ph.D. dissertation that was published before the invention. The dissertation was cited in the application as prior art. The court stated that "invalidity for anticipation requires that all of the elements and limitations of the claim are found within a *single prior art reference.*" If multiple references are necessary to cover all the elements of the claimed invention, then the invention cannot be anticipated and therefore is "novel," but nevertheless may still fail to qualify as nonobvious under section 103.

The justification for novelty requirements is that there is no need to encourage innovation if the invention is already known by people in the relevant field. Patent law should not punish prior users of a product or method by creating a monopoly where there previously was free access and open availability.

To avoid rejection of patent claims on the basis of novelty, an inventor may "swear behind" the date of the use or publication that allegedly anticipates his or her invention. The effective date of a reference is the date on which an ordinary person in the relevant field of art has effective access to the disclosure. Clearly, this may vary from the date of publication to the date of indexing by a library (in the case of a publication that does not circulate widely). The critical date for the inventor is the date on which he or she completed the invention; this date is assumed by the PTO to be the date on which the applicant filed a complete application disclosing the invention. However, if the examiner produces anticipating prior art dated before the inventor's date of filing, the inventor is permitted to establish that she invented the invention before the date of filing. The usual procedure for establishing this invention date is to "swear behind" by filing an affidavit under Patent Office Rule 131 claiming "completion of the invention in this country" before the date of the anticipatory reference.[17] An invention is "completed" when the invention has been "reduced to practice" or the inventor establishes "conception coupled with due diligence" from the date of the reference to reduction to practice.

Statutory Bar—"Loss of Right"

The purpose of the statutory bar or "loss of right" is to encourage inventors to seek patent protection for their inventions diligently.[18] The statutory bar focuses on the activities of the applicant and the public more than one year before the date of filing of the patent application (not the issuance of the patent). Section 102(b) invalidates a patent if the invention was on sale in the United Sates more than one year before the application (the "on-sale bar"). In addition, a patent can be invalidated if the invention is patented or described in a printed publication in the United States or a foreign country one year before the date of the application. Finally, if the invention is in public use by anyone in the United Sates one year before the application, the patent will be invalid ("public use bar"). In general terms, if the inventor or patent owner is responsible for any of these activities, the patent statutes bar the patent even though the invention is novel, and thus the result is a "loss of right." If someone other than the inventor or patent owner is responsible for these activities, then the patent is barred because the invention is not "novel."

Pfaff v. Wells Electronics, Inc.[19]

Pfaff filed a patent application on a computer chip socket invention on April 19, 1982. The statutory bar therefore concerns events occurring prior to April 19, 1981. On March 17, 1981, Pfaff showed the invention to Texas Instruments. On April 8, 1981, Pfaff received written confirmation of a previous oral purchase order. The order was filled in July 1981. The court found that the patent was invalid. The court found that an offer for sale was enough for the product to be considered "on sale" under section 102(b), because an "attempt to commercialize" may be sufficient if the invention was "ready for patenting" at the time of the offer for sale.

Pfaff's two-pronged test governs application of the on-sale bar, although the courts have had some difficulty applying the two tests to the facts of particular cases.

Crystal Semiconductor Corp. v. TriTech Microelectronics Int'l, Inc.[20]

In this case, the Federal Circuit clarified the on-sale bar doctrine. Crystal filed a patent application for its analog-to-digital converter technology on October 2, 1987, thus creating a "critical date" of October 2, 1986, for purposes of the statutory bar. Crystal received a purchase order confirmation for five of its converter chips on September 11, 1986. The court found that the purchase order could

Crystal Semiconductor Corp. v. TriTech Microelectronics Int'l, Inc. (continued)

qualify as a "commercial exploitation" of the patented technology even though Crystal placed the order "on hold" and did not accept the offer until after the critical date. Apparently the fact that the order was capable of being accepted was sufficient to satisfy the commercialization prong of *Pfaff*.

Linear Tech. Corp. v. Micrel, Inc.[21]

Linear Technology filed a complaint against Micrel alleging infringement of Linear Technology's patent pertaining to adaptive transistor drive circuitry used in telecommunications, cell phones, and computers. The District Court held the patent invalid due to the on-sale bar.

The Federal Circuit reversed, holding that none of the activities in question constituted an "offer" to sell. In order to interpret "offer," the court looked to the common law definitions of the term and concluded that an offer must (1) communicate with potential customers, and (2) must indicate that assent by the customer will constitute an agreement (i.e., that Linear Technology intends to be bound by its offer, if accepted). Mere advertising, such as promotional materials sent to distributors, may simply qualify as "an invitation for offers," but not an actual offer.

Finally, *Monon* examines not whether an offer or sale was made, but whether that transaction was commercial in nature.

Monon Corp. v. Stroughton Trailers, Inc.[22]

A sale prior to the critical date does not necessarily establish invalidity; if the sale or public use of the patented device was *primarily experimental* (as opposed to primarily commercial), the patent may survive the statutory bar. In *Monon*, the patentee manufactured trailers. Since the patentee did not also operate its trailers, it completed a sale in order to subject the patented device to conditions of actual use. Specifically, the court heard testimony that the sale was necessary to determine whether the trailer could withstand the stress of heavy loading and long hauls. The Federal Circuit held that this evidence was sufficient to withstand summary judgment because it raised a genuine issue of material fact as to whether the sale was primarily for "commercial" or "experimental" purposes.

Nonobviousness

Section 103 of the Patent Act requires that a patentable invention must not be obvious at the time of the invention to a person of ordinary skill in the relevant art. Prior art must be in the same field, or an "analogous art" (i.e., a field of expertise that would be logical to search if confronted with the particular problem facing the inventor). Where the prior art "teaches away" (i.e., discourages the inventor's approach to the problem, the prior art can be good evidence of nonobviousness). To render an invention obvious, the prior art must provide both an enabling suggestion, teaching, or motivation to combine the prior art in the manner that the invention is claimed in the patent, and must contain a reasonable expectation of success.

Graham v. John Deere Co.[23]

This case sets out the factors to be considered in determining nonobviousness: (1) determine the scope and content of the prior art; (2) determine the differences between the prior art and the patent claims at issue; (3) determine the level of ordinary skill in the art; and (4) determine secondary considerations, such as commercial success, long-felt need, failure of others, and the acquiescence of others to the validity of the patent as demonstrated in licensing or development agreements. The Court first recounts the history leading up to the 1952 Patent Act. The 1952 Act added section 103, requiring nonobviousness (and replaced the earlier "new and useful" tests). The invention at issue in *Graham* was a spring clamp that allowed a plow to be pushed upward if it hits obstructions, thus preventing the plow from breaking as frequently. The defendant who was alleged to infringe Graham's patent claimed the patent would have been obvious. Under the four-pronged test, the Court found that the Graham patent would have been obvious to one skilled in the art at the time of the invention. The difference in structure between the Graham clamp and the prior art was the only other possible effective structure, as the simple inversion of the shank and hinge plate was the only way to increase the flex. Thus, the product would have been obvious and not worthy of patent protection.

PATENT INFRINGEMENT

Section 271 of the Patent Act governs infringement. There are two types of infringement. The first type of infringement is "direct" infringement, which occurs when a person makes, uses, sells, or offers to sell in the United States an apparatus or process encompassed by any claim of a patent. Intent or knowledge of infringement is irrelevant. The second type of infringement is "indirect" infringement, which occurs when the defendant causes another to directly infringe and the defendant actively and knowingly aids in the direct infringement. Indirect infringement also includes "contributory" infringement. Contributory infringement is a subset of indirect infringement; under section 271(c), offers to sell, sale, or import a component that is a "material part" of the patented invention, made with the knowledge that the component will likely result in infringement by the purchaser, constitute contributory infringement. However, if the allegedly infringing component is a "staple article or commodity of commerce suitable for substantial noninfringing use," then the offer to sell, sale, or import the component cannot be the basis for contributory infringement. In other words, if the product incorporating the component could be used in a substantial manner that would not infringe the patent, the courts will not protect the patent owner from its sale.

Infringement is determined by comparing the allegedly infringing, or "accused," product or process with the claims of the "patent in suit." Infringement is "literal" if the product or process falls within the literal meaning of the words of each element of a claim. Section 112, paragraph 6, allows patents to include claims in which some or all of the claimed elements or steps are stated in "means plus function" format, and such claims that may be the basis for literal infringement. A "means plus function" format describes elements in broad terms of what function the element accomplishes rather than reciting the structure of the element. For example, a claim might include "a means of linking *A* to *B*," instead of specifying "a nail." However, "means plus function" elements are limited to the specific structures disclosed in the patent specification and "equivalents" thereof. This proviso acts as a check on potentially broad claim elements.

Infringement can also be shown by the "doctrine of equivalents." Proof of infringement under the doctrine of equivalents requires proof of "substantial equivalency" of all the limitations of a claim that are not "literally" satisfied. A patent owner may sue for infringement under the doctrine of equivalents if the accused device performs "substantially the same function in substantially the same way to obtain the same result."[24] Equivalency considers the type of patent (pioneer invention or improvement), the prior art, the prosecution history, the content of the specification, and other factors. Individual elements, not the invention as a whole, must be considered for application of the doctrine of equivalents.

Graver Tank & Mfg. Co. v. Linde Air Prods. Co.[25]

Graver Tank analyzes infringement under the doctrine of equivalents, examining what constitutes "equivalence." The Court held that equivalency must be determined in the context of the patent, the prior art, and the particular circumstance of

(continues)

Graver Tank & Mfg. Co. v. Linde Air Prods. Co. (continued)

the case. In this case, the Court found that the substitution of manganese for the particular alkaline earth metal used in the patent's welding process was a substitution taught by prior art, and thus still infringed. The purpose for an ingredient, the way in which it serves its function, and the result are all factors that enter an analysis of equivalence. Thus, a patent's protection cannot be circumvented by unimportant or insubstantial alterations to a patented device.

Hilton Davis Chemical Co. v. Warner-Jenkinson Co., Inc.[26]

Hilton Davis presented a slightly different way of analyzing the doctrine of equivalents to establish infringement as compared to the function/way/result test outlined in *Graver Tank*. In *Hilton Davis*, the Federal Circuit emphasized that the doctrine of equivalents applies "if and only if the differences between the claimed and accused products or processes are *insubstantial*."

The factors to be determined in evaluating the "substantiality" of the differences between the products or processes include: (1) whether persons with skill in the relevant art actually knew of the equivalence of the claimed and accused inventions; (2) whether a person with skill in the relevant art could have known of the equivalence; and (3) how the defendant invented or designed her product. This last factor examines whether the defendant intended to copy the patented invention (which could indicate that the differences were only trivial), had intended to design around the patented invention (which might imply that the defendant had attempted to make substantial changes), or had inadvertently arrived at the same invention through independent research (which may neutralize this factor for purposes of the evaluation).

Despite these limitations on applying the doctrine of equivalents, the doctrine is commonly asserted in patent litigation, at least as an alternative grounds for establishing infringement. Many plaintiffs will argue that the defendant infringes both literally and under the doctrine of equivalents, and possibly narrow their theory as discovery progresses. However, a recent Federal Circuit decision appears to place extensive new limits on the use of the doctrine of equivalents to establish infringement.

Festo Corp. v. Shoketsu Kinoki Kogyo Kabushiki[27]

Festo marks a shift in the Federal Circuit's approach to the doctrine of equivalents by limiting the potential applications of the doctrine and thus confirming the court's narrower approach to claim construction. The Federal Circuit held that when a party amended a claim during prosecution of the patent for any reason related to the statutory requirements for a patent, no range of equivalents is available for the amended claimed element. In other words, the patentee must prove that the accused product or process literally satisfies the language of the amended element. The court also found that "voluntary" claim amendments—i.e., those not required by the examiner or made in response to a specific rejection by an examiner—must be treated the same as any other claim amendments if the result of the amendment was to narrow the scope of the claim. Since the patent owner, Festo, had not established explanations unrelated to patentability for its claim amendments, the Federal Circuit found that the doctrine of equivalents was not available to Festo as a theory of infringement.

Since many patent applications go through several amendments, and arguably all amendments are related to meeting the patentability requirements, *Festo* casts a daunting shadow on the scope of the doctrine of equivalents. Many commentators think that the Federal Circuit went too far and essentially eliminated the doctrine of equivalents in all but a few, unusual cases where the patent application did not go through the typical revision and amendment process. Upon appeal of the Federal Circuit's decision, the United States Supreme Court granted cert. and heard oral arguments in early 2002. At the time of drafting and submission of this manuscript to publisher, the authors were awaiting the Supreme Court's decision. The Supreme Court decision issued on May 28, 2002, effectively reaffirmed the importance of the doctrine of equivalents while recognizing its limited application where claims were amended for patentability reasons. However, the Supreme Court rejected a complete bar on infringement by equivalents in those cases in favor of a rebuttable presumption. The first supplement to this book will discuss the Supreme Court decision and its aftershocks in detail.

SUMMARY

This chapter addressed the basic law of patents. It is critical that both attorneys and experts working in the area of patent damages understand the foundation elements of patent law. This chapter described what a patent is, how to read a patent, the requirements of validity, the requirements to demonstrate infringement, and the defenses to infringement. Only after a patent is found to be valid and infringed will damages be awarded. Yet damage experts must undertake their analysis before the resolution of these issues. As a result, damage experts must understand how their arguments impact the liability arguments, and they must be able to make intelligent decisions concerning the breadth of the patent claims. This chapter attempted to lay the foundation for these skills.

ENDNOTES

[1] Great Britain, Statutes at Large, 21 Jam. 1, ch. 3, § 6 (1623).

[2] 35 U.S.C. § 154.

[3] 35 U.S.C. § 271.

[4] Some sources dispute the accuracy of this quotation, especially in light of Duell's 1899 report, which documents an increase of about 3,000 patents over the previous year and nearly 60 times the number granted in 1837. *See* Samuel Sass, *A Patently False Patent Myth*, Skeptical Inquirer 13 (1989), at 310–312. However, the quotation still is popularly attributed to Duell and frequently used as an example of predictions that do not come to pass.

[5] *USPTO Performance and Accountability Report: Fiscal Year 2000*, at 13. The patent was awarded to 3Com Corporation for the HotSync Technology, which allows Palm users to synchronize their information with a computer at a single touch of a button.

[6] 35 U.S.C. § 112.

[7] The particular language used in a claim indicates precise limitations on the scope of the patent. It is important to be aware that words or phrases commonly understood to be synonymous may have distinctly different meanings in the context of a patent. For example, "comprising" indicates that the following terms are a nonexclusive list ("comprising A" thus means "including at least A, and possibly other elements"), while "consisting of" is an exclusive phrase that implies "A and only A." Accordingly, "comprising" is generally appropriate in descriptions of new areas, where the obvious substitutes for certain elements are not yet clear. Patent drafting is a highly particular process, and the lesson for most experts simply is not to make assumptions about the meanings of claim language.

[8] Design and plant patents have slightly different requirements, which are not discussed in detail here. Designs must be new, original, nonobvious, and ornamental in order to receive patent protection. Plant patents are awarded only to distinct, new, asexually reproduced varieties of plants. (Sexually reproduced plants receive protection under the agricultural statutes. *See* Plant Variety Protection Act, 7 U.S.C. § 2402.)

[9] 35 U.S.C. § 101.

[10] Improvements on inventions within any of the four categories are also patentable if they are new, useful, and nonobvious.

[11] *Diamond v. Chakrabarty*, 447 U.S. 303 (1980).

[12] *State Street Bank & Trust Co. v. Signature Financial Group, Inc.*, 149 F.3d 1368 (Fed. Cir. 1998).

[13] 35 U.S.C. § 101.

[14] 35 U.S.C. § 103.

[15] *Brenner v. Manson*, 383 U.S. 519 (1966).

[16] *Scripps Clinic & Research Found., Inc. v. Genentech, Inc.*, 927 F.2d 1565 (Fed. Cir. 1991).

[17] *See* 37 C.F.R. § 1.131.

[18] 35 U.S.C. § 102(b), (c), and (d).

[19] *Pfaff v. Wells Electronics, Inc.*, 525 U.S. 55 (1998).

[20] *Crystal Semiconductor Corp. v. TriTech Microelectronics Int'l, Inc.*, 246 F.3d 1336 (Fed. Cir. 2001).

[21] *Linear Tech. Corp. v. Micrel, Inc.* 275 F.3d 1040 (Fed. Cir. 2001).

[22] *Monon Corp. v. Stoughton Trailers, Inc.*, 239 F.3d 1253 (Fed. Cir. 2001).

[23] *Graham v. John Deere Co.*, 383 U.S. 1 (1966).

[24] *Graver Tank & Mfg. Co. v. Linde Air Prods. Co.*, 399 U.S. 605 (1950).

[25] *Id.*

[26] *Hilton Davis Chemical Co. v. Warner-Jenkinson Co.*, 62 F.3d 1512 (Fed. Cir. 1995).

[27] *Festo Corp. v. Shoketsu Kinoki Kogyo Kabushiki*, 187 F.3d 1381 (Fed. Cir. 1999).

ADDITIONAL READING

Suzanne Scotchmer, *Standing on the Shoulders of Giants: Cumulative Research and the Patent Law*, 5 Journal of Economic Perspectives 29 (Winter 1991).

Kimberly Moore, Paul Michel, and Raphael Lupo, *Patent Litigation and Strategy*, New York: West Publishing (1999).

Margreth Barrett, *Intellectual Property: Cases and Materials*, New York: West Publishing (1995).

Arthur Miller and Michael Davis, *Intellectual Property in a Nutshell*, New York: West Publishing (1990).

Robert Harmon, *Patents and the Federal Circuit*, Washington, D.C.: BNA (2001).

7

How to Calculate Patent Damages

In this chapter, we describe how experts and lawyers should approach the calculation of patent infringement damages. The chapter combines skills in law, economics, and accounting.

THE PATENT STATUTE

The starting point for any analysis of patent damages is Title 35 of the United States Code (U.S.C.), section 284 (the Patent Statute), which provides that:

> Upon finding for the claimant the court shall award the claimant damages adequate to compensate for the infringement, but in no event less than a reasonable royalty, for use made of the invention by the infringer.

Before 1946, the precursor to section 284 went beyond "compensation," allowing for both recovery of compensation and the infringer's profits. The 1946 Amendment Act of August 1, 1946, Ch. 726, § 1, eliminated the language regarding the infringer's profits and added the reference to compensation.[1]

This revision is important. Before 1946, patent owners were awarded damages that included both the lost profits to the patent owner and the infringer's profits.[2] Essentially, a successful plaintiff was placed in a better position than had the infringement not occurred because profits on some sales were counted twice—once as lost profits to the patent owner and again as the actual profits the infringer received. The Supreme Court interpreted the 1946 revision as correcting this situation, holding that the intent of the revised statute was to limit a plaintiff's damages to "compensation for the pecuniary loss [the patent owner] has suffered from the infringement, without regard to the question whether the defendant has gained or lost by his unlawful acts."[3] According to the Court, the statutory reference to compensatory damages means that damages are limited to "the difference between [the patent owner's] pecuniary condition after the infringement, and what his condition would have been if the infringement had not occurred."[4] In other words, "[h]ad the infringer not infringed, what would [the] Patent Holder . . . have made?"[5]

King Instruments, Inc. v. Perego[6]

In *King Instruments*, a manufacturer of machines for loading magnetic tape into cassettes claimed that a competitor was infringing his patent. The Federal Circuit found that the competitor's reel changer infringed the patent and held that the manufacturer was entitled to both lost profits and a reasonable royalty. The Court maintained that the only limitation on the types of harm for which damages may be awarded is that the plaintiff must prove that the injury was caused by the alleged infringement. The Court also upheld the patent owner's right to withhold the subject of the patent where it led to higher profits from manufacturing and marketing nonpatented products that would otherwise compete with the patented product. To compensate for infringement of the right to exclude, damages may include lost profits on competing products not covered by the infringed patent claims.

THE CHOICE BETWEEN LOST PROFITS AND REASONABLE ROYALTIES

The first decision the lawyer or expert must make is to decide which method to use in calculating damages in a particular case: "lost profits," a "reasonable royalty," or a combination of both. The courts view lost profits as the preferred method when it is appropriate for the facts of the case. As stated in *Hansen v. Alpine Valley Ski Area, Inc.*, "If the record permits the determination of actual damages, namely, the profits the patentee lost from the infringement, that determination accurately measures the patentee's loss. If actual damages cannot be ascertained, then a reasonable royalty must be determined."[7]

There are situations in which the patent owner would be better off licensing to others the right to use the patent in exchange for royalties. A classic example is the garage inventor, who has a great idea but lacks the necessary manufacturing, marketing, distribution, or other assets necessary to fully exploit the value of the patent. The best use of the patent is to license the technology to a firm with the requisite manufacturing and marketing assets to develop the product into a commercially successful product. Another example of licensing is when a product requires the use of multiple patents owned by different firms. In this case, since each patent owner can prevent the other from producing the product, it frequently will make sense to break the deadlock by cross-licensing each other.

In each of these licensing examples, the crucial feature is that the patent owner cannot make optimal use of the patent by himself. As discussed subsequently, licensing requires some sharing of the profitability gained from the invention between licensor and licensee. Therefore, when the patent owner can use the patent without licensing, it generally will be more profitable to do so.

The lost profits damages scenario—embodied in the four-part *Panduit* test discussed in the next section—essentially identifies a clear case in which a patent owner can profitably go it alone, producing and selling the patented product without having to recruit the assistance of others. Although subsequent cases have recognized that while the *Panduit* test identifies a clear case where lost profits are appropriate, the criteria may be too narrow and exclude other cases in which lost profits would also be appropriate. Consider the first part of the test, whether there is a market for the patented product. In *Rite-Hite* the court recognized that the real issue is what sales the patent owner has lost, whether those sales are of the patented product.[8] This is because the patent owner's right is to exclude others from using the patent and does not require that the patent owner use the patent. Therefore, *Rite-Hite* established the principle that the patent owner's lost sales need not necessarily be of the patented products, but would include any lost sales that are attributable to the infringement. As discussed below, the practical effect of *Rite-Hite* is to allow a patent owner to claim lost profits on products, including functionally related "convoyed" products, by showing that infringement displaced sales of such products.

LOST PROFITS

Proof of lost profits requires the patent owner to demonstrate that, absent infringement, he would have made the sales that the infringer actually made. The standards for such proof have changed measurably in the last 15 years. Before the establishment of the Federal Circuit, the burden of proof to establish lost profits was substantial. Any possibility that someone other than the patent owner could have made any sales of the infringer completely negated a recovery of lost profits.[9] In contrast, the Federal Circuit has adopted a lower standard of "reasonable probability." Under that standard, the patent owner must show only that it is more probable than not that he would have made the infringer's sales but for the infringement.

Although the Federal Circuit has made it clear that there is no single method by which the patent owner must carry its burden of proving lost profits, by far the most common approach is the four-part test outlined in *Panduit Corp. v. Stahlin Brothers Fibre Works, Inc.*[10] (mentioned previously). The *Panduit* test requires that the plaintiff establish (1) the existence of demand for the patented product; (2) the absence of acceptable noninfringing substitutes; (3) the patent owner's ability to meet demand; and (4) some proof of the amount of profit lost per lost sale.[11] Satisfying these four factors results in the establishment of the fact that, absent infringement, the patent owner would have made the infringer's sales.

The first prong of the *Panduit* test rarely is difficult for the plaintiff to meet. Likewise, the fourth factor may require little more than the production of the plaintiff's income statement. It is not surprising, then, that the key inquiries involved in proving lost profits are the absence of acceptable noninfringing substitutes and the patent owner's ability to produce, market, and sell to the infringer's customers. Both of these questions are well suited for economic analysis, and the Federal Circuit has increasingly incorporated economic analysis when addressing these issues.

Pall Corp. v. Micron Separations, Inc.[12]

In *Pall Corp.*, the court held that, in order to be acceptable, a noninfringing alternative must be free of any pending litigation. The proposed noninfringing alternatives (certain membranes used in microfiltration) were themselves the subject of infringement litigation during the time of Micron's infringement, until they were licensed. The Federal Circuit held that the trial court should have recognized "the distinction between the legal and market situation before and after the licensing," and held that during the period that the proposed design-arounds were not licensed, their presence in the market did not provide an acceptable noninfringing alternative such that would defeat Pall's entitlement to lost profits for all of Micron's infringing sales.

Zygo Corp. v. Wyko Corp.[13]

Zygo, the patent owner, manufactured and sold a patented interferometer. Wyko produced the Wyko 6000 interferometer, which was found to infringe Zygo's patent. As a defense to awarding lost profits, Wyko argued that it could have sold SIRIS instead, a similar product that Wyko had sold before launching the infringing Wyko 6000. Zygo did not contend that SIRIS was infringing. However, the court rejected Wyko's argument, holding that in order to be an acceptable noninfringing alternative, the product must be available in the market. Since Wyko had discontinued production of SIRIS, the court found that SIRIS was only "available on the market" during the period that it was still being marketed by Wyko.

Fiskars, Inc. v. Hunt Manufacturing Co.[14]

Fiskars involved evaluation of a potential noninfringing alternative not disclosed until several years after the conclusion of the trial. The procedural posture of *Fiskars* therefore is somewhat unusual, but it offers informative guidance on the nature of noninfringing alternatives for the purposes of calculating patent damages. The manufacturer Hunt claimed, subsequent to the trial, that he was entitled to relief from the trial court's damages award because of his new, noninfringing alternative to Fiskars's patented paper trimmer. The Federal Circuit rejected the manufacturer's claim, holding that he was not entitled to a second opportunity to present his case.

The manufacturer argued that he could not have introduced evidence of the new product at trial because he lacked sales data at the time to demonstrate the acceptability of the noninfringing product. However, the Court rejected this argument, finding that although sales data could provide significant evidence of an alternative's acceptability, such data "is not the sole means for demonstrating acceptability." The Court held that accused infringers could rely on witness testimony to show that the alternative was acceptable because customers did not require the patented features that were (necessarily to avoid infringement) absent from the substitute product. Although parties must support their positions with "sound economic proof," absolute certainty is not required in constructing the hypothetical but for market.

Accordingly, Hunt was denied relief from the trial verdict because it could have argued the existence of the noninfringing alternative at the time of the damages award.

Initially, the Federal Circuit required proof that noninfringing substitutes did not possess all of the attributes of the patented product.[15] Such a test cannot withstand even cursory scrutiny, however, because substitutes that possess literally all of the attributes of the patented product would be infringing, not "noninfringing." Accordingly, the effect of this early Federal Circuit doctrine was to ensure that patent owners virtually automatically met the critical second prong of the *Panduit* test.

The logical defect in this first approach led the Federal Circuit to focus on the attitudes of consumers toward the patented product and any substitutes rather than on their physical attributes.

Slimfold Mfg. Co. v. Kinkead Indus.[16]

In *Slimfold*, the court denied awarding lost profits to the patent holder because Slimfold was unable to attribute demand for the infringing product to the patented feature. The patent covered a part for a metal door; however, Slimfold could not establish that the defendant's inclusion of the patented part resulted in a change in demand or market share for either Slimfold or the defendant's door. Moreover, Slimfold failed to prove the absence of noninfringing substitutes that would have been equally acceptable to the customers. Accordingly, the defendant could simply have shifted to marketing one of the acceptable substitutes.

The court also affirmed the court's award of a relatively small royalty—0.75 percent—because the advantage of the patented invention primarily was a manufacturing advantage (for which the court awarded damages separately) and did not significantly increase the value of the entire door.

Although this change of focus marked an improvement, the Federal Circuit also held that acceptable noninfringing substitutes are legally absent when some set of customers can be shown to prefer the patented product.[17] The difficulty with this approach is that, if consumer tastes are not uniform, some subset of consumers will always prefer the patented product. As a consequence, this second approach also negated any serious analysis and ensured that the patent owner could satisfy the second *Panduit* prong.

Federal Circuit case law has now advanced significantly. In *State Industries, Inc. v. Mor-Flo Industries, Inc.*, the Federal Circuit held that lost profits are available to the patent owner only for the share of the infringing sales that would have gone to the patent owner absent the infringement.[18] Thus, the Federal Circuit dispensed with the rigid "all or nothing" approach of *Panduit*. Under this new procedure, a court can award lost profits to the patent owner on the portion of the infringer's sales that are equal to the patent owner's market share. For example, assume that there are three competitors in a market: the patent owner, the infringer, and another firm that sells a noninfringing substitute. Each competitor sells 100 units, so the market shares are one-third each. If the infringer were removed from the market and the customers of the infringer were redistributed to the remaining firms (the patent owner and the noninfringing substitute producer), the result would be that the patent owner's "but for" infringement sales would be increased by half the infringer's sales. The resulting damages in such a circumstance would be a "hybrid" of lost profits and a reasonable royalty. A lost profits analysis applies to half of the infringer's sales based on the reasoning in *Mor-Flo*, and a reasonable royalty applies to the remaining sales.

To establish the applicability of a *Mor-Flo*–type analysis, the expert must establish that the customers of the infringer are reasonably likely to redistribute themselves among the other sellers according to market share "but for" the infringement. Examination of marketing, advertising, and historical changes in market share can be useful in this analysis. This approach, although a substantial improvement, is still not without problems. One is likely to find that the *Mor-Flo* approach is accurate only for cases in which the products at issue are "homogeneous," that is, where the products lack significant brand-name recognition or significant physical or quality differences. However, in cases in which products are heterogeneous, the *Mor-Flo* market share approach may still lead to erroneous conclusions.

In applying the *Mor-Flo* approach, consider the following example of infringement in the carbonated soda industry where products theoretically are heterogeneous. Suppose it were found that Pepsi had been infringing the patented formula used by Coca-Cola (in reality the formula is a trade secret). Further assume that the relevant market is defined as branded soda in the United States and includes the sales of 7-Up, Dr. Pepper, several root beer brands, and a few other products sold nationally.[19] Moreover, for purposes of illustration, assume that in this market, Coca-Cola's market share is 30 percent and Pepsi's share is 20 percent. We would now have the situation depicted in Exhibit 7-1.

In this example we assume, following *Mor-Flo*, that once the infringer is removed from the market, consumers will choose products in the same proportions as they did prior to the infringer being removed. This approach makes the calculation of lost sales easy. Lost sales are the difference between Coke's sales in the "but for" world absent the infringer and its sales in the actual world. In this case, lost sales are 37.5 percent of the market less 30 percent of the market, or 7.5 percent of the sales of branded soda.

However, it is evident that consumers of Pepsi may have chosen Coke as a closer substitute than other sodas. If this is true, the *Mor-Flo* approach underestimates Coke's lost sales. In *BIC Leisure Products, Inc. v. Windsurfing Int'l, Inc.*, the Federal Circuit recognized the importance of product differentiation to the lost profits analysis.[20] In that case, the patent owner sold a high-end, high-priced windsurfing board, while the alleged infringer sold a similar, but lower-priced, low-end board. The Federal Circuit reached beyond the standard market share approach to lost profits and held that the two products at issue, while arguably part of the same product market, were sufficiently differentiated that the patent owner probably would have sold to very few of the infringer's

ACTUAL MARKET SHARES		"BUT FOR" MARKET SHARES	
Coke	30%	Coke (30/80×20)	37.5%
Pepsi	20%	Pepsi	0
Dr Pepper	10%	Dr Pepper	12.5%
7-Up	10%	7-Up	12.5%
Private label	0%	Private label	0
Others	30%	Others	37.5%

EXHIBIT 7-1   Market Shares in Soda Brands

customers. This was the court's conclusion despite the fact that the patent owner had a significant overall market share. *BIC Leisure* thus represents a clear advance in economic thinking for the Federal Circuit. Finally, in a recent case, *Grain Processing Corp. v. American Maize-Products Co.*, the Federal Circuit held that a noninfringing substitute need not be "on the market" or "for sale."[21] All that is required is that the substitute be "available" to be included in the market.[22]

In order to be entitled to lost profits damages, the patent owner also must demonstrate that he possesses the marketing, manufacturing, and financing capability to make the infringer's sales. The reason for this requirement is that, even if it could be shown that demand for the patent owner's product would have increased absent the infringement, the patent owner must show that he had the ability to meet the additional demand and actually increase his sales.[23]

Hebert v. Lisle Corp.[24]

In *Hebert*, the patentee admitted that he had never sold one of his patented exhaust manifold spreaders. The court noted that where the patentee does not seek to make and sell the invention, lost profits are not an appropriate measure of damages. However, Hebert presented evidence of his activities that allegedly established his intent to manufacture the tool. Hebert also claimed that Lisle's action in flooding the market with its infringing version of the tool deprived him of the opportunity to market and sell the patented invention. The court found that it would be incorrect to bar a patentee who is not yet manufacturing the product from proving that his actual damages were larger than a reasonable royalty, but that the burden on such a patentee was "commensurately heavy" to prove what he would have earned but for the infringement. "Damage awards cannot be based upon speculation or optimism, but must be established by evidence," concluded the court, and remanded the issue to the trial court for evaluation of the evidence that Hebert would have and could have captured Lisle's profits but for the infringement.

Although in the past, the ability to make the infringer's sales was considered solely from the point of view of manufacturing capacity, courts today also inquire whether the patent owner has the ability to market and service the infringer's customers.[25] This is important because, as any business people know, the ability to procure sales requires much more than merely producing the product. The ability to distribute, market, and service a product is equally as important as the manufacturing capacity to produce it. Other factors that an expert should consider include:

- Is there distribution capacity?
- Are the infringer's sales made to longtime customers?

- Does the patent owner have the required marketing, full line of products, services, or other attributes required to make the infringer's sales?
- Do the cash flow statements indicate any capital constraints?
- Is there sufficient inventory of the product available?

THE CALCULATION OF INCREMENTAL PROFITS

Once the amount of lost sales has been established, all that remains is to determine the amount of profits that would have been earned on those lost sales. Since we are attempting to determine how much better off the patent owner would have been had there been no infringement, an appropriate method is to measure the "incremental" profits or income that would have resulted from the lost sales. As stated in *Paper Converting*:

> [t]he incremental income approach to the computation of lost profits is well established in the law relating to patent damages. The approach recognizes that it does not cost as much to produce unit N + 1 if the first N (or fewer) units produced already have paid the fixed costs. Thus fixed costs—those costs which do not vary with increases in production, such as management salaries, property taxes, and insurance—are excluded when determining profits.[26]

Thus, the patent damages expert is directed to determine how much additional cost is incurred to make the additional sales that would have been made "but for" the infringement. Elements of cost that would have been incurred in either case obviously do not enter into this calculation; only costs that vary with the changes in the sales volume at issue should be deducted from the sales at issue to determine incremental profits.

The determination of incremental costs can be an area of significant contention in a patent damages case. For example, the patent owner may claim that it could produce the additional volume of sales in question without adding any additional plant, equipment, overhead, or infrastructure, so that only the variable cost of goods sold need be subtracted to calculate incremental profitability. The patent owner would argue that the "gross margin" line on his income statements is the appropriate benchmark for calculating incremental profitability. The infringer, however, may claim that in order to produce the incremental output, the patent owner would have to increase all his costs proportionately (i.e., adding to plant, equipment, overhead, and infrastructure as output increases). The infringer would argue that the "net profits" line on the patent owner's income statement more accurately represents the patent owner's incremental profitability. Depending on the facts, the truth could lie anywhere in the range bounded by these two positions.

The expert must carefully examine how costs change with sales of the products in question over the range of output claimed as incremental sales. The most direct approach usually entails a detailed examination of each discrete line item of costs, broken down as finely as possible. For each cost line item, the patent damages expert should determine whether such costs are variable or fixed over the range of the incremental output.[27]

Alternatively, or as a check on the detailed cost item calculation, the expert can examine the historical behavior of total costs at different ranges of output. Changes in the patent owner's output comparable to the claimed incremental sales can yield important information relevant to the amount of incremental costs that would have to be incurred to make those incremental sales. Of course, the patent damages expert should be careful to remove any extraordinary or nonrecurring cost items that would not be expected.

In addition, it may be possible to apply econometric methods to cost and input data to estimate the effect on cost of incremental sales volume. Over the past several decades, the use of the ordinary least squares to estimate cost functions has grown widely. Although this method is a powerful tool for the analysis of data, it is important that the expert have a thorough understanding of when and how the method is appropriately used and of the limitations of the methodology (see Chapter 3).[28]

THE DAMAGE PERIOD

The damage period over which lost profits are available begins at the onset of infringement of an issued patent if the patent owner's products are marked as patented (if such marking is possible).[29] In no case can damages be awarded for infringement committed more than six years prior to the filing of the complaint.[30] If the patent owner's patented products are not marked, the damage period begins when the infringer receives actual notice of infringement. The damage period ends on the date of trial because presumably, if the infringer loses its case on liability, an injunction will be imposed. An interesting issue, however, concerns whether a patent owner can be compensated for an infringer's future impact on the patent owner's sales that results from the market effect of the infringer's past infringement.

PRICE EROSION

Lost profits include not only the loss of sales due to infringement but also the price reduction that results from the unlawful competition from the infringer. This reduction in price, or "price erosion," is now a recognized part of the lost profits damage measure. According to the Federal Circuit:

> lost profits may be in the form of diverted sales, *eroded prices*, or increased expenses. The patent owner must establish causation between his lost profits and the infringement. A factual basis for causation is that, "but for" the infringement, the patent owner would have made the sales that the infringer made, charged higher prices, or incurred lower expenses.[31]

The earliest case to establish a price erosion element of lost profits was *Yale Lock Manufacturing Co. v. Sargent*.[32] In *Yale Lock*, the Supreme Court found that the infringer was selling locks that included the infringing device at a lower price than the patent owner was. As a result, the patent owner was forced to lower his price by one dollar on some types of locks and by two dollars on other types of locks. The Court awarded, as part of the patent owner's lost profits, the erosion of the patent owner's lock price multiplied by the sales on which the lower price had been applied. But *Yale Lock* failed to consider the impact that the hypothetical price increase might have had on output or sales. As some later courts have recognized, it is not consistent for the patent owner to claim that "but for" the infringement, prices would have been higher, while simultaneously contending that total sales would have remained unchanged.[33]

Economic principles teach that there is a direct relationship between the price level and the level of output or sales.[34] Some courts have recognized this connection. For example, in the seminal case of *Panduit Corp. v. Stahlin Bros. Fibre Works*, Judge Markey held for the purposes of calculating lost profits that demand was sufficiently elastic that "any loss in Panduit's profits due to the price reduction was more than compensated by the gain in profits due to the increase in plaintiff's sales volume because of the price reduction."[35] Similarly, in *Polaroid Corp. v. Eastman Kodak Co.*, the Massachusetts District Court concluded that no lost profits from price erosion were justified because "the higher prices Polaroid says it would have charged would have depressed demand so substantially that the strategy they historically pursued is actually the more profitable one."[36] In other words, the court found that price elasticity was already too high to justify an award based on price erosion.

Despite the apparent simplicity of this principle, the majority of courts that have awarded damages for price erosion have done so without adjusting the level of output on which lost profits are calculated. The case of *Micro Motion, Inc. v. Exac Corp.* is illustrative.[37] The case involved Exac's infringement of Micro Motion's patent for flow meters. Before Exac entered the market, Micro Motion was the only supplier of the flow meters at issue. Micro Motion claimed patent damages in the form of lost profits on Exac's sales for which Micro Motion had the capacity to produce and a reasonable royalty on the remainder of Exac's sales. But Micro Motion also claimed that, but for the infringement, its prices on its sales would have been higher. Micro Motion called Professor Daniel Rubinfeld, a nationally recognized economist, who testified that absent infringement, Micro Motion's prices would have been 4 percent higher, and as a result, total output would have been 1 percent lower (thus, elasticity was 0.25). Citing this testimony, the court awarded the plaintiff an additional 4 percent of sales on the lost profits portion of Exac's sales, but surprisingly did not reduce the size of the total output base consistent with Rubinfeld's analysis.

The court was clearly in error. Either output should have been reduced based on the theorized price increase, as plaintiffs' expert conceded, or the court should have refused to grant damages for price erosion altogether. The theory would be that if Micro Motion had licensed Exac (the basis for the reasonable royalty award), Exac would have competed with Micro Motion for all sales (since it had a license), thus eliminating any ability of Micro Motion to raise its prices.

To illustrate the problem with awarding price erosion damages without also adjusting for resulting decreases in the quantity demanded, consider Exhibit 7-2. The original "but for" price and quantity combination, representing total sales of both infringer and patent owner, is denoted P_c, Q_c. A damage award that does not take into account price erosion would award the patent owner profits equal to the area corresponding to P_c, Q_c, less the profits actually earned by the patent owner. However, absent infringement, Micro Motion would have been able to attain even greater profits with the price and quantity combination of P_m, Q_m. Doing so would gain a higher margin on sales that remained despite the higher price, denoted by area a, while losing the margin on sales that are lost due to the higher price, denoted by the area b.[38] Whenever area a is larger than area b, it is profitable to charge the higher price and sell fewer units. Therefore, the typical damage award, not accounting for price erosion, undercompensates the patent owner by the amount of area (a − b). However, in the *Micro Motion* case, in attempting to account for price erosion, the court appears to have awarded profits based on a price and quantity combination of P_m, Q_c. The result is to overcompensate the patent owner by the sum of areas b and c.

THE ENTIRE MARKET RULE

Another issue often raised in patent infringement cases is what product sales are eligible for compensation to the patent owner—that is, can the sale of products not covered by the patent in suit be a basis for lost profits? The contours of the proper legal and economic limitations to recovery on the sales of nonpatented items raises serious legal and

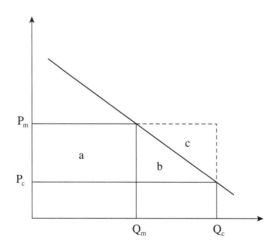

EXHIBIT 7-2   Price Erosion Damages

constitutional issues. Only a brief outline of the pertinent rules is provided here.[39] The Federal Circuit recently addressed this issue in *Rite-Hite Corp. v. Kelley Co., Inc.*[40] There, the Federal Circuit held that lost profits on nonpatented components or complementary products sold with the patented product must satisfy the so-called entire market rule to be compensable. The entire market rule requires that, to be recoverable, the "unpatented components must function together with the patented components in some manner so as to produce a desired end product or result. All the components together must be analogous to components of a single assembly or be parts of a complete machine, or they must constitute a functional unit."[41] Thus, the sale of products that are complements to a patented product (i.e., convoyed sales) but not functionally integrated are not compensable.[42] The court reasoned that the Patent Statute sought to compensate only competitive injury, and products sold with the patented product do not necessarily compete directly with the infringer.

Although this reasoning narrows the lost profits recovery by eliminating awards for convoyed sales, it also expands potential recoveries for lost sales on products that are not covered by the patent in suit, but nonetheless compete with the infringer's products. To illustrate such a situation, suppose that the patent owner sells two products, *A* and *B*. Further assume that the infringer infringes the patent covering product *A*, but sells its product in competition with product *B*. According to *Rite-Hite*, the patent owner can recover for lost profits on its lost sales of product *B*, even though product *B* does not use the patented technology.

The *Rite-Hite* holding is likely to raise future controversy.[43] The foundation of the *Rite-Hite* rule lies in the court's definitions of "competition" and "functional integration." Both concepts are defined narrowly by the Federal Circuit. Functional integration is defined in physical terms rather than economic terms, focusing on how products physically relate to each other in use, rather than the efficiencies or inefficiencies from their complementary features. Likewise, competition is limited to a direct product by product confrontation and does not consider broader strategic rivalry among firms. Economic analysis can be useful in unpacking the logic of the *Rite-Hite* holding as these issues are revisited in the future.

REASONABLE ROYALTY

As an alternative to the lost profits method of calculating damages, the patent owner can claim reasonable royalties for use of the patented technology. This analysis can be used to determine damages for any portion of the infringing sales for which the patent owner cannot establish lost profits. A reasonable royalty analysis seeks to determine the royalty the patent owner would have obtained in a voluntary "hypothetical negotiation" between the patent owner (as a willing licensor) and the infringer (as a willing licensee) just prior to the onset of infringement, assuming that both parties agreed that the patent is valid and that the infringers' products infringe the patent.[44] This analysis is guided by economic principles bearing on the costs and benefits of a license to each participant and the relative bargaining leverage of the parties.

The *Georgia-Pacific* Factors

The case law on reasonable royalties contains valuable guidelines for conducting such an analysis. *Georgia-Pacific Corp. v. U.S. Plywood Corp.*[45] provided a list of 14 factors that should be considered in the analysis. These factors are:

1. The royalties received by the patentee for the licensing of the patent in suit, proving or tending to prove an established royalty.
2. The rates paid by the licensee for the use of other patents comparable to the patent in suit.
3. The nature and scope of the license, as exclusive or nonexclusive; or as restricted or nonrestricted in terms of territory or with respect to whom the manufactured product may be sold.
4. The licensor's established policy and marketing program to maintain his patent monopoly by not licensing others to use the invention or by granting licenses under special circumstances designed to preserve that monopoly.
5. The commercial relationship between the licensor and licensee, such as whether they are competitors in the same territory in the same line of business or whether they are inventor and promoter.
6. The effect of selling the patented specialty in promoting sales of other products of the licensee; the existing value of the invention to the licensor as a generator of sales of his nonpatented item; and the extent of such derivative or convoyed sales.
7. The duration of the patent and the term of the license.
8. The established profitability of the product made under the patent, its commercial success, and its current popularity.
9. The utility and advantages of the patent property over alternative products or methods, if any, that had or could have been used to obtain similar results.
10. The nature of the patented invention, the character of the commercial embodiment of it as owned and produced by the licensor, and the benefits to those who have used the invention.
11. The extent to which the infringer has made use of the invention, and any evidence probative of the value of the use.
12. The portion of the profit or of the selling price that may be customary in the particular business or in comparable businesses to allow for the use of the invention or analogous inventions.
13. The portion of the realizable profits that should be credited to the invention as distinguished from nonpatented elements, services provided in conjunction

with the product, the manufacturing process, business risks, or significant features or improvements added by the infringer.

14. The opinion testimony of qualified experts.

The *Georgia-Pacific* factors identify economically important areas of inquiry and types of evidence that should be considered in an analysis of reasonable royalties sufficient to compensate for alleged infringement. However, as the *Georgia-Pacific* court recognized, the 14 factors necessarily fall short of providing a formula for weighing and quantifying the factors to arrive at a solution to the royalty rate question. Rather, the factors provide an important framework for the analysis and a checklist of information that should be examined in a rigorous economic analysis of reasonable royalty rates.

A Useful Classification of the* Georgia-Pacific *Factors.   For purposes of this discussion, it is convenient to parse the *Georgia-Pacific* factors into five groups corresponding to the major economic considerations they address. Factors 3 and 7 ask us to identify the major parameters of the license at issue. Although we are, by necessity, required to construct a license agreement resulting from "hypothetical negotiations between the patentee and the infringer (both hypothetically willing) at the time infringement began,"[46] this hypothetical construction must nonetheless comport with the market realities and opportunities available at the time of the hypothetical negotiation. For example, the hypothetical license should reflect the number of years remaining in the life of the patent. Chapter 14 discusses the *Georgia-Pacific* factors again in a more practical context.

The *Georgia-Pacific* factors 1, 2, and 4 direct us to examine whether other licenses provide useful information. This is discussed in the subsequent section covering comparable licenses.

Factors 4 and 5 direct us to consider costs to the licensor of granting a license. Considerations such as alternatives to licensing or the potential creation of a competitor through licensing affect the royalty rate that would be acceptable to a patent owner. In particular, a patent owner would not be willing to accept a royalty rate that does not cover his costs of licensing. These "opportunity costs" to the licensor play an important role in defining one of the boundaries of a mutually acceptable license in the hypothetical negotiation.

Factors 6 and 8 to 13 require examination of benefits to the licensee of obtaining a license. Generally, the more profitable the resulting products, the more important the technology is in allowing the production of profitable products and the less the alternatives available to the licensee, the higher the royalty rate. The important point is that a licensee will not willingly pay more than the expected benefits from licensing. This consideration determines the other boundary of a mutually acceptable license agreement in the hypothetical license negotiation.

Finally, the issue of relative bargaining power between licensee and licensor must be addressed. A number of rules of thumb or methods of identifying a likely royalty rate from among mutually acceptable rates have been employed. Having identified the general type of license at issue, the maximum acceptable price to a licensee and the minimum acceptable price to a licensor, and the outcome of bargaining in similar situations, we can draw better inferences about the likely outcome in this particular situation. Considerations such as the risks borne by the licensee in developing a salable product and the importance of other resources that the licensee brings to the process can help to narrow the area of mutually beneficial royalty rates.

Comparable Licenses.   When there is an established industry price for the technology at issue or similar technology, this "prevailing" royalty rate may be a good indicator of the result of a hypothetical royalty negotiation for the subject patent. For example, other licenses for the same patent can be highly instructive. However, it often is the case that there are no established or prevailing royalty rates and that other licenses are not comparable for a variety of reasons.

First, patents are by definition unique. The technology covered by one patent is sufficiently different from the technology covered by another patent; otherwise it would not be patentable.

Second, experience with licensing and examination of publicly available data indicates that license fees for patents exhibit impressive range; most licensed patents are worth little or nothing, while a few command very high fees. Moreover, the terms of actual license agreements are typically complex and do not lend themselves to easy extrapolation to other situations. For example, licenses can contain provisions that require subsequent performance by the parties, contingencies that affect the ultimate payments such as caps, and either lump-sum and running royalties or a combination of royalties. Many licenses border on joint venture agreements to develop future products rather than simple payments for the right to use a technology. Similarly, cross-licenses and licenses for portfolios of patents present difficulties in assigning values to individual patents in the portfolio.

Third, in the typical nonlitigation negotiation between a willing licensee and licensor, there is uncertainty regarding whether the patent is valid or whether it is infringed. Thus, in real-world licenses, there is some discounting of the value of the patent owner's right to prevent infringing use of a valid patent. For example, suppose each party believes there is a 50 percent chance of invalidity. If the royalty agreed upon is 3 percent, then the reasonable royalty at trial arguably must be 6 percent. As the example shows, most nonlitigated patent royalty rate agreements reflect a discount for uncertainty with respect to validity and infringement. In contrast, in the litigation context, the patent damages expert is asked to determine a reasonable royalty for a patent *assuming* that it is both valid and infringed. Thus, there should be no discounting for uncertainty regarding the infringement in a royalty rate established through litigation, because the facts of validity and infringement are known and the parties have borne the risk of find-ing out. A "reasonable royalty" for the purposes of assessing damages for past patent infringement may often be significantly different from (i.e., higher than) royalty rates negotiated outside the litigation context for otherwise comparable patents. The case law recognizes that royalty rates established through litigation are fundamentally not comparable to royalty rates agreed to in nonlitigation negotiation. As stated in *Panduit*,

> The setting of a reasonable royalty after infringement cannot be treated, as it was here, as the equivalent of ordinary royalty negotiations among truly "willing" patent owners and licensees. That view would constitute a pretense that the infringement never happened. It would also make and election to infringe a handy means for competitors to impose a "com-pulsory license" policy on every patent owner. Except for the limited risk that the patent owner, over years of litigation, might meet the heavy burden of proving the four elements required for recovery of lost profits, the infringer would have nothing to lose, and everything to gain, if he could count on paying only the normal, routine royalty noninfringers might have paid. As said by this court in another context, the infringer would be in a "heads I win, tails you lose" position.[47]

Finally, there is a sample bias in comparing licensed patents to the patent in question. Most patents are not licensed, probably because they have little or no market value. Comparing a litigated patent only to licensed patents is comparing the subject patent only to the patents that turn out to be market successes.

Empirical Surveys of Royalty Rates. Sometimes industry data on royalty rates can serve as a useful sanity check. Several surveys of the membership of the Licensing Executives Society (LES) have been conducted and published in the LES journal, *Les Nouvelle*. The first survey, which was conducted by McGavock, Haas, and Patin and published in the March–April 1991 issue,[48] was based on a sample of 118 respondents who filled out questionnaires on a variety of licensing topics. The respondents came from a variety of industries, so the survey allows for a cross-tabulation of industry type and average royalty rate, as well as royalty type, relation to profit, and other informa-tion. Degnan and Horton conducted a second survey of LES members, which involved 428 respondents and was published in the June 1997 issue of *Les Nouvelle*.[49] Finally, McGavock and Lasinski performed a third survey of LES members (186 of whom responded), which was published in the September 1998 issue of *Les Nouvelle*.[50] This last survey focused on intellectual property (IP) policy and strategy employed by LES members. Although far from determinative of the applicable royalty in a particular case, these surveys can provide helpful estimates of a range of reasonable royalties and proffer a good check on outrageously high or low figures.

To qualify as admissible evidence rather than merely internal sanity checks, surveys must meet several judicial criteria. Survey evidence must be "material, more probative on the issue than any other evidence and . . . [have] guarantees of trustworthiness."[51]

The trustworthiness of a survey depends on its conformity to generally accepted survey principles, including sampling "an adequate or proper universe of respondents."[52] To some extent, technical or methodological deficiencies affect the weight accorded a survey, not its admissibility, so long as the survey complies with generally accepted survey principles to establish a proper foundation for admissibility.[53] However, surveys may be excluded where the flaws are so substantial that any probative value of the survey is outweighed by the inaccuracies.[54] Precisely what constitutes a "generally accepted survey principle" is subject to some debate, but the courts have identified certain primary standards as follows:

> The trustworthiness of surveys depends on foundation evidence that (1) the "universe" was properly defined, (2) a representative sample of that universe was selected, (3) the questions to be asked of interviewees were framed in a clear, precise and non-leading manner, (4) sound interview procedures were followed by competent interviewers who had no knowledge of the litigation or the purpose for which the survey was conducted, (5) the data gathered was accurately reported, (6) the data was analyzed in accordance with accepted statistical principles and (7) objectivity of the entire process was assured. *Failure to satisfy one or more of these criteria may lead to exclusion of the survey.*[55]

Courts have criticized unreliable means of selecting the interviewees and found that a sample that is not properly representative warrants exclusion of the survey at trial.[56] Moreover, leading and suggestive questions undermine the legitimacy of the results.[57] The *Les Nouvelle* surveys do not appear to meet these criteria for admissibility other than as a sanity check.

Generally, the proponent of the survey will establish these criteria by using the testimony of the individuals responsible for various parts of the survey.[58] Where the proponent cannot proffer this type of testimony, the survey itself may lack sufficient foundation for admissibility. For example, in *Toys "R" Us, Inc. v. Canarsie Kiddie Shop, Inc.*, the expert witness relying on the survey for evidence of trademark confusion conceded that he had no knowledge of what the interviewers actually did in conducting the interviews, no personal knowledge of whether they followed their instructions, and no knowledge of the accuracy of the content analysis because that work, too, was subcontracted to another company.[59] Based on the expert's lack of the necessary knowledge of the survey's methodology and calculations, the court excluded the survey and the opinions of the experts based on that survey.[60] In concluding that the survey could not be used as evidence at trial, the court noted that the "absence of any testimony by others who were responsible" for the survey raised doubts as to the survey's trustworthiness.[61]

Hypothetical Negotiation: The Boundaries.   A basic economic principle is that a rational economic agent will not willingly enter into an agreement that makes him worse off. As discussed previously, the *Georgia-Pacific* factors include consideration of the cost to the hypothetical licensor (the patent owner) of granting a license to the patent

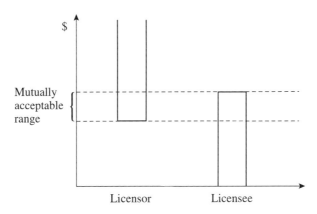

EXHIBIT 7-3   Range of Acceptable Royalty Rates

and the benefits to the hypothetical licensee from taking a license to the patent. These considerations determine the boundaries of a mutually beneficial license; the patent owner will not accept less than his cost of granting the license, while a potential licensee will not pay more than his gain from licensing.

In the willing licensor–willing licensee hypothetical situation, it must be assumed that there are mutual gains from voluntary trade, that is, that both the licensor and the licensee will be better off if a license is granted. If this were not the case, no trade between the parties would occur.

Exhibit 7-3 represents the range of acceptable royalty rates for both licensor and licensee. The area of overlap, the "mutually acceptable range," defines the set of royalty rates that make each party better off by licensing.[62]

Thus, the expert must determine the boundaries of the set of mutually agreeable royalty rates. Typically, the opportunity cost of the patent owner is the amount of profit that could be earned by not licensing (i.e., producing the product himself) or by licensing to somebody else.

On the other side of the hypothetical bargaining table, the potential licensee's benefit from licensing typically is the profit that could be gained by producing and selling products that use the patented technology.[63] In calculating the licensee's profit from using the technology, it is important to consider the licensee's opportunity costs. Opportunity cost means the benefits that could have been derived from the licensee's next best opportunity. Therefore, the appropriate maximum that a licensee would be willing to pay is equal to the profit that the licensee expects to receive from using the new technology net of the profit that it could obtain by utilizing the next-best alternative technology available.

It would be a fundamental error to consider the licensee's potential gains to be the actual accounting profits. Yet some courts have made this error in calculating patent damages.[64] An example will illustrate the problem. Suppose that a licensee can make $5,000 using technology A, but using this technology will infringe a patent covering technology A. In the alternative, the licensee can make $4,000 using a noninfringing technology. Therefore, the licensee will be unwilling to pay more than $1,000 to license the patent to technology A, even though his income statement would show a profit of $5,000 using technology A. Quite simply, paying more than $1,000 for a license to technology A would not be as profitable as simply using technology B. Thus, one must know what the opportunity cost of the infringer is to correctly identify the maximum royalty that the infringer would pay. Most courts have recognized that taking account of opportunity cost is the only correct method.[65]

One open issue is when the expert should consider the bargaining situation as taking place. Although the case law tells us that the bargaining should occur at the "onset" of infringement, an expert must be careful to consider whether the situation is prior to the infringer incurring significant sunk costs. Once sunk costs are incurred, the infringer's opportunity costs will be higher than prior to such commitments. For example, once a company has undertaken a massive investment in a project only to discover on the eve of the product launch that its product infringes, obtaining a license could be a "bet the company" issue. Conversely, had the potential infringement been discovered earlier, the company's willingness to pay would be determined by the value of undertaking the infringing project compared to undertaking the next-best net present value project.

Experts often rely on forecast documents to attempt to understand how the infringer would value a license. Forecast documents can be useful, but they also reflect the hidden assumptions and institutional motives of their author. Such documents cannot be taken at face value. Instead, interviews or discovery should be used to understand their contextual meaning before relying on them.

In any event, there typically will be a range of royalty rates that satisfy the requirements of the mutually acceptable range. A particularly difficult issue in calculating reasonable royalties involves determining where within the mutually acceptable range the negotiating parties would end up. Which amount is the most reasonable royalty? Of course, this also determines the split between the licensor and licensee of the benefits of the patented technology. In the following sections, we discuss several approaches that have been used to address this indeterminacy.

The Rule of Thumb.   One rule of thumb, sometimes used as a starting point in license negotiations, is to set a royalty rate such that 0.25 to 0.33 of the licensee's profits from using the patent go to the patent owner as a license fee. The rationale for leaving 0.75 to 0.66 of the profits to the licensee is because the licensee is expected to assume greater financial risk in commercializing the technology. This is appropriate in situations in which the patent owner is unable to commercialize the technology without significant assistance from a licensee with complementary assets, such as manufacturing, marketing, distribution, or product development skills. Recently, Jarosz, Mulhern, and Vigil of

Analysis Group conducted an empirical survey of royalty rates and concluded that, despite the fact that royalty rates varied significantly, royalty rates tended to range between 21 and 40 percent of successful licensee profits.[66]

Analytical Method.   Another approach is called the "analytical method." The analytical method is based on the premise that any rate of return in excess of normal can be attributed to the patent and constitutes the profits to be divided between the negotiation parties. The analytical method takes the profits of the infringer, subtracts the infringer's "normal" profit, and awards some portion of the remainder to the patent owner. The approach in *Tektronix*[67] is typical. In that case, the court calculated the reasonable royalty as follows. First, the court determined the infringer's sales and subtracted both variable and fixed costs to arrive at gross profits and a gross profit rate. Next, the court subtracted the infringer's rate of profit on his other products from this gross profit rate. Finally, the court divided the remainder among the infringer and the patent owner to provide some return to the infringer for the risks of manufacturing the patented product.

Design-Around Costs.   The "design-around costs" method is based on the observation that a willing licensee will not be willing to pay more for the right to use the patent than it would cost him to "design around" the patent. If the patent owner demands more than the design-around costs, the potential licensee is better off using his own resources to avoid the patent. Of course, there may be some risks associated with attempting to design around a patent, and such risks should be considered when assessing design-around costs. This method pegs the maximum value of a patent as the advantage of the patent over the next-best alternative, consistent with *Georgia-Pacific*'s factor requiring the examination of acceptable noninfringing substitutes.

Other Patent Damages.   In addition to lost profits and reasonable royalties, the patent statute allows for an injunction preventing future sales of the infringing product. When there is a finding of willful infringement, a court can increase damages up to three times the amount and assess attorney fees. "Willfulness" requires that the infringer (1) was aware of the patent, and (2) failed to investigate the patent's scope and form a good-faith belief that the patent was invalid or not infringed by the product or process in question. Finally, the statute makes clear that an infringer will be assessed interest and costs.

Stryker Corp. v. Intermedics Orthopedics, Inc.[68]

Stryker, the patent owner, sued Intermedics for infringement of its patent for a hip implant prosthesis. The court affirmed a finding of willful infringement, noting that "slavish copying" is not required to establish "deliberate" infringement.

(continues)

Stryker Corp. v. Intermedics Orthopedics, Inc. (continued)

Copying is relevant, but not a necessary element of willful infringement, although it could be evidence of a lack of good faith. Moreover, the infringing product need not be "virtually an exact copy of the patentee's product." The court found that Intermedics had failed to investigate the scope of the patent at issue once it knew of its existence and had no good-faith belief that the patent was invalid or not infringed by its prosthesis. Intermedics had an affirmative duty of due care to avoid infringement of the known patent rights of others, including seeking and obtaining competent legal advice before engaging in potentially infringing activity.

Minco provides an example of the available remedies and possible damages enhancements once a court determines that a defendant willfully infringed the patent at issue.

Minco, Inc. v. Combustion Engineering, Inc.[69]

In *Minco*, the district court found willful infringement on the part of Combustion Engineering. Since courts have the discretionary power to increase a damage award up to three times the original amount where willfulness is proven, the court doubled the sum of the lost profits and reasonable royalty that it had awarded, then added attorneys fees and prejudgment interest. Moreover, the royalty was already a "relatively high royalty" of 20 percent based on the fact that the parties were close rivals in the same market, the absence of noninfringing alternatives, the inferiority of Combustion Engineering's product before infringement, and the high rate of profitability enjoyed in the industry.

SUMMARY

This chapter is a core chapter presenting the basic principles that must be employed in the calculation of patent damages. The chapter began where every lawyer and expert must, with the applicable statute. The patent statute sets out a scheme for damage calculation from which courts have developed a methodology that is very compatible with economic theory. This chapter explained how economic principles can be used to satisfy the statutory and judicial aims in devising appropriate remedies for patent infringement. In Chapter 13 we build on and contrast with the principles discussed in this chapter, while discussing the means of calculating damages for other types of IP infringement.

ENDNOTES

[1] The legislative history of the Patent Statute is discussed in *Kori Corp. v. Wilco Marsh Buggies & Draglines, Inc.*, 761 F.2d 649, 654 (Fed. Cir. 1985).

[2] *See Kori Corp.*, 761 F.2d at 655.

[3] *Aro Manufacturing Co. v. Convertible Top Replacement Co.*, 377 U.S. 476, 507 (1964).

[4] *Id.*

[5] *Id.*

[6] *King Instruments, Inc. v. Perego*, 65 F.3d 941 (Fed Cir. 1995).

[7] *Hansen v. Alpine Valley Ski Area, Inc.*, 718 F. 2d 1075, 1078 (Fed. Cir. 1983).

[8] *Rite-Hite Corp. v. Kelley Co., Inc.*, 56 F.3d 1538 (Fed. Cir. 1995).

[9] *See Tektronix, Inc. v. United States*, 552 F.2d 343, 349 (Ct. Cl. 1977) ("if lost profits are ever to be awarded . . . it should be only after the strictest proof that the patentee would actually have earned and retained those sums in its sales").

[10] *Panduit Corp. v. Stahlin Brothers Fibre Works, Inc.*, 575 F.2d 1152 (6th Cir. 1978).

[11] *Id.* at 1156.

[12] *Pall Corp. v. Micron Separations, Inc.*, 66 F.3d 1211 (Fed. Cir. 1995).

[13] *Zygo Corp. v. Wyko Corp.*, 79 F.3d 1563 (Fed. Cir. 1996).

[14] *Fiskars, Inc. v Hunt Manufacturing, Co.*, 279 F.3d 1378 (Fed. Cir. 2002).

[15] *See, e.g., TWM Manufacturing Co., Inc. v. Dura Corp.*, 789 F.2d 895, 901 (Fed. Cir. 1986) ("a product lacking the advantages of the patented [product] can hardly be termed a substitute acceptable to the consumer who wants those advantages").

[16] *Slimfold Mfg. Co. v. Kinkead Indus.*, 932 F.2d 1453 (Fed. Cir. 1991).

[17] *See Standard Havens Products, Inc. v. Gencor Industries, Inc.*, 953 F.2d 1360, 1373 (Fed. Cir. 1991) ("if purchasers are motivated to purchase because of particular features available only from the patented product, products without such features—even if otherwise competing in the marketplace—would not be acceptable noninfringing substitutes").

[18] *State Industries, Inc. v. Mor-Flo Industries, Inc.*, 883 F.2d 1573 (Fed. Cir. 1989)

[19] This is how the Federal Trade Commission has defined the relevant market in this industry.

[20] *BIC Leisure Products, Inc. v. Windsurfing Int'l, Inc.*, 1 F.3d 1214, 1218 (Fed. Cir. 1993).

[21] *Grain Processing Corp. v. American Maize-Products Co.*, 185 F.3d 1341 (Fed. Cir. 1999).

[22] *See also Riles v. Shell Exploration and Prod. Co.*, No. 01-1553 (Fed. Cir. July 31, 2002) (holding that a reasonable royalty rate must consider potential noninfringing alternatives as limit on hypothetical negotiations).

[23] This third *Panduit* prong is connected to the second prong because the size of the patent owner's capacity impacts the number of noninfringing substitutes in the market. If the patent owner cannot meet demand, then the class of acceptable noninfringing substitutes must expand as consumers turn to other products to satisfy their needs. Despite their connection, the two issues can be treated separately.

[24] *Hebert v. Lisle Corp.*, 99 F.3d 1109 (Fed. Cir. 1996).

[25] *See Polaroid Corp. v. Eastman Kodak Co.*, 16 U.S.P.Q. 2d 1481 (D. Mass. 1990).

[26] *Paper Converting Machine Company v. Magna-Graphics Corporation*, 745 F.2d 11, 22 (Fed. Cir. 1984).

[27] Preexisting classifications of costs among "variable," "fixed," and "semivariable" may not be reliable because such classifications may not have been assigned according to the scale of output that is relevant in a particular case.

[28] This topic is too large and technically involved to be adequately discussed here. The reader is advised to consult some of the many texts available on the topic. We list several texts at the end of Chapter 3. *See, e.g.*, Rubinfeld *Reference Guide on Multiple Regression*, in Reference Manual on Scientific Evidence; Fisher, *Multiple Regression in Legal Proceedings*, 80 Columbia Law Review 702 (1980); Rubinfeld, *Econometrics in the Courtroom*, 85 Columbia Law Review 1048 (1985).

[29] 35 U.S.C. § 287.

[30] 35 U.S.C. § 286.

[31] *See LAM, Inc. v. Johns-Manville Corp.*, 718 F.2d 1056, 1065 (Fed. Cir. 1983) (emphasis added); *see also General American Transp. Corp. v. Cryo-Trans, Inc.*, 893 F. Supp. 774, 796 (N.D. Ill. 1995) ("price erosion occurs when a plaintiff is forced to lower prices due to the presence in the market of the defendant's infringing product"); *Saf-Gard Products, Inc. v. Service Parts, Inc.*, 491 F. Supp. 996, 1002 (D. Ariz. 1980) ("Computation of the plaintiff's lost profits also requires determination as to the plaintiff's effective selling price. If the plaintiff's reduced selling prices are used in the computation of lost profits, the defendant would receive a substantial benefit as a result of its infringing competition with the plaintiff.")

[32] *Yale Lock Mfg. Co. v. Sargent*, 117 U.S. 536, 548 (1886).

[33] Courts have granted damages based on a price erosion theory on the basis of a variety of types of evidence. For example, in *TWM Mfg. Co., Inc. v. Dura Corp.*, 789 F.2d 895, 902 (Fed. Cir. 1986), the Federal Circuit upheld an award of damages based on price erosion because of proffered evidence that TWM "had to give special discounts to compete with Dura's pricing practices." *Id.* at 902. The court further dismissed defendant Dura's argument "that there was no correlation between the special discounts and its infringing activity." *Id.* Similarly, in *Brooktree Corp. v. Advanced Micro Devices, Inc.*, 977 F.2d 1555, 1579 (Fed. Cir. 1992), the Federal Circuit upheld an award of lost profits based on price erosion because of evidence presented by Brooktree that "it was forced to reduce its prices when AMD announced its chips at lower prices, and that but for the infringement, Brooktree would have continued to sell its chips at the prices that had already been established." *Id.* at 1579.

[34] As discussed in Chapter 3, this relationship is measured by the concept of "elasticity." Demand for a product is said to be very elastic when consumers are willing to switch to a different good that is only slightly less expensive. In contrast, demand for a product is said to be inelastic when significant increases in price fail to cause equally significant reductions in the quantity purchased.

[35] *Panduit Corp. v. Stahlin Bros. Fibre Works*, 575 F.2d 1152, 1157 (6th Cir. 1978).

[36] *Polaroid Corp. v. Eastman Kodak Co.*, 16 U.S.P.Q. 2d 1481, 1506 (D. Mass. 1990).

[37] *Micro Motion, Inc. v. Exac Corp.*, 761 F. Supp. 1420 (N.D. Cal. 1991).

[38] For simplicity in exposition, this example assumes that costs are zero. However, the conclusion does not depend on assumptions about costs.

[39] Those readers interested in the deeper issues raised by the entire market rule should consult the complete set of opinions cited in *Rite-Hite Corp v. Kelley Co., Inc.*, 56 F.3d 1538 (Fed. Cir. 1995).

[40] *Rite-Hite Corp. v. Kelley Co., Inc.*, 56 F.3d 1538, 35 U.S.P.Q. 2d 1065, 1071 (Fed. Cir. 1995).

[41] *Id.* at 1071.

[42] Prior to *Rite-Hite*, convoyed sales were compensable if they were normally sold with the patented product.

[43] For a discussion, see Lisa C. Childs, *Rite Hite Corp. v. Kelly Co., The Federal Circuit Awards Damages for Harm Done to a Patent Not in Suit*, 1996 Loy. U. Chi. L. Rev. 665.

[44] *See, e.g.*, *Mahurkar v. C.R. Bard Inc.*, 79 F.3d 1572, 1579 (Fed. Cir. 1996) ("Hypothetical results of hypothetical negotiations between the patentee and the infringer (both hypothetically willing) at the time infringement began."); *Georgia-Pacific Corp. v. U.S. Plywood Corp.*, 318 F. Supp. 1116, 1120 (S.D.N.Y. 1970), *modified on other grounds*, 446 F. 2d 295 (2d Cir. 1971), *cert. denied*, 404 U.S. 870 (1971).

[45] *Georgia-Pacific Corp. v. U.S. Plywood Corp.*, 318 F. Supp. 1116, 1120 (S.D.N.Y. 1970), *modified on other grounds*, 446 F. 2d 295 (2d Cir. 1971), *cert. denied*, 404 U.S. 870 (1971).

[46] *Mahurkar v. C.R. Bard, Inc.*, 79 F.3d 1572, 1579 (Fed. Cir. 1996).

[47] *Panduit Corp.*, 575 F.2d at 1158.

[48] Daniel McGavock, David Haas, and Michael Patin, *Factors Affecting Royalty Rates,* Les Nouvelles, March–April 1991 at 205.

[49] Stephen Degnan and Corwin Horton, *A Survey of Licensed Royalties,* Les Nouvelles, June 1997 at 91.

[50] Daniel McGavock and Michael Lasinski, *IP Survey Finds Gap in Information,* Les Nouvelles, September 1998 at 107.

[51] *Harolds Stores, Inc. v. Dillard Dep't Stores, Inc.*, 82 F.3d 1533, 1544 (10th Cir. 1996); *see also Starter Corp. v. Converse, Inc.*, 170 F.3d. 286 (2d Cir. 1999) (affirming exclusion of trademark survey where the survey did not effectively test consumer confusion of the two marks and thus was irrelevant); *C.A. May Marine Supply Co. v. Brunswick Corp.*, 649 F.2d 1049 (5th Cir. 1981); *Simon Prop. Group L.P. v. mySimon, Inc.*, 104 F. Supp. 2d 1033, 1041 (S.D. Ind. 2000) (excluding surveys where flaws are "so fundamental that the court does not believe it would be fair to treat them as matters going only to the weight of the evidence"); Fed. R. Evid. 402; 4 McCarthy on Trademarks § 32:170.

[52] *Id.*

[53] *Id.*; *Indianapolis Colts, Inc. v. Metropolitan Baltimore Football Club, L.P.*, 34 F.3d 410, 416 (7th Cir. 1994) (finding that imperfect survey may still be admissible); *AHP Subsidiary Holding Co. v. Stuart Hale Co.*, 1 F.3d 611, 618 (7th Cir. 1993) (holding that flawed survey is admissible except in "rare" occasions); *McGraw-Edison Co. v. Walt Disney Prods.*, 787 F.2d 1163, 1172 (7th Cir. 1986) (same).

[54] *Simon Property Group, L.P. v. mySimon, Inc.*, 104 F. Supp. 2d 1033, 1039 (S.D. Ind. 2000) (excluding survey regarding Internet home pages because the survey so grossly distorted the marketplace conditions as to strip the survey of any significant probative value); *Starter Corp. v. Converse, Inc.*, 170 F.3d 286, 297 (2d Cir. 1999); *A.H.P. Subsidiary Holding Co. v. Stuart Hale Co.*, 1 F.3d 611, 618 (7th Cir. 1993) (finding that flawed surveys may be completely unhelpful to the trier of fact and therefore inadmissible); *Spraying Systems Co. v. Delavan*, 975 F.2d 387, 394 (7th Cir. 1992) (affirming summary judgment where survey of consumer opinion was too flawed to create a genuine issue of material fact).

[55] *Toys "R" Us, Inc. v. Canarsie Kiddie Shop, Inc.*, 559 F. Supp. 1189, 1205 (E.D.N.Y. 1983) (emphasis added); *see also Ramdass v. Angelone*, 530 U.S. 156, 172 (2000) (excluding death penalty poll and citing *Toys "R" Us, Inc.* for factors to consider in determining survey reliability).

[56] *See Harolds Stores, Inc.*, 82 F.3d at 1544, citing *Bank of Utah v. Commercial Sec. Bank*, 369 F.2d 19, 27 (10th Cir. 1966); *Toys "R" Us, Inc.*, 559 F. Supp. at 1204 (random intercept survey method and inaccuracies in recording the responses might yield unreliable results); *Amstar Corp. v. Domino's Pizza, Inc.*, 615 F.2d 252, 264 (5th Cir. 1980) (noting inadequate universe of survey recipients); *Dreyfus Fund, Inc. v. Royal Bank of Canada*, 525 F. Supp. 1108, 1116 (S.D.N.Y. 1981) (unreliable survey technique); *Kingsford Products Co. v. Kingsfords, Inc.*, 715 F. Supp. 1013, 1016 (Kan. 1989).

[57] *Simon Property Group, L.P. v. mySimon, Inc.*, 104 F. Supp. 2d 1033 (S.D. Ind. 2000); *Sterling Drug, Inc. v. Bayer AG*, 792 F. Supp. 1357, 1373 (S.D.N.Y. 1992) (disapproving of improperly drafted survey questions); *Conagra, Inc. v. Geo. A. Hormel & Co.*, 784 F. Supp. 700, 726 (Neb. 1992) (survey flawed in that failed to inquire regarding reasons certain answers were selected).

[58] *Id.*

[59] *Toys "R" Us, Inc. v. Canarsie Kiddie Shop, Inc.*, 559 F. Supp. 1189, 1203 (E.D.N.Y. 1983).

[60] *Id.* at 1205.

[61] *Id.*

[62] If the analysis determines that there is no royalty rate that makes both parties better off, this probably is a signal that a "lost profits" rather than a "reasonable royalty" is appropriate.

[63] One vexing problem is that the boundaries of the mutually acceptable range are sensitive to when the negotiation takes place. For example, if the negotiation takes place before the potential licensee invests in production facilities to make the product, his potential benefit from taking a license is different than it would be if the licensee had already made "sunk" investments specific to the patented product. The cases simply state that the hypothetical negotiation takes place at the onset of infringement.

[64] *See, e.g., Polaroid Corp. v. Eastman Kodak Co.*, 16 U.S.P.Q. 2d 1481 (D. Mass. 1990); *Fromson v. Western Litho Plate & Supply Co.*, 853 F.2d 1568, 1575 (Fed. Cir. 1988).

[65] *See, e.g., Columbia Wire Co. v. Kokomo Steel & Wire Co.*, 194 F.108, 110, 114 C.C.A. 186 (C.C.A. 1911); *Union Carbide Corp. v. Graver Tank & Mfg. Co.*, 345 F.2d 409, 411, 145 U.S.P.Q. 240 (7th Cir. 1965); *Hanson v. Alpine Valley Ski Area, Inc.*, 718 F.2d 1075, 1078,

219 U.S.P.Q. 679 (Fed. Cir. 1983); *Smith International, Inc. v. Hughes Tool Co.*, 1986 WL 4795, 299 U.S.P.Q. 81, 83 (C.D. Cal. 1986); *Ellipse Corp. v. Ford Motor Co.*, 461 F. Supp. 1354, 1369, 201 U.S.P.Q. 455 (N.D. Ill. 1978); and *Slimfold Mfg. Co., Inc. v. Kinkead Industries, Inc.*, 932 F.2d 1453, 1458, 18 U.S.P.Q. 2d 1842 (Fed. Cir. 1991).

[66] John Jarosz, Carla Mulhern, and Robert Vigil, "Industry Royalty Rates and Profitability: An Empirical Test of the 25% Rule," Presentation to LES Annual Meeting, October 30, 2001.

[67] *Tektronix, Inc. v. United States*, 552 F.2d 343 (Ct. Cl. 1977).

[68] *Stryker Corp. v. Intermedics Orthopedics, Inc.*, 96 F.3d 1409 (Fed. Cir. 1996).

[69] *Minco, Inc. v. Combustion Eng'g, Inc.*, 95 F.3d 1109 (Fed. Cir. 1996).

ADDITIONAL READING

Russell L. Parr, *Intellectual Property Infringement Damages: A Litigation Support Handbook*, New York: John Wiley & Sons (1993).

Everett M. Rogers, *Diffusion of Innovations*, 3rd ed., New York: The Free Press (1995).

Jay B. Abrams, *Quantitative Business Valuation*, New York: McGraw-Hill (2001).

Geoffery A. Moore, Paul Johnson, and Tom Kippola, *The Gorilla Game*, New York: Harper Business (1999).

Clayton M. Christensen, *The Innovator's Dilemma*, New York: Harper Business (2000).

Frederick P. Brooks, Jr., *The Mythical Man-Month*, 20th Anniversary Edition, Addison-Wesley-Longman (1995).

Geoffery A. Moore, *Inside the Tornado*, New York: Harper Perennial (1999).

Damages: Lost Profits on Lost Sales of Unpatented Items, 5 Federal Circuit Bar Journal 242 (Summer 1995).

Dorsey Baker, *Patent Damages—Quantifying the Award*, Journal of the Patent & Trademark Office Society 121 (March 1987).

Jonathan Bloom et al., *Federal Circuit Addresses Patent Infringement Damages Issues*, 7 Journal of Proprietary Rights 21 (Aug. 1995).

Patricia N. Brantley, *Patent Law Handbook* 1993–94 ed., § 604, Clark Boardman Callaghan, Ltd.

Alex Chartove, *Patent Law Developments in the United States Court of Appeals for the Federal Circuit During 1991*, 9 Computer & High Technology Law Journal 109 (1993).

Alex Chartove, *Patent Law Developments in the United States Court of Appeals for the Federal Circuit During 1989*, 39 The American University Law Review 1142 (1990).

Lisa C. Childs, *Rite-Hite Corp. v. Kelley Co.: The Federal Circuit Awards Damages for Harm Done to a Patent Not in Suit*, 27 Loyola University of Chicago Law Journal 665 (Spring 1996).

Ned L. Conley, *An Economic Approach to Patent Damages*, 15 AIPLA Q.J. 354 (1987).

Ronald B. Coolley, *Overview and Statistical Study of the Law on Patent Damages*, Journal of the Patent & Trademark Office Society 515 (July 1993).

Robert J. Cox, *Recent Development: But How Far?: Rite-Hite Corp. v. Kelley Co.'s Expansion of the Scope of Patent Damages*, 3 Journal of Intellectual Property Law 327 (Spring 1996).

John D. Culbertson and Roy Weinstein, *Product Substitutes and the Calculation of Patent Damages*, Journal of the Patent & Trademark Office Society 749 (Nov. 1988).

Robert Goldscheider, *Companion to Licensing Negotiations*, Licensing Law Handbook (1993–1994).

Robert Goldscheider, *Measuring Damages in U.S. Patent Litigation*, 5 Journal of Proprietary Rights 2 (1993).

Robert Goldscheider, *Value of Patents from a Damages Expert's Point of View*, 12 Licensing Law & Business Report 109 (Nov.–Dec. 1989).

Robert L. Harmon, *Damages, Interest, and Costs*, Patents and the Federal Circuit 478 (3rd ed., 1994).

Robert L. Harmon, Patents and the Federal Circuit, § 12.2 (2d ed., 1991).

Robert L. Harmon, *Seven New Rules of Thumb: How the Federal Circuit Has Changed the Way Patent Lawyers Advise Clients*, 14:3 George Mason Law Review 573 (1992).

Paul M. Janicke, *Contemporary Issues in Patent Damages*, 42 The American University Law Review 691 (1993).

Wm. Marshall Lee, *Determining Reasonable Royalty*, Les Nouvelles 124 (Sept. 1992).

Nancy J. Linck and Barry P. Golob, *Patent Damages: The Basics*, 34 IDEA: The Journal of Law & Technology 13 (1993).

Frederick A. Lorig and David J. Meyer, *Maximizing Patent Damages*, 321 Practicing Law Institute 367 (1991).

Timothy J. Malloy and Melissa M. McCaulley, *Rite-Hite: Has the Federal Circuit Expanded the Legal Limits on Damages Awarded in Patent Infringement Actions?* 424 Practicing Law Institute 515 (1995).

Timothy J. Malloy and Robert P. Renke, *Patent Damages Revisited: Recent Issues Before the Federal Court*, 397 Practicing Law Institute 277 (1994).

Daniel M. McGavock and Rochelle Kopp, *Emerging Topics in the Calculation of Economic Damages in Patent Litigation*, 5 Journal of Proprietary Rights 17 (March 1993).

William E. McGowan, *Patent Law—Limiting Infringement Protection for Product-by-Product Claims*, 27 Suffolk University Law Review 300 (1993).

Joel Meyer, *State Industries v. Mor-Flo and the Market Share Approach to Patent Damages: What Is Happening to the Panduit Test?* Wisconsin Law Review 1369 (1991).

George F. Pappas and April J. Sands, *Law of Patent Damages*, CA42 ALI-ABA 1 (Sept. 28, 1995).

Laura B. Pincus, *The Computation of Damages in Patent Infringement Actions*, 5 Harvard Journal of Law & Technology 95 (Fall 1991); reprinted in Journal Business Law (U.K.) (March 1992), 213.

N. Richard Powers, *At the End of the Second Rainbow—Calculation of Damages in Patent Cases*, Delaware Lawyer 18 (March 1989).

Richard T. Rapp and Philip A. Beutel, *Patent Damages: Rules on the Road to Economic Rationality*, 321 Practicing Law Institute 337 (1991).

Charles Shifley, *Upfront and Benchmark Payments as Part of Reasonable Royalty Patent*, 4 Federal Circuit Bar Journal 33 (Spring 1994).

Charles W. Shifley, *Alternatives to Patent Licenses: Real-World Considerations of Potential Licensees Are—and Should Be—a Part of the Courts' Determinations of Reasonable Royalty Patent Damages*, 34 The Journal of Law & Technology 1 (1993).

John M. Skenyon and Frank P. Porcelli, *Patent Damages*, Journal of the Patent & Trademark Office Society 762 (Nov. 1988).

Gerald Sobel, *Damages for Patent Infringement*, 416 Practicing Law Institute 197 (1995).

Stephen I. Willis, *Economic Modeling of Patent Infringement Damages*, 321 Practicing Law Institute 331 (1991).

Harold E. Wurst and Anne Wang, *The Law of Patent Damages*, 376 Practicing Law Institute 7 (1993).

8

Introduction to the Antitrust Laws

This chapter provides a basic overview of the antitrust laws. A working knowledge of antitrust principles is important to the analysis of intellectual property (IP) damages because there are significant areas of overlap between the IP laws and the antitrust laws. In addition, many of the tools developed by the courts in antitrust cases, such as the concept of a relevant market, have been imported into the IP arena. This chapter provides a historical background concerning the two principal antitrust statutes, the Sherman Act and the Clayton Act; describes the evolving goals of the antitrust laws; and discusses the essential components of the major antitrust claims.

THE HISTORICAL FOUNDATIONS OF THE ANTITRUST LAWS

In contrast to the IP laws that find their roots in the U.S. Constitution, the antitrust laws were born in the upheaval of the Industrial Revolution at the end of the nineteenth century. Contemporary descriptions of the time describe it as a period of "excess competition." The increased intensity of competition after the Civil War occurred in part as a result of advances in transportation that brought formerly isolated geographic markets into rivalry with each other. The rising competitive pressure impacted unevenly on large and small firms, and the years following the Civil War coincided with an accelerated process of mechanization, which widened the gap between large and small enterprises.[1] Mechanization had significant consequences for competition. Thorelli states that as a result of "heavy fixed investments" by the new industrial firms:

> Many old enterprises [were] unable or unwilling to expand fast enough and raise the capital necessary to keep abreast in their fields [and] were gradually, or in the recurrent slumps suddenly, forced to the wall. To this extent at least a certain concentration of production to fewer firms became concomitant with the increase in optimum size. . . .[2]

It was under these circumstances that the most dynamic large firms in the economy attempted to avoid the detrimental effects on accelerated competition by organizing profit pools, cartels, and trusts. As a result of these successful efforts to control inter-firm rivalry, major tensions were created between big business and their smaller competitors, farmers, and urban workers.

Before to the Industrial Revolution, traditional firms were insulated from competitive pressure by their small size and the distance from their competitors. As the Industrial Revolution took hold, new technologies led to larger firms with increased capacity and new forms of communication and transportation that broke down old barriers to competition. The result was severe price competition as large firms selling homogeneous commodities clashed in the market. The response to the downward pricing pressure was to form new corporate forms that reduced competition by collective price-setting.

Not surprisingly, other groups in the economy—particularly farmers organized by the granger movement, small businesses that formed the backbone of the progressive movement, and urban workers—vehemently opposed the large trusts. The trusts became an object of ridicule and hatred, and the political pressure mounted to heightened levels prompting action by Congress. Few people deny that Congress passed the Sherman Act because public condemnation of trusts was becoming increasingly violent. In introducing his antitrust bill, Senator John Sherman explained:

> The popular mind is agitated with problems that may disturb social order, and among them all none is more threatening than the inequality of condition, of wealth, and opportunity that has grown within a single generation out of the concentration of capital into vast combinations to control production and trade and to break down competition . . . They had monopolies and mort mains of old, but never before such giants as in our day. You must heed their (the voters') appeal or be ready for the socialist, the communist and the nihilist.[3]

Congressional debate and revision of the antitrust bill represented a condensation of many conflicting political forces caused by the economic upheaval of the Industrial Revolution.

The Origins of the Sherman Act

The original purpose of Sherman's antitrust bill was to protect the small traditional firms.[4] Although Sherman tried to keep the bill in the Finance Committee, which he controlled, the Judiciary Committee, after much debate, obtained jurisdiction and within a week had produced a different bill that employed the language of the old common law of restraints of trade. Many historians contend that the final legislative language was essentially a political compromise between the interests of both large firms and small firms. It was the compromise nature of the Sherman Act and the difficulty of its interpretation that may have fostered its overwhelming support (it was passed with only one dissenting vote in the Senate) and may account for the initial weak enforcement efforts in the first decade following its enactment.

The final draft of the Sherman Act[5] stated:

> An Act To Protest Trade and Commerce Against Unlawful Restraints and Monopolies.
>
> Section 1. Every contract, combination in the form of trust or otherwise, or conspiracy, in restraint of trade or commerce among the several States, or with foreign nations, is declared to be illegal. Every person who shall make any contract or engage in any combination or conspiracy hereby declared to be illegal shall be deemed guilty of a felony. . . .
>
> Section 2. Every person who shall monopolize, or attempt to monopolize, or combine or conspire with any other person or persons, to monopolize any part of the trade or commerce among the several States, or with foreign nations, shall be deemed guilty of a felony. . . .

The final draft that became the Sherman Act replaced Sherman's original words requiring "free competition" with a more ambiguous prohibition on "restraints of trade" and "monopolization." By returning to these older and more malleable common law concepts, a measure of protection for smaller businesses was accomplished, but essentially without sacrificing or stemming the corporate revolution that was transforming the economy. In addition, because of the ambiguous language, the meaning of the Sherman Act at the time was not obvious to lawyers who needed to advise their corporate clients and also was unclear to enforcement officials. Congress had left the arduous task of interpreting and applying the terms of the Sherman Act to the Supreme Court.

It was not until 1897 that the Supreme Court first heard a series of restraint of trade cases and first interpreted the ambiguous language of section 1, which literally stated that "[e]very contract, combination in the form of trust or otherwise, or conspiracy, in restraint of trade . . . is declared to be illegal." The issue first arose in *United States v. Trans-Missouri Freight Association*,[6] in which the government filed a lawsuit, under section 1 of the Sherman Act, against 18 railroads that controlled most of the commerce west of the Mississippi River and that regularly fixed prices. The railroads defended on the grounds that, absent the cartel, the railroads would be destroyed because of "ruinous competition." The railroads contended that the Sherman Act should outlaw only "unreasonable" restraints, and a restraint that prevents ruinous competition must be "reasonable." The majority decision of the Supreme Court rejected the railroad's argument, reasoning that the plain language of the statute makes illegal "every" contract, combination, or conspiracy that is in restraint of trade, not just unreasonable agreements.[7] Therefore, the ruinous competition defense was without merit. The Court further made clear its concern that such restraints of trade as the railroads proposed would "drive out of business all the small dealers in the commodity."[8] Justice White wrote a forceful dissent, to which four members of the Court concurred, supporting the view (which is now prevailing law) that when Congress used the term *restraint of trade* it meant only "unreasonable" restraints of trade, as the term was used in the common law.[9]

The majority's interpretation of the Sherman Act not surprisingly was supported by small business and its political allies in the progressive movement. In contrast, organizations such as the National Civic Federation, which represented big business, lobbied Congress to reject the majority's interpretation and to overturn the *Trans-Missouri* opinion. At the same time, Justice Peckham authored several more opinions holding fast to a narrow interpretation of the Sherman Act and to the interpretation offered in the dissenting opinion in *Trans-Missouri Freight Association*. Specifically, in 1898, Justice Peckham authored *United States v. Joint Traffic Assoc.*[10] and *Hopkins v. United States.*[11]

Between Judge Peckham's opinions in *Trans-Missouri Freight Association* and *Joint Traffic*, Judge Taft rendered his famous and highly lauded opinion in *United States v. Addyston Pipe & Steel Co.*,[12] in which he offered an alternative interpretation of the Sherman Act. The *Addyston Pipe* case involved a challenge by the government to a cartel of six pipe makers that had allocated customers through a bid-rigging arrangement. Under the arrangement, one cartel member was designated as the real bidder and others would submit (phony) high bids. The pipe makers claimed that stricter law applied to the railroad industry than to other industries, and under the common law the pipe makers' agreement should be judged reasonable. Judge Taft disagreed. Judge Taft distinguished between "naked restraints," those not ancillary to any larger legitimate contract, and "ancillary restraints," those reasonably necessary to fulfill the "main and lawful purpose" of a contract. For an ancillary restraint to be legal, it must make the main transaction more effective in accomplishing its legitimate purpose.[13] Taft provided a nonexhaustive list of transactions to which a restraint could be ancillary. The first example Taft recited was "agreements by the seller of property or business not to compete with the buyer in such a way as to derogate from the value of the property or business sold."[14] In Judge Taft's opinion, ancillary restraints are illegal only if they are part of a transaction that involves a general scheme to control a market. The Supreme Court did not adopt Judge Taft's approach.

The Supreme Court also did not reevaluate how the Sherman Act should be applied to horizontal restraints until 1911, when it issued its opinion in *Standard Oil Co. of New Jersey v. United States.*[15] In *Standard Oil*, the United States filed suit against John D. Rockefeller's Standard Oil, contending that Standard Oil had engaged in a series of predatory pricing and cartel activities. Justice White, writing for the new majority on the Court, overturned the earlier broad interpretation of the Sherman Act,[16] stating instead that "it follows that it was intended that the standard of reason which had been applied at the common law and in this country in dealing with subjects of the character embraced by the statute was intended to be the measure used for the purpose of determining whether, in a given case, a particular act had or had not brought about the wrong against which the statute provided."[17] In other words, the Court held for the first time that only "unreasonable" restraints of trade, not "every" restraint of trade, are illegal.

Contrary to Justice Harlan's dissent, Justice White's opinion did not set forth an open-ended rule of reason. Instead, Justice White clearly reasoned that the statute does not mean "all" restraints of trade are illegal, but that Congress intended "to leave it to be determined by the light of reason, guided by the principles of law," which restraints were to be prohibited.[18] White's rule of reason also contained structure. For instance, a restraint on trade that by its inherent nature is anticompetitive should be condemned.[19] This suggests a *per se* concept, even though little guidance is provided for which types of conduct come within this category. If a restraint is not judged by its "inherent nature," the Court was then to examine its "inherent effect" (or market power) and its "evident purpose" (or intent).[20]

The *Standard Oil* decision caused an immediate reaction in Congress. Progressive movement forces feared that a conservative Supreme Court would take the teeth out of the Sherman Act by determining much of the conduct of the trusts and monopolies to be "reasonable." Immediate work began on a new bill in Congress to specifically define what acts would be unreasonable and would violate the law. This new bill eventually would be the Clayton Act in 1914.

The Clayton Act and the Federal Trade Commission

The Clayton Act[21] and the Federal Trade Commission Act[22] were enacted simultaneously in 1914. The Clayton Act aimed at defining specific practices that were anticompetitive and to reach these anticompetitive practices in their incipiency.[23] The Federal Trade Commission (FTC) proscribed "unfair methods of competition" and established an administrative enforcement procedure.[24]

The simultaneous enactment of these acts established a new framework, which some believed to be an additional congressional step toward curbing the power of big business. Other historians disagree. For example, Weinstein advanced the following view:

> The Federal Trade Commission Act of 1914 is most often thought of as a Wilsonian reform embodying a bias against "big business." In fact, the principles underlying the FTC were enunciated by corporation leaders and their lawyers consistently through the Progressive Era in response to a series of legislative and judicial actions stretching over some seventeen years.[25]

As in the case of the Sherman Act, the impact of the Clayton Act depends in part on how it is enforced. According to Wise, with respect to the FTC:

> doing something about the trusts was no longer the central issue of the day. Rather, it was a consensus whose details were being worked out. But the devil is in the details; the form the compromise package took foreshadowed the Commission's almost immediate troubles.[26]

Specifically, the Clayton Act originally contained several loopholes that favored big business. Section 7 of the Clayton Act covered acquisitions of "the whole or any part of the stock or other share capital of another corporation." Use of the term *stock* originally excluded asset acquisitions from regulation. Likewise, the section 8 prohibition on interlocking directors was easily circumvented by indirect interlocks.

Like the Sherman Act, the Clayton Act can be viewed as a political compromise. Representatives of small business supported a law that specified that certain practices were anticompetitive. In contrast, big business was particularly supportive of the FTC, because it satisfied a long-standing desire for an administrative approach to antitrust that would provide some certainty and consistency in enforcement.

The Clayton Act addresses the following practices:

a. Section 3 prohibits tie-in sales, exclusive dealing and requirements contracts where the effect "may be substantially to lessen competition or tend to create a monopoly" in a relevant market.[27]

b. Section 4 allows private plaintiffs to bring treble damages actions under the Sherman Act and Clayton Act.[28]

c. Section 6 exempts labor unions and agricultural cooperatives from the antitrust laws.[29]

d. Section 7 prohibits mergers and acquisitions where the effect "may be substantially to lessen competition or tend to create a monopoly" in any relevant market.[30]

e. Section 8 prohibits interlocking directors of competing companies.[31]

Subsequent to 1914, the Clayton Act was amended several times. For example, the Robinson-Patman Act[32] of 1936 substantially amended section 2 to prohibit price discrimination except in certain defined situations.[33] The Celler-Kefauver[34] Act of 1950 amended section 7 to close the loophole for "stock acquisitions" and generally tightened the antimerger provisions.[35] In 1976, a premerger reporting requirement was added as section 7A.[36] Finally, in 1990, section 8 was amended to prohibit both interlocking directors and officers.[37]

The Federal Trade Commission Act created the FTC and gave it broad powers to enforce the Sherman Act and the Clayton Act concurrent with the Department of Justice (DOJ) and private parties. Section 5 of the Federal Trade Commission Act gave the FTC exclusive authority to prosecute "unfair methods of competition" and "unfair or deceptive acts or practices."[38] Section 5 has been subsequently interpreted to give the FTC wide-ranging enforcement powers.

Antitrust Enforcement from World War I to World War II

Despite passage of the Clayton Act, prosecution of antitrust claims during the 1920s was minimal. In the 1920s, business was encouraged to adopt "scientific management" and to participate in trade associations that could provide industry data. The Supreme Court curbed some abuses, but collaboration and mergers went largely unchecked.

During the Depression, the prominent theory of the collapse was excess competition. As a result, during the first half of the New Deal, the National Recovery Administration (NRA) organized business into industrial groups and suspended antitrust enforcement. The views of Leon Henderson, the chief economist for the NRA, were typical of the 1920s. Henderson stated:

> The Anti-Trust Acts are a throw-back to the Neolithic Age of statesmanship, and their blind sponsorship is a sort of jittering caveman ignorance.[39]

By 1935, however, the NRA was under heavy criticism and was considered by many to be unmanageable. That same year, the NRA was declared unconstitutional. Although the economy certainly was not out of the Depression in 1935, the immediate emergency situation was over, and the time was ripe for more conventional approaches. At the end of the first New Deal, Franklin Roosevelt was tempted to reorganize industries using a scheme similar to that of the NRA, but under private control in the tradition of trade associations of the 1920s. However, he ultimately decided to return to vigorous antitrust enforcement as a method to resolve price flexibility problems. The historian Herbert Stein summarizes Roosevelt's dramatic change in attitude as follows[40]:

> At the same time many of the President's advisors, even the "planners" among them, were afraid of giving so much control to the businessmen [within new "private" codes]. The prevailing view of this subject within the administration ran in the opposite direction—to take steps to curb the "concentration of economic power." Roosevelt went along with this to the extent of sending Congress a special message on the subject in April, 1938. Congress responded by setting up the Temporary National Economic Committee. . . .[41]

The Depression itself had a devastating effect on the traditional sector of industry. The collapse of obsolete firms was a major factor in the long duration of the Depression, but it also is important to stress the other side of the coin: that the Depression also was an important event in the transition to a new economy dominated by large efficient enterprises, both politically and institutionally. Without the rivalry of the traditional small firms, the post–World War II period became an era of reevaluation and revamping of the goals and objectives of the antitrust laws, and an increase in importance of intellectual property.

THE GOALS OF THE ANTITRUST LAWS

In the post–World War II period, four competing goals of the antitrust laws emerged. These goals include the need to protect simple businesses, to encourage allocative efficiency, to prevent wealth transfers from buyers to sellers, and to encourage dynamic or innovative efficiency.

Protection of Small Business

Many earlier antitrust opinions held that the antitrust laws should protect the independence of small, often locally owned, businesses. In attempts to protect small businesses, the courts and commentators alike have relied on various democratic rationales. For example, in *United States v. Trans-Missouri Freight Ass'n,*[42] the Supreme Court's decision, authored by Justice Peckham, stated that large firms and concentrated industries were not in the substantial interest of the country or its citizens. The Court reasoned:

> [I]t is not for the real prosperity of any country that such changes should occur which result in transferring an independent business man, the head of his establishment, small though it might be, into a mere servant or agent of a corporation for selling the commodities which he once manufactured or dealt in, having no voice in shaping the business policy for the company and bound to obey orders issued by others.[43]

In addition, many commentators have suggested that the concentration of wealth would lead to the concentration of political power. Therefore, the argument goes, preservation of small business protects the vitality of democracy.

Allocative Efficiency

The ascendant view of the goals of antitrust laws in the post–World War II period is that antitrust laws are aimed at protecting consumers, not small business. It is conceivable that this change may have been made possible by the destruction of the political power of small business during the Depression. Nonetheless, once the interests of consumers take center stage, microeconomics provides an elegant and powerful tool to analyze the impact of corporate practices on consumer welfare. According to economists, consumer welfare is maximized at the competitive price and output. Any price and output pair other than the competitive price and output generates some "deadweight loss" to society. This means that resources are not deployed to their highest valued use. Some judges, including Judge Robert Bork and Judge Richard Posner, have prominently advocated the view that the only viable goal of the antitrust laws is to maximize consumer surplus.[44]

Wealth Transfers

The result of reducing prices from monopoly pricing to competitive pricing is twofold: it increases consumer surplus and reduces monopoly profits. Lande has argued in response to a pure consumer welfare goal that Congress, in passing various antitrust laws, was more interested in preventing transfers of wealth from consumers to monopolies than in increasing consumer surplus.[45] The DOJ recognizes the need to protect against the transfer of wealth from buyers to sellers and the misallocation of resources as goals in its enforcement statements.[46]

Dynamic Efficiency or Innovation Efficiency

More recently, the antitrust agencies and the courts have recognized that innovation is an important source of consumer welfare. Dynamic efficiency was discussed at length in Chapter 3. As a result of new research on technological change, preventing conduct that reduces competition for future innovation has become an object of antitrust enforcement. The Intellectual Property Guidelines address concerns about innovation efficiency by considering the impact of IP acquisitions and licensing on three types of markets: (1) traditional "goods" markets, (2) "technology" markets that consist of IP and their substitutes, and (3) "innovation" markets that consider the impact of conduct on research and development activities.

ANTITRUST CLAIMS UNDER SECTION 1 OF THE SHERMAN ACT

This section summarizes the primary recognized violations of the antitrust laws. It is not exhaustive, but instead is meant only as an introduction to be used by lawyers and experts in IP cases to identify possible issues for further research.

Section 1 of the Sherman Act[47] prohibits any "contract, combination . . . or conspiracy" that creates an unreasonable restraint of trade.[48] Intellectual property license often involves horizontal restraints. These restraints can take the form of territorial divisions, covenants not to compete, or other restrictions on competition between licensors and licensees. Attorneys and experts must be careful not to allow such restraints, whether in the form of a settlement to infringement litigation or a licensing arrangement to be structured in a manner that violates section 1 of the Sherman Act.

A section 1 claim requires that two elements be proven. First, an agreement between two or more persons must exist ("contract, combination, or conspiracy"). Second, the agreement must involve an "unreasonable" restraint of trade.

An Agreement

An agreement requires either a meeting of the minds to accomplish some goal or the coerced cooperation of several parties under the leadership of a ringleader. An agreement can be demonstrated from either direct evidence or circumstantial evidence. Circumstantial evidence requires such evidence "that tends to exclude the possibility that the alleged conspirators acted independently."[49] In other words, circumstantial evidence consistent with unilateral action is not sufficient to establish an illegal agreement.

Unilateral conduct cannot be a basis for a section 1 claim. This was made clear in 1987 by the Supreme Court in *Copperweld Corp. v. Independence Tube Corp.*[50] There, the Court stated that "Section 1 of the Sherman Act . . . reaches unreasonable restraints of trade effected by a 'contract, combination . . . or conspiracy' between separate entities, and does not reach conduct that is 'wholly unilateral.'"[51] The Court went on to hold that wholly owned subsidiaries of a corporation cannot conspire for section 1 purposes.[52]

Rule of Reason, *Per Se*, and Quick-Look Approaches to Conduct Under Section 1 of the Sherman Act

Once an agreement has been demonstrated, it also must be shown that the restraint at issue is unreasonable. An unreasonable restraint of trade can be established under the *per se* test, the rule of reason test, or more recently the quick-look test. This is one of the most difficult and controversial areas of antitrust jurisprudence, yet it is a critical area for IP licensing and joint development.

Rule of Reason. It is arguable that the full-blown rule of reason approach was established in 1918 by Justice Brandeis in *Board of Trade of Chicago v. United States*,[53] as opposed to being established in *Standard Oil*. *Board of Trade of Chicago* involved a challenge to the Chicago Board of Trade's call rule in which dealers agreed that grain purchased after the trading session ended (in transit to Chicago) would be purchased at the closing price. The case, however, is important not for its facts but for its method. According to the majority decision authored by Justice Brandeis, a restraint on trade violates section 1 of the Sherman Act when it suppresses or destroys competition as opposed to merely regulating and perhaps promoting competition.[54] To determine the effect of a restraint, the Court mandated a full inquiry into the:

> [F]acts peculiar to the business to which the restraint is applied, its condition before and after the restraint was imposed; the nature of the restraint and its effect, actual or probable. The history of the restraint, the evil believed to exist, the reason for adopting the particular remedy, the purpose or end sought to be attained, are all relevant facts.[55]

The Court concluded that these factors were important because intent was relevant to the analysis. Specifically, the Court stated that knowledge of intent may help the Court to interpret facts and predict consequences.[56] There is a simple efficiency explanation for this rule. Large dealers had much better information about grain in transit and could obtain better deals from small dealers after the trading session closed than they could during the day when information was revealed during the bidding process. Justice Brandeis came to the right conclusion, but he never clearly stated why.

Following the *Board of Trade of Chicago* opinion, the prevailing legal opinion was that the rule of reason applied to all or most restraints of trade.[57] The extent of the penetration of the rule of reason analysis can be judged from the Supreme Court's subsequent 1933 opinion in *Appalachian Coals, Inc. v. United States*.[58] In *Appalachian Coals*, the government challenged a classic cartel of coal producers that set prices for the sale of coal through a single selling agency. This "selling agency" was formed in response to the depressed conditions in the coal market due to oversupply and the eroding demand resulting from the Depression. The plan was enjoined by the district court, but the Supreme Court reversed, holding that the serious decline in the industry justified "an honest effort to remove abuses, to make competition fairer, and thus to promote the essential interests of commerce."[59] Thus, the Court applied the rule of reason and upheld a restraint that was nothing more than a price-fixing scheme. The Court did this on the grounds of preventing ruinous competition,[60] an argument that had been consistently rejected since the Supreme Court's 1897 decision in the *Trans-Missouri* case. The *Appalachian Coals* decision shows how strong the prevailing view—that the rule of reason should be widely applied to horizontal restraints—was at that time.

The Rise of the **Per Se** *Rule.* The Supreme Court first articulated a *per se* rule for price-fixing in 1927 in *United States v. Trenton Potteries Co.*[61] *Trenton Potteries* upheld a trial court opinion that a price-fixing scheme involving 82 percent of the market for pottery fixtures for bathrooms and lavatories was conclusively unreasonable without a rule of reason analysis and therefore illegal under the Sherman Act.[62] In upholding the lower court, the Supreme Court held that even if a cartel set a reasonable price today, it is dangerous for the cartel to possess pricing power because that same reasonable price may prove unreasonable in the future.[63] Moreover, the Court reasoned that relying on a judicial determination of what is reasonable independent of the competitive process is a useless endeavor. The Court could have obtained the same result by contending that the agreement was not ancillary to a contract with a lawful purpose. Instead, the Court essentially held that price-fixing was *per se* illegal, ancillary or not.[64]

The tension between *Trenton Potteries* and *Appalachian Coal* was resolved by Justice Douglas's opinion in *United States v. Socony-Vacuum Oil Co. Inc.*[65] *Socony-Vacuum* represents the apex of *per se* condemnation. *Socony-Vacuum* involved a buying scheme that impacted the spot price of gasoline. There was no direct price-fixing as in *Trenton Potteries*. The spot price of gasoline impacted numerous contracts and had a dramatic impact on overall prices. Under the NRA, which repealed the Sherman Act for approved industry coordination, the petroleum industry had attempted to control the spot price of gasoline. However, even after the repeal of the NRA, the petroleum industry continued to try to prevent the decline of spot prices by establishing "dancing partners" between the major oil producers and the independents. Under the plan, the majors would purchase "distress" gas from independents, which provided a floor for the spot price. In now-famous language, the Supreme Court struck down the scheme as *per se* illegal holding:

> Under the Sherman Act a combination formed for the purpose and with the effect of raising, depressing, fixing, pegging, or stabilizing the price of a commodity in interstate or foreign commerce is illegal *per se*.[66]

The language of *Socony-Vacuum* is very broad. The *Socony-Vacuum* Court essentially held that any horizontal constraint that impacts prices is presumed to be unreasonable *per se.*[67] This abbreviated approach stands in stark contrast to the broad application of the rule of reason approach announced in *Board of Trade of Chicago.*

Finally, the Supreme Court returned to articulating the *per se* rule in *Northern Pacific Railway Co. v. United States.*[68] Although the case was a tying case, the Court took the opportunity to explain the rationale behind the *per se* approach:

> However, there are certain agreements or practices which because of their pernicious effect on competition and lack of any redeeming virtue are conclusively presumed to be unreasonable and therefore illegal without elaborate inquiry as to the precise harm they have caused or the business excuse for their use. This principle of *per se* unreasonableness not only makes the type of restraints which are proscribed by the Sherman Act more certain to the benefit of everyone concerned, but it also avoids the necessity for an incredibly complicated and prolonged economic investigation. . . .[69]

To date, *Socony-Vacuum* and *Northern Pacific* are the most widely cited cases advocating a broad application of the *per se* rule.

Recent Erosion of the* Per Se *Rule. The Supreme Court revisited the *per se* rule in *National Society of Professional Engineers v. United States.*[70] In *National Society*, the association of engineers required as a condition of membership that its members not discuss the question of fees until a client had selected an engineer. The United States challenged the restriction as an agreement to suppress price competition. The engineers disagreed, arguing that bidding to the lowest price could threaten public health and safety. The district court rejected the defense, and the Court of Appeals affirmed. The Supreme Court also affirmed, but indicated that, under some conditions, restrictions on certain practices that impact competition might be reasonable.[71] The Court went on to state that only two categories of antitrust analysis exist. The first category involves "agreements whose nature and necessary effect are so plainly anticompetitive that no elaborate study of the industry is needed to establish their illegality—they are 'illegal *per se.*'"[72] The Court identified these agreements as the proper province of the *per se* rule. The second category includes "agreements whose competitive effect can only be evaluated by analyzing the facts peculiar to the business, the history of the restraint, and the reasons why it was imposed."[73] These agreements require treatment under the rule of reason. The Court concluded, however, that a ban on competitive bidding fell within the *per se* category.[74]

A year earlier, the Supreme Court had overturned the rule, announced in *United States v. Arnold Schwinn & Co.*,[75] that all vertical territorial restrains were *per se* illegal. In *Continental T.V., Inc. v. GTE Sylvania, Inc.*, the Court held that such restraints would in the future be governed by the rule of reason.[76] In the opinion, the Court recognized that the rule of reason is the prevailing standard, and thus retreated from *Socony-Vacuum*, stating:

Since the early years of this century a judicial gloss on [Section I] has established the "rule of reason" as the prevailing standard of analysis. Under this rule, the fact finder weighs all of the circumstances of a case in deciding whether a restrictive practice should be prohibited as imposing an unreasonable restraint on competition. *Per se* rules of illegality are appropriate only when they relate to conduct that is manifestly anticompetitive.[77]

The Court went on to claim that the market impact of vertical restrictions "is complex because of their potential for a simultaneous reduction of intrabrand competition and stimulation of interbrand competition."[78] The Court further described the *per se* rule as a "demanding standard" and made clear that any "departure from the rule of reason standard must be based upon demonstratable economic effect rather than . . . upon formalistic line drawing."[79] As a result, the court concluded that vertical nonprice restraints are not an appropriate candidate for *per se* treatment.[80]

The Supreme Court further retreated from *Socony-Vacuum* in three cases involving claims of horizontal price-fixing: *Broadcast Music, Inc. v. Columbia Broadcasting System, Inc. (BMI)*[81]; *Arizona v. Maricopa County Medical Society (Maricopa)*[82]; and *NCAA v. Board of Regents of University of Oklahoma (NCAA)*[83]. *BMI* followed *Sylvania's* assertion that the *per se* rule should be limited to restraints that are clearly or manifestly anticompetitive. For years, BMI and its codefendant (ASCAP) represented composers and holders of copyrights to musical works. Broadcast Music, Inc. offered buyers a blanket license to all of its copyrighted works or a program license for a use of all of its works for a specific program. Columbia Broadcasting System challenged the license as *per se* price-fixing. Under *Socony-Vacuum*, there is no doubt that CBS should have prevailed. Instead, however, the Court upheld BMI's licensing plan. The *BMI* Court introduced a two-step approach to analyzing horizontal restraints in the following passage:

As generally used in the antitrust field, "price-fixing" is a shorthand way of describing certain categories of business behavior to which the *per se* rule has been held applicable. The Court of Appeals' literal approach does not alone establish that this particular practice is one of those types or that it is "plainly anticompetitive" and very likely without "redeeming virtue." Literalness is over simplistic and often over broad. When two partners set the price of their goods or services they are literally "price-fixing," but they are not *per se* in violation of the Sherman Act. . . . Thus, it is necessary to characterize the challenged conduct as falling within or without the category of behavior to which we apply the label "*per se* price-fixing." That will often, but not always be a simple matter. . . .[84]

The *BMI* Court went on to hold that the horizontal price-fixing rule should not be applied to the blanket copyright license at issue, because it "is not a naked restrain[t] of trade with no purpose except stifling of competition, but rather accompanies the integration of sales, monitoring, and enforcement against unauthorized copyright use."[85] The *BMI* opinion linked the concept of ancillary restraint to the effect of an agreement that increased productive efficiency through integration. The Court deemed as significant the fact that without the pricing limitation, it would not be possible to offer the product itself.[86]

The Supreme Court's decision in *Maricopa* is consistent with *BMI*, despite the fact that it reached a different result. In *Maricopa*, the Court dealt with an arrangement in which doctors in Arizona fixed maximum prices. The Court held that these maximum price schedules were simply an invitation to set minimum prices and declared the agreement *per se* illegal.[87] The Court contrasted the arrangement among the independent doctors with the efficiencies that would result from an integration such as a merger or a joint venture:

> If a clinic offers complete medical coverage for a flat fee, the cooperating doctors would have the type of partnership arrangement in which a price-fixing agreement among the doctors would be perfectly proper. But the fee agreements disclosed by the record in this case are among independent competing entrepreneurs. They fit squarely into the horizontal price-fixing mold.[88]

Accordingly, because no production efficiencies were created and because no new product was developed, the Court held that the scheme was a naked constraint that was *per se* illegal.[89]

The Supreme Court's opinion in *NCAA* is also consistent with *BMI* and *Maricopa*. The litigation involved a challenge to the NCAA plan that allocated rights to televise college football games. The *NCAA* Court found that the plan prevented schools from conducting separate price negotiations and artificially limited output.[90] Nevertheless, the Court rejected the *per se* approach because the "case involves an industry in which horizontal restraints on competition are essential if the product is to be available at all."[91] The *NCAA* Court then concluded that the restraint violated the Sherman Act because it was not truly necessary for the production of the product, "college football."[92] Put differently, the Court found potential production efficiencies from the NCAA joint venture, but the output restriction at issue was not be shown to be linked to the attainment of these efficiencies. Had this link been demonstrated, the Court likely would have approved the restraint.

In 1986, the Supreme Court again addressed the issue of *per se* treatment of a group boycott in *FTC v. Indiana Federation of Dentists*.[93] Briefly, the facts involved a joint effort by Indiana dentists to resist insurance company requests for dental X rays as part of the paperwork required for reimbursement. The Court stated as follows:

> [W]e decline to resolve this case by forcing the Federation's policy into the "boycott" pigeonhole and invoking the *per se* rule. As we observed last term in *Northwest Wholesale Stationers, Inc. v. Pacific Stationary Printing Co.*, 472 U.S. 284, 105 S. Ct. 2613, 86 L.Ed.2d 202 (1985), the category of restraints clauses as group boycotts is not to be expanded indiscriminately, and the *per se* approach has generally been limited to cases in which firms with market power boycott suppliers or customers. . . . [W]e have been slow to . . . extend *per se* analysis to restraints imposed in the context of business relationships where the economic impact of certain practices is not immediately obvious. . . .[94]

The Court went on to condemn the dentists' practice under the rule of reason.[95]

The Quick Look. The trend toward erosion of the *per se* rule has continued in the Supreme Court. The *NCAA*, in particular, ushered in an approach to horizontal restraints called the "structured rule of reason" or "quick look."[96] The quick-look approach is applied when the Court is not sufficiently familiar with the specific fact pattern, yet the conduct is suspicious enough that it could fall within a suspect *per se* category.[97] Under the quick look, the plaintiff need prove only that a restraint is a type of agreement that is likely to have anticompetitive effects. After such a showing is made, the burden of proof shifts to the defendant to demonstrate any procompetitive justification for the restraint. If the defendant can make such a showing, then the analysis reverts to a full-scale rule of reason analysis.

In *California Dental Ass'n v. FTC*,[98] the Ninth Circuit used a quick-look analysis to address a restraint by California dentists that limited advertising. The dentists' argument that the restraint prevented false advertising was rejected by the Ninth Circuit.[99] On appeal, the Supreme Court reversed, holding that "the Court of Appeals erred when it held as a matter of law that quick look analysis was appropriate."[100] The Court remanded the case, not for *per se* treatment, but for a full rule of reason analysis.[101] In addition, the Court concluded that there is "no categorical line to be drawn between restraints that give rise to an intuitively obvious inference of anticompetitive effect and those that call for more detailed treatment. What is required, rather, is an enquiry meant for the case, looking to the circumstances, details, and logic of a restraint."[102] "The truth is that our categories of analysis of anticompetitive effect are less fixed than terms like *per se*, quick look, and rule of reason tend to make them appear."[103] The Court, therefore, pushed even farther away from perfunctory *per se* condemnation toward the approach used in *Chicago Board of Trade*.

In the dissent, Justice Breyer agreed with the majority that a rule of reason approach was appropriate but sought to provide guidance and structure to the analysis. To this end, he set forth an approach to horizontal restraints that many commentators believe probably will be adopted by courts in the future:

> I would break that question down into four classical, subsidiary antitrust questions: (1) What is the specific restraint at issue? (2) What are its likely anticompetitive effects? (3) Are there offsetting competitive justifications? (4) Do the parties have sufficient market power to make a difference?[104]

The Views of the Federal Antitrust Enforcement Agencies. Both the FTC and the DOJ (collectively, the Agencies) have specifically rejected a strict *per se* approach in all but the most narrow of circumstances.

In the *Department of Justice Antitrust Enforcement Guidelines for International Operations*, the DOJ adopted an approach where the *per se* rule was restricted to "restraint[s] that [are] inherently likely to restrict output or raise price and [are] not plausibly related to some form of economic integration (by contract or otherwise) of the parties' operations that in general may generate procompetitive efficiencies."[105] More recently, in 1996, then Assistant Attorney General Joel Klein unveiled the DOJ's "stepwise" approach for review of horizontal restraints.[106] Under the stepwise approach, the DOJ first determines whether the restraint clearly falls within a *per se* category. When determining whether an agreement should be subject to *per se* treatment, the DOJ looks to see whether the agreement is ancillary and necessary for accomplishing a lawful agreement. If the agreement is not ancillary, the inquiry ends. If the restraint is ancillary, then the DOJ further inquires into whether there is a procompetitive justification. If there is, then the DOJ will determine whether such procompetitive benefits outweigh any anticompetitive effects. Interestingly, Klein specifically criticized the *Topco* decision for ignoring the clear procompetitive effects that resulted from the private label program. Such efficiencies would have removed the restraint from *per se* scrutiny by the DOJ. William Kolasky, the deputy to the current Assistant Attorney General Charles James, responded to the DOJ's stepwise approach in an article, published in *Antitrust Magazine*, contending that it misplaces the burden on defendants to show efficiencies in the second step.[107] Kolasky's article may or may not be indicative of the current DOJ position after Klein's departure.

The recent United States Department of Justice and Federal Trade Commission Antitrust Guidelines for Collaborations Among Competitors (Joint Venture Guidelines) also counsel that the Agencies will consider efficiencies prior to condemning a restraint as *per se*:

> If, however, participants in an efficiency-enhancing integration of economic activity enter into an agreement that is reasonably related to the integration and reasonably necessary to achieve its procompetitive benefits, the Agencies analyze the agreement under the rule of reason, even if it is of a type that might be considered *per se* illegal.[108]

In the FTC's 1988 decision, *In re Massachusetts Board of Registration in Optometry*, the FTC rejected the *per se* rule of reason dichotomy and replaced it with a three-step decision analysis. The FTC stated:

> First, we ask whether the restraint is "inherently suspect." In other words, is the practice the kind that appears likely, absent an efficiency justification, to "restraint competition and reduce output?". . . If the restraint is not inherently suspect, then the traditional rule of reason, with attendant issues of definition and power, must be employed. But if it is inherently suspect, we must pose a second question: Is there a plausible efficiency justification for the practice? That is, does the practice seem capable of creating or enhancing competition (e.g., by reducing the costs of producing or marketing the product, creating a new product, or improving the operation of the market)? Such an efficiency defense is plausible if it cannot be rejected without extensive factual inquiry. If it is not plausible, then the restraint can be quickly condemned. But if the efficiency justification is plausible, further inquiry—*a third inquiry*—is needed to

determine whether the justification is really valid. If it is, it must be assessed under the full balancing test of the rule of reason. But if the justification is, on examination, not valid, then the practice is unreasonable and unlawful under the rule of reason without further inquiry—there are no likely benefits to offset the threat to competition.[109]

Former chairman Pitofsky has contended that the *per se* approach still exists, but only for restraints that both are "naked" and have no efficiency justification.[110] Nonetheless, the FTC's *Massachusetts Board* decision still provides insight into how the FTC approaches the characterization of horizontal restraints.

Types of Conduct That Can Be *Per Se* Illegal Under Section 1 of the Sherman Act

The potential *per se* categories of conduct include price-fixing (and bid-rigging), market allocation, group boycotts, minimum resale price maintenance, and tying. Because price-fixing has been discussed in the context of the development of the *per se* rule, we begin our discussion with market allocation.

Market Allocation. Intellectual property licenses have sometimes been viewed as a vehicle to divide territories or customers. As a result, it is important to understand the characterization problem in connection with market allocation. In an early case, *National Ass'n of Window Glass Manufacturers v. United States*, Justice Holmes actually upheld an agreement among makers of handblown glass to operate only during half the year.[111] The purpose of the agreement was to allocate scarce labor between the factories.[112] Justice Holmes applied the full-blown rule of reason approach of *Chicago Board of Trade* to uphold the agreement on the grounds that the industry could not survive without it, and massive unemployment would result.[113]

Subsequent to *Window Glass Manufacturers*, the Supreme Court decided the *Socony-Vacuum* case. In 1951, the Court had an opportunity to clarify its view on how to treat horizontal market allocation in *Timken Roller Bearing Co. v. United States*.[114] In *Timken*, the government charged that Timken, British Timken, and French Timken restrained trade in the sale of antifriction bearings. The parties had allocated territories among themselves and attempted to fix prices on the products whenever one firm sold in the territory of another firm. Timken defended its restraints as reasonable, arguing that they were ancillary to a joint venture between the parties that was organized to exploit the Timken trademark. The Supreme Court rejected this argument, holding that the "dominant purpose for the restrictive agreements . . . was to avoid all competition."[115] With respect to the trademark defense, the Court found that the parties had gone far beyond what was necessary for trademark protection.[116] Nevertheless, the Court did not explicitly condemn the market allocation as *per se* illegal.

In 1966, the Supreme Court again addressed the post–*Socony-Vacuum* characterization of market allocation in *United States v. General Motors Corp.*[117] This case involved General Motors' "location clauses" contained in their dealer agreements that prohibited a dealer from moving to or establishing "a new or different location." Dealer associations policed the agreements to prevent discounters. The Court struck down the agreements as *per se* illegal on the grounds that the dealers were openly cooperating to prevent discounters.[118]

Similarly, *United States v. Sealy, Inc.*[119] involved an agreement among mattress manufacturers that created mutually exclusive territories. Sealy retailers themselves monitored and enforced agreements that set exclusive territories, retail prices, advertised prices, and other terms of sale. The Court found concerning these practices that "[t]heir anticompetitive nature and effect are so apparent and so serious that the courts will not pause to assess them in light of the rule of reason."[120] As in *Timken Roller*, the Court rejected Sealy's defense that the territorial allocation was ancillary to the use of the Sealy trademark.[121]

United States v. Topco Associates, Inc.[122] was the first case before the Court in which *horizontal market* division was presented in its *pure form*. The facts of the case were that 25 small regional supermarkets (with market shares all below 10 percent) formed Topco, a cooperative, to distribute to its members "private label" brand-name products. Topco argued that this was required if its members were to compete successfully with large chain stores, such as A&P, that had their own brands. The agreement between the members contained an ancillary restraint that Topco private label products could only be sold in the geographic area assigned to it by Topco. Citing *Northern Pacific*, Justice Marshall wrote that "[o]ne of the classic examples of a *per se* violation of § 1 is an agreement between competitors at the same level of the market structure to allocate territories in order to minimize competition. . . . We think that it is clear that the restraint in this case is a horizontal one, and, therefore, a *per se* violation of § 1.[123] As discussed below, *Topco* is inconsistent with subsequent Supreme Court precedent and has been widely criticized, although it has not been overruled.[124]

Since *Topco*, and following the precedent in *BMI, Maricopa, Sylvania,* and *NCAA*, lower courts that have addressed horizontal market allocation have advocated a flexible, non–*per se* approach.[125] The three most important cases from the appellate courts addressing division of territories are: (1) *General Leaseways, Inc. v. National Truck Leasing Ass'n (General Leaseways)*[126]; (2) *Polk Bros., Inc. v. Forest City Enterprises, Inc. (Polk)*[127]; and (3) *Rothery Storage & Van Co. v. Atlas Van Lines, Inc. (Rothery Storage)*[128]. Each of these cases suggests that the application of the *per se* rule must take into account possible efficiencies that may result from, and justify, any transaction at issue.

In *General Leaseways*, Judge Posner recognized the *per se* rule expressed by *Topco, Sealy,* and *Timken,* but indicated that the rule should not apply where the defendants establish that their agreement facilitates market efficiencies. The defendants in *General Leaseways* consisted of 130 competing trucking companies that had agreed not to operate their leasing or repair businesses within certain designated territories. The agreement also contained a provision that required that participants perform emergency repairs on each others' trucks if the trucks happened to break down in their territories, such repairs being subject to reimbursement from the other party. The Seventh Circuit examined the possibility that the agreement contributed to certain economic efficiencies, but it concluded that the territorial division was broader than necessary (i.e., not the least restrictive means) to achieve the legitimate purpose of creating a nationwide system of truck repairs, and therefore was *per se* illegal.[129] However, by analyzing the relationship between the *per se* rule and the alleged efficiencies of horizontal restraints, the court indicated that the *per se* rule could not be applied without examining potential economic efficiencies.[130]

Judge Posner even suggested that a division of geographic markets might have been justified in *Topco* if Topco had established that its program would have prevented a market inefficiency such as a free-rider problem (i.e., one grocer benefiting unfairly from the promotional investment made by another grocer in a particular market).[131] Regardless of whether the facts of *Topco* support that analysis, Judge Posner's introduction of efficiency considerations into the *per se* characterization problem undercuts the simplified approach of merely classifying a type of transaction as a horizontal market allocation once it is "alleged" and then declaring it *per se* illegal. Accordingly, Judge Posner artfully constructed his analysis to be consistent with *BMI, Maricopa,* and *NCAA*, indicating that those cases might best be explained by the "enormous efficiency" of the arrangements involved therein and the need for those arrangements in order to attain the efficiencies.[132]

In *Polk*, the Seventh Circuit addressed how to characterize market allocation after *BMI, Maricopa,* and *NCAA*. The case involved two stores that agreed to share a single building for the sale of their complementary products (lumber/hardware and home appliances). The two companies also contracted not to sell competing products at that store location. Although the arrangement was construed as a horizontal allocation of market and customers, the *Polk* court examined the market effects of the agreement rather than characterizing it as *per se* illegal.[133] It held that if an agreement arguably "promoted enterprise and productivity at the time it was adopted," then the rule of reason must be applied to distinguish legitimate competition from anticompetitive effects."[134] Moreover, the *Polk* court noted that *per se* characterization is an unusual step that should apply only to classic naked restraints, not ancillary restraints contributing to "productivity through integration of efforts."[135] The court concluded that the noncompetition provisions between the parties were necessary for "productive cooperation," or production efficiencies, and that consumers would benefit from the arrangement.[136] Accordingly, the court held that the *per se* rule did not apply to the agreement at issue and ruled in favor of the defendants.[137]

The last important post-*Topco* market decision case (prior to *Palmer*, which is discussed next) is *Rothery Storage*. In that case, Judge Bork (of the District of Columbia Circuit Court) emphasized the inconsistency between *Topco* and subsequent Supreme

Court decisions, stating: "[R]ecent Supreme Court decisions . . . demonstrate[] . . . that, to the extent *Topco* and *Sealy* stand for the proposition that all horizontal restraints are illegal *per se*, they must be regarded as effectively overruled."[138] *Rothery Storage* concerned a challenge to the Atlas network's policy of terminating its agents (independent moving companies throughout the country) that persisted in handling interstate carriage on its own account as well as for Atlas as a group boycott. The *Rothery Storage* court held that the restraints at issue were ancillary to the joint venture that constituted the Atlas van line.[139] In rejecting application of the *per se* rule, the court stated that "[t]he restraints preserve the efficiencies of the nationwide van line by eliminating the problem of the free ride."[140] The free-rider argument referred to the market efficiencies that result from preventing these agents from benefiting from Atlas's training, services, and equipment without paying Atlas anything.

The court also rejected the *per se* rule because, after evaluating the specific facts, it appeared that there was no possibility that the restraints could suppress market competition or decrease output.[141] The facts showed that Atlas had less than 6 percent of the relevant market and therefore lacked the market power to impact market prices through decreasing output.[142] In addition, the *Rothery Storage* court ruled that a joint venture made more efficient through ancillary restraints was equivalent to a corporate merger and therefore should be evaluated under the rule of reason used in section 2 cases.[143]

Despite the opportunity to do so in its 1990 decision *Palmer v. BRG of Georgia, Inc.*,[144] the Supreme Court did not validate the erosion of *Topco* and the *per se* rule. In *Palmer*, two competing companies offering bar review courses and related materials entered into a noncompetition agreement for certain territories. Part of the agreement provided for one company to license its material and well-known name to the other company for use in Georgia in exchange for a share of the resulting revenue. The two companies argued that the noncompetition provisions were reasonable and were merely ancillary to the IP license. Notwithstanding this argument, the Court found that the revenue-sharing formula, particularly viewed in light of the price increase that took place immediately after the licensor withdrew (as per the agreement) from Georgia, established that the agreement was formed for the illegal purpose of raising prices and thus constituted a *per se* violation.[145]

Group Boycotts.   Another area in which antitrust law is applied to IP is concerted refusals to deal or group boycotts. Boycotts can arise from certain patent pools and cross-licensing agreements. Some types of group boycott and concerted refusals to deal have been held to be *per se* illegal.[146] For instance, in *Klor's, Inc. v. Broadway-Hale Stores, Inc. (Klor's)*, a large San Francisco department store, Broadway-Hale, secured the agreement of several appliance manufacturers to boycott Klor's, a small competitor next door. Broadway defended on the grounds that even if Klor's closed, it would not impact competitors. The Supreme Court held that because the boycott was horizontal and concerted, no analysis of competition was required.[147] Earlier, in *Fashion*

Originators' Guild of America v. FTC (*Fashion Originators*), the Supreme Court struck down an effort by the Fashion Originators' Guild to boycott retailers who sold copies of the guild members' "original creations." The Court noted that the guild had market power and engaged in activities beyond what could be justified by the control of copying.[148] The Court therefore held the boycott to be illegal.[149] *Radiant Burners, Inc. v. Peoples Gas Light and Coke Co.* involved a boycott in a standard-setting situation. In that case, the Supreme Court determined that an agreement among gas companies to sell natural gas only to customers using equipment approved by an industry organization comprised of manufacturers of such equipment to be *per se* illegal.[150]

Not all boycott cases are *per se* cases. Generally, the cases in which the Supreme Court has applied the *per se* rule to group boycotts typically have involved two types of situations. In the first type of situation, a group of sellers or buyers refuses to allow a competitor to participate in a trade association or other type of cooperative. In such cases, the Court generally has held that *per se* treatment is reserved for cases where "the cooperative possesses market power, or exclusive access to an element essential to effective competition."[151] The second type of situation in which the Supreme Court typically applies the *per se* rule involves a group of sellers boycotting customers to enforce a price-fixing cartel. For example, in *Federal Trade Commission v. Superior Court Trial Lawyers Association*,[152] the Court held that an agreement by members of the Superior Court Trial Lawyers Association to refuse representation to indigent criminal defendants until the District of Columbia increased their compensation was subject to analysis under the *per se* rules.[153] The Court stated that the conduct involved "not only a boycott but was also a horizontal price-fixing agreement—a type of conspiracy that has been consistently analyzed as a *per se* violation for many decades."[154] In contrast, in situations in which market power is not present or where important efficiencies can be claimed as a result of the boycott, the Supreme Court has applied a rule of reason approach.[155]

A more difficult fact situation is presented when the group boycott is undertaken by consumers or buyers rather than by sellers. Although there have been numerous cases involving boycotts by buyers, none has articulated a clear basis for distinguishing an unlawful "buyer conspiracy" from a procompetitive joint purchasing arrangement. Typically, if a court concludes that the boycott or joint action by the buyers has a negative impact on competition with little legitimate business justification, it will invoke the *per se* rule and then apply the analysis developed in seller cases.[156] However, if a court finds a plausible justification for the joint buyer activity, it will apply a rule of reason analysis and thereafter require a substantial showing of competitive harm to find liability.[157]

Minimum Resale Price Maintenance. Vertical arrangements that fix minimum resale prices are included among the *per se* violations. The Supreme Court first addressed vertical arrangements in *Dr. Miles Medical Co. v. John Park & Sons Co.*[158] In *Dr. Miles,* the Supreme Court considered a situation in which a manufacturer of proprietary medicines (essentially "snake oil") sought "to maintain certain prices fixed by it for all the sales of its products both at wholesale and retail."[159] The Court likened the facts to horizontal price-fixing, because the impact was the same as if the retailers had fixed prices among themselves.[160] The Court concluded that such vertical price-fixing was *per se* illegal.[161]

Since the *Dr. Miles* decision, the rule against vertical price-fixing has withstood challenge. Many economists have contended that manufacturers must establish retail margins by limiting intraband competition, so that retailers can provide services and quality assurance that allows the manufacturer to compete more effectively with other brands.[162] In contrast to vertical *minimum* price-setting, the Supreme Court has recently held that vertical *maximum* price-setting is not a *per se* offense.[163]

Tying. The last *per se* section 1 category is tying. Tying or bundling the sale of two products together can be a *per se* offense if (1) the seller has market power in the tying product, (2) two separate products exist, (3) the sale of one product is conditioned on the sale of the other product, and (4) substantial commerce in the tied market is affected.[164] In *Jefferson Parish Hosp. Dist. No. 2 v. Hyde*, an anesthesiologist challenged East Jefferson Hospital's practice of requiring all surgery patients to use a single medical group for anesthesiology services. The danger that a tie posed for competition was that the defendant may gain a monopoly in the tying and tied markets, which would harm competition in the tied market. Moreover, tying could make entry more difficult because a new entrant would have to sell in both markets to compete. Conversely, tying could have procompetitive consequences.[165]

Although tying can have anticompetitive, procompetitive, or neutral effects, the black-letter law is that tying is *per se* illegal when each of the abovementioned elements is present. First, the bundle or tie must involve at least two products. Separate products exist when there is separate consumer demand for each product.[166] Second, the defendant must have market power in the tying market.[167] This typically is defined as a large market share in the relevant market. Third, the sale of the separate products must be conditioned (i.e., you cannot reasonably buy one without the other).[168] Fourth, there must be some "not insubstantial" impact on the tied market.[169] In addition, some but not all courts require some showing of an anticompetitive effect of a relevant market.[170]

Although tying is considered a *per se* offense, courts have often considered business justifications for tying. For example, in *United States v. Jerrold Electronics Corp.*,[171] the district court upheld a tie of components of a system and service during a company's development period because it ensured the proper functioning of a complex system. Ties also have been used when it is required to protect trade secrets.[172] Quality control generally is not a defense if less restrictive alternatives are available.[173]

Finally, if a plaintiff cannot prove the elements of a *per se* tying case, tying can be brought under the rule of reason if significant adverse effects on competition can be shown.[174]

Conduct Judged Under the Rule of Reason for Purposes of Section 1

In contrast to the *per se* test, the rule of reason approach requires a full competitive analysis to determine whether a restraint on balance harms competition. According to the Supreme Court, under a rule of reason analysis "the fact finder weighs all of the circumstances of a case in deciding whether a restrictive practice should be prohibited as imposing an unreasonable restraint on competition."[175] The rule of reason does not "open the field" to any argument. Instead, the rule of reason takes into account all of the factors necessary to determine whether the restraint "is one that promotes competition or one that suppresses competition."[176] In other words, the rule of reason requires an analysis of markets and market power, and any direct evidence of prices and output to determine the extent of any anticompetitive impact of a restraint. It then weighs this effect against all procompetitive efficiencies, increased competition, and legitimate business justifications. The rule of reason offenses that could relate to IP include vertical non-price restraints, such as exclusive dealing or exclusive territories. Each of these offenses requires a more complete competitive analysis.

Exclusive Dealing. The early law of exclusive dealing did not involve a full rule of reason analysis. In *Standard Oil Co. of California and Standard Stations, Inc. v. United States* (*Standard Stations*),[177] a full-blown rule of reason analysis was not available because, as the Court reasoned:

> To insist upon such an investigation would be to stultify the force of Congress' declaration that requirements contracts are to be prohibited wherever their effect "may be" to substantially lessen competition. . . . We conclude, therefore, that the qualifying clause of Section 3 [of the Clayton Act] is satisfied by proof that competition has been foreclosed in a substantial share of the line of commerce affected.[178]

Under this so-called "quantitative substantiality test," the aftermarket entrant would need only to demonstrate the existence of foreclosure in the distribution channel, and no effective competitive effects defense would be possible.[179]

In 1961 the Supreme Court revisited the issue of exclusive dealing in *Tampa Electric Co. v. Nashville Coal Co.* (*Tampa*)[180] In *Tampa*, the Court rejected the quantitative substantiality test advocated by the *Standard Stations* Court and instead adopted what has come to be known as the "qualitative substantiality" test.[181] The *Tampa* Court summarized its guidelines for analyzing exclusive dealing arrangements as follows: "First, the line of commerce . . . involved must be determined. . . . Second, the area of effective competition in the known line of commerce must be charted. . . . Third, and last, the competition foreclosed by the contract must be found to constitute a substantial share of the relevant market."[182] The requirement of defining the relevant market was a critical advance.[183]

The Court's decision in *Jefferson Parish Hospital District No. 2 v. Hyde*[184] may have increased the importance of a competitive effects analysis when analyzing an exclusive dealing contract. Although not addressed by the majority opinion, the issue was discussed in Justice O'Connor's concurrence, in which she stated: "[W]hether or not the Hospital-Roux contract is characterized as a tie between distinct products, the contract unquestionably does constitute exclusive dealing. Exclusive dealing arrangements are independently subject to scrutiny under Section 1 of the Sherman Act, and are also analyzed under the Rule of Reason."[185] Justice O'Connor further reasoned that "[e]xclusive dealing arrangements may, in some circumstances, create or extend market power of a supplier of the purchaser party to the exclusive dealing arrangement," and thus may restrain horizontal competition.[186]

In his typical style, Judge Posner, on the heels of the *Jefferson Parish* decision, cut right to the point in *Roland Machinery Co. v. Dresser Industries, Inc.*, stating[187]:

> The exclusion of competitors is cause for antitrust concern only if it impairs the health of the competitive process itself. Hence, a plaintiff must prove two things to show that an exclusive dealing arrangement is unreasonable. First, he must prove that it is likely to keep at least one significant competitor of the defendant from doing business in a relevant market. If there is no exclusion of a significant competitor, the agreement cannot possibly harm competition. Second, he must prove that the probable (not certain) effect of the exclusion will be to raise prices above (and therefore reduce output below) the competitive level, or otherwise injure competition; he must show in other words that the anticompetitive effects (if any) of the exclusion outweigh any benefits to competition from it.[188]

More recently, several lower courts explicitly have given prominence to a competitive effects analysis in exclusive dealing cases through full-blown rule of reason analyses. For example, in *Actom v. Merle Norman Cosmetics Inc.*,[189] the district court introduced its analysis of an exclusive dealing arrangement by stating that "[v]ertical non-price restraints of the type at issue in this case are subject to the Rule of Reason analysis."[190] Citing the Ninth Circuit's opinion in *Thurman Industries v. Pay'N Pak Stores, Inc.*,[191] the district court stated that "in order to prove injury to competition as required by the rule of reason, plaintiffs must prove the relevant product and geographic markets, and demonstrate the effects of the alleged restraints within those markets."[192] Then, combining the three-part test in *Tampa* with the traditional requirements of a rule of reason analysis, the court concluded that "[t]o condemn exclusive dealing arrangements after *Tampa* requires a detailed depiction of circumstances and the most careful weighing of alleged dangers and potential benefits, which is to say the normal treatment afforded by the rule of reason."[193]

A similar approach can be found in *Ryko Manufacturing Co. v. Eden Services.*[194] Extrapolating from *Tampa*, the Eighth Circuit held that the proper "test requires us to examine the character of the relevant market and to assess the competitive impact of the alleged constraints."[195] According to the court, where "the supplier imposing the provisions has substantial market power, we may rely on the foreclosure rate alone to establish the violation."[196] Moreover, "the plaintiff must show that the restraint . . . has a probable adverse affect on interbrand competition."[197]

Vertical Non-Price Restrictions. The rule of reason is also applied to exclusive distributors or exclusive distributor territories. A contract in which a manufacturer appoints a distributor as his sole or exclusive outlet is subject to the rule of reason.[198] In *United States v. Arnold Schwinn & Co.*,[199] the government challenged an exclusive territorial system of Schwinn distributors. The Court held, in a weakly reasoned opinion, that territorial restraints were *per se* illegal. *Schwinn* later was overturned in 1977 in *Continental T.V., Inc. v. GTE Sylvania, Inc.* (*Sylvania*).[200] In *Sylvania*, the Court held that non-price vertical restraints would be governed by the rule of reason.[201] Because vertical restrictions simultaneously reduce competition between dealers of a single brand but may stimulate competition between brands, the Court held that a balancing of the harms and benefits was necessary.[202] In practice, a non-price vertical restraint will be upheld if there exist good business justifications for the restraint, such as control of free riders or to induce fixed investments by dealers. Lower courts have addressed such factors as the purpose of the restrictions, analyzing whether less restrictive alternatives exist and determining the market share of the supplier involved.

ANTITRUST CLAIMS UNDER SECTION 2 OF THE SHERMAN ACT

Although certain IP licensing practices can run afoul of section 2 of the Sherman Act, it is far more likely that IP antitrust challenges will arise under section 1 of the Sherman Act. Nonetheless, this chapter briefly addresses the basic elements of a section 2 antitrust claim. Section 2 of the Sherman Act prohibits unilateral monopolization, attempted monopolization, and conspiracy to monopolize. All section 2 claims are tested under the rule of reason. Monopolization and attempted monopolization require possession of monopoly power (or the dangerous probability of obtaining monopoly power for attempt), plus an element of deliberateness. For example, in *United States v. Grinnell Corp.*,[203] the Supreme Court expressed the elements of a monopolization case as follows:

> The offense of monopoly under § 2 of the Sherman Act has two elements: (1) the possession of monopoly power in the relevant market and (2) the willful acquisition or maintenance of that power as distinguished from growth or development as a consequence of a superior product, business consumer, or historic accident.[204]

The first element, monopoly power, is inferred from evidence of large market shares in the relevant market along with barriers to entry.[205] Typically, market shares at least as large as 70 percent are required.[206] For an attempt to monopolize, case market shares above 60 percent are typically required.[207]

The second element of a monopolization case requires exclusionary or predatory conduct. Various specific types of conduct can support a section 2 claim when monopoly power is present, including predatory pricing, monopolization of an essential facility, other types of exclusionary activity, anticompetitive use of an invalid patent, leveraging monopoly power into another market, and raising rivals' costs.

Predatory Pricing. There is a long and complicated history of the law and economics of predatory pricing. Under current federal law, a predatory pricing claim now requires two elements. First, a competitor must set prices below some level of incremental cost. In addition, the competitor must have a realistic chance to recoup its losses after the target competitor is driven from the market.[208]

Essential Facilities. Monopolization of an essential facility means that a monopolist controls a bottleneck monopoly over some product or service required by others to be viable competitors. In *MCI Communications Corp. v. AT&T*,[209] the Seventh Circuit identified four elements required to establish section 2 liability under the essential facilities doctrine:

> (1) control of the essential facility by a monopolist; (2) a competitor's inability practically or reasonably to duplicate the essential facility; (3) the denial of the use of the facility to a competitor; and (4) the feasibility of providing the facility.[210]

Leveraging. Another type of exclusionary conduct that can support a section 2 claim is leveraging. Leveraging is the use of monopoly power in one market to monopolize or attempt to monopolize another market. In *Alaska Airlines, Inc. v. United Airlines, Inc.*,[211] the Ninth Circuit helped to clarify that a plaintiff alleging leveraging must show that "the monopolist uses its power in the first market to [actually] acquire and maintain a monopoly in the second market, or . . . attempt to do so. . . ."[212]

Raising Rivals' Costs. Raising rivals' costs refers to engaging in conduct that raises a competitor's costs. Such cost increases allow the predatory firm to raise its price and thereby hurt consumers. Firms can raise a rival's costs by causing its input prices to increase, refusals to deal, or other conduct. Such cases often arise when the predator firm is vertically integrated.[213]

ANTITRUST CLAIMS UNDER THE CLAYTON ACT

The only Clayton Act section that is relevant to IP issues is section 7. Section 7 of the Clayton Act is the primary merger statute. It prohibits mergers or acquisitions of stock or assets if their effect "may be substantially to lessen competition, or to tend to create a monopoly." Horizontal mergers increase concentration by reducing the number of competitors in the market. Early cases applying section 7 to mergers interpreted even small increases in concentration as pushing a competitive threat.[214] The Supreme Court also considered the trend in concentration.[215] In *United States v. Philadelphia Nat'l Bank*, the Supreme Court held that an increase in concentration was enough to establish a presumption of illegality.[216]

Later cases have focused on a host of competitive factors such as ease of entry, buyer power, efficiencies, and others. The 1992 Horizontal Merger Guidelines discussed in Chapter 3 are a good indicator of how a court will analyze a merger. These guidelines describe a five-step analytic process to determine whether a merger substantially harms competition. The steps are: (1) define the relevant product and geographic markets that would be impacted by the merger, (2) assess how much additional concentration will be caused in those markets by the merger, (3) assess whether entry barriers into the relevant markets are high, (4) consider the competitive effects of the merger, and (5) consider any merger specific efficiencies that may result. Courts have followed a similar approach to section 7 of the Clayton Act.

SUMMARY

This chapter introduced a brief history and the basic elements of the federal antitrust laws. Intellectual property law is closely akin to antitrust law. Attorneys and experts must be in a position to spot potential antitrust issues, avoid IP arguments that invoke antitrust problems, and structure settlements or damage solutions that are not anticompetitive.

ENDNOTES

[1] In concert with a sudden rise of the labor cost in the first half of the 1880s, these movements resulted in significantly diminished returns on capital despite the increasing size of the production units.

[2] *See* Hans B. Thorelli, *The Federal Antitrust Policy: Organization of an American Tradition,* Baltimore: The Johns Hopkins Press (1955), 66.

[3] Hans B. Thorelli, *The Federal Antitrust Policy,* at 180–85, 226–29.

[4]   The preservation of small producers was an explicit concern in the drafting of the Sherman Antitrust bill. *See id.* at 27.

[5]   Sherman Act of July 2, ch. 647, 26 Stat. 209 (1890).

[6]   166 U.S. 290 (1897).

[7]   *See United States v. Trans-Missouri Freight Ass'n,* 166 U.S. 290, 327-29 1007 (1897).

[8]   *Id.* at 323.

[9]   *See id.* at 353–54 (J. White dissenting).

[10] 171 U.S. 505 (1898).

[11] 171 U.S. 578 (1898).

[12] 85 F. 271 (6th Cir. 1898).

[13] *Id.* at 282.

[14] *Id.* at 281. For an economic analysis, *see generally* Wesley L. Liebeler, *1984 Economic Review of Antitrust Developments: Horizontal Restrictions, Efficiency, and "the* Per Se *Rule,"* 31 UCLA L. Rev. 1019 (1986).

[15] 221 U.S. 1 (1911).

[16] *See id.* at 67–68.

[17] *Id.* at 60.

[18] *Id.* at 63, 64.

[19] *Id.* at 75–77.

[20] *Id.*

[21] Clayton Act, ch. 323, 38 Stat. 730 (1914).

[22] Federal Trade Commission Act, ch. 311, 38 Stat. 717 (1914).

[23] *See generally* 15 U.S.C. §§ 372a (1997).

[24] *See generally* 15 U.S.C. §§ 1-58 (1997).

[25] James Weinstein, *The Corporate Ideal in the Liberal State, 1900–1918,* Boston: Beacon Press (1968), at 62.

[26] Michael Wise, *Robert M. Lafollette's Progressive Wisconsin Idea and the Origin of the Federal Trade Commission,* Antitrust Report (1995) at 20–21.

[27] Currently codified at 15 U.S.C. § 14 (1997).

[28] Currently codified at 15 U.S.C. § 15 (1997).

[29] Currently codified at 15 U.S.C. § 17 (1997).

[30] Currently codified at 15 U.S.C. § 18 (1997).

[31] Currently codified at 15 U.S.C. § 19 (1997).

[32] Robinson-Patman Act, ch. 592, §§ 2–4, 49 Stat. 1526 (1936).

[33] *See* 15 U.S.C. §§ 13a, 13b (1997).

[34] Celler-Kefauver Act, ch. 1184, 64 Stat. 1125 (1950).

[35] *See* 15 U.S.C. §§ 18, 21 (1997).

[36] *See* Pub. L. 94-435, Title II, § 201, 90 Stat. 1390 (1976); section 7 is currently codified at 15 U.S.C. § 18a (1997).

[37] *See* Pub. L. 101-588, § 2, 104 Stat. 2879 (1990); section 8 of the Clayton Act is currently codified at 15 U.S.C. § 19 (1997).

[38] *See* 15 U.S.C. § 45 (1997).

[39] Arthur M. Schlesinger, *The Politics of Upheaval*, Houghton Mifflin Co. (1960), 390.

[40] Leon Henderson also had a dramatic change in attitude. Schlesinger summarizes Henderson's about-face as follows: "Leon Henderson, the vigorous and resourceful chief economist of NRA, viewing the economic future late in 1935 from the rubble of his agency, outlined one program to test the possibilities of competition. . . . The key problem as Henderson saw it, was to restore price competition. He appreciated the strength of the tendency toward economic concentration, and price inflexibility. . . . I favor a positive program for securing laissez faire, said Henderson—a multiple attack on concentration and price rigidity, including the active use of the taxing power; the revision of the patent laws; vigorous antitrust action; encouragement in co-operatives; yardstick competition; tariff reduction, and so on." Schlesinger, *supra* note 147, at 388.

[41] Herbert Stein, *The Fiscal Revolution In America*, American Enterprise Institute for Public Policy Research (1969), 104.

[42] 166 U.S. 290 (1897).

[43] *Id.* at 324.

[44] *See* Robert Bork, *The Antitrust Paradox* 16 (1978); Richard Posner, *Antitrust Law: An Economic Perspective*, Chicago: Univ. of Chicago (1976) at 8.

[45] *See* Robert Lande, *Wealth Transfers as the Original and Primary Concern of Antitrust: The Efficiency Interpretation Challenged*, 34 Hastings L.J. 65 (1982).

[46] *See, e.g.*, 1992 Horizontal Merger Guidelines § 0.1 ("[T]he result of the exercise of market power is a *transfer of wealth* from buyers to sellers or a misallocation of resources") (emphasis added).

[47] *See* 15 U.S.C. §§ 1–7 (1997).

[48] 15 U.S.C. § 1 (1997).

[49] *Matsushira Elec. Indus. Co. v. Zenith Radio Corp.*, 475 U.S. 574, 588 (1986)

[50] 467 U.S. 752, 767–68 (1987).

[51] *Id.* at 753, 104 S. Ct. at 2733.

[52] *Id.* at 771.

[53] 246 U.S. 231, 238–39 (1918).

[54] *Id.* at 238.

[55] *Id.*

[56] *Id.* at 238–39.

[57] One exception was the trial court ruling in *Trenton Potteries*, discussed in the next section.

[58] 288 U.S. 344 (1993), *overruled by Copper Crop. v. Independence Tube Corp.*, 467 U.S. 752, 104 S. Ct. 2731, 81 L. Ed. 2d 623 (1984).

[59] *Id.* at 372.

[60] *Id.* at 372–73.

[61] 273 U.S. 392 (1927).

[62] *Id.* at 400–01.

[63] *Id.* at 397–98.

[64] *Id.* at 401–02, 47 S. Ct. at 381.

[65] 310 U.S. 150 (1940).

[66] *Id.* at 223.

[67] *Id.* at 223–24.

[68] 356 U.S. 1 (1958).

[69] 356 U.S. 1 at 549.

[70] 435 U.S. 679 (1978).

[71] *Id.* at 688.

[72] *Id.* at 692.

[73] *Id.*

[74] *Id.* at 696.

[75] 388 U.S. 365 (1967), *overruled by Continental T.V., Inc. v. GTE Sylvania, Inc.*, 433 U.S. 36 (1977).

[76] 433 U.S. 36, 58 (1997). The Court, however, clarified that the opinion does not foreclose the possibility that particular applications of vertical restrictions might justify *per se* prohibition. See *id.*

[77] *Id.* at 49–50.

[78] *Id.* at 51.

[79] *Id.* at 58–59; *see also Center Video Indus. v. United Media, Inc.*, 995 F.2d 735, 737 (9th Cir. 1993).

[80] *Id.* at 59. In 1997, the Supreme Court ruled that maximum resale price restraints also would no longer be subject to *per se* condemnation. *See State Oil Co. v. Khan*, 522 U.S. 3 (1997).

[81] 441 U.S. 1 (1979).

[82] 457 U.S. 332 (1982).

[83] 468 U.S. 85 (1984).

[84] *BMI*, 441 U.S. at 9.

[85] *Id.* at 2 (citations omitted).

[86] The next year, the Court appeared to somewhat retreat to *Socony-Vacuum* in *Catalano, Inc. v. Target Sales, Inc.*, 446 U.S. 643 (1980). In *Catalano*, the Court held that agreements on credit arrangements were *per se* illegal. *See id.* at 648. The *Catalano* Court apparently had no trouble "characterizing" the arrangement. *See id.*

[87] *See Maricopa County*, 457 U.S. at 348.

[88] *Id.* at 357.

[89] *Id.* at 356–57.

[90] *See NCAA*, 468 U.S. at 106-07.

[91] *Id.* at 103–04.

[92] *Id.* at 118–19.

[93] 476 U.S. 447 (1986).

[94] *Id.* at 458–59.

[95] *Id.* at 459. Following the Supreme Court's line of cases on *per se* conduct, the Third Circuit in *United States v. Brown University*, 5 F.3d 658 (3rd Cir. 1993), found that a cartel of universities that met annually to exchange information and set financial aid amounts was not *per se* illegal. The Court rejected *per se* treatment holding that "the test for determining what constitutes *per se* unlawful price-fixing is one of substance, not semantics . . . the fact that overlap may be said to involve price-fixing in a literal sense therefore does not mean that it automatically qualifies as *per se* illegal price-fixing." Significantly, the Court found that evidence of direct impact was sufficient, and no market power inquiry was necessary.

[96] In fact, the "quick look" approach originated in Chief Justice Berger's dissent in *Topco*. The first judge to use the term *quick look* was Judge Posner in *Vogel v. American Society of Appraisers*, 744 F.2d 598 (7th Cir. 1984).

[97] *See NCAA*, 468 U.S. at 109-10 and n.39, 104 S. Ct. at 2964-65 and n.39; *Law v. NCAA*, 134 F.3d 1010, 1019–21 (10th Cir. 1998); *Chicago Pro. Sports LTD Partnership v. NBA*, 961 F.2d 667, 674 (7th Cir. 1992) (applying quick look); *Lie v. St. Joseph Hosp.*, 964 F.2d 567, 569 (6th Cir. 1992) (stating that quick-look approach applies "when the agreement at issue is very similar to *per se* violations and might, but for prudential constraints, be analyzed under the *per se* presumption").

[98] 128 F.3d 720, 727 (9th Cir. 1997).

[99] *See id.*

[100] *Cal. Dental Ass'n v. FTC*, 526 U.S. 756 (1999).

[101] *Id.* at 769 n.8.

[102] *Id.* at 780–81.

[103] *Id.* at 779.

[104] 526 U.S. at 782 (J. Breyer, dissenting). *See* Stephen Calkins, *California Dental Association: Not a Quick Look But Not the Full Monty*, 67 Antitrust L.J. 495 (2000); Timothy J. Muris, *The Rule of Reason After California Dental*, 68 Antitrust L.J. 527 (2000).

[105] 4 Trade Reg. Rep. (CCH) 13, 109.

[106] *See* Joel I. Klein, *A Stepwise Approach to Antitrust Review of Horizontal Agreements* (Nov. 7, 1996).

[107] William Kolasky, *The Department of Justice's "Stepwise" Approach Imposes Too Heavy a Burden on Parties to Horizontal Agreements*, 12 Antitrust 41 (1998).

[108] Joint Venture Guidelines § 3.2.

[109] *In re Massachusetts Bd. of Registration in Optometry;* 110 F.T.C. 549, 604 (1988) (emphasis added). *See* application of this standard in *Detroit Auto Dealers Ass'n*, 955 F.2d 457, 469-70 (6th Cir.), *cert. denied*, 506 U.S. 972 (1992) (making rule of reason inquiry into defendants' market power and alleged efficiency justifications where defendants had reached agreement limiting showroom hours and impact of that limitation was not immediately apparent).

[110] *See* Muris, *The Rule of Reason After California Dental*, 68 Antitrust L.J. 538 (2000).

[111] 263 U.S. 403, 413 (1923).

[112] *Id.*

[113] *Id.* at 411–12.

[114] 341 U.S. 593 (1951), *overruled by Copperweld Corp. v. Independence Tube Corp.*, 467 U.S. 752 (1984).

[115] *Id.* at 597.

[116] *Id.* at 598.

[117] 384 U.S. 127 (1966).

[118] *Id.* at 145.

[119] 388 U.S. 350.

[120] *Id.* at 355.

[121] *Id.* at 357 n.4.

[122] 405 U.S. 596 (1972).

[123] *Id.* at 608, 92 S. Ct. at 1133.

[124] *See, e.g.*, Herbert Hovencamp, *Federal Antitrust Policy* 190–92 (1994) ("Although *Topco* has never been overruled, it is widely criticized and not infrequently honored").

[125] In applying the rule of reason analysis rather than the *per se* rule, the Eleventh Circuit Court of Appeals stated that:

> [T]he purpose of the *per se* rule is to dispose of cases quickly without the more detailed and costly inquiry required under the rule of reason test. It is to be applied, however, "only when history and analysis have shown that in sufficiently similar circumstances the rule of reason unequivocally results in finding of liability under the Sherman Act. . . ." To use the *per se* rule as a means of avoiding rule of reason analysis when it is unclear what the result would be under the rule would subvert the intention and purpose of the rule.

> *Consultants & Designers, Inc. v. Butler Serv. Group, Inc.*, 720 F.2d 1553, 1562 (11th Cir. 1983). In accord with this logic, the Ninth Circuit applied the rule of reason where the type of contract at issue was a novel agreement with which the judiciary lacked sufficient experience to classify as a *per se* violation. *See Northrop Corp. v. McDonnell Douglas Corp.*, 705 F.2d 1030 (9th Cir. 1983) (analyzing "teaming agreement" between government contractors that allowed the parties to allocate certain military projects between them while pooling their expertise in relevant areas). *But see United States v. Capitol Serv., Inc.*, 568 F. Supp. 134, 151 (E.D. Wash. 1983) (finding that it was not necessary for the court to have had experience with this particular type of agreement, so long as the agreement fell within one of the designated *per se* categories, such as price-fixing). The

Ninth Circuit noted that, "[m]ore important, however, is the fact that . . . not only do the agreements not preclude all competition between the parties' respective variants of the F-18, they actually foster competition by allowing both parties to compete in a market from which they were otherwise foreclosed." *Northrop*, 705 F.2d at 1052–53. Accordingly, the agreements could not constitute naked restraints of trade with the sole purpose of stifling competition. *See id.* at 1053; *see also SCFC ILC, Inc. v. Visa USA, Inc.*, 36 F.3d 958 (10th Cir. 1994) (affirming application of rule of reason to restraints, and concluding that the factors to examine in rejecting the *per se* rule included whether the restriction was ancillary, whether the agreement resulted in decreased output, and whether the prices increased after the agreement).

[126] 744 F.2d 588 (7th Cir. 1984).

[127] 776 F.2d 185 (7th Cir. 1985).

[128] 792 F.2d 210 (D.D.C. 1986).

[129] *General Leaseways*, 744 F.2d at 595.

[130] *Id.* at 595-96.

[131] *Id.* at 592.

[132] *Id.* at 594; *see also Continental T.V., Inc. v. GTE Sylvania, Inc.*, 433 U.S. 36, 54–57 (1977); *NCAA v. Bd. of Regents of the Univ. of Okla.*, 468 U.S. 85 (1984) (suggesting *in dicta* that this kind of balancing would apply in horizontal restraints as well).

[133] *See Polk*, 776 F.2d at 188–89.

[134] *Id.* at 189 (citing *BMI* and *NCAA* in support of horizontal agreements that involve cooperation among rivals and might produce "larger output and more desirable products").

[135] *Id.* at 188–90. For a criticism of *Polk, see* Ross, Principles of Antitrust Law, *Agreements to Divide Markets*, at 57–158.

[136] *Id.* at 189–90.

[137] *Id.* at 191.

[138] *Rothery Storage*, 792 F.2d at 226.

[139] *Id.* at 229.

[140] *Id.*

[141] *Id.* at 229.

[142] *Id.*

[143] *Id.* at 230; *see also* Department of Justice Business Review Letter (Sept. 28, 2000) (analyzing proposed collaboration as a merger and applying the rule of reason to proposed restraints where restraints did not give the parties the ability to raise prices).

[144] 498 U.S. 46 (1990) (*per curiam*).

[145] *Id.* at 49–50.

[146] *See, e.g., Radiant Burners, Inc. v. Peoples Gas Light & Coke Co.*, 364 U.S. 656 (1961); *Klor's, Inc. v. Broadway-Hale Stores, Inc.*, 359 U.S. 207 (1959); *Fashion Originators' Guild of Am. v. FTC*, 312 U.S. 457 (1941).

[147] *See Klor's*, 359 U.S. at 212–13.

[148] *See Fashion Originators*, 312 U.S. at 467–68.

[149] *Id.* at 468.

[150] *See Radiant Burners*, 364 U.S. at 659–60.

[151] *See, e.g., Northwest Wholesale Stationers, Inc. v. Pacific Stationery & Printing Co.*, 472 U.S. 284, 296, 105 S. Ct. 2613-21, 86 L.Ed.2d 202 (1985); *Registered Physical Therapists v. Intermountain Health Care*, 1988-2 Trade Cas. (CCH) and 68, 233 at 9, 484 (Dt. Utah 1988).

[152] 493 U.S. 411 (1990).

[153] *Id.* at 436.

[154] *Id.* at 436 n.19.

[155] *See, e.g., FTC v. Indiana Fed'n of Dentists*, 476 U.S. 447 (1986) (analyzing refusal by a group of dentists to forward X rays to insurance companies for medical reasons under the rule of reason and held anticompetitive on balance); *NCAA v. Bd. of Regents of the Univ. of Okla.*, 468 U.S. 85 (1984) (stating exclusion had efficiency justification because a sports league "would be completely ineffective if there were no rules").

[156] Buyer conspiracies to depress prices have been found illegal *per se* in at least 18 cases. *See, e.g., Mandeville Island Farms, Inc. v. Am. Crystal Sugar Co.*, 334 U.S. 219 (1948); *Harkins Amusement Enters. v. Gen. Cinema Corp.*, 850 F.2d 477, 485-86 (9th Cir. 1988), *cert. denied*, 488 U.S. 1019 (1989); *United States v. Capitol Serv., Inc.*, 756 F.2d 502 (7th Cir.), *cert. denied*, 474 U.S. 945 (1985); *Reid Bros. Logging Co. v. Ketchikan Pulp Co.*, 699 F.2d 1292 (9th Cir.), *cert. denied*, 464 U.S. 916 (1983); *In re Beef Industry Antitrust Litig.*, 600 F.2d 1148 (5th Cir. 1979), *cert. denied*, 449 U.S. 905 (1980), *later appeal*, 907 F.2d 510 (5th Dir. 1990); *United States v. Champion Int'l Corp.*, 557 F.2d 1270 (9th Cir.), *cert. denied*, 434 U.S. 938 (1977); *Cackling Acre, Inc. v. Olson Farms, Inc.*, 541 F.2d 242 (10th Cir. 1976), *cert. denied*, 429 U.S. 1122 (1977); *Nat'l Macaroni Mfrs. Ass'n v. FTC*, 345 F.2d 421 (7th Cir. 1965); *Union Carbide & Carbon Corp. v. Nisely*, 300 F.2d 561 (10th Cir.), *cert. dismissed*, 371 U.S. 801 (1962); *Live Poultry Dealers Protective Ass'n v. United States*, 4 F.2d 840 (2d Cir. 1924); *Transor (Bermuda) Ltd. v. BP N. Am. Petroleum*, 1990-1 Trade Cas. (CCH) and 68,998 (S.D.N.Y. 1990); *United States v. Seville Indus. Mach. Corp.*, 696 F. Supp. 986 (D.N.J. 1988); *Barr v. Dramatists Guild, Inc.*, 575 F. Supp. 555 (S.D.N.Y. 1983); *Gen. Cinema Corp. v. Buena Vista Dist. Co.*, 532 F. Supp. 1244 (C.D. Cal. 1982); *Bray v. Safeway Stores*, 392 F. Supp. 851 (N.D. Cal.), *vacated following settlement*, 1975-2 Trade Cas. (CCH) and 60,533 (9th Cir. 1975); *Robertson v. NBA*, 389 F. Supp. 867 (S.D.N.Y. 1975); *Denver Rockets v. All-Pro Mgmt., Inc.*, 325 F. Supp. 1049 (C.D. Cal 1971); *United States v. Olympia Provision & Baking Co.*, 282 F. Supp. 819 (S.D.N.Y. 1968), *aff'd mem.*, 393 U.S. 480 (1969). *See also Kapp v. NFL*, 586 F.2d 644 (9th Cir. 1978), *cert. denied*, 441 U.S. 907 (1979); *Cinema-Tex Enters. v. Santikos Theaters, Inc.*, 535 F.2d 932 (5th Cir. 1976); *Twentieth Century-Fox Film Corp. v. Goldwyn*, 328 F.2d 190 (9th Cir.), *cert. denied*, 379 U.S. 880 (1964); *United States v. N.Y. Great Atl. & Pac. Tea Co.*, 173 F.2d 79 (7th Cir. 1979).

[157] *See, e.g., White & White v. Am. Hosp. Supply Corp.*, 723 F.2d 495 (6th Cir. 1983); *Webster County Mem'l Hosp. v. UMW*, 536 F.2d 419 (D.C. Cir. 1976); *Langston Corp. v. Standard Register Co.*, 553 F. Supp. 632 (N.D. Ga. 1982); *see also Central Retailer-Owned Grocers, Inc. v. FTC*, 319 F.2d 410 (7th Cir. 1963). In *United States v. Topco Assocs., Inc.*, 405 U.S. 596 (1972), a cooperative association owned by competing retail food chains

had a "basic function [of] serv[ing] as a purchasing agent for its members." *Id.* at 598. Although the government challenged (and the Court condemned) Topco's exclusive *distribution* territories, the joint purchasing aspect of the Topco organization was not challenged and remained intact under the decree. *See* 1973-1 Trade Cas. (CCH) and 74,391 and 74,485 (N.D. Ill.), *aff'd by an equally divided Court*, 414 U.S. 801 (1973).

[158] 220 U.S. 373 (1911).

[159] *Id.* at 383.

[160] *Id.* at 407–08.

[161] *Id.* at 409.

[162] *See, e.g.*, Howard Marrel and Stephen McCafferty, *The Welfare Effects of Resale Price Maintenance*, 28 J. Law Econ. 363 (1985).

[163] *State Oil Co. v. Kahn*, 522 U.S. 3 (1997).

[164] *See generally Jefferson Parish Hosp. Dist. No. 2 v. Hyde*, 466 U.S. 2 (1984). Tying can also be held illegal under section 3 of the Clayton Act if the products involved are "commodities."

[165] *See, e.g.*, Roger Blair and David Kaserman, *Vertical Control with Variable Proportions: Ownership Integration and Contractual Equivalents*, 46 So. Econ. I. 1118 (1980).

[166] *See, e.g.*, *Eastman Kodak Co. v. Image Tech. Servs.*, 504 U.S. 451, 462 (1992) ("there must be sufficient consumer demand so that it is efficient for a firm to provide service separately from parts").

[167] *See, e.g.*, *United States Steel Corp. v. Fortner Enter.*, 429 U.S. 610, 611–12 (1977) ("appreciable economic power" in the tying market is required).

[168] *N. Pac. Ry. v. United States*, 356 U.S. 1, 6 n.4 (1958) (stating "where the buyer is free to take either product by itself there is no tying problem").

[169] *See, e.g.*, *Jefferson Parish*, 466 U.S. at 16.

[170] *See, e.g.*, *Commodore Plaza at Century 21 Condo. Assoc., Inc. v. Saul J. Morgan Enters.*, 746 F.2d 671 (11th Cir.), *cert. denied*, 467 U.S. 1241 (1984).

[171] 187 F. Supp. 543 (E.D. Pa. 1960), *aff'd per curiam*, 365 U.S. 567 (1961).

[172] *See, e.g.*, *Krehl v. Baskin Robbins Ice Cream Co.*, 664 F.2d 1348, 1350, 1353 and n.14 (9th Cir. 1982).

[173] *Id.* at 1353 and n.12.

[174] *See, e.g.*, *Town Sound & Custom Tops, Inc. v. Chrysler Motor Corp.*, 959 F.2d 468 (3rd Cir.), *cert. denied*, 506 U.S. 868 (1992).

[175] *Continental T.V., Inc. v. GTE Sylvania Inc.*, 433 U.S. 36, 49 (1977).

[176] *Nat'l Soc'y of Prof'l Eng'rs v. United States*, 435 U.S. 679, 691 (1978).

[177] 337 U.S. 293 (1949).

[178] *Id.* at 313–14.

[179] In *Standard Stations*, the Court struck down Standard Oil's use of exclusive dealing contracts as a "potential clog on competition," even though, according to the Court, only 6.7 percent of the total gross business was affected.

[180] 365 U.S. 320 (1961).

[181] The Court in *Tampa* analyzed a requirements contract between an electric utility and a coal company that had a 20-year term and involved approximately $128 million of coal sales. The Court held that the relevant market to be analyzed was the coal market in approximately seven states. The coal, subject to the requirements contract, was found to be approximately 0.77 percent of that market.

[182] *Id.* at 327–28.

[183] *Queen City Pizza, Inc. v. Domino's Pizza, Inc.*, 124 F.3d 430, 443-44 (3d Cir. 1997) (dismissing an exclusive dealing action for failure to define the relevant market).

[184] 466 U.S. 2 (1984).

[185] *Id.* at 44–45 (J. O'Connor, concurring).

[186] *Id.* at 45 (J. O'Connor, concurring).

[187] 749 F.2d 380 (7th Cir. 1984).

[188] *Id.* at 394 (citation omitted).

[189] 1995-1 Trade Cas. (CCH) ¶ 71,025 (C.D. Cal. 1995).

[190] *Id.* at 74,818.

[191] 875 F.2d 1369, 1373 (9th Cir. 1989).

[192] *Actom*, 1995-1 Trade Cas. (CCH) ¶ 71,025, at 74,818. *See also Kaplin v. Burroughs Corp.*, 611 F.2d 286, 291 (9th Cir. 1979) (proof that the defendant's activities had an impact upon competition in a relevant market is an absolutely essential element of a rule of reason case).

[193] *Actom*, 1995-1 Trade Cas. (CCH) ¶ 71,025, at 74,819.

[194] 823 F.2d 1215 (8th Cir. 1987)

[195] *Id.* at 1233.

[196] *Id.*

[197] *Id.* at 1234; *see also Queen City Pizza, Inc. v. Domino's Pizza, Inc.*, 124 F.3d 430 (3d Cir. 1997).

[198] *See, e.g., Packard Motor Car Co. v. Webster Motor Car Co.*, 243 F.2d 418 (D.C. Cir. 1957).

[199] 388 U.S. 365 (1967), *overruled by Continental T.V., Inc. v. GTE Sylvania, Inc.*, 433 U.S. 36 (1977).

[200] 433 U.S. 36 (1977).

[201] *Id.* at 58–59.

[202] *Id.*

[203] 384 U.S. 563 (1966).

[204] *Id.* at 570–71.

[205] *Id.*

[206] *United States v. Aluminum Co. Am.*, 148 F.2d 416, 424 (2d Cir. 1945) (stating 90 is enough, 60 or 64 percent may not be).

[207] *See, e.g., Am. Tobacco Co. v. United States*, 328 U.S. 781, 797 (1946).

[208] *Brooke Group, LTD. v. Brown & Williamson Tobacco Corp.*, 509 U.S. 209 (1993).

[209] 708 F.2d 1081 (7th Cir.), *cert. denied*, 464 U.S. 891 (1983).

[210] *Id.* at 1132–33.

[211] 948 F.2d 536 (9th Cir. 1991), *cert. denied*, 503 U.S. 977 (1992).

[212] *Id.* at 548.

[213] *See, e.g., Premier Elec. Constr. Co. v. Nat'l Elec. Contractors Ass'n, Inc.*, 814 F.2d 358 (7th Cir. 1987).

[214] *See, e.g., Brown Shoe Co. v. United States*, 370 U.S. 294 (1962).

[215] *See, e.g., United States v. Von's Grocery Co.*, 384 U.S. 270 (1966).

[216] 374 U.S. 321, 365.

ADDITIONAL READING

Antitrust Developments (Fifth), Section of Antitrust Law, ABA.

Stephen Ross, *Principles of Antitrust Law*, New York: Foundation Press (1993).

Lawrence Sullivan and Warren Grimes, *The Law of Antitrust: An Integrated Handbook*, New York: West Publishing (2000).

Herbert Hovenkamp, *Federal Antitrust Policy: The Law of Competition and Its Practice*, New York: West Publishing (1994).

9

The Intellectual Property–
Antitrust Interface

Chapter 8 described how patent law is closely related to antitrust law. Because intellectual property (IP) and the antitrust laws have similar theoretical foundations, the tools of analysis overlap and concrete cases often involve claims in both areas. At first blush, patent law and antitrust law appear to be direct opposites. Antitrust laws seek to reduce abuse of market power, while IP laws grant legal monopolies. One recent court has remarked: "[w]hile the antitrust laws proscribe unreasonable restraints of competition, the patent laws reward the inventor with a temporary monopoly that insulates him from competit[ion]. . . . [T]he patent and antitrust laws necessarily clash."[1] To the extent that the goals of antitrust laws are interpreted as "allocative" efficiency (i.e., the movement of resources to their highest valued use by competitive prices as described in Chapter 3), IP laws and antitrust laws are indeed antithetical. However, to the extent that the goals of antitrust laws are to increase "dynamic" or "innovation" efficiency, i.e., growth through innovation, the two bodies of law are quite complementary. The Federal Circuit has taken the latter position, noting that "the two bodies of law are actually complementary, as both are aimed at encouraging innovation, industry and competition."[2]

BACKGROUND

The patent–antitrust interface has evolved over time. The interrelationship between IP and antitrust emerged from the development of the doctrine of patent misuse. The term *patent misuse* refers to an affirmative defense to patent infringement based on a claim that the patent owner has attempted to extend the scope of the patent. Under the patent misuse doctrine, until the misuse has been "purged," a patent is unenforceable against an infringer.

Early attempts by defendants to use antitrust laws as a defense to a patent infringement claim were largely unsuccessful. Until World War II, the Supreme Court and many lower courts rejected claims by alleged infringers that the patent owner was illegally extending his monopoly by, for example, placing restrictions on unpatented products tying.

This is an aversion to a legal concept of patent misuse changed as patent owners began to assert contributory infringement claims. The misuse concept developed to limit contributory infringement claims. Contributory infringement (described in Chapter 6) occurs when an infringer supplies an unpatented input with the intent that it be used with an infringing product or process. By selling the unpatented product, the defendant is inducing others to infringe. The contributory infringement doctrine arose to protect patents from joint infringement where several parties sell aspects of a product, but each sale taken separately does not infringe. Taken together, however, the sum of the parts infringe once they are used in combination.[3] To combat such joint infringement, patent owners began to include licensing terms restricting the sale of necessary but unpatented products. In response, infringers contended that the restriction of the sale of unpatented products extended the patent grant beyond its legal monopoly.

The Supreme Court attempted to strike a balance between the extension of the patentor's rights and genuine protection from contributory infringement in *Morton Salt Co. v. G.S. Suppiger Co.*[4] Morton Salt had a patent on a salt tablet machine. Morton required that lessees of its patented machines purchase unpatented salt from Morton. The Supreme Court viewed the restraint on the salt as "misuse of the patent," which rendered the patent unenforceable until the practice was abandoned.[5] The Court reasoned that the patent on the machine should not be extended to cover salt.[6] *Morton Salt* and cases that followed balanced misuse and contributory negligence, but generally to the detriment of the contributory negligence claim. Congress then joined the debate and, in 1952, enacted section 271(c) of the Patent Act, which created a statutory cause of action for contributory infringement when nonstaple goods are involved. Nonstaple goods are products that have no use other than an infringing one.

The question naturally arose whether patent misuse and antitrust law are coextensive. In *Zenith Radio Corp. v. Hazeltine Research, Inc.*,[7] the Supreme Court suggested a possible relationship between patent misuse and an antitrust violation. The Court in *Zenith* held that, while the doctrines were related, misuse could be found from conduct that *does not* rise to the level of an antitrust violation and, conversely, that a finding of misuse does not mean that an antitrust violation has occurred.[8]

Although elegant in theory, the line between misuse and violations of the antitrust law was unclear and without a reasoned foundation. As a result, the misuse doctrine began to slowly merge with antitrust law. In *USM Corp. v. SPS Technologics, Inc.*,[9] for example, Judge Posner, writing for the Seventh Circuit, addressed the issue of whether discriminatory royalties constitute misuse. Judge Posner concluded that discriminatory royalties do not extend the patent monopoly (since the patent owner need not even license the patent); however, he explicitly recognized that traditional patent misuse situations might have to be judged by a different standard than the antitrust laws.[10] Posner resolved the problem by applying antitrust principles to *all* but the so-called convention applications of misuse including tying nonstaple goods and selling minimum prices.[11] The Federal Circuit in *Windsurfing International, Inc. v. AMF, Inc.*,[12] appeared to follow suit, albeit in dicta.

Congress again intervened on this issue in 1988 by amending section 271(d) of the Patent Act.[13] Congress added sections (4) and (5), which provided that misuse cannot be found from a refusal to license and that no misuse can result from tying, absent market power in the tying market.[14] The 1988 amendment brought the misuse and antitrust doctrines into even closer alignment. Hoerner offers a concise summary of what remains of the patent misuse doctrine. In summary, his main conclusions are:

- In all patent misuse cases, an anticompetitive effect must be proved.
- The anticompetitive effect is demonstrated by the antitrust rule of reason concept, which requires a market.
- If a restriction is reasonably within the patent grant, it is not misuse.[15]

In sum, the patent–antitrust interface arose out of the patent misuse doctrine, which was intended to curb abuses of contributory infringement. Over time, misuse and antitrust have become to a large extent coextensive.

OVERLAP OF PATENT AND ANTITRUST PRINCIPLES

In addition to the evolution of the patent misuse concept, antitrust jurisprudence has developed an independent analysis of the IP–antitrust interface. An excellent summary source for IP lawyers and experts confronting IP–antitrust interface issues is the *Antitrust Guidelines for the Licensing of Intellectual Property*, promulgated by the Federal Trade Commission (FTC) and the Department of Justice (DOJ) in 1995 (the IP Guidelines).[16] The IP Guidelines apply to patent, copyright, and trade secret law, but they expressly exclude trademark licenses.[17] The IP Guidelines diligently attempt to reconcile antitrust and IP principles. The IP Guidelines describe their originating principle as treating IP like any other form of tangible property for antitrust purposes. This is a bit of a misnomer because IP actually is *not* like other forms of property in one critical respect. Compare a patent owner with a homeowner. A homeowner's property right allows the homeowner to exclude others from enjoyment of the home. But a patent owner can exclude others not only from the home he or she builds, but also from reproducing the home. The IP Guidelines implicitly recognize the additional dimension of IP rights (but incompletely) by making clear that IP may or may not confer market power. Market power is not conferred if a sufficient number of substitutes exist for the patented product such that the patent alone cannot give the patent owner the ability to raise prices above competitive levels.[18]

The general theme of the IP Guidelines might best be described as follows. The antitrust laws aim to restrict the patent owner to his legal patent grant and no more. If through some additional transaction the patent owner seeks to extend the legal monopoly, the antitrust laws are triggered. In practice, however, application of this principle can be difficult. This chapter provides a sample of current examples. Nonetheless, the DOJ's guiding principles are a useful guide to IP lawyers and experts who must navigate through competitive issues in IP cases.

ANTITRUST LAW AND SPECIFIC PATENT PRACTICES

The IP Guidelines and antitrust case law have applied antitrust analysis to several specific patent practices. Lawyers and experts confronted with a specific IP–antitrust issue should consult the abundant literature and case law addressing the practice at issue in their case.

Intellectual Property Obtained by Fraudulent Means

A direct application of the principle that antitrust laws attempt to prevent the exercise of market power beyond the statutory grant is the antitrust treatment of fraudulently procured patent rights. A patent obtained by fraud involves the exercise of market power obtained by illegitimate means. For example, in *Walker Process Equipment, Inc. v. Food Machinery & Chemical Corp.*,[19] the Supreme Court found that enforcement of a patent obtained by fraud can form the basis for a cause of action under section 2 of the Sherman Act.[20] In *Walker*, the defendant alleged that the patent owner filed a false oath and did not disclose a statutory bar. The Court held that these allegations were enough to satisfy the conduct element of a section 2 claim.[21] The elements of a so-called *Walker* antitrust claim are:

> a. Fraud in the procurement of the patent. Fraud satisfies the "willful acquisition" element of a Section 2 claim. In the case of attempted monopolization, fraud is sufficient to satisfy "specific intent." Courts have emphasized that the deception must be deliberate; a mistake or so-called "technical fraud" is not enough.[22] A misrepresentation can consist of either a misstatement or a purposeful withholding of information, however, the misrepresentation must be material. This means, absent the misrepresentation, the patent would not have issued and, therefore, patent is invalid.[23] The standard for demonstrating fraud is high, specifically a plaintiff must demonstrate fraud by clear and convincing evidence.[24]
>
> b. As in all Section 2 claims, a plaintiff asserting a *Walker* claim must show market power in the relevant market.[25]
>
> c. Finally, the plaintiff must also show that he/she was injured as a proximate cause of some conduct based upon the invalid patent. As discussed below, *Walker* claims are often barred as an IP counterclaim because good faith litigation by a patent owner is immunized from antitrust liability under the *Noerr* doctrine.[26] A successful counterclaim would require both a showing of "sham" litigation as well as fraud on the patent office.[27]

Even if no fraud exists, a patent owner who attempts to injure competition by enforcing a patent that he or she knows is invalid (often called a *Handguards* claim), or in other words in "bad faith," may violate section 2 of the Sherman Act.[28] The elements of a section 2 claim based on bad-faith enforcement of a patent are:

1. The patent owner must have knowledge that would prevent him or her from having a good-faith belief that the patent was valid. Moreover, the patent must in fact be invalid. There will be an initial presumption that a patent infringement case was brought in good faith. This presumption must be rebutted by clear and convincing evidence.
2. A plaintiff must show every other element of a section 2 claim, for example, market power, standing, etc.

Again, because the conduct supporting the antitrust claim in a section 2 claim based on "bad-faith" enforcement of a claim is the filing of a lawsuit, the plaintiff in such a case must overcome the defendant's *Noerr* immunity under the First Amendment by showing that the lawsuit itself was a "sham."

As discussed previously, claims asserted under *Walker* and *Handguards* must overcome the *Noer–Pennington* doctrine. In *Professional Real Estate Investors,* the Supreme Court set forth the two elements to demonstrate that litigation is not protected under the First Amendment. First, a plaintiff must prove that the litigation was not "objectively reasonable," that "no reasonable litigant could realistically expect success in the merits."[29] Second, a plaintiff must also show that the litigation is "subjectively" baseless (i.e., it was brought for an improper purpose and was known to be baseless).[30] The Ninth Circuit has limited application of *Professional Real Estate* to situations in which there is *no* series of cases or a broader pattern of anticompetitive conduct.[31]

Refusal to License Intellectual Property

The antitrust laws generally do not require that a patent owner either use or license a patented technology. The right to refuse to license is also part of the patent grant. However, the right can have limits. This is one of the most controversial areas of antitrust law. For example, it is unclear whether a patent owner can use patent rights to exclude a competitor from an essential technology required to compete in an unpatented product. Antitrust laws prohibit the refusal of access to an "essential facility" required for competition.[32] Courts, however, have not applied this concept to a patent. Nonetheless, in *Image Technical Servs., Inc. v. Eastman Kodak Co.,*[33] the Ninth Circuit stated that the Sherman Act prohibits a monopolist from refusing to sell products covered by patents when it will "create or maintain a monopoly absent a legitimate business justification."[34] The Ninth Circuit forced Kodak to provide independent service organizations with numerous patented parts required to service Kodak photocopy equipment.[35] Similarly, a federal district court in Alabama followed the Ninth Circuit's reasoning. In *Intergraph Corp. v. Intel Corp.,*[36] however, the Federal Circuit has come down squarely against this approach.[37] As a result, the bounds of a patent owner's ability to reduce competition by refusal to license IP are not yet clear.

> ### Can a Patent Be Used to Protect a Monopolist's Aftermarket?
>
> Several courts have addressed this issue with conflicting answers. In *Data General Corp. v. Grumman Systems Support Corp.*, 36 F.3d 1147, 1187 (1st Cir. 1994), the First Circuit held that copyrighted software can be withheld from independent service providers only if valid business justifications exist. In contrast, the Ninth Circuit, in *Image Technical Services, Inc. v. Eastman Kodak Co.*, 125 F.3d 1195, 1226–27 (9th Cir. 1997), held that Kodak could not withhold parts from independent service organizations even though many of the parts were patented. The Federal Circuit, in *In re: Independent Service Organization Antitrust Litigation*, 203 F.3d 1322, 1328 (Fed. Cir. 2000), held that Xerox did not violate the antitrust law by refusing to sell necessary patented parts to independent service organizations.

Price and Quantity Limitations

The present case law and the IP Guidelines deviate in a few areas from the general principle that a patent owner can conduct business within the bounds of this statutory monopoly free of antitrust scrutiny. One such area involves resale price maintenance. Resale price maintenance means that the patent owner sets the prices by which his licensees sell the licensed product. Such a practice arguably does not exceed the patent grant, because the patent owner could set the price directly to the end user by eliminating the licensee. Early on, the Supreme Court analyzed price restrictions in this way. In *United States v. General Electric Co.*,[38] the Supreme Court concluded that a provision in a license setting the price at which a licensee can sell the patented product "is reasonably within the reward which the patentee by the grant of the patent is entitled to secure.[39] Because of the strong judicial history of application of *per se* illegality to vertical price-fixing, the *General Electric* rule has been challenged twice before the Supreme Court. In both cases, the Court upheld the rule.[40] Although not overruled, *General Electric* has been severely limited and is now honored in its breach. As a result, in practice, price restrictions in an IP license are likely to be violative of the antitrust law even though the *General Electric* rule is still good law and makes intuitive sense.[41]

Output restrictions in patent licenses have also been held to be unlawful because price and quantity are simultaneously determined.[42] This rule makes sense in light of the effective prohibition on vertical price-fixing.

Acquisition of Patents

The assignment, licensing, or purchase of patents may raise antitrust concerns under section 2 of the Sherman Act or section 7 of the Clayton Act if the patent owners' acquisition of additional patents creates market power. This is clearly the law today despite some early Supreme Court pronouncements to the contrary.[43] This current rule is a straightforward application of the principle discussed previously. If the combination of technologies can create market power *beyond the individual patent grants*, and is not offset by efficiencies resulting from the combination, it violates the antitrust laws. The IP Guidelines reaffirm this intuition by indicating that acquisition of IP will be analyzed under the merger guidelines used to analyze mergers of tangible assets. Thus, the typical step-by-step analysis of whether the acquisition substantially harms competition will be undertaken.

Patent Pools

The pooling of patents through cross-licensing or other agreements also may violate section 1 of the Sherman Act. A patent pool covers a variety of arrangements in which patent owners combine patents. Regardless of structure, the patent owners typically agree to jointly exercise rights under the pooled patents. The structure, however, may differ. Patent pools can be exclusive, restricting third-party licensing, or they can be open. The precise nature of the arrangement and the market must be analyzed to determine whether there is injury to competition beyond the patent grants. In some cases, pools are necessary to resolve conflicts involved in complex technologies requiring multiple licenses. A patent pool can be an effective way of resolving conflicting rights. This is the situation, for example, in the production of many high-tech products such as computer chips and other computer hardware. Patent pooling in such cases is scrutinized to determine whether the provisions are the least restrictive method of achieving efficiencies. In *Standard Oil Co. v. United States*,[44] the Supreme Court upheld a patent pool by several oil companies. The Court applied a rule of reason analysis and concluded that the competing companies held blocking patents and that without the pool each company would be precluded from practicing its own technology.[45] Issues of patent pooling often arise in a settlement context.

Conversely, patent pools can also have anticompetitive effects.[46] A patent pool can dampen incentives to invest in research and development and the discovery and use of design-around alternatives.[47] Patent pools can also simply constitute anticompetitive horizontal restraints. For example, two competitors with nonblocking patents could pool their rights to block competitors from entering the market using a combination of blocking patents. A patent pool could be used both to restrict licensing and reduce competition between the patent owners and to fix prices in downstream markets.[48]

To determine the type of patent pool at issue, courts and agencies define the relevant market that includes all the technologies that compete with the patent pool. Next, the share of that market occupied by the patent pool is assessed. Then the intent of the pool and the degree of access to the pool are considered.[49] Courts and agencies judge open pools to be far less dangerous than closed pools. An open pool eliminates the danger that the parties involved in the patent pool are creating a monopoly or facilitating a cartel. The full competitive analysis of a patent pool considers additional factors such as the relevant market, the parties' intent, the degree of access, and the pro- and anti-competitive effects.

In sum, patent pools can serve important procompetitive purposes. In some cases, however, a patent pool can cause anticompetitive harm. In these later cases, because patent pools often involve agreements between competitors, patent pools likely will violate section 1 of the Sherman Act.

Royalties

There is no antitrust violation when a very high royalty is charged. However, competitors who coordinate royalties could be engaged in illegal price-fixing.[50] Moreover, any attempt to extend the royalty beyond the patent term is illegal.[51] In addition, royalty discrimination among licensees that clearly harms competition could rise to the level of an antitrust case. In several early cases involving shrimp-cleaning machines, some courts condemned price discrimination using different royalties.[52] Subsequent commentary and decisions, however, have criticized these cases.[53] The basis of the criticism is that the patent grant allows the patent owner to refuse to license altogether. Licensing at a high price or at different prices is therefore a less restrictive practice than the legal monopoly allows. As a result, unless a strong showing of injury to competition can be made out, price discrimination among licenses is likely to be upheld.

Non-Price Restrictions

The Patent Statute allows exclusive licensing of a patent to the whole or any specified part of the United States. This implies that Congress has approved territorial restrictions in patent licensing. This is limited by the exhaustion principle, which provides that patent rights end at first sale. As limited by the exhaustion principle, territorial restrictions are legal.

Field of use restrictions refer to the restrictions of a licensee to use the invention in one or more fields. Field of use restrictions generally are legal because they merely divide the original market power granted by the patent. Numerous cases and agency opinions have approved field of use restrictions in patent licenses.[54] Only in the rare case in which a field of use restriction somehow extends the patent grant will it raise antitrust concerns.[55]

Grant-Back Clauses

A grant-back clause requires the licensee to grant back to the licensor patent rights that the licensee later develops. A grant-back clause may be exclusive or nonexclusive.

Grant-backs can dilute the incentive of the licensee to innovate. For example, if a grant-back is exclusive, which requires the licensee to assign all future patents to the licensor, it will reduce the incentive of the licensee to engage in research and development. Moreover, it potentially could give the licensor monopoly power. For this reason, grant-backs of long duration and wide scope may violate the antitrust laws. This is another case in which the general principle of limiting patent owners to the legal patent monopoly is violated. In a grant-back situation, the driving principle is preventing dilution of incentives to discover improvement patents, not limiting market power.[56] However, nonexclusive grant-backs cause little competitive concern. Even exclusive grant-back provisions that are limited in time or involve circumscribed areas of technology will have little anticompetitive impact.

Tying

Conditioning the sale of a patented product on the sale of an unrelated unpatented product violates the antitrust law. There is, however, a gray area. When several licenses are packaged together for a single royalty, there may be significant cost savings that can justify the practice. A tying arrangement involving a patent will violate the antitrust laws only when each of the four elements of a tying claim is satisfied: (1) market power in the tying market where no presumption of market power exists because of the patent, (2) two separate products, (3) a conditioned sale, and (4) substantial commerce in the tied market affected. The tying law applied to IP is the same as that described in the previous chapter. However, when the tying product is covered by a patent or copyright, courts often presume that the market power element was satisfied. This presumption was eliminated by section 271(d) of the Patent Act. As a result, a plaintiff alleging tying in the IP context must demonstrate all of the elements of tying under section 1 of the Sherman Act or section 3 of the Clayton Act.

Tying claims often arise when package licenses are offered. In a package license one patent is offered only on the condition that several others are accepted. The general rule is that voluntary packages are legal, whereas compulsory packages are illegal.[57] Mandatory packages can be procompetitive when blocking patents are involved. In these cases, courts have upheld the package.[58]

SUMMARY

Intellectual property cases often bleed over into antitrust concerns when the patent owner engages in some form of restrictive practice. This chapter presented a skeletal outline of the antitrust laws and attempted to familiarize IP experts and attorneys with some of the common overlap areas they may encounter.

ENDNOTES

[1] *SCM Corp. v. Xerox Corp.*, 645 F.2d 1195, 1203 (2d Cir. 1981), *cert. denied*, 455 U.S. 1016 (1982).

[2] *Atari Games Corp. v. Nintendo of America, Inc.*, 897 F.2d 1572, 1577 (Fed. Cir. 1990).

[3] *See, e.g., Heaton-Peninsular Button-Fastener Co. v. Eureka Specialty Co.*, 77 F. 288 (6th Cir. 1896), discussed in George Gordon and Robert Hoernes, *Overview and Historical Development of the Misuse Doctrine, in Intellectual Property Misuse: Licensing and Litigation*, 2000 A.B.A. Sec. Antitrust Law.

[4] 314 U.S. 488, 62 S. Ct. 402, 86 L. Ed. 363 (1942), *cert. denied*, 315 U.S. 826 (1942).

[5] *Id.* at 491–93, 62 S. Ct. at 404–06.

[6] *See id.* at 491–92, 62 S. Ct. at 404–05.

[7] 395 U.S. 100, 89 S. Ct. 1562, 23 L. Ed. 2d 129 (1969), *judgment rev'd by* 401 U.S. 321 (1971).

[8] *See id.* at 134–35, 89 S. Ct. at 1533.

[9] 694 F.2d 505 (7th Cir. 1982).

[10] *See id.* at 510–11.

[11] *See id.* at 511–12.

[12] 782 F.2d 995 (Fed. Cir. 1986).

[13] 35 U.S.C. § 271(d) (2001).

[14] *See id.* § 271(d)(4), (5) (2001). Amended by 1988, Pub. L. 100-418, Title IX, § 9003, 102 Stat. 1564 (Aug. 23, 1988).

[15] Robert J. Hoerner, *The Decline (and Fall?) of the Patent Misuse Doctrine in the Federal Circuit*, 69 Antitrust L. J. 669 (2002).

[16] *See* Appendix C.

[17] *See* Guidelines at 1.0, included in Appendix C.

[18] *See, e.g., Jefferson Parish*, 466 U.S. at 37 n. 7, 104 S. Ct. at 1571–72 n. 7 (O'Connor, J., concurring); *C.R. Bard, Inc. v. M3 Systems, Inc.*, 157 F.3d 1340, 1367 (Fed. Cir. 1998).

[19] 382 U.S. 172, 86 S. Ct. 347, 15 L. Ed. 2d 247 (1965).

[20] *See id.* at 178, 86 S. Ct. at 351.

[21] *See id.* at 177–78, 86 S. Ct. at 350–51; (*see also* Chapter 8).

[22] *See Cataphote Corp. v. De Soto Chemical Coatings, Inc.*, 450 F.2d 769, 772 (9th Cir. 1971), *cert. denied*, 408 U.S. 929 (1972) ("affirmative dishonesty" required).

[23] *Litton Indus. Prod., Inc. v. Solid State Sys. Corp.*, 755 F.2d 158, 166 (Fed. Cir. 1985).

[24] *Vetiker v. Jurid Werke GMH*, 671 F.2d 596, 600 (D.C. Cir. 1982) ("A finding that a patent was procured by fraud must be based on 'clear, unequivocal and convincing' evidence.").

[25] *See American Hoist & Derrick Co. v. Sowa & Sons, Inc.*, 725 F.2d 1350, 1366 (Fed. Cir.), *cert. denied*, 469 U.S. 831 (1984).

[26] *See, e.g., United Mine Workers of America v. Pennington*, 381 U.S. 657, 659–70, 85 S. Ct. 1585, 1593, 14 L. Ed. 2d 626 (1965).

[27] *See, e.g., Professional Real Estate Investors, Inc. v. Columbia Pictures Indus., Inc.*, 508 U.S. 49, 61–62, 113 S. Ct. 1920, 1928–30, 123 L. Ed. 2d 611 (1993). Recent Federal Circuit Law on Walker Process Claims can be gleaned from *C.R. Bard, Inc. v. M3 Systems, Inc.*, 157 F.3d 1340 (Fed. Cir. 1998).

[28] *See, e.g., Handguards, Inc. v. Ethicon, Inc.*, 743 F.2d 1282, 1289 (9th Cir. 1984).

[29] *See Professional Real Estate Investors*, 508 U.S. at 60, 113 S. Ct. at 1928.

[30] *See id.* at 61, 113 S. Ct. at 1928–29.

[31] *See, e.g., USS-POSCO Indus. v. Contra Costa County Bldg. & Const. Trades Council*, 31 F.3d 800, 810–11 (9th Cir. 1994).

[32] *See, e.g., Otter Tail Power Co. v. United States*, 410 U.S. 366, 93 S. Ct. 1022, 35 L. Ed. 2d 359 (1973), *United States v. Terminal R.R. Ass'n*, 224 U.S. 383, 32 S. Ct. 507, 56 L. Ed. 810 (1912).

[33] 125 F.3d 1195 (9th Cir. 1997).

[34] *Id.* at 1209.

[35] *See id.* at 1226–27.

[36] 3 F. Supp. 3d 1255 (M.D. Ala. 1998).

[37] See *In re Independent Service Organization Antitrust Litigation*, 203 F.3d 1322 (Fed. Cir. 2000).

[38] 272 U.S. 476, 47 S. Ct. 192, 71 L. Ed. 362 (1926).

[39] *Id.* at 490, 47 S. Ct. at 197.

[40] *United States v. Huck Mfg. Co.*, 382 U.S. 197, 86 S. Ct 385, 15 L. Ed. 2d 268 (1965); *United States v. Line Materials Co.*, 333 U.S. 287, 68 S. Ct. 550, 92 L. Ed. 701 (1948).

[41] *See* Guidelines § 5.2, included in Appendix C.

[42] *See United States v. E.I. DuPont de Nemours & Co.*, 118 F. Supp 41 (D. Del. 1953), *aff'd* 351 U.S. 377 (1956).

[43] *See, e.g., Automatic Radio Mfg. Co. v. Hazeltine Research, Inc.*, 339 U.S. 827, 834, 70 S. Ct. 894, 898, 94 L. Ed. 1312 (1950), *overruled in part by Lear, Inc. v. Adkins*, 395 U.S. 653, 89 S. Ct. 1902, 23 L. Ed 2d 610 (1969).

[44] 283 U.S. 163, 51 S. Ct. 421, 75 L.Ed. 926 (1931).

[45] *See id.* at 174–79, 51 S. Ct. at 425–28.

[46] *See, e.g.,* Business Review Letter from Department of Justice to Gerrard R. Beeney, Esq. (June 26, 1997) (approving pooling of MPEG-2 technologies).

[47] *See United States v. Manufacturers Aircraft Ass'n, Inc.*, 1976-1 Trade Cas. (CCH) ¶ 60,810 (S.D.N.Y. 1975).

[48] *See Standard Oil*, 283 U.S. at 174, S. Ct. at 425.

[49] *See, e.g., Cutter Laboratories, Inc. v. Lyophile-Cryochem Corp.*, 179 F.2d 80, 93–94 (9th Cir. 1949).

[50] *See In re Yarn Processing Patent Validity Litigation*, 541 F.2d 1127, 1136–37 (5th Cir. 1976), *cert. denied*, 433 U.S. 910 (1977).

[51] *See Brulotte v. Thys Co.*, 379 U.S. 29, 32–33, 85 S. Ct. 176, 179, 13 L.Ed. 2d 99 (1964).

[52] *See, e.g., Peelers Co. v. Wendt*, 260 F. Supp. 193 (W.D. Wash. 1966); *Laitran v. King Crab, Inc.*, 244 F. Supp. 9 (D. Ala.), *modified*, 245 F. Supp. 1019 (1965).

[53] *See, e.g., Official Airline Guides, Inc. v. FTC*, 630 F.2d 920 (2d Cir. 1980), *cert. denied*, 450 U.S. 917 (1981).

[54] *See e.g., United States v. Studiengesellschaft Kohl, m.b.H.*, 670 F.2d 1122 (D.C. Cir. 1981).

[55] *See, e.g., Ethyl Gasoline Corp. v. United States*, 309 U.S. 436, 60 S. Ct. 618, 84 L. Ed. 852 (1940).

[56] *See* Appendix C.

[57] *See, e.g., United States v. Paramount Pictures, Inc.*, 334 U.S. 131, 63 S. Ct. 915, 92 L. Ed. 1260 (1948).

[58] *See, e.g., International Mfg. Co., Inc. v. Landon, Inc.*, 336 F.2d 723 (9th Cir. 1964), *cert. denied, sub nom. Iacuzzi Bros. Inc. v. Landon, Inc.*, 379 U.S. 988 (1965).

ADDITIONAL READING

Peter Boyle, Penelope Lister, and J. Clayton Everett Jr., *Antitrust Law at the Federal Circuit: Red Light or Green Light at the IP-Antitrust Intersection*, 69 Antitrust Law Journal 739 (2002).

Herbert Horenkampe, Mark Janis, and Mark Lemley, *IP and Antitrust*, New York: Aspen Law and Business (2002).

William C. Holmes, *Intellectual Property and Antitrust Law*, New York: West Publishing (2001).

Robert J. Hoerner, *Innovation Markets: Old Wine in New Bottles*, 64 Antitrust Law Review 1 (1995).

American Bar Association Section of Antitrust Law, *Understanding and Refining the Role of Misuse in Intellectual Property Licensing and Litigation* (March 28, 1996).

Washington, DC, Spring Meeting 1997, *Intellectual Property Committee Meeting: The Aftermath of Professional Real Estate Investors: New Directions and New Alternatives for Bad Faith Litigation of Intellectual Property* (April 9, 1997).

American Bar Association Section of Antitrust Law, *Intellectual Property Committee Program: An Intensive Look at Technology and Innovation Markets* (April 5, 1995).

Richard J. Gilbert, *The 1995 Antitrust Guidelines for the Licensing of Intellectual Property: New Signposts for the Intersection of Intellectual Property and the Antitrust Laws* (April 6, 1995).

Norman E. Rosen, *Current Intellectual Property Antitrust Issues* (August 9, 1993).

Part Three

Copyright, Trademark, and Trade Secret Damages

10

Introduction to Copyright Law

The copyright laws can be understood as a system of legal protections designed to balance the incentives for authors with the need for public access to new works. Copyright protection is designed to reward authors for their original, creative expressions of ideas to encourage further such creation. However, the creation of endless original works would be meaningless to society at large if there were no means of guaranteeing some degree of access to those works. Copyright law is meant to encourage dissemination of expressive works by compensating authors for the costs of creation. Without copyrights, authors would be systematic losers, incurring all costs related to creation and dissemination, while enjoying a return on those investments only for the limited time that it took others to copy the work. Copycat publishers could expend only the price of replication and massively undercut the author's prices until the original work lost most of its fiscal worth. In contrast, if there were no limit on an author's rights, the public might be deprived of access to artistic works indefinitely. Copyright law attempts to balance the incentives for creation and publication with the access costs related to restricting the free use of an author's work.

A BRIEF HISTORY OF COPYRIGHT LAW

The law of copyright grew out of the conflict between authors and publishers in England during the seventeenth and eighteenth centuries. Before the development of the printing press, copying a work of literature was a time-intensive labor. However, as the printing industry became more established, duplicating literary works became a relatively inexpensive and simple matter.[1] Fearing the prevalence of copying, some authors opted to withhold new literature from publication, opting instead to disseminate privately their works in small, exclusive circles. The arrangement resulted in poor incentives for authors and inadequate dissemination of new works of art and science to the public. In the early eighteenth century, the British Parliament struck a balance between the rights of publishers and the rights of the public by recognizing copyright protection of a literary work for only a finite period. This legislation was known as the Statute of Anne.[2] Although the statute provided for an author's copyright, the benefit to authors was short-lived because most publishers required the author to assign their rights to the publisher as a condition of publication. Accordingly, the publishers generally had exclusive rights to publish, copy, and sell the work during the term of the copyright. However, once the copyright expired, a work entered the "public domain." This structure prevented an unlimited monopoly on the part of the booksellers and preserved the incentives for authors to publish their works.[3]

When the English common law was imported to the United States at the time of the American Revolution, English common law copyright notions were also adopted.[4] The U.S. Congress derives its power to regulate copyrights from the same section of the Constitution that authorizes patent statutes. This clause, often referred to as the "Patent and Copyright Clause," states that: "The Congress shall have Power . . . to promote the Progress of Science and useful Arts, by securing for limited Times to Authors and Inventors the exclusive Right to their respective Writings and Discoveries."[5] Accordingly, the stated purpose of U.S. copyright law is the promotion of science and the "useful arts."[6] The mechanism selected to accomplish this purpose was legislation that secured the exclusive rights of authors for a limited time.

Like the patent statute, the copyright statute has been revised several times; the major revisions were made in 1831, 1870, 1909, 1976, and 1989. These revisions were driven primarily by new forms of expression that gained economic importance over time. The current governing copyright statute is the Copyright Act of 1976, as amended.[7] Although works created before 1976 are governed by earlier statutes, this chapter focuses only on the 1976 statutory scheme, as modified by the Berne Convention in 1989.

STANDARDS FOR COPYRIGHT PROTECTION

Copyrightable expressions can occur in many mediums; although copyright commonly is associated with literary works, copyright protection can apply to everything from computer code to sculptures, from oil paintings to music. Under the Copyright Act, copyright protection is available for "original works of authorship fixed in any tangible medium of expression."[8] Moreover, copyright protection cannot apply to "any idea, procedure, process, system, method of operation, concept, principle or discovery."[9] Thus, there are three primary standards for copyright protection; copyright protection applies to works that are (1) original, (2) fixed, and (3) expressions of ideas rather than the ideas themselves.

Originality

Originality requires that the author created his or her work through independent intellectual or artistic effort. Although the requirement is not as rigorous as the "novelty" requirement in patent law, it does have some bite. The work must be independently created by the author; merely copying another source of information or expression is precluded.[10] Theoretically, two authors could compose identical sonnets, completely independent of each other, and neither sonnet would be "novel," yet both could be original and subject to copyright protection.[11]

Moreover, borrowing some elements of a copyrighted work may be permissible if the overall result is sufficiently original to qualify as a "derivative work."[12] Derivative works are discussed in detail in a subsequent section of this chapter; for purposes of understanding originality, it simply is noteworthy that not all aspects of a work must be original for the work to deserve copyright protection.

Eden Toys, Inc. v. Florelee Undergarment Co., Inc.[13]

Eden Toys involved the popular children's book character, Paddington Bear. Eden Toys had an exclusive license to market Paddington merchandise in North America. In order to capitalize on that license, Eden Toys had a series of drawings made based on the copyrighted Paddington Bear illustrations. Eden Toys then registered those drawings as derivative works, properly made with the permission of the Paddington copyright holder. Florelee subsequently began selling nightshirts featuring a print of Paddington Bear that was nearly identical to Eden Toys' copyrighted drawings. The district court found that Eden Toys' copyright was invalid because it was insufficiently original given the preexisting illustrations.

On appeal, the Second Circuit held that the lower court's standard for originality was too high. The proper standard for sufficient originality is "whether a work contains 'some substantial, not merely trivial, originality.'" In this case, the minor variations to the original sketch were substantial enough to satisfy the originality requirement. These changes included "the changed proportions of the hat, the elimination of individualized fingers and toes, and the overall smoothing of lines." These cumulative effect was a "different, cleaner 'look'" than the illustrations on which the drawings were based. Accordingly, the Eden Toys drawings were sufficiently original and worthy of copyright protection.

Beyond merely requiring that a work be original, the originality requirement implies the presence of "at least some minimal degree of creativity" in the authorship process.[14] Works of meager artistic merit or minimum creativity may not be proper subject matter for a copyright. Although "original" may appear to encompass "creative" (after all, the fact that a work is an original implies some degree of creativity), a work may be original and still lack the minimal creativity necessary for a copyright.[15] For example, the difference in appearance between a two-dimensional symbol and a three-dimensional version of that symbol may be insufficiently original to merit copyright protection, even as a derivative work.[16] Copyright protection can apply only to works that are more than a "trivial variation of previous work."[17]

Magic Marketing, Inc. v. Mailing Services of Pittsburgh, Inc.[18]

Magic Marketing was a designer of mass mailing advertising campaigns that contracted with Mailing Services to supply it with basic supplies and printing work. Magic Marketing alleged that Mailing Services infringed its copyrighted envelopes by selling copies of the envelopes to other companies. In response, Mailing Services argued that Magic Marketing's envelopes were insufficiently original to be copyrighted.

The envelopes in question were typical of the unsolicited "junk mail" that many individuals receive in their mail every day. The envelopes were conventional in size and contained the words "PRIORITY MESSAGE: CONTENTS REQUIRE IMMEDIATE ATTENTION" and other similar instructions on the front of the envelope. The court agreed with Mailing Services, calling the lack of originality "lethal" to the claim of copyright infringement. The terse phrases on the envelopes merely described the contents and/or instructed the recipient as to the desired use ("open immediately"). The phrases were "generic in nature and lack[ed] the minimal degree of creativity necessary for copyright protection."

Certain terms have been excluded from copyright protection because their very brevity implies a lack of creativity. This latter category includes words and "short phrases such as names, titles, and slogans."[19] Copyright protection does not extend to blank forms and common property such as calendars and area code maps.[20] Clichéd language and stereotypical expressions also are not copyrightable.[21] Even directions and instructions, which arguably are more than generic, are insufficiently creative to merit protection because they are dictated solely by functional considerations.[22]

Fixation

An author's expression must be "fixed in any tangible medium" to be protected under the Copyright Act.[23] Section 101 defines "fixed" as "when its embodiment in a copy or phonorecord, by or under the authority of the author, is sufficiently permanent or stable to permit it to be perceived, reproduced, or otherwise communicated for a period of more than transitory duration."[24] Under the law, the medium of fixation includes a wide range of media, including print materials, film, microfilm, CDs, DVDs, audiotapes, and so on. Moreover, the statute anticipates the continuing progression of technology, explicitly including within "copies" any work fixed "by any method now known or later developed."[25] Broadcasting, or other means of "simultaneous transmission" of the work, also qualifies as adequate fixation.[26]

However, improvised live performances or unrecorded speeches cannot be copyrighted. For example, in 1972, performance artist Vito Acconci developed a work that he called "Seedbed." Seedbed consisted of Acconci lying under a wooden ramp that rose up from the gallery floor and masturbating for eight hours a day over a two-week period. During Acconci's performance, he would voice his sexual fantasies about the audience into a microphone as the audience walked around the gallery and over Acconci.[27] Regardless of its questionable artistic merit, Acconci's work could not qualify for copyright protection because it was not "fixed" as required by the Copyright Act.

The requirement that fixation occur "by or under the authority of the author" can be explained by the advantage to the author of knowing where any and all copies of his or her work are (at least when they are first made). This knowledge offers the author some modicum of control over the uses and dissemination of his or her work. However appealing this rationale might be, it does not explain why the author whose work is recorded without permission has created less of a "fixed" work or is less deserving of copyright protection. Possibly the better explanation is that the requirement of authorized fixation places a premium on the value of preserving original works for future audiences by giving authors an incentive to ensure that their works are fixed.

Copyright Protection Does Not Extend to Ideas

Ideas are not a proper subject for copyright protection; only a particular *expression* of an idea can be protected.[28] For example, an article describing a new treatment for cancer could be copyrighted, but the underlying drug or process could not be copyrighted. Patents are the appropriate means for protecting new and nonobvious ideas.[29]

Homan v. Clinton[30]

Homan filed suit for copyright infringement against Bill Clinton (then president of the United States), Al Gore, and the Democratic Party, among others. Homan alleged that he authored a copyrighted article entitled "Bridge Village," which contained "the central theme and motto about BUILDING BRIDGES TO THE FUTURE." Homan claimed that Clinton's presidential campaign infringed on that article when it adopted the slogan "Building Bridges to the 21st Century" during the 1996 election. The court held that Homan's complaint should be dismissed as frivolous because it was merely an attempt to copyright an idea or general concept, which cannot be protected under copyright law. Moreover the court noted that there was no evidence that the Clinton campaign had expressed the idea in precisely the same way that Homan did in his copyrighted article. Accordingly, Homan could not establish copyright infringement.

Consistent with the copyright laws' resistance to extending protection to ideas, the existence of only a limited means of expression may preclude infringement because copyright protection effectively would allow a few parties to control the idea.[31] Moreover, a work that can be expressed in only one way cannot be given copyright protection because it would remove the underlying idea from the public domain.[32] This principle is known as the merger doctrine.[33]

The merger doctrine can be understood as simply an extension of the idea–expression dichotomy; the concern with copyrighting a work that reflects the only possible expression of an idea probably is that the work is likely to be more of a factual work than a creative expression. In other words, the merger doctrine and the idea–expression requirements may really be another way of getting at the requirement of minimal creativity. Moreover, with a generic work, the access costs of restricting public use (particularly of ideas) probably outweigh the costs to the author of creating the work; this imbalance weighs in favor of reducing the legal protections of the work and encouraging the author to seek protection under the patent laws. Finally, the merger doctrine operates in favor of certainty and judicial efficiency—if purely factual ideas could be copyrighted, it would be nearly impossible to know whether infringement had taken place or merely independent creation.

Feist Publications v. Rural Telephone Service Co.[34]

In *Feist*, the Supreme Court considered whether a telephone book could be protected by a copyright, despite the factual nature of the contents. Feist had copied thousands of listings from Rural's white pages, including four fictitious listings that Rural had included in order to detect copying. Rural filed suit against Feist alleging copyright infringement and arguing that the effort necessary to compile the entries in the book rendered the work more than purely factual.

The Court began with the established law that "facts" alone are not copyrightable, while certain compilations of facts are. The Court also rejected the "sweat of the brow" doctrine—a common law notion that a significant effort alone established copyrightable material. Instead, the Ccourt recognized that compilations may involve choices as to selection and arrangement that merit copyright protection. According to the Court, "the requisite level of creativity is extremely low, even a slight amount will suffice." A directory can be copyrighted even if it contains only facts if it features "an original selection or arrangement." However, the simple compilation of telephone numbers in alphabetical order by surname did not meet this low standard.

Post-*Feist*, some courts have struggled to determine exactly what kinds of works are uncopyrightable because they are primarily factual and lack sufficient creativity.[35] Other cases have established that compilations are copyrightable where the bundling of facts or distinct components creates a whole that has a greater value to consumers than simply the sum of the parts.[36]

In the context of computer software and technology, the idea–expression principle can become more muddled. The basic functions of a software program cannot be protected by copyright for the very reasons that the merger doctrine exists—software may be both expressive and functional—but technological progress would stall if programmers were able to co-opt large chunks of code that are the only means of achieving certain functionality.[37]

Lotus Development Corp. v. Borland International, Inc.[38]

Borland's Quattro Pro spreadsheet copied the Lotus 123 command hierarchy so that Quattro Pro could remain compatible with the Lotus product. The issue was whether user interface command hierarchy is entitled to copyright protection. The court found that the Lotus menu command hierarchy is a "method of operation," making it uncopyrightable under section 102(b). The menu commands are not merely expression, but the method by which the program is operated and controlled. Without access to these commands, macros designed for use on Lotus could not be transferred to Quattro Pro. This is distinct from the screen layout itself which contains expressive elements that could be accomplished by many means. Similarly, the underlying source code is expression because many different strings of code could be used to accomplish the same Lotus operations.

Under the court's analysis, copyright protection applied when the purpose for the menu commands was explanatory expressions, but such protection could not be extended to those commands with a purpose of enabling use.

SUBJECT MATTER OF COPYRIGHTS

Section 102(a) of the copyright statute specifies eight categories of works that can be protected by copyright: (1) literary works, (2) musical works, (3) dramatic works, (4) pantomimes and choreographic works, (5) pictorial, graphic, or sculptural works, (6) motion pictures and other audiovisual works, (7) sound recordings, and (8) architectural works.[39] Each of these categories is defined by statute, with the exception of musical works, dramatic works, and pantomimes and choreographic works.[40] When dealing with a case involving a statutorily defined category of work, the specific definition should be closely examined. Moreover, the requirements discussed in the preceding section, including the legal distinction between ideas and expression, must be applied to each category to determine whether a copyright would be valid. For example, utilitarian aspects of sculptured works or articles are not copyrightable.[41] Blueprints of buildings are copyrightable, but until 1990 the building itself was not copyrightable and could be copied.[42]

Section 103 extends copyright protection to compilations and derivative works, both of which were mentioned earlier.[43] Derivative works require a bit more explanation.

Derivative Works

Derivative works achieve copyright status by making some creative addition to underlying material (which material may or may not be copyrighted). A derivative work is defined as:

> a work based upon one or more preexisting works, such as a translation, musical arrangement, dramatization, fictionalization, motion picture version, sound recording, art reproduction, abridgment, condensation, or any other form in which a work may be recast, transformed or adapted.[44]

Derivative works consisting of "editorial revisions, annotations, elaborations or other modifications" (such as new editions of books) must, *as a whole*, represent an original work of authorship in order to be copyrighted as a derivative work.[45]

An overly broad interpretation of derivative works (or a restrictive approach to the creativity requirement) might swamp both the courts and the copyright system. Arguably, nearly every work is "derivative" in some sense of preexisting works. In fact, Henry Louis Mencken once said of Shakespeare, "After all, all he did was string together a lot of old, well-known quotations." For this reason, derivative works must be subject to some limitation. The Seventh Circuit has explicitly addressed this potential problem:

> Defined too broadly, "derivative work" would confer enormous power on the owners of copyrights in preexisting works. The Bernstein–Sondheim musical *West Side Story*, for example, is based loosely on Shakespeare's *Romeo and Juliet*, which in turn is based loosely on Ovid's *Pyramus and Thisbe*, so that if "derivative work" were defined broadly enough (and copyright were perpetual) *West Side Story* would infringe *Pyramus and Thisbe* unless authorized by Ovid's heirs. We can thus imagine the notion of pervasiveness being used to distinguish a work fairly described as derivative from works only loosely connected with some ancestral work claimed to be their original.[46]

In other words, a derivative work must be more than simply "loosely connected" to the preexisting work, but not so similar as to lack an insubstantial variation from the original. A derivative work must possess a degree of originality in order to prevent overlapping claims.[47] For example, merely employing a different medium from that used by the copyright holder does not constitute a novel addition to the underlying work.[48] Moreover, the courts are split regarding copyright treatment of allegedly derivative works that make actual physical use of a copyrighted work, such as pasting a copy of a painting onto a tile.[49]

A derivative work may be based on a copyrighted preexisting work or a work that resides in the public domain. Works in the public domain may be the basis for copyright protection in a derivative work so long as the latter has more than a trivial amount of variation from the original.[50] The degree of skill required to make the derivative work may also influence judicial treatment of the "variation" from the preexisting work.[51]

An author has the exclusive right to prepare derivative works of his or her copyrighted material unless that right has been transferred.[52] "A work which makes non-trivial contributions to an existing one may be copyrighted as a derivative work and yet, because it retains the 'same aesthetic appeal' as the original work, render the holder liable for infringement of the original copyright if the derivative work were to be published without permission from the owner of the original copyright."[53] Accordingly, unauthorized derivative works can be the subject of infringement actions.

Pickett v. Prince[54]

The singer Prince changed his name to an unpronounceable symbol, which was not only his trademark, but also a copyrighted work of visual art that Prince's licensees embodied in various forms, including jewelry, clothing, and musical instruments. Pickett designed a guitar in the shape of Prince's unpronounceable symbol. Shortly after Pickett showed his guitar to Prince, Prince began performing with a very similar guitar. Pickett brought suit for copyright infringement, claiming that he had created a derivative work worthy of copyright protection and that Prince's suspiciously similar guitar infringed that derivative work.

The Seventh Circuit held that Pickett had no right to make a derivative work without Prince's permission, as only the copyright owner and his licensees have that right. The court explained that the justification for concentrating the right to make derivative works in the copyright owner was avoiding the potential for infinite disputes between competing authors of extremely similar derivative works. For example, it would be nearly impossible to resolve whether Prince's guitar was a copy of Pickett's version or simply a derivative work of his own symbol. Accordingly, the law and public policy supported dismissal of Pickett's claim against Prince because Pickett had no rights in an unauthorized derivative work.

A classic example of a derivative work is the second edition of a treatise. The second edition is copyrightable even though it makes only minor changes and additions to the original edition. However, if someone were to publish a second edition of the treatise without the permission of the copyright owners, the second edition would infringe on the original copyrighted work.[55] Only the copyright owner (or his or her assignees) has the right to make derivative works.[56]

The justification for this allocation of rights is simple: if there were no limitation on who could create derivative works, there would be a proliferation of copyright disputes that could not be resolved by reference to standard copyright principles.[57] For example, two scholars could independently draft translations of a copyrighted foreign-language novel. The translations necessarily would be very similar (unless one author was considerably less skilled as a translator than his compatriot), and both would be sufficiently original. Without an initial allocation of authority to the author of the original work, the courts would have a difficult time resolving which derivative author should acquire the copyright.[58]

Regardless of the nature of the underlying work, the scope of a derivative work copyright is limited to the extent of the material contributed to the preexisting work; it does not confer a copyright on the underlying work.[59] Authors of derivative works are entitled to copyright protection only for any "novel additions" made by their work to the existing copyrighted work.[60]

Computer Programs

Original computer programs, regardless of the computer language used, are copyrightable. It is now settled law that at least the source code and object code of a computer program are copyrightable under section 102 as "literary works."[61] The code itself is equivalent to the "writing" element present in a literary work, while the typical storage media (software, diskettes, and computer chips) constitute tangible media that satisfy the fixation requirement.[62] However, the basic functions of a computer program cannot be protected by copyright because they constitute more "ideas" than "expressions."[63] Courts struggle with whether certain aspects of software are expressions, and thus subject to copyright protection, or ideas that should be covered by patent law, if at all. The following case defined "idea" in the context of a computer program and established a three-pronged test of possible infringement.

Computer Associates International v. Altai, Inc.[64]

In *Altai*, the owner of a copyrighted computer program brought suit for infringement of the nonliteral elements of its operating system's compatibility components. The program at issue concerned a scheduling function that specified when the computer should run various tasks. The plaintiff also marketed an adapter program which translates a given computer program's language into the computer's operating system. The court refers to this program as a "common system interface." Altai used some of the adapter source code to create its own interface system. Altai then modified its interface to excise the copied adapter source code. Nonetheless, Altai's program was similar to the copyrighted program.

The court explained that it wanted to strike a balance between "incentives to create" and "monopolistic stagnation." After finding that the literal elements of computer programs such as source and object code are copyrightable, the court framed the problem as whether "ideas" or "expression" were at issue. The court defined "ideas" as components that are (1) necessarily incidental to the function of the program;

Computer Associates International v. Altai, Inc. (continued)

(2) dictated by efficiency or externalities; (3) merged with the idea of the program; (4) stock components that are commonly used; or (5) taken from the public domain.

The court then adopted a three-step test, commonly referred to as "Abstraction-Filtration-Comparison" or "Successive Filtration" test. First, break down the alleged infringing program into its parts, starting with the lowest level of abstractions and moving toward the most general level. Next, through a process of "filtration," separate protectable expression from nonprotectable ideas. This step utilizes the definition of "ideas" outlined above. Finally, compare the remaining alleged infringing aspects with the copyrighted expression, and consider the relative importance of the copied portions to the overall program. The similarity between the elements remaining in the final comparison determines whether infringement exists. In this case, the similar, nonliteral aspects of the programs were essential ideas dictated by the nature of the programs and thus could not be protected by copyright.

As *Altai* illustrates, the merger doctrine is vital to assessing copyright protection for computer software.[65] Where there are only limited ways to effectively interface the user with a computer, such as a printer icon or the word "print" to indicate the print function, such interfaces are not likely to be copyrightable.[66]

Authors of copyrighted computer programs have an important restriction on their exclusive rights. Section 117 of the Copyright Act states that it is not infringement for the owner of a copy of a program to make a copy of that program for archival purposes (i.e., as backup) or if that copy is created as an essential step in the use of the program on a computer.[67] Moreover, it is not an infringement for the owner of a computer to make (or authorize making) a copy of the program "for purposes only of maintenance or repair of that machine."[68] These "repair copies" can be used only for those purposes and must be destroyed immediately after the maintenance or repair is completed.[69]

These exceptions are narrowly tailored in an attempt to prevent rampant software copying. For example, none of these exceptions authorizes the owner of a program to post or download a copy of that program to or from the Internet. Additionally, any archival copy prepared under section 117 can be transferred to another person only if the original copy is also transferred and the transfer is part of the sale of all rights in the program.[70] The limitations of section 117 represent the copyright law's continuing attempt to adjust to the particular facts of new and evolving mediums.

Characters

Characters, such as David Copperfield or Papa Smurf, are protected by the copyright laws if they are developed with sufficient specificity so as to constitute protectable expression.[71] Some courts adopt a more restrictive approach, requiring the character to "constitute [ ] the story being told" in order to be copyrightable.[72] The latter approach has been increasingly criticized, and limited in its application.[73] Under either test, stock characters are not likely to be copyrightable because they are merely vehicles of the story.[74] On the other hand, where the character *is* the story, copyright protection generally adheres.[75]

Several courts appear to limit the more stringent requirements for copyright protection to purely literary characters rather than those characters that are visually depicted in a movie or a comic book, as well as sketched out by the written word.[76] Where the author adds a visual, physical image to his concept of the character, the courts may be more likely to find that the character contains the requisite unique elements of expression.[77] For example, comic book characters have satisfied even the more stringent test for copyright protection of characters due, in part, to their identifying visual characteristics.[78]

Anderson v. Stallone[79]

Anderson v. Stallone involved a dispute regarding the authorship of the script for the movie *Rocky IV*. A screenwriter, Anderson, claimed that Sylvester Stallone and the MGM Studios had stolen his ideas from a sample screenplay and used that screenplay as the basis for Stallone's script. Stallone owned the copyright for the first three "Rocky" movies, but Anderson argued that the Rocky characters did not merit copyright protection as they were merely "stock characters." Accordingly, Anderson claimed that he had every right to use the Rocky characters—including the boxer Rocky Balboa, his loyal wife Adrienne, tough but loving coach Mick, and competitor-turned-coach Apollo Creed—in a sequel.

The court rejected this argument, describing the character of Rocky Balboa as "such a highly delineated character that his name is the title of all four of the Rocky movies." In fact, the court stated that "if any group of movie characters is protected by copyright, surely the Rocky characters are protected from bodily appropriation into a sequel." The court concluded that the Rocky characters meet either test for copyright protection, and thus Anderson's script was merely a derivative work. Since the script was an unauthorized derivative work, Anderson's claim to authorship of *Rocky IV* was dismissed.

It is interesting that the court treated the "Rocky" characters with such deference. Arguably, the characters were recognizable primarily because they are such simple, stock characters—the tough, blue-collar boxer from the streets, his loyal and constantly worried wife, and even the hard-nosed coach who ends up loving Rocky like a son— these characters are present in many boxing films. In fact, the traits cited by the court as evidence of Rocky's highly developed character (his speaking mannerisms and physical characteristics) are primarily associated with the actor who played the character, Sylvester Stallone, rather than evident from the printed page. The court's decision implicitly recognizes that an actor's characteristics may blur with the script to form a total character for copyright purposes. Other courts certainly have also recognized that "speech is only a small part of a dramatist's means of expression."[80] However, where the primary "expressive" features of a character are contributed by the well-known actor who portrays the character, the traditional justifications for awarding copyright protection to the author of the screenplay do not seem to apply.

Music

There are two statutory categories of music that may be subject to copyright protection: "musical works, including any accompanying words" and "sound recordings."[81] The former category covers the actual piece of sheet music or fixation of the lyrics rather than the sounds themselves. The latter category proffers protection to the audible works that result from the fixation of "a series of musical, spoken or other sounds, but not including the sounds accompanying a motion picture or other audiovisual work. . . ."[82] The same requirements of originality and fixation discussed previously apply to both categories of copyrightable music. The Copyright Act uses the term *phonorecord* in the context of fixation of music. Despite its apparently dated meaning, "phonorecord" is defined by the Act as any material object in which sounds are fixed "by any method now known or later developed, and from which the sounds can be perceived, reproduced, or otherwise communicated. . . ."[83] Accordingly, "phonorecords" can refer to CDs, audio-cassette tapes, or any future means of recording sounds.

Unlike other copyrightable works, musical works are subject to a compulsory licensing scheme.[84] Essentially, the author's "exclusive" rights to make and distribute phonorecords under sections 106(1) and 106(3) are subject to compulsory licensing of covers of nondramatic musical works. The compulsory licensing allows any artist to pay a fee and make his or her own recording of the musical work, but not to simply reproduce another's copyrighted sound recording.[85] The would-be cover artist must notify the copyright holder of intent to produce a licensed recording and pay a royalty rate established by federal arbitration panels.[86] The royalty rate is adjusted periodically; for example, in 1999, the royalty rate was 7.1 cents per recording or 1.35 cents per minute, whichever amount was larger.[87]

There are limits on the compulsory licensing scheme. The highly technical distinctions and requirements are beyond the scope of this discussion, but there are a few basic parameters. First, the primary purpose of the cover must be public distribution of the sound recording for private use.[88] Second, a compulsory licensee can rearrange the work to conform to individual style, but he or she cannot change the "basic melody or fundamental character of the work" and thus shall not be independently copyrightable as a derivative work.[89] Third, it is important to remember that audiovisual works are excluded from compulsory licensing and the written lyrics may be independently copyrighted as a literary work.[90]

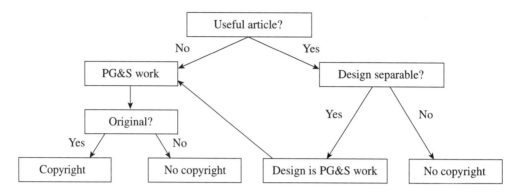

EXHIBIT 10-1   Design of a Useful Article

Pictorial, Graphic, and Sculptural Works

Under section 101, copyright protection may apply to "two-dimensional and three-dimensional works of fine, graphic and applied art. . . ."[91] Moreover, copyright protection can apply to the form of an object, but only to those aspects that are neither mechanical nor utilitarian (see Exhibit 10-1).[92] This means that it is possible to copyright the design of a useful article where that design incorporates "pictorial, graphic, or sculptural features that can be identified separately from, and are capable of existing independently of, the utilitarian aspects of the article."[93]

The practical analysis of copyright protection for pictorial, graphic, and sculptural works can be broken down as follows:

First, the practitioner must determine whether an article qualifies as "useful." "Useful articles" are defined as objects with an intrinsic utility beyond portraying the appearance of conveying information.[94] If the article is "useful," then the question becomes whether there are design aspects that can be separated from the utilitarian functions of the article. If not, then the article cannot be copyrighted. Finally, if the overall design or at least certain aspects of the design qualify as a pictorial, graphic, or sculptural work, then the standard originality analysis must be applied to determine whether copyright protection can apply.

For example, a lamp base shaped like a Balinese dancer holding the bulb functions both as a structural lighting support and as a sculptural work. The dancer is both physically and conceptually separate from the rest of the lamp. Accordingly, the dancer design aspects of the lamp probably could be copyrighted.[95] Of course, the copyright owner could not prevent others from using the idea of human figures supporting light, but he could preclude competitors from copying his particular copyrighted dancers.[96]

In contrast, where the allegedly artistic features are dictated by the function of the article, the features probably are inseparable from the utility and thus are not copyrightable. For example, a mannequin's torso is not copyrightable, despite the superficial similarity to sculptural works, because the artistic features are inseparable from the utility of facilitating clothing display.[97] Moreover, the wavy design of a bike rack has also been assessed merely as "form following function" and thus is not a proper sculptural work.[98]

Patents are also available to protect designs. In fact, there may be some overlap between the two legal regimes in this area. Design patents offer greater protection than copyrighted designs because they bar *any* copy of the design, even those that are independently created. However, it may be more difficult to satisfy the legal requirements for a patent than for a copyright. Furthermore, design patents have shorter duration than copyrights (see subsequent discussion of copyright duration). Accordingly, in some cases, copyright protection is more attractive and cost-effective than undergoing the technical proceedings associated with acquiring a design patent.

Finally, authors of pictorial, graphic, and sculptural works have unique rights under the Copyright Act that do not apply to the authors of other types of copyrighted works. In 1990, Congress added the Visual Artists Rights Act (VARA) to the Copyright Act to protect the moral rights of authors.[99] The VARA provides two distinct rights to the authors of visual art: the right of attribution and the right of integrity.[100] The right of attribution ensures that the author shall always have the right to take credit for authorship of the work and deny credit for work that either (a) the author did not create, or (b) has been so mutilated that attribution would be prejudicial to the author's honor or reputation.[101] The right of integrity allows the author to prevent any intentional "distortion, mutilation or other modification" of the visual work that would be prejudicial to the author's honor or reputation.[102] The right of integrity may also allow an author to prevent the destruction of a work of "recognized statute."[103]

This discussion simply outlines the VARA; any particular claims raised under this section of the Copyright Act should spur careful review of the statutory requirements. Moreover, VARA rights have some important limitations, a few of which bear mention here. First, the rights adhere only to the author, even if the author is no longer the owner of the copyright (due to transactions transferring the copyright to another party). Second, the rights of attribution and integrity are subject to the fair use defense (discussed later in this chapter).[104] Finally, if the work is a part of a building and the author consented to that incorporation, then the rights are curtailed.[105]

PUBLICATION

Under common law and early federal law, publication was a significant act triggering or ending the legal protection of copyrighted works. Initially, publication marked a transition from common law protection to the federal protection scheme. Prior to the 1976 Act, federal law did not protect unpublished works. Instead, such works were covered by common law copyright. In contrast, common law copyright protection expired upon publication. "Published" signifies the point at which copies of the work were first distributed to the public by sale or other transfer of ownership.[106]

Currently, the issue of publication is less significant because it affects only the duration of copyrights preceding 1978 and copyrights of works for hire. Fixation in a tangible medium is sufficient to invoke federal copyright protection for original works.

COPYRIGHT FORMALITIES

The primary formal requirements for copyright protection are notice and registration. Before 1976, works had to carry a notice of copyright to preserve statutory rights upon publication. This requirement was weakened by the 1976 Act, which allowed a correction to be made within five years of publication, and eliminated altogether in 1989. After 1989, the federal law ceased requiring formal notice.[107] The importance of notice today is that when the work does include a notice of copyright, an infringer cannot assert the defense of "innocent" infringement.[108]

Registration of the copyright (with the Copyright Office of the Library of Congress) also is optional under the current regime.[109] However, registration within five years of first publication gives rise to prima facie evidence that the copyright is valid; also, registration is a prerequisite for a copyright infringement suit under the act.[110] Although registration is not a precondition for copyright protection (i.e., the rights of the owner are still in effect), it is necessary to register before bringing an action under the act.[111] Moreover, since a work that falls within the subject matter of federal copyright cannot receive common law protection, the unregistered owner may be without *any* legal recourse until he or she registers the work.[112] Registration can occur after the infringement begins, but this type of tardy action by the copyright owner affects the damages available. As discussed in subsequent chapters, statutory damages and attorney fees are available only after registration occurs.[113]

OWNERSHIP

Ownership of a copyright is conceptually distinct from ownership of a copyrighted object.[114] Transferring ownership of a copyrighted object does not transfer the copyright embodied in that object.[115] For example, purchasing a Picasso painting does not transfer the copyright from Picasso (or his heirs) to the purchaser. Ownership of a copyright resides in the author of the work in question.[116] The analysis becomes more complicated if more than one individual contributed to the work.

Two or more authors are treated as co-owners of the copyright if their intention was that their contributions be "merged into inseparable or interdependent parts of a unitary whole."[117] The product of this type of collaboration is called a "joint work."[118] Where this standard of intentional intermingling is not met, the resulting work is deemed a "collective work."[119] Each author of a collective work is presumed to have acquired a copyright only as to his or her contribution and may copy and distribute copies only of that portion of the collective work.[120] In contrast, joint authors have rights to the entire work and may transfer the copyright only upon reaching an agreement among a majority of the authors.[121]

But what happens when a company hires a programmer to produce new software? The statute considers this situation under the "work for hire" doctrine.[122] Although the statute has a lengthy definition of a "work for hire," essentially when a work is prepared by a regular employee acting within the scope of employment, the work is considered a work for hire, and the copyright in that work belongs to the person for whom the work was prepared.[123] With independent contractors, the copyright belongs to the creator *unless* the work was created under a contract that explicitly indicates that the work being specially ordered or commissioned will be treated as a work for hire.[124] In other words, the parties may contract to treat any work as a work for hire, resulting in the employer or the commissioning party being considered the author of the work and the owner of the copyright.

Community for Creative Non-Violence v. Reid[125]

This case lays out the factors for determining copyright ownership of a work produced as part of a job. CCNV hired Reid to create a statue depicting the plight of the homeless. After completion of the statue, the parties filed competing copyright registrations. CCNV argued that the work was a work for hire under the statutory definition, while Reid claimed that he had been merely an independent contractor and thus retained the copyright as author.

To resolve this conflict, the court looked to whether the artist was an employee within common law definitions of the master–servant relationship. The court rejected CCNV's argument that the hiring party's right to control or actual control tests should determine whether the statue was a work for hire. In fact, the court concluded that Reid was not an employee as he was hired only for a single, well-defined task, worked in his own studio, provided his own materials for the statue, and was a skilled sculptor. These factors indicated that Reid was an independent contractor, and therefore owned the copyright.

COPYRIGHT HOLDER'S RIGHTS

Unlike the limited right of exclusion granted to a patentee, a copyright owner is entitled to several affirmative rights. The Copyright Act grants six categories of basic rights to the copyright holder[126]:

1. Only the copyright holder can grant permission to copy the work.
2. Only a copyright owner can create a derivative work.
3. Only a copyright owner can sell or distribute copies of the work.

4. Only the copyright owner can grant permission to publicly perform his or her work.
5. Only the copyright owner has the right to display the work in public.
6. Only the copyright owner can perform a sound recording by means of a digital audio transmission.

Copyrights have a limited duration, varying based on the type of work at issue. With standard, single-author works, copyright protection runs for the life of the author plus 70 years.[127] In the case of joint works, the copyright covers the life of the last surviving author plus 70 years.[128] If the work is anonymous, pseudonymous, or a "work for hire," the duration of protection runs for 120 years from the date of fixation or 95 years from the date of publication, whichever is shorter.[129] Finally, the public can presume that the author is dead 95 years after the year of the first publication of the work, or 120 years after the year of the work's creation (whichever expires first), unless the author indicates otherwise.[130] Reliance in good faith on the presumption of an author's death is a complete defense to infringement.[131]

INFRINGEMENT

Infringement is the unauthorized exercise of one of the copyright holder's exclusive rights.[132] Frequently, the issue is whether copying actually occurred. It is possible that the alleged infringer merely came up with the same work without copying; so-called "independent creation" or "accidental duplication" is a defense to copyright infringement.[133] Copying typically is proven either by showing direct copying (e.g., a photocopy of the copyrighted work) or by circumstantial evidence that (1) the defendant had *access* to the protected work, and (2) that the accused work is *substantially similar*.[134] Substantial similarity can be seen in overall structure, specific wording, or elements composing important fragments of the infringing work.[135] An inference of copying (generally established by probable access) in conjunction with substantial similarity can establish infringement.[136] Overall, the courts appear to be engaged in a constant balancing of the trade-off between striking similarity of the two works and likelihood of access; the finding of infringement must appear reasonable in light of all the evidence, but some courts place a greater emphasis on similarity, while others seem to want evidence of access before finding liability for infringement.

Ty, Inc. v. GMA Accessories[137]

Ty involved alleged infringement of the popular "Beanie Babies" toy animals, particularly a bean bag pig and cow. The court analyzed infringement by a two-step test—access and similarity. The court determined that access could be inferred "when two works are so similar to each other and not to anything in the public domain that it is likely that the creator of the second work copied the first, but the inference

Ty, Inc. v. GMA Accessories (continued)

can be rebutted by disproving access or otherwise showing independent creation. . . ." Accordingly, establishing lack of access could overcome substantial similarity. However, the court held that "similarity so close as to be highly unlikely to have been an accident of independent creation *is* evidence of access."

This analysis works best where the copyrighted work is both unusual and dissimilar to anything in the public domain. In those cases, extremely close similarity can establish infringement despite protestations of independent creation.

An alternative interpretation of the access requirement is the theory of subconscious copying, as first explained in the following case.

Bright Tunes Music Corp. v. Harrisongs Music, Ltd.[138]

Bright Tunes alleged that former Beatle George Harrison's song "My Sweet Lord" infringed the copyrighted song "He's So Fine," originally recorded by a group known as the Chiffons. Bright Tunes owned the copyright to "He's So Fine" and argued that the musical motifs and harmonies in the songs were virtually identical. Harrison conceded the possibility of access, given the popularity of "He's So Fine" and his own musical background, but contended that he came up with his song while "vamping" some guitar chords after a concert. Several witnesses observed Harrison while the idea was germinating and the basic structure of the song evolved.

The court concluded that Harrison had engaged in "subconscious copying." Specifically, the court found that while Harrison experimented with different musical combinations, he hit upon a combination that he felt would be appealing to an audience. The court decided that, at that moment, Harrison's "subconscious knew it already had worked in a song his conscious mind did not remember." Despite Harrison's lack of awareness that he was utilizing the theme to "He's So Fine," the two songs were virtually identical, other than the difference in lyrics.

Accordingly, the court found that Harrison infringed Bright Tunes's copyright "no less so even though subconsciously accomplished." Access plus substantial similarity were sufficient evidence of infringement, despite the conceded absence of intent.

Although not every court accepts the theory of subconscious copying, the theory does suggest that courts may be increasingly skeptical about the independent creation defense, particularly in a world where information travels so quickly and access can be easily attained. However, damages may be reduced in these cases to account for the possibility of independent creation and credit the defendant's lack of bad faith.

COPYRIGHT IN THE DIGITAL AGE

Copyright law is being brought into the digital age as individuals attempt to apply copyright protection where patents are unavailable, particularly to software code. The increasing presence of copyrights in the technology context has produced several interesting developments. First, the legal debate over computer code's dual role as command and expression continues, even as new code threatens to undermine technical copyright protections erected by copyright owners. As discussed earlier in this chapter, the idea–expression dichotomy breaks down to some extent when dealing with computer code, as it can be both command and expression. If the code itself is copyrighted, then the copyright owners exclusive right to copy and distribute that code may conflict with other copyright owners' attempts to protect their works from that code. *Universal City Studios v. Corley* exemplifies these dilemmas and the interaction between copyright law and First Amendment concerns.

Universal City Studios v. Corley[139]

Universal City Studios examines First Amendment law in the digital age, and its interaction with copyright protection. Corley appealed from an injunction barring him from posting a decryption program known as "DeCSS" on his web site or from knowingly linking his web site to any other web site on which DeCSS was posted. DeCSS was designed to circumvent CSS, the encryption technology that motion picture studios place on DVDs to prevent unauthorized viewing and copying. Corley argued that the decryption program was protected speech under the First Amendment and that those constitutional concerns trumped the copyright protections threatened by DeCSS.

The court determined that although "computer code is not likely to be the language in which a work of literature is written," computer code and programs are "speech" and therefore protected under the First Amendment. However, since computer code causes a computer to accomplish tasks with minimal human action, computer code should be treated as combining nonspeech and speech elements (sometimes referred to as functional and expressive elements) for purposes of free speech analysis. The court concluded that the prohibition on posting and linking to DeCSS was constitutional because it was targeted only at the nonspeech component of the code, as the injunction was concerned solely with DeCSS's capacity to instruct a computer, not the limited information it might convey to a human reader. Furthermore, the court maintained that encryption undertaken to protect economic interests, such as the interest of the moviemakers in protecting their copyrighted DVDs, was lawful and making deciphering software available for the primary purpose of circumventing encryption was *not* protected by the same law it sought to undermine.

Second, the congressional response to copyright problems in cyberspace resulted in the Digital Millenium Copyright Act (DMCA).[140] The DMCA has two purposes: (1) the prevention of copyright infringement by banning technologies that allow circumvention of copyright protections such as encryption; and (2) the creation of a "safe harbor" for on-line service providers (OSPs) for certain types of copyright infringement. The former provisions are highly technical and have been the subject of recent criminal prosecutions. The latter provides OSPs with immunity from monetary liability for direct, vicarious, and contributory copyright infringement so long as the OSP has complied with certain procedural requirements and had no *actual knowledge* of the infringement.[141] To take advantage of the safe harbor provisions, OSPs must develop and post a policy regarding the termination of accounts of repeat offenders and general compliance with copyright laws. Moreover, the OSPs must comply with specific notification requirements for disabling and restoring access to allegedly infringing material. If the OSP has complied with the statutory requirements, then it cannot be held liable in any monetary sense for unknowing storage of infringing materials, links or referrals to infringing materials, caching of infringing materials, or removing access to infringing materials.

Hendrickson v. eBay, Inc.[142]

In a matter of first impression in the federal courts, the Internet auction company eBay successfully used the safe harbor provisions of the DMCA as a defense to allegations of copyright infringement. Hendrickson sued eBay because the company refused to take down DVDs and videotapes of his 1972 documentary *Manson* that he alleged were pirated copies. Hendrickson refused to submit a sworn, written statement in compliance with eBay's "Verified Rights Owner Program" and the DMCA's requirement of *written* notification of the copyright infringement claim before filing suit. Absent such notification, the court held that although eBay may have facilitated the sale of infringing material, eBay did not have the right or ability to exert control over those sales. eBay is not required to proactively monitor the postings on its site or affirmatively search for infringing material. Accordingly, the court granted eBay's motion for summary judgment.

FAIR USE DEFENSE

There are several possible defenses to copyright infringement. Many of them have been discussed already, including: invalidity of the copyright (because it is asserted by a nonowner, applies to inappropriate subject matter, is insufficiently original, or not fixed); independent creation; and the section 117 defenses for uses of computer software. The remaining primary defense, "fair use," immunizes an alleged infringer from liability for the "fair use" of a copyrighted work.[143] Fair use of copyrighted works can be made for criticism, comment, news reporting, scholarship, or research. These "fair uses" share the trait of being productive uses, not simply duplicative of the original, copyrighted work. The following statutory factors determine whether use of a copyrighted work is "fair use" or infringement[144]:

1. The purpose and character of the use. In general, transformative uses of copyrighted works, such as a parody of a copyrighted song, are favored.[145] Moreover, uses that are of a commercial nature are less likely to be deemed a fair use than uses that are purely nonprofit or educational. For example, including a copyrighted poster in the background of a television sitcom is simply a decorative use, not "incidental" or transformative. Accordingly, it probably will not qualify for a fair use defense.[146]

2. The nature of the copyrighted work. This factor examines whether the work is derived more from facts or fantasy. The closer a work is to being factual, the more likely an unauthorized use of that work is to be found a fair use. The courts may also consider whether the work is rare or out of print. If a work is hard to find, the use may be justified on the basis of increasing the public access to an otherwise unattainable work.

3. The amount of the work used relative to the copyrighted work as a whole. Courts determine the amount and substantiality of the portion of the copyrighted work used, relative to the copyrighted work as a whole. Minimal uses are more likely fair uses than those uses that excerpt the heart of the work. Penalizing uses of a small amount of the work merely increases transaction costs and diminishes the probability that there will be any substantial effect on the market for the original work.[147]

4. The impact of the use on the market or value of the copyrighted work. Generally, this is the most important factor, as where the use will result in a loss of sales or licensing of the copyrighted material through substitution, the use is disfavored and the fair use defense probably will not prevail. Courts examine the market effects of the conduct taken to its logical extreme, for example, the crucial factor is the impact of allowing *everyone* to engage in the conduct, not simply ignoring an isolated act of infringement that, by itself, lacks significant market effects.[148]

Harper & Row v. Nation Enterprises[149]

The case involved publication by *Nation* magazine of a portion of the unpublished autobiography of Gerald Ford that was scheduled to appear in *Time* magazine. *Time* canceled its publication after the *Nation* article appeared and sued for copyright infringement. The issue was whether the *Nation* article constituted "fair use."

Harper & Row v. Nation Enterprises (continued)

The Court addressed the section 107 factors. It found that an author makes implied consent to "reasonable and customary" use of a released work. However, in this case the *Nation* article preempted the value of the *Time* article. The significant market effect of the use, as well as the fact that a substantial portion of the work was used, precluded the fair use defense. Moreover, it does not matter that the issue was newsworthy, although this can be a factor.

The Court described the unpublished status of the autobiography as a "key but not determinative factor." Fair use is less persuasive when the copyrighted work is unpublished because use by any other person irrevocably destroys the author's right of first publication. Focusing on the section 107 factors, the Court found that the *Nation* had infringed and did not come within the fair use doctrine.

The "market effect" factor has spawned a slightly different fair use defense, that of a "substantial noninfringing use."[150] In *Sony Corp. of America v. Universal City Studios*, the Supreme Court examined the use of VCRs to record copyrighted shows as a possible fair use of those copyrighted works. The Court determined that there was the possibility of a substantial noninfringing use, for example, that many television shows would have no objection to being recorded, particularly educational programs, sporting matches, religious services, and so on.[151] Moreover, the home recording was not a commercial use of the copyrighted shows, nor did it appear that there were any substantial market effects related to the practice. The Court did not appear concerned with whether the primary uses actually would be the substantial noninfringing uses that fell under the fair use defense, but focused on the fact that the technology was "merely capable" of those uses. Accordingly, the Court refused to hold Sony liable for marketing VCRs that enabled their users to infringe others' copyrights because the technology also allowed fair uses.

SUMMARY

Copyright law seeks to grant the copyright owner the right to restrict others from reproducing, distributing, publicly performing or displaying, transmitting, or creating derivative works of the owner's protected work. The exclusive rights serve as incentives and rewards for the creation of unique expressions in art, literature, and nearly any other medium, including computer code. Whatever the medium, works must be "original" and "fixed" in order to qualify for copyright protection, and the legal protection extends only to that particular expression, not to the underlying idea or concept itself. An alleged copyright infringer may raise several defenses, including independent creation, fair use, and the invalidity of the copyright itself.

ENDNOTES

[1]   *See* David L. Bainbridge, *Intellectual Property* 28, 3rd ed. Pitman Publishing (1996) (discussing ancient roots of copyright laws).

[2]   *See generally* Matthew D. Bunker, *Eroding Fair Use: The Use Doctrine After Campbell*, 7 Comm. L. Pol'y 1 (2002) (discussing history of copyright laws).

[3]   *See generally* Roberta Rosenthal Kwall, *Author-Stories: Narrative's Implications for Moral Rights and Copyright's Joint Authorship Doctrine*, 75 Cal. L. Rev. 1, 17–20 (2001) (discussing history of copyright laws).

[4]   *See id.* at 20–21.

[5]   U.S Const., art. I, § 8, cl. 8.

[6]   *Constant v. Advanced Micro-Devices, Inc.*, 848 F.2d 1560, 1564 n.4 (Fed. Cir. 1988). ("The power to grant patents to inventors is for the promotion of the useful arts, while the power to grant copyrights to authors is for the promotion of 'Science,' which had a much broader meaning in the 18th Century than it does today.")

[7]   17 U.S.C.A. §§ 101-1332 (1998 and Supp. 2000).

[8]   *Id.* §102.

[9]   *Id.* § 102(b).

[10] *Harper & Row Publishers, Inc. v. Nation Enterprises*, 471 U.S. 539, 547–49 (1985); 1 M. Nimmer and D. Nimmer, *Copyright* §§ 2.01[A], [B] (1990).

[11] *See Feist Publications, Inc. v. Rural Telephone Svc.*, 499 U.S. 340 (1991), citing *Sheldon v. Metro-Goldwyn Pictures Corp.*, 81 F.2d 49, 54 (2d Cir. 1936).

[12] 17 U.S.C. § 101; *United States v. Taxe*, 540 F.2d 961, 965 n.2 (9th Cir. 1976), *cert. denied*, 429 U.S. 1040 (1977).

[13] *Eden Toys, Inc. v. Florelee Undergarment Co.*, 697 F.2d 27 (2d Cir. 1982).

[14] *Feist Publications*, 499 U.S. 340; *see also Eden Toys*, 697 F.2d at 34.

[15] *See* 1 Nimmer on Copyright § 20.01[B] at 2-13 (illustrating class of cases where even independent efforts may be too trivial or insignificant to merit a copyright).

[16] *Pickett v. Prince*, 207 F.3d 402, 405 (7th Cir. 2000) (noting that plaintiff's guitar built in the shape of the symbol adopted by the artist formerly known as Prince probably lacked the requisite incremental originality, even if plaintiff had obtained Prince's permission to build the guitar (which he had not)); *see also* 1 Nimmer on Copyright § 2.15 (identifying line of cases holding that types of lettering and typefaces are not copyrightable).

[17] *Magic Marketing, Inc. v. Mailing Services of Pittsburgh, Inc.*, 634 F. Supp. 769 (W.D. Pa. 1986); *Woods v. Bourne Co.*, 60 F.3d 978, 990 (2d Cir. 1995) (quoting *L. Batlin & Son, Inc. v. Snyder*, 536 F.2d 486, 491 (2d Cir.) (en banc), *cert. denied*, 429 U.S. 857, 97 S. Ct. 156 (1976)).

[18] *Magic Marketing*, 634 F. Supp. 769.

[19] 37 C.F.R. § 202.1(a); *Shaw v. Lindheim*, 919 F.2d 1353, 1362 (9th Cir. 1990); *Sem-Torq, Inc. v. K Mart Corp*, 936 F.2d 851, 854–55 (6th Cir. 1991); *Arthur Retlaw & Assocs., Inc. v. Travenol Labs, Inc.*, 582 F. Supp. 1010, 1014 (N.D. Ill. 1984).

[20] *See, e.g., Harper House, Inc. v. Thomas Nelson, Inc.*, 889 F.2d 197 (9th Cir. 1989).

[21] *Magic Marketing*, 634 F. Supp. at 772; *Merritt Forbes & Co. v. Newman Investment Securities, Inc.*, 604 F. Supp. 943, 951 (S.D.N.Y. 1985); *Perma Greetings v. Russ Berrie & Co.*, 598 F. Supp. 445, 448 (E.D. Mo. 1984).

[22] *See Kitchens of Sara Lee, Inc. v. Nifty Foods, Corp.*, 266 F.2d 541 (2d Cir. 1959) (declining to apply copyright protection to serving directions on a frozen dessert package); 1 Nimmer on Copyright § 2.01[B] at 2-13–14. This logic parallels the treatment of pictorial, graphic, and sculptural works discussed later in this chapter.

[23] 17 U.S.C. § 102(a). If a work is not fixed, it falls within common law copyright protection, or any applicable state law. *See* 17 U.S.C. § 301(b)(1) (regarding scope of federal preemption of other copyright laws).

[24] 17 U.S.C. § 101.

[25] *Id.*

[26] *Id.* ("A work consisting of sounds, images, or both, that are being transmitted, is 'fixed' for purposes of this title if a fixation of the work is being made simultaneously with its transmssion.")

[27] *See* R. R. Kwall, *Copyright and the Moral Right: Is an American Marriage Possible?* 38 Vand. L. Rev. 1, 75 (1985).

[28] 17 U.S.C. § 102(b); *see, e.g. Mazer v. Stein,* 347 U.S. 201, 217 (1954); *Mihalek Corp. v. Michigan,* 814 F.2d 290, 294 (6th Cir. 1987); *Arica Institute, Inc. v. Palmer*, 761 F. Supp. 1056, 1062 (S.D.N.Y. 1991); *Wickham v. Knoxville Int'l Energy Exposition, Inc.*, 739 F.2d 1094, 1097 (6th Cir. 1984).

[29] *See* Chapter 6; *see also Baker v. Selden*, 101 U.S. 99 (1879) (finding that idea for bookkeeping system was more properly within the purview of patent law than copyright).

[30] *Homan v. Clinton*, No. 98-3844, 1990 U.S. App. LEXIS 13401 (6th Cir. June 14, 1999).

[31] *See, e.g., Morrissey v. Procter & Gamble Co.*, 379 F.2d 675 (1st Cir. 1967) (finding that sweepstakes rules were not copyrightable).

[32] *See, e.g., Kregos v. Assoc. Press*, 937 F.2d 700 (2d Cir. 1991); *Consumers Union v. Hobart Mfg. Co.*, 199 F. Supp. 860 (S.D.N.Y. 1961) (quotations from *Consumer Reports* were "bald statement[s] of fact" that could not have been stated in a different fashion); *see also* 37 C.F.R. § 202.1(d) (copyright protection does not extent do common property such as standard calendars and area code maps).

[33] Some courts treat the merger doctrine as a principle best evaluated in the context of determining whether infringement has occurred, rather than as an issue of copyright validity. *See Kregos v. Assoc. Press*, 937 F.2d 700 (2d Cir. 1991); 3 Nimmer on Copyright § 13.03[B][3] at 13–58 (1990).

[34] *Feist Publications,* 499 U.S. 340.

[35] *See, e.g., Key Publications, Inc. v. Chinatown Today Publishing Enters., Inc.*, 945 F.2d 509 (2d Cir. 1991) (finding selective yellow pages to merit copyright protection); *BellSouth Advertising & Publishing Corp. v. Donnelly Information Publishing, Inc.*, 999 F.2d 1436 (11th Cir. 1993) (finding yellow pages were not copyrightable); *Transwestern Pub. v. Multimedia Marketing Assoc.*, 133 F.3d 773 (10th Cir. 1998) (declining to protect yellow pages under copyright law).

[36] See *Roth Greeting Cards v. United Card Co.*, 429 F.2d 1106, 1109 (9th Cir. 1970); *Sem-Torq, Inc. v. K Mart Corp*, 936 F.2d 851, 854–55 (6th Cir. 1991) (bundling several un-original signs together for sale did not create a copyrightable work where the bundling did not add anything of value to the work of authorship); *Apple Computer v. Microsoft*, 779 F. Supp. 133, 136 (N.D. Cal. 1991) (upholding copyright for original combination of independently unprotectable elements); *Barris Fraser v. Goodson-Todman*, 5 U.S.P.Q. 2d 1887, 1891 (S.D.N.Y. 1988); *Baldine v. Furniture Comfort Corporation*, 956 F. Supp. 580, 587 (M.D.N.C. 1996).

[37] *See, e.g., Gates Rubber Co. v. Bando Chem. Indus., Ltd.*, 9 F.3d 823 (10th Cir. 1993).

[38] *Lotus Dev. Corp. v. Borland Int'l, Inc.*, 49 F.3d 807 (1st Cir. 1995), *aff'd* 516 U.S. 233 (1996).

[39] 17 U.S.C. § 102(a).

[40] *See id* § 101.

[41] *See e.g. Mazer v. Stein*, 347 U.S. 201, 217 (1954).

[42] *See, e.g., Imperial Homes Corp. v. Lamont*, 458 F.2d 895, 899 (5th Cir. 1972); 17 U.S.C. §§ 101,102; *see also* Architectural Works Copyright Protection Act (AWCPA), Pub. L. No. 101-650, tit. 7, § 706(1), (2), 104 Stat. 5133, 5134 (1990).

[43] 17 U.S.C. § 103(a), (b).

[44] *Id.* § 101.

[45] *Id.*

[46] *Pickett v. Prince*, 207 F.3d 402, 407 (7th Cir. 2000).

[47] *Gracen v. The Bradford Exchange*, 698 F.2d 300, 304 (7th Cir. 1982).

[48] *See Pickett*, 207 F.3d at 405 (noting that copyright was not limited to two-dimensional version of defendant's unpronounceable symbol); *see also Eden Toys*, 697 F.2d at 35 (finding the fact that one drawing was printed on gift wrap while the other was printed on clothing was irrelevant); *Entertainment Research Group, Inc. v. Genesis Creative Group, Inc.*, 122 F.3d 1211 (9th Cir. 1997), *cert. denied*, 118 S. Ct. 102 (1998) (finding that inflatable versions of copyrighted characters for use in a parade lacked sufficient originality to be derivative works); *L. Batlin & Son, Inc.*, 536 F.2d 486 (2d Cir. 1976); *Davis v. E.I. DuPont deNemours & Co.*, 240 F. Supp. 612 (S.D.N.Y. 1965).

[49] *See Mirage Editions, Inc. v. Albuquerque A.R.T. Co.*, 856 F.2d 1341 (9th Cir. 1988) (finding that mounting pictures on tiles constituted a derivative work); *Lee v. A.R.T. Co.*, 125 F.3d 580 (7th Cir. 1997) (criticizing *Mirage* and holding that pictures mounted on tiles could not be a derivative work because they did not differ from simply changing the means of display, as with a frame).

[50] *Alfred Bell & Co. v. Catalda Fine Arts, Inc.*, 191 F.2d 99 (2d Cir. 1951) (recognizing copyright for mezzotint engravings of public domain paintings).

[51] *Id.; see also L. Batlin & Son, Inc. v. Snyder*, 536 F.2d 486 (2d Cir. 1976) (denying copyright protection as a derivative work for plastic version of metal "Uncle Sam" piggy bank).

[52] 17 U.S.C. § 106(2).

[53] *Eden Toys*, 697 F.2d at 34.

[54] *Pickett*, 207 F.3d 402.

[55] *Eden Toys*, 697 F.2d at 34.

[56] *Pickett*, 207 F.3d 402.

[57] *Pickett*, 207 F.3d at 406-7.

[58] *Id.*

[59] 17 U.S.C. §103(b).

[60] *Eden Toys*, 697 F.2d at 33; *G. Ricordi & Co. v. Paramount Pictures*, 189 F.2d 469, 471 (2d Cir. 1951).

[61] *See Whelan Assoc. v. Jaslow Dental Lab., Inc.*, 797 F.2d 122, 1233 (3d Cir. 1986); *Apple Computer, Inc. v. Franklin Computer Corp.*, 714 F.2d 1240, 1249 (3d Cir. 1983).

[62] *Id.*

[63] *Gates Rubber Co. v. Bando Chem. Indus., Ltd.*, 9 F.3d 693, 705 (2d Cir. 1993).

[64] *Computer Associates International v. Altai, Inc.*, 982 F.2d 693 (2d Cir. 1992).

[65] *See also Apple Computer, Inc. v. Microsoft Corp.*, 35 F.3d 1435 (9th Cir. 1994); *ILOG, Inc. v. Bell Logic, LLC.*, 181 F. Supp.2d 3 (D. Mass. 2002).

[66] *Computer Associates*, 982 F.2d at 706–10; *see also Lotus Dev. Corp. v. Borland Int'l, Inc.*, 49 F.3d 807 (1st Cir. 1995), *aff'd* 116 S. Ct. 804 (1996) and the discussion of *Lotus supra*.

[67] 17 U.S.C. §117 (a).

[68] *Id.* §117 (c).

[69] *Id.* §117 (c)(1).

[70] *Id.* §117 (b).

[71] *Nichols v. Universal Pictures*, 45 F.2d 119, 121 (2d Cir. 1930), *cert. denied*, 282 U.S. 902 (1931).

[72] *Warner Bros. v. Columbia Broadcasting System, Inc.*, 216 F.2d 945, 950 (9th Cir. 1954).

[73] *See, e.g., Metro-Goldwyn-Mayer, Inc. v. American Honda Motor Co.*, 900 F. Supp. 1287 (C.D. Cal. 1995); *Anderson v. Stallone*, 11 U.S.P.Q. 2d (BNA) 1161 (C.D. Cal. 1989); *Walt Disney Prods. v. Air Pirates*, 581 F.2d 751, 755 (9th Cir. 1978).

[74] *See, e.g., Nichols*, 45 F.2d 119; *cf. Sheldon v. Metro-Goldwyn Pictures Corp.*, 81 F.2d 49 (2d Cir. 1936).

[75] *Anderson v. Stallone*, 11 U.S.P.Q.2d (BNA) 1161 (C.D. Cal. 1989).

[76] *See, e.g., Anderson*, 11 U.S.P.Q.2d (BNA) 1161; *Walt Disney Prods*, 345 F. Supp. 108.

[77] *Walt Disney Prods*, 345 F. Supp. 108; *see also Anderson,* 11 U.S.P.Q.2d (BNA) 1161 (noting that a less stringent test may apply to the copyright protection of graphic characters).

[78] *Walt Disney Prods*, 345 F. Supp. 108 (finding that lewd comic book portrayal of the Mickey Mouse character infringed Walt Disney's copyright because it mimicked Mickey Mouse's physical characteristics too closely).

[79] *Anderson*, 11 U.S.P.Q.2d (BNA) 1161.

[80] *Sheldon*, 81 F.2d 49.

[81] *See* 17 U.S.C. § 102(2), (7).

[82] *Id.* § 101.

[83] *Id.*

[84] *Id.* § 115.

[85] *Id.* § 114 (copyright owner of sound recording only has exclusive rights to the actual sounds of the original recording, not to independent fixation of other sounds, even if they sound identical).

[86] *Id.* § 115(b), (c).

[87] *Id.* § 115(c).

[88] *Id.* § 115(a)(1).

[89] *Id.* § 115(a)(2).

[90] *Id.* §115; *ABKCO Music, Inc. v. Stellar Records, Inc.*, 96 F.3d 60 (2d Cir. 1996) (finding that karaoke machines infringed music copyrights because they were audiovisual works and incorporated written copy of lyrics).

[91] 17 U.S.C. § 101.

[92] *Id.*

[93] *Id.*; *Mazer v. Stein*, 347 U.S. 201 (1954).

[94] 17 U.S.C. § 101.

[95] *See Mazer*, 347 U.S. 201 (affirming the validity of copyrights on similar lamps); *see also Kieselstein-Cord* (finding designer belt buckle copyrightable because the buckle had conceptually separate sculptural elements that made it more akin to jewelry worn on the waist than simple pants support).

[96] *Mazer*, 347 U.S. 201.

[97] *See Carol Barnhart, Inc. v. Economy Cover Corp.*, 594 F.Supp. 364 (E.D.N.Y. 1984).

[98] *Brandir Int'l, Inc. v. Cascade Pac. Lumber Co.*, 834 F.2d 1142 (2d Cir. 1987).

[99] *See* 17 U.S.C. § 106A.

[100] *Id.* § 106A(a); *see Quality King Distrib., Inc. v. L'Anza Research Int'l, Inc.*, 523 U.S. 135, 149 n.21 (1998).

[101] 17 U.S.C. § 106A(a).

[102] *Id.*

[103] *Id.*; *but see Martin v. Indianapolis*, 192 F.3d 608 (7th Cir. 1999) (rejecting artist's claim under VARA because the destruction of his sculpture was due to bureaucratic failure rather than willful destruction).

[104] *Id.* § 107.

[105] *Id.* § 113(d).

[106] *Id.* § 101.

[107] *See Id.* §§ 405.

[108] *Id.* § 401(d).

[109] *See Id.* §§ 408, 409, 410.

[110] *Id.* § 411; *See, e.g., Store Decor Div. of Jas Int'l, Inc. v. Stylex Worldwide Indus., Ltd.*, 767 F. Supp. 181, 184 (N.D. Ill. 1991); *Tree Pub. Co. v. Warner Bros. Records Div. of Time-Warner, Inc.*, 785 F. Supp. 1272, 1274 (M.D. Tenn. 1991); *Pristine Indus., Inc. v. Hallmark Cards, Inc.*, 753 F. Supp 14, 148 (S.D.N.Y. 1990).

[111] *See Pickett*, 207 F.3d at 403; *See* 17 U.S.C. § 408(a).

[112] *See Om v. Weathers*, No. 91 C 4005, 1992 U.S. Dist. LEXIS 8915 (N.D. Ill. June 19, 1992). Federal preemption doctrine is beyond the scope of this chapter; however, it is important to realize that common law or state protection should not be presumed available as a backup for failure to comply with federal registration requirements.

[113] *See also* Chapter 14 for a more complete discussion of the impact of nonregistration on available remedies.

[114] 17 U.S.C. § 202.

[115] *Id.*

[116] *Id.* § 201(a).

[117] *Id.* § 101.

[118] *Id.*

[119] *Id.* §§ 101, 201(c).

[120] *Id.* § 201(c).

[121] *Id.* §§ 201(a), 203(a)(1).

[122] *Id.* §§ 101, 201(b).

[123] *Id.* § 201(b).

[124] *Id.* § 101.

[125] *Community for Creative Non-Violence v. Reid*, 490 U.S. 730 (1989).

[126] 17 U.S.C. § 106. These rights are subject to the compulsory licensing for audio recordings set forth in section 115.

[127] *Id.* § 302(a). These durations apply only to works fixed after January 1, 1978. Older works have different calculations of their copyright duration that are increasingly less relevant to most litigation taking place today.

[128] *Id.* § 302(b).

[129] *Id.* § 302(c).

[130] *Id.* § 302(e).

[131] *Id.*

[132] *Id.* § 501(a).

[133] Note that the act does not define "infringement" *per se*, but merely states that anyone who violates the exclusive rights is an infringer. *See* 17 U.S.C. §§ 106, 501.

[134] *See, e.g., Columbia Pictures Industries, Inc. v. Redd Horne, Inc.*, 749 F.2d 154 (3d Cir. 1984); *Gaste v. Kaiserman*, 863 F.2d 1061 (2d Cir. 1988); *Selle v. Gibb*, 741 F.2d 896 (7th Cir. 1984).

[135] *Id.*

[136] *Id.*

[137] *Ty, Inc. v. GMA Accessories*, 132 F.3d 1167 (7th Cir. 1997).

[138] *Bright Tunes Music Corp. v. Harrisongs Music, Ltd.*, 420 F. Supp. 177 (S.D.N.Y. 1976).

[139] *Universal City Studios, Inc. v. Corley*, 2001 WL 1505495 (2d Cir. 2001).

[140] 17 U.S.C. § 512.

[141] *Id.* §512.

[142] *Hendrickson v. eBay, Inc.*, 2001 U.S. Dist. LEXIS 14420 (C.D. Cal. Sept. 4, 2001).

[143] 17 U.S.C. § 107.

[144] *See id.*

[145] *Campbell v. Acuff-Rose Music, Inc.*, 114 S. Ct. 1164 (1994).

[146] *Ringgold v. Black Entertainment Television, Inc.*, 126 F.3d 70 (2d Cir. 1997).

[147] *Harper & Row v. Nation Enterprises*, 471 U.S. 539 (1985).

[148] *Princeton University Press v. Michigan Document Svcs., Inc.*, 99 F.3d 1381 (6th Cir. 1996) (en banc), *cert. denied*, 117 S.Ct. 1336 (1997).

[149] *Harper & Row*, 471 U.S. 539.

[150] *Sony Corp. v. Universal City Studios*, 464 U.S. 417 (1984).

[151] The Court's analysis on this point may have hinged more on the lack of harm to those copyright owners from the recording than on a theory of implied consent.

ADDITIONAL READING

Michael G. Anderson and Paul F. Brown, *The Economics Behind Copyright Fair Use: A Principled and Predictable Body of Law*, 24 Loyola University of Chicago Law Journal 143 (1993).

Richard Colby, *The First Sale Doctrine: The Defense That Never Was?* 32 J. Copyright Society 77 (1984).

Copyright Symposium Parts I and II: Copyright Protection for Computer Databases, CD-ROMs and Factual Compilations, 17 Univ. Dayton Law Review 323–629, 731–1018 (1992).

2 *Goldstein on Copyrights*, 2nd ed. (1998).

Pamela Hobbs, *Methods of Determining Substantial Similarity in Copyright Cases Involving Computer Programs*, 67 Univ. Detroit Law Review 393 (1990).

Intellectual Property and the Construction of Authorship, 10 Cardozo Arts & Entertainment Law Journal 277–720 (1992).

Bernard Korman & I. Fred Koenigsberg, *Performing Rights in Music and Performing Rights Societies*, 33 Journal of the Copyright Soc'y of the USA 332 (1987).

Leslie A. Kurtz, *Speaking to the Ghost: Idea and Expression in Copyright*, 47 Univ. Miami Law Review 1221 (1993).

Leslie A. Kurtz, *The Independent Legal Lives of Fictional Characters*, 1986 Wisconsin Law Review 429 (1986).

William M. Landes, *Copyright, Borrowed Images and Appropriation Art: An Economic Approach.* 9 George Mason Law Review 1 (2000).

William M. Landes and Richard A. Posner, *"An Economic Analysis of Copyright Law,"* 18 Journal of Legal Studies 325 (June 1989).

Laura G. Lape, *Transforming Fair Use: The Productive Use Factor in Fair Use Doctrine*, 58 Albany Law Review 677 (1995).

Laura G. Lape, *The Metaphysics of the Law: Bringing Substantial Similarity Down to Earth*, 98 Dickinson Law Review 181 (1996).

Alan Latman, *"Probative Similarity" as Proof of Copying: Toward Dispelling Some Myths in Copyright Infringement*, 90 Columbia Law Review 1187 (1990).

Karen Burke LeFevre, *The Tell-Tale "Heart": Determining "Fair" Use of Unpublished Texts*, 55 Law & Contemporary Problems 153 (1992).

Mark A. LoBello, *The Dichotomy Between Artistic Expression and Industrial Design: To Protect or Not to Protect*, 13 Whittier Law Review 107 (1992).

Jessica Litman, *Copyright and Information Policy*, 55 Law & Contemporary Problems 185 (1992).

Raymond T. Nimmer & Patricia Ann Krauthaus, *Software Copyright: Sliding Scales and Abstracted Expression*, 32 Houston Law Review 317 (1995).

NOTE: Copyright Implications of "Unconventional Linking" on the World Wide Web: Framing, Deep Linking and Inlining +, 49 Case Western Reserve Law Review 181 (1998).

Mark Sableman, *Link Law Revisited: Internet Linking Law at Five Years*, 16 Berkeley Technology Law Journal 1273 (Fall 2001).

Edward Samuels, *The Idea–Expression Dichotomy in Copyright Law*, 56 Tennessee Law Review 321 (1989).

David E. Shipley, *Copyright Law and Your Neighborhood Bar and Grill: Recent Developments in Performance and the Section 110(5) Exemption*, 29 Arizona Law Review 475 (1987).

Symposium on Industrial Design Law and Practice, 19 University of Baltimore Law Review 160 (1989).

11

Introduction to Trademark Law and Trade Secret Law

This chapter outlines the basics of trademark and trade secret law, including the elements of proof to prevail on a trade secret case or a trademark infringement claim. Where trade secrets maintain their value through a lack of public discovery, the value of a trademark lies in its potential for permanent public use and the accompanying brand recognition.

Although commonly thought of merely as logos and catchphrases, legally enforceable trademarks actually include a much broader array of devices. Any mark or device that is sufficiently distinctive to identify the owner's product or services can be a trademark. Trademarks range from slogans like "Just do it" (Nike's popular advertising slogan) to the colorful packaging of a children's cereal. In fact, a single product may be associated with more than one trademark. For example, in the case of a children's cereal, the cereal company potentially could trademark the name of the cereal, the designs on the cereal box, and the shape of the cereal itself. Of course, this assumes that these product traits meet all of the requirements for legally enforceable marks, which are discussed in detail in subsequent sections. Essentially, a trademark must be more than a generic or purely descriptive name for the goods to which it is affixed. Accordingly, "Shredded Wheat" probably would not qualify as a trademarked cereal name, but "Captain Crunch" probably is sufficiently fanciful to meet at least the basic requirements.[1]

BRIEF HISTORY OF TRADEMARK PROTECTION

Trademarks initially were protected under the common law, which permitted a firm to obtain rights in a distinctive mark simply by designing the mark and applying it to the firm's products. The actual use requirement prevented the waste of resources that might otherwise be expended protecting marks not in use and precluded firms from simply stockpiling trademarks to limit the marks available to their competitors. The common law did not require registration of the mark as a prerequisite to legally enforceable rights in the mark. The lack of a registration requirement could make it difficult to resolve priority disputes under the common law because it is often difficult to tell which firm actually used a mark first.

The common law distinguished between "trademarks" and "trade names." The former referred to arbitrary or distinctive marks that identified the user's goods, while the latter generally had a primary meaning other than as an identifying mark created for the purpose of distinguishing the goods. For example, the name of the producer might qualify as a trade name, such as "Swensen's Raspberry Jam." In order to enforce rights to a trade name, the owner was required to establish that the mark had attained a "secondary meaning" or special significance in the eyes of the potential customer that distinguished the goods to which it was affixed. In other words, Ms. Swensen could not simply trademark her own surname without having proven that it had acquired a distinctive market meaning when affiliated with Ms. Swensen's delicious raspberry jam.

Currently, trademarks are also protected by the Lanham Act.[2] The Lanham Act is a federal statute that provides for a right of action for trademark infringement, as well as the possibility of statutory damages in some cases (discussed later). Many states also have trademark registration acts that are largely modeled after the Lanham Act. As under the common law, a merchant must affix the mark at issue to her goods and sell the goods in commerce in order to attain enforceable rights to the mark. In other words, whether considering a common law regime or the statutory requirements, no trademark rights can accrue without use of the mark. One distinction from the common law treatment of marks is that under the Lanham Act, once the mark is in use, the mark owner must file a formal registration application to qualify for trademark protection. Additionally, the distinction between trademarks and trade names was eliminated under the federal trademark statute, which includes trade names in its definition of trademarks.

TYPES OF MARKS

The Lanham Act allows the registration of four types of marks: trademarks, service marks, certification marks, and collective marks.[3] A trademark is any "word, name, symbol or device, or any combination thereof" used to distinguish goods from those manufactured by others and to indicate the source of the goods.[4] A service mark is similar, but it identifies a particular owner's services, as opposed to products.[5] Trademarks and service marks probably represent the types of marks that the public commonly considers to be protected marks, such as Pepsi and AAA Auto Repair.

Certification marks identify goods that satisfy a particular standard or originate from a particular geographic region. For example, a certification mark might be an indication that a product has passed an underwriter's laboratory standard or that the balsamic vinegar is an authentic product of Modena, Italy. The owner of a certification mark cannot be the producer of the goods to which the mark is attached; clearly, if a certification mark could be affixed in a purely subjective manner, the mark would lose its informative value and sheen of legitimacy.[6] Moreover, if a producer owned the certification mark, the mark could be used by the producer as a barrier to entry in the market in order to reduce competition. The Lanham Act provides legislative support for the aura of legitimacy attached to certification marks, as it provides for the cancellation of marks that are applied in a discriminatory or uncontrolled manner.[7] In other words, certification marks cannot be withheld from producers who meet the qualifications for the particular certification mark, or awarded without any control over the recipients.

Finally, a collective mark identifies a member of "a cooperative, an association, or other collective group or organization."[8] Like certification marks, collective marks are owned and controlled by an organization, but used by actual producers. Collective marks are adopted by organizations to identify their members or the goods and services of their members, such as the Opticians Association of America. Although the Lanham Act defines the two types of marks separately, it is unclear how distinct they really are. It appears that if an organization has certain prerequisites or standards for membership, then joining the organization truly is indistinct from receiving a certification mark indicating that those standards have been met.[9]

A mark that identifies merely the business itself, rather than its goods or services, is known as a trade name. Trade names are not entitled to protection under the Lanham Act, although they are protected under the common law against confusingly similar uses.[10] Moreover, in some situations, a mark functions as both a trademark and a trade name. AAA Auto Repair, as mentioned previously, may operate as a service mark because it identifies the services provided, but it also may be the name of the business, and thus a trade name.[11] This issue of whether a trade name qualifies for protection as a service mark is a question of fact resolved by the courts by evaluating the way in which the mark is used and the possible impact of that use on potential consumers.[12]

Owners register a mark by submitting an application to the United States Patent and Trademark Office (commonly referred to as the PTO). Applications are screened for the requirements of registration, and approved marks are published in the Trademark Office's Official Gazette. This publication notifies the public that a mark is registered and identifies the owner of that mark.

Registration affords several competitive advantages. First, registration entitles the owner to a presumption that the mark is valid.[13] Second, only registered marks can carry the commonly recognized symbol of the "r in the circle," "®." Third, registration provides nationwide constructive notice of the mark, even in areas where the merchant does not do business.[14] As is discussed later in this chapter, this prevents an alleged infringer from avoiding liability by simply claiming that he or she did not know the mark belonged to someone else.

Finally, after continuous and exclusive use for five years, a registrant may apply to have the mark declared incontestable.[15] An incontestable mark cannot be challenged by accused infringers on the basis of invalidity. Although some defenses remain, an incontestable mark has more value in litigation than a mark that will have to defend its status as a legitimately issued trademark as well as establish the facts of infringement.

To be deemed incontestable, the registrant must satisfy several other requirements in addition to the prerequisite continuous and exclusive use. First, there must also be no final decision in existence that was adverse to the registrant's claim. Second, there can be no pending proceedings involving the registrant's rights. Third, the registrant must file an affidavit setting forth the goods or services connected with the mark and swearing to the absence of the aforementioned adverse decision and pending proceedings. Finally, the mark cannot have become a "generic" name for the goods or services. Generic marks are discussed in detail in the next section.

Incontestable marks are not invincible. They can be attacked on several fronts, as outlined in section 33(b) of the Lanham Act. Section 33 indicates that an incontestable mark can be defeated if the defendant establishes that the mark itself is generic or has been abandoned by the owner.[16] Additionally, fraud in the owner's application, flaws in the issuance of a certification mark, or abuse of the mark may be defenses to infringement.[17] Finally, the alleged infringer may assert defenses justifying his or her own conduct, such as that the use of the mark was a "fair use" in that it was purely descriptive, or that no confusion resulted from the use.[18]

PRIMARY CLASSIFICATIONS OF TRADEMARKS

Marks are classified by the distinctiveness of the association they create with the product or service. In descending order of legal strength, a mark is either fanciful, arbitrary, suggestive, or descriptive. "Fanciful" means that the mark was made up purely for the purpose of this brand and lacks any independent meaning. Examples of fanciful marks include Jeep and Xerox. The difficulty with fanciful marks is that they can become generic terms for the type of product. For example, many people use "Xerox" simply to mean "photocopy," and "Band-Aid" has become nearly synonymous with adhesive bandages. As mentioned above, a mark that becomes a generic description for the general category of product or service may be cancelled.[19] This presents owners with an interesting dilemma—the more successful their marketing of the fanciful brand is, the more likely it is to become simply a description of the product that lacks legal significance. Of course, the trademark owner can stave off this sort of pyrrhic victory by vigilantly enforcing the mark against infringers and preserving the distinctive association of that brand with a particular producer. Moreover, new drugs are often designated with both a brand name and a generic name to avoid losing their trademark status for the brand name.

"Arbitrary" marks are terms in common parlance, but their common usage is neither inherently descriptive nor suggestive of the goods or services to which the mark is affixed. An easy example of a successful arbitrary mark is Apple computers. Although "apple" is a common word, it was not (prior to Steve Jobs' efforts) associated with personal computing. "Apple" remains a mark that could not be legally enforceable as a trademark for a seller of apple fruit, but it is arbitrary with relation to computers, and hence appropriate for trademark protection.

"Suggestive" marks require the audience to "think about" the connection in order to perceive the link between the mark and the related product or service. In other words, suggestive marks may bring to mind a good or service, although they are not straightforward descriptions of the underlying products. For example, Coppertone tanning lotion is suggestive of the pleasant brown glow that might accompany successful use of the product, but it is not a generic description such as "sunscreen."

"Descriptive" marks indicate an important quality or characteristic of the related product. Vision Center and Raisin Bran are examples of descriptive marks. Empirically, courts (and scholars) have great difficulty distinguishing between suggestive marks and descriptive marks. The Fifth Circuit has provided one example of the interesting, and often subjective, analysis that goes into making this distinction:

> [T]he trier of fact must be aware of, or informed of, common, up-to-date usage of the word or phrase. Furthermore, even were usage not constantly changing, the context in which a word or phrase appears is relevant to determining the proper category for purposes of trademark eligibility. The word or phrase must be compared to the product or service to which it is applied. For example . . . [u]sed in the phrase "FishWear" for dive clothing, "fish" may be suggestive if the intent is to suggest that divers who wear this clothing will be able to "swim like a fish." On the other hand, with respect to clothing worn while fishing, "FishWear" might be descriptive.[20]

This discussion indicates the type of reasoning that courts apply to questions of trademark eligibility, although it cannot provide a definitive answer as to what will and will not be deemed "suggestive" versus "descriptive."[21] "Raisin Bran" cereal has been found to be descriptive, while "Orange Crush" orange drink was deemed suggestive.[22] The creative litigant can find ample support for arguments going either way on the fine line between these two categories of trademarks.

Finally, generic terms are not entitled to any legal protection because they are necessary to indicate a product or service. In fact, generic terms or names do not function as "marks" at all. Generic terms may have begun as protectable marks, but the marks decline to generic status once the common usage is simply a generic reference to the product. Examples of generic terms include "aspirin," "trampoline," and "thermos." These terms are also examples of trademarks that lost their distinctiveness status and become generic. "Kleenex" may soon become generic. The following case exemplifies the judicial treatment of generic terms and the analytical factors that go into finding a mark "generic."

Genesee Brewing Co. v. Stroh Brewing Co.[23]

The issue in this case was whether the term "honey brown" could be a valid trademark for lager beer. The court found that "honey brown" was a generic name incapable of receiving trade protection. The honey brown title was generic because its principal significance was an indication of a class of beers rather than a particular source. The rationale for this holding is that it would contravene public policy to allow an individual to gain exclusive rights over terms necessary to describe a characteristic of the good. If there is no equally efficient means of describing a good, then the terms are "necessary" and the mark incorporating the terms is generic.

Any trademark must be distinctive in order to receive legal protection. This means that the mark identifies goods in an unambiguous way. Fanciful, arbitrary, and suggestive marks are deemed inherently distinctive because they have no other common meaning. For example, the term "Two Gods" has no relationship to a pencil and therefore could be an inherently distinctive designation for a pencil. Moreover, a trademarked phrase may contain elements of varying distinctiveness, and the courts may opt to give greater weight to certain portions of that phrase. Accordingly, "Blue Gods" as a trademark for pencils arguably could infringe the "Two Gods" mark if the facts indicated that the Blue Gods company was banking on resulting confusion of the two marks. The following recent case presents a similar type of analysis involving only "partial" infringement of a trademarked phrase.

Ty, Inc. v. The Jones Group, Inc.[24]

This case demonstrates that certain parts of a mark may be stronger, and thus more likely the basis for an infringement action, than others. Ty, Inc. manufactured popular plush bean bag toys under the name "Beanie Babies" and similar marks. The Jones Group, a NASCAR licensee, made bean bag toys that replicated NASCAR racecars. The racecar beanbags utilized similar materials and had similar dimensions to the Beanie Babies. The Jones Group marketed these toys as "Beanie Racers." Ty brought suit, claiming that the use of "beanie" in the toy's name confused customers as to the source of the toys and the possible affiliation with Ty's Beanie Babies. Ty did not have a registered trademark for "beanie," but argued that common law trademark rights protected its use of the word "beanie." The court ruled that, given the arguable similarity of the products themselves, the use of the word "beanie" referred to the composite "beanie babies" mark and thus infringed on that mark.

Ty, Inc. v. The Jones Group, Inc. (continued)

The court rejected The Jones Group's argument that the entire phrase should be compared (i.e., "Beanie Babies" to "Beanie Racers"), because "if one word or feature of the composite trademark is the salient portion of the mark, it may be given greater weight than the surrounding elements." Arguably, "beanie" is merely descriptive of the type of materials used in the toys, but the court found that partial infringement, even of an arguably descriptive mark, constituted a plausible infringement claim. The court noted that Ty marketed other toys featuring the word "Beanie," such as "Beanie Buddies" and "Beanie Kids," and may also have been influenced by Ty's survey indicating that 70 percent of the respondents identified the words "Beanies" and "Beanie" with Beanie Babies and Ty. Accordingly, the court denied defendant's motion for summary judgment, holding that Ty had presented sufficient evidence of infringement to go before a jury.

Generic names and descriptive marks fall at the other end of the distinctiveness spectrum from the first three types of marks. Although generic names can never acquire trademark protection, descriptive marks can qualify for trademark if (and only if) they obtain "secondary meaning." Secondary meaning attaches to a mark when the primary significance of that mark is that it identifies the source, or producer, of a good rather than merely describing the good itself. If a mark has become incontestable, secondary meaning is presumed. Otherwise, the mark owner must establish that consumers associate the mark with the producer, commonly either through the testimony of actual customers or through surveys that purport to indicate the overall impressions from taking a scientific sample. Secondary meaning is not immutable; like other types of marks, if a descriptive mark becomes synonymous with the type of product to which it is affixed, it has lost its secondary meaning and will no longer be enforceable. "Elevator" is an example of a descriptive mark that has evolved into the generic term for that type of apparatus, even though once it may have possessed secondary meaning.

Protection for secondary meaning marks generally is weak, as other firms can still use the mark in its nontrademark (i.e., purely descriptive) sense. This potential defense is fertile ground for alleged infringers.

Car-Freshner Corp. v. S.C. Johnson & Son, Inc.[25]

Car-Freshner emphasizes that the key to defending against allegations of infringing a secondary meaning mark is not how the owner uses the mark, but how the alleged infringer uses the mark. Car-Freshner sells tree-shape car fresheners that dangle from rearview mirrors in a variety of colors and scents, including pine.

(continues)

Car-Freshner Corp. v. S.C. Johnson & Son, Inc. (continued)

Johnson sells a seasonal pine-tree-shaped plug-in for use with an electrical socket; the plug-in came in a scent called "Holiday Pine Potpourri." Although the products were ostensibly in different markets, Car-Freshner claimed that the plug-in infringed its exclusive right to a pine-tree shape for the purpose of air freshening. The court found that "it should make no difference whether the plaintiff's mark is to be classed on the descriptive tier of the trademark ladder. . . . *What matters is whether the defendant is using the protected word or image descriptively, and not as a mark.*" Accordingly, the court examined the plug-in, and found that the pine-tree shape refers to the scent, as well as the Christmas season during which it is sold. Moreover, the packaging for the plug-ins prominently displayed Johnson's marks and corporate logo, rather than attempting to pass off the product as something made by Car-Freshner.

Car-Freshner's complaint was dismissed.

Certain types of names are explicitly excluded from trademark protection. These names include: (1) deceptive terms (such as "glass wax"); (2) geographic terms that are primarily geographically descriptive with no secondary meaning; and (3) surnames that have not acquired a secondary meaning. The latter exclusion is justified by the judicial reluctance to prevent people from using their own name simply because they were preceded in the market by someone with the same surname. However, surnames are subject to an exception where they have achieved significant renown as mark, although later competitors seeking to use the same or a similar surname must take "reasonable precautions."

Taylor Wine Co. v. Bully Hill Vineyards[26]

This case indicates that a surname may become a trademark if and only if it has achieved secondary meaning. In this case, the trademark owner was a winery founded 100 years earlier by the defendant's grandfather. The winery marketed wine under the Taylor label since 1880 and registered 13 trademarks. Defendant Walter S. Taylor founded a competing winery and began marketing a line of "Walter S. Taylor" wine, prominently displaying the Taylor name on the wine bottles. Taylor argued that his use of his surname did not infringe because his wines were "better" and not in actual competition with the Taylor Wine Company.

The court rejected this argument, finding that "the average American who drinks wine on occasion can hardly pass for a connoisseur of wines . . . [and] remains an easy mark for an infringer." Finding that "subtlety of taste" did not

Taylor Wine Co. v. Bully Hill Vineyards (continued)

protect Taylor's infringing use of the Taylor trademarks, the court held that confusion was likely and an injunction appropriate. However, the court noted that it would not completely forbid Taylor from using the family name so long as he included an appropriate disclaimer that he was not connected with, or a successor to, the Taylor Wine Company. In other words, his continued use was contingent on preventing confusion of the two marks.

TRADE DRESS

The courts' unease with applying trademark protection to generic or necessary aspects of goods is evident in their approach to trade dress protection. The shape, color, and art style of goods may be trademarked as "trade dress" if they indicate source and are not merely "utilitarian." "Utilitarian" aspects are defined as those qualities that are superior in function or economy in light of a competitive necessity to copy. Even secondary meaning is insufficient if the design is primarily functional. The product or packaging design must be evaluated as a whole; the presence of some functional features does not mean that the entire design is unprotectable.

Qualitex offers one example of the judicial treatment of nonfunctional elements under a trademark analysis, specifically colors.

Qualitex v. Jacobson Products[27]

The issue in this case was whether color could serve as a trademark, specifically the green-gold dry cleaning press pads sold by Owens-Corning. The Court found that color could be protected as a trademark, as can a distinctive nonutilitarian shape. However, to qualify for protection, the color must not be functional and must obtain a secondary meaning. The Court noted that "over time, customers may come to treat a particular color on a product or its packaging . . . as signifying a brand." Moreover, colors can never be inherently distinctive.

The Court examined, and rejected, defendant's "color depletion theory." The "theory" was that allowing trademarks on colors would limit the colors available to competitors and eventually preclude effective competition altogether. The Court indicated that this scenario was avoidable by requiring courts to examine whether the color is a necessary, nontrademark part of the product. If it is, then the color depletion theory might preclude enforcement of an allegedly trademarked color.

Another example of protectable trade dress is the décor and various elements making up the ambience of a restaurant.

Two Pesos v. Taco Cabana[28]

The Supreme Court found that the trade dress of the Mexican restaurant Taco Cabana was protected despite lacking evidence of the trade dress having acquired secondary meaning. The Court decided that the trade dress in question was "inherently distinctive" and thus did not require evidence of secondary meaning. Trade dress was defined as the "total image of the business," including the shape and general appearance of the exterior, the identifying sign, the décor, the menu, and the server's uniforms. In this case, Taco Cabana's vivid color scheme, festive eating atmosphere, and neon stripes on the exterior of the restaurant were all part of its inherently distinctive trade dress. One stated justification was that the trademark laws should protect new products and expansions into new markets where there has not yet been an opportunity to establish secondary meaning.

One further interesting note about this case: After the Supreme Court's decision affirming the jury verdict of $3.7 million, Taco Cabana brought a second suit against Two Pesos alleging damages of $5 million. Shortly thereafter, Two Pesos signed a letter of intent to sell its entire chain of 34 restaurants to Taco Cabana.[29]

Subsequent cases have clarified that the ruling of *Two Pesos* is limited in application to product packaging rather than product design. This distinction appears sustainable based on the less functional nature of the trade dress involved in packaging rather than the design of the actual product.

Wal-Mart Stores v. Samara Brothers[30]

In *Wal-Mart*, the Court had the opportunity to overrule *Two Pesos*, but opted instead to draw a distinction between product design trade dress and product packaging trade dress. Samara Brothers sued Wal-Mart for selling "knockoff" versions of its children's clothing designs. The main product at issue was a line of one-piece seersucker outfits decorated with appliqués of flowers, hearts, and so on. Wal-Mart intentionally developed a clothing line based on the Samara Brothers' designs with only minor modifications. The Court treated the clothing design as a form of trade dress (specifically product design trade dress) and found that without evidence of secondary meaning, Samara Brothers could not prevail on its claim.

The Court held that trade dress, like other trademarks, must be distinctive in order to merit protection. Accordingly, trade dress must either be inherently

Wal-Mart Stores v. Samara Brothers (continued)

distinctive or have acquired secondary meaning. Product design, unlike product packaging, can never be inherently distinctive because it is not reasonable to assume "customer predisposition to equate the feature with the source." Customers are aware that even the most unusual product designs, such as a cocktail shaker shaped like a penguin, are intended primarily to render the product itself more appealing rather than to identify the source of the product. Since product design will always be serving these alternative purposes, it would be detrimental to the public to eliminate competition among producers with regard to particular utilitarian and aesthetic features.

Two Pesos thus survives *Wal-Mart*, but only because the trade dress at issue was not treated as product design. Restaurant décor, to the judicial eye, is more akin to packaging (and hence more likely to be accepted by customers as an indication of source) than product design. Furthermore, the Court left open the possibility that *Two Pesos* could be further narrowed as it noted that the décor was either product packaging or "some tertium quid that is akin to product packaging."[31] Accordingly, it is possible that this undefined third category could evolve into the sole appropriate ground for application of "inherent distinctiveness" to trade dress. Moreover, the increased evidentiary burden on design owners seeking protection under the Lanham Act may encourage the owners to apply for protection under copyright laws or design patents instead.

PRIORITY

Where ownership of a mark is contested by multiple parties, the courts evaluate which party should be granted "priority" over the others and awarded full legal rights of enforcement. The common law and the Lanham Act have contrasting definitions of priority. Under the common law, the first merchant to use a mark on a minimal number of sales has priority over all subsequent users in the area where the first use occurred. Furthermore, the mark must be physically attached to the goods or their container, thus preventing firms from making use of the mark before the related product is on the market. This is known as the "affixation" requirement, and the date of affixation can establish priority under the common law.

There are some weaknesses in the common law's approach to priority. For example, because product development often requires significant time, a company could be without protection until it is capable of meeting the affixation requirement. This dilemma creates incentives for an inefficient race to be the first to market, regardless of any corresponding trade-offs in product quality. Moreover, as mentioned earlier in the chapter, the regime can lead to uncertainties in the priority context because of the possible difficulties in establishing first use. In one case, three separate companies began using the mark "Kimberly" for clothing on May 9, May 10, and May 11, respectively.[32] This near-simultaneous use of the same mark forces courts to either award the mark to the user who preceded the others by a matter of days, or even hours, or construct an equitable alternative. In this particular case, the Second Circuit held that the uses were close enough in time to make awarding priority inequitable, so henceforth each company would be required to differentiate its product from that of the other companies.

Near-simultaneous use causes less uncertainty where a claim is brought under the Lanham Act. The Lanham Act awards priority to the first user to register the mark, regardless of the date of the first use.[33] The affixation requirement is somewhat looser than the common law interpretation, as the statute defines a use in commerce "on goods" as being when:

> [the mark] . . . is placed in any manner on the goods or their containers or the displays associated therewith or on the tags or labels affixed thereto, or if the nature of the goods makes such placement impracticable, then on documents associated with the goods or their sale.[34]

Similarly, the affixation requirement is met as to services when the mark is "displayed in the sale or advertising of services."[35] This relaxed requirement still prevents the establishment of trademark priority through advertising use alone, even where services are concerned.[36] Accordingly, use is necessary, but not sufficient, for priority under the Lanham Act.

The only exception to this rule allows an applicant to file for registration before actual commercial use. In that case, the applicant must file an "intent-to-use" (ITU) statement with his or her application for registration.[37] The ITU application must indicate a "bona fide intention, under circumstances showing the good faith of such a person, to use a trademark in commerce."[38] An ITU applicant has up to six months from the date of the notice of allowance to file a statement verifying actual commercial use. The six-month deadline may be extended for up to two years upon written request and a showing of good cause for the extension and continuing bona fide intent to use the mark in commerce.[39] The significant advantage offered by an ITU (versus simply waiting to apply) is that priority is retroactive to the date that the ITU application was filed.

The Lanham Act's treatment of the priority issue essentially allows an ITU to constitute constructive notice of use.[40] This approach successfully addresses the flaws in the common law system by offering a clear test of priority. Moreover, the ITU protects premarket investments by firms in their trademarks and avoids inefficient races to market.

INFRINGEMENT

In general, the unauthorized use of a valid trademark by a party who competes in the same market with the trademark owner constitutes infringement. Section 32 of the Lanham Act provides the statutory definition of infringement of a registered mark:

> Any person who shall, without consent of the registrant—use in commerce any reproduction, counterfeit, copy or colorable imitation of a registered mark in connection with the sale, offering for sale, distribution or advertising of any goods or services on or in connection with which such use is likely to cause confusion, or to cause mistake, or to deceive . . . shall be liable in a civil action by the registrant for the remedies hereinafter provided.[41]

Most infringement cases turn on whether the unauthorized use results in a "likelihood of confusion."

Plaintiffs typically demonstrate a likelihood of confusion through a survey or other evidence that the use of the mark confuses customers as to the source or sponsorship of the goods. Factors considered in determining the likelihood of confusion can include the similarities between the sound, sight, and meaning of the allegedly confusing marks; the strength of plaintiff's mark; survey information; consumer sophistication; whether the goods are cheap or expensive; and actual instances of confusion.[42] Courts will not simply examine the products side by side, but will consider the circumstances of their sale, such as where they usually are sold, their sale price, the wrapping or packaging, any relevant promotions, and so on.[43] Moreover, confusion of noncustomers may be relevant where an indirect experience with the product, such as observing it in public, leads to an inaccurate attribution of source.[44] In short, any factor that points to confusion regarding the actual source of a product or service may be considered as indicative of likelihood of confusion, and thus possible causation of damages.[45] However, the most important factors generally are the similarity of the marks, the intent of the claimed infringer, and evidence of any actual confusion.[46]

Apart from contesting the likelihood of confusion, the alleged infringer has several potential defenses available to him or her.[47] Although we do not provide a complete list of possible defenses, the following discussion does outline the bases on which an infringement action may be defeated.

First, the infringer can attack the validity of the mark, either by arguing that it has become a functional or generic term, or that the registration or right to use the mark was obtained through fraud.

Second, the infringer can argue that the mark has been abandoned by the owner, and thus has entered the public domain and cannot be infringed. Abandonment is defined as discontinuing use made in the ordinary course of trade with the intent not to resume such use.[48] The intent can be inferred from the circumstance, and the nonuse will not be defeated by a purely nominal use made merely to reserve the owner's rights in the mark.[49] Nonuse for three consecutive years constitutes prima facie evidence of abandonment.[50]

Third, the Lanham Act stipulates that evidence that the mark "has been or is being used to violate the antitrust laws of the United States" is a defense to infringement.[51] We discuss trademark misuse in detail in Chapter 12. Finally, use of the mark in a nontrademark manner cannot be infringement.[52] This defense is sometimes referred to as a "fair use" defense. In essence, good faith use of the mark only to describe the goods and services of owner is a use "otherwise than as a mark" and does not violate the owner's trademark rights.[53] Nontrademark uses of a mark might include uses that identify the owner for purposes of comparative advertising or parody.[54] The fair use defense is consistent with the definition of infringement, since there should not be a likelihood of confusion when the use distinguishes the mark owner, rather than conflating the owner's product with a competing product.

There are several variations on a straightforward infringement action, including infringement of an unregistered mark, false advertising, and metatag infringement.

Infringement of an Unregistered Mark

Another type of unauthorized trademark use is the false designation of the product's origin or false descriptions of its qualities. Section 43(a)(1)(A) of the Lanham Act prohibits "any false designation of origin, false or misleading description of fact, or false or misleading representation of fact," that is likely to cause confusion or mistake as to the affiliation of such person with another person, or as to the "origin, sponsorship or approval of his or her goods, services or commercial activities by another person."[55] Essentially, section 43(a)(1)(A) is directed at those individuals who attempt to "pass off" their products as those of the trademark owner, an aim that arguably overlaps with the protection already available to the registered trademark owner. However, unlike section 32, section 43(a)(1)(A) does not require registration as a prerequisite to bringing suit. This may be the primary difference between actions brought under the two statutory sections and may help explain the need for the section.[56]

False Advertising

The Lanham Act's concern with the deception of consumers is further exemplified in its prohibition of false advertising, a short statutory provision that goes beyond the regulation of trademarks to address more general misrepresentations to the public.[57] Although this cause of action arguably goes beyond the protection of intellectual property, we address it briefly here as a corollary to the trademark laws. The Lanham Act proscribes any commercial advertising or promotion that "misrepresents the nature, characteristics, qualities, or geographic origin of his or her or another person's goods, services, or commercial activities."[58] This provision is the statutory basis for "false advertising" claims.

To prevail on a false advertising claim, the misrepresentation in question must be "material" to consumers. A misrepresentation is material if it has deceived more than an insubstantial number of consumers and consumers actually relied on the misrepresented fact in making their purchasing decisions. Materiality may be established through survey evidence of customer confusion or evidence that the defendant knew the advertising was misleading.[59] Moreover, courts presume that evidence of expenditures on willfully deceptive advertising implies that the defendant thought the misrepresentation would affect customers' purchasing decisions.[60] "Willfully deceptive" advertisements are those that are facially false and egregiously misleading (even if actually true).[61] However, if a statement is literally true, the plaintiff must present evidence that the advertisement has a tendency to mislead based on how the intended audience would perceive the message.

Avis Rent A Car System v. Hertz[62]

In this battle between car rental services, the court's decision provides a helpful example of how courts examine the "falsity" of alleged false advertising in context rather than taking a strictly literal approach. Hertz placed a print advertisement that read "Hertz has more new cars than Avis has cars." At the time that the advertisement was published, the number of cars that Hertz had available for rental *was* slightly larger than the number of Avis's available rental cars, but Avis's total fleet of cars was much larger than Hertz's total fleet. The trial court found that the literal language of the advertisement clearly referred to total cars, not merely rental cars, and thus was false. However, on appeal, the Second Circuit reversed and held that the full context of the advertisement—including other references to rentals, both parties' reputations as car renters, and consumer studies supporting the narrower interpretation—indicated that the phrase accurately referred to the number of rental cars owned by each company. Accordingly, the Second Circuit ordered the trial court to dismiss the complaint against Hertz.

A false advertising plaintiff must also establish that he is "likely to be damaged" by the defendant's advertising.[63] If the plaintiff is asking a court to enjoin a defendant's promotional activities, there is a lower threshold for injury than if the plaintiff is seeking to recover damages for the conduct.[64] Where the advertising in question singles out a particular competitor, as in comparative advertising, it generally is easier for the plaintiff to demonstrate a likelihood of injury.[65] Moreover, if the products are competing in the relevant market and it appears likely that the advertising will decrease the plaintiff's sales, it is not necessary for the plaintiff to establish more than a "logical causal connection."[66] In contrast, where the products are not in obvious, direct competition, the plaintiff must show that consumers view the products as comparable substitutes for each other in order to establish a likelihood of injury.[67]

The plaintiff does not need to establish any particular state of mind on the part of the advertiser making misrepresentations; false advertising is a strict liability offense, meaning that intentional conduct is sufficient, regardless of whether the consequences were intended. Although evidence that the defendant is intentionally making misrepresentations in her advertising is relevant to the materiality of the statements and also possibly to causation, it is not necessary for the plaintiff to recover on her claim. The absence of a requisite mental state reduces the costs to plaintiffs of bringing suit, decreases administrative costs, and may increase consumer trust in the information function of advertisements. However, the lack of this element may be overly harsh, because it makes litigation easier, and thus more likely. Additionally, making false advertising a strict liability offense reduces the victim's incentives to take reasonable and efficient precautions because the defendant will be liable for all harm caused by his actions. Some courts might respond to this criticism by noting that the real "victim" of a false advertising claim is the consumer who is misled, not the competitor who may lose some sales. Unlike the competitor, the consumer victim does not recover any money from a successful false advertising suit, so regardless of the legal elements for false advertising, consumers have full incentives to be informed and take precautions to avoid being duped.

Metatag Infringement

Metatags are words inserted in each web page that ordinarily are visible to search engines, but not to the visitor who accesses the site with a standard browser. The metatags are intended to function as an index of the site's content. Because search engines read metatags to determine the potential relevancy of a site to users' queries, some companies have begun using a competitors' trademarks in their metatags to increase the prominence of their site in response to queries for the competing product or company. The unauthorized use of a trademark in metatags constitutes trademark infringement.[68] Faced with increasing allegations of trademark infringement through use of the marks in metatags, the courts created a new doctrine, specific to the Internet context, to address their concern with the potential for consumer confusion—"initial interest confusion."[69]

Brookfield Communications v. West Coast Entertainment[70]

In *Brookfield*, the plaintiff had a registered trademark for "MovieBuff" as a mark designating both goods and services related to providing entertainment industry news and information via computer software. However, West Coast Entertainment, a chain of video rental stores, registered the domain name "moviebuff.com" before Brookfield applied for its trademark registration. West Coast allegedly picked that name because it is part of its own service mark, "The Movie Buff's Movie Store." Brookfield sued for trademark infringement and unfair competition under the Lanham Act and sought an injunction precluding West Coast from using the mark "moviebuff" in their domain name or in their metatags.

The court found that traditional understandings of a "likelihood of confusion" did not capture the potential for confusion on the Internet, noting that "Web surfers are more likely to be confused as to the ownership of a web site than traditional patrons of a brick-and-mortar store would be of a store's ownership." The court was particularly concerned with the unique confusion that can result from manipulation of search engine results, since search engines are the primary means of navigating the Internet. Accordingly, the court developed the theory of initial interest confusion.

Brookfield Communications v. West Coast Entertainment (continued)

The theory of initial interest confusion recognizes that a trademark owner may be harmed by the alleged infringement, even if once the user actually accesses the site it becomes clear that the site is not affiliated in any sense with the trademark owner. Supposedly, by diverting the user to its site, the infringer improperly benefits from the goodwill associated with the mark, even if the user is only distracted for a moment and no actual sale is completed as a result of the infringement. The rationale for the theory is that the infringer has at least increased the chance that the user will give up trying to find the actual site he was searching for and settle for the one that he has accessed.

Accordingly, the court held that the Lanham Act barred West Coast from including in its metatags any term confusingly similar with Brookfield's mark, unless that term was necessary for a good faith index of the content of the site.

A related tactic, "cyberstuffing," occurs when a mark is inserted repeatedly in a metatag (e.g., Apple, Apple, Apple, Apple, Apple) so that the site may appear higher on a search engine's hit list.[71] Alternatively, competitors may achieve the same result by placing excessive references to their competitors in the *content* of their sites rather than in the metatags.

J.K. Harris v. Steven Kassel[72]

In this recent case, J.K. Harris, a tax firm, accused its competitor, taxes.com, of unfair competition, false advertising, and a slew of other related claims. On one claim, J.K. Harris alleged that taxes.com manipulated search engine results by using J.K. Harris's trade name up to 75 times in headlines, header tags, and underlined tags. The resulting "keyword density" allegedly resulted in taxes.com appearing first on the list of results compiled by search engines when a user searched for "J.K. Harris." This high placement on search engines allowed taxes.com to lure consumers away from their search for J.K. Harris's site.

The court was persuaded that this conduct presented a potential for irreparable harm to the plaintiff and issued a preliminary injunction barring taxes.com from using the trade name more than reasonably necessary to identify J.K. Harris, including excessive use in headers and as underlined words.

Arguably, this opinion expands the initial interest confusion theory by applying it to the excessive use of a mark in the content of the site, rather than the more subtle use in the invisible metatags.

Liability for metatag trademark infringement is still subject to the fair use defense (e.g., comparative advertising, nondescriptive use, parody, etc.).[73] Metatags must be allowed if they constitute a good faith index of the content of the site and no confusion is likely.[74] However, evidence of repetitious usage or of the defendant's general intent to harm the mark owner may defeat the argument that the use is merely a good faith effort to index site content.[75]

Playboy Enterprises v. Terri Welles, Inc.[76]

Terri Welles, a former Playboy "Playmate of the Year," established a web site that included the terms "playboy" and "playmate" in the metatags for the site. Playboy Enterprises sued Welles for trademark infringement, unfair competition, and dilution of trademark. The court found that although initial interest confusion is actionable, it does not guarantee a finding of infringement or bar a fair use defense. A plaintiff seeking to prevail on this theory must develop facts that indicate whether the initial interest confusion is "damaging and wrongful," whether the confusion between the products will cause consumers to mistakenly believe there is a connection between the two products, or evidence that the confusion "offers an opportunity for sale not otherwise available" to the defendant.

In this case, the court found no evidence that any of these factors were established, and there was no evidence that Ms. Welles had intended to divert Playboy Enterprises' customers through her use of the metatags. Rather, Ms. Welles wished to benefit from her fame and recognition as the Playboy Playmate of the Year 1981, and the logical way for a consumer to find her site on the web is by entering those key words on a search engine. The court also noted that Playboy Enterprises had not suggested any alternative, nonoffending words to properly identify Ms. Welles and her web site. Ms. Welles's use of the marks was *descriptive* and beyond the scope of trademark law. Since the use of Playboy's marks was a nominative, fair use of the terms to describe Ms. Welles's goods and services, summary judgment was awarded to the defendants.

TRADEMARKS AND DOMAIN NAME DISPUTES

One by-product of the proliferation of Internet sites has been the problem often referred to as "cybersquatting." Cybersquatting refers to the bad faith registration of a domain name that includes or consists entirely of a well-known trademark in order to sell the domain name to the mark owner at a tidy profit. Other problems arise when two or more companies appear to have equal rights to use a particular phrase as their web site address. Either situation can be classified as a domain name dispute.

There are three statutory means of resolving domain name disputes: (1) the Lanham Act (as already discussed), (2) the Uniform Dispute Resolution Procedures (UDRP), and (3) the Anti-Cybersquatting Consumer Protection Act (ACPA).

The UDRP was implemented in December 1999, proffering an administrative dispute resolution process that can reach a decision much faster, and for less cost, than litigating the matter in court. Most proceedings take less than two months. However, the only remedies available to the complaining party are transfer or cancellation of the domain name. Damages or monetary awards are not an option. Arguably, this structure provides inadequate deterrence for the would-be cybersquatter. The losing party has 10 days after the UDRP decision is posted (on the Internet) to file a complaint in court; otherwise the transfer or cancellation will be implemented automatically. Not all domain names disputes use the UDRP because it must be invoked by a contractual provision; it does not simply kick in whenever trademark laws might be violated by a domain name. Generally, the UDRP applies where the contract with the Internet service provider provided for all disputes to be resolved under the rules and regulations of the UDRP.

The ACPA also targets cybersquatting and was implemented around the same time as the UDRP. Unlike the UDRP, the ACPA provides for statutory damages, capped at $100,000 per domain name, and anticipates proceedings in court.[77] Despite the availability of monetary damages under the ACPA, it appears that most trademark owners prefer the faster and less expensive resolution of the UDRP. The ACPA also contains a safe harbor provision, protecting defendants who both "believed and had reasonable grounds to believe that the use of the domain name was fair use or otherwise lawful."[78]

Virtual Works, Inc. v. Volkswagen of America Inc.[79]

In *Virtual Works*, the Fourth Circuit examined the intent element of the ACPA, which requires the defendant to have had a bad faith intent to profit from the domain name registration. Virtual Works, an Internet service provider, registered the domain name "vw.net" in October 1996. Approximately three years later, Volkswagen filed a protest seeking to have the domain name put on hold because it allegedly infringed their trademark, "VW." The trial court found that Virtual Works was cybersquatting, relying in part on the fact that Volkswagen was the only entity with rights in the mark since Virtual Works never registered the VW mark or conducted business under that mark. Moreover, the use of vw.net caused confusion and disparaged Volkswagen by describing it as a Nazi enterprise supported by slave labor. The differences between the two companies' products was irrelevant because "both parties use the Internet as a facility to provide goods and services."

On appeal, the court found sufficient evidence of bad faith on the part of Virtual Works in registering the domain name vw.net to affirm summary judgment in

(continues)

Virtual Works, Inc. v. Volkswagen of America Inc. (continued)

favor of Volkswagen. The court's analysis focused on three factors: (1) evidence that Virtual Works was aware of Volkswagen; (2) Virtual Works' attempt to make a significant profit by selling the domain name to Volkswagen (until Volkswagen initiated the action to claim the domain name); and (3) Virtual Works' threat to sell the domain name to the highest bidder unless Volkswagen purchased the name. The Fourth Circuit was not convinced that Virtual Works' legitimate business uses of the mark outweighed the evidence of bad faith intent. Accordingly, the court upheld the award of summary judgment for Volkswagen.

The following case also examines the "bad faith" requirement of cybersquatting. However, unlike *Virtual Works*, the following case did not involve a famous mark and was resolved in arbitration rather than in the courtroom.

Broadcom Corp. v. Becker[80]

Broadcom recently attempted to clarify the meaning of "bad faith" in the context of domain name disputes. In *Broadcom*, the arbitration panel stated that putting a fairly generic domain name such as <cyberbroadcomm.com> up for open sale qualifies as a legitimate interest in and use of that domain name. When the domain name in question is also a well-known trademark, the same actions can constitute bad faith, particularly where the domain name is offered for sale to the trademark owner or a competitor of that owner. However, the domain name in this case was not famous, nor was there any evidence that the defendant knew of Broadcom or its trademark (Broadcom) when he registered the domain name and offered it for sale to the public.

The fact that the domain name in question differed slightly from the trademark was not a determining factor. If the defendant had registered the domain name to prevent the trademark owner from obtaining a domain name that would reflect her mark, even though the name was not identical to the mark, such registration might be found to be in bad faith. In short, if the trademark owner proves that defendant's registration was done primarily to disrupt the business of the trademark owner, or so that the registrant might benefit from the likely resulting confusion, the owner has demonstrated bad faith.

Several individuals have attempted to satisfy the "legitimate use" requirement with less than fully developed web sites. However, the courts do not appear willing to blindly accept that any use of the domain name on a web site qualifies the registrant's actions as legitimate use.

Hewlett-Packard Co. v. Rayne[81]

Mike Rayne registered the domain names <hpcopier.com> and <hewlettpackard-fax.com> with Network Solutions, Inc. As a contractual condition of the registration, Rayne was required to resolve any domain name disputes related thereto under the UDRP. Accordingly, when Hewlett-Packard complained about the domain names infringing its famous trademarks "Hewlett-Packard" and "HP," the matter was heard by an arbitration panel. The arbitration not only found the domain names to be confusingly similar to the plaintiff's trademark, but also stated that the unsupported claim that the web site was "under construction" did not constitute legitimate use of the domain. Ten months after registering the domain names, Rayne still had not made any use of the site, despite the posted claim that it was "soon to be" a consumer chat web site. This passive holding of the disputed domain name, without significant use, permitted an inference of bad faith on Rayne's part.

Another factor considered by the panel in *Hewlett-Packard v. Rayne* was Rayne's pattern of registering infringing domain names and then offering them for sale to the trademark owner. Rayne also owned the domain names: <cannoncopiers.com>, <fujitsu fax.com>, <hitachifax.com>, and <xeroxfax.com>, among others. This type of repeated registration of domain names that incorporate well-known marks is coming under great scrutiny from the judiciary. Similarly, transparent attempts to sell the domain names rather than use them can indicate bad faith by the alleged infringer.

PRIMEDIA Magazine Finance, Inc v. Manzo[82]

The WIPO arbitrator examined claims that Richard Manzo's registration of <powerandmotoryacht.com> and <powerandmotoryachts.com> infringed the registered trademark "Power & Motoryacht" for magazines dealing with boating. The arbitrator found that it was clear from the web sites that the primary purpose of the sites were to offer the domain names for sale. Manzo could not claim that he had a legitimate use for the marks, as his web site did not offer any goods or services, but simply provided a link to an unaffiliated web site. The arbitrator rejected Manzo's argument that he was simply using the links until he had the "time and motivation" to set up a permanent web site, particularly in light of Manzo's inability to provide any information about the site he claimed he would develop or any other evidence of legitimate use. Accordingly, the arbitrator required the domain names to be transferred to the trademark owner.

As the reader may have already noticed from cases cited in this chapter, web sites with sexual content have been a driving force in shaping the law applicable to trademarks in cyberspace. Playboy, in particular, has been very active in enforcing its marks. Accordingly, several of the seminal cases involving metatag infringement and domain name disputes stem from litigation involving the venerable "Playboy" and "Playmate" marks.

Playboy Enterprises International v. Tonya Flynt Foundation[83]

Despite Playboy's well-known and registered "Playboy" mark (in connection with adult entertainment in various media), Playboy had difficulty registering the domain name <playboyonline.com>. Tonya Flynt, the daughter of Larry Flynt and publisher of *Hustler* magazine, registered the domain and refused to transfer it to Playboy, despite entering negotiations at one point. Instead, Flynt used the site to advertise various goods, including videos. The arbitrator agreed with Playboy that Flynt was well acquainted with the adult entertainment industry and the mark was sufficiently famous for Flynt's actions to be construed as being in "bad faith." Moreover, the panel was satisfied that Flynt's use of the disputed domain name web site to sell products that are also products the public would expect Playboy to sell indicated bad faith and did not constitute a legitimate use of the mark.

Moreover, trademark owners who are not involved in the adult entertainment industry tend to be extremely concerned about infringing uses of their marks that appear to affiliate them with pornography.

Trump v. olegevtushenko a/k/a/ Oleg Evtushenko[84]

This case involved another pornography dispute, in particular a dispute involving Donald Trump and an individual, Oleg Evtushenko, who registered the domain name <porntrumps.com>. Donald Trump had used and registered the TRUMP service mark in connection with high-class casino and entertainment services, while Evtushenko had used the domain name for a pornographic video web site offering "extreme XXX" pornography and membership in a pornographic video club. Despite the international recognition of Donald Trump, the arbitration panel noted that the *common use* of the word "trump" both as a noun and a verb predated Mr. Trump. Moreover, the panel found that there was no likelihood of confusion between TRUMP and <porntrumps.com>. The use of "trumps" as a verb was meant to suggest that pornography "gets the better of" things. This particular use was not a trademark use and therefore did not infringe Trump's rights as a mark owner. The complaint was therefore dismissed.

The Internet has forced trademark law to evolve in ways that recognize the particular harms and types of infringement possible only in cyberspace. Traditional doctrines of likelihood of confusion and infringement have given rise to judicial concepts such as initial interest confusion and metatag misuse. Another doctrine that has found new life since the advent of the World Wide Web is the cause of action for dilution.

DILUTION AND REVERSE CONFUSION

Under section 43(c) of the Lanham Act, a trademark owner may sue for a commercial use of his or her mark when the use dilutes the mark's value. In 1995, Congress enacted the Federal Trademark Anti-Dilution Act (FTDA) to establish a uniform set of standards for the common law claim of dilution.[85] Dilution commonly takes two forms: blurring and tarnishment. "Blurring" causes customers to pause and think for a moment as to what source is being identified by the mark (sort of a temporary confusion), whereas "tarnishment" refers to negative effects on a mark's positive meanings or associations (often by linking it with sexual matters or by other means of reducing its prestige value). The cause of action for dilution allows a trademark owner to preclude use of a mark on noncompeting goods if the use of the mark could dilute the mark's distinctiveness or tarnish the brand association.

Mead Data Central, Inc. v. Toyota Motor Sales, U.S.A. Inc.[86]

Mead Data provides an example of a dilution claim under the *blurring theory*. The case dealt with two similar marks: "Lexis" (in connection with Mead Data's legal research service) and "Lexus" (in connection with Toyota's luxury cars). Ultimately, the court determined that there could be no blurring because the relevant consumers for each product were very sophisticated and would easily distinguish between the marks. Moreover, the "Lexis" mark circulated only in a very limited market, so it lacked recognition among the general population and was unlikely to be associated with a dissimilar product. Moreover, given the vastly different product contexts, there was no reason to think that consumers would forge even a brief mental link between the two products. Accordingly, the court held that it was unlikely that there would be any significant amount of blurring between the Lexis and Lexus marks in Mead Data's market.

Ford Motor Co. v. Lapertosa[87]

This case held that use of a famous trademark in the domain name of a pornographic site tarnished the mark and constituted dilution. Lapertosa registered a

(continues)

Ford Motor Co. v. Lapertosa (continued)

domain name for <fordrecalls.com>, which it used for an adult entertainment web site. Ford naturally took offense at this use and sued Lapertosa, alleging that the use of the famous mark "Ford" in the domain name of a pornographic web site tarnished the mark and diluted its value. The court found that Lapertosa's use of the mark was "fundamentally inconsistent with the otherwise wholesome and commercial nature of the mark" and preliminarily enjoined Lapertosa from using the domain name. Moreover, the court forbade Lapertosa from auctioning, selling, or transferring the domain name to another user other than Ford, and ordered the defendant to transfer the <fordrecalls.com> to the trademark owner.

Although blurring and tarnishment remain the primary theories of dilution, courts have recognized that dilution encompasses more than actions that fall into those two categories. As elsewhere, the Internet has forced courts to consider new twists on the traditional cause of action.

Panavision Int'l, L.P. v. Toeppen[88]

In this case of dilution on the Internet, the defendant had registered <panavision.com> as his domain name. "Panavision" was the plaintiff's registered trademark in connection with motion picture camera equipment. Toeppen used the web site to display photographs of the City of Pana, Illinois—ostensibly his "Panavision." Although that might have provided some sort of legitimate use defense, Toeppen's subsequent conduct undermined that position. After Panavision demanded that he cease using their trademark, Toeppen offered to sell the domain name to Panavision. When Panavision declined, he registered Panavision's other trademark, "panaflex," as the domain name <panaflex.com>; that web page displayed only the word "Hello." Moreover, Toeppen had registered domain names incorporating the trademarks of over 100 other companies and offered to sell those names to the mark owners.

The court found that both the Lanham Act and California law provide for injunctive relief for the owner of a famous mark if an unauthorized commercial use causes "dilution of the distinctive quality of the mark." Toeppen claimed that use of a mark as a domain name is not commercial use. The court disagreed, particularly because it found that Toeppen misstated his use of the panavision mark. The court described Toeppen's actual business as the registration and sale of domain names that incorporate famous marks. Accordingly, Toeppen's use "traded on the value of Panavision's marks," limiting Panavision's ability to

Panavision Int'l, L.P. v. Toeppen (continued)

exploit the value of its trademarks on the Internet until and unless Panavision paid Toeppen for the domain name. The courtheld that it did not matter that the mark was not attached to a particular product, because his attempt to sell the trademarks themselves constituted a commercial use.

Although the court noted that Toeppen's conduct varied from the two classic dilution theories of "blurring" and "tarnishment," it held that these traditional definitions were not necessary to find a defendant liable for dilution. Toeppen's conduct constituted dilution because it diminished "the capacity of the Panavision marks to identify and distinguish Panavision's goods and services on the Internet."

Regardless of the particular theory of dilution, the mark at issue must be "famous." In determining whether a mark is famous, the courts consider multiple factors, including those set forth by the FTDA:

    a. the degree of inherent or acquired distinctiveness of the mark;

    b. the duration and extent of use of the mark in connection with the goods or services with which the mark is used;

    c. the duration and extent of advertising and publicity of the mark;

    d. the geographical extent of the trading area in which the mark is used;

    e. the channels of trade for the goods or services with which the mark is used;

    f. the degree of recognition of the mark in the trading areas and channels of trade used by the marks' owner and the person against whom the injunction is sought;

    g. the nature and extent of use of the same or similar marks by third parties; and

    h. whether the mark was registered. . . .[89]

Despite these guidelines and the enactment of the FTDA, courts still vary greatly in their approach to dilution claims. Some courts have attempted to limit the applicability of a dilution claim by taking a narrow view as to the type of mark that qualifies for protection.

TCPIP Holding Co. v. Haar Comm, Inc.[90]

Plaintiff operated a chain of stores that sold children's clothing and accessories under the registered trademark "The Children's Place." Haar registered the domain name <thechildrensplace.com> as a web site for children. Plaintiff brought suit claiming dilution of its mark. The court found that in order to be protectable, the mark had to possess a certain degree of inherent distinctiveness to satisfy the act's requirement of "distinctive quality." "The Children's Place" was not inherently

(continues)

TCPIP Holding Co. v. Haar Comm, Inc. (continued)

distinctive, and so could not qualify for protection under the FTDA. Moreover, the court found that a mark must also have achieved a sufficient degree of consumer recognition ("acquired distinctiveness" or secondary meaning) to satisfy the act's requirement of fame. Merely acquiring secondary meaning would not satisfy the distinctiveness requirement and thus would be insufficient to qualify the mark for protection; a mark must be both inherently distinctive and famous.

There are already several circuit splits concerning crucial elements of a claim under the FTDA. For example, there is a split between the circuits regarding whether the mark must be famous in a broad sense or merely acquire niche fame. Some jurisdictions hold that the plaintiff need only prove the famousness of the mark within the particular market in which it is used, and not the market in a broader sense.[91] Other courts find that niche market fame is not sufficient to render the mark famous under the FTDA unless the allegedly diluting use is directed toward the same market.[92]

Furthermore, the courts differ over whether the plaintiff must demonstrate actual dilution of his or her mark or whether a likelihood of dilution is adequate to maintain an action. The Fourth and Fifth Circuits have interpreted the Dilution Act to require actual dilution in order to prevail on a cause of action under the Act.[93] In contrast, the Second, Third, Seventh, Eighth, and Ninth Circuits merely require evidence of a likelihood to cause dilution.[94] Since the Supreme Court has not resolved this split, Congress may implement some type of legislative clarification in the near future.

Defenses to dilution include: fair use of the mark in comparative advertising; noncommercial use; use in all forms of news or news commentary; and the nominative use defense.[95] Use of a mark in comparative advertising, as discussed earlier, is not a use of a mark as a trademark and thus is not actionable. Use of a mark in a noncommercial context (e.g., as nonprofit parody or news reports) is protected by free speech concerns from qualifying as infringement. "Nominative use" is a defense where (1) the product is not readily identifiable without the mark; (2) the mark is used only as much as is reasonably necessary; and (3) the user does not suggest sponsorship by, or affiliation with, the mark's owner.[96]

Hormel Foods Corp. v. Jim Henson Productions, Inc.[97]

Hormel Foods involves the parody defense to a dilution action. Hormel sued Jim Henson Productions over the creation of a new Muppet—an exotic wild boar named "Spa'am." Henson thought that the association between the crazy boar and the tame, familiar pork blend known as SPAM would be humorous. Hormel

Hormel Foods Corp. v. Jim Henson Productions, Inc. (continued)

apparently could see nothing funny about Spa'am, and alleged that the "grotesque" and "untidy" wild boar would inspire "negative and unsavory associations with SPAM® luncheon meat." However, the court found that Spa'am was a likable character, unlikely to tarnish the SPAM mark. The court also noted that the Muppet merchandise would not directly compete in any sense with SPAM meat. In fact, the defendant had no incentive to diminish SPAM sales, as SPAM was vital to the humor of the new Muppet's name. Finally, the court held that "parody inheres in the product" so there was no likelihood of dilution under a tarnishment theory.

Even if the use is open criticism of the trademark owner, rather than lighthearted parody, courts have recognized that such uses are not commercial uses of the mark, and thus cannot qualify as dilution.

Ford Motor Co. v. 2600 Enterprises[98]

This case involved an unauthorized use of a registered trademark that the court found to be permissible, as it merely directed web users to the official Ford site. 2600 Enterprises had incorporated "Ford" into their code so that any user who entered their web site would be automatically redirected to the web site operated by Ford at <www.ford.com>. The catch, at least from Ford's perspective, was that defendant's web site had the domain name <www.fuckgeneralmotors.com>. Ford complained that the public might believe that the obscene domain name was sponsored or approved by Ford, and that the association with obscenity tarnished Ford's famous mark.

The court rejected Ford's motion for a preliminary injunction, finding that Ford was unlikely to prevail on its claim for dilution because the mark was not being used in commerce. The decision stated, "This court does not believe that Congress intended the FTDA to be used by trademark holders as a tool for eliminating Internet links that, in the trademark holder's subjective view, somehow disparage its trademark. Trademark law does not permit Plaintiff to enjoin persons from linking to its homepage simply because it does not like the domain name or other content of the linking web page." The court also noted that the offending web site neither sold products or services nor linked to a page (other than plaintiff's own page) that engaged in e-commerce.

A recent visit to the web site at issue in *Ford Motor Co. v. 2600 Enterprises* revealed a new addition—just before the web user is automatically transferred to the official

Ford site, there is an optional link, "To learn more about FuckGeneralMotors.com, click here." Clicking on that link takes you to a new page with the web address www.fordreallysucks.com, and information about the site owners' legal battle with Ford. Although much more obvious than the use of Ford's trademark already addressed by the court, this use of "Ford" in the domain name probably falls even more clearly within protected speech or commentary, and thus permissible use.

Finally, a related cause of action recognized by some courts is the doctrine of reverse confusion. With reverse confusion, the junior user of the mark saturates the market with a similar mark and overwhelms the senior user.[99] Instead of attempting to trade off of the renown of the original mark user, the junior user overtakes the senior user in popularity, thus destroying the value of the mark for the senior user.

A&H Sportswear, Inc. v. Victoria's Secret Stores, Inc.[100]

This case involved a dispute between the plaintiff, owner of the registered trademark "The Miraclesuit" in connection with swimwear, and Victoria's Secret, who used its own trademark "The Miracle Bra" in connection with lingerie and swimwear. The court had already determined that there was no likelihood of direct confusion between the products and found that Victoria's Secret was causing reverse confusion of the marks through its extremely successful marketing of its own swimwear under the confusingly similar mark. The sole issue at this stage was the appropriate remedy for reverse confusion.

Victoria's Secret initially had only used the mark in connection with lingerie, and the court noted that the extension into swimwear was merely a legitimate good faith attempt to capitalize on its own success. Accordingly, the court found that there was no bad faith or malicious intent on the part of Victoria's Secret, so awarding a portion of the profits on Miracle Bra swimwear was not appropriate. However, the court entered a permanent injunction forbidding Victoria's Secret from using the mark in connection with swimwear. Because a partial injunction permitting the mark to be used in conjunction with a disclaimer would be difficult to enforce, the court opted to completely enjoin use of the mark in the specific line of products that threatened reverse confusion.

SUMMARY OF TRADEMARK LAW

The trademark laws attempt to benefit both consumers and producers by offering legal protection of certain marks. Consumers benefit from the increased reliability of marks indicating the source of specific products or services, while firms benefit from the increased efficiency of their advertising and precluding imitators from free-riding on the firms' accumulated goodwill. To be protected as a trademark, a mark must be distinctive, either inherently so (because it is fanciful or arbitrary) or because it has acquired secondary meaning that affiliates it with its owner or product. A trademark owner can establish infringement where the defendant used the mark in commerce, in connection with the sale or promotion of goods or services, and the particular use is likely to confuse potential customers as to the origin of the goods or services.

INTRODUCTION TO TRADE SECRET LAW

Unlike patents, copyrights, and trademarks, trade secrets are governed exclusively by state law. Therefore, as an expert or attorney in a trade secret case, it is important to read the relevant state's trade secret statute and any seminal case law relating to remedies. Currently, approximately 40 states and the District of Columbia have adopted some version of the Uniform Trade Secrets Act (the Uniform Act)[101]; 2 states—Massachusetts and Alabama—afford protection under separate statutes, and 8 states—Michigan, Missouri, New Jersey, New York, Pennsylvania, Tennessee, Texas, and Wyoming—protect trade secrets under common law.[102] Nonetheless, almost all states follow or find persuasive the definitions stated in the Restatement of Torts[103] and the Restatement (Third) of Unfair Competition.[104] Despite the various attempts to define a trade secret, courts and commentators alike have remarked on the difficulty in defining "trade secret," primarily because almost any subject matter can be claimed as a trade secret.[105] In fact, what constitutes a trade secret is "one of the most elusive and difficult concepts in law to define."[106] This section will help elucidate the different definitions and factors used in determining whether certain information may be protected as a trade secret.

WHAT IS A TRADE SECRET?

Whether certain information qualifies as a trade secret depends on the type of information, the applicable state law, and the measures taken to ensure secrecy. The identification of trade secrets is a dynamic process. Information that a business may consider a trade secret is constantly changing—some information becomes obsolete and may no longer be commercially valuable, while new, developing information gains value. In addition, given that trade secrets today may appear in either paper or electronic form, the rules governing protection of trade secrets are evolving, and companies are, or should be, careful about identifying and protecting their trade secrets.

Providing a precise definition of a trade secret that applies in every situation may not be possible. The most commonly accepted sources, the Uniform Act, the Restatement of Torts, and the Restatement (Third) of Unfair Competition, provide varied, yet similar, approaches to defining a trade secret.

The Uniform Trade Secrets Act

The definition of a trade secret likely will vary from jurisdiction to jurisdiction. The majority of jurisdictions, however, accept some form of the definition stated by the Uniform Act:

> "Trade Secret" means information, including a formula, pattern, compilation, program, devise, method, technique or process that: (i) derives independent economic value, actual or potential, from not being generally known to, and not being readily ascertainable by proper means by, other persons who can obtain economic value from its disclosure or use, and (ii) is the subject of efforts that are reasonable under the circumstances to maintain secrecy.[107]

Under the Uniform Act, there are three defining characteristics of a trade secret: (1) the information must not be generally known or readily ascertainable by competitors or the general public through proper means, (2) it must derive actual or potential commercial or economic value from being unknown, and (3) it is kept confidential through affirmative steps to maintain secrecy.

The Common Law: Restatement of Torts and Restatement (Second) of Unfair Competition

The common law also provides substantial guidance in defining and identifying trade secrets. In fact, the common law is the exclusive authority in jurisdictions that are not governed by any particular trade secret statute. The Restatement of Torts, originally published in 1939, provides one of the first cogent definitions of a trade secret. While recognizing that "[a]n exact definition of a trade secret is not possible," the Restatement of Torts provides:

> A trade secret may consist of any formula, pattern, device or compilation of information which is used in one's business, and which give him an opportunity to obtain an advantage over competitors who do not know or use it. It may be a formula for a chemical compound, a process of manufacturing, treating or preserving materials a process, a pattern for a machine or other device, or a list of customers. . . . Generally it relates to the production of goods, as, for example, a machine or formula for the production of an article. It may, however, relate to the sale of goods or to other operations in the business, such as a code for determining discounts, rebates or other concessions in a price list or catalogue, or a list of specialized customers, or a method of bookkeeping or other office management. . . . A trade secret is a process or device for continuous use in the operation of a business.[108]

In addition, the Restatement of Torts identified several factors useful in considering whether certain information constitutes a trade secret, including: (1) the extent to which the information is known outside the business, (2) the extent to which it is known by employees and others involved in the business, (3) the extent of measures taken to guard the secrecy of the information, (4) the value of the information to the business and to competitors, (5) the amount of effort or money expended to develop the information, and

(6) the ease or difficulty with which the information could be properly acquired or duplicated by others.[109]

In 1995, trade secret law principles were refined by the Restatement (Third) of Unfair Competition. The Restatement (Third) of Unfair Competition defines a trade secret as "any information that can be used in the operation of a business or other enterprise and that is sufficiently valuable and secret to afford an actual or potential economic advantage over others."[110] Arguably, the Restatement (Third) of Unfair Competition expands the definition of trade secret. Notably, the new definition proffers trade secret protection to "any information" rather than focusing on the form in which it is presented (e.g., formula, pattern, device, etc.). In addition, there is no requirement that the trade secret be in "continuous use in the operation of a business." In fact, the new Restatement definition extends trade secret protection to "blind alleys" or "dead ends," because negative information, such as knowing the failures involved in developing a process or method, can have value and may provide an economic advantage in competition.[111]

Although there are some differences between the definitions of trade secret articulated by the Uniform Act, the Restatement of Torts, and the Restatement (Second) of Unfair Competition, the common thread that runs through all three is that a trade secret is something that is confidential, provides some value to the business, and whose value would be reduced if it were known by competitors. The distinctions between the three definitions often are blurred by the courts. In interpreting and applying the Uniform Act and various state statutes, courts often look to the Restatement of Torts and the Restatement (Second) of Unfair Competition for guidance. As one court stated, "Although all of the Restatement's factors no longer are required to find a trade secret, those factors still provide helpful guidance to determine whether the information in a given case constitutes 'trade secrets' within the definition of the statute."[112]

FACTORS INDICATIVE OF TRADE SECRETS

Various factors have been used by courts to resolve the ultimate issue in a trade secret case: Is the valuable information secret? The sine qua non of trade secret status is, of course, secrecy. While certain factors may be given different weight throughout the different jurisdictions, most courts view the following factors as persuasive in determining whether specific identified information can be protected as a trade secret.

Public Awareness

To be protected as a trade secret, the information must not be generally known or readily ascertainable by competitors or the general public through proper means. The law makes clear that a company can have no legitimate interest in restricting the use of easily accessible information or information readily accessible by a reasonably diligent competitor.[113] A trade secret is not "readily ascertainable" if the replication or acquisition of alleged trade secret information requires a substantial investment of time, expense, or effort.[114]

Although a competitor may be reasonably diligent, the Uniform Act makes clear that there are proper and improper means by which to obtain trade secret information. For instance, "proper means" to obtain information might include independent discovery, observation in public use, obtaining information from published materials, and, in some instances, reverse engineering. Indeed, the United States Supreme Court has declared: "A trade secret law . . . does not offer protection against discovery by fair and honest means, such as by independent invention, accidental disclosure, or by so-called reverse engineering, that is by starting with the known product and working backward toward to divine the process which aided in its development or manufacture."[115] By contrast, "improper means" include "theft, bribery, misrepresentation, breach or inducement of a breach of duty to maintain secrecy or espionage through electronic or other means."[116] Although the Supreme Court has approved of reverse engineering (because the information is obtainable), some state courts have held reverse engineering to be an improper means of obtaining information because of the expense and time involved in obtaining the otherwise "secret" information.[117] The bottom line is the more extensively the information is known or the easier it is to access the information outside the company, the less likely it will be regarded as a trade secret.

Intracompany Awareness

The greater the number of employees who know the information at issue, the less likely it is that the information is a protected trade secret. Although limiting the number of employees who have access to or know the trade secret information may be important, of particular importance are the measures taken by the company to protect the trade secret information and prevent its dissemination to other employees, competitors, and the public.

Reasonable Measures

In virtually every jurisdiction and under the Uniform Act, the trade secret owner must take some affirmative steps to protect the trade secret. In particular, the Uniform Act will not protect information unless its owners have taken reasonable measures to protect its secrecy. Specifically, the Uniform Act provides: "The efforts required to maintain secrecy are those 'reasonable under the circumstances.' The courts do not require that extreme and unduly expensive procedures be taken to protect trade secrets against flagrant industrial espionage."[118] Although what is "reasonable under the circumstances" will vary from case to case, several basic measures commonly are discussed as reasonable protections of trade secrets:

a. Marking documents and materials as "confidential";
b. Use of confidentiality and nondisclosure agreements with employees, contractors, suppliers, and all parties given access to confidential information;
c. Restricting access to physical facilities;
d. Securing confidential information within a facility and limiting access to those only with a "need to know";
e. Requiring special passwords to gain access to confidential computerized information and databases;
f. Policies to track and retrieve copies of documents containing sensitive information; and
g. Employee exit interviews and document return procedures.[119]

Absolute secrecy, however, is not required, and would in fact make most trade secrets devoid of value inside the company. Generally, some employees must be allowed to know the "secret" in order for it to be of value to the company. However, reasonable steps to preserve secrecy must be taken, with "reasonableness" evaluated in light of the business, the type of secret, the feasibility of certain measures, and the circumstances of the situation. For example, the most famous trade secret is the formula for Coca-Cola. According to certain sources, the Coca-Cola Company protects the secrecy of its formula by limiting disclosure of the ingredients to only two people within the company.[120] The names of these individuals are not publicly known, and they are not allowed to travel together. The written formula is stored in a bank vault that can be released only by approval of the Coca-Cola Company's Board of Directors.[121]

The type of measures that are appropriate will vary from case to case and likely will be dependent on the type of business involved and the information sought to be protected. However, trade secrets law clearly does not require the company to take every possible precaution to ensure the security of its trade secrets, nor does it require that the steps taken be foolproof. Rather, the "owner of the secret must take reasonable, though not extravagant, measures to protect the secrecy."[122]

Degree of Competitive Value

To qualify for trade secret protection, not only must the information be secret, but also the company must derive actual or potential commercial or economic value from keeping the information relatively unknown. The value can be derived from the amount of time, money, or effort invested in the development of the information, whether positive (it works) or negative (it does not work). Value also can be derived from the detail, complexity, or sophistication of the knowledge. Nonetheless, the greater the value, the more likely that the information will be protected as a trade secret.

Effort to Create the Information

The more time, effort, and money invested in developing the information, the more likely it is that the information is a protected trade secret.[123]

Ease of Replication

The easier the information is to replicate or properly obtain, the less likely the information will be considered a protected trade secret.

TYPICAL PROTECTABLE TRADE SECRETS

In general, several types of subject matter have traditionally been protected as trade secrets. These types of traditional trade secrets include (1) manufacturing processes; (2) prepatented disclosures; (3) software (object code or source code), software equipment, and documentation; (4) designs, drawings, and models; (5) internal specifications and testing procedures; (6) strategic plans; (7) marketing, development, and research plans; (8) novel techniques, ideas, concepts, discoveries, or inventions; (9) negative information (i.e., procedures, processes, methods, etc., that did not work); (10) customer lists; (11) client information; (12) vendor and supplier information; and (13) pricing and cost information. Unique compilations or combinations of information, even if the underlying information is known in the trade, may be subject to trade secret protection. In fact, "a trade secret can exist in a combination of characteristics and components, each of which, by itself, is in the public domain, but the unified process, design and operation of which, in unique combination, affords a competitive advantage and is a protectable trade secret."[124]

Interestingly, a trade secret can be the proper subject matter for a patent. However, the disclosure requirements of a patent force the trade secret owner to make a conscious choice between protection through secrecy or through the patent. It certainly is not a given that a trade secret would qualify for a patent. The subject matter for a trade secret is not the same as the novelty requirement for patentability. In *Kewanee Oil Co. v. Bicron Corp.*, the Supreme Court held that a trade secret requires only "minimal novelty," for example, a trade secret will not necessarily meet the novelty requirements for a patent.[125] At a minimum, however, a trade secret must have some utility and competitive significance.

INFORMATION NOT PROTECTED AS A TRADE SECRET AND TREATMENT OF CONFIDENTIAL INFORMATION

Information that a company does not attempt to keep secret is not considered a trade secret.[126] In addition, merely labeling information as a "trade secret" does not guarantee such protection. Generally, there is no trade secret protection for information that merely constitutes general business knowledge or experience. For example, a company cannot prevent a former employee from using information that is generally known or available in the industry by merely having the employee agree in writing that the information is a trade secret. There also is no trade secret protection over an employee's general knowledge of how to do his or her jobs (although the employee could be enjoined from developing or using information revealed in confidence and under a confidentiality agreement). Finally, there is no trade secret protection for information that is already in the public domain.[127]

Although information deemed "confidential" does not necessarily rise to the level of a trade secret, courts often afford protection for such information. In fact, both courts and commentators recognize that certain information need not rise to the level of a trade secret to be considered valuable and confidential.[128] For example, one court has acknowledged: "Although given information is not a trade secret, one who receives the information in a confidential relationship is under a duty not to disclose or use that information."[129] Moreover, if the owner of the information fails to take reasonable steps to keep the information secret, the information may not be protected under the Uniform Act, despite the fact that the information still may be unknown to the public, and the owner may well consider the information confidential and valuable. Under such circumstances, the information may be protected under certain confidentiality agreements.

MISAPPROPRIATION OF TRADE SECRETS

The Uniform Act prohibits the actual or threatened "misappropriation" of trade secrets through "improper means." As stated previously, "improper means" includes theft, bribery, misrepresentation, breach or inducement to breach a duty to maintain secrecy, or espionage through electronic means or otherwise. The Uniform Act defines "misappropriation" as:

> (1) the acquisition of a trade secret by a person who knows or has reason to know that the trade secret was acquired by improper means, or (2) the disclosure or use of a trade secret without the express or implied consent of the owner by a person who: (a) used improper means to acquire the trade secret; or (b) knew or had reason to know that the knowledge of the trade secret that the person acquired was derived from or through a person who had utilized improper means to acquire it, was acquired under circumstances giving rise to a duty to maintain its secrecy or limit its use, or was derived from or through a person who owed a duty to the person seeking relief to maintain its secrecy or its use; or (c) before a material change of their position, knew or had reason to know that it was a trade secret and that knowledge of it had been acquired by accident or mistake.

Appropriation of a trade secret by improper or unauthorized means by someone who knows that such information is proprietary constitutes a violation of trade secret law. In addition, the disclosure of a trade secret by someone who legally possesses the secret and has a duty of confidentiality (by contract or otherwise) also is a violation. In fact, hiring a competitor's former employee in order to gain trade secret information, despite the employee's nondisclosure agreement, can qualify as misappropriation of a trade secret. Courts may consider it "inevitable" that the new employee would use the trade secret in the new job,[130] or weigh the fact that the employee was less than forthcoming with his former employer regarding the new job as an indicator of the likelihood that the trade secret will be disclosed in determining whether the secret was in fact "misappropriated."[131]

Chemetall GBMH v. ZR Energy, Inc.[132]

Chemetall sued ZR for misappropriation of its trade secrets for the manufacture, marketing, and sale of zirconium metal powder products. The court found that ZR had, in fact, acted maliciously, but also that ZR had asked Chemetall on several occasions whether the alleged trade secret was confidential information, and Chemetall assured ZR that it was not. However, despite these assurances, the court found that ZR *should have known* that it was acquiring trade secrets when it hired one of Chemetall's former employees. The court also decided that ZR's actions were more akin to recklessness than deliberate misappropriation.

The court held that Chemetall's disputed process was not a trade secret in many respects and therefore denied fees, as injunctive relief constituted a sufficient deterrent. The decision also affirmed the right of a business to enforce existing employee confidentiality agreements when acquiring all or part of another company, since Chemetall had acquired a specialty metals division of Morton International and sought to prevent a former Morton employee from using the trade secrets when he joined ZR.

If, however, the secret is acquired by proper means, then there is no violation. For example, if the secret is disclosed in a patent, then there cannot be liability for misappropriation of a trade secret because the invention has been disclosed to the public. Similarly, obtaining a trade secret from a publication of the secret, disclosure to the public (even accidental disclosure) or reverse engineering is not misappropriation.

Generally speaking, the available remedies for misappropriation of a trade secret may include actual damages, punitive damages, and, in some cases, attorneys' fees. Injunctive relief may also be available—to prevent either the competitor or the former employee from using or disclosing the protected trade secret. The available remedies are discussed in more detail in later chapters.

SUMMARY OF TRADE SECRET LAW

Trade secret law allows a company or individual to protect confidential information from unauthorized disclosure or use. In contrast to patents, trade secrets exist only until they are disclosed to the public. A trade secret relies on private security measures such as nondisclosure agreements and restricted access to preserve the status of the valuable information as a trade secret. The law only becomes involved after there has been a misappropriation of that information, generally through theft or breach of a confidentiality agreement. Defendants can be held liable for uses or disclosures of the information, particularly where their use is in direct competition with the trade secret owner's products or services and places the continuing existence of the owner's products or services in jeopardy.

ENDNOTES

[1] *See Kellogg Co. v. Nat'l Biscuit Co.*, 305 U.S. 111 (1938) (finding that "Shredded Wheat" was a purely generic term for the cereal and thus could not afford its owner an exclusive right to use the name).

[2] 15 U.S.C. § 1051 et seq.

[3] *See* Lanham Act § 45.

[4] *Id.*

[5] *Id.*

[6] *See id.* § 14(5)(D) (providing for the cancellation of any certification mark abused in this way).

[7] *Id.* § 14(5)(D), (A).

[8] *Id.* § 45.

[9] *See also Opticians Assoc. v. Independent Opticians, Inc.*, 920 F.2d 187 (3d Cir. 1990).

[10] *Id.; see also Lawyers Title Ins. Co. v. Lawyers Title Ins. Corp.*, 109 F.2d 35 (D.C. Cir. 1939), *cert. denied*, 309 U.S. 684 (1940) (noting that both confusion of the public and injury to the public generally will be found where a trade name is used by a second company).

[11] *See In re Amex Holding Corp.*, 163 U.S.P.Q. 558 (TTAB 1969); *Communications Satellite Corp. v. Comcet, Inc.*, 429 F.2d 1245 (4th Cir. 1970), *cert. denied*, 400 U.S. 942 (1971).

[12] *Id.* It should also be noted that the Lanham Act does provide protection to foreign nationals for trade names "without the obligation of filing or registration *whether or not they form parts of marks.*" Lanham Act § 44(g) (emphasis added). This chapter deals primarily with domestic filings, but the reader should be aware that there are separate provisions for foreign applicants. *See* Lanham Act § 44.

[13] Lanham Act § 7(b).

[14] *Id.* § 7(c).

[15] *Id.* § 15.

[16] *Id.* § 33(b).

[17] *Id.; see also id.* § 14 (flaws in certification process).

[18] *Id.* §§ 33(b), 32.

[19] *Id.* § 14(3).

[20] *Union Nat'l Bank of Texas, Laredo v. Union Nat'l Bank of Texas*, 909 F.2d 839 (5th Cir. 1990).

[21] *See* J. Thomas McCarthy, Trademarks and Unfair Competition §§ 11.24, 11.72 (providing examples of marks found descriptive and marks held suggestive).

[22] *See id.*

[23] *Genesee Brewing Co., Inc. v. Stroh Brewing Co.*, 124 F.3d 137 (2d Cir. 1997).

[24] *Ty, Inc. v. The Jones Group, Inc.*, No. 99 C 2057, 2001 WL 1414232 (N.D. Ill. Nov. 9, 2001).

[25] *Car-Freshner Corp. v. S.C. Johnson & Son, Inc.*, 70 F.3d 267 (2d Cir. 1995).

[26] *Taylor Wine Co., Inc. v. Bully Hill Vineyards, Inc.*, 569 F.2d 731 (2d Cir. 1978).

[27] *Qualitex Co. v. Jacobson Prods Co., Inc.*, 514 U.S. 159 (1995).

[28] *Two Pesos, Inc. v. Taco Cabana, Inc.*, 505 U.S. 763 (1992).

[29] *Wall Street Journal*, p. B8, col. 1, Jan. 14, 1993.

[30] *Wal-Mart Stores, Inc. v. Samara Bros., Inc.*, 529 U.S. 205 (2000).

[31] *Id.* Note that "tertium quid" simply means "a third something."

[32] *Manhattan Industries, Inc. v. Sweater Bee by Banff, Ltd.*, 627 F.2d 628 (2d Cir. 1980). The sudden interest in the mark was due to the fact that the previous mark owner had formally abandoned the mark on May 7 of the same year. *Id.*

[33] *See* Lanham Act § 33 ("Any registration issued . . . and owned by a party to an action shall be admissible in evidence and shall be prima facie evidence of the validity of the registered mark and of the registration of the mark, of the registrant's ownership of the mark, and of the registrant's *exclusive right* to use the mark in commerce . . .").

[34] *See* Lanham Act § 45.

[35] *See* Lanham Act § 33.

[36] *See In re Sanger Telecasters, Inc.*, 1 U.S.P.Q. 2d 1589 (TTAB 1986) (finding that extensive advertising does not constitute "use" for purposes of registration where the actual services had not yet been rendered).

[37] *See* Lanham Act § 1(b)–(d).

[38] *Id.* § 1(b)(1).

[39] *Id.* § 1(d)(2).

[40] *See Warnervision Entertainment, Inc. v. Empire of Carolina, Inc.*, 101 F.3d 259 (2d Cir. 1996) (refusing to enjoin ITU applicant's use of a mark despite subsequent use by third party). Constructive use can also be obtained by a foreign filing for registration under certain circumstances. *See* Lanham Act § 44(d).

[41] Lanham Act § 32(1)(a).

[42] *See Smith Fiberglass Prods., Inc. v. Ameron, Inc.*, 7 F.3d 1327 (7th Cir. 1993); *Dr. Seuss Enters. v. Penguin Books USA, Inc.*, 109 F.3d 1394, 1404 (9th Cir. 1997); *Dreamwerks Prod. Group v. SKG Studio*, 142 F.3d 1127 (9th Cir. 1998).

[43] *Libman Co. v. Vining Indus., Inc.*, 69 F.3d 1360 (1995), *cert. denied*, 116 S. Ct. 1878 (1996) (comparing two brooms to determine whether the similar contrast-coloring of the bristles infringed a trademark).

[44] *Ferrari S.P.A. Esercizio v. Roberts*, 944 F.2d 1235 (6th Cir. 1991), *cert. denied*, 112 S. Ct. 3028 (1992).

[45] *Eli Lilly & Co. v. Natural Answers, Inc.*, No. IP 99-1600-CH/G, 2000 U.S. Dist. LEXIS 1930 (S.D. Ind. Jan. 20, 2000) (list of factors not intended to be a mechanical checklist, "myriad of variables" must be considered); *Dorr-Oliver, Inc. v. Fluid-Quip, Inc.*, 94 F.3d 376 (7th Cir. 1996).

[46] *G. Heileman Brewing Co., Inc. v. Anheuser-Busch, Inc.*, 873 F.2d 985 (7th Cir. 1989).

[47] *See* Lanham Act § 33(b)(1)–(9) (listing potential defenses to infringement, even of incontestable marks).

[48] *Id.* § 45.

[49] *Id.*

[50] *Id.*

[51] *Id.* § 33(b)(7).

[52] *Id.* § 33(b)(4).

[53] *Id.*

[54] *See, e.g., New Kids on the Block v. News America Publ., Inc.*, 971 F.2d 302 (9th Cir. 1992); *Playboy Enterprises, Inc. v. Netscape Communications Corp.*, 5 F. Supp.2d 1070 (C.D. Cal. 1999).

[55] Lanham Act § 43(a)(1)(A).

[56] *See Wal-Mart Stores, Inc. v. Samara Bros., Inc.*, 529 U.S. 205 (2000) (recognizing that section 43(a) is the appropriate framework for owners of unregistered trademarks to seek damages or injunctive relief).

[57] *See* Jean Wegman Burns, *Confused Jurisprudence: False Advertising Under the Lanham Act*, 79 B.U. L. Rev. 807, 808 (1999).

[58] Lanham Act § 43(a)(1)(B).

[59] *Johnson & Johnson v. Carter-Wallace, Inc.*, 631 F.2d 186 (2d Cir. 1980) (finding plaintiff's case supported by the "logical causal connection" between the ads and plaintiff's sales, the testimony of a consumer witness, and surveys regarding people's reaction to the ads); *see also Ortho Pharmaceutical Corp. v. Cosprophar, Inc.*, 32 F.3d 690 (2d Cir. 1994).

[60] *Johnson & Johnson * Merck Consumer Pharmaceuticals Co. v. Smithkline Beecham Corp.*, 960 F.2d 294 (2d Cir. 1992).

[61] *U-Haul Int'l, Inc. v. Jartran, Inc.*, 793 F.2d 1034 (9th Cir. 1986).

[62] *Avis Rent A Car System, Inc. v. Hertz Corp.*, 782 F.2d 381 (2d Cir. 1986).

[63] Lanham Act § 43(a)(1).

[64] *Johnson & Johnson*, 631 F.2d 186 (actual loss is not a prerequisite to § 43(a) injunctive relief).

[65] *Ortho Pharmaceutical Corp. v. Cosprophar, Inc.*, 32 F.3d 690 (2d Cir.) (requiring a more substantial showing of injury and causation where plaintiff's products were not in direct competition with defendant's products and the advertisements in question did not draw direct comparisons between the two); *Johnson & Johnson*, 631 F.2d 186.

[66] *See Johnson & Johnson, supra.*

[67] *See Ortho Pharm. Corp., supra.*

[68] *Brookfield Communications, Inc. v. West Coast Entertainment Corp.*, 174 F.3d 1036 (9th Cir. 1999).

[69] *Id.*; *Paccar, Inc. v. Telescan Techn., L.L.C.*, 115 F. Supp.2d 772 (E.D. Mich. 2000); *Nitron Corp. v. Radiation Monitoring Devices, Inc.*, 27 F. Supp.2d 102 (D. Mass. 1998); *but see Bigstar Entertainment, Inc. v. Next Big Star, Inc.*, 105 F. Supp.2d 185 (S.D.N.Y. 2000) (declining to apply initial interest confusion in an Internet context for seven reasons, including that the dispute did not involve competitors or metatag misuse); *The Network Network v. CBS, Inc.*, No. CV 98-1349 NM, 2000 U.S. Dist. LEXIS 4751 (C.D. Cal. Jan. 16, 2000) (distinguishing initial interest confusion from the instant case).

[70] *Brookfield Communications, Inc. v. West Coast Entertainment Corp.*, 174 F.3d 1036 (9th Cir. 1999).

[71] *See Trans Union LLC v. Credit Research, Inc.*, 142 F. Supp.2d 1029 (N.D. Ill. 2001).

[72] *J.K. Harris v. Kassell*, No. 02-0400 (N.D. Cal. March 2002).

[73] *Bihari v. Gross*, 119 F. Supp.2d 309 (S.D.N.Y. 2000); *Trans Union LLC v. Credit Research, Inc.*, 142 F. Supp.2d 1029 (N.D. Ill. 2001); *but see Eli Lilly & Co. v. Natural Answers, Inc.*, No. IP-99-160-CH/G, 2000 U.S. Dist. LEXIS 1930 (S.D. Ind Jan. 20, 2000) (noting that it is difficult to see how manipulative metatag use of a mark could ever be a fair use, except in "unusual situations").

[74] *Playboy Enterprises, Inc. v. Welles*, 7 F. Supp.2d 1098 (S.D. Cal. 1998); *Playboy Enterprises, Inc. v. Terri Welles, Inc.*, No. 98-CV-0413-K, 1999 U.S. Dist. LEXIS 21047 (S.D. Cal. Dec. 1, 1999).

[75] *SNA, Inc. v. Array*, 51 F. Supp.2d 554 (E.D. Penn. 1999).

[76] *Playboy Enterprises, Inc. v. Terri Welles, Inc.*, No. 98-CV-0413-K, 1999 U.S. Dist. LEXIS 21047 (S.D. Cal. Dec. 1, 1999).

[77] There are some other, more subtle distinctions between the two schemes that are not discussed here.

[78] 15 U.S.C. § 1125(d)(1)(B)(ii).

[79] *Virtual Works, Inc. v. Volkswagen of America, Inc.*, CV 99-1289-A, 2001 U.S. App. LEXIS 831 (4th Cir. Jan. 22, 2001).

[80] *Broadcom Corp. v. Becker*, Claim No. FA0108000098819, Oct. 22, 2001 (Hill, Arb.), *available at www.arbitration-forum.com/domains/decisions/98819.htm.*

[81] *Hewlett-Packard Co. v. Rayne*, Claim No. FA0110000101465, Dec. 17, 2001 (Johnson, Arb.), *available at www.arbitration-forum.com/domains/decisions/101465.htm.*

[82] *PRIMEDIA Magazine Finance, Inc. v. Manzo*, No. D2001-1258, Dec. 13, 2001 (Thompson, Arb.), *available at: http://arbiter.wipo.int/domains/decisions/html/2001/ d2001-1258.html.*

[83] *Playboy Enterprises Int'l, Inc. v. Tonya Flynt Found.*, Case No. D2001-1002, Nov. 16, 2001 (Foster, Arb.), *available at http://arbiter.wipo.int/domains/decisions/html/2001/ d2001-1002.html.*

[84] *Trump v. olegevtushenko*, Claim No. FA0110000101509, Dec. 11. 2001 (Carmody, Arb.), *available at www.arbforum.com/domains/decisions/101509.html.*

[85] 15 U.S.C. § 1125(c) (1995).

[86] *Mead Data Central, Inc. v. Toyota Motor Sales, U.S.A. Inc.*, 875 F.2d 1026 (2d Cir. 1989).

[87] *Ford Motor Co. v. Lapertosa*, 2001 U.S. Dist. LEXIS 253 (E.D. Mich. January 3, 2001).

[88] *Panavision Int'l, L.P. v. Toeppen*, 1998 WL 178553 (9th Cir. 1998).

[89] Lanham Act § 43(c)(1).

[90] *TCPIP Holding Co. v. Haar Comm, Inc.*, 244 F.3d 88 (2d Cir. 2001).

[91] *Advantage Rent-A-Car, Inc. v. Enterprise Rent-A-Car Co.*, 238 F.3d 378 (5th Cir. 2001); *Syndicate Sales Inv. v. Hampshire Paper Corp.*, 192 F.3d 464 (7th Cir. 1999).

[92] *Hartog & Co. AS v. Swix.com*, 136 F. Supp.2d 531 (E.D. Va. 2001).

[93] *See, e.g., Ringling Bros.-Barnum & Bailey Combined Shows Inc. v. Utah Div. of Travel Development*, 170 F.3d 449 (4th Cir. 1999); *Westchester Media Co. v. PRL USA Holdings Inc.*, 214 F.3d 658 (5th Cir. 2000).

[94] *Nabisco Inc. v. PF Brands Inc.*, 191 F.3d 208 (2d Cir. 1999); *Times Mirror Magazines, Inc. v. Las Vegas Sports News, L.L.C.*, 212 F.3d 157 (3d Cir. 2000), *cert. denied*, 69 U.S.L.W. 3259 (2001); *Eli Lilly & Co. v. Natural Answers, Inc.*, 2000 WL 1735075 (7th Cir. 2000); *Luigino's, Inc. v. Stouffer Corp.*, 170 F.3d 827 (8th Cir. 1999); *Panavision Int'l, L.P. v. Toeppen*, 141 F.3d 1316 (9th Cir. 1998).

[95] *See* 15 U.S.C. § 1125(c)(4).

[96] *New Kids on the Block v. News America Publ., Inc.*, 971 F.2d 302 (9th Cir. 1992).

[97] *Hormel Foods Corp. v. Jim Henson Prods., Inc.*, 73 F.3d 497 (2d Cir. 1996).

[98] *Ford Motor Co. v. 2600 Enterprises*, 177 F. Supp.2d 661 (E.D. Mich. 2001).

[99] *A&H Sportwear, Inc. v. Victoria's Secret Stores, Inc.*, 237 F.3d 198, 228 (3d Cir. 2000); *Fisons Horticulture, Inc. v. Vigoro Indus., Inc.*, 30 F.3d 466, 475 (3d Cir.1994); *Ameritech, Inc. v. American Info. Techs. Corp.*, 811 F.2d 960, 964 (6th Cir. 1987).

[100] *A&H Sportwear, Inc. v. Victoria's Secret Stores, Inc.*, No. 94-cv-7408 (E.D. Pa. Jan. 9, 2002), *available at www.paed.uscourts.gov/documents/opinions/02D0027P.htm*.

[101] Uniform Trade Secrets Act, 14 U.L.A. 437 (1990) (hereinafter UTSA).

[102] *See* William G. Porter II and Michael C. Griffaton, *Identifying and Protecting Employers' Interests in Trade Secrets and Proprietary Information*, 68 Def. Couns. J. 439, 439 (2001); Linda K. Stevens, *Trade Secrets and Inevitable Disclosure*, 36 Tort & Insur. L. J. 917, 918 (2001).

[103] *See generally* Restatement of Torts §§ 757–59 (1939).

[104] *See generally* Restatement (Third) of Unfair Competition §§ 39–45 (1995).

[105] *See* 2 Rudolph Callman, The Law of Unfair Competition, Trademarks and Monopolies, § 14.06, 14-35 (4th ed. 1992); James Chapman, *California Uniform Trade Secrets Act: A Comparative Analysis of the Act and the Common Law*, 2 Computer High Tech. L.J. 389, 392 (1986) (stating trade secrets are "extraordinarily difficult to define").

[106] *Lear Siegler Inc. v. Ark-Ell Springs, Inc.*, 569 F.2d 286, 288 (5th Cir. 1978).

[107] UTSA § 1(4).

[108] Restatement of Torts § 757, cmt. b (1939).

[109] *See id.*

[110] Restatement (Third) of Unfair Competition § 39 (1995).

[111] *See id.* § 39 cmt. e; *see also* Stevens, *supra* at 919; Porter and Griffaton, *supra* at 440.

[112] *Optic Graphics Inc. v. Agee*, 591 A.2d 578, 585 (Md. App. 1991); *see also Minuteman, Inc. v. Alexander*, 434 N.W.2d 773 (1989).

[113] *See Primo Enter. v. Bachner*, 539 N.Y.S.2d 320, 321 (N.Y. App. Div. 1989); *see also Surgidev Corp. v. Eye Tech. Inc.*, 648 F. Supp. 661, 682 (D. Minn. 1986).

[114] *See Amoco Prod. Co. v. Laird*, 622 N.E.2d 912, 196 (Ind. 1993).

[115] *Kewanee Oil Co. v. Bicron Corp.*, 415 U.S. 470, 476 (1974); *Banito Boats, Inc. v. Thunder Craft Boats, Inc.*, 489 U.S. 141, 155 (1989).

[116] UTSA § 1(1) & § 1 cmt.

[117] *See, e.g., Hamer Holding Group, Inc. v. Elmore*, 560 N.E.2d 907, 918 (Ill. Ct. App. 1990). ("Conversely, information which can be duplicated only by an expensive and time-consuming method of reverse-engineering, for instance, could be secret, and the ability to duplicate it would not constitute a defense.")

[118] UTSA § 1 cmt.

[119] *See* Stevens, *supra* at 920 and n.17 (citing various cases requiring certain "reasonable" steps to protect trade secrets); *see also* Gary E. Weiss, *Biting the Hand That Stops Feeding: How to Protect Trade Secrets from Misappropriation by Laid Off Employees*, 661 Prac. L. Inst./Lit. 469, 487–89 (2001).

[120] *See, e.g.,* The Trade Secret Handbook: Protecting Your Franchise System's Competitive Advantage 23, American Bar Association, Michael J. Lockerby, ed., Chicago, IL: 2000.

[121] *See id.*

[122] *Flotec, Inc. v. Southern Research, Inc.*, 16 F. Supp.2d 992, 999–1000 (S.D. Ind. 1998).

[123] *See, e.g., Public Sys. Inc. v. Towry*, 587 So.2d 969, 972 (Ala. 1991).

[124] *See* Restatement of Torts § 757 (1939).

[125] *See Kewanee Oil*, 416 U.S. at 476.

[126] *See, e.g., Motorola Inc. v. Fairchild Camera & Instruments. Corp.*, 366 F. Supp. 1173 (D. Ariz. 1973) (rejecting trade secret protection where company failed to take rudimentary steps to secure what it claimed to be a trade secret); *Gordon Employ., Inc. v. Jewell*, 356 N.W.2d 738 (Minn. Ct. App. 1984) (rejecting trade secret protection to unsecured client lists, where there was no secrecy program and no discussion with employees not to disclose).

[127] *See generally* Porter II and Griffaton, *supra* at 443.

[128] *See generally* Stevens, *supra* at 923 (discussing difference between trade secret and confidential information); *see also* Robert Unikel, *Bridging the "Trade Secret" Gap: Protecting "Confidential Information" Not Rising to the Level of Trade Secrets*, 29 Loy. U. Chi. L. J. 841, 860–62 (1998).

[129] *Digital Dev. Corp. v. International Memory Sys.*, 185 U.S.P.Q. 136, 141 (S.D. Cal. 1973).

[130] For a more thorough discussion of the "inevitable disclosure doctrine," *see generally* Porter II and Griffaton, *supra* at 444–45 (stating at least 20 states recognize doctrine, which restricts former employees' post-employment activities when the employees will inevitably disclose the former employer's trade secrets in their new position, by nature of

the new employment); *see also PepsiCo v. Redmond*, 54 F.3d 1262, 1271 (7th Cir. 1995). ("PepsiCo finds itself in the position of a coach, one of whose players has just left, playbook in hand, to join the opposing team before the big game").

[131] *PepsiCo., Inc. v. Redmond*, 54 F.3d 1262 (7th Cir. 1995).

[132] *Chemetall GMBH v. ZR Energy, Inc.,* 2002 U.S. Dist LEXIS 158 (N.D. Ill. Jan. 8, 2002).

ADDITIONAL READING

Trademark Reading

A Practical Guide to Monetary Relief in Trademark Infringement Cases, 85 Trademark Reporter 263 (May–June 1995).

Remedies, 85 Trademark Reporter 263 (May–June 1995).

Roger D. Blair and Thomas F. Cotter, *An Economic Analysis of Damages Rules in Intellectual Property Law*, 39 William and Mary Law Review 1585 (May 1998).

Sheri A. Byrne, *Nintendo of America, Inc. v. Dragon Pacific International: Double Trouble—When Do Awards of Both Copyright and Trademark Damages Constitute Double Recovery?* 31 University of San Francisco Law Review 257 (Fall 1996).

Stephen L. Carter, *The Trouble with Trademark*, 99 Yale Law Journal 759 (January 1990).

Dennis S. Corgill, *Measuring the Gains of Trademark Infringement*, 65 Fordham Law Review 1909 (April 1997).

Robert C. Denicola, *Some Thoughts on the Dynamics of Federal Trademark Legislation and the Trademark Dilution Act of 1995*, 59 Law and Contemporary Problems 75 (1996).

Terrell W. Mills, *METATAGS: Seeking to Evade User Detection and the Lanham Act*, 6 Richmond Journal of Law and Technology 22 (Spring 2000).

Rachel Jane Posner, *Manipulative Metatagging, Search Engine Baiting, and Initial Interest Confusion*, 33 Columbia Journal of Law and Social Problems 439 (Summer 2000).

Keith M. Stolte, *Remedying Judicial Limitations on Trademark Remedies: An Accounting of Profits Should Not Require a Finding of Bad Faith*, 87 Trademark Reporter 271 (1997).

Trade Secret Reading

Annotation: Use of Idea or Invention—Remedies, 170 ALR 449 (1947).

American Law Institute, Restatement of Torts, Miscellaneous Trade Practices §§ 757, 758 (1939).

Uniform Trade Secrets Act § 2, 1990 Comments.

Uniform Trade Secrets Act § 3, 1990 Comments.

Restatement (Third) of Unfair Competition §§ 44, 45 (1993).

Jonathan Bloom, et al., *Seventh Circuit Affirms Jury Award in Trade Secret Case*, 4 Journal of Proprietary Rights 31 (April 1994).

David D. Friedman, et al., *Some Economics of Trade Secret Law*, 5 Journal of Economic Perspectives 61 (Winter 1991).

Wayne A. Hoeberlein, *Trade Secrets: Damages*, 340 Practicing Law Institute 599 (1992).

Craig N. Johnson, *Assessing Damages for Misappropriation of Trade Secrets*, 27 Colorado Lawyer 71 (August 1998).

Christopher S. Marchese, *Patent Infringement and Future Lost Profits Damages*, 26 Arizona State Law Journal 747 (Fall 1994).

Patricia A. Meier, *Looking Back and Forth: The Restatement (Third) of Unfair Competition and Potential Impact on Texas Trade Secret Law*, 4 Texas Intellectual Property Law Journal 415 (Spring 1996).

Roger M. Milgrim, Milgrim on Trade Secrets § 1.02 (1967).

Roger M. Milgrim, Milgrim on Trade Secrets § 15.02[1][d] (1967).

Gale R. Peterson, *Recent Developments in Trade Secret Law in an Information Age*, 507 Practicing Law Institute 351 (February 1998).

Felix Prandl, *Damages for Misappropriation of Trade Secret*, 22 Tort & Insurance Law Journal 447 (Spring 1987).

Michael A. Rosenhouse, *Proper Measure and Elements of Damages for Misappropriation of Trade Secret*, 11 ALR 4th 12 (1982).

Ferdinand S. Tinio, *Propriety of Permanently Enjoining One Guilty of Unauthorized Use of Trade Secret From Engaging in Sale or Manufacture of Device in Question*, 38 ALR 3d 572 (1971).

Stephen I. Willis, *An Economic Evaluation of Trade Secrets*, 269 Practicing Law Institute 737 (1989).

Donald M. Zupanec, *Annotation: Disclosure of Trade Secret*, 92 ALR 3d 138 § 2[b] (1979).

12

Misuse of Copyrights, Trademarks, and Trade Secrets

Like patent owners, the owners of copyrights and trademarks can forfeit their rights where the alleged infringer successfully establishes that the owner has misused his or her intellectual property (IP) rights, particularly in ways that mimic violations of antitrust law. We have already discussed this defense as it applies to patent infringement (see Chapter 9). However, the misuse defense applies slightly differently to copyrights and trademarks. In part, the distinctions between patent misuse and misuse of copyrights or trademarks exist because the latter types of IP offer a lesser degree of exclusivity than patents. Patent rights are limited only by time, not by the popularity of the underlying work or possible defenses such as independent creation. During the term of a patent, the owner has a nearly complete monopoly on the patented work. Additionally, the enforcement process differs from proving patent infringement. These differences have made some courts leery of extending the misuse defense beyond the patent context. In fact, although copyright misuse appears to be gaining credibility as a defense, the misuse argument is far from accepted as a defense to trademark infringement.[1]

Accordingly, this chapter discusses the misuse defense separately in the context of each area. Readers should keep in mind that this area of law is not settled and probably will evolve further as the courts find increasing occasion to apply the defense.

COPYRIGHT MISUSE

The defense of copyright misuse was first accepted by a U.S. court in 1948. The federal district court in Minnesota found that a copyright owner's blanket licensing practices (requiring would-be users of the copyrighted work to purchase a license covering every work owned by the owner, instead of simply a license for the desired work) were an impermissible use of the owner's copyright, creating a monopoly beyond the intended scope of copyright protection. Accordingly, the court refused to enforce the copyright against the alleged infringers, holding that "[o]ne who unlawfully exceeds his copyright monopoly and violates the anti-trust laws is not outside the pale of the law, but where the Court's aid is requested, . . . and the granting thereof would tend to serve the plaintiffs in their plan . . . to extend their copyrights in a monopolistic control beyond their proper scope, it should be denied."[2] It would be another 42 years before a court applied the copyright misuse doctrine again to bar an infringement action.[3]

During those 42 years, the Supreme Court did hear antitrust cases dealing with copyright misuse such as tying arrangements, but it did not deal with the defense directly. The Supreme Court has affirmed injunctions prohibiting a party from conditioning one license upon the purchase of additional licenses, but it has yet to go beyond enjoining the offending practice. The language of the Court's decisions is rooted in classic analysis of tying arrangements under antitrust law, not copyright infringement. In other words, the Court has yet to find a copyright unenforceable or require mandatory licensing based on the owner's misuse of the copyright.[4]

Since the Supreme Court has not yet provided controlling guidance on the judicial response to copyright misuse, the primary case for understanding the current judicial treatment of copyright misuse is probably *Lasercomb America, Inc. v. Reynolds.*[5]

Lasercomb America, Inc. v. Reynolds

Lasercomb addressed the impact of certain clauses in the copyright owner's licensing agreement that precluded licensees of the protected work (computer-assisted die-making software) from competing with the copyright owner. These extremely broad noncompetition clauses prevented any licensee, its directors, and employees from directly or indirectly writing, developing, producing, or selling competing software for 99 years. However, the defendant in the case had refused to sign the licensing agreement. Accordingly, although the Court found that the defendant had intentionally infringed the copyright, the Court had to consider whether the misuse defense would apply even where the defendant had not itself been affected by the alleged misuse.

The Court examined whether the copyright owner was using its copyright in a manner *contrary to the public policies* that justify granting a copyright in the first place. The alleged misuse does not need to constitute an antitrust violation in order to provide the defendant with a viable defense. Theoretically, copyrights are issued to promote and reward new expressions of ideas; the broad restrictions in plaintiff's licenses operated to restrict and stifle any new expressions related to the subject matter of the copyrighted work. This function directly violated the public policies behind copyright protection, and therefore constituted copyright misuse, even though the defendant had not personally been harmed by the misuse.

Subsequent cases have held that even less explicit restrictions on licensees may constitute copyright misuse. For example, the Fourth Circuit determined that a clause requiring licensees to use their "best efforts" to promote the copyright owner's work implicitly prohibited independent development of a competing product, and thus created a misuse defense.[6] Moreover, using copyright licenses to indirectly gain control over a noncopyrighted element of the product or service also has been found to be a misuse of copyright, regardless of whether the conduct rises to the level of an illegal tying arrangement under antitrust law.

Alcatel USA, Inc. v. DGI Technologies[7]

In *Alcatel*, DGI Technologies wanted to develop software that would operate on telephone switches protected by the plaintiff's copyright. The software, contained in microprocessor cards, did not infringe any copyright. However, the copyright owner effectively prohibited all licensees from testing microprocessor cards other than those purchased from the copyright owner. The Fifth Circuit held that by prohibiting that type of conduct, the owner effectively gained a commercial advantage over noncopyrighted products. This type of unauthorized (albeit limited) monopoly formed the basis for a misuse defense.

It should be noted that many other courts that have considered this issue have found that similar unilateral refusals to license certain technology or products are *not* misuse.[8]

Although an antitrust violation is not necessary for a successful copyright misuse defense, if the defendant cannot establish an antitrust violation, he or she must prove some other illegal extension of the copyright monopoly or other violation of public policy.[9] For example, misrepresentations by a copyright owner as to the scope of his or her rights may create a misuse defense. In *qad., Inc. v. ALN Assoc., Inc.*, the court agreed with the defendant's argument that the owner's failure to disclose in its copyright registrations that its software was a derivative work was a misuse of copyright.[10] The owner had been engaged in litigation with the defendant for years, asserting that the software was a completely original work. Accordingly, the court declined to enforce the copyright on the basis of the owner's improper use of legal proceedings to protect an illegitimate extension of the copyright. Similarly, a plaintiff's attempt to enforce copyrights that he or she acquired through registering works that were copied from others constitutes copyright misuse.[11] Essentially, it appears that fraud by the copyright owner in acquiring or enforcing the copyright can raise a misuse defense to any infringement action.

Several courts have recognized copyright misuse as a potential defense, even though they refrained from applying it in the particular cases at hand. These decisions at least indicate that the defense might find a receptive judiciary in those jurisdictions, given appropriate facts.[12]

Some courts have been more reluctant than others to bar infringement actions based on copyright misuse. Some courts may be waiting for explicit approval of the doctrine from the Supreme Court before they will apply it in their jurisdictions.[13] Other courts have taken a narrow view of the copyright misuse defense, finding that an antitrust violation is required to establish misuse. For example, the rationale of the Seventh Circuit's approach surfaces in many courts' interpretations of the standards applicable to establishing the defense. In *Saturday Evening Post Co. v. Rumbleseat Press, Inc.,* the Court found it too difficult to examine misuse claims without incorporating conventional antitrust principles, stating "[o]ur law is not rich in alternative concepts of monopolistic abuse; and it is rather late in the day to try to develop one without in the process subjecting the rights of patent holders to debilitating uncertainty."[14] In the context of copyright misuse, the Seventh Circuit found that the need for using established antitrust principles was even more pronounced, given that substantial market power is rarely inherent in a copyright. The threat of holding copyright owners to an uncertain and possibly shifting standard has motivated a number of courts to require an antitrust violation as evidence of copyright misuse.[15]

Even if the court does not require the defendant to establish a violation of antitrust laws, the principles that govern antitrust analysis likely will impact judicial discussions of copyright misuse. One way that antitrust jurisprudence shows up in copyright misuse cases is the analysis of the copyright owner's market power. Clearly, market power will be an issue if a court relies on patent misuse principles in analyzing tying allegations as a defense to copyright infringement. However, some commentators claim that the copyright owner's market power should be a relevant consideration in every case, even where the misuse allegations are not based on an antitrust violation. The theoretical justification for examining the copyright owner's market power in the latter category of cases is that where the copyright owner is unable to coerce third parties through exercise of the copyright, there is a decreased likelihood of significant harm and a greater likelihood that the alleged misconduct has some economic or social benefits.[16] Arguably, the presence or absence of market power often distinguishes coercive behavior from allegedly offending contractual terms that are the product of consensual conduct, and therefore less troubling to the courts.[17]

However, market power appears to be less closely tied to copyright ownership than it is to patent ownership. As discussed at the outset of this chapter, patents generally are thought to grant broader rights of exclusivity than copyrights or trademarks. A patent awards the patent owner monopoly power over a particular product or process that is limited only by the term of the patent. Being in essence a legal monopoly, a patent thus can be seen as granting potential market power through its right to exclude others. Since the legal monopoly awarded to copyright owners is not as sweeping as the scope of a patent, a copyright seldom confers market power on its owner.

In re: Napster, Inc. Copyright Litigation[18]

In the much-publicized litigation concerning Napster's music file-sharing service, Napster asserted copyright misuse as a defense to the infringement action. Napster's ability to get licenses for the music on its computer system was restricted by its exclusive contract with plaintiff MusicNet. MusicNet's conditions included requiring Napster to go through MusicNet for all licenses, even licenses to third-party works that were not held by MusicNet. Additionally, there were extensive financial penalties if Napster failed to use MusicNet as its exclusive licensor for content. This resulted in a de facto expansion of MusicNet's copyrights to cover the music catalogs of the other plaintiffs.

The court noted that copyright misuse, if proven, prevented plaintiff from enforcing its rights; misuse does not simply limit the period during which damages are available. Moreover the court rejected the argument that Napster's own unclean hands should bar the defense, as the focus of the misuse doctrine is preventing copyright owners from thwarting the public policies behind copyright law, not the protection of individual defendants. Similarly, the court found it irrelevant to the misuse claim that Napster had voluntarily signed the contract with MusicNet. Accordingly, the court denied summary judgment for MusicNet on the misuse claim and ordered further discovery into the facts of the misuse.

Legally, there is no recognized presumption of market power for copyrights, trademarks, *or* patents. The Federal Trade Commission and the Department of Justice take the position that IP rights do not create a presumption of market power in the antitrust context.[19] Despite the potential rights of exclusivity conferred by IP, the agencies explain that "there will often be sufficient actual or potential close substitutes for such product, process, or work to prevent the exercise of market power."[20] In other words, the right to exclude others lacks significance in the context of market power if the exclusivity applies to a product market where consumers have several noninfringing alternatives available to them. It follows that no presumption of market power should exist where there is, in fact, no market power. At any rate, the government's position clearly is that market power is an issue to be proven, not assumed from the existence of a copyright or trademark.

DEFENSES TO COPYRIGHT MISUSE

Judicial reluctance to extend the misuse defense to copyright infringement may affect both the ultimate outcome of the litigation and the availability of interim relief such as preliminary injunctions. For example, in *Data Gen. Corp. v. Grumman Sys. Support Corp.,* the court opted to grant temporary relief to the copyright holder, despite the defendant's allegations of copyright misuse, because of uncertainty regarding the defense's viability.[21]

In addition to bearing the initial burden of convincing the court to accept misuse as a defense, the proponent of the theory must overcome several potential arguments that may be raised by the alleged misuser. For example, the party asserting misuse must not itself have "unclean hands." The "unclean hands" doctrine is legal shorthand for an equitable defense based on an opponent's misconduct. In the presence of unclean hands, a court may refuse to enforce certain rights because of the right holder's own misconduct. For example, a party asserting breach of contract against another party will have a difficult time obtaining full damages if he or she has also failed to meet contractual obligations. Generally, the unclean hands defense can be asserted only where: (1) the offending act of the other party has an immediate and necessary relation to the matter in controversy, and (2) the party asserting unclean hands has been personally injured by the other party's conduct.[22]

The misuse defense itself may be seen as an extension of the unclean hands doctrine, as it protects alleged infringers where the IP owner has abused his rights, thereby dirtying his hands and forfeiting judicial protection. However, the two defenses are distinct in that copyright misuse generally relies on an analysis of the misconduct's relationship to the public policy foundation of copyright law; the mere presence of some general misconduct does not in itself give rise to the misuse defense. Market power and antitrust principles are extraneous factors in most cases where unclean hands are raised as a defense.

Generally, if the court observes that both parties have unclean hands, it will not enforce an equitable defense against either party. However, several courts, including the Fourth Circuit in *Lasercomb* (discussed earlier in this chapter), have held that a copyright owner who abused the copyright is barred from enforcing that copyright under the misuse doctrine, *even where* the alleged infringer also has unclean hands. In other words, some courts allow equity to turn a blind eye to the "unworthiness" of the alleged infringer when the infringer asserts a misuse defense. The underlying justification for this judicial stance may be that the copyright owner has abused the legal system to a greater extent than the infringer by asking for judicial assistance in increasing the scope of IP rights already stretched beyond the intended legal limits.[23]

However, other jurisdictions have declined to recognize misuse as a defense to infringement of copyrights where the defendant infringer has its own unclean hands (beyond the fact of the alleged infringement itself). The following case exemplifies this judicial stance.

Atari Games Corp. v. Nintendo of America, Inc.[24]

In *Atari*, the alleged infringer lied to the Copyright Office to acquire a copy of its competitor's copyrighted program. When the competitor sued for copyright infringement, the alleged infringer asserted the misuse defense. However, the Federal

Atari Games Corp. v. Nintendo of America, Inc. (continued)

Circuit found that the alleged infringer could not prevail on the misuse defense because of its own misconduct (the fraud on the Copyright Office) and, hence, its unclean hands. The court emphasized that copyright misuse is not a defense established by statute, but "solely an equitable doctrine." Without the misuse defense in the picture, the copyright owner prevailed on its copyright infringement claim at summary judgment.[25]

In short, some courts must be satisfied not only with the evidence of misuse by the copyright owner, but also with the defendant's "worthiness" before they will apply the misuse defense.

Given the judicial reluctance to apply the copyright misuse defense, it is not surprising that misuse generally is limited to use as a defense, not an affirmative claim for relief. Most courts have not indicated an interest in recognizing copyright misuse as a basis for bringing suit or recovering damages.[26] Arguably, conduct causing harm unrelated to possible infringement litigation is more likely to rise to the level of an antitrust violation. In such a case, the antitrust laws, not equitable theories and the public policy surrounding the copyright misuse defense, offer superior potential for personal recovery from the overreaching copyright owner. However, a small number of courts have indeed allowed a party to prevail using copyright misuse as a claim for relief, rather than simply a defense for their own alleged infringement. This approach is similar to the usual judicial approach to patent misuse claims.[27] *Electronic Data Systems* provides an example of the minority view.

Electronic Data Systems Corp. v. Computer Assoc., Inc.[28]

In *Electronic Data Systems,* copyright misuse was raised as an affirmative claim by the licensee of certain software. The licensee alleged copyright misuse, using principles of antitrust law, and asked the court to award damages and a declaratory judgment that the licensor's copyright misuse rendered the copyrights themselves invalid. The licensee alleged restraints of competition, restrictions of the use of copyrighted software beyond the valid rights granted by copyright laws, and tying arrangements that linked purchases of copyrighted software to purchases of other products sold by the licensor. Although the licensor argued that copyright misuse did not give rise to a claim for affirmative relief such as damages and declaratory judgment, the court found that the misuse claim should be permitted to the extent that the licensee sought a declaration of noninfringement due to misuse, and held that the misuse allegations concerning software tying arrangements rose to the level of an antitrust violation under section 2 of the Sherman Act.

A final limit on the application and acceptance of the copyright misuse defense is the time elapsed following the alleged misuse by the copyright owner. The factual requirements of this argument are unsettled, but the gist of the argument is that misuse does not preclude all enforcement of copyrights postdating the misuse. In other words, there must be a limit on the period during which a copyright owner's rights are restricted by their misuse of the copyright.[29] After some period of "purging," a copyright owner, in essence, washes off the taint of misuse and regains full status as a copyright owner accorded certain rights of enforcement under the law.[30] Like the unclean hands argument, this position is rooted in equity and the need for a connection between the alleged misuse and the punishment of nonenforcement.

The patent misuse defense recognizes the same types of temporal restrictions on the life of a misuse defense. Accordingly, the factors that indicate that patent misuse has been "purged" probably also will influence a court evaluating the copyright misuse defense. For example, evidence that the copyright owner has abandoned the practice allegedly constituting copyright misuse and that the deleterious effects of the misuse have dissipated may be sufficient for a court to reject misuse as a defense to infringement. Ultimately, the extent to which a copyright owner's misuse is removed from the infringement at issue, and the effect of that distance on the misuse defense, will be a factual issue to be resolved at the court's discretion.[31]

TRADEMARK MISUSE

The doctrine of unclean hands plays an even more prominent role in the trademark misuse analysis than it does in copyright or patent misuse. In fact, unclean hands was the early basis for the trademark misuse defense, rather than the market analysis and examination of public policy that misuse involves in patent or copyright contexts.[32] As one court noted, "it is inappropriate to predicate trademark misuse upon the same anticompetitive practices which constitute patent misuse . . ." because a trademark use analysis examines the significance that a mark has to the public more than the anticompetitive practices of stifling original works or preempting matter that should be in the public domain.[33] One court expressed the judicial hesitance to recognize trademark misuse thusly:

> [A] trademark, unlike other intellectual property rights, does not confer a legal monopoly on any good or idea; it confers rights to a name only. Because a trademark merely enables the owner to bar others from the use of the mark, as distinguished from competitive manufacture and sale of identical goods bearing another mark, the opportunity for effective antitrust misuse of a trademark . . . is so limited that it poses a far less serious threat to the economic health of the nation [than patent misuse].[34]

Despite these distinctions between trademark rights and other IP rights, as early as the nineteenth century, courts refused to enforce trademarks where it appeared that the trademark owner had engaged in misconduct, despite the defendant's intentional infringement of the protected mark. In *Manhattan Medicine Co. v. Wood,*[35] the plaintiff manufactured medicine for jaundice and bottled it in distinctive glass containers with the name of the product (Atwood's Vegetable Physical Jaundice Bitters) and a notation that the product was made "by Moses Atwood, Georgetown, Massachusetts, and sold by his agents throughout the United States." The latter notation was false, although Mr. Atwood had *originally* created and marketed the medicine in Georgetown, Mass-achusetts. The defendants began to market a knockoff elixir that they sold in packaging nearly identical to Manhattan's glass bottles and labels. The Supreme Court found that the trademark owner (Manhattan) could not enjoin the defendants from selling the imi-tation medicine because of Manhattan's own misconduct in deceptively labeling the medicine. The Court held that the false label constituted a misrepresentation to the pub-lic and declined to assist the trademark owner in perpetuating that fraud.

The Court's concern was that the trademark laws exist to protect the public from fraud, and neither potential unfairness to this particular defendant nor the market im-plications of the trademark owner's actions entered into the analysis. This approach is consistent with the theoretical function of trademark laws (i.e., not to protect new and unique ideas or novel expressions of ideas, but instead to guard against public con-fusion). The protection of individual interests such as a trademark owner's possible investment in establishing goodwill affiliated with its mark is only a secondary concern. Although trademark rights preserve the trademark owners' incentives to invest in mar-keting, develop goodwill, and maintain quality control, these benefits are valued by the courts and the case law only to the extent that they serve the public's interest in improved knowledge regarding products and their source.

Similarly, the Lanham Act is not entirely clear on the role of a misuse defense in trademark infringement actions. Section 1115(b)(7) states that use of a mark to violate the antitrust laws is a defense to the incontestability of a mark.[36] However, it is unclear whether misuse affects only a trademark owner's ability to assert incontestability or whether it also might be a general defense to trademark infringement. It may be that trademark misuse constitutes a general defense when the misuse violates antitrust laws.[37] Consistent with that approach, some cases place a greater emphasis on antitrust principles than on equitable analysis.[38]

From the available case law, it appears that a trademark misuse defense is applicable where (1) the trademark owner's conduct severely compromises the significance of a mark; or (2) the trademark owner wrongfully seeks to exclude others from using generic words or functional features, and the possible effect of that exclusion would be a sub-stantial restriction of competition in a relevant product or service market.[39] Practices that frequently are argued to constitute trademark misuse involve franchise tying arrangements.[40] It is common practice for a franchise to require would-be franchisees to purchase not only a license for use of their mark but also recipes, supplies, building and training plans, and other goods from the franchiser. Although these arrangements probably are tying agreements, the franchisee still must establish that the franchise trademark has market power in a relevant economic market, and this can be difficult to demonstrate. Most franchises face strenuous competition from other franchises in the same market. For example, even McDonald's competes with Burger King and several other restaurants, which makes it hard to show that the McDonald's trademarks confer any significant degree of control over the relevant product market. In other words, requiring McDonald's franchisees to purchase their ground beef and chicken parts from the franchiser will not grant McDonald's the ability to dominate any relevant markets. Moreover, there are multiple significant procompetitive effects of the franchise tying arrangements that weigh against punishing the franchiser for trademark misuse. The franchiser has an interest in maintaining quality control over the products associated with its marks, and the public benefits from arrangements that allow the franchise to monitor and control the conduct of its franchisees.[41] Accordingly, although tying arrangements frequently are alleged to be the basis for trademark misuse, the misuse claim may not be successful in the face of an efficiency defense.[42]

Since the trademark laws exist to prevent confusion of the public, nonenforcement is not the preferred remedy for trademark misuse. Clearly, prohibiting trademark owners from enforcing their mark where they have misused their IP rights could undermine the very purpose for legal protection of those marks as it would allow infringing uses to continue unabated. Accordingly, the preferred remedy for trademark misuse is to restrict the trademark owner's ability to recover for the infringement or predicate injunctive relief on the cessation of the misuse by the trademark owner.[43] For example, the court might limit relief to damages, or the ability to terminate a particular license, rather than allowing the trademark owner to enjoin all unauthorized users of the protected mark.

Recent cases have indicated that trademark misuse might provide an affirmative claim where tying arrangements were the basis for the alleged misuse. As in antitrust cases, the claim revolves around the definition of the relevant market. This focus is clear in the cases dealing with allegations of franchise tying arrangements. Where the relevant market is defined as the market for a franchiser's trademarked goods (such as demand for a McDonald's franchise), the law favors the franchisees because the franchiser appears to have complete control in the relevant market. In contrast, defining the market as the demand for franchises in general, or even franchises simply in the same line of business (such as all burger joints), allows the franchisers to argue that they lacked sufficient market power to affect competition through their alleged misuse of trademarks.

Queen City Pizza v. Domino's Pizza[44]

Queen City Pizza addressed the definition of the relevant market in an alleged franchise tying arrangement. The plaintiffs complained that they could have sup-

Queen City Pizza v. Domino's Pizza (continued)

plied Domino's franchisees with supplies, and would have done so for a lesser price, but for Domino's allegedly abusive restrictions on its trademark licensees. The Third Circuit defined the relevant market as all franchises originally available to the franchisees rather than simply the franchise that they ultimately selected. The court held that the "aftermarket" is a valid definition of the market only if it consists of unique goods or services. Since that was not the case with pizza restaurants, the market was defined as all the franchises potentially available to a would-be franchisee at the time of entering the franchise relationship. Accordingly, the court upheld Domino's practice of requiring its franchisees (i.e., trademark licensees) to buy up to 90 percent of their supplies from Domino's.[45]

Another trademark misuse claim rooted in antitrust law involves the use of a trademark licensing agreement to facilitate the allocation of territories or markets between competitors. The key identification of such agreements is that they delineate where the parties will sell all of a particular good or service, extending beyond simply the use of the mark itself. The Supreme Court addressed such a scenario in *Timken Roller Bearing Co. v. United States*.[46] The Court found that a license agreement, ostensibly for trademarks, actually was primarily the means of illegally dividing the market, with the trademarks transferred merely to facilitate that division. The Court's decision emphasized that the trademark license was only *secondary* to the main purpose of illegal market allocation; if the trademark license had been the primary goal of the agreement, a resulting territory division might be only "ancillary" and therefore acceptable.[47]

Recent cases have reevaluated whether trademark misuse can form the basis of an affirmative claim. In *Juno Online Svcs, L.P. v. Juno Lighting, Inc.*, the court considered Juno Online's claim that it was entitled to damages (as well as declaratory relief, injunctive relief, and cancellation of Juno Lighting's Internet registration) for Juno Lighting's trademark misuse.[48] Juno Lighting had tried to have Juno Online's Internet domain name "juno.com" cancelled and registered the domain name "juno-online.com" for itself. The court concluded that although it might be possible to recover for trademark misuse "where the mark holder does attempt to destroy its competitors through the use of its mark," Juno Online's case was not an appropriate case to establish the doctrine.[49] Although Juno Online alleged that Juno Lighting's domain name was misleading and false, it did not establish that Juno Lighting had "used" the domain name. Apparently, Juno Lighting never created a web page for the domain name, so the court found that merely registering the address could not be a "use in commerce" under section 43(a) of the Lanham Act. Without an allegation of "use," the court dismissed the claim in its entirety.

Indeed, the Internet may provide the catalyst for a new line of cases examining the potential for misuse of trademarks. However, some plaintiffs have discovered that the courts are unwilling or unable to extend their rights in the context of cyberspace. The following explanation of the interrelationship between courts, the Internet, and trademark law indicates that the doctrine of trademark misuse faces even more of an uphill battle in cyberspace than it does in bricks-and-mortar commerce. Or it may simply reflect the unwillingness of one judge to compensate for perceived failures in the relevant technologies.

> If the Internet were a technically ideal system for commercial exploitation, then every trademark owner would be able to have a domain name identical to its trademark. But the parts of the Internet that perform the critical addressing functions still operate on the 1960s and 1970s technologies that were adequate when the Internet's function was to facilitate academic military research. Commerce has entered the Internet only recently. In response, the Internet's existing addressing systems will have to evolve to accommodate conflicts among holders of intellectual property rights, and conflicts between commercial and non-commercial users of the Internet. . . . No doubt trademark owners would like to make the Internet safe for their intellectual property rights by reordering the allocation of existing domain names so that each trademark owner automatically owned the domain name corresponding to the owner's mark. . . . Various solutions to this problem are being discussed, such as a graphically based Internet directory that would allow the presentation of trademarks in conjunction with distinguishing logos, new top-level domains for each class of goods, or a new top-level domain for trademarks only. *The solution to the current difficulties faced by trademark owners on the Internet lies in this sort of technical innovation,* not in attempts to assert trademark rights over legitimate non-trademark uses of this important new means of communication.[50]

TRADE SECRET MISUSE

The federal antitrust agencies have indicated that they will apply the same antitrust principles to trade secrets that they apply to patents and copyrights.[51] Trade secrets, by their nature, have the power to effectively limit competition. Like patent owners, trade secret owners have monopolies over certain information. Unlike patents, however, trade secrets probably will always be commercially significant, as without a link to substantial profits, there is no incentive to engage in the type of secrecy and confidentiality necessary to preserve the information's status as a trade secret. Moreover, trade secret owners cannot cite the public policies underlying patent law as justification for allegedly anticompetitive actions. Accordingly, misuse of trade secrets, through bad faith assertion of trade secret claims or overly restrictive licensing terms, may constitute a violation of the antitrust laws.[52]

Bad faith assertion of trade secrets entails claiming that certain information is subject to trade secret protection when the alleged owner knows that no such trade secrets exist. Such conduct can support a violation of either section 1 or section 2 of the Sherman Act.[53] In *CVD, Inc. v. Raytheon, Co.,* the court held that "the threat of unfounded trade secrets litigation in bad faith is sufficient to constitute a cause of action under the antitrust laws."[54] Other factors that influence whether a bad faith assertion of trade secrets constitutes misuse may include the potential impact of the threatened litigation on the purported defendant and whether the assertion would foreclose competition.[55]

Unreasonable restrictions in trade secret licenses may also constitute trade secret misuse. Restrictive licensing arrangements are particularly troubling in the trade secret context because trade secrets, unlike patents, have no expiration date. Even eventual disclosure of the trade secret may not nullify payment obligations under a licensing arrangement.[56] The primary issue for a court will be whether the restrictions are ancillary to a legitimate purpose, such as protection of the trade secret, or whether they are merely an attempt to extend control over the competition.[57] For example, territorial restrictions that are not part of a trade secret owner's plan to suppress competition may be lawful,[58] while the same type of territorial restraints are unlawful where they function merely as part of a larger conspiracy to allocate geographic markets.[59] Similarly, using trade secret licenses to leverage the trade secret into power in other competitive areas will be problematic. Examples of this type of leverage could include package licenses where the trade secret owner conditions the trade secret license upon licensing other IP from him or her, as well as tying arrangements and refusals to deal.[60]

SUMMARY

The doctrines of copyright and trademark misuse are available as defenses for alleged infringers, particularly where the misuse threatens to undermine the public policies that favor legal enforcement of copyrights and trademarks. However, courts are reluctant to grant the same recognition to the misuse defense in these contexts (particularly trademark misuse) that they award to patent misuse, at least in part because of the different rationales behind the legal protection of patented ideas versus mere expressions or marks. Moreover, courts are not likely to view either doctrine as a basis for recovery of damages, at least not without a significant competitive injury that can be attributed to the alleged misuse. In the trade secret context, misuse lacks significant public policy standards apart from the antitrust laws' concern with anticompetitive actions. Accordingly, trade secret misuse probably will be successful only where the claims parallel, or even rise to the level of, antitrust violations.

Many of the recent misuse cases deal with the computer industry and copyrighted computer code. In fact, the increasing recognition of copyright misuse probably is directly attributable to the fact that the computer industry is one of the few venues where a copyright may grant market power to the owner. If the courts begin to recognize the Internet as a similar venue for purposes of trademark misuse (i.e., since trademarked domain names may confer greater market power than simply the mark itself in a non–e-commerce context), we may see a similar increase in the recognition of trademark misuse.

ENDNOTES

[1] The Fourth, Fifth, and Ninth Circuits accept the doctrine of copyright misuse, as do some lower courts from other circuits. Among the district courts that have not applied it are several that appear to be uncertain about the defense's status in their circuits.

[2] *M. Witmark & Sons v. Jensen,* 80 F. Supp. 843, 850 (D. Minn. 1948).

[3] *See Lasercomb,* 911 F.2d 970.

[4] *See United States v. Loew's, Inc.,* 371 U.S. 38 (1962); *United States v. Paramount Pictures, Inc.,* 334 U.S. 131 (1948).

[5] *Lasercomb America, Inc. v. Reynolds,* 911 F.2d 970 (4th Cir. 1990).

[6] *See PRC Realty Systems v. National Assoc. of Realtors,* 1992 U.S. App. LEXIS 18017 (4th Cir. 1992).

[7] *Alcatel USA, Inc. v. DGI Technologies,* 166 F.3d 772 (5th Cir. 1999).

[8] *In re Independent Serv. Orgs,* 203 F.3d 1322 (Fed. Cir. 2000); *Service & Training, Inc. v. Data Gen. Corp.,* 963 F.2d 680 (4th Cir. 1992); *Triad Sys. Corp. v. Southeastern Express Co.,* 64 F.3d 1330 (9th Cir. 1995); *Advanced Computer Servs. v. MAI Sys. Corp.,* 845 F. Supp. 356 (E.D. Va. 1994); *Warner/Chappel Music, Inc. v. Pilz Compact Disc, Inc.,* 52 U.S.P.Q.2d 1942 (E.D. Pa. 1999).

[9] Several courts have indicated that a defendant may assert a copyright misuse defense based on violations of public policy underlying the copyright laws, rather than an antitrust violation such as a tying arrangement. *See K-91, Inc. v. Gershwin Pub. Corp.,* 372 F.2d 1 (9th Cir. 1967); *Broadcast Music, Inc. v. Moor-Law, Inc.,* 527 F. Supp. 758 (D. Del. 1981); *Nat'l Cable Television Ass'n, Inc. v. Broadcast Music, Inc.,* 772 F. Supp. 614 (D.D.C. 1991); *Sega Enterprises v. Accolade, Inc.,* 785 F. Supp. 1392 (N. D. Cal. 1991); *Atari Games Corp. v. Nintendo of Am., Inc.,* 975 F.2d 832 (Fed. Cir. 1992); *Microsoft Corp. v. BEC Computer Co.,* 818 F. Supp. 1313 (C.D. Cal. 1992); *Advanced Computer Servs. v. MAI Sys. Corp.,* 845 F. Supp. 356 (E.D. Va. 1994).

[10] *qad., Inc. v. ALN Assoc., Inc.,* 770 F. Supp. 1261 (N.D. Ill. 1991).

[11] *See Michael Anthony Jewelers, Inc. v. Peacock Jewelry, Inc.,* 795 F. Supp. 639 (S.D.N.Y. 1992).

[12] *See, e.g., Practice Mgmt. Info. Corp. v. American Med. Assoc.,* 121 F.3d 516 (9th Cir. 1997) (following reasoning of 4th circuit and explicitly adopting copyright misuse as a defense); *Religious Tech. Ctr. v. Lerma,* 40 U.S.P.Q.2d 1569 (E.D. Va. 1996) (finding copyright owner's alleged intent to harass the defendant with infringement litigation did not establish a misuse defense); *In re: Independent Servs. Orgs. Antitrust Litig.,* 989 F. Supp. 1131 (D. Kan. 1997) (recognizing copyright misuse as a possible defense, but holding unilateral refusal to license was not misuse); *F.E.L. Publications, Ltd. v. Catholic Bishop of Chicago,* 214 U.S.P.Q. 409 (7th Cir. 1982) (refusing to apply copyright misuse defense because equities favored the copyright owner in case at issue); *Triad Sys. Corp. v. Southeastern Express Co.,* 64 F.3d 1330 (9th Cir. 1995); *Mastercraft Fabrics Corp. v. Dickson Elberton Mills, Inc.,* 821 F. Supp. 1503 (M.D. Ga. 1993); *LucasArts Entertainment Co. v. Humongous Entertainment Co.,* 870 F. Supp. 1503 (N.D. Cal. 1993).

[13] *See Rural Telephone Svc. Co., Inc. v. Feist Publications, Inc.,* 663 F. Supp. 214 (D. Kan. 1987), *aff'd,* 916 F.2d 718 (10th Cir. 1990), *rev'd on other grounds,* 499 U.S. 340 (1991) (not addressing the issue of the copyright misuse defense).

[14] *Saturday Evening Post Co. v. Rumbleseat Press, Inc.,* 816 F.2d 1191, 1200 (7th Cir. 1987).

[15] *See Edward B. Marks Music Corp. v. Colorado Magnetics, Inc.,* 497 F.2d 285 (10th Cir. 1973); *Saturday Evening Post Co.,* 816 F.2d 1191; *United Tel. Co. v. Johnson Publishing Co.,* 855 F.2d 604 (8th Cir. 1988); *Bell South Advertising & Publishing Corp. v. Donnelley Info. Publishing, Inc.,* 933 F.2d 952 (11th Cir. 1991); *Basic Books, Inc. v. Kinko's Graphics Corp.,* 758 F. Supp. 1522 (S.D.N.Y. 1991); *Electronic Data Sys. Corp. v. Computer Assoc. Int'l, Inc.,* 802 F. Supp. 1463 (N.D. Tex 1992).

[16] *See* Troy Parades, *Copyright Misuse and Tying: Will Courts Stop Misusing Misuse?* 9:2 High Tech. L. J. 271, 303–09 (1994); James Kobak, Jr., *A Sensible Doctrine of Misuse for Intellectual Property Cases,* 2 Alb. L. J. Sci. Tech. 1, 34–35, 45 (1992).

[17] Courts are not in agreement over whether market power should be presumed as an inherent product of the right to exclude granted with a patent or copyright. In 1962, the Supreme Court found that copyrights give rise to a presumption of market power given the necessarily unique nature of a copyrighted work. *See United States v. Loew's, Inc.,* 371 U.S. 38 (1962); *see also MCA Television, Ltd. v. Public Interest Crp.,* 171 F.3d 1265 (11th Cir. 1999) (following *Loew's* presumption). However, recent cases have moved away from presuming market power simply from the existence of a copyright. One reason to question the presumption of market power is the presence of close substitutes for the copyrighted work. If another uncopyrighted work would be satisfactory to the consumers, then that substitutability indicts the theory that holds copyrights are tantamount to market power. *See Abbot Lab. v. Brennan,* 952 F.2d 1346 (Fed. Cir. 1991); *Xeta, Inc. v. Atex, Inc.,* 852 F.2d 1280 (Fed. Cir. 1988); *Mozart Co. v. Mercedes Benz of N. Am., Inc.,* 833 F.2d 1342 (9th Cir. 1987); *A.I. Root Co. v. Computer/Dynamics, Inc.,* 806 F.2d 673 (6th Cir. 1986); *Ralph C. Wilson Indus., Inc. v. Chronicle Broadcasting, Co.,* 794 F.2d 1359 (9th Cir. 1986); *SCM Corp. v. Xerox Corp.,* 645 F.2d 1196 (2d Cir. 1981); *Broadcast Music, Inc. v. Hearst/ABC Viacom Entertainment Svcs.,* 746 F. Supp. 320, 328 (S.D.N.Y. 1990).

[18] *In re: Napster, Inc. Copyright Litig.,* No. MDL 00-1369 MHP (N.D. Calif. Feb 21, 2002), *available at* <http://news.findlaw.com/hdocs/docs/napster/napster022102ord.pdf>.

[19] U.S. Department of Justice and Federal Trade Commission, Antitrust Guidelines for the Licensing of Intellectual Property § 2.0 (1995).

[20] *Id.* at § 2.2.

[21] *Data Gen. Corp. v. Grumman Sys. Support Corp.,* 1988 U.S. Dist. LEXIS 16427 (D. Mass. Dec. 29, 1988). Ultimately, the copyright misuse defense failed on appeal as well. *See Data Gen. Corp. v. Grumman Sys. Support Corp.,* 36 F.3d 1147 (1st Cir. 1994); *see also Orth-O-Vision v. Home Box Office,* 474 F. Supp. 672 (S.D.N.Y. 1979) (holding that violations of the antitrust laws were not a defense to copyright infringement, and noting the Supreme Court's lack of express holdings concerning copyright misuse as a defense).

[22] *Intellectual Property Misuse: Licensing and Litigation,* Chicago, IL: American Bar Association Section of Antitrust Law (2000), at 187.

[23] *See Alcatel USA, Inc. v. DGI Techs., Inc.,* 166 F.3d 772 (5th Cir. 1999); *Lasercomb Am., Inc. v. Reynolds, Inc.,* 911 F.2d 970 (4th Cir. 1990); *qad. Inc.,* 770 F. Supp. 1261, 1266 n. 16 (N. D. Ill. 1991).

[24] 975 F.2d 832, 846 (Fed. Cir. 1992).

[25] *See Atari Games Corp. v. Nintendo of America, Inc.,* 1993 U.S. Dist. LEXIS 6786 (N.D. Cal. May 18, 1993).

[26] *See Broadcast Music, Inc. v. Hearst/ABC Viacom Entertainment Servs.,* 746 F. Supp. 320, 328 (S.D.N.Y. 1990); *Warner/Chappel Music Inc. v. Pilz Compact Disc, Inc.,* 52 U.S.P.Q.2d 1942, 1947, n.3 (E.D. Pa. 1999); *Juno Online Servs. L.P. v. Juno Lighting, Inc.,* 979 F. Supp. 684, 688–90 (N.D. Ill. 1997) (rejecting affirmative claim for trademark misuse); Susan G. Braden, *Copyright Misuse: If Not a Shield, a Sword, Practicing Law Institute, Patents, Copyrights, Trademarks and Literary Property,* Practicing Law Institute: Intellectual Property/Antitrust (1993).

[27] *See, e.g., B. Braud Med. Inc. v. Abbot Lab.,* 124 F.3d 1419 (Fed. Cir. 1997).

[28] *Electronic Data Systems Corp. v. Computer Assoc., Inc.,* 802 F. Supp. 1463 (N.D. Tex. 1992).

[29] *Lasercomb Am., Inc. v. Reynolds,* 911 F.2d 970, 979 n.22 (4th Cir. 1990); *Budish v. Gordon,* 784 F. Supp. 1320, 1337, n.12 (N.D. Ohio 1992) (noting in dicta that a plaintiff will not be precluded from enforcing the copyright if any alleged misuse is purged).

[30] *See Preformed Line Prods. Co. v. Fanner Mfg. Co.,* 328 F.2d 265 (6th Cir. 1964); *McCullough Tool Co. v. Well Surveys, Inc.,* 343 F.2d 381, 410 (10th Cir. 1965).

[31] *See United States v. United States Gypsum Co.,* 340 U.S. 76, 89 (1950); *International Salt Co., Inc. v. United States,* 332 U.S. 392, 400–01 (1947); *Preformed Line Prods.,* 328 F.2d at 279.

[32] *Carl Zeiss Stiftung v. V.E.B. Carl Zeis, Jena,* 298 F. Supp. 1309, 1314 (S.D.N.Y. 1969) (noting that a "sharp distinction must be drawn between the antitrust misuse defense in patent infringement suits, on the one hand, and trademark suits, on the other.").

[33] *Northwestern Corp. v. Gabriel Mfg. Co.,* 48 U.S.P.Q.2d 1902, 1908 (N.D. Ill. 1998).

[34] *Clorox Co. v. Sterling Winthrop, Inc.,* 117 F.3d 50, 56 (2d Cir. 1997) (quoting *Carl Zeiss Stiftung v. V.E.B. Carl Zeiss, Jena,* 298 F. Supp. 1309, 1315 (S.D.N.Y. 1969)).

[35] *Manhattan Medicine Co. v. Wood,* 108 U.S. 218 (1883).

[36] 15 U.S.C. 1115(b)(7) (1946, as amended).

[37] *Carl Zeiss Stiftung v. V.E.B. Carl Zeiss, Jena,* 298 F. Supp. 1309 (S.D.N.Y. 1969).

[38] *See id.; Phi Delta Theta Fraternity v. J.A. Buchroeder & Co.,* 251 F. Supp. 968, 974–78 (W.D. Mo. 1966) (examining legislative history and determining that trademark misuse with anticompetitive effects could be a general defense to infringement).

[39] *Intellectual Property Misuse: Licensing and Litigation,* "Copyright and Trademark Misuse" at 202; *see also* Restatement of Unfair Competition (Third) § 31(e) (1995).

[40] *See Valley Prods. v. Landmark,* 128 F.3d 398, 405 (6th Cir. 1997); *Mozart Co. v. Mercedes-Benz of N. M.,* 833 F.2d 1342, 1346 (9th Cir. 1987); *Queen City Pizza v. Domino's Pizza,* 124 F.3d 430 (3d Cir. 1997).

[41] Apart from the market incentives to police uses of its trademarks, the trademark owner risks invalidation of the marks if it engages in unsupervised or "naked" licensing. *See Stanfield v. Osborne Indus.,* 52 F.3d 867 (10th Cir. 1995); *Dawn Donut Co. v. Hart's Food Stores,* 267 F.2d 358 (2d Cir. 1959) (Lumbard, J., dissenting); 3 J. Thomas McCarthy, McCarthy on Trademarks and Unfair Competition § 26.14.

[42] *See also* Ben Klein and Larry Saft, *The Law and Economics of Franchise Tying Contracts,* 28 J. L. Econ. 345 (1985).

[43] *See Colt Beverage Corp. v. Canada Dry Ginger Ale,* 146 F. Supp. 300, 303 (S.D.N.Y. 1956).

[44] *See, e.g., Queen City Pizza v. Domino's Pizza,* 124 F.3d 430 (3d Cir. 1997).

[45] *But see Collins v. Int'l Dairy Queen, Inc.,* 980 F. Supp. 1252 (M.D. Ga. 1997) (disagreeing with *Queen City*'s definition of the market to the extent that it limited the aftermarket to those markets consisting of unique goods or services); *see also* Alan H. Silberman, *The Myths of Franchise "Market Power,"* 65 Antitrust L.J. 181 (1996).

[46] *Timken Roller Bearing Co. v. United States,* 341 U.S. 593 (1951).

[47] *See also United States v. Sealy,* 388 U.S. 350 (1967); *United States v. Topco Assoc.,* 405 U.S. 596 (1972); *Palmer v. BRG,* 498 U.S. 46 (1990) (*per curiam*). These cases also deal with trademark licenses that became the basis for alleged antitrust violations.

[48] *Juno Online Svcs, L.P. v. Juno Lighting, Inc.,* 979 F. Supp. 684 (N.D. Ill. 1997).

[49] *Id.* at 690.

[50] *Lockheed Martin Corp. v. Network Solutions, Inc.,* 985 F. Supp. 949, 967–68 (C.D. Calif. 1997) (emphasis added).

[51] *See* Antitrust Law Developments (5th), *Intellectual Property,* 1107.

[52] *CVD, Inc. v. Raytheon, Co.,* 769 F.2d 842 (1st Cir. 1985), *cert. denied,* 475 U.S. 1016 (1986).

[53] *Id.* at 851.

[54] *Id.*

[55] *Id.* (noting that litigation would have been "ruinous" to new competitor in the market and would have "effectively foreclosed competition").

[56] *See, e.g., Aronson v. Quick Point Pencil Co.,* 440 U.S. 257 (1979); *Warner-Lambert Pharm. Co. v. John J. Reynolds, Inc.,* 178 F. Supp. 655 (S.D.N.Y. 1959).

[57] *A. & E. Plastik Pak Col. v. Monsanto Co.,* 396 F.2d 710, 715 (9th Cir. 1968).

[58] *See, e.g., Shin Nippon Koki Co. v. Irvin Indus.,* 186 U.S.P.Q. (BNA) 296 (N.Y. Sup. Ct. 1975); *United States v. E.I. duPont de Nemours & Co.,* 118 F. Supp. 41, 219 (D. Del. 1953); *Foundry Servs. v. Beneflux Corp.,* 110 F. Supp. 857 (S.D.N.Y.), *rev'd on other grounds,* 206 F.2d 214 (2d Cir. 1953); *Thoms v. Sutherland,* 52 F.2d 592 (3d Cir. 1931).

[59] *See, e.g., United States v. Pilkington plc.,* 1994-2 Trade Cas. (CCH) ¶ 70,842 (D. Ariz. 1994); *United States v. Imperial Chem. Indus.,* 100 F. Supp. 504 (S.D.N.Y. 1951); *United States v. Timken Roller Bearing Co.,* 83 F. Supp. 284, 315–16 (N.D. Ohio 1949).

[60] *See, e.g., In re Data General Corp. Antitrust Litig.,* 529 F. Supp. 801 (N.D. Cal. 1981), *aff'd in part and rev'd in part sub nom, Digidyne Corp. v. Data Gen. Corp.,* 734 F.2d 1336 (9th Cir. 1984); *Technograph Printed Circuits, Ltd. v. Bendix Aviation Corp.,* 218 F. Supp. 1, 50 (Md. 1963), *aff'd per curiam,* 327 F.2d 497 (4th Cir.), *cert. denied,* 379 U.S. 826 (1964).

ADDITIONAL READING

Intellectual Property Misuse: Licensing and Litigation, Chicago IL: American Bar Association Section of Antitrust Law (2000).

Troy Paredes, *Copyright Misuse and Tying: Will Courts Stop Misusing Misuse?* 9:2 High Technology Law Journal 271, 324–25 (1994).

Alan H. Silberman, *The Myths of Franchise "Market Power,"* 65 Antitrust Law Journal 181 (1996).

Stephen A. Stack, Jr., *Recent and Impending Developments in Copyright and Antitrust*, 61 Antitrust Law Journal 331 (1993).

Jere M. Webb and Lawrence A. Locke, *Intellectual Property Misuse: Developments in the Misuse Doctrine*, 4 Harvard Journal of Law & Technology 257 (Spring 1991).

Leslie Wharton, *Misuse and Copyright: A Legal Mismatch*, 8:3 Computer Law 1 (1991).

13

How to Calculate Copyright, Trademark, and Trade Secret Damages

Although the preceding chapters dealt with copyrights, trademarks, and trade secrets as separate and distinct bodies of law, the damage principles applicable to those forms of intellectual property (IP) are quite similar. Our approach is to build on the foundations developed in Chapter 6, on patent infringement damages. For each IP area, we point out similarities and differences with patent damages. Many of the differences will apply to all three areas, and therefore, after reading this chapter's explanation of calculating copyright damages, the reader should have an excellent foundation for understanding trademark and trade secret damages. Recurring themes such as "actual damages" and "infringer's profits" will resurface throughout the chapter. However, the reader should be careful not to allow the similarities to blur the vital distinctions between the remedies available under each type of infringement or the evidentiary requirements for obtaining those remedies. For example, although defendant's profits and actual damages are recoverable for both copyright infringement and trademark infringement, under the trademark regime a plaintiff must establish willfulness in order to merit monetary damages at all. That said, approaching this chapter in sequence should render each successive damage theory slightly easier to understand, culminating in a discussion of trade secret damages that amounts to reviewing old concepts in a new context (with one important exception).

COPYRIGHT DAMAGES

As in patent law, the starting point for determining damages in a copyright case is the relevant federal statute. Section 504(b) of the Copyright Act provides that:

> The copyright owner is entitled to recover the actual damages suffered by him or her as a result of the infringement, and any profits of the infringer that are attributable to the infringement and are not taken into account in computing the actual damages. In establishing the infringer's profits, the copyright owner is required to present proof only of the infringer's

gross revenue, and the infringer is required to prove his or her deductible expenses and the elements of profit attributable to factors other than the copyrighted work.

As outlined by the statute, a copyright owner who establishes infringement may recover not only his or her actual damages, but also any profits that the infringer accrued as a result of the infringement (so long as there is no double-counting; i.e., the copyright owner may not recover the profits that the infringer made *and* the profits that the owner would have made, except to the extent that those two categories do not overlap). Because of the practical difficulties in accurately calculating actual damages and lost profits, a subsequent section of the statute provides that a successful copyright plaintiff may elect to forgo the estimation of damages altogether and accept statutory damages as compensation for their injury.

Frequently, plaintiffs in copyright infringement actions are more concerned with stopping the offending behavior than with recovering any amount of money. Even a large sum of money may be inadequate compensation to a copyright owner who has lost exclusive control over his or her work and possibly faces the difficulty of making any profits in a market overrun by cheap or poor-quality copies. Accordingly, the Copyright Act allows copyright owners to obtain injunctive relief (i.e., a court order preventing or restraining the infringing behavior). Infringing copies already in existence may also be impounded and/or destroyed under the authority of the Copyright Act. Actual damages, statutory damages, and injunctive relief are discussed in greater detail in subsequent sections.

In addition to any of these remedies, the Copyright Act permits the prevailing party to recover attorneys' fees as well as other costs that the court has the discretion to award.[1] However, where the copyright owner prevails on liability but recovers nothing in damages, the court may decline to award any costs.[2] The award of costs and fees is within the courts' discretion, allowing courts to take into account the particular facts and circumstances regarding the infringement at issue and reimburse the plaintiff where those facts and circumstances warrant additional compensation. In particular, several circuits look to the "objective reasonableness" of the factual and legal components of the case in determining whether to award attorneys' fees.[3] The award of attorneys' fees is not necessarily insubstantial—recently, a court awarded $2.7 million in what may be the largest award of attorneys' fees ever in a copyright case.[4]

Similarities and Differences with the Patent Scheme

As in patent law, the plaintiff is entitled to lost profits from the infringement. Lost profits should be determined in the same manner as under patent law, with one notable exception. In a copyright case, a reasonable royalty calculation can be used to approximate the copyright owner's lost profits if the facts so warrant. Moreover, unlike the patent statute, the Copyright Act makes no mention of treating a reasonable royalty as a form of minimum damages.[5] Instead, the Copyright Act allows the plaintiff to elect to receive statutory damages as a substitute for actual damages if the copyright was registered.[6] Thus, statutory damages are the true equivalent to a reasonable royalty in the patent situation, in that such damages generally are the minimum amount recoverable (assuming prior registration). Another significant difference between the types of damages available in copyright cases and patent cases is that the Copyright Act allows for recovery of the infringer's profits.[7] The infringer's profits are explicitly disallowed as a measurement of the appropriate remedy under patent law. However, to recover the infringer's profits, section 504(b) of the Coypright Act requires an allocation of the infringer's profits into those profits due to the copyright right infringement and those that are not caused by the infringement. The copyright owner may recover only those profits that are caused by the use or sale of the infringing product.

These three possible measures of damages—actual damages, infringer's profits, and statutory damages—form the framework for damage analysis under the Copyright Act. Each of the three damage theories has specific evidentiary requirements, some of which may be more difficult to establish than others. In general, most copyright owners will attempt to prove both actual damages and an entitlement to at least a portion of the infringer's profits. However, statutory damages can be a valuable remedy, particularly where neither the infringer nor the copyright owner had profits attributable to the copyrighted work, such as where the copyright owner had not yet published the work. Each of these three theories is discussed in the following sections.

Actual Damages

The actual damages suffered by a copyright owner may be actual lost profits (from sales or licensing of the copyrighted work) or some other measure of the extent that the market value of the work was diminished, in part or entirely, by the infringement. As with any damage theory, copyright damages must be caused by the alleged bad act (here, the infringement of the copyrighted work) and be calculable without undue speculation. Once the copyright owner establishes a causal link between the infringement and some loss of anticipated revenue, the court may allow limited speculation as to the precise amount lost. Uncertainty as to the precise amount of damages does not preclude recovery of damages where the causal relationship—and thus the *fact* of damages—is established.

Neither the Copyright Act nor its legislative history defines "actual damages," leaving a substantial amount of discretion to the courts for evaluating damages calculations.[8] Actual damages may be measured by lost profits, a reasonable royalty, or a "market value" test. Each of these measures attempts to capture the value of the copyright owner's loss attributable to the infringement. Lost profits represent the profits that the copyright owner failed to achieve as a result of the infringement. One means of computing a plaintiff's lost profits involves calculating the average revenue for a period before infringement and then subtracting the revenue earned during the period of infringement.[9] The lost profit test typically will apply only where the copyright owner and the infringer were actual or potential competitors; otherwise the infringement could not have caused the copyright owner to lose sales. Where the infringing work and the copyrighted work compete at the same price in the same market, the infringer's sales could be used as a measure of sales lost by the copyright owner. (However, the copyright owner's overhead expenses may need to be deducted from the amount of sales to determine the lost *profits*.)

Faced with this type of damage theory, a defendant can argue that his sales of the allegedly infringing product are not an adequate measure of lost sales because of the differences in marketing, manufacturing costs, and pricing, as well as other aspects that differentiate the sales of the two products. In fact, a one-to-one sales comparison usually is unsupported by adequate evidence of similarity. For example, a defendant may argue that is not reasonable to assume that sales of an infringing product directly trade off with sales of the copyrighted work if the infringing product is sold at a significantly lower price than the price at which the copyrighted work is actually sold. This argument would assume completely inelastic demand. To justify a one-to-one substitution of the infringer's sales for the copyright owner's lost sales, the copyright owner must show that all of the infringer's customers would have bought the copyrighted work "but for" the availability of the infringing product. Significant differences in retail price may render such a showing extremely difficult, or even impossible, because an inexpensive product may acquire some customers who were precluded from buying the original product at its higher price. Although the copyright owner may be entitled to recover the infringer's profits from some of those sales to prevent the infringer from profiting from his or her bad act, the profits are not a simple substitute for lost sales on the owner's part. Put succinctly, the infringing sales eventually may be part of the remedy for infringement, but they do not always represent actual damages to the copyright owner.

Where the court decides that a reasonable royalty is appropriate, the court will attempt to determine the amount that the infringer would have paid for the right to legally use the copyrighted work. As in patent cases, any preexisting licenses may offer a measure of the appropriate reasonable royalty. However, a defendant may attempt to distinguish preexisting licenses on the basis of the types of uses that they authorized, the amount of the copyrighted work that was used, the changing value of the copyrighted work over time, and so forth. The reasonable royalty might take the form of a lump sum representing the reasonable value of the work, or the royalty might be a percentage of the licensee's profits. A copyright owner may testify as to the value of the copyrighted work, but the owner's testimony generally should be corroborated by some other evidence.

Stevens Linen Assoc., Inc. v. Mastercraft, Corp.[10]

Stevens Linen involved the determination of a reasonable damages award to compensate for Mastercraft's infringement of Stevens Linen's copyrighted fabric designs. The trial court declined to award compensatory damages because Mastercraft had lost money on its infringing fabrics, and therefore no profits

Stevens Linen Assoc., Inc. v. Mastercraft, Corp. (continued)

could be awarded. Moreover, the court refused to award any actual damages to Stevens Linen because it found that although it was "reasonable to assume that the infringement affected plaintiff's sales," the damages were too speculative.

On appeal, the appellate court held that there were two alternative measures of damages and that the trial court should have awarded whichever of the two sums proved to be the greater. The trial court was correct that Stevens Linen could not simply assume that it would have sold the entire amount of fabric sold by Mastercraft, in part because the infringing fabric was sold at a discounted price. However, the appellate court found that damages should be measured either (1) by lost profits that Stevens Linen would have realized from sales to customers who, during the infringement, bought from both Stevens Linen and Mastercraft (minus those sales that Mastercraft could prove Stevens Linen would not have made); or (2) based on the difference between Stevens Linen's actual sales of the infringed fabric and the average sales of all Stevens's other fabrics during the period in question. Both theories attempted to account for changes in the market and for changes in the value of the copyrighted work over time.

Films, songs, and software are most often licensed by their creators. Such transactions provide industry benchmarks from which to establish an estimated royalty amount. If the industry practice is to license the use of a copyrighted product, a reasonable royalty might be used to estimate damages. Consider the following examples.

Assume that an architect designs a home and creates a copyrighted plan. The architect sells the plan for $500 per home. The amount charged by the architect is consistent with the amounts charged by other architects for other home designs. Assume that a builder buys one copy and then proceeds to build two homes using the plan. Further assume that the builder usually makes a profit of $10,000 per home. Finally, assume that the builder has built many other homes of a similar size with a different design and also made a $10,000 profit per home. The property damage amount is $500 per infringement. Although some plaintiffs may claim that they lost $10,000 per infringement, the total profit is attributed to many things beyond the design (i.e., building costs, labor, equipment, etc.). This is proven by the fact that the home builder makes the same profit on homes that do not use the copyrighted plans. All methods of calculating damages lead to the same set of conclusions:

- The architect's lost profits are $500. Because there are no incremental costs associated with using the same design, the revenue and the profits are equivalent.
- The unjust enrichment is $500. The builder avoided paying $500 by stealing the design. The builder would be expected to make $10,500 on the home with

the stolen design ($10,000 of normal profit plus the $500 of saved expense). Of that amount, only the $500 is "unjust enrichment."
- The fact that the architect regularly sells the design for $500 could constitute an "established royalty rate."

Next assume that a widget maker copyrights a design for an assembly line. Through improved efficiencies, the design allows the widget maker to save one dollar per widget made. The designer has never shared the plans with any other firm (nor licensed them). A competitor misappropriates the design and duplicates it in its own facility. Finally, assume that the competitor experiences a $1.75 per widget savings after infringing on the design.

- The designer's lost profits are zero, so they did not lose any sales as a result of the theft.
- The unjust enrichment is $1.75 per unit based on the infringer's profits.
- A reasonable royalty would be an amount less than one dollar. Although there is no established royalty, the infringer is likely to have expected a one-dollar savings (royalty ceiling) and the designer would not be afraid of losing any sales (zero royalty floor). Other factors (such as the *Georgia-Pacific* factors) could determine where within the range the reasonable royalty lies.

Accordingly, the facts of the case are critical to the damage calculation in a copyright case.

Where neither lost sales nor a reasonable royalty have any empirical basis, the copyright owner may employ the "market value test" as an alternative measure of actual damages. The market value test requires determining the copyright's fair market value by determining what a willing buyer would have freely paid to a willing seller for the use of the work.[11] This is the same approach sometimes applied in patent cases for determining a reasonable royalty—the court assumes that hypothetical negotiations took place, and the resulting award represents the probable outcome of those negotiations if undertaken at the onset of infringement. Some courts attempt to determine the value to the infringer of his use of the copyrighted work. This determination is simply another attempt to approximate the result of the hypothetical negotiations between a willing buyer and a willing seller. Alternatively, the copyright owner or her expert witnesses may testify as to the detrimental effect of the infringement on the copyright's market value.[12]

As mentioned previously, copyright owners can employ the market value test where they cannot prove that they lost sales and where a reasonable royalty would be difficult to calculate given the lack of preexisting licenses or other reasons. The market value test can apply where the infringement detracted from the reputation of the copyrighted work, decreased its value in a particular market, or harmed the copyright owner's goodwill, without necessarily resulting in lost sales or profits to the infringer. At times, the infringer may have been unsuccessful in marketing his infringing product, yet the presence of the unauthorized copies still damages the copyright owner by reducing the market value of the copyright. (This scenario is similar to the trademark actions brought for "blurring" or dilution of the value of a particular brand due to the promotion and sale of low-quality knockoffs, which are discussed in subsequent sections.) The market value test may also be useful to a copyright owner where the particular market factors make it unlikely that a license would be negotiated (e.g., where the copyright owner wishes only to preserve exclusive use of the work rather than to create licensees and permissible uses by other parties).

Deltak v. Advanced Systems, Inc.[13]

In *Deltak*, the infringing material was used in defendant's marketing brochures, but there was no evidence that any profits were garnered from these brochures. Nonetheless, the court found that the infringer obtained value from its use of a marketing tool. The value was equal to "the acquisition cost saved by infringement instead of purchase, which [defendant] was then free to put to other uses." As the court recognized, the "value in use" measure is very close to "what a willing buyer would have been reasonably required to pay to a willing seller for plaintiff's work." Nonetheless, the court contended that the concept is not identical to a reasonable royalty. Value is used as a measure of actual damage, not a substitute for lost profits. Moreover, not mentioned by the court is the fact that value of use does not depend on what the infringer would have been willing to pay, but only on the likely acquisition price.

Some courts have declined to expand the definition of damages in accordance with *Deltak* (see case study), holding that the copyright statutes provide adequate remedies to a copyright owner in the absence of actual damages or profit to the infringer.[14] However, the "value in use" appears to be a viable estimation of damages where statutory damages and other methods of calculating actual damages are unavailable.[15]

Finally, copyright law recognizes that lost sales, reasonable royalty, market value, or any combination of those theories may not fully compensate the copyright owner for actual damages. Accordingly, there are several categories of additional recoverable damages in the copyright context. First, a copyright owner may recover damages for loss of the value of receiving credit as the author of the work and any related loss of goodwill. Courts are aware that damage to an author's professional reputation may not be captured by lost sales and may be completely unrelated to the value to the infringer of using the copyrighted work. Second, a copyright owner may also recover the value of sales lost on noninfringed goods. In other words, where the copyright owner sells goods that are linked to the copyrighted good, the owner may have suffered a decrease in those sales as well as the sales of the copyrighted work itself. This theory of damages parallels the line of thought in patent law that allows recovery for lost sales of noninfringed goods that are related to the patented product, such as the sales of rewritable CDs that are compatible with a specific type of CD burner. Third, the copyright owner may recover additional miscellaneous expenses directly related to infringement. For example, any changes in the work necessitated by the infringement may be compensated. Furthermore, some courts have awarded the monetary value of time spent working on the copyrighted work, travel and research expenses, and other similar costs.

Measuring the Infringer's Profits

As explained at the outset of this chapter, a copyright owner may recover not only actual damages, but also the infringer's profits attributable to the infringement. The clear purpose of this statutory scheme is to prevent the infringer from unfairly benefiting from a wrongful act. In other words, the Copyright Act aims to remove the incentives for an "efficient breach," for example, an unauthorized act that is economically rational in that the infringer has the ability to profit more from the illegal act than the copyright owner does from the legal exercise of his or her rights. Absent the possibility of recovering the infringer's profits, the infringer could rationalize that the unauthorized use of the copyrighted work would be on net profitable (discounting the potential for protracted litigation and its related expenses) if he or she stands to lose only the profit for those sales that would have been made by the copyright owner. The argument against this approach, of course, is that it may result in a windfall to the copyright owner, particularly the owner who has done nothing to market or profit from the copyrighted work.

   Although the copyright owner is entitled to both lost profits and the infringer's profits, the copyright owner's damage calculations must exclude any double-counting. It is evident from the case law and the Copyright Act that the phenomenon of "double-counting" must be avoided in copyright damage calculations. Section 504(b) of the Copyright Act explicitly states that a copyright owner is entitled to collect only that portion of the infringer's profits that was not already "taken into account in computing the actual damages."[16] As an example of what is meant by double-counting, consider

Customers

Copyright owner	1	2	3	4	5	6
Infringer	5	6	7	8	9	10

EXHIBIT 13-1   Customers of the Copyright Owner and the Infringer

the following hypothetical case. Suppose that Exhibit 13-1 depicts the customers of the copyright owner and the infringer.

Assume that the infringer made sales to all 10 customers, but absent the infringement, the copyright owner and the infringer would have sold to their own customers. In this case, the copyright owner would be entitled to lost profits on customer sales 1 through 4, and the infringer's profits on customer sales 7 through 10, but only lost profits *or* the infringer's profits on customer sales 5 and 6, *not on both*.

The Copyright Act clearly places the burden on the plaintiff/copyright owner of proving the size of the infringer's revenue from infringement. The burden of establishing the expenses related to producing and selling the infringing work is on the defendant/alleged infringer. From an economic standpoint, only avoided costs should be deducted. The case law supports this view by stating that only costs related to the infringing work itself can be deducted.[17] Such costs can include royalties, advertising, marketing, production and selling costs, and overhead. Overhead expenses should be subtracted only if they would not have been incurred absent the infringement. Any doubt regarding the amount of deductible expenses and profits will be resolved in favor of the copyright owner. In fact, if the infringer failed to present evidence supporting his argument that not all of the profits were attributable to the infringement, or indicating the existence of certain deductible expenses, the court could assume that the infringer's entire gross revenues are profits recoverable by the copyright owner (at least to the extent that they have not been taken into account in lost sales calculations).

Infringers can also be liable for profits on related goods or works that are proximately caused by the infringement; sometimes this class of profits is referred to as "indirect profits." Courts can consider any enhancements of the infringer's business that are directly attributable to the infringement. If the indirect profits are only remotely or speculatively attributable to the infringement, the copyright owner may not recover those profits. The *Knitwaves* case offers an example of the type of indirect profits that may be recoverable.

Knitwaves v. Lollytogs, Ltd., Inc.[18]

Knitwaves was a clothing manufacturer that owned a copyright on the design of its sweaters. Knitwaves sold its sweater designs separately as matching sets, a top sweater and a bottom. Lollytogs began marketing an infringing version of the sweater, but sold it as a complete outfit with top and bottom. Knitwaves was able to recover all of Lollytog's profits on the sweater outfits because the court found that the value of Lollytog's entire product (i.e., the complete sweater set, even the noninfringing parts) was derived from its infringing aspects.

Allocating the Infringer's Profits

The copyright statute requires that damages be limited to the portion of the infringer's profits caused by the infringement. This presents a difficult allocation problem. In *Sheldon v. Metro-Goldwyn Pictures Corp.*, the Supreme Court held that "what is required is not mathematical exactness but only a reasonable approximation."[19] Causation is a very important element of an expert damage analysis in a copyright case.

Frank Music Corp. v. Metro-Goldwyn-Mayer Inc.[20]

The case involved the copyright infringement of five songs that were part of a musical revue staged at the MGM Grand Hotel called "Hallelujah Hollywood." One issue in the case was how much of the revue's profits could be attributed to the five infringing songs. The infringing portion constituted six minutes of music in a 100-minute musical revue. The court made clear that an allocation is required by law and some reasoned method based on the facts of each case must be undertaken. Because the district court did not provide an explanation for its allocation, the case was remanded. The court also allowed for the apportionment of not only the direct profits from the revue, but also the indirect profits from the hotel and casino that sponsored the show. Although mathematical certainty was not necessary, "a reasonable and just apportionment of profits is required."

Statutory Damages

Unlike in patent cases, the Copyright Act provides for statutory damages. (Since statutory damages are available only when the copyright was registered, cases may still exist in which no damages are available.) However, the owner of a registered copyright may elect to recover statutory damages in any event, even where there is evidence of lost profits or infringer's profits. In fact, the copyright owner may choose statutory damages at any time before final judgment. The Supreme Court has even permitted the election of statutory damages *after* the copyright owner sees the jury's verdict and award of actual damages.[21] Once the copyright owner has elected to collect statutory damages, he or she may no longer seek actual damages, even on appeal. Given the low mathematical range of possible awards under the statutory scheme (relative to the sums available under the other damages schemes) and the irreversible nature of the decision, copyright owners generally will elect statutory damages only where neither their use nor the infringing use was very profitable.

As set forth in section 412 of the Copyright Act, the availability of statutory damages is conditioned on registration of the copyright.[22] Although a suit may be brought for infringement that took place before the registration (e.g., where the copyright owner becomes aware of the infringement and registers the copyright as a precursor to litigation), section 412 limits the ability of a copyright owner to claim statutory damages for infringement that took place before the effective date of the copyright registration.[23] For an unpublished work, statutory damages are not available for any infringement that predates the work's registration. For a published work, copyright owners may not seek statutory damages for any "infringement of copyright commenced after first publication of the work and before the effective date of its registration, unless [the] registration is made within three months after the first publication of the work."[24] This provision perpetuates the incentives for authors to register their copyrights; even though registration is no longer mandatory for an author to claim a copyright, registration is a prerequisite to suits brought under the Copyright Act and to the recovery of statutory damages.[25] It also limits the recoverable damages where a copyright owner neglects to register until immediately preceding litigation.[26]

Once the initial hurdle of registration is cleared, the statute prescribes a floor and a ceiling for the amount of statutory damages available in any given case. All infringement actions arising from January 1, 1978, to March 1, 1989, are governed by a range of statutory damages from $250 to $10,000 per work. However, on March 1, 1989, the Berne Implementation Act allowed for a doubling of statutory damage awards in an attempt to increase the incentives for registration. Aside from certain limited exceptions, the current statutory minimum damage award for copyright infringement is $700 per work, while the maximum statutory damage award is $30,000 per work.[27] This heightened range of damages applies to works both created and registered after March 1, 1989. However, it is not clear whether the Berne Implementation Act applies to works created, published, or registered before that date, where the complaint was not filed or a verdict entered until after March 1, 1989.

Within that statutory range of possibilities, the court has the discretion to award any amount, adjusted appropriately for the facts of the particular case. In exceptional circumstances, the court may even award an amount outside the statutory range where the defendant's actions merit a departure from the guidelines. Courts consider several factors in determining statutory damages, including the infringer's state of mind (e.g., whether the infringement was deliberate and in bad faith), the infringer's profits, the copyright owner's lost profits, and the expenses the infringer managed to avoid by his infringement. In other words, actual damages become a factor even in the calculation of statutory damages. Courts also may consider the fair market value of the copyrighted work, the amount and type of the infringement (e.g., whether it was technical or substantive), and defendants' conduct after becoming aware of the copyright owner's objections (usually in the form of a cease and desist letter or a request that the defendant obtain a license for use of the copyrighted work).

Where there is little evidence of actual damages, substantial profits by the infringer, or bad faith, the courts commonly award the statutory minimum amount.

Additionally, the Copyright Act allows courts to award less than the statutory minimum award where the infringer proves that he "was not aware and had no reason to believe that his or her acts constituted an infringement of copyright."[28] To meet this evidentiary burden, the infringer must prove that: (1) his infringing actions were based on a good faith belief that the actions in question did not constitute copyright infringement; and (2) the good faith belief that the actions were not infringing was a reasonable belief. When a valid notice appeared on published copies to which the infringer had access, the infringer cannot rely on the innocent infringer defense to mitigate statutory damages. Moreover, the decision as to what amount of damages to award is still a discretionary one, and the court could elect to award the maximum statutory amount despite proof that the infringement was "innocent." After March 1, 1989, generally even an innocent infringer cannot mitigate statutory damages below $700 unless the original work was unpublished, had an invalid notice, or was inaccessible to the infringer.

Storm Impact, Inc. v. Software of the Month Club[29]

The *Storm Impact* case demonstrates the courts' discretion when awarding statutory damages. Storm Impact developed a copyrighted computer game called "MacSki" that it distributed over the Internet as "shareware." Shareware generally is free to users for testing and review, subject to payment if the user would like to play the full version of the game, including higher levels, additional features, and so on. In this case, MacSki would stop when the virtual skier was halfway down the ski slope and ask the user to register with Storm Impact and purchase a "key" if the user wanted to continue. Software of the Month Club (SOMC) collected shareware programs on CD-ROMs and sold them to its subscribers as the "latest and greatest" shareware. SOMC included MacSki on one of its monthly CDs, apparently without reading the express restrictions on MacSki requiring Storm Impact's permission before mass distribution of the program.

Storm Impact successfully established that this use infringed its copyright on MacSki and requested the greater of actual or statutory damages. The actual damages were quite low, so the court calculated statutory damages. Without a finding of willful infringement, the court noted that the damages could range from $500 to $20,000 for each program, subject to the court's discretion. The court found that SOMC did not willfully infringe the copyrighted material because it made a plausible (although ultimately unsuccessful) argument of implied consent and removed MacSki from its monthly compilations once it was notified of the alleged infringement. However, the court also held that an absence of willfulness did not merit merely minimal damages. Storm Impact had suffered some damage

---

Storm Impact, Inc. v. Software of the Month Club (continued)

to its goodwill from the use of its product (although it was difficult to quantify), and it was impossible to determine precisely how much of SOMC's profits were due to Storm Impact's product. Accordingly, the court awarded $10,000 per infringement, for a total of $20,000 (there was one other copyrighted work besides MacSki that was included on the disk).

Where the copyright owner establishes that the infringer "willingly" infringed (i.e., that the infringer's state of mind was not merely innocent), the court may award damages above the $30,000 maximum, up to a sum of not more than $150,000. Section 504(c)(2) authorizes such a departure from the statutory range of damages. The culpable state of mind may be proven by the infringer's conduct after being asked to stop, repeated unauthorized uses, and so on. To have acted willfully, an infringer must have had actual knowledge that the infringing conduct constituted copyright infringement. In other words, the infringer must have personal knowledge of the infringement, not merely knowledge imputed by an employee or agent who was aware of the infringement. An infringer may negate willfulness by showing that he received legal advice indicating that the conduct was not infringement. Thus, an infringer who received notice from the copyright owner that his conduct was infringing, but received a contrary opinion from his counsel, may assert a good faith defense to the "willfulness" aspect of the infringement. Courts also have awarded damages above the statutory maximum to punish an infringer whose conduct directly led to the copyright owner's inability to establish or reasonably calculate actual damages. For example, an infringer's refusal to answer questions about the volume of their infringing sales, or their profits from those sales, may entitle the copyright owner to maximum statutory damages.[30]

Where an infringer copied from multiple works owned by the same owner, the statutory damages will be multiplied by the number of infringed copyrights. For example, where the infringer copied three copyrighted works, the copyright owner is entitled to statutory damages of at least $1,500 and up to $60,000. If the infringer had unauthorized use of several different versions of a copyrighted work, the Act suggests that only a single statutory damages award is available. The test for whether more than one "work" has been infringed for the purpose of deciding whether to multiply the statutory damages is whether "all the parts of a compilation or derivative work constitute one work."[31]

An infringer frequently will infringe a single copyrighted work by several different acts. The Copyright Act provides for a single award for "all infringements involved in the actions, with respect to any one work. . . ."[32] This means that an infringer will be liable for a single statutory award whether the infringer made 1 copy or 99 copies.

However, courts will take into account the number of individual infringements when determining the appropriate award within the statutory range.

Summary of Copyright Damages

The Copyright Act allows a plaintiff to recover damages where he or she can establish ownership of the copyright and copying by the defendant. Under the statute, a successful plaintiff may recover both actual damages and the defendant's profits attributable to the infringement. Since actual damages may be difficult to calculate and the defendants have not always profited from infringement, the Copyright Act also allows a plaintiff to elect statutory damages (instead of actual damages) as compensation for the harm to the protected work. Courts also have the power to enjoin the defendant from further infringing acts, impound the infringing items, and award attorneys' fees and costs to the copyright owner.

TRADEMARK DAMAGES

The three primary sources of law concerning trademark damages are:

1. Section 35 of the Lanham Act
2. Section 36 of the Restatement of Unfair Competition Third (the Restatement)
3. The case law

Availability of Monetary Damages

An important difference between the law of damages in the patent and copyright areas and the damages available for trademark infringement is the judicial reluctance in trademark cases to award monetary damages rather than simply enjoining the infringement. Some courts, in accord with pre–Lanham Act case law, require a trademark owner to make an initial showing of either willful infringement or actual lost profits before monetary damages will be awarded for trademark infringement. Sections 36(3) and 37(2) of the Restatement appear to codify this threshold requirement by offering factors that should be considered before "damages for pecuniary loss are appropriate" or "defendant's profits" can be awarded.

The historical basis for this reluctance can be traced to the old divisions between the different types of courts. Originally, trademark infringement was brought in equity courts, and the remedy was an injunction and an accounting of the infringer's profits. Actual damages were an available remedy only in a court of law, and thus were unavailable to the trademark owner. After the merger of courts of law and equity courts, many courts continued the tradition of awarding only an injunction and the infringer's profits. It was not until the passage of the Lanham Act in 1946 that a plaintiff's actual damages became available.

Although the Lanham Act allows trademark owners to recover both the defendant's profits and the owner's actual damages, the extent of an owner's recovery is explicitly "subject to the principles of equity. . . ."[33] Consistent with this codified consideration of equitable factors, shortly after the Lanham Act was enacted, the Supreme Court held that damages for trademark infringement would not be automatic.[34] Moreover, infringers who merely reproduce a registered mark on labels or packaging "intended to be used in commerce" (as opposed to actually used in commerce) are not liable for profits or actual damages unless their acts were committed "with knowledge that such imitation is intended to cause confusion."[35] Lower courts have justified awarding an injunction without monetary damages because trademark infringement can be innocent (when the infringer is aware of the mark) and may not cause actual consumer confusion.

Injunctive relief is the standard remedy for trademark infringement, requiring only a demonstration of a *likelihood* of confusion.[36] In general, damages are available when (1) actual confusion exists, or (2) the infringement is willful.[37] Despite this general rule, some courts have awarded damages when actual confusion is lacking (typically a reasonable royalty)[38] and where infringement is innocent (often the innocent infringer benefits from the infringement).[39]

Types of Damages Available

Assuming that monetary damages are available, section 35 of the Lanham Act provides for the recovery of: (1) "any damages sustained by the plaintiff"; (2) "defendants' profits"; and (3) "the costs of the action."[40] The Lanham Act also gives the courts discretion to increase the actual damages up to three times such amount, whichever is greater, so long as the increase represents "compensation and not a penalty."[41] In "exceptional cases," the courts may also award attorneys' fees to the prevailing party.[42] Moreover, if the infringement consists of "intentionally using a mark or designation, knowing such mark or designation is a counterfeit mark," courts are required to award attorneys' fees as well as trebled damages or trebled profits, whichever is greater.[43] Finally, statutory damages are available for use of counterfeit marks, as defined by the statute.[44]

As an IP expert or attorney, it is important to be familiar with the means of calculating plaintiff's actual damages, defendant's profits, and statutory damages.

Plaintiff's Actual Damages

A trademark owner's actual damages can be measured by at least three types of harm: (a) lost profits on sales, (b) price erosion, and (c) lost goodwill or future sales because of harm to reputation.[45] Moreover, plaintiffs may recover their expenditures on advertising necessary to rectify the market confusion resulting from the infringing use of plaintiff's mark. The costs of this "corrective advertising" are another recognized type of actual damage to the mark owner. Finally, a reasonable royalty may be available to the trademark owner where actual damages exist but are difficult to calculate.

Lost Profits.   Lost profits are the profits that the trademark owner would have made absent the infringement. As in the copyright damages context, the plaintiff's lost profits and the defendant's profits can be duplicative, and any double-count must be eliminated from the total damages award. The other principles for calculating lost profits generally do not differ from those already explained in the discussion of damages for patent infringement. However, there is no authority to use the *Panduit* factors explicitly to establish lost sales in trade infringement cases. Instead, lost sales in trademark cases typically are determined directly by using the plaintiff's noninfringed products that use the same mark as a yardstick or estimating lost sales from a pre- and postinfringement analysis of the trademark owner's sales.[46] In a two-supplier market, the defendant's infringing sales may be used as a good proxy for the plaintiff's lost sales.[47] After lost sales have been identified, the lost profits are determined by applying the trademark owner's profit margin to the number of lost sales. The authors believe that a credible market analysis performed in accordance with the case law on patent damages likely will render acceptable results in a trademark case.

Price Erosion.   As with other types of IP, the erosion of a plaintiff's prices resulting from the alleged infringement constitutes another form of actual damages available for trademark infringement.[48] Price erosion in the trademark context must be proven in the same manner that it would be established in a patent infringement case. However, credible proof that prices would be higher "but for" the infringement of plaintiff's mark is difficult, and damage awards for price erosion are rare in trademark cases.

Damage to Reputation and Goodwill.   A plaintiff may recover for damage to its goodwill or reputation associated with the infringed trademark. Since the purpose of a trademark is to signal information to consumers about the quality or the characteristics of the trademark owners' products, infringement by an inferior good or forms of false advertising can undermine the trademark owner's investment in the mark. The Lanham Act recognizes this potential harm from trademark infringement and allows recovery for damage to the mark owner's goodwill or reputation.

Measuring injury to reputation can be difficult. One method of estimation is to compare the performance of the trademark owner before and after the infringement began. However, damage to reputation may overlap with lost profits and corrective advertising, although it is not coextensive with those amounts. Damage to goodwill can affect a mark owner's future performance, not simply past sales, and lost profits may fail to account for the negative effect of the infringement on future sales, even once the infringing use has ceased. Moreover, although corrective advertising expenses may indicate an owner's concern with (and possibly their valuation of) their diminished goodwill, the corrective advertising ultimately may be unable to completely repair the damage. Accordingly, any overlap between the amount determined to represent the damage to plaintiff's goodwill and the amounts of any lost profits and corrective advertising should be subtracted as duplicative damages; the difference constitutes an independent amount of recoverable damages.

Corrective Advertising.   A trademark owner may undertake corrective advertising in an attempt to restore the brand value of his mark. The cost of this advertising may be recoverable as a type of actual damage to the plaintiff. For example, in *Big O Tire Dealers, Inc. v. Goodyear Tire & Rubber Co.*, the district court upheld a jury verdict of $2.8 million based on a need for corrective advertising.[49] The jury based its verdict on the ratio of states in which infringement occurred to all states where Big O sold tires and multiplied this percentage by the defendant's advertising budget. The Tenth Circuit upheld the concept of corrective advertising damages, but reduced the percentage to 25 percent based on a formula used by the Federal Trade Commission.[50]

Corrective advertising also is available for prospective advertising. In other words, although the plaintiff may not yet have undertaken any corrective advertising, he or she may be able to recover the estimated amount that the advertising will cost. In cases where the damage to reputation is very difficult to measure, the cost of corrective advertising, established through the testimony of advertising personnel and sufficient expert analysis, may be a means of proving the amount of actual damage to the mark's reputation. There is a danger of undue speculation in this approach, and several commentators have criticized this use of corrective advertising.[51]

Reasonable Royalty.   Another means of determining the appropriate damages for trademark infringement is the calculation of a reasonable royalty.

Sands, Taylor & Wood v. Quaker Oats Co.[52]

This case involved an advertising battle between sports drinks, specifically the trademarks "Gatorade" and "Thirst Aid." Gatorade began using the slogan "Gatorade is Thirst Aid for That Deep Down Body Thirst," which plaintiffs alleged infringed their Thirst Aid mark. Somewhat surprisingly (given the arguably descriptive use of the term *thirst aid*), the district court granted summary judgment for Sands and awarded it 10 percent of Quaker's pretax profits on Gatorade—a total award of nearly $43 million. In an appeal of that award, the Seventh Circuit rejected the award of defendant's profits because the profits were insufficiently related to the use of plaintiff's mark. Since the plaintiff had not marketed a sports drink under the Thirst Aid mark for several years, there were no possible lost sales, so the appeals court remanded with instructions to calculate a reasonable royalty.

(continues)

Sands, Taylor & Wood v. Quaker Oats Co. (continued)

On remand, the district court noted that the hypothetical determination of a reasonable royalty in the trademark context is "a form of restitution designed to prevent unjust enrichment." The defendant had knowingly and in bad faith infringed the incontestable Thirst Aid mark, so the court wanted to award an amount that would act as a deterrent to future infringement. In other words, the reasonable royalty may strike a balance between a "windfall" to the plaintiff in the form of profits unrelated to its mark and the perceived undercompensation of pure injunctive relief. Moreover, the court was concerned with the potential failure of a reasonable royalty to discourage infringement if the royalty was simply the "normal, routine royalty, noninfringers might have paid." Accordingly, the court exercised its discretion under the Lanham Act and doubled the amount of the hypothetical royalty. After the application of prejudgment interest (to the original, undoubled award only), this resulted in a royalty of over $26 million.

As in patent infringement cases, a court first will determine whether an established royalty exists.[53] If no established royalty exists, then a reasonable royalty in a trademark infringement case is determined (just as in a patent infringement case) by use of the "willing licensor, willing licensee" test.[54] The same analysis discussed in connection with the calculation of a reasonable royalty in a patent infringement case applies to a trademark infringement case. As reflected in *Sands*, the courts also may consider the efficacy of the selected royalty as a deterrent to future misconduct, particularly in light of the defendant's profits from the infringing use.[55]

Defendant's Profits

The Lanham Act and the Restatement, like the Copyright Act, provide for the plaintiff to recover the defendant's profits.[56] Moreover, the burdens of proof and the calculations of defendant's profits in a trademark case are the same as in a copyright case. Essentially, the plaintiff attempts to calculate (or "account for") the defendant's profits attributable to the infringing use of plaintiff's mark.

George Basch Co., Inc. v. Blue Coral, Inc.[57]

Blue Coral marketed a metal polish with a trade dress similar to that of Basch's metal polish. The district court denied Basch's claim for actual damages because it found no evidence of consumer confusion or intent to deceive; however, the court awarded Basch Blue Coral's profits on the metal polish.

George Basch Co., Inc. v. Blue Coral, Inc. (continued)

On appeal, the court considered the requirements for awarding the infringer's profits as a remedy. The court held that, under section 35(a) of the Lanham Act, a plaintiff must prove that the infringer acted with "willful deception" in order for the plaintiff to recover the infringer's profits by way of an accounting. This "bad intent" requirement operates to limit the frequency with which a plaintiff might recover a windfall and precludes the "innocent" or "good faith" infringer from being unduly penalized.

A finding of willful deceptiveness is necessary but not sufficient to warrant an accounting for the infringer's profits. The other factors that should be considered include the egregiousness of the fraud; the degree of certainty that the defendant benefited from the infringement; the adequacy of other available remedies; the role of a particular defendant in the infringement; plaintiff's laches arguments; and any evidence of plaintiff's own unclean hands that might mitigate against a generous award. In this case, the court reversed the award of profits because there was no showing that sales had been diverted by the infringing use, nor were the failed negotiations between the parties before the infringement sufficient evidence of bad faith on Blue Coral's part.

There is little judicial guidance for determining the infringer's profits under an accounting theory of damages. Typically, the trademark owner will obtain the infringer's financial records in discovery and use the revenue or sales line of the income statement as a rough cut at estimating profits. The burden then shifts to the defendant to prove the "deductions" that must be made to arrive at actual profit. Acceptable deductions have included cost of goods sold, depreciation, utilities, advertising, commissions, administrative costs, discounts, start-up costs, maintenance, rent, insurance, nonlitigation legal expenses, returns, and taxes.[58] Opportunity costs are also a category of costs that have been allowed by courts. In a competitive market, opportunity costs will equal the infringer's profits. However, presumably the infringement led to increased profits over the competitive level. Deduction of opportunity costs allows for the measurement of the incremental contribution of the infringement itself. Practically, however, opportunity costs are difficult to measure, and the risk-free rate of return might be considered as a proxy for "normal" profits.

Another judicial controversy involves whether the infringer should be allowed to deduct fixed costs. The correct rule is that only incremental costs (fixed and variable) should be deducted. As discussed in Chapter 4, incremental costs are those costs that would have been avoided if the infringement had not occurred. However, different circuits have adopted different rules on this topic, and courts within the same circuit have rendered conflicting decisions. In short, it is important to check controlling law before deciding which deductions are appropriate.

Statutory Damages

Section 35(c) of the Lanham Act provides for statutory damages as an alternative to other damages when use of a counterfeit mark has occurred. Counterfeit marks are defined as unauthorized counterfeits of a registered mark that is in use or "a spurious designation that is identical with, or substantially indistinguishable from," designations specifically protected by the Trademark Counterfeiting Act of 1984.[59] An example of the latter category is designations identified in the Olympic Charter Act.[60] Election of statutory damages can occur any time before the final judgment. The statutory amount ranges between $500 and $1,000 per counterfeit mark per type of good or service sold when the infringement is not willful and up to $1 million per counterfeit mark per good or service sold if infringement is willful.[61]

Summary of Trademark Damages

Trademark damages have a lot in common with patent and copyright infringement damages, and the underlying methods used in those two areas of the law can and should be imported to the trademark damage arena. Some important differences also exist. By nature, a trademark conveys information to consumers concerning the nature of a product or services brand. As a result, damage to reputation that impacts future sales can result in damage beyond lost profits. Corrective advertising is one approach to measuring lost reputation, but other methods may be more appropriate under a particular fact scenario. Depending on the factual context, corrective advertising and damage to reputation may only partially overlap. Finally, experts and attorneys must be careful to identify the appropriate statute and the controlling law of the jurisdiction in which the litigation takes place in order to pin down the precise standards for recovery of monetary damages.

TRADE SECRET DAMAGES

Trade secret damages seek to address the ethical concerns and basic fairness principles at the heart of trade secret protection. "The necessity of good faith and honest, fair dealing, is the very life and spirit of the commercial world."[62] To fully discourage the misappropriation of trade secrets, the case law generally requires wrongdoers to compensate the trade secret owner for the value of the trade secret, including, but not necessarily limited to, all of their gains. Moreover, although the trade secret genie can never be completely returned to the bottle, the courts often genuinely attempt to restore the trade secret owner to as near his or her pretheft position as possible.[63]

Trade secret damages, like the cause of action itself, generally are governed by state law. However, the principles already discussed with reference to the calculation of damages for patent and copyright infringement influence trade secret damages as well. In general, "the proper measure of damages in the case of a trade secret appropriation is to be determined by reference to the analogous line of cases involving patent infringement, just as patent infringement cases are used by analogy to determine the damages for copyright infringement."[64] As a result, trade secret damages mirror patent damages to some extent, while varying depending on the relevant jurisdiction. Most states (43 at last count) have adopted some form of the rules for damages contained in the Uniform Trade Secret Act (Uniform Act), while the remaining states generally follow the principles contained in the Restatement of Unfair Trade (Restatement). These resources are provided in Appendices I and J. Although both the Uniform Act and the Restatement discuss the remedies for misappropriation of a trade secret, the two sources take different approaches to calculating the appropriate amount of damages. A brief overview of the types of damages available may provide a helpful foundation for the following discussion of particular calculations.

Under section 3 of the Uniform Act, a plaintiff can recover (1) damages for the trade secret owner's actual losses, and (2) damages reflecting the amount of the defendant's unjust enrichment from use of the misappropriated trade secret, so long as double-counting is eliminated. In other words, to the extent that the defendant's profits capture the trade secret owner's losses, that number should be counted only once, but both the defendant's gains and the plaintiff's losses may be recovered. Moreover, "in lieu of damages measured by any other methods, the damages caused by misappropriation may be measured by imposition of liability for a reasonable royalty. . . ."[65] This means that a reasonable royalty is also available as an alternative measure of damages. The case law under the Uniform Act appears to adopt the Patent Statute standard for calculating lost profits and the reasonable royalty.[66] If misappropriation is willful, the Uniform Act also allows for increasing the damage award up to twice the original amount, including attorneys' fees.[67] The Uniform Act also allows for injunctive relief.[68]

Under section 45 of the Restatement, monetary damages are measured as "the pecuniary loss to the [trade secret owner] caused by the appropriation *or* . . . the [infringer's] own pecuniary gain resulting from the appropriation, *whichever is greater. . . .*" Accordingly, under the Restatement approach, the damages are the larger of lost profits or the infringer's total profits. This is a distinct departure from the typical rule of summing the lost profits and the infringer's profits and eliminating the double-count.[69] Moreover, while the text of section 45 does not mention a reasonable royalty, comment d to the text makes it clear that a reasonable royalty is available and should be measured as "the price that would be agreed upon by a willing buyer and a willing seller for use made of the trade secret by the defendant."

Keeping these differences in mind, this section outlines the available damages for misappropriation of trade secrets.

Losses to the Trade Secret Owner

Both the Uniform Act and the Restatement provide for lost profits due to the misappropriation. Generally, calculating the loss to the trade secret owner is essentially a valuation where the misappropriation has destroyed the value of the secret, often through public disclosure of the confidential information.[70] In contrast, where the misappropriator preserved the secrecy of the trade secret (beyond the fact of the initial misappropriation) but used the trade secret for personal benefit, the owner's losses may be an inadequate measure of damages. Under that scenario, the owner's losses fail to reflect harm resulting from changes in the relative positions of the owner and the misappropriator in the relevant market.[71] At least the following four categories have been identified as potential factors in measuring the trade secret owner's losses.

Lost Profits. The Restatement specifically refers to recovery of lost profits.[72] Lost profits in a trade secret case should be calculated as they are calculated in a patent infringement case. Although the authors are not aware of authority for use of market analysis instead of directly identifying diverted sales, in principle the two methods have the same objective. The Restatement refers to both "specific customers diverted" and "a general decline in sales."[73] In a two-firm market, the sales of the misappropriator probably can be safely used as a proxy for lost sales. Although the more sophisticated approaches used in patent infringement cases should also be applicable in trade secret cases, we have not seen them in reported cases to date.

DSC Communications Corp. v. Next Level Communications[74]

Next Level Communications was formed by former employees of DSC Communications. DSC sued Next Level for misappropriation of trade secrets, specifically the technology for DSC's new broadband access product, switched digital video (SDV). The jury found Next Level liable for misappropriation and awarded damages of $369,200,000 premised on Next Level's developing an SDV system that competed with DSC's system.[75]

On appeal, Next Level argued that the lost profits award was overly speculative given that DSC had yet to sell its SDV product and there was no established market for the product. However, the court affirmed the damage award, finding that DSC adequately established lost sales through extensive market research, known history of the telecommunications industry, empirical success of a precursor product to the SDV system, and DSC's history of strong performance. The court held that "Even if a product is not yet fully developed, a plaintiff is not prevented from recovering future profits if it was hindered in developing that product, and the evidence shows the eventual completion and success of that product is probable."

Price Erosion.   As in other IP cases, price erosion is a potential basis for damages attributable to trade secret misappropriation. Price erosion should be measured in the same manner that it is measured in patent, copyright, and trademark infringement cases.

Value of the Trade Secret.   A trade secret's value varies depending on the chosen perspective. The trade secret may have a much greater value to the owner who developed it than to the misappropriator. Once a trade secret enters the public domain, its value is destroyed. Where the trade secret's value has been destroyed, the secret should be valued from the owner's perspective.[76] Conversely, the value of the secret to the misappropriator usually is the appropriate measure where the secret has not been destroyed and specific injury to the plaintiff is not evident.[77]

A trade secret can be valued like other forms of intangible property, or when informational difficulties exist, the owner's investment in the trade secret can be used as a proxy for the trade secret's minimum value. Such a proxy can be based on the "cost approach" discussed in Chapter 4. The cost approach requires more than just consideration of the out-of-pocket expenses. Consider the following example:

Imagine that a plaintiff has developed a trade secret that allows him to dry his company's product very quickly. The plaintiff developed the product in his spare time over three years. He is the founder and CEO of the company. Finally, assume that he developed the process in a spare room on-site at the company. By stealing the trade secret, the defendant is able to duplicate the drying process. In discovery, the defendant obtains the trial balance (see Chapter 4 for a discussion of the trial balance) of the plaintiff and discovers that it has a line item titled "Drying Process Costs." According to the trial balance, the plaintiff spent $200,000 on developing the drying process. This amount spent by plaintiff is the *minimum* value of the trade secret for several reasons.

First, the plaintiff's cost likely does not include all of the costs incurred during the process of creating the trade secret. For instance, most companies would not allocate any cost of the CEO's salary or a proportionate share of rent to such a project. Thus, if the defendant had to create the trade secret on its own, the actual costs probably would be higher than the amount recorded on the trial balance.

Second, the plaintiff, on its trial balance, would *never* record the costs that should be considered in valuing the trade secret (e.g., the value of avoiding failed invention attempts). As with any invention, the defendant may have had to go through more attempts than the plaintiff did to duplicate the secret. With each failed attempt, the defendant would incur labor costs, material costs, etc.

Third, the cost approach requires that the value of the asset also include a return on the investment that was made to create the asset. In other words, the value of the trade secret is not just the materials, labor, and risk of failure. It also includes a return on the investment in materials, labor, and risk of failure. The rate of return can best be determined using the techniques described in Chapter 5.

Head Start Damages. In trade secret cases, the damage period typically includes a "head start" period. The head start period is the period of time required to eliminate any competitive advantage obtained by the misappropriator. The head start, or "lead time," approach allows defendants to argue that damages should be limited to that period in which the defendant could have become aware of those secrets through legitimate business procedures.[78]

Kilbarr Corp. v. Business Systems, Inc.[79]

The trade secrets at issue in this case concerned an electric typewriter. The court determined that in order to adequately compensate the plaintiff, it was necessary to consider factors such as the impact of the defendant's refusal to return the trade secret to the plaintiff. Because of that refusal, plaintiff was completely precluded from also manufacturing electromechanical typewriters. Not only was plaintiff precluded from licensing others, and entering the market individually, but also the plaintiff still (at the time of the decision) was unable to enter the market because the defendant refused to comply with the court orders requiring the return of the critical information. Nevertheless, the defendant argued that its liability should be limited by the head start rule to that period during which it could have learned the proprietary information through reverse engineering or independent research.

Given the knowing misappropriation and defendant's "grossly improper" conduct, the court refused to limit the monetary remedy by a lead time valuation.

The head start rule is well established in trade secret cases.[80] The Uniform Act also contains a comment endorsing the head start concept:

> Like injunctive relief, a monetary recovery for trade secret misappropriation is appropriate only for the period in which information is entitled to protection as a trade secret, plus the additional period, if any, in which a misappropriator retains an advantage over good faith competitors because of misappropriation. Actual damage to a complainant and unjust benefit to a misappropriator are caused by misappropriation during this time period alone.[81]

The Restatement contains a similar limitation:

> Monetary remedies, whether measured by the loss to the plaintiff or the gain to the defendant, are appropriate only for the period of time that the information would have remained unavailable to the defendant in the absence of the appropriation. This period may be measured by the time it would have taken the defendant to obtain the information by proper means such as reverse engineering or independent development.[82]

However, strict application of the head start rule risks potential undervaluation of the trade secret and the impact of its misappropriation. Specifically, it is important to note any aspects of the relevant market that might render a "head start" completely preclusive of subsequent entrants. In other words, in industries that change very rapidly or that quickly standardize the first product to market, the first to market may be the *only* competitive force in the market. Under that scenario, the value of the trade secret to the defendant may be the better measure of damages.[83]

The Misappropriator's Gain

Using the value of the trade secret to the defendant is an appropriate calculation where the value of the trade secret is destroyed and the plaintiff cannot show specific injury, such as lost sales.[84] In fact, it is not necessary for the trade secret owner to have ever profited from the trade secret in order to recover damages from the misappropriator.[85] There are many possible variations in the means of calculating a defendant's benefit from the stolen trade secret.[86] Under both the Restatement and the Uniform Act, damages can be calculated as the unjust enrichment or the profits of the misappropriator. Although the misappropriator's profits can be awarded even when the trade secret owner has incurred actual losses, if the owner has been awarded lost profits, no duplicative damages are appropriate.[87] Moreover, as mentioned earlier, the Restatement requires plaintiffs to elect which type of damages they prefer rather than taking both.

As in other IP cases, the plaintiff bears the burden of proving the misappropriator's revenue. However, with trade secrets cases, the courts tend to be less stringent in enforcing the requirement that damages must not be unduly speculative.[88] Doubts are resolved against the wrongdoer to preserve disincentives to steal confidential information.[89] In response to plaintiff's numbers, the misappropriator can seek to reduce her liability by establishing sales not caused by the misappropriation and proving that some expenses must be deducted from revenue. The categories of expenses that may be excluded differ by state, so state law should be consulted on this issue.

When a trade secret contributes to a reduction in costs by the misappropriator, the difference between costs incurred with the trade secret and costs incurred without the trade secret constitutes the unjust enrichment. As previously discussed, another possible measure of the misappropriator's gains are the costs saved by not having to develop the trade secret independently. However, when the trade secret results in a reduction of costs, it often is very difficult to determine reasonably a date at which the damages end. For example, assume that the trade secret relates to the organization of an assembly line. The trade secret reduces operating costs. Once the defendant knows how to more efficiently arrange its assembly line, it would be nearly impossible to take back the trade secret. In such cases, it typically is more appropriate to compute damages based on the value of the technology. By taking a trade secret that effectively cannot be returned, the defendant has effectively "bought" the secret. Damages based on the value of the trade secret compensate the plaintiff for the defendant's use of the trade secret in perpetuity.[90]

Reasonable Royalty

When lost profits and unjust enrichment cannot be measured, the Uniform Act and the Restatement authorize a court to determine a reasonable royalty as the appropriate remedy for the misappropriation of a trade secret.[91] "[T]he lack of actual profits does not insulate the defendants from being obliged to pay for what they have wrongfully obtained in the mistaken benefit their theft would benefit them."[92] The Restatement defines a reasonable royalty by the "willing licensor, willing licensee" test, which we have discussed at some length. However, the reasonable royalty in a trade secret context may be increased to adequately punish the defendant.[93] This is sometimes referred to as placing the risk on the wrongdoer rather than on the trade secret owner. The legal system also has an interest in discouraging would-be misappropriators from gambling on escaping with merely a minimum royalty payment equivalent to what they would have paid absent any wrongdoing.

Moreover, some factors in the patent context that operate as checks on the amount of a reasonable royalty are notably absent in trade secret cases. For example, patent licenses often account for uncertainties regarding the patentee's ability to prove infringement and validity of the patent. The technical natures of these questions can prolong litigation and mitigate in favor of a reduced royalty rate. Moreover, patent cases typically assume that the patent owner is a willing licensor. Although this certainly is not always true in a patent case either, in the trade secret context, the assumption is virtually always wrong. The very nature of a trade secret requires that the owner is unwilling to disclose the secret to others, even for a price.[94] Otherwise, the trade secret owner might simply apply for a patent on the secret process and rely on the patent laws to protect his or her rights.

University Computing Co. v. Lykes-Youngstown Corp.[95]

In *University Computing Co.*, the defendant (LYC) bribed an employee to steal the trade secret information related to Universal Computing Co.'s (UCC's) computer system. The facts could be the script for a Hollywood version of a trade secret theft: the bribed employee delivered a suitcase filled with computer tapes and other materials to LYC, then later was paid to fly to Atlanta from Dallas with additional tapes and documents when the original materials were found to be insufficient. On appeal, LYC did not contest the fact of liability for misappropriation, but it disputed the amount of the damages awarded. Despite its best efforts, LYC had not been able to sell the trade secret computer system at a profit and thus had no actual profits to indicate the value of the secret to LYC.

The Fifth Circuit emphasized that the absence of profits should not insulate the defendant's conduct from liability and affirmed the royalty awarded by the district

University Computing Co. v. Lykes-Youngstown Corp. (continued)

court. The court described the factors for determining a reasonable royalty as follows:

"In calculating what a fair licensing price would have been had the parties agreed, the trier of fact should consider such factors as the resulting and foreseeable changes in the parties' competitive posture; the prices past purchasers or licensees may have paid; the total value of the secret to the plaintiff, including the plaintiff's development costs and the importance of the secret to the plaintiff's business; the nature and extent of the use the defendant intended for the secret; and finally whatever other unique factors in the particular case which might have affected the parties' agreement, such as the ready availability of alternative processes."

The court upheld UCC's estimation of the value of the trade secret. UCC's expert calculated the value of the trade secret information by multiplying UCC's costs in developing the materials by a multiple of 2.5. Despite recognizing "a certain amount of speculation" involved in the calculation, the court affirmed that the expert had the expertise to determine the proper means for estimating sales price as a function of costs.

Royalties also may be awarded as a lump sum by considering the defendant's sales projections over the useful life of the product and discounting to present value. This approach is utilized in several patent cases.[96]

Interactive Pictures Corp. v. Infinite Pictures, Inc.[97]

Interactive Pictures involved infringement of a patented image viewing system. The court affirmed a lump sum royalty award as damages based on Infinite Pictures's sales projections made shortly before the infringement began. Despite the fact that the actual performance of Infinite Pictures's product was substantially below the projections (only $66,500 in sales versus the $1 million of projected sales), the court agreed that the sales projections provided a snapshot of the defendant's valuation of the technology at that time. The court stated that while "Infinite's subsequent failure to meet its projections may simply illustrate the 'element of approximation and uncertainty' inherent in future projections," the lump sum royalty based on those projections was not unduly speculative or grossly excessive.

Summary of Trade Secret Damages

Trade secret damages are governed by state law. Most states have adopted in some form the rules contained in the Uniform Trade Secret Act and the Restatement (Third) of unfair competition. Both of these sources provide for remedies similar or identical to those available in patent, copyright, and trademark infringement cases. However, in a trade secret case, no statutory damages exist. Moreover, trade secrets are the only area of IP damage law in which the head start doctrine may limit the available damages.

ENDNOTES

[1] 17 U.S.C. § 505; *see also Fogerty v. Fantasy*, 510 U.S. 517 (1994) (holding that standard governing award of attorneys' fees under section 505 should be identical for prevailing plaintiffs and prevailing defendants).

[2] *See Marobie-FL. v. Nat'l Assoc. of Fire Equipment Distrib.*, No. 96 C 2966, 2002 U.S. Dist. LEXIS 2350 (N.D. Ill. Feb. 13, 2002) (requiring each party to bear costs and attorneys' fees where jury awarded $0 for infringement of plaintiff's copyrighted works).

[3] *See Lotus Dev. Corp. v. Borland Int'l, Inc.*, 140 F.3d 728 (7th Cir. 1998); *Maljack Prods., Inc. v. GoodTimes Home Video Corp.*, 81 F.3d 881 (9th Cir. 1996); *Diamond Star Bldg. Corp. v. Freed*, 30 F.3d 503 (4th Cir. 1994).

[4] David Horrigan, *Compaq Wins $2.7M Fee Award in Copyright Case*, Nat'l Law J., May 1, 2002 (the court cited numerous discovery abuses and even ordered the attorneys to reimburse Compaq $101,822 for their "unreasonable and vexatious conduct" during discovery).

[5] 17 U.S.C. § 504.

[6] *Id.* §§ 412, 504(c).

[7] *Id.* § 504(a), (b).

[8] *Storm Impact, Inc. v. Software of the Month Club*, 13 F. Supp.2d 782 (N.D. Ill. 1998); *Joseph J. Legat Architects, P.C. v. United States Dev. Corp.*, 1991 U.S. Dist. LEXIS 3358 (N. D. Ill.).

[9] *Taylor v. Meirick*, 712 F.2d 1112 (7th Cir. 1983).

[10] *Stevens Linen Assoc., Inc. v. Mastercraft Corp.*, 656 F.2d 11 (2d Cir. 1981).

[11] *Big Seven Music Corp. v. Lennon*, 554 F.2d 504 (2d Cir. 1977) (comparing sales of infringed Lennon album with sales of his other contemporary albums).

[12] *See, e.g., Stevens Linen Assoc., Inc. v. Mastercraft Corp.*, 656 F.2d 11 (2d Cir. 1981).

[13] *Deltak, Inc. v. Advanced Systems, Inc.*, 767 F.2d 357 (7th Cir. 1985).

[14] *See, e.g., Business Trends Analysts, Inc. v. Freedonia Group, Inc.*, 887 F.2d 399 (2d Cir. 1989); *Quinn v. City of Detroit*, 23 F. Supp. 2d 741 (E.D. Mich. 1998).

[15] *Storm Impact, Inc. v. Software of the Month Club*, 17 F. Supp.2d 782, 791 (N.D. Ill. 1998).

[16] *See also Blackman v. Hustler Magazine, Inc.*, 585 F.2d 274, 281 (6th Cir. 1988).

[17] *See Stevens Linen Assocs. v. Mastercraft Corp.,* 656 F.2d 11 (2d Cir. 1981) (discussed previously).

[18] *Knitwaves, Inc. v. Lollytogs, Ltd.,* 71 F.3d 996 (2d Cir. 1995).

[19] *Sheldon v. Metro-Goldwyn Pictures Corp.,* 309 U.S. 390 (1940).

[20] *Frank Music Corp. v. Metro-Goldwyn-Mayer Inc.,* 772 F.2d 505 (9th Cir. 1985).

[21] *See Feltner v. Columbia Pictures Television, Inc.,* 523 U.S. 340, 343–344 (1998).

[22] 17 U.S.C. § 412.

[23] *Id.* § 412.

[24] *Id.* § 412(2).

[25] Because of earlier legislation, causes of action arising before January 1, 1978, permit the owner to seek statutory damages even if there was no registration at the time of infringement, so long as the owner registers the copyright prior to filing a complaint. Cases involving this older legislation seldom occur anymore, so we will not discuss the particular laws and requirements of registration that attach to those causes of action.

[26] *See, e.g., Eden Toys, Inc. v. Florelee Undergarment Co.,* 697 F.2d 27, 33 (2d Cir. 1982).

[27] Copyright Damages Improvement Act of 1999 (Pub. L.106-160), signed into law December 9, 1999 (the "normal" and "maximum" statutory damages were increased by 50 percent; previously, the normal range of statutory damages was $500 to $20,000 for each work).

[28] 17 U.S.C. § 504(c)(2).

[29] *Storm Impact, Inc. v. Software of the Month Club,* 17 F. Supp.2d 782 (N.D. Ill. 1998).

[30] *See Dive N' Surf, Inc. v. Anselozitz,* 834 F. Supp. 379 (M.D. Fla. 1993).

[31] 17 U.S.C. § 504(c)(1).

[32] *Id.*

[33] 15 U.S.C. § 35(a).

[34] See *Champion Spark Pkg. Co. v. Sanders,* 331 U.S. 125 (1947); *Intel Corp. v. Terabyte Inter. Inc.,* 6 F.3d 614 (9th Cir. 1993).

[35] 15 U.S.C. § 32(1).

[36] *See id.* § 34; *see also* Brown, *Civil Remedies for Intellectual Property Invasions: Themes and Variations,* 55 L. Contemp. Probs. 45, 51, 65 (1992).

[37] *See, e.g., George Basch Co., Inc. v. Blue Coral, Inc.,* 968 F.2d 1532 (2d Cir. 1992); *see also Texas Pig Stands, Inc. v. Hard Rock Café Int'l,* 951 F.2d 684 (5th Cir. 1992).

[38] *See, e.g., Taco Cabana International, Inc. v. Two Pesos, Inc.,* 932 F.2d 1113 (5th Cir. 1991).

[39] *See, e.g., Maltina Corp. v. Cawx Bottling Co., Inc.,* 613 F.2d 582, 585 (5th Cir. 1980).

[40] 15 U.S.C. § 35(a).

[41] *Id.*

[42] *Id.*

[43] *Id.* § 35(b).

[44] *Id.* § 35(c).

[45] *Id.* § 36(2)(a), (b), (c).

[46] *See, e.g., BASF Corp. v. Old World Trading Co., Inc.,* 41 F.3d 1081 (7th Cir. 1994).

[47] *See, e.g., Intel Corp. v. Terabyte Int., Inc.,* 6 F.3d 614 (9th Cir. 1993).

[48] *See, e.g., Burndy Corp. v. Teledyne Industries, Inc.,* 748 F.2d 767 (2d Cir. 1984).

[49] *Big O Tire Dealers, Inc. v. Goodyear Tire & Rubber Co.,* 408 F. Supp. 1219 (D. Colo. 1976).

[50] *Big O Tire Dealers, Inc. v. Goodyear Tire & Rubber Co.,* 561 F.2d 1365 (10th Cir. 1977).

[51] *See, e.g.,* James E. Heald, *Money Damages and Corrective Advertising: An Economic Analysis,* 55 U. Chi. L. Rev. 629 (1988); Restatement (Third) of Unfair Competition § 36 (1995).

[52] *Sands, Taylor & Wood v. Quaker Oats Co.,* 34 F.3d 1340 (7th Cir. 1994).

[53] *Bandag, Inc. v. Al Bulser's Tire Stores, Inc.,* 750 F.2d 903 (Fed. Cir. 1984); Restatement (Third) of Unfair Competition § 36 (1995).

[54] *Sands, Taylor & Wood,* 34 F.3d 1340.

[55] *Id.*

[56] 15 U.S.C. § 35(a); Restatement (Third) of Unfair Competition § 37.

[57] *George Basch Co., Inc. v. Blue Coral, Inc.,* 968 F.2d 1532 (2d Cir. 1992).

[58] *See* discussion in James M. Koelemay, Jr., *A Practical Guide to Monetary Relief in Trademark Infringement Cases,* 85 Trademark Rep. 263 (1995).

[59] 15 U.S.C. §§ 35(c), 34(d)(1)(B).

[60] 18 U.S.C. § 2320(e)(1).

[61] 15 U.S.C. § 35(c).

[62] *Kewanee Oil Corp. v. Bicron Corp.,* 416 U.S. 470, 482 (1974) (citations omitted) (emphasizing the importance of trade secret law to maintaining commercial ethics).

[63] *Telex Corp. v. IBM Corp.,* 510 F.2d 894 (10th Cir.), *cert. denied,* 423 U.S. 802 (1975) (identifying as a common thread throughout trade secret cases that "the plaintiff should be made whole").

[64] *University Computing Co. v. Lykes-Youngstown Corp.,* 504 F.2d 518, 535 (5th Cir. 1974) (*quoting Int'l Indus., Inc. v. Warren Petroleum Corp.,* 248 F.2d 696, 699 (3rd Cir. 1957)).

[65] Uniform Trade Secrets Act § 3(a).

[66] *See Metallurgical Industries, Inc. v. Fourtek, Inc.,* 790 F.2d 1995 (5th Cir. 1986).

[67] Uniform Trade Secrets Act § 3(b); *See, e.g., Jannotta v. Subway Sandwich Shops, Inc.,* 125 F.3d 503 (7th Cir. 1997) (awarding punitive damages against a corporation for acts of its employees where employee was acting in a managerial capacity or the corporation ratified the employee's acts); *Weibler v. Universal Technologies, Inc.,* 61 U.S.P.Q.2d (BNA) 1599 (10th Cir. 2002) (declining to award attorneys' fees for trade secret misappropriation where the conduct lacked an element of "meaningful control and deliberate action" normally associated with willful and malicious acts); *Mangren Research and Dev. Corp. v. Nat'l Chemical Co., Inc.,* 87 F.3d 937 (7th Cir. 1996) (finding exemplary

damages appropriate where actions indicated "conscious disregard of the rights of another"); *RKI, Inc. v. Grimes*, No. 01 C 8542, 2002 U.S. Dist. LEXIS 7974 (N.D. Ill. May 2, 2002) (awarding $150,000 in exemplary damages where intentional misappropriation and attempted cover-up).

[68] Uniform Trade Secrets Act § 2.

[69] *See, e.g., Brown v. Ruallam Ents., Inc.*, 44 S.W.3d 740 (Ark. App. 2001) (applying Arkansas trade secret law to preclude the recovery of both plaintiff's lost profits and defendant's profits); *see also Saforo & Assocs., Inc. v. Porocel Corp.*, 991 S.W.2d 117 (Ark. 1999) (comparing two veins of authority on this topic).

[70] *University Computing Co. v. Lykes-Youngstown Corp.*, 504 F.2d 518, 535 (5th Cir. 1974); *Precision Plating v. Martin Marietta*, 435 F.2d 1262 (5th Cir. 1970) (holding that the value of a trade secret process had been completely destroyed upon public disclosure).

[71] *Id.* (distinguishing defendant's use of the trade secret from a disclosure that would destroy the value of the secret to plaintiff); *see also Servo Corp. v. General Elec. Co.*, 393 F.2d 551 (4th Cir. 1968) (outlining aspects of disclosure in a trade secrets context).

[72] Restatement § 45(1) (trade secret damages include liability for "the pecuniary loss to the other"); *see also* related comments.

[73] *See* comments to Restatement § 45.

[74] *DSC Comm. Corp. v. Next Level Comm.*, 107 F.3d 322 (5th Cir. 1997).

[75] After posttrial reductions and interest, the award amounted to approximately $140.7 million. *See also DSC Comm. Corp. v. Next Level Comm.*, 929 F. Supp. 239, 246 (E.D. Tex. 1996) (noting that since neither party had produced a product ready for sale to customers, the purchase price of Next Level itself [whose assets consisted almost exclusively of DSC's allegedly stolen ideas] might be the least speculative method of deriving the value of the trade secrets).

[76] *University Computing*, 504 F.2d at 535–36.

[77] *Id.*

[78] *See, e.g. Abernathy-Thomas Eng. Co. v. Pall Corp.*, 103 F. Supp. 2d 582, 607 (E.D. N.Y. 2000) (limiting appropriate measure of damages to the lost profits during that period from the date the misuse began until the date that the defendant could have compiled the stolen customer list independently); *Schiller & Schmidt, Inc. v. Nordisco Corp.*, 969 F.2d 410, 415–16 (7th Cir. 1992).

[79] *Kilbarr Corp. v. Bus. Systems, Inc.*, 679 F. Supp. 422 (D.N.J. 1988), *aff'd* 869 F.2d 589 (3d Cir. 1989).

[80] *See, e.g., Sokol Crystal Products v. DSC Communications Corp.*, 15 F.3d 1427, 1422 (7th Cir. 1994) ("[W]here a misappropriation of a trade secret only gives a competitor a 'head start' in developing a product, damages should be limited to the injury suffered in that 'head start' period"); *Micro Lithography, Inc. v. Inko Indus., Inc.*, 20 U.S.P.Q. 2d 1347, 1353 (Cal. St. App. 1991) ("The duration of the accounting period is generally limited in two ways: the disclosure of the trade secret itself or application of the 'headstart' rule."); *Molinaro v. Burnbaum*, 201 U.S.P.Q. 150, 163 (D. Mass 1978) ("The award for damages compensates the plaintiff for the head start that the defendants obtained through its misappropriation."); *Carboline Co. v. Jarboe*, 454 S.W.2d 549, 552 (Mo. 1970) ("Plas-Chem

should be given the opportunity to establish the 'head start' time as to these products, and the injunction should be limited to that period of time if shown").

[81] Uniform Trade Secrets Act comment to § 3.

[82] Restatement (Third) of Unfair Competition § 45 cmt. H.

[83] *See, e.g., Kilbarr Corp. v. Bus. Systems, Inc.,* 679 F. Supp. 422 (D.N.J. 1988), *aff'd* 869 F.2d 589 (3d Cir. 1989); *Sikes v. McGraw-Edison Co.,* 665 F.2d 731, 736–37 (5th Cir. 1982); *USM Corp. v. Marson Fastener Corp.,* 467 N.E.2d 1271, 1285 (Mass. 1984).

[84] *University Computing Co.,* 504 F.2d at 536; Uniform Trade Secrets Act § 3(a).

[85] *Perdue Farms, Inc. v. Hook,* 777 So.2d 1047 (Fla. App. 2001) (affirming $25 million award despite fact that plaintiff had never profited or received any royalty for the trade secret).

[86] *Id.*

[87] Uniform Trade Secrets Act § 3(a) ("Damages can include both the actual loss caused by misappropriation and the unjust enrichment caused by misappropriation that is not taken into account in computing actual loss."); *Telex v. IBM,* 510 F.2d 894, 931–32 (10th Cir.) (*per curiam*), *cert. dismissed,* 423 U.S. 802 (1975).

[88] *See University Computing,* 504 F.2d at 539; *see also Olson v. Nieman's, Ltd.,* 579 N.W.2d 299 (Iowa 1998) (allowing plaintiff "considerable leeway" on speculation involving damages in order to prevent unfair competitors to profit from their misdeeds); *Koehler v. Cummings,* 380 F. Supp. 1294 (M.D. Tenn. 1974).

[89] *See, e.g., BE&K Constr. Co. v. Will & Grundy Counties Bldg Trades Council, AFL–CIO,* 156 F.3d 756, 770 (7th Cir. 1998) (holding that damages need not be proven "with the certainty of calculus" and doubts should be resolved against the wrongdoer); *Sunds Defibrator Ab v. Beloit Corp.,* 930 F.2d 564 (7th Cir. 1991); *Weston v. Buckley,* 677 N.E.2d 1089 (Ind. App. 1997).

[90] *But see Sonoco Prods. Co. v. Johnson,* 23 P.3d 1287 (Colo. App. 2001) (rejecting plaintiff's model based on the misappropriator's "cost of capital" savings from use of the trade secret process for manufacturing toilet paper rolls).

[91] *See American Sales Corp. v. Adventure Travel, Inc.,* 862 F. Supp. 1476 (E.D. Va. 1994); *RKI, Inc. v. Grimes,* No. 01 C 8542, 2002 U.S. Dist. LEXIS 7974 (N.D. Ill. 2002); *Perdue Farms, Inc. v. Hook,* 777 So.2d 1047 (Fla. App. 2001).

[92] *University Computing Co.,* 504 F.2d at 536.

[93] *Id.; King Instruments Corp. v. Perego,* 65 F.3d 941 (Fed. Cir. 1995) (approving awards higher than reasonable royalty in a patent context in order to discourage infringers from "heads-I-win, tails-you-lose" tactics); *Panduit Corp. v. Stahlin Bros. Fibre Works,* 575 F.2d 1152 (6th Cir. 1978) (same).

[94] *See University Computing Co.,* 504 F.2d at 544 (noting that one should take into account the reasons the seller is unprepared to sell and consider the plaintiff's interest in preserving its competitive positions, possibly by diminishing the focus on a royalty that the defendant actually would have accepted).

[95] *University Computing Co. v. Lykes-Youngstown Corp.,* 504 F.2d 518 (5th Cir. 1974).

[96] *See, e.g., Interactive Pictures Corp. v. Infinite Pictures, Inc.,* 274 F.3d 1371 (Fed. Cir.
      2001); *Snellman v. Ricoh Co., Ltd.,* 862 F.2d 283 (Fed. Cir. 1988); *TWM Mfg. Co. v. Dura
      Corp.,* 789 F.2d 895 (Fed. Cir.), *cert. denied,* 479 U.S. 852 (1986).

[97] *Interactive Pictures Corp. v. Infinite Pictures, Inc.,* 274 F.3d 1371 (Fed. Cir. 2001).

ADDITIONAL READING

Copyright Reading

David Nimmer, *Infringement Actions—Remedies,* 4 Nimmer on Copyright ch. 14 (1963,
1999).

Sheri A. Byrne, *Nintendo of America, Inc. v. Dragon Pacific International: Double Trouble—
When Do Awards of Both Copyright and Trademark Damages Constitute Double Recovery?*
31 University of San Francisco Law Review 257 (Fall 1996).

Andrew Coleman, *Copyright Damages and the Value of the Infringing Use: Restitutionary
Recovery in Copyright Infringement Actions,* 21 American Intellectual Property Law
Association Quarterly Journal 91 (1993).

Charles Ossola, *Registration and Remedies: Recovery of Attorney's Fees and Statutory
Damages Under the Copyright Reform Act,* 13 Cardozo Arts & Entertainment Law Journal
559 (1995).

Barry I. Slotnick, *Copyright Damages, Statutory Damages and the Right to a Jury Trial,*
533 Practicing Law Institute 655 (1998).

Trademark Reading

Ralph S. Brown, *Civil Remedies for Intellectual Property Invasions: Themes and Variations,* 55 Law & Contemporary Problems 45, 51, 65 (1992).

McCarthy on Trademarks, Chapter 30.

James M. Koelemay, Jr., *A Practical Guide to Monetary Relief in Trademark Infringement
Cases,* 85 Trademark Reporter 263 (1995).

James M. Koelemay, Jr., *Monetary Relief for Trademark Infringement Under the Lanham
Act,* 22 Trademark Reporter 458 (1982).

Terence P. Ross, *Trademark Infringement Damages,* in Intellectual Property Law: Damages
and Remedies, Chapter 4 (2000).

Siegrum D. Kane, *Trademark Law: A Practitioner's Guide,* PLI, Chapter 16 (2001).

Trade Secret Reading

Patricia A. Meier, *Looking Back and Forth: The Restatement (Third) of Unfair Competition
and Potential Impact on Texas Trade Secret Law,* 4 Texas Intellectual Property Law
Journal 415 (1996).

Michael A. Rosenhouse, *Proper Measure and Elements of Damages for Misappropriation
of Trade Secret,* 11 ALR 4th 12.

Craig N. Johnson, *Assessing Damages for Misappropriation of Trade Secrets,* 27 Colorado Lawyer (1998).

Wayne A. Hoeberlein, *Trade Secrets: Damages,* 340 PLI/Pat 599 (1992).

Felix Prandl, *Damages for Misappropriation of Trade Secret,* 22 Tort & Insurance Law Journal 447 (1987).

Milgram on Trade Secrets, Chapter 3.

Christopher Marchese, *Patent Infringement and Future Lost Profits Damages,* 26 Arizona State Law Journal 747 (1994).

Stephen I. Willis, *An Economic Evaluation of Trade Secrets,* 269 PLI/Pat 737 (1989).

14

The Nuts and Bolts
of Intellectual Property
Damage Calculation

This final chapter focuses on the actual process or "nuts and bolts" of determining intellectual property (IP) damages. When actually faced with the need to develop a coherent damage theory in an IP dispute, the sophisticated practitioner should undertake several steps. First, it is necessary to address whether the calculation of damages in a particular case will consist of a reasonable royalty, lost profits, or a combination of both. Then the focus should shift to the means of determining a reasonable royalty and/or lost profits related to an established product. Finally, this chapter guides the practitioner through the process of determining lost profits related to an unestablished product. These steps should provide a pragmatic outline of a reasonable approach to IP damage calculations. The following outline is intended to provide a format for the thought process behind determining damages as well as a general description of some of the mechanics of preparing such an analysis. The authors, in conjunction with many other experts in damage analysis, are currently working on a supplement to the book. The supplement deals almost exclusively with the mechanics of a damage calculation. We are optimistic that court rulings and advancements in financial analysis will have a lesser effect on this chapter than on the chapters in the supplement. However, since new rulings are made every day, we encourage readers to make sure they are considering rulings that have been made since the printing of this book.

THE PROCESS OF DETERMINING WHETHER THE PROPER DAMAGES CONSIST OF A REASONABLE ROYALTY, LOST PROFITS, OR A COMBINATION OF BOTH

All infringing sales ultimately must be considered in determining damages. As a consequence, the first practical step in a damage analysis is to identify the sales of both parties that are generated by the IP at issue. As will be discussed in detail, the sales of the owner (referred to herein as "the plaintiff") must be considered to determine capacity and profitability. The infringer's sales are needed to determine the number of infringing units.

As a practical matter, access to the detailed sales ledger is extremely important to the successful completion of this first step. The detailed sales ledger is likely to contain sales sufficiently detailed to allow the practitioner to cull the alleged infringing sales from other sales. However, because sales ledgers typically record only the dollar amount of the sales (as opposed to the number of units), it is likely that either production reports (a non-accounting document generated by the manufacturing department which will detail units) or invoices (which detail prices so that one can estimate the number of units by dividing sales by price) also will be needed. It also is helpful to obtain information concerning the customer's name and the location at which the sale was made, as well as the sales channel and the date of the sale. All such data should be gathered from both parties if possible.

Once identified, the defendant's sales can be divided into two broad categories: (1) the infringing sales that would have been made by the plaintiff absent infringement, and (2) the infringing sales that would not have been made by the infringed party absent infringement. (see Exhibit 14-1). The plaintiff is entitled to lost profits on all of the sales in the first category and a reasonable royalty on the sales in the second category.[1]

As discussed in Chapter 7 of this book, an important component in determining whether a plaintiff is entitled to lost profits or reasonable royalties is the determination of whether there is a market or demand for the infringing product. Typically, the defendant would not have infringed if there were no demand for the infringing product. Companies often generate marketing materials that can be useful in establishing whether market demand existed. However, in rare instances, a product can be infringed on in a manner that does not require market demand for the product. Where there is no market demand for the product, there can be no lost profits because the "but for" causation is lost.

Once the practitioner determines that market demand exists (or existed), the next step is examining whether the defendant had a noninfringing substitute available to it at the time the infringement began. The size and importance of noninfringing substitutes is key

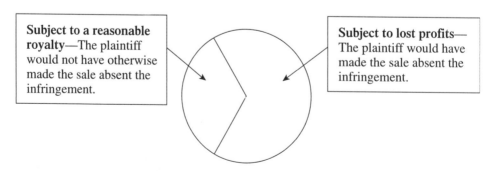

EXHIBIT 14-1   Total Infringing Sales by Defendant

to both the lost profits and reasonable royalty analyses. The defendant's noninfringing alternatives to the technology must be considered in the hypothetical royalty negotiation. No economically rational, self-interested party would pay a royalty amount that is greater than the cost to design around the technology at issue. This notion is consistent with valuation theory. The "cost approach" (described in Chapter 5) often is depicted as a methodology based on estimating value by quantifying the amount of money that would be required to replace the future service capability. Moreover, the availability of noninfringing substitutes may prevent the plaintiff from receiving lost profits. If the defendant had noninfringing substitutes available that would not have substantially affected sales volumes, prices, production costs, or product quality, the plaintiff would not have obtained any infringing sales in the "but for" world. Accordingly, many defendants initially claim that such a substitute existed. Proof of an acceptable substitute typically requires testimony by persons with personal knowledge or technical expertise concerning the design-around prospects. There typically is an economic disadvantage to using a noninfringing substitute over the patented product. In other words, it usually costs money to switch to the noninfringing substitute because the alternative may not perform as well as the patented technology. The quantification of this potential disadvantage can, in some cases, represent the proper amount of damages.

A third issue is whether the plaintiff had the capacity to make the defendant's sales. The analysis of capacity has several dimensions. Determining the plaintiff's capacity to make the infringing sales requires an analysis of the plaintiff's manufacturing, selling, and financing ability.

Manufacturing Capacity

The ability to physically produce the patented product often is determined through interviews with production managers and an analysis of production documents. Even companies that are operating at their plants' physical limits may still have additional capacity through expansion. However, expansion is possible only through incurring increased costs. These costs are not solely the cost of increasing the manufacturing capacity. For example, if the plaintiff claims that it would have had increased manufacturing capacity by leasing additional space, adding a shift, and so on, the additional building costs, supervisor pay, and overtime expense must be considered. Of course, if the plaintiff argues that it would have built a facility to create additional capacity, the time necessary to complete the facility and the risk that the plant will not operate properly are additional costs and should be considered. If a single additional shift is needed, the cost of adding manufacturing capacity may involve additional overtime. Finally, if the plaintiff already had excess capacity in place, there may be little or no cost to expansion. The actual analysis of capacity expansion is performed in the same manner as in a valuation exercise. The cost of adding capacity can be determined either through the creation of projections (the income approach) or by examining competitors' costs (the market approach).

Financing Capacity

Additional sales require additional investment in working capital. As described earlier, working capital represents the difference between current assets (cash, receivables, and other like items) and current liabilities (accounts payable, accrued liabilities, etc.). The plaintiff must have the financial ability to provide the working capital necessary to make the infringing sales and thus obtain lost profits. The analysis of a plaintiff's ability to finance lost sales is most often performed in two steps. The practitioner must determine (1) the amount of investment that is needed, and (2) the plaintiff's ability and the costs of obtaining the required funds.

Determining the Amount of Investment Needed.　　The methodology for determining the necessary investment is similar to the manner in which working capital requirements are determined in conducting a business valuation. Nearly all firms with increasing sales must make some investment in working capital. For example, imagine a new law firm that is composed of two attorneys, one being the owner and the other an associate. The lawyers have good reputations that cause their practice to have billable work beginning on the first day of operation. By the end of the first month, both attorneys worked 200 hours and billed $200 per hour ($80,000 dollars, $200 \times 200 \times 2$). On the first day of the second month, the firm sends its clients a bill for the work done during the first month of operation. The clients pay within 30 days. Accordingly, 2 months pass before the attorneys begin receiving any revenue. During that time, light bills, the associate's salary, rent, and other expenses must be paid by the law firm. As a result, the owner must resort to savings (equity) or borrowed funds (debt) to pay the bills. Some expenses can be deferred beyond the two-month period. Thus, the amount of financing capacity needed is defined as the *difference* between the total expenses incurred and the portion of total expenses that did not have to be paid in the first 60 days.

A firm's financial statements make it relatively easy to calculate the firm's financing capacity. Working capital is calculated from the balance sheet as the "total current assets" less the "total current liabilities." The difference between these quantities must be financed. If balance sheet information is not relevant for use in a "but for" scenario, it may be necessary to estimate the amount of working capital needed based on industry averages or historical changes in working capital. The "liquidity" ratios discussed in Chapter 4 are a common approach to determining the amount of working capital a firm requires.

Determining the Plaintiff's Ability to Obtain the Required Amount of Financing. Once the necessary *amount* of financing is determined, a firm's *ability* to finance such an amount must be established. The easiest way to establish a firm's ability to finance is by identifying existing credit lines. Many businesses have credit lines on which they can draw funds. Alternatively, an analysis that compares the debt level of the plaintiff to the levels of its similarly situated competitors may provide evidence concerning the amount a firm can borrow and the likely cost of borrowing. The leverage ratios discussed in Chapter 4 are also a common means of analyzing a firm's ability to obtain funds.

Marketing Ability

Finally, the plaintiff must be able to have access to the defendant's customers in order to make the defendant's sales. If the plaintiff has a sales relationship with the defendant's customers, it often is safe to assume that the sale could have been made by the plaintiff. Marketing plans often provide data necessary to estimate the number of new clients per week, the number of salespeople that are required to generate the sales, and so on. Moreover, sales ledgers often list customer names. In some cases, service or warranties are a necessary requirement to sell a product. If the plaintiff does not have the ability to provide the relevant service and warranties, it would be inappropriate to include the sale in lost profits.

Once the ability to make the infringer's sales has been determined, lost profits should be applied only to those sales for which all the aforementioned prerequisites are met.

CALCULATING LOST PROFITS

One frequently used approach to calculating lost profits involves the following essential steps:

- Determine the number of unit sales that would have been made by the plaintiff during the damage period.
- Determine the net sales price of the units that would have been sold by the plaintiff.
- Determine the plaintiff's incremental costs of producing and selling the units.
- Determine whether it is appropriate to discount the resulting profits for the time value of money and the risks connected to such sales.

The proper lost profits damage amount is calculated by multiplying the number of units that the plaintiff would have sold "but for" the infringement by the incremental profits that would have been generated by the sale. This incremental profit is calculated as the difference between the net selling price of the units sold and the incremental costs of producing and selling the same units. A closer inspection of the steps in this calculation reveals that they are essentially the same steps involved in the income approach to valuation.

Determine the Number of Unit Sales That Would Have Been Made by the Plaintiff During the Damage Period for a Firm with a Proven Track Record

Even where the plaintiff possessed the capacity to make certain sales, it does not necessarily follow that the plaintiff would have actually made the sales. The ultimate lost sales amount is determined by analyzing the critical factors that determine sales of the infringing product. It may be that sales are driven by factors other than the patented technology. For instance, customers often purchase from a particular firm because of sales relationships, the ability to access a full line of products, maintenance contracts, service, brand recognition, warranties, or any of a number of reasons other than the product itself. In situations in which the plaintiff has a long operating history, the number of lost sales is most easily determined by using a "before-and-after" approach. Under this approach, the plaintiff's sales activity before infringement is compared with its sales activity after infringement. Market factors also must be considered, including industry-wide sales expectations, the overall state of the economy, etc.

Determining "But for" Sales for a Firm with an Unproven Track Record

One of the most difficult issues that a damage expert must grapple with is determining the "but for" sales of a product that incorporates a technology with an unproven track record. In this situation, the expert should specify the growth trajectory that the product could take in the future. Although there are several approaches to this problem, one approach that is gaining popularity relies on the body of research related to the "diffusion" of a technology to hypothesize that the future growth of a technology will follow an S-shaped pattern. An S shape can be the result of numerous functional forms, and the expert must attempt to establish both a factual basis for application of diffusion theory and a basis for a particular functional form of the S curve that is adopted.

The diffusion literature is a multidisciplinary analysis of how an innovation is communicated through certain channels and adopted by the population. For example, the advent of refrigerators ushered in a process of rapid replacement of the old iceboxes. Diffusion theorists have studied the time path of the replacement of the old technology with the new technology and the factors involved in this replacement process. Empirical research on the diffusion of innovations has resulted in a body of literature consisting of hundreds of published books and articles (see Additional Reading at the end of this chapter). A central principle in this literature is that technology is adopted by distinct groups and diffuses through these groups at varying times and speeds. Theoretically, the process begins with a small set of "innovators," proceeds to "early adopters," and then picks up speed as groups called the "early majority" and the "late majority" slowly adopt the technology. Finally, a population group called the "laggards" adopt the technology. The size of these population groups, their adoption speed, and their sequence of adoption typically result in an observed overall pattern of diffusion of a technology that looks like an S-shaped curve.

The diffusion literature posits a complex set of factors that appear to determine the rate of adoption of a new technology. These factors include attributes of the innovation, attributes of the adopting population, promotion efforts, and the nature of communication channels.[2] Moreover, several assumptions underlie the various diffusion models. Most models assume a single monopoly producer. The presence of competition adds significant complexity to these models. Also, the models often assume a binary diffusion process, where only one adoption per household is possible. Other assumptions adopted for tractability include a fixed population ceiling and the absence of change in the innovation over time.

With these caveats, diffusion theory may be a useful tool when grounded in the facts of the particular case. For example, consider the use of diffusion theory in damage analysis for a technology with an unproven track record. Initially, the practitioner should determine the categorization of the future customers of this technology.

Innovators. Innovators represent the type of buyers who quickly experiment with new technology. These consumers often enjoy buying the technology, disassembling it, and learning how it runs as much as they enjoy its actual use. Innovators often are employed in research and development departments. The IP that is being purchased by innovators typically generates sales at prices below the ultimate expected sales price. In fact, it often is given away by technology companies in the hope of future sales. Furthermore, sales typically are made in sporadic, small amounts. Although innovators frequently want to pay only a modest amount for the technology, they usually have very low demands for performance. In fact, their reactions to problems with the product often make significant contributions to the debugging process.

Many technology products fail to ever develop past this stage of adoption. Other technologies linger in this stage for many years as they are being developed and the market "catches up" to the developers. Plaintiffs whose technology is in this stage must consider the significant risk that the product will never gain market acceptance. Additionally, plaintiffs selling into markets made up of innovators must consider the risk that the product will not even work to the consumers' expectations.

Early Adopters. Early adopters represent the second stage in the market life cycle. These individuals typically are motivated by the desire to gain a competitive advantage through the use of the new technology. Early adopters commonly pay a price that is below the ultimate expected sales price. In fact, they are offered lower prices to compensate for the additional risk of using the product at this early stage in its marketing and development. Early adopters expect the product to work properly. However, they often are comfortable with a developer that has not fully completed the support network for the technology. For example, imagine an early adopter who purchases a new software product. He or she probably will expect the software to work relatively bug-free. However, they likely would be unconcerned that the packaging was not elaborate or colorful or that the user manual was incomplete. Early adopters typically incur costs of implementing the technology that are greater than the costs that ultimately will be paid by the market. This happens as the early adopters actually figure out the best way to use the technology in their businesses.

At this point in the market life cycle, the technology company may be focused on establishing a customer base with adequate size to act as a reference point for the next market stage—the "early majority." Generally, the developer attempts to create the proper reference point by focusing sales efforts on a relatively small niche to garner a large share of the niche market.

Unfortunately, it is not unusual for an inventor to sell to early adopters in many different niches. For early adopters, part of the attraction of the product is its newness (i.e., the fact that it is *unknown*). In contrast, as discussed below, customers in the next stage generally *will not* buy a product *if it is unknown*. If inventors cannot resist the opportunity to sell to early adopters, they may use up their resources (remember that the sales price is lower than expected) before they can push the technology into the next stage of development. This situation creates a potentially confusing scenario in which sales are increasing rapidly and yet the company is not effectively moving toward the next stage of development. Technology in this stage of development is very susceptible to revenue overestimations. It is easy for the expert to spot the ramp-up in sales and then mistakenly conclude that the company's products are in great demand. Unfortunately for the expert, a company that is successfully moving toward the next stage (early majority) also has rapidly increasing sales. Thus, the appraiser must obtain an understanding of the motivations of the customer base. Increasing sales into a customer base within the same niche represent evidence that the technology is progressing properly toward the next stage of acceptance.

The sample case study below illustrates some of the issues that arise when valuing technology that is in the early adopter stage. The example is based on a January 2001 newspaper article from the *New York Times* discussing a product that is in the early adopter stage of the market development life cycle.

Case Study—Segway Human Transporter[3]

Moving Transportation—It is not a hovercraft, a helicopter backpack, or a teleportation pod. The mystery transportation device being developed by the award-winning inventor Dean Kamen that has been the subject of continuous fevered speculation since provocative clues and predictions surfaced in media reports last January (2001) is not hydrogen-powered, a favored theory in Internet discussions. Nor does it run on a superefficient Stirling engine (yet). But if the public's collective yearning for Jetsonian travel technology must remain unrequited this week, at least the speculators will have their curiosity satisfied.

Kamen plans to demonstrate today a two-wheeled, battery-powered device designed for a single standing rider. Its chief novelty lies in the uncanny effect, produced by a finely tuned gyroscopic balancing mechanism, of intuiting where its rider wants to go and going there.

The device, the Segway Human Transporter, better known by its former code name, Ginger, can go up to 12 miles per hour and has no brakes. Its speed and direction are controlled solely by the rider's shifting weight and a manual turning mechanism on one of the handlebars.

Case Study—Segway Human Transporter (continued)

"You might ask, 'How does it work?'" said Kamen, mounting one of the devices last week on a test track at his company's headquarters in Manchester, New Hampshire. "Think forward," he said, inclining his head ever so slightly and zooming toward a reporter. "Think back," he continued, effortlessly reversing course.

It is clear from the article that the potential customer base for "Ginger" is not certain of the impact of the device. The device apparently works, yet its future is not known. The next article refers to early adopters. Note that the early adopters are purchasing the equipment in small amounts to test the product. It also is evident that at least one early adopter, USPS, is not paying for the device. Segway needs the early adopters to act as a reference source for the next stage of development, the early majority.

USPS Will Test New Transportation Device—12/13/01

The U.S. Postal Service said that it plans to test a new two-wheeled, battery-powered device designed to help increase the efficiency of mail carriers.

The two-wheeled device, called the Segway Human Transporter but better known by its code name of Ginger, was invented by Dean Kamen. The device, which looks like a push lawnmower, is a gyroscope-stabilized, battery-powered vehicle that Kaman says will revolutionize short-distance travel. Its speed and direction are controlled solely by the rider's shifting weight and a manual turning mechanism on one of the handlebars. It moves at an average speed of 8 miles per hour, or three times walking pace.

The Segway can go 15 miles on a 6-hour charge for less than a dime's worth of electricity from a standard wall socket. The first models, which are expected to be available to consumers in about a year, will cost about $3,000.

The USPS said that it plans to try 20 units on mail routes in Concord, New Hampshire, and Fort Myers, Florida, starting in January. The agency hopes the devices can reduce reliance on trucks and enable mail carriers to cover more ground.

The USPS is not paying for the scooters, a USPS spokesman said, during the test phase. Besides the USPS, the National Park Service and the city of Atlanta plan to begin limited field tests of the devices early next year. Amazon.com and several companies that make parts for the Segway, including GE Plastics and Michelin North America, also plan to use the devices to try to save money by reducing the time it takes employees to move around corporate campuses and large warehouses.

This article depicts much of the expected behavior from technologies in the early adopter stage. If sales increase because the companies that currently are testing the device begin to buy larger quantities and incur the expense necessary to roll out the Segway, the expert may reasonably conclude that the technology will make it to the next stage. However, if the product continues to be "sold" to companies that really are only testing the product, the practitioner should have serious doubts as to the long-term viability of the product. Moving past this stage has been characterized as "crossing the chasm." Failure to cross the chasm may be the biggest risk that a new technology faces. The primary risk of IP at this stage relates to the chance of the marketplace not showing enough interest in the technology. Technology that currently is struggling to make it past this stage includes videophones, the Linux operating system, and voice-recognition software. Many people might refer to the technology that fails at this stage as an experimental "gadget," while others support the technology. Success in the early adopter stage is critical to the successful development of a market. Thus, it is very unlikely that a product can survive if the market does not develop past this stage.

Early Majority.   Consumers comprising the early majority stage of development represent those buyers that wish to obtain a product that works properly and is easy to assimilate into their business. Intellectual property that is selling into this stage typically generates revenues at an increasing rate. Prices are likely to be relatively close to the IP's target price. Sales are more likely to be made in quantities sufficient to roll out into the entire business. Additionally, the technology is likely to be sold to larger companies. Furthermore, the technology at this stage often can be found in industry magazines and/or consumer surveys. Trade magazines are likely to discuss the technology and the consumers generally should have an awareness of the technology. Firms in this stage are likely to generate revenue in markets beyond the original niche to which the product was marketed. Furthermore, the technology is likely to have penetrated a substantial portion of the firms in the niche originally targeted. Additionally, the expert should expect to see competing firms entering the marketplace. The competitors are likely to consist of established firms that are threatened with being displaced, as well as other firms with competing disruptive technology. The firms that own the established technology are likely to respond to the new technology with lower prices or added features. Also, other firms are likely to offer competing forms of the innovative technology. At this point in the market's development, it is typical that a standard has not yet been established. Thus, firms in this stage are trying to garner a large enough portion of the market to become the standard. During the early majority stage, disruption of the old technology is likely. One of the biggest questions at this stage is which of the new technologies will become the "standard" and how effectively established competitors (with the old technology) will respond. Technology that is in this stage usually is being sold by enough companies that industry data are available to estimate sales even for unestablished firms.

Late Majority. By this stage in market development, a "standard" has been established. As a result, the competition often is limited to firms making incremental improvements to the "standard" and/or from competing firms with similar IP.

Laggards. Customers in this category are simply reluctant to buy technology. Frequently, laggards buy the technology only because its adoption has made it difficult to work without the new technology. For example, most businesses today buy a fax machine in order to have a reasonable ability to communicate with its clients. One of the characteristics of technology in this stage is that the IP is being displaced by other technology. Alternatively, the IP has become outdated by a series of incremental improvements. Examples of this type of technology include zip™ disk drives, cell phones, and so on.

In sum, in appropriate cases, a diffusion approach or market life cycle approach can be used to estimate sales in the "but for" world even where the business has no established track record.

Determination of the Net Sales Price of the Units That Would Have Been Sold by the Plaintiff

To determine the sales price of the units sold, invoices, price lists, and marketing plans are helpful starting points. However, the market life cycle also should be considered because the price of the unit may be expected to change over time. Furthermore, the impact of the infringer must be considered. Possibly the infringer has caused prices to remain low due to its competition. Conversely, technology in the laggard stage may experience price decreases over time. However, by definition, an actual sales price has already been received by the defendant. Thus, that amount should be used to determine the reasonableness of the price estimated by the analyst.

Determine the Plaintiff's Incremental Costs of Producing and Selling the Product

The appropriate costs to be considered are the "incremental costs." Such costs consist of any costs that would have been incurred in generating the lost revenues. Accountants and economists typically divide costs into "fixed" expenses and "variable" expenses. Fixed expenses do not change as volumes change, whereas variable expenses change directly with volume changes. Incremental costs are somewhere between the two. For example, supervisor salaries usually are considered "fixed" expenses, because the salary is the same regardless of the production level. However, if the company had manufacturing capacity (as discussed previously) based on the assumption that the plaintiff would have added a third shift, the supervisor salary must be included as an incremental cost because an additional supervisor is needed. A good starting place for the determination of the total incremental costs is to ask the plaintiff's accountant to identify all variable and semivariable expenses. Next, obtain the trial balance for several periods of time.

As discussed earlier, the trial balance is a detailed summary of the accounts that create the financial statements.[4] Then, identify the expenses that are correlated with sales. The variable costs usually should have the highest correlation, whereas the fixed costs usually have the lowest correlation. This process allows the identification of incremental expenses. If the expense is strongly correlated with revenue, it should be considered as incremental.

Once the expense categories have been identified, the total amount of the expense must be estimated. This determination is most often made using the historical per unit cost. While this approach is usually effective, sometimes there may not be an adequate historical basis. In such cases, it usually is best to use the expense levels of competitors as a basis. Chapter 5 discussed the market approach and the methodology for identifying such competitors. If the expense level of competitors is used as a proxy for estimating incremental costs, it is important to know the respective business stage of the comparable company. For example, imagine that the plaintiff is a gas station owner with 12 locations. If the expert uses competitors as a proxy for estimating expenses, she should consider only very small chains. The expense structure of Exxon, for instance, would be an improper proxy in this example.

Consider Whether It Is Appropriate to Discount Such Profits and Determine the Appropriate Discount Rate

As with a valuation, the risk of obtaining the lost profits must be considered. Also like a valuation, the level of risk sometimes can be very high or very low. Consider the following scenarios.

- The plaintiff is a direct competitor with the defendant. Both parties have been in business several years. The capacity to make the lost sales is already in place. The technology is proven and has a long track record.
- The plaintiff is a small player in the industry and the defendant is a very large competitor. The plaintiff claims that it would have had the capacity to make the sales by building a new facility and hiring sales personnel in the East Coast.
- The plaintiff is in the process of building its first manufacturing plant. The defendant is also a small company with a short history. The industry is very new and industry standards are yet to be established.

Each of these situations implies a different level of risk. Thus, the discount rate should be different in each case. Please refer to Chapter 5 regarding the method of establishing discount rates for a detailed discussion of the process. Chapter 5 also discusses how to apply the discount rate.

The lost profits should be discounted to the date damages begin. After discounting, the lost profits calculation is complete. Interest at a risk-free (or statutory) rate should apply from the date damages began through the date of the trial. This calculation properly accounts for the plaintiff not facing risk after an award is given. As discussed throughout this book, the plaintiff may be entitled to a reasonable royalty in lieu of lost profits (or in conjunction with them).

CALCULATION OF A REASONABLE ROYALTY

Most analyses of reasonable royalties are based on a theory of estimating what royalty rate the parties would have negotiated prior to infringement. This often is referred to as performing a "hypothetical negotiation." Of course, the valuation of a business is nothing more than a "hypothetical negotiation" between the seller of a business and an unidentified buyer.

The definition of fair market value in IRS Revenue Ruling 59-60[5] highlights some important similarities between the valuation exercise and a "hypothetical negotiation." For instance:

1. "The price"—Just as with any valuation, the reasonable royalty must also ultimately be *a price*.
2. "At which the property would change hands"—Just as with a valuation, the value must an amount great enough to convince the seller to sell and yet small enough to persuade the buyer to enter into a transaction.
3. "Both parties having reasonable knowledge of the facts"—Just as with a valuation, the reasonable royalty calculation is based primarily on knowledge known as of the valuation date. However, with respect to both valuations and hypothetical negotiations, information created after the negotiation date also can be useful in indicating expectations and knowledge at the time of the negotiation.

However, a review of this language reveals some differences between the "hypothetical negotiation" and a typical fair market valuation. Most notably:

(a) Valuation Date

Just as the date of any valuation can affect the asset's value, the date of the "hypothetical negotiation" can affect the outcome of a reasonable royalty calculation. Although courts typically expect the hypothetical negotiation to have taken place just prior to infringement, the law is not clear as to whether the "hypothetical negotiation" is to have taken place immediately prior to infringement (i.e., the day before) or generally prior to infringement (i.e., during some unknown time period prior to infringement). The problem this causes can be easily understood considering the following example. If the negotiation were expected to happen the day prior to infringement and the infringing party had already built a $10 million production facility, the patent holder would have very high leverage and thus would likely garner a higher royalty. If the negotiation took place before the plant was built, the converse would be true. Fortunately, valuation practitioners are well versed in the importance of the valuation date. The same holds true in a reasonable royalty calculation.

(b) Standard of Value

Fair market value does not assume a particular buyer of the asset. In a hypothetical negotiation, both parties are known. Accordingly, the specifics of how they would use the technology is available and must be considered. The business valuation community refers to this standard of valuation as the investment value standard. The same mind-set must be used in performing a "hypothetical negotiation." The "hypothetical negotiation" must be based on the specific circumstances regarding the two known parties, that is, ability to finance, competitive position, respective market strategies, and so on. In other words, if the defendant had a source through which it could easily sell the technology in large quantities, it may pay higher royalty to get the quick sales. This type of specific information is properly considered in the reasonable royalty analysis.

(c) "Between a willing buyer and a willing seller when the former is not under any compulsion to buy and the latter is not under any compulsion to sell."

In the hypothetical negotiation, both parties are *compelled* to conduct a transaction. In some instances, the seller of an asset would reasonably demand more than a specific buyer would reasonably be willing to pay. When this happens in the typical valuation setting, it does not cause a problem. No transaction is made, because fair market value is based on neither party being under any compulsion to perform a transaction. However, the "hypothetical negotiation" effectively forces the parties to enter into such an agreement even if they would not otherwise be likely to do so. This factor is perhaps the most significant difference between a "hypothetical negotiation" and a valuation. When the situation arises, the expert must treat the parties as rational actors and consider their respective economic incentives.

Thus, the reasonable royalty calculation should be approached with a similar mind-set as a valuation of any business. Chapter 7 discussed the *Georgia-Pacific* factors and grouped them according to the economic issues they address. Below, the same factors are discussed with a focus on practical considerations:

1. The royalties received by the patentee for the licensing of the patent in suit, proving or tending to prove an established royalty.
2. The rates paid by the licensee for the use of other patents comparable to the patent in suit.

As discussed in Chapter 5, the market approach is a widely accepted method of valuation that is based on the theory that the fair market value of an asset can be determined by analyzing the actual transaction price of similar assets. In Chapter 5, an example was used to illustrate the approach. It is repeated here for convenience. Assume that a person wanted to buy a house in an exclusive neighborhood ("subject" home). The person would obtain the recent actual sales prices of similar homes in the same neighborhood ("guideline" homes). The person also would consider the physical differences between the "subject" home and the "guideline" homes. For instance, if the "guideline" home had a swimming pool and the "subject" home did not, an adjustment would be made to reflect the anticipated difference in the price of each home. Similarly, the person may make price adjustments for other significant features (e.g., size, style, etc.).

Similarly, it is conventional to consider the market approach in conducting a hypothetical reasonable royalty analysis. The amount at which others have licensed "guideline" technology can provide a basis as to the reasonable royalty for the "subject" technology. An increasing number of web sites are dedicated to capturing licensing transactions. Such web sites are similar to the multiple listing services for home purchasers as they provide a central forum for buyers and sellers to find each other. Furthermore, licensing associations publish studies of royalty rates. Although such surveys can provide a useful reasonableness check, great care must be taken to avoid relying heavily on data with which the practitioner is unfamiliar.

Some of the specific aspects that must be considered are as follows:

- *Is the guideline license from the relevant time period?* Just as one would not buy a home based on outdated "guideline" home sales, the "guideline" technology must be from a relevant period. Considerations such as earning growth prospects, number of competitors, and expectations of economic growth, all of which influence the value of a technology and therefore the royalty, change over time.
- *Does the guideline license provide similar rights to the technology?* Factors such as exclusivity, cross-licensing, usefulness, availability of alternatives, remaining life, and the like significantly affect the license rate and must be considered.
- *Does use of the technology require the same level of investment from the licensor?* Licenses of technology with large up-front investment requirements (such as the construction of a building) generally are associated with lower royalties than the same technology being sold into the same market without any need for a large capital expenditure.
- *Is the guideline technology used in a similar industry?* Each industry faces different forces, such as the number of competitors, profit margins, elasticity of demand, risk of disruptive technology, and the size of the market. These forces affect the profitability and growth prospects of the industry participants and therefore the economic benefits derived from the technology.

Licenses of similar technology that share similar characteristics, including but not limited to those mentioned, may be suitable "guideline" licenses.

3. The nature and scope of the license, as exclusive or nonexclusive; or as restricted or nonrestricted in terms of territory or with respect to whom the manufactured product may be sold.

Typically, a nonexclusive license will command a smaller royalty than an exclusive license will. Furthermore, a license that limits markets is worth less than one that the licensee can use anywhere. If the plaintiff is seeking lost profits, they should assume that the license would be nonexclusive. If it were an exclusive royalty, the plaintiff could not have used the technology.

4. The licensor's established policy and marketing program to maintain his patent monopoly by not licensing others to use the invention or by granting licenses under special conditions designed to preserve that monopoly.

A party that made a strategic decision never to license its IP to competitors would likely demand a higher royalty than a party that was accustomed to competing and interacting with competitors unless this behavior is irrational.

5. The commercial relationship between the licensor and licensee, such as whether they are competitors in the same territory in the same line of business; or whether they are inventor and promoter.

Direct competitors (those competing for the same customers) usually command a premium over indirect competitors (those in the same market, but for different customers) or noncompetitors.

6. The effect of selling the patented specialty in promoting sales of other products of the licensee; the existing value of the invention to the licensor as a generator of sales of his nonpatented items; and the extent of such derivative or convoyed sales.

Products that result in "add-on" sales or the sale of related nonpatented products demand a higher royalty than those products that do not generate such sales. In fact, in some instances, the profit related to the patented product is less than the related products (imagine a patented razor and an unpatented razor blade). Such sales are called convoyed sales in the lost profit analysis.

7. The duration of the patent and the term of the license.

This factor is not consistent in the impact it has on a reasonable royalty. In some instances, a long patent life will raise the royalty as the licensee has a long time to recover their investment. Other times, a long life will not raise the royalty rate. Most high-technology companies are in fields where products have a short life cycle anyway. Consider that it is not likely that a patent on a computer processor is going to be in great demand for more than a few years. In other words, it does not matter when the patent will expire if the product life is such that nobody will want the product after a few years.

8. The established profitability of the product made under the patent; its commercial success; and its current popularity.

A very profitable product is likely to command a much higher royalty than a less profitable product. "Profitability" is best determined based on an expectation of the license's incremental profits.

9. The utility and advantages of the patent property over the old modes or devices, if any, that had been used for working out similar results.

The practitioner must consider noninfringing substitutes. If there are noninfringing substitutes available, the cost of using the substitute essentially acts as a ceiling on the royalty. "Cost" in this instance can mean the cost of switching to the noninfringing technology, lost revenue, or increased expenses as a result of using the noninfringing substitutes. As the cost of using the noninfringing technology rises, so does the reasonable royalty rate.

10. The nature of the patented invention; the character of the commercial embodiment of it as owned and produced by the licensor; and the benefits to those who have used the invention.

This is similar to factor 9. A product that is used to a great extent by the infringer is likely to command a relatively high royalty rate.

11. The extent to which the infringer has made use of the invention; and any evidence probative of the value of that use.

A patent that is widely incorporated usually is more valuable than one that is not used very often.

12. The portion of the profit or of the selling price that may be customary in the particular business or in comparable businesses to allow for the use of the invention or analogous inventions.

When comparing two patents, it is intuitive that a patent that generates high gross margins is more valuable than a patent that results in lower margins.

13. The portion of the realizable profit that should be credited to the invention as distinguished from nonpatented elements, the manufacturing process, business risks, or significant features or improvements added by the infringer.

Many products incorporate more than one patent. The profits of the product must pay for all of the patents. Thus, a patent that is one of several required to sell a product will command a smaller royalty than a patent that requires no other technology to create the same margin.

Moreover, evidence of the value of the patented technology may be reflected in the cost incurred by the plaintiff to acquire and develop the technology. If the technology at dispute represents only a small fraction of the total technology that is necessary for the sale of the defendant's products, it may be that the technology is not very important to the defendant.

14. The opinion testimony of qualified experts.
15. The amount that a licensor (such as the patentee) and a licensee (such as the infringer) would have agreed upon (at the time the infringement began) if both had been reasonably and voluntarily trying to reach an agreement; that is, the amount which a prudent licensee—who desired, as a business proposition, to obtain a license to manufacture and sell a particular article embodying the patented invention—would have been willing to pay as a royalty and yet be able to make a reasonable profit and which amount would have been acceptable by a prudent patentee who was willing to grant a license.

This book provides the relevant factors in both effective expert testimony and constructing a hypothetical negotiation.

We can group the factors using valuation theory as follows (in contrast to our grouping in Chapter 7). Factors 4 and 5 both describe factors that typically are addressed in a valuation assignment as part of the customary research performed in determining the competitive landscape. This is a typical procedure performed in a valuation regardless of the approach. Factors 4 and 5 are consistent with the notion that in performing a reasonable royalty calculation or a valuation, the competitive environment should be understood.

In his book *Valuing a Business: The Analysis and Appraisal of Closely Held Companies*, Shannon Pratt defines the market approach as "a general way of determining a value indication of a business, business ownership interest or security using one or more methods that compare the subject to similar businesses, business ownership interests or securities that have been sold." This definition effectively is duplicated in factors 1, 2,

3, and 12, which all suggest that an appropriate royalty rate can be determined by looking at similar transactions in the marketplace.

Factors 6, 7, 8, 9, 10, 11, and 13 all represent the core of the income approach. Such factors deal with the notion that the amount of profits generated by an asset impact its value.

Finally, factor 14 is consistent with the highest level of valuation theory. Valuation theory is based on the notion that although practitioners may disagree on the exact value of an asset, if they apply a standardized approach, the differences in value conclusions will be the reasonable differences that result from personal preferences. Likewise, the opinions of qualified experts would not be useful without an assumption that the experts are applying standardized approaches to their areas of expertise.

Most frequently, experts begin a reasonable royalty calculation by performing a search for comparable licenses and past transactions entered into by the plaintiff. Next, they estimate a royalty based on any rules of thumb within the industry. After obtaining those data points, the practitioner considers the cost to design around the technology. This calculation establishes a ceiling on the royalty. The royalty "floor" is the amount of money the plaintiff could get for the technology by licensing it to someone other than the defendant. For instance, the plaintiff could compete with defendant, license to a third party, sell the patent to a third party, and so on. Finally, the practitioner considers the "subjective" *Georgia-Pacific* factors and reaches a reasoned, well-supported decision as to the reasonable royalty amount.

SUMMARY

This chapter builds on earlier chapters and presents a high-level "nuts-and-bolts" overview of the process by which an expert might calculate IP damages. The specifics within this chapter must be read in concert with the information presented in other chapters and applied appropriately to the specific facts of each case.

ENDNOTES

[1] A key element of the damage calculation discussed throughout this text is that *all sales must be considered only once in the calculation.*

[2] *See* Everett Rogers, *Diffusion of Innovations*, New York: The Free Press (1995), at 206–207.

[3] *See* article at *www.psdmag.com.*

[4] *See* Chapter 4 in this book for more detail regarding accounting documents.

[5] In Revenue Ruling 59–60, fair market value is defined as "the price at which the property would change hands between a willing buyer and a willing seller when the former is not under any compulsion to buy and the latter is not under any compulsion to sell, both parties having reasonable knowledge of relevant facts."

ADDITIONAL READING

Vijay Mahajan and Robert Peterson, *Models for Innovation Diffusion*, Beverly Hills: CA, Sage Publications (1985).

Vijay Mahajan and Yoram Wind, *Innovation Diffusion Models of New Product Acceptance*, Cambridge, MA: Ballinger (1986).

Everett Rogers, *Diffusion of Innovations*, New York: The Free Press (1995).

Part Four

Appendices

Appendix A

Sample Requests for Production of Documents and Interrogatories

FIRST SET OF REQUESTS
FOR PRODUCTION OF DOCUMENTS TO GAMMA

Pursuant to Rule 34 of the Federal Rules of Civil Procedure, Gamma is requested to produce and make available for inspection and/or copying the following documents within thirty (30) days at the offices of Alpha's counsel.

DEFINITIONS AND INSTRUCTIONS

1. The term "Gamma" shall mean Gamma, Inc., its employees, agents, representatives, and anyone acting on its behalf or at its request, including attorneys, expert witnesses, or other individuals employed in any way in connection with any matter concerning or alleged in the Complaint, Answer, or Counterclaim filed in this action.
2. The term "Alpha" shall mean Alpha Incorporated.
3. The term "Widget patent" shall mean United States Patent No. 1,010,010.
4. The term "documents" shall mean and include any and all written, recorded, printed, and graphic matter, however produced or reproduced, of any kind and description, including but not limited to all communications, correspondence, letters, telegrams, notes, memoranda of meetings, reports, directives, intercompany communications, documents, diaries, logs, contracts, licenses, ledgers, books of account, vouchers, checks, invoices, charge slips, receipts, freight bills, working papers, desk calendars, appointment books, maps, plats, engineering studies, drawings, photographs, and writings of every kind or description, tape recordings, computer printouts, computer programs, magnetic cards, microfilm, microfiches, or other electronic or mechanical information or data of any kind or description, including both originals and copies.

5. The pronoun "you" or "your" shall be synonymous with the term "Gamma."

6. Unless otherwise stated, the discovery period covered by these document requests shall be the period commencing January 1, 1998 to the date of Gamma's response to these document requests.

7. The conjunctions "and" and "or" shall be construed both conjunctively and disjunctively.

8. The singular form of a word shall include its plural form and vice versa whenever such dual construction will make the request more comprehensive in its scope.

9. The term "person" shall be understood to refer to all natural persons, as well as corporations, unincorporated associations, partnerships, joint ventures, and other artificial persons or groups of persons of any kind no matter how identified or how organized.

10. If any document is withheld under a claim of privilege or the attorney work product doctrine, provide the following information:

   a. Identifying information for each document, including the date of the document, the number of pages, the type of information it contains (*e.g.*, text, graphs, statistics), the title of the document, the type of document (*e.g.*, memorandum, letter, brief, transcript, report), the author(s), the addressee(s), and the person(s) copied. In addition to providing these names, identify the positions or titles of all persons mentioned in the document whether or not they are attorneys; and

   b. A specification of which privilege applies and, where more than one privilege is asserted for a document, the portions of that document to which each specified privilege applies.

11. With respect to any requested document that has been destroyed, describe:

   a. The date or dates the document bore or, if undated, the date it was written or created or both;

   b. The name and address of each person who wrote it or created it, or both;

   c. The name and address of each person who may have received a copy of the document;

   d. A description of the document as, for instance, "letter," "memorandum," etc.;

   e. The document's last known location or custodian; and

   f. The circumstances or the reason for the destruction of the document, and the date the document or thing was destroyed.

DOCUMENT REQUESTS

The following are continuing requests. Whenever you become aware of any additional documents following your response to any of the following requests, you are requested to notify Alpha of such additional documents and to produce them.

Request No. 1: Produce all documents and things (including samples of any devices) referring, relating, or pertaining to the research, development, design, construction, testing, manufacture, use, operation in the field, promotion, marketing, operation, offer for sale, sale, offer to lease, or lease of Gamma's Widgets, including any promotional materials supplied to prospective clients and customers.

Request No. 2: Produce audited financial statements for the last five years. Produce balance sheets, income statements, and cash flow statements for the periods covering the calendar years 1993 to 1998.

Request No. 3: Produce all documents that refer, relate, or pertain to your current inventory of the Gamma Widgets.

Request No. 4: Produce all documents reflecting any understanding, agreements, or communications between Gamma and any contractors or subcontractors concerning the supply of liners to Gamma for any of the Gamma Widgets, including the volumes of such liners supplied or to be supplied, and documents that constitute or relate to any indemnification or hold-harmless agreement given by Gamma to any such contractor or subcontractor relating to any of the Gamma Widgets.

Request No. 5: Produce all documents reflecting any understanding, agreements, or communications between Gamma and any third party concerning the supply of liners by Gamma for any of the Gamma Widgets, including the volumes of such liners supplied or to be supplied, and documents that constitute or relate to any indemnification or hold-harmless agreement given by Gamma to any such third party relating to any of the Gamma Widgets.

Request No. 6: Produce all documents that describe, summarize, reflect, or otherwise refer or relate to the volume of sales of Gamma Widgets since January 1, 1998.

Request No. 7: Produce all documents that describe the price, history of prices, pricing policies, pricing forecasts, pricing strategies, and pricing decisions relating to Gamma Widgets since January 1, 1998.

Request No. 8: Produce all documents that describe the incremental costs, cost of goods sold, depreciation, gross profits, overhead costs, profits or net income before taxes, or profit margins of Gamma associated with the sale of the Gamma Widgets since January 1, 1998, including but not limited to subsidiary ledgers for Gamma Widgets, profit and loss statements, sales invoices, sales reports, cost of sales reports, marketing reports, customer lists, product brochures, and profit or market projections.

Request No. 9: Produce all documents that describe, summarize, reflect, or otherwise refer or relate to the sales volume and pricing of any ancillary or convoyed product sold and/or leased with the Gamma Widgets since January 1, 1998, including but not limited to financial statements, balance sheets, cash flow statements, subsidiary ledgers by product, profit and loss statements, sales invoices, sales reports, cost of sales reports, marketing reports, customer lists, product brochures, and profit or market projections.

Request No. 10: Produce all documents discussing the history and operations of Gamma, including major milestones and the current nature of the business, including copies of Gamma brochures or marketing literature that describe Gamma and/or its products.

Request No. 11: Produce all documents reflecting, referring to or discussing the projected annual capital expenditures required to achieve projected revenues and/or profits.

Request No. 12: Produce a current detailed copy of the fixed asset ledger, including description, date of acquisition, original cost, location codes and account codes.

Request No. 13: Produce copies of any and all recent appraisals of Gamma, including but not limited to insurance, Ad-Valorem, and financing appraisals.

Request No. 14: Produce a detail of your current backlog, including but not limited to customer names, product descriptions, quantity, sale prices, etc.

Request No. 15: Produce any available market value information for fixed assets of Gamma, including but not limited to any previous real or personal property appraisals, insurance appraisals, or earlier offers to purchase the property or assets.

Request No. 16: Produce all of Gamma's corporate charts of accounts, income statements, and forecasts or budgets of operations since January 1, 1998.

Request No. 17: Produce all documents relating to competition in the production or sale of the Gamma Widgets since January 1, 1998, including but not limited to market studies, forecasts and surveys, and all other documents relating to market share or competitive position of Gamma or any of its competitors, supply and demand conditions, and attempts to win customers.

Request No. 18: Produce all documents related to the sales, market share, profits, costs, productivity, or prices for the widgets of any competitor of Gamma since January 1, 1998.

Request No. 19: Produce all documents that constitute or relate to any indemnification or hold-harmless agreement given by Gamma to any purchaser or prospective purchaser of any of the Gamma Widgets.

Request No. 20: Produce all documents relating, referring, or pertaining to Gamma's first awareness of the Widget patent.

Request No. 21: Produce all documents constituting, relating, referring or pertaining to: (1) any study or analysis of the Widget patent; or (2) any prior art of relevance to that patent.

Request No. 22: Produce all documents constituting or relating, referring, or pertaining to the validity, invalidity, infringement, noninfringement, enforceability, and/or unenforceability of the Widget patent.

Request No. 23: Produce all patents, publications, or other documents relating to, pertaining to, or in any way supporting Gamma's contentions in this lawsuit, including but not limited to Gamma's contentions of noninfringement, invalidity, and/or unenforceability of the Widget patent.

Request No. 24: Produce all documents referring or relating to any patent application filed by you, whether or not a patent on such application has subsequently been issued to you, regarding any of the Gamma Widgets.

Request No. 25: Produce all documents referring or relating to any patent application or other intellectual property licensed, acquired, or otherwise obtained by Gamma from any third party relating to any of the Gamma Widgets.

Request No. 26: Produce all documents that constitute, refer or relate to communications with any third party regarding the Widget patent or your Complaint.

Request No. 27: Produce all documents reflecting, referring or relating to any communication between you and Alpha regarding the Widget patent or widgets.

Request No. 28: Produce all documents comprising, referring or relating to any oral or written report of any expert witness who may testify at trial.

Request No. 29: Produce all documents to which any expert witness who may testify on your behalf at trial referred or was supplied in connection with his or her work relating to this matter.

FIRST SET OF INTERROGATORIES

Interrogatory No. 1: Identify the shareholders of Gamma, as of January 1, 1998, including shares held (by class) and a discussion of the effective voting rights of each class.

Interrogatory No. 2: Identify and describe the accounting software used by Gamma from January 1, 1998 to the present date.

Interrogatory No. 3: Describe Gamma's product line of widgets, and the uses for the widgets.

Interrogatory No. 4: Describe Gamma's marketing of widgets and their convoyed products, including the geographic market, any cyclical or seasonal nature of the market, and the nature of Gamma's customer base for widgets from January 1, 1998 to the present date.

Interrogatory No. 5: Identify Gamma's primary competitors for widgets, including each company's market share, from January 1, 1998 to the present date.

Interrogatory No. 6: Discuss the impact of any new products and/or technologies on Gamma's widget line from January 1, 1998 to the present date.

Interrogatory No. 7: Identify Gamma's major facilities, including but not limited to locations, brief description of their size and layout, function, limitations, if any, and whether they are owned or leased, original cost, net book values, and approximate ages, if known.

Interrogatory No. 8: Describe any property, plant or equipment owned by Gamma that is not presently used in Gamma's operations, including but not limited to the original cost and approximate fair market value, if known, of that property, plant or equipment.

Interrogatory No. 9: Estimate the maximum production capacity of Gamma given the current facilities, equipment, etc.

DATED this ____ day of ____, 2001.

_____

Attorneys for Plaintiffs
Alpha, Inc.

Appendix B

Sample Expert Report
of John Smith

NOTE: This sample is intended only to demonstrate the form and layout of a typical expert report. The analysis discussed within may or may not be appropriate, depending on the facts in the case.

I. ASSIGNMENT

I have been engaged to calculate damages that Alpha, Inc. ("Alpha") incurred as a result of alleged patent infringement by Gamma, Inc. ("Gamma"). Alpha is the owner of U.S. Patent Number 1,010,010 (the "010 Patent") entitled "A method for producing a widget."

This report describes my work to date and summarizes my opinions and the bases for those opinions. The opinions and findings expressed in this report are based upon my work to date and the facts that I have gleaned from my review of the information itemized in Appendix A. I may, pursuant to Rule 26(e)(1), supplement, update or otherwise modify this report at a later date based on additional documents or information.

This report has been prepared solely in connection with the litigation and is intended for no other use.

II. QUALIFICATIONS

I am currently an economist in private practice with Microeconomists Corporation, a consulting firm in Moab, Utah. I received a Ph.D. in economics from Harvard University at age 16, and since that time I have worked consistently and exclusively in the area of patent damage economics. I have published 45 professional papers in the last five years, and I have testified in 106 cases. My billing rate is $100 an hour. My vitae providing more detail on my qualifications is attached as Appendix A to this report.

III. SUMMARY OF CONCLUSIONS

My understanding is that a patent owner is entitled to either the lost profits or a reasonable royalty on every infringing sale made by an infringer. For this reason, in calculating damages I have divided the total infringing sales by Gamma into two categories: 1) infringing sales that would have otherwise been made by Alpha, and 2) infringing sales that Alpha would not have made, even absent Gamma's infringement. I have therefore computed lost profits on the sales in the first category and a reasonable royalty on the sales in the second category. No sales were double-counted. Lost profits are the incremental profits that Alpha would have made on Gamma's sales absent the infringement. The reasonable royalty is the likely royalty that Gamma and Alpha would have agreed to at the onset of infringement.

In sum, my opinion is that Alpha has lost $1.2 million in lost profits and $.8 million in reasonable royalties. Total compensatory damages are $2 million. I have not considered willfulness, interest or attorneys' fees.

In preparing my report of findings, I have read and/or analyzed certain records and documents of Alpha and Gamma and various other documents pertaining to the widget industry. These documents are detailed in Exhibit B.

IV. INDUSTRY BACKGROUND

The following chronology of events is based on information obtained through review of documents filed in this case. I was given access to the complete set of documents produced in discovery on both sides. I have also conducted extensive independent research. No attempt has been made to assess the internal validity of any of these documents.

Alpha produces widgets that are used to complete oil wells produced in soft hydrocarbon formations. In 1995 Alpha's '010 patent issued in the United States. The patent discloses a method to produce a widget. I assume for purposes of this report that throughout the damage period Gamma produced and sold widgets throughout the world using the method covered by the '010 patent. Gamma produces all their widgets in Houston, Texas. Since Alpha only sells its widgets in the United States the area of geographic competition between Alpha and Gamma is the United States. No other producers of widgets sell their product in the United States.

Alpha does not mark its patented product, but provided Gamma with actual notice of its patent on January 1, 1998. As a result, my calculation of damages is undertaken for the period January 1, 1998 to the date of this report. I may be asked to update my calculation at the time of the trial.

V. BASIS FOR OPINIONS

My understanding from counsel is that patent infringement damages are governed by the Patent Statute:

> Upon finding for the claimant the court shall award the claimant damages adequate to compensate for the infringement, but in no event less than a reasonable royalty, for use made of the invention by the infringer.

35 U.S.C. § 284. Counsel has further informed me that "compensation" or lost profits is defined as the difference between what profits the plaintiff would have made absent the alleged infringement and what profits the plaintiff actually made. Such a legal framework is amenable to economic analysis since economists frequently analyze what a firm or market would look like absent some event or structural characteristic. In this case, the damage issue can be framed as what additional revenue Alpha would have realized from sales of the widgets, absent the infringing use of the widget by Gamma, and what incremental profits Alpha would have made on any such revenue. In conducting the lost profits analysis I have considered the four factors set forth in *Panduit Corp. v. Stahlin Brothers Fibre Works, Inc.*, 575 F.2d 1152 (6th Cir. 1978): (1) The existence of demand for the patented product, (2) the absence of acceptable non-infringing substitutes, (3) the patent owner's ability to meet demand, and (4) some proof of the amount of lost profit per sale.

1)   There is demand for Alpha's patented products

Significant *evidence* exists to indicate that there was significant demand for Alpha's widgets. The evidence from third-party sources indicates that both Alpha widgets were a leader in their respective industry sectors. Other independent market data indicates that during the relevant damage period, Alpha's widget held approximately 72% of the share of sales to oil service firms. Based on Alpha's name recognition and market presence, consumers are well informed about Alpha's product and they consider them to be high-quality products.

2)   No noninfringing substitute products exist

The purpose of *analyzing* the available non-infringing substitutes is to determine what products consumers of Gamma's infringing widgets would have purchased had Gamma's widget not been available. Gamma and Alpha documents, as well as industry publications, suggest that Alpha's widget is by far the closest substitute for Gamma's product and would therefore be the likely second choice for the vast majority of Gamma customers.

My analysis of *Alpha*, Gamma and industry data indicates that Alpha's widget and Gamma's widgets were considered to be the two main competitors for each other within their industry sector.

After reviewing the *documents* produced by Gamma, it was evident that Gamma viewed Alpha's widget as its main competition. The products were often compared side by side. A Gamma document titled *Widget Alternatives* was devoted to market comparisons of Gamma and Alpha. Another document, *Gamma Systems Inc. Company Overview*, referred to Alpha as "the primary competition for Gamma." This same document indicated that Alpha was leading in the widget market, and this would create a "broad acceptance" for Gamma.

Like Gamma, *Alpha* documents also showed that Alpha viewed Gamma's widget as a close substitute. Typically, rather than identifying specific competing companies and products, Alpha focuses on market data from the various industry sectors. However, on six occasions, *MD Productions* prepared reports for Alpha, which were done specifically to compare the two companies and their products. In addition to these reports, Alpha's 2000 operating plan specifically identified Gamma's widget as its sole competition.

My review of industry reports and trade journal articles provided further confirmation that industry analysts and *columnists* viewed Alpha and Gamma's products as each other's only real competitors. The *Widget Market Forecast and Analysis, 2000–2004* stated that after the closure of competitors such as Omega, "Alpha and Gamma were the sole participants in this market." In the article *Widgets,* the Alpha and Gamma drives were said to "both offer the identical qualities." My analysis revealed many cases, such as the previously mentioned examples, where Alpha and Gamma products were the only products mentioned in their industry sector.

Pricing

The similarity in *pricing* between the Alpha and Gamma widgets also shows the sales that would be captured by Alpha absent infringement. Over the course of the damage period, Alpha's widget was selling for roughly $1,000. Gamma widget costs $999.

3)   Alpha had the capacity to make the sales made by Gamma

For Alpha to be entitled to lost profits, Alpha must have the ability to supply the sales to customers who would have purchased an Alpha product rather than a Gamma product absent infringement. I have classified the potential capacity constraints into three categories: 1) marketing, 2) manufacturing, and 3) financing.

1)   **Marketing:** In determining whether or not Alpha had the marketing capacity to make the Gamma sales, I considered the channels through which each com-

pany was selling its products. My analysis of each company's sales detail and marketing channels indicated that Alpha sold products into the same distribution channels and to nearly all the same customers as Gamma. Based on my analysis of each company's customers and due to Alpha's prominence, I believe Alpha would have been in position to market to all of Gamma's customers.

2) **Manufacturing:** Alpha must also demonstrate that it had the manufacturing capacity to produce the additional units. Gamma sold 10,000 units in the U.S. during the damage period. Over that same period, Alpha sold 50,000 widgets. However, over the course of the damage period Alpha manufactured approximately 18,000 more widgets than it sold. This excess inventory would be sufficient to supply all of Gamma's domestic sales.

3) **Financing:** I also analyzed Alpha's financial capacity, to determine whether or not the capital resources existed to manufacture and sell the 10,000 units sold by Gamma in the U.S. My analysis includes an assessment of Alpha's 1) available credit, 2) working capital and 3) its debt to asset ratio.

To determine the amount of financing that would be required by Alpha to finance the additional sales, I analyzed the total incremental cost of the additional drives to Alpha. I also analyzed Alpha's average accounts payable outstanding period, accounts receivable outstanding period and its inventory period.

According to my calculation of incremental costs below, the total incremental cost of the additional units would be approximately $100,000. Alpha would not incur the full $100,000 in additional costs at one time; rather, supplies would have been purchased periodically throughout the year to meet the additional demand. As sales were made, revenue from previous sales would have been used to finance future sales. Therefore, Alpha would have been required to finance only the additional unit's cost for the period between when Alpha paid suppliers, employees, etc. and when it collected the cash made on sales. My analysis indicates that Alpha's accounts payable period averaged 53 days over the course of the damage period and its cash collection period averaged 91 days. Thus, Alpha had to pay for 38 days (91–53) worth of the costs of goods sold. The damage period is approximately one and one-half years, or 548 days. Alpha's cash conversion cycle represents 6.9% (38/548) of the total damage period. Based on these calculations, Alpha would require approximately $6,900 of existing funds to finance the additional sales.

Available Credit
As of the year ended 1998, Alpha had $150,000,000 in secured credit available from Morgan Guarantee Trust. In 1999 this amount was reduced to $75,000,000. At the end of each year, the full credit line was available to Alpha. By drawing on its available credit, Alpha could have easily financed the lost sales.

Working Capital

Working capital is measured by subtracting current liabilities from current assets. A firm with positive working capital would be better able to service the additional inventory and accounts payable that would accompany production of additional units. As of the years ended 1998 and 1999, Alpha's working capital was $200,000,000 and $190,000,000 respectively. These figures indicate that Alpha had the available short-term financial liquidity to finance the production and sale of these units.

After consideration of the above, I have determined that Alpha had the capacity to make all the infringing sales in the United States.

4) The amount of Alpha's lost profits

A) *Total Lost Widget Units*

Based on my analysis and the available market data, I believe Alpha would have made approximately 100% of the Gamma sales. There were 62,243 units sold by Gamma during the damage period.

B) *Alpha Lost Widget Revenue*

Through the damage period, I measured the average quarterly sales price for Alpha's drives. I multiplied the actual average sales prices by the respective monthly units Alpha would have sold, but-for Gamma's infringement, to determine the total lost widget revenue to Alpha. Based on this calculation, lost widget revenue to Alpha was $10,000,000.

C) *Alpha Incremental Widget Cost*

To determine the incremental cost per unit for Alpha's drives, I analyzed Alpha's product cost reports generated during the damage period.

An incremental cost can be defined as a cost that varies in some direct relationship or proportion to a change in production or sales. Costs that do not fall within the scope of this definition are excluded from the calculation. For example, since Alpha could manufacture all the Gamma U.S. sales without expansion, building rent is not considered an incremental cost. It remains constant despite the increased level of production.

As such, I analyzed the pertinent information and identified the average material, labor, freight and other incremental costs for Alpha's widgets, by quarter for the damage period. Based on this calculation, the incremental cost relating to the lost widget sales totaled $100.

D) *Total Lost Drive Profits*

Based on the above analysis, I have determined that over the damage period, Alpha's average incremental profit per unit was $100, and in total $100,000. Therefore, the total lost incremental widget profits due Alpha are $9,900,000.

VI. REASONABLE ROYALTIES

This section describes the bases for my opinion concerning the size of a reasonable royalty that Gamma should pay to Alpha for use of its '010 patented method for widgets it sold outside the United States.

A. Economic Basis for a Reasonable Royalty

I understand from Counsel that a reasonable royalty is determined as the "hypothetical results of hypothetical negotiations between the patentee and the infringer (both hypothetically willing) at the time infringement began." *Makurkar v. C.R. Bard, Inc.*, 79 F.3d 1572 (Fed. Cir. 1966). In other words, what royalty would have resulted from a voluntary negotiation between the patent owner and the infringer prior to the onset of the infringement. I understand this test is called the "willing licensor/willing licensee" test. It is useful to consider the fourteen factors listed with *Georgia-Pacific Corp. v. United States Plywood Corp.*, 318 F. Supp. 1116 (S.D.N.Y. 1970), *modified*, 446 F.2d 295 (2d Cir. 1970), *cert. denied*, 404 U.S. 870 (1971), in determining what Gamma would have been willing to pay and what Alpha would be willing to accept in a hypothetical license negotiation for the '010 patent in 1998. The *Georgia-Pacific* factors are:

1. *The royalties received by the patentee for the licensing of the patent in suit, proving or tending to prove an established royalty.* Alpha has licensed its '010 patent to a Gamma competitor in the EU at a 5% gross royalty.
2. *The rates paid by the licensee for the use of other patents* comparable to the patent in suit. The evidence is that Gamma offered to sublicense the '010 patent from its EU competitor for 6%.
3. *The nature and scope of the license, as exclusive or non-exclusive; or as restricted or non-restricted in terms of territory or with respect to whom the manufactured product may be sold.* The one known license was exclusive with a right to sublicense.
4. *The licensor's established policy and marketing program to maintain his patent monopoly by not licensing others to use the invention or by granting licenses under special conditions designed to preserve that monopoly.* Alpha was unwilling to license anyone in the United States.
5. *The commercial relationship between the licensor and licensee, such as whether they are competitors in the same territory in the same line of business; or whether they are inventor and promoter.* Alpha and Gamma are each other's primary competitors.
6. *The extent to which the infringer has made use of the invention; and any evidence probative of the value of that use.* Every Gamma Widget uses the patented technology.

7. *The portion of the profit or of the selling price that may be customary in the particular business or in comparable businesses to allow for the use of the invention or analogous inventions.* I do not have information on analogous inventions.

8. *The portion of the realizable profit that should be credited to the invention as distinguished from non-patented elements, the manufacturing process, business risks, or significant features or improvements added by the infringer.* I do not have information on this division.

9. *The opinion testimony of qualified experts.*

My understanding is that the *Georgia-Pacific* factors are only to be used as a guide. The critical issue is what Gamma would have been willing to pay for a license to the '010 patent. Since a buyer (a licensee) will not pay more for a product (such as a license to a technology) than it expects to receive in benefit from the purchase of that product, the benefit to the buyer is a cap on the price (in the case of a license—the royalty) that the buyer will pay. In this case, Gamma could not sell its widgets outside the U.S. without use of the '010 patented method. My inspection of Gamma's European financials and documents shows an incremental profit of approximately 20% over the next best method for producing widgets (the old grind-it-out method).

The rule of thumb that approximately 25% to 33% of incremental profits are paid to a patent owner in royalties coincides remarkably with the 5% royalty Alpha has offered and others accepted in the EU. I conclude therefore that the reasonable royalty in this case is 5%.

_____

Signature

Appendix C

Antitrust Guidelines for the Licensing of Intellectual Property

Issued by the
U.S. Department of Justice[1]
and the
Federal Trade Commission
April 6, 1995

1. INTELLECTUAL PROPERTY PROTECTION AND THE ANTITRUST LAWS

1.0   These Guidelines state the antitrust enforcement policy of the U.S. Department of Justice and the Federal Trade Commission (individually, "the Agency," and collectively, "the Agencies") with respect to the licensing of intellectual property protected by patent, copyright, and trade secret law, and of know-how.[2] By stating their general policy, the Agencies hope to assist those who need to predict whether the Agencies will challenge a practice as anticompetitive. However, these Guidelines cannot remove judgment and discretion in antitrust law enforcement. Moreover, the standards set forth in these Guidelines must be applied in unforeseeable circumstances. Each case will be evaluated in light of its own facts, and these Guidelines will be applied reasonably and flexibly.[3]

In the United States, patents confer rights to exclude others from making, using, or selling in the United States the invention claimed by the patent for a period of seventeen years from the date of issue.[4] To gain patent protection, an invention (which may be a product, process, machine, or composition of matter) must be novel, nonobvious, and useful. Copyright protection applies to original works of authorship embodied in a tangible medium of expression.[5] A copyright protects only the expression, not the underlying ideas.[6] Unlike a patent, which protects an invention not only from copying but also from independent creation, a copyright does not preclude others from independently creating similar expression. Trade secret protection applies to information whose economic value depends on its not being generally known.[7] Trade secret protection is conditioned upon efforts to maintain secrecy and has no fixed term. As with copyright protection, trade secret protection does not preclude independent creation by others.

The intellectual property laws and the antitrust laws share the common purpose of promoting innovation and enhancing consumer welfare.[8] The intellectual property laws provide incentives for innovation and its dissemination and commercialization by establishing enforceable property rights for the creators of new and useful products, more efficient processes, and original works of expression. In the absence of intellectual property rights, imitators could more rapidly exploit the efforts of innovators and investors without compensation. Rapid imitation would reduce the commercial value of innovation and erode incentives to invest, ultimately to the detriment of consumers. The antitrust laws promote innovation and consumer welfare by prohibiting certain actions that may harm competition with respect to either existing or new ways of serving consumers.

2. GENERAL PRINCIPLES

2.0   These Guidelines embody three general principles: (a) for the purpose of antitrust analysis, the Agencies regard intellectual property as being essentially comparable to any other form of property; (b) the Agencies do not presume that intellectual property creates market power in the antitrust context; and (c) the Agencies recognize that intellectual property licensing allows firms to combine complementary factors of production and is generally procompetitive.

2.1   Standard Antitrust Analysis Applies to Intellectual Property

The Agencies apply the same general antitrust principles to conduct involving intellectual property that they apply to conduct involving any other form of tangible or intangible property. That is not to say that intellectual property is in all respects the same as any other form of property. Intellectual property has important characteristics, such as ease of misappropriation, that distinguish it from many other forms of property. These characteristics can be taken into account by standard antitrust analysis, however, and do not require the application of fundamentally different principles.[9]

Although there are clear and important differences in the purpose, extent, and duration of protection provided under the intellectual property regimes of patent, copyright, and trade secret, the governing antitrust principles are the same. Antitrust analysis takes differences among these forms of intellectual property into account in evaluating the specific market circumstances in which transactions occur, just as it does with other particular market circumstances.

Intellectual property law bestows on the owners of intellectual property certain rights to exclude others. These rights help the owners to profit from the use of their property. An intellectual property owner's rights to exclude are similar to the rights enjoyed by owners of other forms of private property. As with other forms of private property, certain types of conduct with respect to intellectual property may have anticompetitive effects against which the antitrust laws can and do protect. Intellectual property is thus neither particularly free from scrutiny under the antitrust laws, nor particularly suspect under them.

The Agencies recognize that the licensing of intellectual property is often international. The principles of antitrust analysis described in these Guidelines apply equally to domestic and international licensing arrangements. However, as described in the 1995 Department of Justice and Federal Trade Commission Antitrust Enforcement Guidelines for International Operations, considerations particular to international operations, such as jurisdiction and comity, may affect enforcement decisions when the arrangement is in an international context.

2.2   Intellectual Property and Market Power

Market power is the ability profitably to maintain prices above, or output below, competitive levels for a significant period of time.[10] The Agencies will not presume that a patent, copyright, or trade secret necessarily confers market power upon its owner. Although the intellectual property right confers the power to exclude with respect to the *specific* product, process, or work in question, there will often be sufficient actual or potential close substitutes for such product, process, or work to prevent the exercise of market power.[11] If a patent or other form of intellectual property does confer market power, that market power does not by itself offend the antitrust laws. As with any other tangible or intangible asset that enables its owner to obtain significant supracompetitive profits, market power (or even a monopoly) that is solely "a consequence of a superior product, business acumen, or historic accident" does not violate the antitrust laws.[12] Nor does such market power impose on the intellectual property owner an obligation to license the use of that property to others. As in other antitrust contexts, however, market power could be illegally acquired or maintained, or, even if lawfully acquired and maintained, would be relevant to the ability of an intellectual property owner to harm competition through unreasonable conduct in connection with such property.

2.3   Procompetitive Benefits of Licensing

Intellectual property typically is one component among many in a production process and derives value from its combination with complementary factors. Complementary factors of production include manufacturing and distribution facilities, workforces, and other items of intellectual property. The owner of intellectual property has to arrange for its combination with other necessary factors to realize its commercial value. Often, the owner finds it most efficient to contract with others for these factors, to sell rights to the intellectual property, or to enter into a joint venture arrangement for its development, rather than supplying these complementary factors itself.

Licensing, cross-licensing, or otherwise transferring intellectual property (hereinafter "licensing") can facilitate integration of the licensed property with complementary factors of production. This integration can lead to more efficient exploitation of the intellectual property, benefiting consumers through the reduction of costs and the introduction of new products. Such arrangements increase the value of intellectual property to consumers and to the developers of the technology. By potentially increasing the expected returns from intellectual property, licensing also can increase the incentive for its creation and thus promote greater investment in research and development.

Sometimes the use of one item of intellectual property requires access to another. An item of intellectual property "blocks" another when the second cannot be practiced without using the first. For example, an improvement on a patented machine can be blocked by the patent on the machine. Licensing may promote the coordinated development of technologies that are in a blocking relationship.

Field-of-use, territorial, and other limitations on intellectual property licenses may serve procompetitive ends by allowing the licensor to exploit its property as efficiently and effectively as possible. These various forms of exclusivity can be used to give a licensee an incentive to invest in the commercialization and distribution of products embodying the licensed intellectual property and to develop additional applications for the licensed property. The restrictions may do so, for example, by protecting the licensee against free-riding on the licensee's investments by other licensees or by the licensor. They may also increase the licensor's incentive to license, for example, by protecting the licensor from competition in the licensor's own technology in a market niche that it prefers to keep to itself. These benefits of licensing restrictions apply to patent, copyright, and trade secret licenses, and to know-how agreements.

Example 1[13]

Situation: ComputerCo develops a new, copyrighted software program for inventory management. The program has wide application in the health field. ComputerCo licenses the program in an arrangement that imposes both field-of-use and territorial limitations. Some of ComputerCo's licenses permit use only in hospitals; others permit use only in group medical practices. ComputerCo charges different royalties for the different uses. All of ComputerCo's licenses permit use only in specified portions of the United States and in specified foreign countries.[14] The licenses contain no provisions that would prevent or discourage licensees from developing, using, or selling any other program, or from competing in any other good or service other than in the use of the licensed program. None of the licensees are actual or likely potential competitors of ComputerCo in the sale of inventory management programs.

Discussion: The key competitive issue raised by the licensing arrangement is whether it harms competition among entities that would have been actual or likely potential competitors in the absence of the arrangement. Such harm could occur if, for example, the licenses anticompetitively foreclose access to competing technologies (in this case, most likely competing computer programs), prevent

Example 1 (continued)

licensees from developing their own competing technologies (again, in this case, most likely computer programs), or facilitate market allocation or price-fixing for any product or service supplied by the licensees. (*See* section 3.1.) If the license agreements contained such provisions, the Agency evaluating the arrangement would analyze its likely competitive effects as described in parts 3–5 of these Guidelines. In this hypothetical, there are no such provisions and thus the arrangement is merely a subdivision of the licensor's intellectual property among different fields of use and territories. The licensing arrangement does not appear likely to harm competition among entities that would have been actual or likely potential competitors if ComputerCo had chosen not to license the software program. The Agency therefore would be unlikely to object to this arrangement. Based on these facts, the result of the antitrust analysis would be the same whether the technology was protected by patent, copyright, or trade secret. The Agency's conclusion as to likely competitive effects could differ if, for example, the license barred licensees from using any other inventory management program.

3. ANTITRUST CONCERNS AND MODES OF ANALYSIS

3.1   Nature of the Concerns

While intellectual property licensing arrangements are typically welfare-enhancing and procompetitive, antitrust concerns may nonetheless arise. For example, a licensing arrangement could include restraints that adversely affect competition in goods markets by dividing the markets among firms that would have competed using different technologies. *See, e.g.*, Example 7. An arrangement that effectively merges the research and development activities of two of only a few entities that could plausibly engage in research and development in the relevant field might harm competition for development of new goods and services. *See* section 3.2.3. An acquisition of intellectual property may lessen competition in a relevant antitrust market. *See* section 5.7. The Agencies will focus on the actual effects of an arrangement, not on its formal terms.

The Agencies will not require the owner of intellectual property to create competition in its own technology. However, antitrust concerns may arise when a licensing arrangement harms competition among entities that would have been actual or likely potential competitors[15] in a relevant market in the absence of the license (entities in a "horizontal relationship"). A restraint in a licensing arrangement may harm such competition, for example, if it facilitates market division or price-fixing. In addition, license restrictions with respect to one market may harm such competition in another market by anticompetitively foreclosing access to, or significantly raising the price of, an important input,[16] or by facilitating coordination to increase price or reduce output. When it appears that such competition may be adversely affected, the Agencies will follow the analysis set forth below. *See generally* sections 3.4 and 4.2.

3.2   Markets Affected by Licensing Arrangements

Licensing arrangements raise concerns under the antitrust laws if they are likely to affect adversely the prices, quantities, qualities, or varieties of goods and services[17] either currently or potentially available. The competitive effects of licensing arrangements often can be adequately assessed within the relevant markets for the goods affected by the arrangements. In such instances, the Agencies will delineate and analyze only goods markets. In other cases, however, the analysis may require the delineation of markets for technology or markets for research and development (innovation markets).

3.2.1   Goods Markets

A number of different goods markets may be relevant to evaluating the effects of a licensing arrangement. A restraint in a licensing arrangement may have competitive effects in markets for final or intermediate goods made using the intellectual property, or it may have effects upstream, in markets for goods that are used as inputs, along with the intellectual property, to the production of other goods. In general, for goods markets affected by a licensing arrangement, the Agencies will approach the delineation of relevant market and the measurement of market share in the intellectual property area as in section 1 of the U.S. Department of Justice and Federal Trade Commission Horizontal Merger Guidelines.[18]

3.2.2   Technology Markets

Technology markets consist of the intellectual property that is licensed (the "licensed technology") and its close substitutes—that is, the technologies or goods that are close enough substitutes significantly to constrain the exercise of market power with respect to the intellectual property that is licensed.[19] When rights to intellectual property are marketed separately from the products in which they are used,[20] the Agencies may rely on technology markets to analyze the competitive effects of a licensing arrangement.

Example 2

Situation: Firms Alpha and Beta independently develop different patented process technologies to manufacture the same off-patent drug for the treatment of a particular disease. Before the firms use their technologies internally or license them

Example 2 (continued)

to third parties, they announce plans jointly to manufacture the drug, and to assign their manufacturing processes to the new manufacturing venture. Many firms are capable of using and have the incentive to use the licensed technologies to manufacture and distribute the drug; thus, the market for drug manufacturing and distribution is competitive. One of the Agencies is evaluating the likely competitive effects of the planned venture.

Discussion: The Agency would analyze the competitive effects of the proposed joint venture by first defining the relevant markets in which competition may be affected and then evaluating the likely competitive effects of the joint venture in the identified markets. (*See* Example 4 for a discussion of the Agencies' approach to joint venture analysis.) In this example, the structural effect of the joint venture in the relevant goods market for the manufacture and distribution of the drug is unlikely to be significant, because many firms in addition to the joint venture compete in that market. The joint venture might, however, increase the prices of the drug produced using Alpha's or Beta's technology by reducing competition in the relevant market for technology to manufacture the drug.

The Agency would delineate a technology market in which to evaluate likely competitive effects of the proposed joint venture. The Agency would identify other technologies that can be used to make the drug with levels of effectiveness and cost per dose comparable to that of the technologies owned by Alpha and Beta. In addition, the Agency would consider the extent to which competition from other drugs that are substitutes for the drug produced using Alpha's or Beta's technology would limit the ability of a hypothetical monopolist that owned both Alpha's and Beta's technology to raise its price.

To identify a technology's close substitutes and thus to delineate the relevant technology market, the Agencies will, if the data permit, identify the smallest group of technologies and goods over which a hypothetical monopolist of those technologies and goods likely would exercise market power—for example, by imposing a small but significant and nontransitory price increase.[21] The Agencies recognize that technology often is licensed in ways that are not readily quantifiable in monetary terms.[22] In such circumstances, the Agencies will delineate the relevant market by identifying other technologies and goods which buyers would substitute at a cost comparable to that of using the licensed technology.

In assessing the competitive significance of current and likely potential participants in a technology market, the Agencies will take into account all relevant evidence. When market share data are available and accurately reflect the competitive significance of market participants, the Agencies will include market share data in this assessment. The Agencies also will seek evidence of buyers' and market participants' assessments of the competitive significance of technology market participants. Such evidence is particularly important when market share data are unavailable, or do not accurately represent the competitive significance of market participants. When market share data or other indicia of market power are not available, and it appears that competing technologies are comparably efficient,[23] the Agencies will assign each technology the same market share. For new technologies, the Agencies generally will use the best available information to estimate market acceptance over a two-year period, beginning with commercial introduction.

3.2.3   Research and Development: Innovation Markets

If a licensing arrangement may adversely affect competition to develop new or improved goods or processes, the Agencies will analyze such an impact either as a separate competitive effect in relevant goods or technology markets, or as a competitive effect in a separate innovation market. A licensing arrangement may have competitive effects on innovation that cannot be adequately addressed through the analysis of goods or technology markets. For example, the arrangement may affect the development of goods that do not yet exist.[24] Alternatively, the arrangement may affect the development of new or improved goods or processes in geographic markets where there is no actual or likely potential competition in the relevant goods.[25]

An innovation market consists of the research and development directed to particular new or improved goods or processes, and the close substitutes for that research and development. The close substitutes are research and development efforts, technologies, and goods[26] that significantly constrain the exercise of market power with respect to the relevant research and development, for example by limiting the ability and incentive of a hypothetical monopolist to retard the pace of research and development. The Agencies will delineate an innovation market only when the capabilities to engage in the relevant research and development can be associated with specialized assets or characteristics of specific firms.

In assessing the competitive significance of current and likely potential participants in an innovation market, the Agencies will take into account all relevant evidence. When market share data are available and accurately reflect the competitive significance of market participants, the Agencies will include market share data in this assessment. The Agencies also will seek evidence of buyers' and market participants' assessments of the competitive significance of innovation market participants. Such evidence is particularly important when market share data are unavailable or do not accurately represent the competitive significance of market participants. The

Agencies may base the market shares of participants in an innovation market on their shares of identifiable assets or characteristics upon which innovation depends, on shares of research and development expenditures, or on shares of a related product. When entities have comparable capabilities and incentives to pursue research and development that is a close substitute for the research and development activities of the parties to a licensing arrangement, the Agencies may assign equal market shares to such entities.

Example 3

Situation: Two companies that specialize in advanced metallurgy agree to cross-license future patents relating to the development of a new component for aircraft jet turbines. Innovation in the development of the component requires the capability to work with very high tensile strength materials for jet turbines. Aspects of the licensing arrangement raise the possibility that competition in research and development of this and related components will be lessened. One of the Agencies is considering whether to define an innovation market in which to evaluate the competitive effects of the arrangement.

Discussion: If the firms that have the capability and incentive to work with very high tensile strength materials for jet turbines can be reasonably identified, the Agency will consider defining a relevant innovation market for development of the new component. If the number of firms with the required capability and incentive to engage in research and development of very high tensile strength materials for aircraft jet turbines is small, the Agency may employ the concept of an innovation market to analyze the likely competitive effects of the arrangement in that market, or as an aid in analyzing competitive effects in technology or goods markets. The Agency would perform its analysis as described in parts 3–5.

If the number of firms with the required capability and incentive is large (either because there are a large number of such firms in the jet turbine industry, or because there are many firms in other industries with the required capability and incentive), then the Agency will conclude that the innovation market is competitive. Under these circumstances, it is unlikely that any single firm or plausible aggregation of firms could acquire a large enough share of the assets necessary for innovation to have an adverse impact on competition.

If the Agency cannot reasonably identify the firms with the required capability and incentive, it will not attempt to define an innovation market.

Example 4

Situation: Three of the largest producers of a plastic used in disposable bottles plan to engage in joint research and development to produce a new type of plastic that is rapidly biodegradable. The joint venture will grant to its partners (but to no one else) licenses to all patent rights and use of know-how. One of the Agencies is evaluating the likely competitive effects of the proposed joint venture.

Discussion: The Agency would analyze the proposed research and development joint venture using an analysis similar to that applied to other joint ventures.[27] The Agency would begin by defining the relevant markets in which to analyze the joint venture's likely competitive effects. In this case, a relevant market is an innovation market—research and development for biodegradable (and other environmentally friendly) containers. The Agency would seek to identify any other entities that would be actual or likely potential competitors with the joint venture in that relevant market. This would include those firms that have the capability and incentive to undertake research and development closely substitutable for the research and development proposed to be undertaken by the joint venture, taking into account such firms' existing technologies and technologies under development, R&D facilities, and other relevant assets and business circumstances. Firms possessing such capabilities and incentives would be included in the research and development market even if they are not competitors in relevant markets for related goods, such as the plastics currently produced by the joint venturers, although competitors in existing goods markets may often also compete in related innovation markets.

Having defined a relevant innovation market, the Agency would assess whether the joint venture is likely to have anticompetitive effects in that market. A starting point in this analysis is the degree of concentration in the relevant market and the market shares of the parties to the joint venture. If, in addition to the parties to the joint venture (taken collectively), there are at least four other independently controlled entities that possess comparable capabilities and incentives to undertake research and development of biodegradable plastics, or other products that would be close substitutes for such new plastics, the joint venture ordinarily would be unlikely to adversely affect competition in the relevant innovation market (*cf.* section 4.3). If there are fewer than four other independently controlled entities with similar capabilities and incentives, the Agency would consider whether the joint venture would give the parties to the joint venture an incentive and ability collectively to reduce investment in, or otherwise to retard the pace or scope of, research and development efforts. If the joint venture creates a significant risk of anticompetitive effects in the innovation market, the Agency would proceed to consider efficiency justifications for the venture, such as the potential for combining complementary R&D assets in such a way as to make successful innovation more

> **Example 4 (continued)**
>
> likely, or to bring it about sooner, or to achieve cost reductions in research and development.
>
> The Agency would also assess the likelihood that the joint venture would adversely affect competition in other relevant markets, including markets for products produced by the parties to the joint venture. The risk of such adverse competitive effects would be increased to the extent that, for example, the joint venture facilitates the exchange among the parties of competitively sensitive information relating to goods markets in which the parties currently compete or facilitates the coordination of competitive activities in such markets. The Agency would examine whether the joint venture imposes collateral restraints that might significantly restrict competition among the joint venturers in goods markets, and would examine whether such collateral restraints were reasonably necessary to achieve any efficiencies that are likely to be attained by the venture.

3.3   Horizontal and Vertical Relationships

As with other property transfers, antitrust analysis of intellectual property licensing arrangements examines whether the relationship among the parties to the arrangement is primarily horizontal or vertical in nature, or whether it has substantial aspects of both. A licensing arrangement has a vertical component when it affects activities that are in a complementary relationship, as is typically the case in a licensing arrangement. For example, the licensor's primary line of business may be in research and development, and the licensees, as manufacturers, may be buying the rights to use technology developed by the licensor. Alternatively, the licensor may be a component manufacturer owning intellectual property rights in a product that the licensee manufactures by combining the component with other inputs, or the licensor may manufacture the product, and the licensees may operate primarily in distribution and marketing.

In addition to this vertical component, the licensor and its licensees may also have a horizontal relationship. For analytical purposes, the Agencies ordinarily will treat a relationship between a licensor and its licensees, or between licensees, as horizontal when they would have been actual or likely potential competitors in a relevant market in the absence of the license.

The existence of a horizontal relationship between a licensor and its licensees does not, in itself, indicate that the arrangement is anticompetitive. Identification of such relationships is merely an aid in determining whether there may be anticompetitive effects arising from a licensing arrangement. Such a relationship need not give rise to an anticompetitive effect, nor does a purely vertical relationship assure that there are no anticompetitive effects.

The following examples illustrate different competitive relationships among a licensor and its licensees.

Example 5

Situation: AgCo, a manufacturer of farm equipment, develops a new, patented emission control technology for its tractor engines and licenses it to FarmCo, another farm equipment manufacturer. AgCo's emission control technology is far superior to the technology currently owned and used by FarmCo, so much so that FarmCo's technology does not significantly constrain the prices that AgCo could charge for its technology. AgCo's emission control patent has a broad scope. It is likely that any improved emissions control technology that FarmCo could develop in the foreseeable future would infringe AgCo's patent.

Discussion: Because FarmCo's emission control technology does not significantly constrain AgCo's competitive conduct with respect to its emission control technology, AgCo's and FarmCo's emission control technologies are not close substitutes for each other. FarmCo is a consumer of AgCo's technology and is not an actual competitor of AgCo in the relevant market for superior emission control technology of the kind licensed by AgCo. Furthermore, FarmCo is not a likely potential competitor of AgCo in the relevant market because, even if FarmCo could develop an improved emission control technology, it is likely that it would infringe AgCo's patent. This means that the relationship between AgCo and FarmCo with regard to the supply and use of emissions control technology is vertical. Assuming that AgCo and FarmCo are actual or likely potential competitors in sales of farm equipment products, their relationship is horizontal in the relevant markets for farm equipment.

Example 6

Situation: FarmCo develops a new valve technology for its engines and enters into a cross-licensing arrangement with AgCo, whereby AgCo licenses its emission control technology to FarmCo and FarmCo licenses its valve technology to AgCo. AgCo already owns an alternative valve technology that can be used to achieve engine performance similar to that using FarmCo's valve technology and at a comparable cost to consumers. Before adopting FarmCo's technology, AgCo was using its own valve technology in its production of engines and was licensing (and continues to license) that technology for use by others. As in Example 5, FarmCo does

Example 6 (continued)

not own or control an emission control technology that is a close substitute for the technology licensed from AgCo. Furthermore, as in Example 5, FarmCo is not likely to develop an improved emission control technology that would be a close substitute for AgCo's technology, because of AgCo's blocking patent.

Discussion: FarmCo is a consumer and not a competitor of AgCo's emission control technology. As in Example 5, their relationship is vertical with regard to this technology. The relationship between AgCo and FarmCo in the relevant market that includes engine valve technology is vertical in part and horizontal in part. It is vertical in part because AgCo and FarmCo stand in a complementary relationship, in which AgCo is a consumer of a technology supplied by FarmCo. However, the relationship between AgCo and FarmCo in the relevant market that includes engine valve technology is also horizontal in part, because FarmCo and AgCo are actual competitors in the licensing of valve technology that can be used to achieve similar engine performance at a comparable cost. Whether the firms license their valve technologies to others is not important for the conclusion that the firms have a horizontal relationship in this relevant market. Even if AgCo's use of its valve technology were solely captive to its own production, the fact that the two valve technologies are substitutable at comparable cost means that the two firms have a horizontal relationship.

As in Example 5, the relationship between AgCo and FarmCo is horizontal in the relevant markets for farm equipment.

3.4   Framework for Evaluating Licensing Restraints

In the vast majority of cases, restraints in intellectual property licensing arrangements are evaluated under the rule of reason. The Agencies' general approach in analyzing a licensing restraint under the rule of reason is to inquire whether the restraint is likely to have anticompetitive effects and, if so, whether the restraint is reasonably necessary to achieve procompetitive benefits that outweigh those anticompetitive effects. *See Federal Trade Commission v. Indiana Federation of Dentists*, 476 U.S. 447 (1986); *NCAA v. Board of Regents of the University of Oklahoma*, 468 U.S. 85 (1984); *Broadcast Music, Inc. v. Columbia Broadcasting System, Inc.*, 441 U.S. 1 (1979); 7 Phillip E. Areeda, *Antitrust Law* §1502 (1986). *See also* part 4.

In some cases, however, the courts conclude that a restraint's "nature and necessary effect are so plainly anticompetitive" that it should be treated as unlawful per se, without an elaborate inquiry into the restraint's likely competitive effect. *Federal Trade Commission v. Superior Court Trial Lawyers Association*, 493 U.S. 411, 433 (1990);

National Society of Professional Engineers v. United States, 435 U.S. 679, 692 (1978). Among the restraints that have been held per se unlawful are naked price-fixing, output restraints, and market division among horizontal competitors, as well as certain group boycotts and resale price maintenance.

To determine whether a particular restraint in a licensing arrangement is given per se or rule of reason treatment, the Agencies will assess whether the restraint in question can be expected to contribute to an efficiency-enhancing integration of economic activity. *See Broadcast Music*, 441 U.S. at 16–24. In general, licensing arrangements promote such integration because they facilitate the combination of the licensor's intellectual property with complementary factors of production owned by the licensee. A restraint in a licensing arrangement may further such integration by, for example, aligning the incentives of the licensor and the licensees to promote the development and marketing of the licensed technology, or by substantially reducing transactions costs. If there is no efficiency-enhancing integration of economic activity and if the type of restraint is one that has been accorded per se treatment, the Agencies will challenge the restraint under the per se rule. Otherwise, the Agencies will apply a rule of reason analysis.

Application of the rule of reason generally requires a comprehensive inquiry into market conditions. (*See* sections 4.1–4.3.) However, that inquiry may be truncated in certain circumstances. If the Agencies conclude that a restraint has no likely anticompetitive effects, they will treat it as reasonable, without an elaborate analysis of market power or the justifications for the restraint. Similarly, if a restraint facially appears to be of a kind that would always or almost always tend to reduce output or increase prices,[28] and the restraint is not reasonably related to efficiencies, the Agencies will likely challenge the restraint without an elaborate analysis of particular industry circumstances.[29] *See Indiana Federation of Dentists*, 476 U.S. at 459–60; *NCAA*, 468 U.S. at 109.

Example 7

Situation: Gamma, which manufactures Product *X* using its patented process, offers a license for its process technology to every other manufacturer of Product *X*, each of which competes worldwide with Gamma in the manufacture and sale of *X*. The process technology does not represent an economic improvement over the available existing technologies. Indeed, although most manufacturers accept licenses from Gamma, none of the licensees actually uses the licensed technology. The licenses provide that each manufacturer has an exclusive right to sell Product *X* manufactured using the licensed technology in a designated geographic area and that no manufacturer may sell Product *X*, however manufactured, outside the designated territory.

Example 7 (continued)

Discussion: The manufacturers of Product X are in a horizontal relationship in the goods market for Product X. Any manufacturers of Product X that control technologies that are substitutable at comparable cost for Gamma's process are also horizontal competitors of Gamma in the relevant technology market. The licensees of Gamma's process technology are technically in a vertical relationship, although that is not significant in this example because they do not actually use Gamma's technology.

The licensing arrangement restricts competition in the relevant goods market among manufacturers of Product X by requiring each manufacturer to limit its sales to an exclusive territory. Thus, competition among entities that would be actual competitors in the absence of the licensing arrangement is restricted. Based on the facts set forth above, the licensing arrangement does not involve a useful transfer of technology, and thus it is unlikely that the restraint on sales outside the designated territories contributes to an efficiency-enhancing integration of economic activity. Consequently, the evaluating Agency would be likely to challenge the arrangement under the per se rule as a horizontal territorial market allocation scheme and to view the intellectual property aspects of the arrangement as a sham intended to cloak its true nature.

If the licensing arrangement could be expected to contribute to an efficiency-enhancing integration of economic activity, as might be the case if the licensed technology were an advance over existing processes and used by the licensees, the Agency would analyze the arrangement under the rule of reason applying the analytical framework described in this section.

In this example, the competitive implications do not generally depend on whether the licensed technology is protected by patent, is a trade secret or other know-how, or is a computer program protected by copyright; nor do the competitive implications generally depend on whether the allocation of markets is territorial, as in this example, or functional, based on fields of use.

4. GENERAL PRINCIPLES CONCERNING THE AGENCIES' EVALUATION OF LICENSING ARRANGEMENTS UNDER THE RULE OF REASON

4.1 Analysis of Anticompetitive Effects

The existence of anticompetitive effects resulting from a restraint in a licensing arrangement will be evaluated on the basis of the analysis described in this section.

4.1.1 Market Structure, Coordination, and Foreclosure

When a licensing arrangement affects parties in a horizontal relationship, a restraint in that arrangement may increase the risk of coordinated pricing, output restrictions, or the acquisition or maintenance of market power. Harm to competition also may occur if the arrangement poses a significant risk of retarding or restricting the development of new or improved goods or processes. The potential for competitive harm depends in part on the degree of concentration in, the difficulty of entry into, and the responsiveness of supply and demand to changes in price in the relevant markets. *Cf.* 1992 Horizontal Merger Guidelines §§1.5, 3.

When the licensor and licensees are in a vertical relationship, the Agencies will analyze whether the licensing arrangement may harm competition among entities in a horizontal relationship at either the level of the licensor or the licensees, or possibly in another relevant market. Harm to competition from a restraint may occur if it anticompetitively forecloses access to, or increases competitors' costs of obtaining, important inputs, or facilitates coordination to raise price or restrict output. The risk of anticompetitively foreclosing access or increasing competitors' costs is related to the proportion of the markets affected by the licensing restraint; other characteristics of the relevant markets, such as concentration, difficulty of entry, and the responsiveness of supply and demand to changes in price in the relevant markets; and the duration of the restraint. A licensing arrangement does not foreclose competition merely because some or all of the potential licensees in an industry choose to use the licensed technology to the exclusion of other technologies. Exclusive use may be an efficient consequence of the licensed technology having the lowest cost or highest value.

Harm to competition from a restraint in a vertical licensing arrangement also may occur if a licensing restraint facilitates coordination among entities in a horizontal relationship to raise prices or reduce output in a relevant market. For example, if owners of competing technologies impose similar restraints on their licensees, the licensors may find it easier to coordinate their pricing. Similarly, licensees that are competitors may find it easier to coordinate their pricing if they are subject to common restraints in licenses with a common licensor or competing licensors. The risk of anticompetitive coordination is increased when the relevant markets are concentrated and difficult to enter. The use of similar restraints may be common and procompetitive in an industry, however, because they contribute to efficient exploitation of the licensed property.

4.1.2 Licensing Arrangements Involving Exclusivity

A licensing arrangement may involve exclusivity in two distinct respects. First, the licensor may grant one or more *exclusive licenses*, which restrict the right of the licensor to license others and possibly also to use the technology itself. Generally, an exclusive license may raise antitrust concerns only if the licensees themselves, or the licensor and its licensees, are in a horizontal relationship. Examples of arrangements involving exclusive licensing that may give rise to antitrust concerns include cross-licensing by parties collectively possessing market power (*see* section 5.5), grantbacks (*see* section 5.6), and acquisitions of intellectual property rights (*see* section 5.7).

A non-exclusive license of intellectual property that does not contain any restraints on the competitive conduct of the licensor or the licensee generally does not present antitrust concerns even if the parties to the license are in a horizontal relationship, because the non-exclusive license normally does not diminish competition that would occur in its absence.

A second form of exclusivity, *exclusive dealing*, arises when a license prevents or restrains the licensee from licensing, selling, distributing, or using competing technologies. *See* section 5.4. Exclusivity may be achieved by an explicit exclusive dealing term in the license or by other provisions such as compensation terms or other economic incentives. Such restraints may anticompetitively foreclose access to, or increase competitors' costs of obtaining, important inputs, or facilitate coordination to raise price or reduce output, but they also may have procompetitive effects. For example, a licensing arrangement that prevents the licensee from dealing in other technologies may encourage the licensee to develop and market the licensed technology or specialized applications of that technology. *See, e.g.*, Example 8. The Agencies will take into account such procompetitive effects in evaluating the reasonableness of the arrangement. *See* section 4.2.

The antitrust principles that apply to a licensor's grant of various forms of exclusivity to and among its licensees are similar to those that apply to comparable vertical restraints outside the licensing context, such as exclusive territories and exclusive dealing. However, the fact that intellectual property may in some cases be misappropriated more easily than other forms of property may justify the use of some restrictions that might be anticompetitive in other contexts.

As noted earlier, the Agencies will focus on the actual practice and its effects, not on the formal terms of the arrangement. A license denominated as non-exclusive (either in the sense of exclusive licensing or in the sense of exclusive dealing) may nonetheless give rise to the same concerns posed by formal exclusivity. A non-exclusive license may have the effect of exclusive licensing if it is structured so that the licensor is unlikely to license others or to practice the technology itself. A license that does not explicitly require exclusive dealing may have the effect of exclusive dealing if it is structured to increase significantly a licensee's cost when it uses competing technologies. However, a licensing arrangement will not automatically raise these concerns merely because a party chooses to deal with a single licensee or licensor, or confines his activity to a single field of use or location, or because only a single licensee has chosen to take a license.

Example 8

Situation: NewCo, the inventor and manufacturer of a new flat panel display technology, lacking the capability to bring a flat panel display product to market, grants BigCo an exclusive license to sell a product embodying NewCo's technology. BigCo does not currently sell, and is not developing (or likely to develop), a product that would compete with the product embodying the new technology and does not control rights to another display technology. Several firms offer competing displays, BigCo accounts for only a small proportion of the outlets for distribution of display products, and entry into the manufacture and distribution of display products is relatively easy. Demand for the new technology is uncertain and successful market penetration will require considerable promotional effort. The license contains an exclusive dealing restriction preventing BigCo from selling products that compete with the product embodying the licensed technology.

Discussion: This example illustrates both types of exclusivity in a licensing arrangement. The license is exclusive in that it restricts the right of the licensor to grant other licenses. In addition, the license has an exclusive dealing component in that it restricts the licensee from selling competing products.

The inventor of the display technology and its licensee are in a vertical relationship and are not actual or likely potential competitors in the manufacture or sale of display products or in the sale or development of technology. Hence, the grant of an exclusive license does not affect competition between the licensor and the licensee. The exclusive license may promote competition in the manufacturing and sale of display products by encouraging BigCo to develop and promote the new product in the face of uncertain demand by rewarding BigCo for its efforts if they lead to large sales. Although the license bars the licensee from selling competing products, this exclusive dealing aspect is unlikely in this example to harm competition by anticompetitively foreclosing access, raising competitors' costs of inputs, or facilitating anticompetitive pricing because the relevant product market is unconcentrated, the exclusive dealing restraint affects only a small proportion of the outlets for distribution of display products, and entry is easy. On these facts, the evaluating Agency would be unlikely to challenge the arrangement.

4.2   Efficiencies and Justifications

If the Agencies conclude, upon an evaluation of the market factors described in section 4.1, that a restraint in a licensing arrangement is unlikely to have an anticompetitive effect, they will not challenge the restraint. If the Agencies conclude that the restraint has, or is likely to have, an anticompetitive effect, they will consider whether the restraint is reasonably necessary to achieve procompetitive efficiencies. If the restraint is reasonably necessary, the Agencies will balance the procompetitive efficiencies and the anticompetitive effects to determine the probable net effect on competition in each relevant market.

The Agencies' comparison of anticompetitive harms and procompetitive efficiencies is necessarily a qualitative one. The risk of anticompetitive effects in a particular case may be insignificant compared to the expected efficiencies, or vice versa. As the expected anticompetitive effects in a particular licensing arrangement increase, the Agencies will require evidence establishing a greater level of expected efficiencies.

The existence of practical and significantly less restrictive alternatives is relevant to a determination of whether a restraint is reasonably necessary. If it is clear that the parties could have achieved similar efficiencies by means that are significantly less restrictive, then the Agencies will not give weight to the parties' efficiency claim. In making this assessment, however, the Agencies will not engage in a search for a theoretically least restrictive alternative that is not realistic in the practical prospective business situation faced by the parties.

When a restraint has, or is likely to have, an anticompetitive effect, the duration of that restraint can be an important factor in determining whether it is reasonably necessary to achieve the putative procompetitive efficiency. The effective duration of a restraint may depend on a number of factors, including the option of the affected party to terminate the arrangement unilaterally and the presence of contract terms (e.g., unpaid balances on minimum purchase commitments) that encourage the licensee to renew a license arrangement. Consistent with their approach to less restrictive alternative analysis generally, the Agencies will not attempt to draw fine distinctions regarding duration; rather, their focus will be on situations in which the duration clearly exceeds the period needed to achieve the procompetitive efficiency.

The evaluation of procompetitive efficiencies, of the reasonable necessity of a restraint to achieve them, and of the duration of the restraint, may depend on the market context. A restraint that may be justified by the needs of a new entrant, for example, may not have a procompetitive efficiency justification in different market circumstances. *Cf. United States v. Jerrold Electronics Corp.*, 187 F. Supp. 545 (E.D. Pa. 1960), *aff'd per curiam*, 365 U.S. 567 (1961).

4.3   Antitrust "Safety Zone"

Because licensing arrangements often promote innovation and enhance competition, the Agencies believe that an antitrust "safety zone" is useful in order to provide some degree of certainty and thus to encourage such activity.[30] Absent extraordinary circumstances, the Agencies will not challenge a restraint in an intellectual property licensing arrangement if (1) the restraint is not facially anticompetitive[31] and (2) the licensor and its licensees collectively account for no more than twenty percent of each relevant market significantly affected by the restraint. This "safety zone" does not apply to those transfers of intellectual property rights to which a merger analysis is applied. *See* section 5.7.

Whether a restraint falls within the safety zone will be determined by reference only to goods markets unless the analysis of goods markets alone would inadequately address the effects of the licensing arrangement on competition among technologies or in research and development.

If an examination of the effects on competition among technologies or in research development is required, and if market share data are unavailable or do not accurately represent competitive significance, the following safety zone criteria will apply. Absent extraordinary circumstances, the Agencies will not challenge a restraint in an intellectual property licensing arrangement that may affect competition in a technology market if (1) the restraint is not facially anticompetitive and (2) there are four or more independently controlled technologies in addition to the technologies controlled by the parties to the licensing arrangement that may be substitutable for the licensed technology at a comparable cost to the user. Absent extraordinary circumstances, the Agencies will not challenge a restraint in an intellectual property licensing arrangement that may affect competition in an innovation market if (1) the restraint is not facially anticompetitive and (2) four or more independently controlled entities in addition to the parties to the licensing arrangement possess the required specialized assets or characteristics and the incentive to engage in research and development that is a close substitute of the research and development activities of the parties to the licensing agreement.[32]

The Agencies emphasize that licensing arrangements are not anticompetitive merely because they do not fall within the scope of the safety zone. Indeed, it is likely that the great majority of licenses falling outside the safety zone are lawful and procompetitive. The safety zone is designed to provide owners of intellectual property with a degree of certainty in those situations in which anticompetitive effects are so unlikely that the arrangements may be presumed not to be anticompetitive without an inquiry into particular industry circumstances. It is not intended to suggest that parties should conform to the safety zone or to discourage parties falling outside the safety zone from adopting restrictions in their license arrangements that are reasonably necessary to achieve an efficiency-enhancing integration of economic activity. The Agencies will analyze arrangements falling outside the safety zone based on the considerations outlined in parts 3–5.

The status of a licensing arrangement with respect to the safety zone may change over time. A determination by the Agencies that a restraint in a licensing arrangement qualifies for inclusion in the safety zone is based on the factual circumstances prevailing at the time of the conduct at issue.[33]

5. APPLICATION OF GENERAL PRINCIPLES

5.0   This section illustrates the application of the general principles discussed above to particular licensing restraints and to arrangements that involve the cross-licensing, pooling, or acquisition of intellectual property. The restraints and arrangements identified are typical of those that are likely to receive antitrust scrutiny; however, they are not intended as an exhaustive list of practices that could raise competitive concerns.

5.1   Horizontal Restraints

The existence of a restraint in a licensing arrangement that affects parties in a horizontal relationship (a "horizontal restraint") does not necessarily cause the arrangement to be anticompetitive. As in the case of joint ventures among horizontal competitors, licensing arrangements among such competitors may promote rather than hinder competition if they result in integrative efficiencies. Such efficiencies may arise, for example, from the realization of economies of scale and the integration of complementary research and development, production, and marketing capabilities.

Following the general principles outlined in section 3.4, horizontal restraints often will be evaluated under the rule of reason. In some circumstances, however, that analysis may be truncated; additionally, some restraints may merit per se treatment, including price fixing, allocation of markets or customers, agreements to reduce output, and certain group boycotts.

Example 9

Situation: Two of the leading manufacturers of a consumer electronic product hold patents that cover alternative circuit designs for the product. The manufacturers assign their patents to a separate corporation wholly owned by the two firms. That corporation licenses the right to use the circuit designs to other consumer product manufacturers and establishes the license royalties. None of the patents is blocking; that is, each of the patents can be used without infringing a patent owned by the other firm. The different circuit designs are substitutable in that each permits the manufacture at comparable cost to consumers of products that consumers consider to be interchangeable. One of the Agencies is analyzing the licensing arrangement.

Discussion: In this example, the manufacturers are horizontal competitors in the goods market for the consumer product and in the related technology markets. The competitive issue with regard to a joint assignment of patent rights is whether the assignment has an adverse impact on competition in technology and goods

(continues)

Example 9 (continued)

markets that is not outweighed by procompetitive efficiencies, such as benefits in the use or dissemination of the technology. Each of the patent owners has a right to exclude others from using its patent. That right does not extend, however, to the agreement to assign rights jointly. To the extent that the patent rights cover technologies that are close substitutes, the joint determination of royalties likely would result in higher royalties and higher goods prices than would result if the owners licensed or used their technologies independently. In the absence of evidence establishing efficiency-enhancing integration from the joint assignment of patent rights, the Agency may conclude that the joint marketing of competing patent rights constitutes horizontal price fixing and could be challenged as a per se unlawful horizontal restraint of trade. If the joint marketing arrangement results in an efficiency-enhancing integration, the Agency would evaluate the arrangement under the rule of reason. However, the Agency may conclude that the anticompetitive effects are sufficiently apparent, and the claimed integrative efficiencies are sufficiently weak or not reasonably related to the restraints, to warrant challenge of the arrangement without an elaborate analysis of particular industry circumstances (*see* section 3.4).

5.2   Resale Price Maintenance

Resale price maintenance is illegal when "commodities have passed into the channels of trade and are owned by dealers." *Dr. Miles Medical Co. v. John D. Park & Sons Co.*, 220 U.S. 373, 408 (1911). It has been held per se illegal for a licensor of an intellectual property right in a product to fix a licensee's *resale* price of that product. *United States v. Univis Lens Co.*, 316 U.S. 241 (1942); *Ethyl Gasoline Corp. v. United States*, 309 U.S. 436 (1940).[34] Consistent with the principles set forth in section 3.4, the Agencies will enforce the per se rule against resale price maintenance in the intellectual property context.

5.3   Tying Arrangements

A "tying" or "tie-in" or "tied sale" arrangement has been defined as "an agreement by a party to sell one product . . . on the condition that the buyer also purchases a different (or tied) product, or at least agrees that he will not purchase that [tied] product from any other supplier." *Eastman Kodak Co. v. Image Technical Services, Inc.*, 112 S. Ct. 2072, 2079 (1992). Conditioning the ability of a licensee to license one or more items of intellectual property on the licensee's purchase of another item of intellectual property or a good or a service has been held in some cases to constitute illegal tying.[35] Although tying arrangements may result in anticompetitive effects, such arrangements can also result in significant efficiencies and procompetitive benefits. In the exercise of their prosecutorial discretion, the Agencies will consider both the anticompetitive effects and the efficiencies attributable to a tie-in. The Agencies would be likely to challenge a tying arrangement if: (1) the seller has market power in the tying product,[36] (2) the arrangement has an adverse effect on competition in the relevant market for the tied product, and (3) efficiency justifications for the arrangement do not outweigh the anticompetitive effects.[37] The Agencies will not presume that a patent, copyright, or trade secret necessarily confers market power upon its owner.

Package licensing—the licensing of multiple items of intellectual property in a single license or in a group of related licenses—may be a form of tying arrangement if the licensing of one product is conditioned upon the acceptance of a license of another, separate product. Package licensing can be efficiency enhancing under some circumstances. When multiple licenses are needed to use any single item of intellectual property, for example, a package license may promote such efficiencies. If a package license constitutes a tying arrangement, the Agencies will evaluate its competitive effects under the same principles they apply to other tying arrangements.

5.4   Exclusive Dealing

In the intellectual property context, exclusive dealing occurs when a license prevents the licensee from licensing, selling, distributing, or using competing technologies. Exclusive dealing arrangements are evaluated under the rule of reason. *See Tampa Electric Co. v. Nashville Coal Co.*, 365 U.S. 320 (1961) (evaluating legality of exclusive dealing under section 1 of the Sherman Act and section 3 of the Clayton Act); *Beltone Electronics Corp.*, 100 F.T.C. 68 (1982) (evaluating legality of exclusive dealing under section 5 of the Federal Trade Commission Act). In determining whether an exclusive dealing arrangement is likely to reduce competition in a relevant market, the Agencies will take into account the extent to which the arrangement (1) promotes the exploitation and development of the licensor's technology and (2) anticompetitively forecloses the exploitation and development of, or otherwise constrains competition among, competing technologies.

The likelihood that exclusive dealing may have anticompetitive effects is related, *inter alia*, to the degree of foreclosure in the relevant market, the duration of the exclusive dealing arrangement, and other characteristics of the input and output markets, such as concentration, difficulty of entry, and the responsiveness of supply and demand to changes in price in the relevant markets. (*See* sections 4.1.1 and 4.1.2.) If the Agencies determine that a particular exclusive dealing arrangement may have an anticompetitive effect, they will evaluate the extent to which the restraint encourages licensees to develop and market the licensed technology (or specialized applications of that technology), increases licensors' incentives to develop or refine the licensed technology, or otherwise increases competition and enhances output in a relevant market. (*See* section 4.2 and Example 8.)

5.5　　Cross-Licensing and Pooling Arrangements

Cross-licensing and pooling arrangements are agreements of two or more owners of different items of intellectual property to license one another or third parties. These arrangements may provide procompetitive benefits by integrating complementary technologies, reducing transaction costs, clearing blocking positions, and avoiding costly infringement litigation. By promoting the dissemination of technology, cross-licensing and pooling arrangements are often procompetitive.

Cross-licensing and pooling arrangements can have anticompetitive effects in certain circumstances. For example, collective price or output restraints in pooling arrangements, such as the joint marketing of pooled intellectual property rights with collective price setting or coordinated output restrictions, may be deemed unlawful if they do not contribute to an efficiency-enhancing integration of economic activity among the participants. *Compare NCAA* 468 U.S. at 114 (output restriction on college football broadcasting held unlawful because it was not reasonably related to any purported justification) with *Broadcast Music*, 441 U.S. at 23 (blanket license for music copyrights found not per se illegal because the cooperative price was necessary to the creation of a new product). When cross-licensing or pooling arrangements are mechanisms to accomplish naked price-fixing or market division, they are subject to challenge under the per se rule. *See United States v. New Wrinkle, Inc.*, 342 U.S. 371 (1952) (price-fixing).

Settlements involving the cross-licensing of intellectual property rights can be an efficient means to avoid litigation and, in general, courts favor such settlements. When such cross-licensing involves horizontal competitors, however, the Agencies will consider whether the effect of the settlement is to diminish competition among entities that would have been actual or likely potential competitors in a relevant market in the absence of the cross-license. In the absence of offsetting efficiencies, such settlements may be challenged as unlawful restraints of trade. *Cf. United States v. Singer Manufacturing Co.*, 374 U.S. 174 (1963) (cross-license agreement was part of broader combination to exclude competitors).

Pooling arrangements generally need not be open to all who would like to join. However, exclusion from cross-licensing and pooling arrangements among parties that collectively possess market power may, under some circumstances, harm competition. *Cf. Northwest Wholesale Stationers, Inc. v. Pacific Stationery & Printing Co.*, 472 U.S. 284 (1985) (exclusion of a competitor from a purchasing cooperative not per se unlawful absent a showing of market power). In general, exclusion from a pooling or cross-licensing arrangement among competing technologies is unlikely to have anticompetitive effects unless (1) excluded firms cannot effectively compete in the relevant market for the good incorporating the licensed technologies and (2) the pool participants collectively possess market power in the relevant market. If these circumstances exist, the Agencies will evaluate whether the arrangement's limitations on participation are reasonably related to the efficient development and exploitation of the pooled technologies and will assess the net effect of those limitations in the relevant market. *See* section 4.2.

Another possible anticompetitive effect of pooling arrangements may occur if the arrangement deters or discourages participants from engaging in research and development, thus retarding innovation. For example, a pooling arrangement that requires members to grant licenses to each other for current and future technology at minimal cost may reduce the incentives of its members to engage in research and development because members of the pool have to share their successful research and development and each of the members can free ride on the accomplishments of other pool members. *See generally United States v. Mfrs. Aircraft Ass'n, Inc.*, 1976-1 Trade Cas. (CCH) ¶ 60,810 (S.D.N.Y. 1975); *United States v. Automobile Mfrs. Ass'n*, 307 F. Supp. 617 (C.D. Cal 1969), *appeal dismissed sub nom. City of New York v. United States*, 397 U.S. 248 (1970), *modified sub nom. United States v. Motor Vehicle Mfrs. Ass'n*, 1982-83 Trade Cas. (CCH) ¶ 65,088 (C.D. Cal. 1982). However, such an arrangement can have procompetitive benefits, for example, by exploiting economies of scale and integrating complementary capabilities of the pool members, (including the clearing of blocking positions), and is likely to cause competitive problems only when the arrangement includes a large fraction of the potential research and development in an innovation market. *See* section 3.2.3 and Example 4.

Example 10

Situation: As in Example 9, two of the leading manufacturers of a consumer electronic product hold patents that cover alternative circuit designs for the product. The manufacturers assign several of their patents to a separate corporation wholly owned by the two firms. That corporation licenses the right to use the circuit designs to other consumer product manufacturers and establishes the license royalties. In this example, however, the manufacturers assign to the separate corporation only patents that are blocking. None of the patents assigned to the corporation can be used without infringing a patent owned by the other firm.

Discussion: Unlike the previous example, the joint assignment of patent rights to the wholly owned corporation in this example does not adversely affect competition in the licensed technology among entities that would have been actual or likely potential competitors in the absence of the licensing arrangement. Moreover, the licensing arrangement is likely to have procompetitive benefits in the use of the technology. Because the manufacturers' patents are blocking, the manufacturers are not in a horizontal relationship with respect to those patents. None of the patents can be used without the right to a patent owned by the other firm, so the patents are not substitutable. As in Example 9, the firms are horizontal

(continues)

Example 10 (continued)

competitors in the relevant goods market. In the absence of collateral restraints that would likely raise price or reduce output in the relevant goods market or in any other relevant antitrust market and that are not reasonably related to an efficiency-enhancing integration of economic activity, the evaluating Agency would be unlikely to challenge this arrangement.

5.6   Grantbacks

A grantback is an arrangement under which a licensee agrees to extend to the licensor of intellectual property the right to use the licensee's improvements to the licensed technology. Grantbacks can have procompetitive effects, especially if they are nonexclusive. Such arrangements provide a means for the licensee and the licensor to share risks and reward the licensor for making possible further innovation based on or informed by the licensed technology, and both promote innovation in the first place and promote the subsequent licensing of the results of the innovation. Grantbacks may adversely affect competition, however, if they substantially reduce the licensee's incentives to engage in research and development and thereby limit rivalry in innovation markets.

A nonexclusive grantback allows the licensee to practice its technology and license it to others. Such a grantback provision may be necessary to ensure that the licensor is not prevented from effectively competing because it is denied access to improvements developed with the aid of its own technology. Compared with an exclusive grantback, a nonexclusive grantback, which leaves the licensee free to license improvements technology to others, is less likely to have anticompetitive effects.

The Agencies will evaluate a grantback provision under the rule of reason, *see generally Transparent-Wrap Machine Corp. v. Stokes & Smith Co.*, 329 U.S. 637, 645–48 (1947) (grantback provision in technology license is not per se unlawful), considering its likely effects in light of the overall structure of the licensing arrangement and conditions in the relevant markets. An important factor in the Agencies' analysis of a grantback will be whether the licensor has market power in a relevant technology or innovation market. If the Agencies determine that a particular grantback provision is likely to reduce significantly licensees' incentives to invest in improving the licensed technology, the Agencies will consider the extent to which the grantback provision has offsetting procompetitive effects, such as (1) promoting dissemination of licensees' improvements to the licensed technology, (2) increasing the licensors' incentives to disseminate the licensed technology, or (3) otherwise increasing competition and output in a relevant technology or innovation market. *See* section 4.2. In addition, the Agencies will consider the extent to which grantback provisions in the relevant markets generally increase licensors' incentives to innovate in the first place.

5.7   Acquisition of Intellectual Property Rights

Certain transfers of intellectual property rights are most appropriately analyzed by applying the principles and standards used to analyze mergers, particularly those in the 1992 Horizontal Merger Guidelines. The Agencies will apply a merger analysis to an outright sale by an intellectual property owner of all of its rights to that intellectual property and to a transaction in which a person obtains through grant, sale, or other transfer an exclusive license for intellectual property (i.e., a license that precludes all other persons, including the licensor, from using the licensed intellectual property).[38] Such transactions may be assessed under section 7 of the Clayton Act, sections 1 and 2 of the Sherman Act, and section 5 of the Federal Trade Commission Act.

Example 11

Situation: Omega develops a new, patented pharmaceutical for the treatment of a particular disease. The only drug on the market approved for the treatment of this disease is sold by Delta. Omega's patented drug has almost completed regulatory approval by the Food and Drug Administration. Omega has invested considerable sums in product development and market testing, and initial results show that Omega's drug would be a significant competitor to Delta's. However, rather than enter the market as a direct competitor of Delta, Omega licenses to Delta the right to manufacture and sell Omega's patented drug. The license agreement with Delta is nominally nonexclusive. However, Omega has rejected all requests by other firms to obtain a license to manufacture and sell Omega's patented drug, despite offers by those firms of terms that are reasonable in relation to those in Delta's license.

Discussion: Although Omega's license to Delta is nominally nonexclusive, the circumstances indicate that it is exclusive in fact because Omega has rejected all reasonable offers by other firms for licenses to manufacture and sell Omega's patented drug. The facts of this example indicate that Omega would be a likely potential competitor of Delta in the absence of the licensing arrangement, and thus they are in a horizontal relationship in the relevant goods market that includes drugs for the treatment of this particular disease. The evaluating Agency would apply a merger analysis to this transaction, since it involves an acquisition of a likely potential competitor.

6. ENFORCEMENT OF INVALID INTELLECTUAL PROPERTY RIGHTS

The Agencies may challenge the enforcement of invalid intellectual property rights as antitrust violations. Enforcement or attempted enforcement of a patent obtained by fraud on the Patent and Trademark Office or the Copyright Office may violate section 2 of the Sherman Act, if all the elements otherwise necessary to establish a section 2 charge are proved, or section 5 of the Federal Trade Commission Act. *Walker Process Equipment, Inc. v. Food Machinery & Chemical Corp.*, 382 U.S. 172 (1965) (patents); *American Cyanamid Co.*, 72 F.T.C. 623, 684–85 (1967), *aff'd sub. nom. Charles Pfizer & Co.*, 401 F.2d 574 (6th Cir. 1968), *cert. denied*, 394 U.S. 920 (1969) (patents); *Michael Anthony Jewelers, Inc. v. Peacock Jewelry, Inc.*, 795 F. Supp. 639, 647 (S.D.N.Y. 1992) (copyrights). Inequitable conduct before the Patent and Trademark Office will not be the basis of a section 2 claim unless the conduct also involves knowing and willful fraud and the other elements of a section 2 claim are present. *Argus Chemical Corp. v. Fibre Glass-Evercoat, Inc.*, 812 F.2d 1381, 1384–85 (Fed. Cir. 1987). Actual or attempted enforcement of patents obtained by inequitable conduct that falls short of fraud under some circumstances may violate section 5 of the Federal Trade Commission Act, *American Cyanamid Co., supra.* Objectively baseless litigation to enforce invalid intellectual property rights may also constitute an element of a violation of the Sherman Act. *See Professional Real Estate Investors, Inc. v. Columbia Pictures Industries, Inc.*, 113 S. Ct. 1920, 1928 (1993) (copyrights); *Handguards, Inc. v. Ethicon, Inc.*, 743 F.2d 1282, 1289 (9th Cir. 1984), *cert. denied*, 469 U.S. 1190 (1985) (patents); *Handguards, Inc. v. Ethicon, Inc.*, 601 F.2d 986, 992–96 (9th Cir. 1979), *cert. denied*, 444 U.S. 1025 (1980) (patents); *CVD, Inc. v. Raytheon Co.*, 769 F.2d 842 (1st Cir. 1985) (trade secrets), *cert. denied*, 475 U.S. 1016 (1986).

ENDNOTES

[1] These Guidelines supersede section 3.6 in Part I, "Intellectual Property Licensing Arrangements," and cases 6, 10, 11, and 12 in Part II of the U.S. Department of Justice 1988 Antitrust Enforcement Guidelines for International Operations.

[2] These Guidelines do not cover the antitrust treatment of trademarks. Although the same general antitrust principles that apply to other forms of intellectual property apply to trademarks as well, these Guidelines deal with technology transfer and innovation-related issues that typically arise with respect to patents, copyrights, trade secrets, and know-how agreements, rather than with product-differentiation issues that typically arise with respect to trademarks.

[3] As is the case with all guidelines, users should rely on qualified counsel to assist them in evaluating the antitrust risk associated with any contemplated transaction or activity. No set of guidelines can possibly indicate how the Agencies will assess the particular facts of every case. Parties who wish to know the Agencies' specific enforcement intentions with respect to any particular transaction should consider seeking a Department of Justice busi-

ness review letter pursuant to 28 C.F.R. §50.6 or a Federal Trade Commission Advisory Opinion pursuant to 16 C.F.R. §§1.1–1.4.

[4] *See* 35 U.S.C. §154 (1988). Section 532(a) of the Uruguay Round Agreements Act, Pub. L. No. 103-465, 108 Stat. 4809, 4983 (1994) would change the length of patent protection to a term beginning on the date at which the patent issues and ending twenty years from the date on which the application for the patent was filed.

[5] *See* 17 U.S.C. §102 (1988 & Supp. V 1993). Copyright protection lasts for the author's life plus 50 years, or 75 years from first publication (or 100 years from creation, whichever expires first) for works made for hire. *See* 17 U.S.C. §302 (1988). The principles stated in these Guidelines also apply to protection of mask works fixed in a semiconductor chip product (*see* 17 U.S.C. §901 *et seq.* (1988)), which is analogous to copyright protection for works of authorship.

[6] *See* 17 U.S.C. §102(b) (1988).

[7] Trade secret protection derives from state law. *See generally Kewanee Oil Co. v. Bicron Corp.*, 416 U.S. 470 (1974).

[8] "[T]he aims and objectives of patent and antitrust laws may seem, at first glance, wholly at odds. However, the two bodies of law are actually complementary, as both are aimed at encouraging innovation, industry and competition." *Atari Games Corp. v. Nintendo of America, Inc.*, 897 F.2d 1572, 1576 (Fed. Cir. 1990).

[9] As with other forms of property, the power to exclude others from the use of intellectual property may vary substantially, depending on the nature of the property and its status under federal or state law. The greater or lesser legal power of an owner to exclude others is also taken into account by standard antitrust analysis.

[10] Market power can be exercised in other economic dimensions, such as quality, service, and the development of new or improved goods and processes. It is assumed in this definition that all competitive dimensions are held constant except the ones in which market power is being exercised; that a seller is able to charge higher prices for a higher-quality product does not alone indicate market power. The definition in the text is stated in terms of a seller with market power. A buyer could also exercise market power (e.g., by maintaining the price below the competitive level, thereby depressing output).

[11] The Agencies note that the law is unclear on this issue. *Compare Jefferson Parish Hospital District No. 2 v. Hyde*, 466 U.S. 2, 16 (1984) (expressing the view *in dictum* that if a product is protected by a patent, "it is fair to presume that the inability to buy the product elsewhere gives the seller market power") *with id.* at 37 n.7 (O'Connor, J., concurring) ("[A] patent holder has no market power in any relevant sense if there are close substitutes for the patented product."). *Compare also Abbott Laboratories v. Brennan*, 952 F.2d 1346, 1354–55 (Fed. Cir. 1991) (no presumption of market power from intellectual property right), *cert. denied*, 112 S. Ct. 2993 (1992) *with Digidyne Corp. v. Data General Corp.*, 734 F.2d 1336, 1341–42 (9th Cir. 1984) (requisite economic power is presumed from copyright), *cert. denied*, 473 U.S. 908 (1985).

[12] *United States v. Grinnell Corp.*, 384 U.S. 563, 571 (1966); *see also United States v. Aluminum Co. of America*, 148 F.2d 416, 430 (2d Cir. 1945) (Sherman Act is not violated by the attainment of market power solely through "superior skill, foresight and industry").

[13] The examples in these Guidelines are hypothetical and do not represent judgments about, or analysis of, any actual market circumstances of the named industries.

[14] These Guidelines do not address the possible application of the antitrust laws of other countries to restraints such as territorial restrictions in international licensing arrangements.

[15] A firm will be treated as a likely potential competitor if there is evidence that entry by that firm is reasonably probable in the absence of the licensing arrangement.

[16] As used herein, "input" includes outlets for distribution and sales, as well as factors of production. *See, e.g.*, sections 4.1.1 and 5.3–5.5 for further discussion of conditions under which foreclosing access to, or raising the price of, an input may harm competition in a relevant market.

[17] Hereinafter, the term "goods" also includes services.

[18] U.S. Department of Justice and Federal Trade Commission, Horizontal Merger Guidelines (April 2, 1992) (hereinafter "1992 Horizontal Merger Guidelines"). As stated in section 1.41 of the 1992 Horizontal Merger Guidelines, market shares for goods markets "can be expressed either in dollar terms through measurement of sales, shipments, or production, or in physical terms through measurement of sales, shipments, production, capacity or reserves."

[19] For example, the owner of a process for producing a particular good may be constrained in its conduct with respect to that process not only by other processes for making that good, but also by other goods that compete with the downstream good and by the processes used to produce those other goods.

[20] Intellectual property is often licensed, sold, or transferred as an integral part of a marketed good. An example is a patented product marketed with an implied license permitting its use. In such circumstances, there is no need for a separate analysis of technology markets to capture relevant competitive effects.

[21] This is conceptually analogous to the analytical approach to goods markets under the 1992 Horizontal Merger Guidelines. *Cf.* §1.11. Of course, market power also can be exercised in other dimensions, such as quality, and these dimensions also may be relevant to the definition and analysis of technology markets.

[22] For example, technology may be licensed royalty-free in exchange for the right to use other technology, or it may be licensed as part of a package license.

[23] The Agencies will regard two technologies as "comparably efficient" if they can be used to produce close substitutes at comparable costs.

[24] *E.g.*, *Sensormatic*, FTC Inv. No. 941-0126, 60 Fed. Reg. 5428 (accepted for comment Dec. 28, 1994); *Wright Medical Technology, Inc.*, FTC Inv. No. 951-0015, 60 Fed. Reg. 460 (accepted for comment Dec. 8, 1994); *American Home Products*, FTC Inv. No. 941-0116, 59 Fed. Reg. 60,807 (accepted for comment Nov. 28, 1994); *Roche Holdings Ltd.*, 113 F.T.C. 1086 (1990); *United States v. Automobile Mfrs. Ass'n*, 307 F. Supp. 617 (C.D. Cal. 1969), *appeal dismissed sub nom. City of New York v. United States*, 397 U.S. 248 (1970), *modified sub nom. United States v. Motor Vehicles Mfrs. Ass'n*, 1982–83 Trade Cas. (CCH) ¶ 65,088 (C.D. Cal. 1982).

[25] *See* Complaint, *United States v. General Motors Corp.*, Civ. No. 93–530 (D. Del., filed Nov. 16, 1993).

[26] For example, the licensor of research and development may be constrained in its conduct not only by competing research and development efforts but also by other existing goods that would compete with the goods under development.

[27] *See, e.g.*, U.S. Department of Justice and Federal Trade Commission, Statements of Enforcement Policy and Analytical Principles Relating to Health Care and Antitrust 20–23, 37–40, 72–74 (September 27, 1994). This type of transaction may qualify for treatment under the National Cooperative Research and Production Act of 1993, 15 U.S.C.A §§4301–05.

[28] Details about the Federal Trade Commission's approach are set forth in *Massachusetts Board of Registration in Optometry*, 110 F.T.C. 549, 604 (1988). In applying its truncated rule of reason inquiry, the FTC uses the analytical category of "inherently suspect" restraints to denote facially anticompetitive restraints that would always or almost always tend to decrease output or increase prices, but that may be relatively unfamiliar or may not fit neatly into traditional per se categories.

[29] Under the FTC's *Mass. Board* approach, asserted efficiency justifications for inherently suspect restraints are examined to determine whether they are plausible and, if so, whether they are valid in the context of the market at issue. *Mass. Board*, 110 F.T.C. at 604.

[30] The antitrust "safety zone" does not apply to restraints that are not in a licensing arrangement, or to restraints that are in a licensing arrangement but are unrelated to the use of the licensed intellectual property.

[31] "Facially anticompetitive" refers to restraints that normally warrant per se treatment, as well as other restraints of a kind that would always or almost always tend to reduce output or increase prices. *See* section 3.4.

[32] This is consistent with congressional intent in enacting the National Cooperative Research Act. *See* H.R. Conf. Rpt. No. 1044, 98th Cong., 2d Sess., 10, *reprinted in* 1984 U.S.C.C.A.N. 3105, 3134–35.

[33] The conduct at issue may be the transaction giving rise to the restraint or the subsequent implementation of the restraint.

[34] *But cf. United States v. General Electric Co.*, 272 U.S. 476 (1926) (holding that an owner of a product patent may condition a license to manufacture the product on the fixing of the *first* sale price of the patented product). Subsequent lower court decisions have distinguished the *GE* decision in various contexts. *See, e.g., Royal Indus. v. St. Regis Paper Co.*, 420 F.2d 449, 452 (9th Cir. 1969) (observing that *GE* involved a restriction by a patentee who also manufactured the patented product and leaving open the question whether a nonmanufacturing patentee may fix the price of the patented product); *Newburgh Moire Co. v. Superior Moire Co.*, 237 F.2d 283, 293–94 (3rd Cir. 1956) (grant of multiple licenses each containing price restrictions does not come within the *GE* doctrine); *Cummer-Graham Co. v. Straight Side Basket Corp.*, 142 F.2d 646, 647 (5th Cir.) (owner of an intellectual property right in a process to manufacture an unpatented product may not fix the sale price of that product), *cert. denied*, 323 U.S. 726 (1944); *Barber-Colman Co. v. National Tool Co.*, 136 F.2d 339, 343–44 (6th Cir. 1943) (same).

[35] *See, e.g., United States v. Paramount Pictures, Inc.*, 334 U.S. 131, 156–58 (1948) (copyrights); *International Salt Co. v. United States*, 332 U.S. 392 (1947) (patent and related product).

[36] *Cf.* 35 U.S.C. §271(d) (1988 & Supp. V 1993) (requirement of market power in patent misuse cases involving tying).

[37] As is true throughout these Guidelines, the factors listed are those that guide the Agencies' internal analysis in exercising their prosecutorial discretion. They are not intended to circumscribe how the Agencies will conduct the litigation of cases that they decide to bring.

[38] The safety zone of section 4.3 does not apply to transfers of intellectual property such as those described in this section.

Appendix D

Sample Patent

US005301760A

United States Patent [19]

Graham

[11]   **Patent Number:**   **5,301,760**

[45]   **Date of Patent:**   **Apr. 12, 1994**

[54]   **COMPLETING HORIZONTAL DRAIN HOLES FROM A VERTICAL WELL**

[75]   Inventor: **Stephen A. Graham**, Bellaire, Tex.

[73]   Assignee: **Natural Reserves Group, Inc.,** Houston, Tex.

[21]   Appl. No.:   **943,448**

[22]   Filed: **Sep. 10, 1992**

[51]   Int. Cl.^{5} E21B 7/06
[52]   U.S. Cl. **175/61;** 166/285; 166/386
[58]   Field of Search 175/61, 62, 45; 166/379, 267, 421, 285, 386

[56]   **References Cited**

U.S. PATENT DOCUMENTS

2,839,270	6/1958	McCune et al.	175/61
4,397,360	8/1983	Schmidt	175/61
4,402,551	9/1983	Wood et al.	175/61
4,407,367	10/1983	Kydd	166/267
4,420,049	12/1983	Holbert	175/61
4,601,353	7/1986	Schuh et al.	175/62
4,699,224	10/1987	Burton	175/61
4,762,186	8/1988	Dech et al.	175/61
4,880,067	11/1989	Jelsma	175/61

OTHER PUBLICATIONS

"Reservoir Simulation of Horizontal Wells in the Holder Field", by Zagalai et al., Aug., 1991, JPT.

Primary Examiner—Ramon S. Britts
Assistant Examiner—Frank S. Tsay
Attorney, Agent, or Firm—G. Turner Moller

[57]   **ABSTRACT**

A horizontal bore hole is sidetracked through a window cut in a cased vertical well or from a vertical open hole shaft extending below the kickoff point. In one embodiment, a whipstock is used. In another embodiment, the cased vertical well provides a drillable joint so the window can be cut with a conventional bent housing mud motor from a cement plug located adjacent the drillable joint at the kickoff point. In yet another embodiment, a cement plug is dressed down to the kickoff point in a vertical open hole and is used to start the curved well bore. After drilling at least the curved bore hole, a production string extending into the vertical well is cemented in the curved bore hole and then cut off inside the vertical cased hole with a conventional burning shoe/wash pipe assembly. The whipstock or cement plug is removed to clear the vertical well to a location below the entry of the horizontal well bore. Multiple horizontal wells may be drilled. Any open hole portions of the vertical well are cased with a liner. A downhole pump may be provided in the vertical well below the entry of the horizontal well bore. In addition to one or more horizontal completions, one or more productive intervals can be perforated through the vertical well to provide vertical completions.

21 Claims, 3 Drawing Sheets

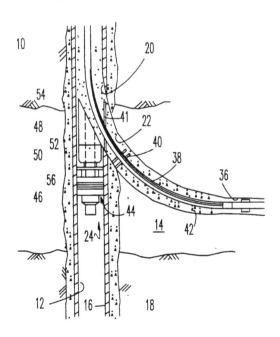

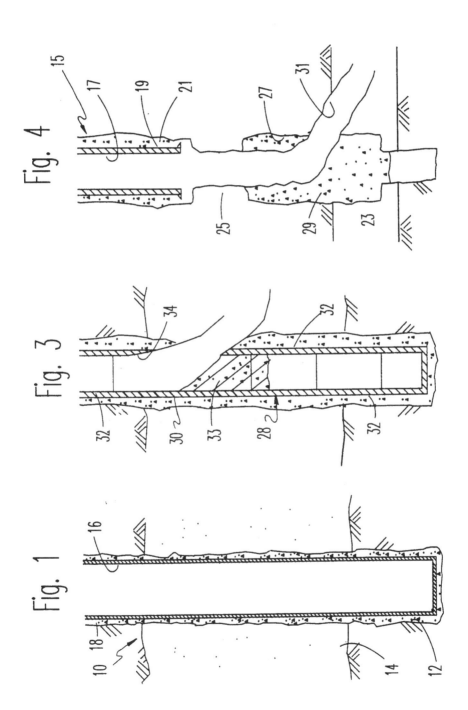

U.S. Patent   Apr. 12, 1994   Sheet 2 of 3   5,301,760

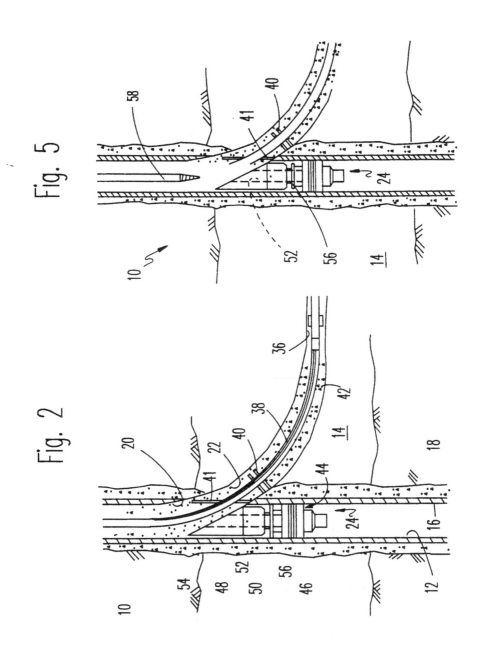

U.S. Patent   Apr. 12, 1994   Sheet 3 of 3   5,301,760

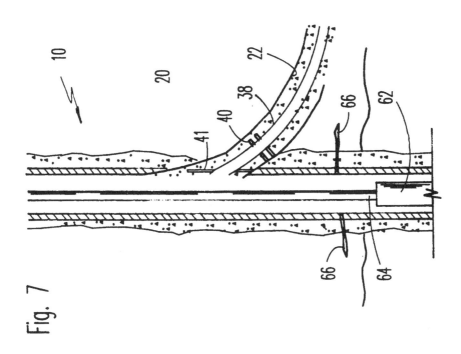

Fig. 7

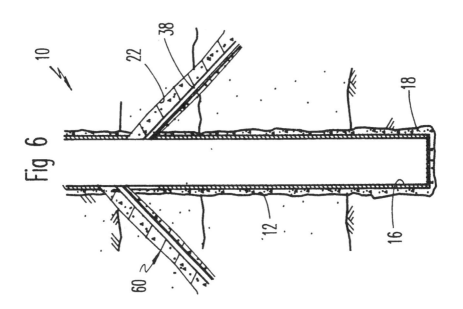

Fig 6

5,301,760

1

COMPLETING HORIZONTAL DRAIN HOLES FROM A VERTICAL WELL

This invention relates to completing one or more horizontal drain holes from a new or existing vertical well.

Horizontally drilled wells have recently become quite popular in attempting to make commercial wells in vertically fractured formations, such as the Austin Chalk or Bakken Shale. Horizontally drilled wells also have many advantages in conventional sandstone reservoirs because of the much improved linear flow characteristics rather than the radial flow characteristics inherent in vertical wells. Horizontal wells typically exhibit greater productivity than vertical wells because more of the formation is exposed to the well bore.

Conventional horizontal completions leave much to be desired in a variety of respects. Because of the way most of the horizontal well bore sections are currently drilled, mechanical pumps are commonly located in the vertical or near vertical portion of the well at a substantial vertical distance above the horizontal well bore. This leads to inefficiencies in pumping liquids from the well. It is much more desirable to position the pump at a location in the well below any producing horizon. In addition, it is desirable in some situations to combine horizontal and vertical completions from the same formation and have them produce into the same vertical well bore. This configuration would enable a formation to be produced to a lower bottomhole pressure than would be possible if the pump were located near the horizontal kickoff point in the vertical portion of the well. It is also desirable in some situations to complete multiple horizontal completions and have them produce into the same vertical well bore. Completing a vertical well in one or more formations in a conventional manner together with horizontal drain hole completions extending from the same vertical well bore is advantageous in many circumstances because it maximizes the efficiency of the downhole and surface equipment associated with the vertical well.

In accordance with this invention, a window is cut in a cased vertical well and a bore hole is sidetracked through the window or a curved well bore is kicked off from a vertical open hole. Angle is built up in a curved well bore until the bore hole is more-or-less horizontal. The horizontal well bore is drilled a substantial distance into a hydrocarbon bearing formation. A production string is run into the well so it extends from adjacent the horizontal well bore, through the curved well bore section and into the vertical cased hole or vertical open hole. The well is cemented so at least the curved portion of the well bore includes an impermeable sheath around the production string isolating the production string from permeable formations above the pay zone and isolating the top of the pay zone. After the cement cures, that portion of the production string extending into the vertical cased hole or vertical open hole is cut off by the use of a conventional full gauge burning shoe/wash pipe assembly, leaving a relatively clean intersection between the curved and vertical well bore sections. Another horizontal well bore section may be drilled and completed off the vertical hole into the same or a different hydrocarbon bearing formation. If a horizontal well bore is drilled from a vertical open hole, the vertical open hole may be cased with a liner after completing the horizontal drilling operation. It will be seen

2

that a pump may be run into the vertical cased well and placed below all of the entries between the horizontal and vertical well bores. In addition, it will be seen that one or all of the hydrocarbon bearing formations may also be perforated in the vertical well to provide both vertical and horizontal completions producing into the same vertical cased well.

One object of this invention is to provide an improved technique for completing horizontal well bores.

A further object of this invention is to provide a technique for completing horizontal well bores in which a mechanical pump may be placed below the entry of the horizontal well bore into the vertical well.

Another object of this invention is to provide a technique for completing hydrocarbon wells so there are both vertical and horizontal completions producing into the same vertical cased well.

These and other objects of this invention will become more fully apparent as this description proceeds, reference being made to the accompanying drawings and appended claims.

IN THE DRAWINGS

FIG. 1 is a schematic cross-sectional view of a vertical cased well extending through a subterranean hydrocarbon bearing formation;

FIG. 2 is a schematic cross-sectional view showing a technique of drilling and completing a horizontal drain hole in accordance with this invention;

FIGS. 3 and 4 are schematic cross-sectional views showing alternate techniques for sidetracking the hole and drilling the curved well bore;

FIG. 5 is a schematic cross-sectional view of a subsequent stage of drilling and completing a horizontal drain hole in accordance with this invention;

FIG. 6 is a schematic cross-sectional view of a second horizontal well bore drilled from a cased vertical well; and

FIG. 7 is a schematic cross-sectional view of a completed well having both horizontal and vertical completions.

Referring to FIG. 1, a vertical cased well 10 comprises a well bore 12 drilled into the earth to penetrate a subterranean hydrocarbon bearing formation 14. Typically, the well bore 12 is logged to provide reliable information about the top and bottom, porosity, fluid content and other petrophysical properties of the formations encountered. A relatively large casing string 16, e.g. 7″ O.D. or greater, is cemented in the well bore 12 in any suitable manner so an impermeable cement sheath 18 prevents communication between formations in the annulus between the well bore 12 and the casing string 16.

Referring to FIG. 2, a window 20 is cut in the casing string 16 and a curved bore hole 22 is drilled, preferably on a short or medium radius, to intersect the formation 14. In accordance with one technique, the window 20 is cut by using a whipstock 24 set in the vertical cased well 10 where the well is to be sidetracked and the window 20 is conventionally cut with a mill (not shown).

In the alternative, if the vertical cased well 10 is drilled and cased with this in mind, as opposed to reentering an old well or conventionally completing the well 10, the window may be cut in a different manner. As shown in FIG. 3, a well 26 includes a casing string 28 having a drillable joint 30 made of a carbon/glass-/epoxy composite material and a plurality of conven-

5,301,760

3

tional steel joints **32**. Because the joint **30** is much easier to drill than the steel joints **32**, a cement plug **33** is placed in the well **26** and then dressed down to the kickoff point. A window **34** is then cut in the joint **30** with a conventional bent housing mud motor assembly (not shown). It may be advantageous in some situations to initiate the kickoff with a whipstock/packer assembly (not shown) instead of the cement plug **33**.

Referring to FIG. **4**, a somewhat different situation is illustrated. A well **15** includes a vertical bore hole **17** having steel casing **19** cemented therein by a cement sheath **21** above a target hydrocarbon bearing formation **23**. A vertical open hole **25** is drilled below the casing string **19** to a point below the formation **23**. After logging the open hole **25** for formation evaluation purposes, a portion **27** of the vertical open hole **25** is enlarged using conventional underreaming techniques. A cement plug **29** is pumped into the enlarged open hole **27** adjacent the kickoff point and then dressed off after the plug has hardened. A conventional bent housing mud motor assembly (not shown) is then used to drill the curved bore hole **22** in a conventional manner.

In any event, the curved portion of the well bore is begun. Referring back to FIG. **2**, a curved bore hole section **22** is drilled toward the hydrocarbon bearing formation **14**. Either before or after drilling a horizontal well bore **36** into the formation **14**, a pipe string **38** is run through the window **20** at least into the curved bore hole **22** so it extends upwardly into the well **10**. The pipe string **38** provides thereon a plurality of centralizers **40** and a plurality of reinforcing members **41**. The centralizers **40** support the pipe string **38** off of the bottom of the curved bore hole **22** and the members **41** act to reinforce cement adjacent the window **20** as will be more fully apparent hereinafter. The reinforcing members **41** are positioned on the pipe string **38** so they partially fill the annulus between the curved bore hole **22** and the string **38** in the immediate area of the window **20**. The reinforcing members **41** may comprise lengths of the same type wire as used in wire casing scratchers. For reasons more fully apparent hereinafter, the pipe string **38** may wholly or partially comprise joints of drillable material such as a carbon/fiberglass/epoxy composite.

Cement **42** is pumped through the pipe string **38** to surround the pipe string **38**, close off the window **20** and extend upwardly into the cased vertical well **10**. This prevents formations above the hydrocarbon bearing formation **14** from sloughing off through the window **20** into the vertical well **10**, prevents water from formations above the formation **14** from entering the cased vertical well **10** and prevents gas or steam from entering the well **10** from adjacent the top of the formation **14**.

The horizontal well bore **36** may be completed in a conventional manner, such as in the open hole or through perforations, or as shown in copending U.S. application Ser. No. 07/920,804, filed Jul. 24, 1992, the disclosure of which is incorporated herein by reference.

After the cement **42** sets up, that portion of the cement **42** and the production string **38** inside the vertical cased well **10** is drilled up. Preferably, the production string **38** is filled with a viscous, low residue, high gel strength water based, temporary blocking agent to minimize the amount of cement and pipe cuttings that enter the curved and horizontal sections of the well.

Drilling of the cement **42** and production string **38** is accomplished by use of a conventional full bore burning shoe/washpipe assembly. Although any suitable burn-

4

ing shoe may be used, a typical choice would be a Type D Rotary Shoe from Tri-State Oil Tools which cuts on the bottom of the shoe and on the inside. Basically, the burning shoe cuts away the periphery of the cement **42** and production string **38**, leaving a core shaped remnant which is caught by an internal catch device (not shown) located above the washpipe or with a conventional fishing tool run after the burning shoe/wash pipe assembly is retrieved. If a cement plug is used to initiate the curved bore hole section **22** as in FIGS. **3** and **4**, then the vertical cased well or the vertical open hole **25** is configured to drill another horizontal drain hole using similar techniques or a production liner is run.

If a whipstock is used to initiate the curved bore hole section **22** as in FIG. **2**, the preferred whipstock **24** is a modified version of that shown in U.S. Pat. No. 5,113,938. In this type whipstock, a lower assembly **44** includes a packer **46** for anchoring the whipstock **24** at a desired location. A wedge shaped upper end **48** is pivoted by a pair of short pins **50** to the lower assembly **44**. An axial passage **52** extends through the upper end **48** past the pivot pins **50** to receive a setting tool (not shown). The setting tool (not shown) holds the upper end **48** in alignment with the lower assembly **44** as the whipstock **24** is run into the well **10**. When the packer **46** is set and the setting tool (not shown) removed, the upper end **48** pivots about the pin **50** into engagement with the casing **16**.

The whipstock **24** has been modified in two respects. First, a drillable shoulder **54** has been provided to position the upper end **48** away from the casing **16**. Second, a locator ring **56** of a drillable metal is incorporated in the lower assembly **44**. As the cement **42** and production string **38** are being cut away by the burning shoe (not shown), the drillable shoulder **54** allows the burning shoe to get behind the wedge shaped upper end **48** to cut the cement **42** and production string **38** below the top of the wedge shaped upper end **48**. The locator ring **56** provides an indication to the driller that the burning shoe is past the window **20** and the location of the bottom of the burning shoe is immediately above the packoff elements of the packer **46**. When the burning shoe completes drilling of the production string **38**, only cement will be drilled for a somewhat variable distance, e.g. two-three feet, between the bottom of the production string **38** and the locator ring **56**. Because the locator ring **56** is a drillable metal, the driller will realize that metal is being cut again by the burning shoe. The thickness of the locator ring **56** is known, so the driller can recognize when it has been drilled through. It will be seen that the reinforcing elements **41** act, much as rebar in poured concrete, to reinforce the cement **42** adjacent the window **20**. In addition, fibrous material, such as Halliburton's TUF cement additive disclosed in U.S. Pat. No. 3,774,683, may be added to the cement to make the hardened cement less brittle with more resiliency to shock and vibration loading.

After the locator ring **56** is drilled up, the hole is circulated to remove all cement and pipe cuttings and the burning shoe/wash pipe assembly and its captive cement-pipe remnant is removed from the well leaving the situation as shown in FIG. **5**. The whipstock **24** is then removed from the vertical cased well **10** using any suitable fishing tool such as a taper tap **58**. The axial passage **52** is partially cleaned out by advancing and rotating the taper tap **58** into the passage **52** and pumping therethrough. The taper tap **58** is lowered into the passage **52** until it torques up and catches or anchors in

5,301,760

5

the whipstock **24**. Picking up on the taper tap **58** unseats the packer **46**. If the packer **46** is an inflatable packer, as is preferred, picking up on the taper tap **58** shears the packer deflation pin thereby allowing the packer **46** to deflate. The whipstock **24** is thereby released from securement to the casing **16** and is removed from the cased vertical well **10**.

As shown in FIG. **6**, another horizontal completion **60** may be provided to produce into the vertical cased well **10**, using the same techniques as previously discussed.

As shown in FIG. **7**, the well **10** may then be completed by running a downhole pump **62** on the end of a tubing string **64** below the entry of the production string **38** into the vertical well **10**. If desired, perforations **66** may be shot through the casing **16** to complete the formation into the vertical cased well **10** as a vertical completion as well as the horizontal completion through the production string **38**.

Although this invention has been disclosed and described in its preferred forms with a certain degree of particularity, it is understood that the present disclosure of the preferred forms is only by way of example and that numerous changes in the details of construction and operation and in the combination and arrangement of parts may be resorted to without departing from the spirit and scope of the invention as hereinafter claimed.

I claim:

1. In a process of completing a horizontal well in a hydrocarbon formation comprising the steps of providing a vertical well, drilling a curved well bore from the vertical well, drilling a horizontal well bore into the formation through the curved well bore, positioning a first section of a pipe string in the curved well bore and a second section of the pipe string in the vertical well, and cementing the pipe string in the curved well bore, the improvement comprising comminuting the pipe string in the vertical well and thereby providing a passage between the horizontal well bore section and the vertical well and then producing hydrocarbons from the horizontal well bore section through the passage into the vertical well.

2. The process of claim **1** wherein the providing step comprises drilling a vertical open hole and then drilling the curved well bore by sidetracking from the vertical open hole at a location above the bottom of the vertical open hole.

3. The process of claim **1** wherein the providing step comprises providing a vertical cased well and cutting a window through the vertical cased well and then drilling the curved well bore through the window.

4. The process of claim **1** wherein the step of drilling the curved well bore comprises setting a plug in the vertical well and then drilling the curved well bore at a location starting above the bottom of the plug and further comprising the steps of removing the plug from the vertical well to provide a sump below an intersection of the curved well bore and the vertical well, placing a pump in the sump and the producing step comprises pumping liquid hydrocarbons from the sump upwardly through the vertical well.

5. The process of claim **4** wherein the plug is a hardened pumpable impermeable material.

6. The process of claim **4** wherein the plug is a whipstock and the removing step comprises retrieving the whipstock upwardly through the vertical well.

6

7. The process of claim **6** wherein the whipstock includes a drillable locator and the retrieving step includes drilling the locator.

8. The process of claim **6** wherein the whipstock includes a lower assembly including means for anchoring the whipstock to the vertical cased well, a wedge shaped upper assembly, means pivoting the upper assembly on the lower assembly and a drillable shoulder on the upper assembly for standing the upper assembly away from the vertical cased well and the retrieving step includes drilling the drillable shoulder.

9. The process of claim **1** wherein the vertical well extends substantially into the subterranean formation and further comprising the step of establishing a radial flow pattern from the formation into the vertical well at a location below an intersection of the curved well bore and the vertical well.

10. The process of claim **9** wherein the vertical well is a vertical cased well and the establishing step comprises perforating the vertical cased well at a vertical elevation corresponding to the formation.

11. The process of claim **1** wherein the cementing step comprises affixing a plurality of radial metallic elements to the pipe string along a predetermined zone, running the pipe string into the well and positioning the zone at a location below an intersection of the curved well bore and the vertical well, and filling up an annulus between the pipe string and the curved well bore with a hardenable impermeable material and the comminuting step comprises comminuting the pipe string and cement in the vertical well.

12. The process of claim **1** wherein the vertical well comprises a multiplicity of joints of hard-to-drill metal joints and at least one joint of a drillable material substantially easier to drill than the hard-to-drill metal, and wherein the step of drilling a curved well bore comprises cutting a window through the joint of drillable material.

13. The process of claim **1** wherein the comminuting step comprises drilling up the pipe string and cement in the vertical well and circulating cuttings of the pipe string and cement upwardly out of the vertical well.

14. The process of claim **13** wherein the drilling up step comprises cutting an annulus through the pipe string and cement in the vertical well to produce a remnant of pipe string and cement and removing the remnant upwardly through the vertical well.

15. A process comprising drilling a well bore into the earth, running a casing string into the well bore including a plurality of first joints of hard-to-drill metal pipe and at least one second joint of pipe of a material easier-to-drill than the first joints, and cutting window in the casing string through the second joint.

16. A well having a first vertical cased section extending into and communicating with a subterranean hydrocarbon bearing formation, a curved well bore section extending away from the first vertical cased section at a location above the bottom of the formation, a horizontal well bore section extending away from the curved well bore section and into the formation, a second vertical cased section extending below the curved well bore section and means for producing a first stream of hydrocarbons from the horizontal well bore section and a second stream of hydrocarbons from the second vertical cased section.

17. The well of claim **16** further comprising means commingling the first and second streams in the vertical cased section at a location above an intersection be-

5,301,760

7

tween the vertical cased well and the curved well bore section.

18. The well of claim **16** wherein the vertical cased section communicates with the formation through perforations.

19. The well of claim **16** wherein the formation is in a radial flow pattern with the vertical cased section and

8

is in a second flow pattern with the horizontal well bore different than the radial flow pattern.

20. The well of claim **19** further comprising a pump in the vertical cased section below the top of the formation.

21. The well of claim **20** wherein the pump is below the bottom of the formation.

* * * * *

5

10

15

20

25

30

35

40

45

50

55

60

65

Appendix E

United States Code (U.S.C.) Title 35—Patents

PART III—PATENTS AND PROTECTION OF PATENT RIGHTS

**CHAPTER 29—REMEDIES FOR INFRINGEMENT OF PATENT,
AND OTHER ACTIONS**

Sec. 283. Injunction
The several courts having jurisdiction of cases under this title may grant injunctions in accordance with the principles of equity to prevent the violation of any right secured by patent, on such terms as the court deems reasonable.

(July 19, 1952, ch. 950, 66 Stat. 812.)

Sec. 284. Damages
Upon finding for the claimant the court shall award the claimant damages adequate to compensate for the infringement, but in no event less than a reasonable royalty for the use made of the invention by the infringer, together with interest and costs as fixed by the court.

When the damages are not found by a jury, the court shall assess them. In either event the court may increase the damages up to three times the amount found or assessed. Increased damages under this paragraph shall not apply to provisional rights under section 154(d) of this title.

The court may receive expert testimony as an aid to the determination of damages or of what royalty would be reasonable under the circumstances.

(July 19, 1952, ch. 950, 66 Stat. 813; Pub. L. 106-113, div. B, Sec. 1000(a)(9) [title IV, Sec. 4507(9)], Nov. 29, 1999, 113 Stat. 1536, 1501A-566.)

AMENDMENTS

1999—Second par. Pub. L. 106–113 inserted at end "Increased damages under this paragraph shall not apply to provisional rights under section 154(d) of this title."

Effective Date of 1999 Amendment
Amendment by Pub. L. 106–113 effective on date that is 1 year after Nov. 29, 1999, and applicable to all applications filed under section 111 of this title on or after that date, and all applications complying with section 371 of this title that resulted from international applications filed on or after that date, see section 1000(a)(9) [title IV, Sec. 4508] of Pub. L. 106–113, set out as a note under section 10 of this title.

Sec. 285. Attorney fees
The court in exceptional cases may award reasonable attorney fees to the prevailing party.
   (July 19, 1952, ch. 950, 66 Stat. 813.)
   This section is referred to in sections 154, 157, 271, 273, 287, 296 of this title.

Sec. 286. Time limitation on damages
Except as otherwise provided by law, no recovery shall be had for any infringement committed more than six years prior to the filing of the complaint or counterclaim for infringement in the action.
   In the case of claims against the United States Government for use of a patented invention, the period before bringing suit, up to six years, between the date of receipt of a written claim for compensation by the department or agency of the Government having authority to settle such claim, and the date of mailing by the Government of a notice to the claimant that his claim has been denied shall not be counted as part of the period referred to in the preceding paragraph.
   (July 19, 1952, ch. 950, 66 Stat. 813.)
   Section Referred to in Other Sections
   This section is referred to in section 157 of this title.

Sec. 287. Limitation on damages and other remedies; marking and notice

   (a) Patentees, and persons making, offering for sale, or selling within the United States any patented article for or under them, or importing any patented article into the United States, may give notice to the public that the same is patented, either by fixing thereon the word "patent" or the abbreviation "pat.", together with the number of the patent, or when, from the character of the article, this can not be done, by fixing to it, or to the package wherein one or more of them is contained, a label containing a like notice. In the event of failure so to mark, no damages shall be recovered by the patentee in any action for infringement, except on proof that the infringer was notified of the infringement and continued to infringe thereafter, in which event damages may be recovered only for infringement occurring after such notice. Filing of an action for infringement shall constitute such notice.

(b) (1) An infringer under section 271(g) shall be subject to all the provisions of this title relating to damages and injunctions except to the extent those remedies are modified by this subsection or section 9006 of the Process Patent Amendments Act of 1988. The modifications of remedies provided in this subsection shall not be available to any person who—

(A) practiced the patented process;

(B) owns or controls, or is owned or controlled by, the person who practiced the patented process; or

(C) had knowledge before the infringement that a patented process was used to make the product the importation, use, offer for sale, or sale of which constitutes the infringement.

(2) No remedies for infringement under section 271(g) of this title shall be available with respect to any product in the possession of, or in transit to, the person subject to liability under such section before that person had notice of infringement with respect to that product. The person subject to liability shall bear the burden of proving any such possession or transit.

(3) (A) In making a determination with respect to the remedy in an action brought for infringement under section 271(g), the court shall consider—

(i) the good faith demonstrated by the defendant with respect to a request for disclosure,

(ii) the good faith demonstrated by the plaintiff with respect to a request for disclosure, and

(iii) the need to restore the exclusive rights secured by the patent.

(B) For purposes of subparagraph (A), the following are evidence of good faith:

(i) a request for disclosure made by the defendant;

(ii) a response within a reasonable time by the person receiving the request for disclosure; and

(iii) the submission of the response by the defendant to the manufacturer, or if the manufacturer is not known, to the supplier, of the product to be purchased by the defendant, together with a request for a written statement that the process claimed in any patent disclosed in the response is not used to produce such product.

The failure to perform any acts described in the preceding sentence is evidence of absence of good faith unless there are mitigating circumstances. Mitigating circumstances include the case in which, due to the nature of the product, the number of sources for the product, or like commercial circumstances, a request for disclosure is not necessary or practicable to avoid infringement.

 (4) (A) For purposes of this subsection, a "request for disclosure" means a written request made to a person then engaged in the manufacture of a product to identify all process patents owned by or licensed to that person, as of the time of the request, that the person then reasonably believes could be asserted to be infringed under section 271(g) if that product were imported into, or sold, offered for sale, or used in, the United States by an unauthorized person. A request for disclosure is further limited to a request—

  (i) which is made by a person regularly engaged in the United States in the sale of the same type of products as those manufactured by the person to whom the request is directed, or which includes facts showing that the person making the request plans to engage in the sale of such products in the United States;

  (ii) which is made by such person before the person's first importation, use, offer for sale, or sale of units of the product produced by an infringing process and before the person had notice of infringement with respect to the product; and

  (iii) which includes a representation by the person making the request that such person will promptly submit the patents identified pursuant to the request to the manufacturer, or if the manufacturer is not known, to the supplier, of the product to be purchased by the person making the request, and will request from that manufacturer or supplier a written statement that none of the processes claimed in those patents is used in the manufacture of the product.

  (B) In the case of a request for disclosure received by a person to whom a patent is licensed, that person shall either identify the patent or promptly notify the licensor of the request for disclosure.

  (C) A person who has marked, in the manner prescribed by subsection (a), the number of the process patent on all products made by the patented process which have been offered for sale or sold by that person in the United States, or imported by the person into the United States, before a request for disclosure is received is not required to respond to the request for disclosure. For purposes of the preceding sentence, the term "all products" does not include products made before the effective date of the Process Patent Amendments Act of 1988.

(5) (A) For purposes of this subsection, notice of infringement means actual knowledge, or receipt by a person of a written notification, or a combination thereof, of information sufficient to persuade a reasonable person that it is likely that a product was made by a process patented in the United States.

(B) A written notification from the patent holder charging a person with infringement shall specify the patented process alleged to have been used and the reasons for a good faith belief that such process was used. The patent holder shall include in the notification such information as is reasonably necessary to explain fairly the patent holder's belief, except that the patent holder is not required to disclose any trade secret information.

(C) A person who receives a written notification described in subparagraph (B) or a written response to a request for disclosure described in paragraph (4) shall be deemed to have notice of infringement with respect to any patent referred to in such written notification or response unless that person, absent mitigating circumstances—

(i) promptly transmits the written notification or response to the manufacturer or, if the manufacturer is not known, to the supplier, of the product purchased or to be purchased by that person; and

(ii) receives a written statement from the manufacturer or supplier which on its face sets forth a well grounded factual basis for a belief that the identified patents are not infringed.

(D) For purposes of this subsection, a person who obtains a product made by a process patented in the United States in a quantity which is abnormally large in relation to the volume of business of such person or an efficient inventory level shall be rebuttably presumed to have actual knowledge that the product was made by such patented process.

(6) A person who receives a response to a request for disclosure under this subsection shall pay to the person to whom the request was made a reasonable fee to cover actual costs incurred in complying with the request, which may not exceed the cost of a commercially available automated patent search of the matter involved, but in no case more than $500.

(c) (1) With respect to a medical practitioner's performance of a medical activity that constitutes an infringement under section 271(a) or (b) of this title, the provisions of sections 281, 283, 284, and 285 of this title shall not apply against the medical practitioner or against a related health care entity with respect to such medical activity.

(2) For the purposes of this subsection:

(A) the term "medical activity" means the performance of a medical or surgical procedure on a body, but shall not include (i) the use of a patented machine, manufacture, or composition of matter in violation of such patent, (ii) the practice of a patented use of a composition of matter in violation of such patent, or (iii) the practice of a process in violation of a biotechnology patent.

(B) the term "medical practitioner" means any natural person who is licensed by a State to provide the medical activity described in subsection (c)(1) or who is acting under the direction of such person in the performance of the medical activity.

(C) the term "related health care entity" shall mean an entity with which a medical practitioner has a professional affiliation under which the medical practitioner performs the medical activity, including but not limited to a nursing home, hospital, university, medical school, health maintenance organization, group medical practice, or a medical clinic.

(D) the term "professional affiliation" shall mean staff privileges, medical staff membership, employment or contractual relationship, partnership or ownership interest, academic appointment, or other affiliation under which a medical practitioner provides the medical activity on behalf of, or in association with, the health care entity.

(E) the term "body" shall mean a human body, organ or cadaver, or a nonhuman animal used in medical research or instruction directly relating to the treatment of humans.

(F) the term "patented use of a composition of matter" does not include a claim for a method of performing a medical or surgical procedure on a body that recites the use of a composition of matter where the use of that composition of matter does not directly contribute to achievement of the objective of the claimed method.

(G) the term "State" shall mean any state or territory of the United States, the District of Columbia, and the Commonwealth of Puerto Rico.

(3) This subsection does not apply to the activities of any person, or employee or agent of such person (regardless of whether such person is a tax exempt organization under section 501(c) of the Internal Revenue Code), who is engaged in the commercial development, manufacture, sale, importation, or distribution of a machine, manufacture, or composition of matter or the provision of pharmacy or clinical laboratory services (other than clinical laboratory services provided in a physician's office), where such activities are:

    (A) directly related to the commercial development, manufacture, sale, importation, or distribution of a machine, manufacture, or composition of matter or the provision of pharmacy or clinical laboratory services (other than clinical laboratory services provided in a physician's office), and

    (B) regulated under the Federal Food, Drug, and Cosmetic Act, the Public Health Service Act, or the Clinical Laboratories Improvement Act.

  (4) This subsection shall not apply to any patent issued based on an application the earliest effective filing date of which is prior to September 30, 1996.

(July 19, 1952, ch. 950, 66 Stat. 813; Pub. L. 100-418, title IX, Sec. 9004(a), Aug. 23, 1988, 102 Stat. 1564; Pub. L. 103-465, title V, Sec. 533(b)(5), Dec. 8, 1994, 108 Stat. 4989; Pub. L. 104-208, div. A, title I, Sec. 101(a) [title VI, Sec. 616], Sept. 30, 1996, 110 Stat. 3009, 3009-67; Pub. L. 106-113, div. B, Sec. 1000(a)(9) [title IV, Sec. 4803], Nov. 29, 1999, 113 Stat. 1536, 1501A-589.)

AMENDMENTS

1999—Subsec. (c)(4). Pub. L. 106-113 substituted "based on an application the earliest effective filing date of which is prior to September 30, 1996" for "before the date of enactment of this subsection".

1996—Subsec. (c). Pub. L. 104-208 added subsec. (c).

1994—Subsec. (a). Pub. L. 103-465, Sec. 533(b)(5)(A), substituted "making, offering for sale, or selling within the United States" for "making or selling" and inserted "or importing any patented article into the United States," after "under them,".

Subsec. (b)(1)(C). Pub. L. 103-465, Sec. 533(b)(5)(B)(i), substituted "use, offer for sale, or sale" for "use, or sale".

Subsec. (b)(4)(A). Pub. L. 103-465, Sec. 533(b)(5)(B)(ii), substituted "sold, offered for sale, or" for "sold or" in introductory provisions.

Subsec. (b)(4)(A)(ii). Pub. L. 103-465, Sec. 533(b)(5)(B)(iii), substituted "use, offer for sale, or sale" for "use, or sale".

Subsec. (b)(4)(C). Pub. L. 103-465, Sec. 533(b)(5)(B)(iv), (v), substituted "have been offered for sale or sold" for "have been sold" and "United States, or imported by the person into the United States, before" for "United States before".

1988—Pub. L. 100-418 inserted "and other remedies" in section catchline, designated existing provisions as subsec. (a), and added subsec. (b).

Effective Date of 1994 Amendment

Amendment by Pub. L. 103-465 effective on date that is one year after date on which the WTO Agreement enters into force with respect to the United States [Jan. 1, 1995], with provisions relating to earliest filed patent application, see section 534(a), (b)(3) of Pub. L. 103-465, set out as a note under section 154 of this title.

Effective Date of 1988 Amendment

Amendment by Pub. L. 100-418 effective 6 months after Aug. 23, 1988, and, subject to enumerated exceptions, applicable only with respect to products made or imported after such effective date, see section 9006 of Pub. L. 100-418, set out as a note under section 271 of this title.

Section Referred to in Other Sections

This section is referred to in section 157 of this title.

Appendix F

Copyright Act of 1976

§502. REMEDIES FOR INFRINGEMENT: INJUNCTIONS

(a) Any court having jurisdiction of a civil action arising under this title may, subject to the provisions of section 1498 of title 28, grant temporary and final injunctions on such terms as it may deem reasonable to prevent or restrain infringement of a copyright.

(b) Any such injunction may be served anywhere in the United States on the person enjoined; it shall be operative throughout the United States and shall be enforceable, by proceedings in contempt or otherwise, by any United States court having jurisdiction of that person. The clerk of the court granting the injunction shall, when requested by any other court in which enforcement of the injunction is sought, transmit promptly to the other court a certified copy of all the papers in the case on file in such clerk's office.

§503. REMEDIES FOR INFRINGEMENT: IMPOUNDING AND DISPOSITION OF INFRINGING ARTICLES

(a) At any time while an action under this title is pending, the court may order the impounding, on such terms as it may deem reasonable, of all copies or phonorecords claimed to have been made or used in violation of the copyright owner's exclusive rights, and of all plates, molds, matrices, masters, tapes, film negatives, or other articles by means of which such copies or phonorecords may be reproduced.

(b) As part of a final judgment or decree, the court may order the destruction or other reasonable disposition of all copies or phonorecords found to have been made or used in violation of the copyright owner's exclusive rights, and of all plates, molds, matrices, masters, tapes, film negatives, or other articles by means of which such copies or phonorecords may be reproduced.

§504. REMEDIES FOR INFRINGEMENT: DAMAGES AND PROFITS

(a) In General—Except as otherwise provided by this title, an infringer of copyright is liable for either—

 (1) the copyright owner's actual damages and any additional profits of the infringer, as provided by subsection (b); or

 (2) statutory damages, as provided by subsection (c).

(b) Actual Damages and Profits—The copyright owner is entitled to recover the actual damages suffered by him or her as a result of the infringement, and any profits of the infringer that are attributable to the infringement and are not taken into account in computing the actual damages. In establishing the infringer's profits, the copyright owner is required to present proof only of the infringer's gross revenue, and the infringer is required to prove his or her deductible expenses and the elements of profit attributable to factors other than the copyrighted work.

(c) Statutory Damages—

 (1) Except as provided by clause (2) of this subsection, the copyright owner may elect, at any time before final judgment is rendered, to recover, instead of actual damages and profits, an award of statutory damages for all infringements involved in the action, with respect to any one work, for which any one infringer is liable individually, or for which any two or more infringers are liable jointly and severally, in a sum of not less than $750 or more than $30,000 as the court considers just. For the purposes of this subsection, all the parts of a compilation or derivative work constitute one work.

 (2) In a case where the copyright owner sustains the burden of proving, and the court finds, that infringement was committed willfully, the court in its discretion may increase the award of statutory damages to a sum of not more than $150,000. In a case where the infringer sustains the burden of proving, and the court finds, that such infringer was not aware and had no reason to believe that his or her acts constituted an infringement of copyright, the court in its discretion may reduce the award of statutory damages to a sum of not less than $200. The court shall remit statutory damages in any case where an infringer believed and had reasonable grounds for believing that his or her use of the copyrighted work was a fair use under section 107, if the infringer was: (i) an employee or agent of a nonprofit educational institution, library, or archives acting within the scope of his or her employment who, or such institution, library, or archives itself, which infringed by reproducing the work in copies or phonorecords; or (ii) a public broadcasting entity which or a person who, as a regular part of the nonprofit activities of a public broadcasting entity

(as defined in subsection (g) of section 118) infringed by performing a published nondramatic literary work or by reproducing a transmission program embodying a performance of such a work.

(d) Additional Damages in Certain Cases—In any case in which the court finds that a defendant proprietor of an establishment who claims as a defense that its activities were exempt under section 110(5) did not have reasonable grounds to believe that its use of a copyrighted work was exempt under such section, the plaintiff shall be entitled to, in addition to any award of damages under this section, an additional award of two times the amount of the license fee that the proprietor of the establishment concerned should have paid the plaintiff for such use during the preceding period of up to 3 years.

§505. REMEDIES FOR INFRINGEMENT: COSTS AND ATTORNEY'S FEES

In any civil action under this title, the court in its discretion may allow the recovery of full costs by or against any party other than the United States or an officer thereof. Except as otherwise provided by this title, the court may also award a reasonable attorney's fee to the prevailing party as part of the costs.

§512. LIMITATIONS ON LIABILITY RELATING TO MATERIAL ONLINE

(a) Transitory Digital Network Communications—A service provider shall not be liable for monetary relief, or, except as provided in subsection (j), for injunctive or other equitable relief, for infringement of copyright by reason of the provider's transmitting, routing, or providing connections for, material through a system or network controlled or operated by or for the service provider, or by reason of the intermediate and transient storage of that material in the course of such transmitting, routing, or providing connections, if—

(1) the transmission of the material was initiated by or at the direction of a person other than the service provider;

(2) the transmission, routing, provision of connections, or storage is carried out through an automatic technical process without selection of the material by the service provider;

(3) the service provider does not select the recipients of the material except as an automatic response to the request of another person;

(4) no copy of the material made by the service provider in the course of such intermediate or transient storage is maintained on the system or network in a manner ordinarily accessible to anyone other than anticipated recipients, and no such copy is maintained on the system or network in a manner ordinarily accessible to such anticipated recipients for a longer period than is reasonably necessary for the transmission, routing, or provision of connections; and

(5) the material is transmitted through the system or network without modification of its content.

(b) System Caching—

   (1) Limitation on Liability—A service provider shall not be liable for monetary relief, or, except as provided in subsection (j), for injunctive or other equitable relief, for infringement of copyright by reason of the intermediate and temporary storage of material on a system or network controlled or operated by or for the service provider in a case in which—

      (A) the material is made available online by a person other than the service provider;

      (B) the material is transmitted from the person described in subparagraph (A) through the system or network to a person other than the person described in subparagraph (A) at the direction of that other person; and

      (C) the storage is carried out through an automatic technical process for the purpose of making the material available to users of the system or network who, after the material is transmitted as described in subparagraph (B), request access to the material from the person described in subparagraph (A), if the conditions set forth in paragraph (2) are met.

   (2) Conditions—The conditions referred to in paragraph (1) are that—

      (A) the material described in paragraph (1) is transmitted to the subsequent users described in paragraph (1)(C) without modification to its content from the manner in which the material was transmitted from the person described in paragraph (1)(A);

      (B) the service provider described in paragraph (1) complies with rules concerning the refreshing, reloading, or other updating of the material when specified by the person making the material available online in accordance with a generally accepted industry standard data communications protocol for the system or network through which that person makes the material available, except that this subparagraph applies only if those rules are not used by the person described in paragraph (1)(A) to prevent or unreasonably impair the intermediate storage to which this subsection applies;

      (C) the service provider does not interfere with the ability of technology associated with the material to return to the person described in paragraph (1)(A) the information that would have been available to that person if the material had been obtained by the subsequent users described in paragraph (1)(C) directly from that person, except that this subparagraph applies only if that technology—

(i) does not significantly interfere with the performance of the provider's system or network or with the intermediate storage of the material;

(ii) is consistent with generally accepted industry standard communications protocols; and

(iii) does not extract information from the provider's system or network other than the information that would have been available to the person described in paragraph (1)(A) if the subsequent users had gained access to the material directly from that person;

(D) if the person described in paragraph (1)(A) has in effect a condition that a person must meet prior to having access to the material, such as a condition based on payment of a fee or provision of a password or other information, the service provider permits access to the stored material in significant part only to users of its system or network that have met those conditions and only in accordance with those conditions; and

(E) if the person described in paragraph (1)(A) makes that material available online without the authorization of the copyright owner of the material, the service provider responds expeditiously to remove, or disable access to, the material that is claimed to be infringing upon notification of claimed infringement as described in subsection (c)(3), except that this subparagraph applies only if—

(i) the material has previously been removed from the originating site or access to it has been disabled, or a court has ordered that the material be removed from the originating site or that access to the material on the originating site be disabled; and

(ii) the party giving the notification includes in the notification a statement confirming that the material has been removed from the originating site or access to it has been disabled or that a court has ordered that the material be removed from the originating site or that access to the material on the originating site be disabled.

(c) Information Residing on Systems or Networks at Direction of Users.—

(1) In General—A service provider shall not be liable for monetary relief, or, except as provided in subsection (j), for injunctive or other equitable relief, for infringement of copyright by reason of the storage at the direction of a user of material that resides on a system or network controlled or operated by or for the service provider, if the service provider—

(A) (i) does not have actual knowledge that the material or an activity using the material on the system or network is infringing;

(ii) in the absence of such actual knowledge, is not aware of facts or circumstances from which infringing activity is apparent; or

(iii) upon obtaining such knowledge or awareness, acts expeditiously to remove, or disable access to, the material;

(B) does not receive a financial benefit directly attributable to the infringing activity, in a case in which the service provider has the right and ability to control such activity; and

(C) upon notification of claimed infringement as described in paragraph (3), responds expeditiously to remove, or disable access to, the material that is claimed to be infringing or to be the subject of infringing activity.

(2) Designated Agent—The limitations on liability established in this subsection apply to a service provider only if the service provider has designated an agent to receive notifications of claimed infringement described in paragraph (3), by making available through its service, including on its website in a location accessible to the public, and by providing to the Copyright Office, substantially the following information:

(A) the name, address, phone number, and electronic mail address of the agent.

(B) other contact information which the Register of Copyrights may deem appropriate.

The Register of Copyrights shall maintain a current directory of agents available to the public for inspection, including through the Internet, in both electronic and hard copy formats, and may require payment of a fee by service providers to cover the costs of maintaining the directory.

(3) Elements of Notification—

(A) To be effective under this subsection, a notification of claimed infringement must be a written communication provided to the designated agent of a service provider that includes substantially the following:

(i) A physical or electronic signature of a person authorized to act on behalf of the owner of an exclusive right that is allegedly infringed.

(ii) Identification of the copyrighted work claimed to have been infringed, or, if multiple copyrighted works at a single online site are covered by a single notification, a representative list of such works at that site.

(iii) Identification of the material that is claimed to be infringing or to be the subject of infringing activity and that is to be removed or access to which is to be disabled, and information reasonably sufficient to permit the service provider to locate the material.

(iv) Information reasonably sufficient to permit the service provider to contact the complaining party, such as an address, telephone number, and, if available, an electronic mail address at which the complaining party may be contacted.

(v) A statement that the complaining party has a good faith belief that use of the material in the manner complained of is not authorized by the copyright owner, its agent, or the law.

(vi) A statement that the information in the notification is accurate, and under penalty of perjury, that the complaining party is authorized to act on behalf of the owner of an exclusive right that is allegedly infringed.

(B) (i) Subject to clause (ii), a notification from a copyright owner or from a person authorized to act on behalf of the copyright owner that fails to comply substantially with the provisions of subparagraph (A) shall not be considered under paragraph (1)(A) in determining whether a service provider has actual knowledge or is aware of facts or circumstances from which infringing activity is apparent.

(ii) In a case in which the notification that is provided to the service provider's designated agent fails to comply substantially with all the provisions of subparagraph (A) but substantially complies with clauses (ii), (iii), and (iv) of subparagraph (A), clause (i) of this subparagraph applies only if the service provider promptly attempts to contact the person making the notification or takes other reasonable steps to assist in the receipt of notification that substantially complies with all the provisions of subparagraph (A).

(d) Information Location Tools—A service provider shall not be liable for monetary relief, or, except as provided in subsection (j), for injunctive or other equitable relief, for infringement of copyright by reason of the provider referring or linking users to an online location containing infringing material or infringing activity, by using information location tools, including a directory, index, reference, pointer, or hypertext link, if the service provider—

(1) (A) does not have actual knowledge that the material or activity is infringing;

(B) in the absence of such actual knowledge, is not aware of facts or circumstances from which infringing activity is apparent; or

(C) upon obtaining such knowledge or awareness, acts expeditiously to remove, or disable access to, the material;

(2) does not receive a financial benefit directly attributable to the infringing activity, in a case in which the service provider has the right and ability to control such activity; and

(3) upon notification of claimed infringement as described in subsection (c)(3), responds expeditiously to remove, or disable access to, the material that is claimed to be infringing or to be the subject of infringing activity, except that, for purposes of this paragraph, the information described in subsection (c)(3)(A)(iii) shall be identification of the reference or link, to material or activity claimed to be infringing, that is to be removed or access to which is to be disabled, and information reasonably sufficient to permit the service provider to locate that reference or link.

(e) Limitation on Liability of Nonprofit Educational Institutions—(1) When a public or other nonprofit institution of higher education is a service provider, and when a faculty member or graduate student who is an employee of such institution is performing a teaching or research function, for the purposes of subsections (a) and (b) such faculty member or graduate student shall be considered to be a person other than the institution, and for the purposes of subsections (c) and (d) such faculty member's or graduate student's knowledge or awareness of his or her infringing activities shall not be attributed to the institution, if—

(A) such faculty member's or graduate student's infringing activities do not involve the provision of online access to instructional materials that are or were required or recommended, within the preceding 3-year period, for a course taught at the institution by such faculty member or graduate student;

(B) the institution has not, within the preceding 3-year period, received more than 2 notifications described in subsection (c)(3) of claimed infringement by such faculty member or graduate student, and such notifications of claimed infringement were not actionable under subsection (f); and

(C) the institution provides to all users of its system or network informational materials that accurately describe, and promote compliance with, the laws of the United States relating to copyright.

(2) For the purposes of this subsection, the limitations on injunctive relief contained in subsections (j)(2) and (j)(3), but not those in (j)(1), shall apply.

(f) Misrepresentations—Any person who knowingly materially misrepresents under this section—

(1) that material or activity is infringing, or

(2) that material or activity was removed or disabled by mistake or misidentification, shall be liable for any damages, including costs and attorneys' fees, incurred by the alleged infringer, by any copyright owner

or copyright owner's authorized licensee, or by a service provider, who is injured by such misrepresentation, as the result of the service provider relying upon such misrepresentation in removing or disabling access to the material or activity claimed to be infringing, or in replacing the removed material or ceasing to disable access to it.

(g) Replacement of Removed or Disabled Material and Limitation on Other Liability—

   (1) No Liability for Taking Down Generally—Subject to paragraph (2), a service provider shall not be liable to any person for any claim based on the service provider's good faith disabling of access to, or removal of, material or activity claimed to be infringing or based on facts or circumstances from which infringing activity is apparent, regardless of whether the material or activity is ultimately determined to be infringing.

   (2) Exception—Paragraph (1) shall not apply with respect to material residing at the direction of a subscriber of the service provider on a system or network controlled or operated by or for the service provider that is removed, or to which access is disabled by the service provider, pursuant to a notice provided under subsection (c)(1)(C), unless the service provider—

      (A) takes reasonable steps promptly to notify the subscriber that it has removed or disabled access to the material;

      (B) upon receipt of a counter notification described in paragraph (3), promptly provides the person who provided the notification under subsection (c)(1)(C) with a copy of the counter notification, and informs that person that it will replace the removed material or cease disabling access to it in 10 business days; and

      (C) replaces the removed material and ceases disabling access to it not less than 10, nor more than 14, business days following receipt of the counter notice, unless its designated agent first receives notice from the person who submitted the notification under subsection (c)(1)(C) that such person has filed an action seeking a court order to restrain the subscriber from engaging in infringing activity relating to the material on the service provider's system or network.

   (3) Contents of Counter Notification—To be effective under this subsection, a counter notification must be a written communication provided to the service provider's designated agent that includes substantially the following:

      (A) A physical or electronic signature of the subscriber.

      (B) Identification of the material that has been removed or to which access has been disabled and the location at which the material appeared before it was removed or access to it was disabled.

(C) A statement under penalty of perjury that the subscriber has a good faith belief that the material was removed or disabled as a result of mistake or misidentification of the material to be removed or disabled.

(D) The subscriber's name, address, and telephone number, and a statement that the subscriber consents to the jurisdiction of Federal District Court for the judicial district in which the address is located, or if the subscriber's address is outside of the United States, for any judicial district in which the service provider may be found, and that the subscriber will accept service of process from the person who provided notification under subsection (c)(1)(C) or an agent of such person.

(4) Limitation on Other Liability—A service provider's compliance with paragraph (2) shall not subject the service provider to liability for copyright infringement with respect to the material identified in the notice provided under subsection (c)(1)(C).

(h) Subpoena to Identify Infringer—

(1) Request—A copyright owner or a person authorized to act on the owner's behalf may request the clerk of any United States district court to issue a subpoena to a service provider for identification of an alleged infringer in accordance with this subsection.

(2) Contents of Request—The request may be made by filing with the clerk—

(A) a copy of a notification described in subsection (c)(3)(A);

(B) a proposed subpoena; and

(C) a sworn declaration to the effect that the purpose for which the subpoena is sought is to obtain the identity of an alleged infringer and that such information will only be used for the purpose of protecting rights under this title.

(3) Contents of Subpoena—The subpoena shall authorize and order the service provider receiving the notification and the subpoena to expeditiously disclose to the copyright owner or person authorized by the copyright owner information sufficient to identify the alleged infringer of the material described in the notification to the extent such information is available to the service provider.

(4) Basis for Granting Subpoena—If the notification filed satisfies the provisions of subsection (c)(3)(A), the proposed subpoena is in proper form, and the accompanying declaration is properly executed, the clerk shall expeditiously issue and sign the proposed subpoena and return it to the requester for delivery to the service provider.

(5) Actions of Service Provider Receiving Subpoena—Upon receipt of the issued subpoena, either accompanying or subsequent to the receipt of a notification described in subsection (c)(3)(A), the service provider shall expeditiously disclose to the copyright owner or person authorized by the copyright owner the information required by the subpoena, notwithstanding any other provision of law and regardless of whether the service provider responds to the notification.

(6) Rules Applicable to Subpoena.—Unless otherwise provided by this section or by applicable rules of the court, the procedure for issuance and delivery of the subpoena, and the remedies for noncompliance with the subpoena, shall be governed to the greatest extent practicable by those provisions of the Federal Rules of Civil Procedure governing the issuance, service, and enforcement of a subpoena duces tecum.

(i) Conditions for Eligibility—

(1) Accommodation of Technology—The limitations on liability established by this section shall apply to a service provider only if the service provider—

(A) has adopted and reasonably implemented, and informs subscribers and account holders of the service provider's system or network of, a policy that provides for the termination in appropriate circumstances of subscribers and account holders of the service provider's system or network who are repeat infringers; and

(B) accommodates and does not interfere with standard technical measures.

(2) Definition—As used in this subsection, the term "standard technical measures" means technical measures that are used by copyright owners to identify or protect copyrighted works and—

(A) have been developed pursuant to a broad consensus of copyright owners and service providers in an open, fair, voluntary, multi-industry standards process;

(B) are available to any person on reasonable and nondiscriminatory terms; and

(C) do not impose substantial costs on service providers or substantial burdens on their systems or networks.

(j) Injunctions—The following rules shall apply in the case of any application for an injunction under section 502 against a service provider that is not subject to monetary remedies under this section:

(1) Scope of Relief—(A) With respect to conduct other than that which qualifies for the limitation on remedies set forth in subsection (a), the court may grant injunctive relief with respect to a service provider only in one or more of the following forms:

        (i) An order restraining the service provider from providing access to infringing material or activity residing at a particular online site on the provider's system or network.

        (ii) An order restraining the service provider from providing access to a subscriber or account holder of the service provider's system or network who is engaging in infringing activity and is identified in the order, by terminating the accounts of the subscriber or account holder that are specified in the order.

        (iii) Such other injunctive relief as the court may consider necessary to prevent or restrain infringement of copyrighted material specified in the order of the court at a particular online location, if such relief is the least burdensome to the service provider among the forms of relief comparably effective for that purpose.

(B) If the service provider qualifies for the limitation on remedies described in subsection (a), the court may only grant injunctive relief in one or both of the following forms:

        (i) An order restraining the service provider from providing access to a subscriber or account holder of the service provider's system or network who is using the provider's service to engage in infringing activity and is identified in the order, by terminating the accounts of the subscriber or account holder that are specified in the order.

        (ii) An order restraining the service provider from providing access, by taking reasonable steps specified in the order to block access, to a specific, identified, online location outside the United States.

(2) Considerations—The court, in considering the relevant criteria for injunctive relief under applicable law, shall consider—

(A) whether such an injunction, either alone or in combination with other such injunctions issued against the same service provider under this subsection, would significantly burden either the provider or the operation of the provider's system or network;

(B) the magnitude of the harm likely to be suffered by the copyright owner in the digital network environment if steps are not taken to prevent or restrain the infringement;

(C) whether implementation of such an injunction would be technically feasible and effective, and would not interfere with access to noninfringing material at other online locations; and

(D) whether other less burdensome and comparably effective means of preventing or restraining access to the infringing material are available.

(3) Notice and Ex Parte Orders—Injunctive relief under this subsection shall be available only after notice to the service provider and an opportunity for the service provider to appear are provided, except for orders ensuring the preservation of evidence or other orders having no material adverse effect on the operation of the service provider's communications network.

(k) Definitions—

(1) Service Provider—(A) As used in subsection (a), the term "service provider" means an entity offering the transmission, routing, or providing of connections for digital online communications, between or among points specified by a user, of material of the user's choosing, without modification to the content of the material as sent or received.

(B) As used in this section, other than subsection (a), the term "service provider" means a provider of online services or network access, or the operator of facilities therefor, and includes an entity described in subparagraph (A).

(2) Monetary Relief—As used in this section, the term "monetary relief" means damages, costs, attorneys' fees, and any other form of monetary payment.

(l) Other Defenses Not Affected—The failure of a service provider's conduct to qualify for limitation of liability under this section shall not bear adversely upon the consideration of a defense by the service provider that the service provider's conduct is not infringing under this title or any other defense.

(m) Protection of Privacy—Nothing in this section shall be construed to condition the applicability of subsections (a) through (d) on—

(1) a service provider monitoring its service or affirmatively seeking facts indicating infringing activity, except to the extent consistent with a standard technical measure complying with the provisions of subsection (i); or

(2) a service provider gaining access to, removing, or disabling access to material in cases in which such conduct is prohibited by law.

(n) Construction—Subsections (a), (b), (c), and (d) describe separate and distinct functions for purposes of applying this section. Whether a service provider qualifies for the limitation on liability in any one of those subsections shall be based solely on the criteria in that subsection, and shall not affect a determination of whether that service provider qualifies for the limitations on liability under any other such subsection.

Appendix G

Trademark Act of 1946 ("Lanham Act"), as Amended

PUBLIC LAW 79-489,
CHAPTER 540, APPROVED JULY 5, 1946; 60 STAT. 427
TITLE VI—REMEDIES

§32 (15 U.S.C. §1114). REMEDIES; INFRINGEMENT; INNOCENT INFRINGERS

(1) Any person who shall, without the consent of the registrant—

(a) use in commerce any reproduction, counterfeit, copy, or colorable imitation of a registered mark in connection with the sale, offering for sale, distribution, or advertising of any goods or services on or in connection with which such use is likely to cause confusion, or to cause mistake, or to deceive; or

(b) reproduce, counterfeit, copy or colorably imitate a registered mark and apply such reproduction, counterfeit, copy or colorable imitation to labels, signs, prints, packages, wrappers, receptacles or advertisements intended to be used in commerce upon or in connection with the sale, offering for sale, distribution, or advertising of goods or services on or in connection with which such use is likely to cause confusion, or to cause mistake, or to deceive,

shall be liable in a civil action by the registrant for the remedies hereinafter provided. Under subsection (b) hereof, the registrant shall not be entitled to recover profits or damages unless the acts have been committed with knowledge that such imitation is intended to be used to cause confusion, or to cause mistake, or to deceive.

As used in this paragraph, the term "any person" includes the United States, all agencies and instrumentalities thereof, and all individuals, firms, corporations, or other persons acting for the United States and with the authorization and consent of the United States, and any State, any instrumentality of a State, and any officer or employee of a State or instrumentality of a State acting in his or her official capacity. The United States, all agencies and instrumentalities thereof, and all individuals, firms, corporations, other persons acting for the United States and with the authorization and consent of the United States, and any State, and any such instrumentality, officer, or employee, shall be subject to the provisions of this Act in the same manner and to the same extent as any nongovernmental entity.

(2) Notwithstanding any other provision of this Act, the remedies given to the owner of a right infringed under this Act or to a person bringing an action under section 43(a) or (d) shall be limited as follows:

(A) Where an infringer or violator is engaged solely in the business of printing the mark or violating matter for others and establishes that he or she was an innocent infringer or innocent violator, the owner of the right infringed or person bringing the action under section 43(a) shall be entitled as against such infringer or violator only to an injunction against future printing.

(B) Where the infringement or violation complained of is contained in or is part of paid advertising matter in a newspaper, magazine, or other similar periodical or in an electronic communication as defined in section 2510(12) of title 18, United States Code, the remedies of the owner of the right infringed or person bringing the action under section 43(a) as against the publisher or distributor of such newspaper, magazine, or other similar periodical or electronic communication shall be limited to an injunction against the presentation of such advertising matter in future issues of such newspapers, magazines, or other similar periodicals or in future transmissions of such electronic communications. The limitations of this subparagraph shall apply only to innocent infringers and innocent violators.

(C) Injunctive relief shall not be available to the owner of the right infringed or person bringing the action under section 43(a) with respect to an issue of a newspaper, magazine, or other similar periodical or an electronic communication containing infringing matter or violating matter where restraining the dissemination of such infringing matter or violating matter in any particular issue of such periodical or in an electronic communication would delay the delivery of such issue or transmission of such electronic communication after the regular time for such delivery or transmission, and such delay would be due to the method by which publication and distribution of such periodical or transmission of such electronic communication is customarily conducted in accordance with sound business practice, and not due to any method or device adopted to evade this section or to prevent or delay the issuance of an injunction or restraining order with respect to such infringing matter or violating matter.

(D)   (i)   (I)   A domain name registrar, a domain name registry, or other domain name registration authority that takes any action described under clause (ii) affecting a domain name shall not be liable for monetary relief or, except as provided in subclause (II), for injunctive relief, to any person for such action, regardless of whether the domain name is finally determined to infringe or dilute the mark.

          (II)   A domain name registrar, domain name registry, or other domain name registration authority described in subclause (I) may be subject to injunctive relief only if such registrar, registry, or other registration authority has—

(aa) not expeditiously deposited with a court, in which an action has been filed regarding the disposition of the domain name, documents sufficient for the court to establish the court's control and authority regarding the disposition of the registration and use of the domain name;

(bb) transferred, suspended, or otherwise modified the domain name during the pendency of the action, except upon order of the court; or

(cc) willfully failed to comply with any such court order.

   (ii) An action referred to under clause (i)(I) is any action of refusing to register, removing from registration, transferring, temporarily disabling, or permanently canceling a domain name—

     (I) in compliance with a court order under section 43(d); or

     (II) in the implementation of a reasonable policy by such registrar, registry, or authority prohibiting the registration of a domain name that is identical to, confusingly similar to, or dilutive of another's mark.

   (iii) A domain name registrar, a domain name registry, or other domain name registration authority shall not be liable for damages under this section for the registration or maintenance of a domain name for another absent a showing of bad faith intent to profit from such registration or maintenance of the domain name.

   (iv) If a registrar, registry, or other registration authority takes an action described under clause (ii) based on a knowing and material misrepresentation by any other person that a domain name is identical to, confusingly similar to, or dilutive of a mark, the person making the knowing and material misrepresentation shall be liable for any damages, including costs and attorney's fees, incurred by the domain name registrant as a result of such action. The court may also grant injunctive relief to the domain name registrant, including the reactivation of the domain name or the transfer of the domain name to the domain name registrant.

(v) A domain name registrant whose domain name has been suspended, disabled, or transferred under a policy described under clause (ii)(II) may, upon notice to the mark owner, file a civil action to establish that the registration or use of the domain name by such registrant is not unlawful under this Act. The court may grant injunctive relief to the domain name registrant, including the reactivation of the domain name or transfer of the domain name to the domain name registrant.

(E) As used in this paragraph—

(i) the term "violator" means a person who violates section 43(a); and

(ii) the term "violating matter" means matter that is the subject of a violation under section 43(a).

(Amended Oct. 9, 1962, 76 Stat. 773; Nov. 16, 1988, 102 Stat. 3943; Oct. 27, 1992, 106 Stat. 3567; Oct. 30, 1998, 112 Stat. 3069; Aug. 5, 1999, 113 Stat. 218; Nov. 29, 1999, 113 Stat. 1501A-549.)

§34 (15 U.S.C. §1116). INJUNCTIONS; ENFORCEMENT; NOTICE OF FILING SUIT GIVEN DIRECTOR

(a) The several courts vested with jurisdiction of civil actions arising under this Act shall have power to grant injunctions, according to the principles of equity and upon such terms as the court may deem reasonable, to prevent the violation of any right of the registrant of a mark registered in the Patent and Trademark Office or to prevent a violation under subsection (a), (c), or (d) of section 43. Any such injunction may include a provision directing the defendant to file with the court and serve on the plaintiff within thirty days after the service on the defendant of such injunction, or such extended period as the court may direct, a report in writing under oath setting forth in detail the manner and form in which the defendant has complied with the injunction. Any such injunction granted upon hearing, after notice to the defendant, by any district court of the United States, may be served on the parties against whom such injunction is granted anywhere in the United States where they may be found, and shall be operative and may be enforced by proceedings to punish for contempt, or otherwise, by the court by which such injunction was granted, or by any other United States district court in whose jurisdiction the defendant may be found.

(b) The said courts shall have jurisdiction to enforce said injunction, as herein provided, as fully as if the injunction had been granted by the district court in which it is sought to be enforced. The clerk of the court or judge granting the injunction shall, when required to do so by the court before which application to enforce said injunction is made, transfer without delay to said court a certified copy of all papers on file in his office upon which said injunction was granted.

(c) It shall be the duty of the clerks of such courts within one month after the filing of any action, suit, or proceeding involving a mark registered under the provisions of this Act to give notice thereof in writing to the Director setting forth in order so far as known the names and addresses of the litigants and the designating number or numbers of the registration or registrations upon which the action, suit, or proceeding has been brought, and in the event any other registration be subsequently included in the action, suit, or proceeding by amendment, answer, or other pleading, the clerk shall give like notice thereof to the Director, and within one month after the judgment is entered or an appeal is taken, the clerk of the court shall give notice thereof to the Director, and it shall be the duty of the Director on receipt of such notice forthwith to endorse the same upon the file wrapper of the said registration or registrations and to incorporate the same as a part of the contents of said file wrapper.

(d) (1) (A) In the case of a civil action arising under section 32(1)(a) of this Act or section 110 of the Act entitled "An Act to incorporate the United States Olympic Association", approved September 21, 1950 (36 U.S.C. 380) with respect to a violation that consists of using a counterfeit mark in connection with the sale, offering for sale, or distribution of goods or services, the court may, upon ex parte application, grant an order under subsection (a) of this section pursuant to this subsection providing for the seizure of goods and counterfeit marks involved in such violation and the means of making such marks, and records documenting the manufacture, sale, or receipt of things involved in such violation.

(B) As used in this subsection the term "counterfeit mark" means—

(i) a counterfeit of a mark that is registered on the principal register in the United States Patent and Trademark Office for such goods or services sold, offered for sale, or distributed and that is in use, whether or not the person against whom relief is sought knew such mark was so registered; or

(ii) a spurious designation that is identical with, or substantially indistinguishable from, a designation as to which the remedies of this Act are made available by reason of section 110 of the Act entitled "An Act to incorporate the United States Olympic Association", approved September 21, 1950 (36 U.S.C. 380);

but such term does not include any mark or designation used on or in connection with goods or services of which the manufacturer or producer was, at the time of the manufacture or production in question authorized to use the mark or designation for the type of goods or services so manufactured or produced, by the holder of the right to use such mark or designation.

(2) The court shall not receive an application under this subsection unless the applicant has given such notice of the application as is reasonable under the circumstances to the United States attorney for the judicial district in which such order is sought. Such attorney may participate in the proceedings arising under such application if such proceedings may affect evidence of an offense against the United States. The court may deny such application if the court determines that the public interest in a potential prosecution so requires.

(3) The application for an order under this subsection shall—

   (A) be based on an affidavit or the verified complaint establishing facts sufficient to support the findings of fact and conclusions of law required for such order; and

   (B) contain the additional information required by paragraph (5) of this subsection to be set forth in such order.

(4) The court shall not grant such an application unless—

   (A) the person obtaining an order under this subsection provides the security determined adequate by the court for the payment of such damages as any person may be entitled to recover as a result of a wrongful seizure or wrongful attempted seizure under this subsection; and

   (B) the court finds that it clearly appears from specific facts that—

      (i) an order other than an ex parte seizure order is not adequate to achieve the purposes of section 32 of this Act;

      (ii) the applicant has not publicized the requested seizure;

      (iii) the applicant is likely to succeed in showing that the person against whom seizure would be ordered used a counterfeit mark in connection with the sale, offering for sale, or distribution of goods or services;

      (iv) an immediate and irreparable injury will occur if such seizure is not ordered;

      (v) the matter to be seized will be located at the place identified in the application;

      (vi) the harm to the applicant of denying the application outweighs the harm to the legitimate interests of the person against whom seizure would be ordered of granting the application; and

(vii) the person against whom seizure would be ordered, or persons acting in concert with such person, would destroy, move, hide, or otherwise make such matter inaccessible to the court, if the applicant were to proceed on notice to such person.

(5) An order under this subsection shall set forth—

(A) the findings of fact and conclusions of law required for the order;

(B) a particular description of the matter to be seized, and a description of each place at which such matter is to be seized;

(C) the time period, which shall end not later than seven days after the date on which such order is issued, during which the seizure is to be made;

(D) the amount of security required to be provided under this subsection; and

(E) a date for the hearing required under paragraph (10) of this subsection.

(6) The court shall take appropriate action to protect the person against whom an order under this subsection is directed from publicity, by or at the behest of the plaintiff, about such order and any seizure under such order.

(7) Any materials seized under this subsection shall be taken into the custody of the court. The court shall enter an appropriate protective order with respect to discovery by the applicant of any records that have been seized. The protective order shall provide for appropriate procedures to assure that confidential information contained in such records is not improperly disclosed to the applicant.

(8) An order under this subsection, together with the supporting documents, shall be sealed until the person against whom the order is directed has an opportunity to contest such order, except that any person against whom such order is issued shall have access to such order and supporting documents after the seizure has been carried out.

(9) The court shall order that service of a copy of the order under this subsection shall be made by a Federal law enforcement officer (such as a United States marshal or an officer or agent of the United States Customs Service, Secret Service, Federal Bureau of Investigation, or Post Office) or may be made by a State or local law enforcement officer, who, upon making service, shall carry out the seizure under the order. The court shall issue orders, when appropriate, to protect the defendant from undue damage from the disclosure of trade secrets or other confidential information during the course of the seizure, including, when appropriate, orders restricting the access of the applicant (or any agent or employee of the applicant) to such secrets or information.

(10) (A) The court shall hold a hearing, unless waived by all the parties, on the date set by the court in the order of seizure. That date shall be not sooner than ten days after the order is issued and not later than fifteen days after the order is issued, unless the applicant for the order shows good cause for another date or unless the party against whom such order is directed consents to another date for such hearing. At such hearing the party obtaining the order shall have the burden to prove that the facts supporting findings of fact and conclusions of law necessary to support such order are still in effect. If that party fails to meet that burden, the seizure order shall be dissolved or modified appropriately.

(B) In connection with a hearing under this paragraph, the court may make such orders modifying the time limits for discovery under the Rules of Civil Procedure as may be necessary to prevent the frustration of the purposes of such hearing.

(11) A person who suffers damage by reason of wrongful seizure under this subsection has a cause of action against the applicant for the order under which such seizure was made, and shall be entitled to recover such relief as may be appropriate, including damages for lost profits, cost of materials, loss of goodwill, and punitive damages in instances where the seizure was sought in bad faith, and, unless the court finds extenuating circumstances, to recover a reasonable attorney's fee. The court in its discretion may award prejudgment interest on relief recovered under this paragraph, at an annual interest rate established under section 6621 of the Internal Revenue Code of 1954, commencing on the date of service of the claimant's pleading setting forth the claim under this paragraph and ending on the date such recovery is granted, or for such shorter time as the court deems appropriate.
(Amended Jan. 2, 1975, 88 Stat. 1949; Oct. 12, 1984, 98 Stat. 2179; Nov. 16, 1988, 102 Stat. 3945; July 2, 1996, 110 Stat. 1386; Aug. 5, 1999, 113 Stat. 218; Nov. 29, 1999, 113 Stat. 1501A-548.)

§35 (15 U.S.C. §1117). RECOVERY OF PROFITS, DAMAGES, AND COSTS

(a) When a violation of any right of the registrant of a mark registered in the Patent and Trademark Office, a violation under section 43(a), (c), or (d) or a willful violation under section 43(c), shall have been established in any civil action arising under this Act, the plaintiff shall be entitled, subject to the provisions of sections 29 and 32 and subject to the principles of equity, to recover (1) defendant's profits, (2) any damages sustained by the plaintiff, and (3) the costs of the action. The court shall assess such profits and damages or cause the same to be assessed under its direction. In assessing profits the plaintiff shall be required to prove defendant's sale only; defendant must prove all elements of cost or deduction claimed. In assessing damages the court may enter judgment, according to the circumstances of the case, for any sum above the amount found as actual damages, not exceeding three times such amount. If the court shall find that the amount of the recovery based on profits is either inadequate or excessive the court may in its discretion enter judgment for such sum as the court shall find to be just, according to the circumstances of the case. Such sum in either of the above circumstances shall constitute compensation and not a penalty. The court in exceptional cases may award reasonable attorney fees to the prevailing party.

(b) In assessing damages under subsection (a), the court shall, unless the court finds extenuating circumstances, enter judgment for three times such profits or damages, whichever is greater, together with a reasonable attorney's fee, in the case of any violation of section 32(1)(a) of this Act (15 U.S.C. 1114(1)(a)) or section 110 of the Act entitled "An Act to incorporate the United States Olympic Association", approved September 21, 1950 (36 U.S.C. 380) that consists of intentionally using a mark or designation, knowing such mark or designation is a counterfeit mark (as defined in section 34(d) of this Act (15 U.S.C. 1116(d)), in connection with the sale, offering for sale, or distribution of goods or services. In such cases, the court may in its discretion award prejudgment interest on such amount at an annual interest rate established under section 6621 of the Internal Revenue Code of 1954, commencing on the date of the service of the claimant's pleadings setting forth the claim for such entry and ending on the date such entry is made, or for such shorter time as the court deems appropriate.

(c) In a case involving the use of a counterfeit mark (as defined in section 1116(d) of this title) in connection with the sale, offering for sale, or distribution of goods or services, the plaintiff may elect, at any time before final judgment is rendered by the trial court, to recover, instead of actual damages and profits under subsection (a) of this section, an award of statutory damages for any such use in connection with the sale, offering for sale, or distribution of goods or services in the amount of—

   (1) not less than $500 or more than $100,000 per counterfeit mark per type of goods or services sold, offered for sale, or distributed, as the court considers just; or

   (2) if the court finds that the use of the counterfeit mark was willful, not more than $1,000,000 per counterfeit mark per type of goods or services sold, offered for sale, or distributed, as the court considers just.

(d) In a case involving a violation of section 43(d)(1), the plaintiff may elect, at any time before final judgment is rendered by the trial court, to recover, instead of actual damages and profits, an award of statutory damages in the amount of not less than $1,000 and not more than $100,000 per domain name, as the court considers just.

(Amended Oct. 9, 1962, 76 Stat. 774; Jan. 2, 1975, 88 Stat. 1949; Jan. 2, 1975, 88 Stat. 1955; Oct. 12, 1984, 98 Stat. 2182; Nov. 16, 1988, 102 Stat. 3945; July 2, 1996, 110 Stat. 1386; Aug. 5, 1999, 113 Stat. 218; Nov. 29, 1999, 113 Stat. 1501A-549.)

§36 (15 U.S.C. §1118). Destruction of infringing articles

In any action arising under this Act, in which a violation of any right of the registrant of a mark registered in the Patent and Trademark Office, a violation under section 43(a), or a willful violation under section 43(c), shall have been established, the court may order that all labels, signs, prints, packages, wrappers, receptacles, and advertisements in the possession of the defendant, bearing the registered mark or, in the case of a violation of section 43(a) or a willful violation under section 43(c), the word, term, name, symbol, device, combination thereof, designation, description, or representation that is the subject of the violation, or any reproduction, counterfeit, copy, or colorable imitation thereof, and all plates, molds, matrices, and other means of making the same, shall be delivered up and destroyed. The party seeking an order under this section for destruction of articles seized under section 34(d) (15 U.S.C. 1116(d)) shall give ten days' notice to the United States attorney for the judicial district in which such order is sought (unless good cause is shown for lesser notice) and such United States attorney may, if such destruction may affect evidence of an offense against the United States, seek a hearing on such destruction or participate in any hearing otherwise to be held with respect to such destruction.

(Amended Jan. 2, 1975, 88 Stat. 1949; Oct. 12, 1984, 98 Stat. 2182; Nov. 16, 1988, 102 Stat. 3945; Aug. 5, 1999, 113 Stat. 218.)

Appendix H

Uniform Trade Secrets Act with 1985 Amendments

SECTION 1: DEFINITIONS

As used in this [Act], unless the context requires otherwise:
(1) "Improper means" includes theft, bribery, misrepresentation, breach or inducement of a breach of a duty to maintain secrecy, or espionage through electronic or other means;
(2) "Misappropriation" means:
    (i) acquisition of a trade secret of another by a person who knows or has reason to know that the trade secret was acquired by improper means; or
    (ii) disclosure or use of a trade secret of another without express or implied consent by a person who
        (A) used improper means to acquire knowledge of the trade secret; or
        (B) at the time of disclosure or use, knew or had reason to know that his knowledge of the trade secret was
            (I) derived from or through a person who had utilized improper means to acquire it;
            (II) acquired under circumstances giving rise to a duty to maintain its secrecy or limit its use; or
            (III) derived from or through a person who owed a duty to the person seeking relief to maintain its secrecy or limit its use; or
        (C) before a material change of his [or her] position, knew or had reason to know that it was a trade secret and that knowledge of it had been acquired by accident or mistake.
(3) "Person" means a natural person, corporation, business trust, estate, trust, partnership, association, joint venture, government, governmental subdivision or agency, or any other legal or commercial entity.

(4) "Trade secret" means information, including a formula, pattern, compilation, program, device, method, technique, or process, that:

   (i) derives independent economic value, actual or potential, from not being generally known to, and not being readily ascertainable by proper means by, other persons who can obtain economic value from its disclosure or use, and

   (ii) is the subject of efforts that are reasonable under the circumstances to maintain its secrecy.

SECTION 2: INJUNCTIVE RELIEF

(a) Actual or threatened misappropriation may be enjoined. Upon application to the court an injunction shall be terminated when the trade secret has ceased to exist, but the injunction may be continued for an additional reasonable period of time in order to eliminate commercial advantage that otherwise would be derived from the misappropriation.

(b) In exceptional circumstances, an injunction may condition future use upon payment of a reasonable royalty for no longer than the period of time for which use could have been prohibited. Exceptional circumstances include, but are not limited to, a material and prejudicial change of position prior to acquiring knowledge or reason to know of misappropriation that renders a prohibitive injunction inequitable.

(c) In appropriate circumstances, affirmative acts to protect a trade secret may be compelled by court order.

SECTION 3: DAMAGES

(a) Except to the extent that a material and prejudicial change of position prior to acquiring knowledge or reason to know of misappropriation renders a monetary recovery inequitable, a complainant is entitled to recover damages for misappropriation. Damages can include both the actual loss caused by misappropriation and the unjust enrichment caused by misappropriation that is not taken into account in computing actual loss. In lieu of damages measured by any other methods, the damages caused by misappropriation may be measured by imposition of liability for a reasonable royalty for a misappropriator's unauthorized disclosure or use of a trade secret.

(b) If willful and malicious misappropriation exists, the court may award exemplary damages in the amount not exceeding twice any award made under subsection (a).

SECTION 4: ATTORNEY'S FEES

If (i) a claim of misappropriation is made in bad faith, (ii) a motion to terminate an injunction is made or resisted in bad faith, or (iii) willful and malicious misappropriation exists, the court may award reasonable attorney's fees to the prevailing party.

SECTION 5: PRESERVATION OF SECRECY

In an action under this [Act], a court shall preserve the secrecy of an alleged trade secret by reasonable means, which may include granting protective orders in connection with discovery proceedings, holding in-camera hearings, sealing the records of the action, and ordering any person involved in the litigation not to disclose an alleged trade secret without prior court approval.

SECTION 6: STATUTE OF LIMITATIONS

An action for misappropriation must be brought within 3 years after the misappropriation is discovered or by the exercise of reasonable diligence should have been discovered. For the purposes of this section, a continuing misappropriation constitutes a single claim.

SECTION 7: EFFECT ON OTHER LAW

(a) Except as provided in subsection (b), this [Act] displaces conflicting tort, restitutionary, and other law of this State pertaining to providing civil liability remedies for misappropriation of a trade secret.

(b) This [Act] does not affect:
  (1) contractual or other civil liability or relief that is remedies, whether or not based upon misappropriation of a trade secret; or
  (2) criminal liability for other civil remedies that are not based upon misappropriation of a trade secret; or
  (3) criminal remedies, whether or not based upon misappropriation of a trade secret.

Appendix I

Restatement of the Law, 3rd, Unfair Competition

§38 APPROPRIATION OF TRADE VALUES

One who causes harm to the commercial relations of another by appropriating the other's intangible trade values is subject to liability to the other for such harm only if:
    (a) the actor is subject to liability for an appropriation of the other's trade secret under the rules stated in §§39-45; or
    (b) the actor is subject to liability for an appropriation of the commercial value of the other's identity under the rules stated in §§46-49; or
    (c) the appropriation is actionable by the other under federal or state statutes or international agreements, or is actionable as a breach of contract, or as an infringement of common law copyright as preserved under federal copyright law.

Copyright 1995, American Law Institute

§39 DEFINITION OF TRADE SECRET

A trade secret is any information that can be used in the operation of a business or other enterprise and that is sufficiently valuable and secret to afford an actual or potential economic advantage over others.

Copyright 1995, American Law Institute

§40 APPROPRIATION OF TRADE SECRETS

One is subject to liability for the appropriation of another's trade secret if:
    (a) the actor acquires by means that are improper under the rule stated in §43 information that the actor knows or has reason to know is the other's trade secret; or

(b) the actor uses or discloses the other's trade secret without the other's consent and, at the time of the use or disclosure,

    (1) the actor knows or has reason to know that the information is a trade secret that the actor acquired under circumstances creating a duty of confidence owed by the actor to the other under the rule stated in §41; or

    (2) the actor knows or has reason to know that the information is a trade secret that the actor acquired by means that are improper under the rule stated in §43; or

    (3) the actor knows or has reason to know that the information is a trade secret that the actor acquired from or through a person who acquired it by means that are improper under the rule stated in §43 or whose disclosure of the trade secret constituted a breach of a duty of confidence owed to the other under the rule stated in §41; or

    (4) the actor knows or has reason to know that the information is a trade secret that the actor acquired through an accident or mistake, unless the acquisition was the result of the other's failure to take reasonable precautions to maintain the secrecy of the information.

Copyright 1995, American Law Institute

§41 DUTY OF CONFIDENCE

A person to whom a trade secret has been disclosed owes a duty of confidence to the owner of the trade secret for purposes of the rule stated in §40 if:

    (a) the person made an express promise of confidentiality prior to the disclosure of the trade secret; or

    (b) the trade secret was disclosed to the person under circumstances in which the relationship between the parties to the disclosure or the other facts surrounding the disclosure justify the conclusions that, at the time of the disclosure,

        (1) the person knew or had reason to know that the disclosure was intended to be in confidence, and

        (2) the other party to the disclosure was reasonable in inferring that the person consented to an obligation of confidentiality.

Copyright 1995, American Law Institute

§42 BREACH OF CONFIDENCE BY EMPLOYEES

An employee or former employee who uses or discloses a trade secret owned by the employer or former employer in breach of a duty of confidence is subject to liability for appropriation of the trade secret under the rule stated in §40.

Copyright 1995, American Law Institute

§43 IMPROPER ACQUISITION OF TRADE SECRETS

"Improper" means of acquiring another's trade secret under the rule stated in §40 include theft, fraud, unauthorized interception of communications, inducement of or knowing participation in a breach of confidence, and other means either wrongful in themselves or wrongful under the circumstances of the case. Independent discovery and analysis of publicly available products or information are not improper means of acquisition.

Copyright 1995, American Law Institute

§44 INJUNCTIONS: APPROPRIATION OF TRADE SECRETS

(1) If appropriate under the rule stated in Subsection (2), injunctive relief may be awarded to prevent a continuing or threatened appropriation of another's trade secret by one who is subject to liability under the rule stated in §40.

(2) The appropriateness and scope of injunctive relief depend upon a comparative appraisal of all the factors of the case, including the following primary factors:

    (a) the nature of the interest to be protected;

    (b) the nature and extent of the appropriation;

    (c) the relative adequacy to the plaintiff of an injunction and of other remedies;

    (d) the relative harm likely to result to the legitimate interests of the defendant if an injunction is granted and to the legitimate interests of the plaintiff if an injunction is denied;

    (e) the interests of third persons and of the public;

    (f) any unreasonable delay by the plaintiff in bringing suit or otherwise asserting its rights;

    (g) any related misconduct on the part of the plaintiff; and

    (h) the practicality of framing and enforcing the injunction.

(3) The duration of injunctive relief in trade secret actions should be limited to the time necessary to protect the plaintiff from any harm attributable to the appropriation and to deprive the defendant of any economic advantage attributable to the appropriation.

Copyright 1995, American Law Institute

§45 MONETARY RELIEF: APPROPRIATION OF TRADE SECRETS

(1) One who is liable to another for an appropriation of the other's trade secret under the rule stated in §40 is liable for the pecuniary loss to the other caused by the appropriation or for the actor's own pecuniary gain resulting from the appropriation, whichever is greater, unless such relief is inappropriate under the rule stated in Subsection (2).

(2) Whether an award of monetary relief is appropriate and the appropriate method of measuring such relief depend upon a comparative appraisal of all the factors of the case, including the following primary factors:

(a) the degree of certainty with which the plaintiff has established the fact and extent of the pecuniary loss or the actor's pecuniary gain resulting from the appropriation;

(b) the nature and extent of the appropriation;

(c) the relative adequacy to the plaintiff of other remedies;

(d) the intent and knowledge of the actor and the nature and extent of any good faith reliance by the actor;

(e) any unreasonable delay by the plaintiff in bringing suit or otherwise asserting its rights; and

(f) any related misconduct on the part of the plaintiff.

Copyright 1995, American Law Institute

§46 APPROPRIATION OF THE COMMERCIAL VALUE OF A PERSON'S IDENTITY: THE RIGHT OF PUBLICITY

One who appropriates the commercial value of a person's identity by using without consent the person's name, likeness, or other indicia of identity for purposes of trade is subject to liability for the relief appropriate under the rules stated in §§48 and 49.

Copyright 1995, American Law Institute

§47 USE FOR PURPOSES OF TRADE

The name, likeness, and other indicia of a person's identity are used "for purposes of trade" under the rule stated in §46 if they are used in advertising the user's goods or services, or are placed on merchandise marketed by the user, or are used in connection with services rendered by the user. However, use "for purposes of trade" does not ordinarily include the use of a person's identity in news reporting, commentary, entertainment, works of fiction or nonfiction, or in advertising that is incidental to such uses.

Copyright 1995, American Law Institute

§48 INJUNCTIONS: APPROPRIATION OF THE COMMERCIAL VALUE OF A PERSON'S IDENTITY

(1) If appropriate under the rule stated in Subsection (2), injunctive relief may be awarded to prevent a continuing or threatened appropriation of the commercial value of another's identity by one who is subject to liability under the rule stated in §46.

(2) The appropriateness and scope of injunctive relief depend upon a comparative appraisal of all the factors of the case, including the following primary factors:

(a) the nature of the interest to be protected;

(b) the nature and extent of the appropriation;

(c) the relative adequacy to the plaintiff of an injunction and of other remedies;

(d) the relative harm likely to result to the legitimate interests of the defendant if an injunction is granted and to the legitimate interests of the plaintiff if an injunction is denied;

(e) the interests of third persons and of the public;

(f) any unreasonable delay by the plaintiff in bringing suit or otherwise asserting his or her rights;

(g) any related misconduct on the part of the plaintiff; and

(h) the practicality of framing and enforcing the injunction.

Copyright 1995, American Law Institute

§49 MONETARY RELIEF: APPROPRIATION OF THE COMMERCIAL VALUE OF A PERSON'S IDENTITY INJUNCTIONS: APPROPRIATION OF THE COMMERCIAL VALUE OF A PERSON'S IDENTITY

(1) One who is liable for an appropriation of the commercial value of another's identity under the rule stated in §46 is liable for the pecuniary loss to the other caused by the appropriation or for the actor's own pecuniary gain resulting from the appropriation, whichever is greater, unless such relief is precluded by an applicable statute or is otherwise inappropriate under the rule stated in Subsection (2).

(2) Whether an award of monetary relief is appropriate and the appropriate method of measuring such relief depend upon a comparative appraisal of all the factors of the case, including the following primary factors:

(a) the degree of certainty with which the plaintiff has established the fact and extent of the pecuniary loss or the actor's pecuniary gain resulting from the appropriation;

(b) the nature and extent of the appropriation;

(c) the relative adequacy to the plaintiff of other remedies;

(d) the intent of the actor and whether the actor knew or should have known that the conduct was unlawful;

(e) any unreasonable delay by the plaintiff in bringing suit or otherwise asserting his or her rights; and

(f) any related misconduct on the part of the plaintiff.

Copyright 1995, American Law Institute

Index